'*How To Grow A Navy* is a wonderfully or
and advocacy. Sweeping across the centu
from the maritime story of Ancient Athen
Naval Powers of Asia, the Spanish and t
Navy and the sea empires of the future, Geoffrey Till makes the case again and
again for why naval force counts. And he does this with a lightness and surety of
touch, a clarity of exposition, and a firm grasp of his subject. Far too often, and
with far less reason, are other books on military and naval themes recommended
to policy-makers. This book really deserves to be read by those states who possess
a navy, and even more by those who would like to grow one.'

Paul Kennedy, *Yale University, USA, author of*
The Rise and Fall of the Great Powers

'Professor Geoffrey Till skilfully derives concepts for building and sustaining a
navy as he examines the exercise of sea power over a large historical and
geographical canvas. A 'must read' for practitioners from navies, large and small,
in order to draw useful lessons and avoid pitfalls from the rich trove of case
studies.'

Admiral (Retd) Nirmal Verma, *former Chief of Naval Staff, Indian Navy and*
former High Commissioner of India to Canada

'In this thoughtful and wide-ranging analysis, Geoff Till explores the sources and
character of maritime ascendency and its relationship to national power and
influence. In casting a broad net from ancient Athens to an emergent China in the
21st century, Till illuminates the interconnectedness of national culture and
maritime supremacy with lessons that are both historic and immediate.'

Craig L. Symonds, *author of World War II at Sea*

'Professor Till's latest study into the enduring dynamics and drivers of maritime
power through history, and how navies develop, is an important and timely
addition to the body of analysis on the contemporary maritime domain. It needs
to be read and absorbed by all those seeking to understand and influence the sea
change now underway in the global maritime arena, not least modern China's
maritime trajectory, and by those national policymakers aiming to grow or
rebuild their own navies.'

Nick Childs, *Senior Fellow for Naval Forces and Maritime Security,*
International Institute for Strategic Studies

'Speaking from real-world strategy formulation experience, Geoff Till's prescrip-
tion is spot on. He correctly argues that naval forces require, first and foremost, a
clear explanation of purpose to justify national funding—a frequently overlooked
and surprisingly misunderstood principle. In this essential volume, Till shows how
governments and navies can build, maintain or revive their maritime forces for the
demands of the current maritime century.'

Bruce B. Stubbs, SES, *Director Navy Strategy and Strategic Concepts,*
The Pentagon, Washington, DC

'*How to Grow a Navy* analyses the complex and sometimes irreconcilable problems of creating, maintaining and operating naval forces in an extremely clear and effective way. The author's deep expertise in maritime strategy and naval history, as well as his global reach and long experience of close interactions with the world's navies, big and small, give him a special authority. This apparently arcane subject is in fact a critical element of not only defence strategies but national security strategies as a whole.'

Rear Admiral James Goldrick, *Royal Australian Navy (ret)*

'Professor Geoffrey Till's understanding of maritime power is essential reading and has inspired navy and coast guard leaders around the world to build naval forces for cooperation and security, providing prosperity and safety for their countries. Through history he asks the question: why do nations need a navy? In today's "blue century", the sea remains important for almost any country's security and prosperity and the quest for the blue commons will be a "heritage for all" or increasingly a frontier in great power competition.'

Lars Saunes, *Professor/Rear Admiral (ret) Chief of the Royal Norwegian Navy*

How to Grow a Navy

This book examines the large but neglected topic of the development of maritime power from both a historical and a contemporary point of view.

Navies have never been more important than they are now, in a century becoming, as widely expected, increasingly and profoundly maritime. The growing competition between China and Russia with the United States and its allies and partners around the world is essentially sea-based. The sea is also central to the world's globalised trading system and to its environmental health. Most current crises are either sea-based or have a critical maritime element to them. What happens at sea will help shape our future. Against that background, this book uses both history and contemporary events to analyse how maritime power and naval strength have been, and are being, developed. In a reader-friendly way, it seeks to show what has worked and what has not, and to uncover the recurring patterns in maritime and naval development which explain past, present and future success – and failure. It reflects on the historical experience of all navies, but in particular it poses the question of whether China is following the same pattern of naval development illustrated by Britain at the start of the 18th century, which led to two centuries of naval dominance.

This book will be of much interest to students of maritime power, naval studies and strategic studies, as well as to naval professionals around the world.

Geoffrey Till is Emeritus Professor of Maritime Studies at King's College London and Chairman of the Corbett Centre for Maritime Policy Studies. Once Dean of Academic Studies at the UK Joint Services Command and Staff College, he is the author of over 300 books, chapters and articles. He now holds the Dudley W. Knox Chair for Naval History and Strategy at the US Naval War College.

Cass Series: Naval Policy and History

Series Editor: Geoffrey Till

ISSN 1366-9478

This series consists primarily of original manuscripts by research scholars in the general area of naval policy and history, without national or chronological limitations. It will from time to time also include collections of important articles as well as reprints of classic works.

60 **Modern Maritime Piracy**
    Genesis, Evolution and Responses
    Robert C. McCabe

61 **Seapower**
    A Guide for the Twenty-First Century (Fourth Edition)
    Geoffrey Till

62 **Maritime Strategy and Sea Denial**
    Theory and Practice
    Milan Vego

63 **India-China Maritime Competition**
    The Security Dilemma at Sea
    Edited by Rajesh Basrur, Anit Mukherjee, and TV Paul

64 **Chinese Maritime Power in the 21st Century**
    Strategic Planning, Policy and Predictions
    Hu Bo

65 **Exercising Control of the Sea**
    Theory and Practice
    Milan Vego

66 **Navies in Multipolar Worlds**
    From the Age of Sail to the Present
    Edited by Paul Kennedy and Evan Wilson

67 **How to Grow a Navy**
    The Development of Maritime Power
    Geoffrey Till

For more information about this series, please visit: https://www.routledge.com/Cass-Series-Naval-Policy-and-History/book-series/CSNPH

How to Grow a Navy
The Development of Maritime Power

Geoffrey Till

LONDON AND NEW YORK

Cover image: © Getty Images

First published 2023
by Routledge
4 Park Square, Milton Park, Abingdon, Oxon OX14 4RN

and by Routledge
605 Third Avenue, New York, NY 10158

Routledge is an imprint of the Taylor & Francis Group, an informa business

British Library Cataloguing-in-Publication Data
A catalogue record for this book is available from the British Library

Library of Congress Cataloging-in-Publication Data
Names: Till, Geoffrey, author.
Title: How to grow a navy : the development of maritime power / Geoffrey Till.
Other titles: Development of maritime power
Description: Abingdon, Oxon ; New York : Routledge, [2023] | Series: Naval policy
& history | Includes bibliographical references and index. |
Identifiers: LCCN 2022012456 (print) | LCCN 2022012457 (ebook) | ISBN
9780367607975 (hardback) | ISBN 9780367607968 (paperback) | ISBN
9781003100553 (ebook)
Subjects: LCSH: Sea-power. | Sea-power--History. | Navies--Organization. |
Navies--History.
Classification: LCC VA10 .T538 2023 (print) | LCC VA10 (ebook) | DDC 359/
.03--dc23/eng/20220613
LC record available at https://lccn.loc.gov/2022012456
LC ebook record available at https://lccn.loc.gov/2022012457

ISBN: 978-0-367-60797-5 (hbk)
ISBN: 978-0-367-60796-8 (pbk)
ISBN: 978-1-003-10055-3 (ebk)

DOI: 10.4324/9781003100553

Typeset in Times New Roman
by MPS Limited, Dehradun

This book is dedicated to the sad absence of my late wife, Cherry and the very real presence of our three offspring (Simon, Philippa and Christopher plus their partners, Ruth, Chiff and Beth) and our four grandchildren (Barney, Martha, Violet and Elowen).

Contents

List of Illustrations   xi
Preface   xii
List of Abbreviations   xv

1 Maritime Matters   1

2 A Predisposition towards the Maritime?   19

3 Henry Maydman, His Context, Maritime Power and a Strategy
  of Means   45

4 The Vision Thing   60

5 Willing the Means: Establishing and Resourcing Strategic
  Priorities   81

6 Going Joint: The Maritime Mix   100

7 Establishing Naval Policy and Setting Strategy   121

8 All of One Maritime Company: The Search for Synergy   143

9 Coastguards and the Assertion of Maritime Authority   165

10 Naval Power: The Administrative Angle   186

11 Delivering a Navy's People   204

12 Designing the Fleet   230

13 Nothing Is for Ever: Maintaining the Fleet   259

14 A Conclusion with Chinese Characteristics   276

    Selected Bibliography   305
    Index   315

Illustrations

Figures

1.1	The Virtuous Circle of Maritime Power	3
2.1	The Framework for Maritime Power	20
2.2	The Island Chains	21
2.3	Power and Economics	38
3.1	Generating Maritime Power	50
8.1	Unit Cost and Complexity	151
8.2	Chinese Fishing Objectives	161
11.1	The Levels of PME	221
12.1	The Battlefleet 1924	241
12.2	A Matrix of Time and Mission	248
13.1	Naval Cost Distribution	265
13.2	The Naval Life Cycle	266
13.3	A Battle System	270

Preface

It all began, one rainy day, in the library of the ancient Cathedral of Salisbury in the county of Wiltshire, England. On a previous visit, I had noticed, quite by chance, that they unexpectedly had a copy of Henry Maydman's book, *Naval Speculations,* published in 1691. Having only vaguely heard of it, I resolved one day to go back and read it. It rained heavily the day I chose and caused a widespread electricity outage in much of Salisbury, including the Cathedral. Nonetheless, the Archivist Librarian, Emily Naish, was waiting for me in the North Porch as arranged and she conducted me to the Cathedral Treasury which had its own energy supply and so I settled down to read it, mini-laptop in hand.

The language was frequently a challenge, if often hilarious. It didn't take me long, though, to realise that *Naval Speculations* was a book of real substance. Maydman was concerned not with what England should do with the Royal Navy, or what sort of war it should prepare for. He was much more interested in how its Navy should be developed and maintained. Implicitly he was making the basic point that a navy's operational effectiveness in the field of battle depended absolutely on how well it was prepared and supported at home. He also grasped the need to take a wider view of this support. His canvas wasn't merely naval; he was as concerned about the broader maritime scene. He had very definite ideas about what needed to be done in the process of growing the navy that England needed.

Then I realised that, stripped of its arcane language and references, Maydman was dealing with universals. He was looking at issues in the development of maritime power and the growth and maintenance of navies that spanned both time and individual countries. For all their historical uniqueness, all navies have faced, and still do, the sort of challenges he was writing about in his own inimitable way. By the end of a long day, with more to come, the idea behind this book was conceived. It would be a review of the past, present and future development of maritime power, with a special focus on the growth and maintenance of navies as part of that power, taking Maydman as a guiding inspiration. Given the state of the world today, it could hardly be more topical.

Four anonymous reviewers at Routledge gave the project their blessing although one hinted that its scope was ambitious, perhaps to the point of lunacy. It didn't take me long to realise how right he or she was. A book, taking the development or maritime power and the growth of navies as its theme, that aims to cover all of naval history as well as review the current and future of the maritime world certainly doesn't want for a demanding agenda. But at least it makes no claim to being the kind of authoritative meta maritime history such as David Abulafia's deeply impressive *The*

Boundless Ocean.[1] Nor does it aim to provide a strategy for the development of navies and maritime power, to be set alongside the likes of Mahan and Corbett. Neither is it a work of deep analysis of any particular navy or period. Instead it is an effort at synthesis, a tentative review of an enormous topic of absolute importance. Taking a phrase from Maydman's own book, it is an attempt at building a cottage where others might afterwards be able to construct a mansion.[2]

Even so, as I darted about from navy to navy and time to time, I needed the help of innumerable people, and this is the place to acknowledge them. First has to be Emily Naish, the Librarian at Salisbury Cathedral that rainy day. In a sense, it's all her fault. Then come my special colleagues at the US Naval War College, especially John Hattendorf, Evan Wilson, Craig Symonds, Peter Dutton, John Kuehn, Cdr Christopher Green (Chilean Navy) and 'J' Dancy. I inflicted early drafts on them and treasured their responses. From the wider Newport community John Maurer, Anna Davis, and Bruce Ellerman all helped in their various ways, usually without realising it. Once a student, then a colleague Lt Col Aaron Bright, helped me with countless illustrations and much encouragement. Ryan Kelley, U.S. Coast Guard was a great source of material help as well.

Elsewhere, in the United States, long-term colleagues Peter Swartz and Bruce Stubbs supplied me with endless material and general inspiration about the contemporary scene, as did Paul Kennedy at Yale, while Patrick Bratton reminded me usefully of the pioneering work of the Indian navalist P.M. Panikkar. In Singapore my colleagues at the Rajaratnam School of International Studies (RSIS), especially Jane Chan, Kwa Chong Guan, John Bradford, Anit Mukherjee and Zhang Hongzhu provided much support, while Mohd Nizam Basiron and Ian Storey helped from outside. The insights of Steve Raaymaker and Admiral Tim Barrett (former Chief of the Royal Australian Navy) on the prospects and problems of taking the wider maritime view were salutary. Brian Farrell, Malcolm Murfett and Fumhito Yamamoto from the National University in Singapore were a great source of historical help, especially on the Malaya campaign. Above all, in some ways, there was the endless inspiration and great friendship provided by the sadly departed Commodore Sam Bateman, whose loss is a tragedy for all who knew him. The remembered inspirations of all my colleagues at the UK Command and Staff College – my old stamping ground – were always in the background. The same applies to my many visits to many navies over the years; all different in countless ways, but the same in others, not least in their never-ending hospitality. I would also like to acknowledge the help of Admiral Claudio Macedo (Brazilian Navy), Col Todd Fredericks, Christopher O'Dea, Richard Longworth and John Pay.

Sarah Kirchberger's pioneering work on the modern Chinese navy, naval engineering expertise and generosity in supplying me with material were tremendously helpful. I am particularly grateful for permission to use some of the illustrations in her admirable book.[3] My son Christopher was helpful on the environmental side of things and was unwittingly inspirational in taking me to the Orkneys, a place dripping with maritime endeavour and Viking memorials.

Students never really believe it when they are told that teaching is essentially a two-way process in which the lecturer's ideas are also refined by exposure, but so it is. I owe a lot to my students at Newport who bravely volunteered to take my 'How to Grow a Navy' Elective and so who were in a sense present at the creation and whether they knew it or not helped shape the project. In a similar fashion, my students over the years from 2006 in Singapore both at the RSIS and the SAFTI Military Institute contributed a great deal and so did the many staff and students from all manner of European navies who assembled every year at the Belgian Defence Academy for a workshop on maritime strategy. The questions they asked and the points they made as real-world practitioners were invaluable. It is invidious to pick out particular students from of an inspirational bunch but I particularly need to acknowledge the help and ideas of Andy Rhodes and Jon Welch for their insights into Chinese naval experience and D Max Jones' for his engaging enthusiasm on defence innovation. The practical help of Ryan Kelley, US Coast Guard greatly eased the burden. Lt Cdr Matthijs Ooms, Royal Netherlands Navy was a reminder of just how bright these people are.

I began this preface by acknowledging my debt to one library but must include my special debt to another. When the Covid lockdown struck I was staying at Ocean View on Bellevue Avenue, Newport, the then home for the last century of the very hospitable Dick family. During those long months, before I bolted back to the UK, I was blessed by the library, with its legion of maritime books, they had accumulated over the years that I could use as I wished. That enforced period of concentration providentially got me off to the best of starts on this project.

Of course, none of these people is responsible for any egregious mistakes I have made in this book. The views expressed are mine and should not be taken to represent those of any official authority with which I am associated. Of course, responsibility for any mistakes and misjudgements that follow are mine alone.

Notes

1 Abulafia, David, *The Great Sea: A Human History of the Mediterranean* (Oxford: University Press, 2011).
2 Maydman, Henry, *Naval Speculations,* 116.
3 Kirchberger, Sarah, *Assessing China's Naval Power: Technological Innovation, Economic Constraints and Strategic Implications* (Heidelberg: Springer, 2015).

Abbreviations

ASW	Antisubmarine Warfare
BRI	(Chinese) Belt and Road Initiative
CCG	China Coast Guard
CMC	(Chinese) Central Military Commission
CIMSEC	Center for International Maritime Security
DWP	Defence White Paper
EEZ	Exclusive Economic Zone
GDP	Gross Domestic Product
IT	Information Technology
LPD	Landing Platform Dock
MDIB	Maritime Defence Industrial Base
MLEA	Maritime Law Enforcement Agency
MOD	Ministry of Defence
NATO	North Atlantic Treaty Organisation
NPP	(US) Naval Planning Process
NSC	National Security Council
O&M	Operations and Management
OT&E	Operational Testing and Evaluation
PME	Professional Military Education
PLAN	(Chinese) Peoples Liberation Army Navy
RCN	Royal Canadian Navy
SOE	State Owned Enterprise
SRF	(Russian) Strategic Rocket Force
SSN	Nuclear Propelled Submarine
SSBN	Ballistic Missile Firing SSN
STUFT	Ships Taken Up From Trade
UAV	Unmanned Aerial Vehicle
UNCLOS	UN Convention on the Law of the Sea

1 Maritime Matters

1.1 Introduction: Why Maritime Power Matters

For centuries developing maritime power and growing navies has had its advocates , many of whom have suspected that there's more to it than building a few ships and drafting in some fisherman and soldiers to operate them. Exploring what it takes to grow a navy was the central theme of Henry Maydman's long-neglected *Naval Speculations* in 1691. Tellingly though, its full title (long even for the customs of the time), was *Naval Speculations and Maritime Politicks, being a modest and brief discourse of the Royal Navy of England, of its Oeconomy and Government: and a Projection for an everlasting Seminary of Seamen by a Royal Maritime Hospital.* This shows that, apart from clearly needing the guiding hand of a literary agent, Maydman realised if you wanted to grow a navy you needed to understand and work with the domestic and international context in which it was to operate. The context posed problems to be overcome as well as opportunities to be exploited. The context helped shape the navy but the reverse was equally true. The two shouldn't be separated and had to be developed together. Accordingly, Maydman wanted to make his points about both.

His recommendations and his context will be reviewed in more detail in Chapter 3, but broadly he had in mind what a much later Chief of Navy would call a 'national enterprise.'[1] Developing maritime power, Maydman said, 'was of such consequence that the very Welfare of the Politick Body of this nation does hang upon it' and those responsible '...require Help of all People of the Nation.'[2] This unity of effort meant properly developing and exploiting all sectors of the country's maritime economy, having a navy, being clear about what it was for and efficient in its development and direction. He insisted on high standards of performance in everyone involved in growing the navy, from top to bottom and discussed their various roles in detail. He had a lot to say about the supply and administration of the navy, about the running of the dockyards, about the treatment of the navy's people and about fleet design. If all this was properly done, Britain ('our island') would have its rightful '... Dominion ... in these Northern and Western Seas from the Baltick to Cape Finister'[3]; peace and prosperity would surely follow.

What clearly drove Maydman was his sense of how important what he called the 'maritime affair' was to his own country and his own times. Nonetheless his recommendations transcend his time and place because the incentives to develop maritime interests and power and to grow the navies these need are universal; maritime power matters everywhere and always has.

K.M. Panikkar was another such advocate of the development of maritime power, 250 years nearer our own time. Panikkar was a leading Indian historian, public servant

DOI: 10.4324/9781003100553-1

and influential geo-strategic thinker. Although he delved much less into the mechanics of exactly how to do it, Panikkar, like Maydman, was convinced that his country needed to develop maritime power – as it approached the resumption of its independence, before, during and after the Second World War. That sovereignty had been lost when Alburquerque and the Portuguese had turned up on the Malabar coast in the early 16th Century. 'India,' Panikkar wrote in his first book *India and the Indian Ocean*, 'never lost her independence till she lost the command of the sea in the first decade of the 16th century.'[4] From then on, India had not been in charge of its own destiny. For hundreds of years there had been a beneficial Indo-Pacific trading system of free and open trading connections, linking the Persians and the Arabs to the West and the Chinese and Southeast Asians to the East. Indian merchants and mariners from the south of the country especially Kerala (where Panikkar grew up) were in the very centre of the system, and benefitted accordingly. No one actually sought to 'command' the sea but everyone wanted to use it for the common benefit.

The arrival of the powerful Europeans, who *were* interested in ideas of 'command' disrupted all this. Increasingly, access to the resources of the sea and its use for commerce was now subject to foreign approval and protection. Since Panikkar wrote, modern historians have shown that in fact the Europeans were in no position actually to bludgeon themselves ashore; initially they largely operated with the guarded consent of local potentates.[5] Nonetheless for local rulers, an ominous direction of travel had been set, which resulted from the mid-18th Century onwards in their losing sovereignty, and many of the earlier benefits they had derived from unimpeded trade in a largely un-commanded ocean. Panikkar recognised that the clock couldn't simply be pushed back and that concepts of 'command' were here to stay. To reverse the disadvantages, India needed to develop maritime power, in a manner perhaps reminiscent of the glory days of the Chola sea-based empire.

The problem was that sea-based invaders weren't India's only problem. The country's sovereignty in the past had been threatened from land-based invaders as well. Moreover, the British, secure in their command of the Indian Ocean from the mid-18th Century onwards, had also been inclined to focus on northern land-based threats to British India particularly in the era of the 'Great Game' against Russia. Their successors, Indian leaders pushing for independence, had largely inherited such habits of thought. Since then, the country's differences with Pakistan and China (and also continuing concerns about internal security) have further reinforced these more continental pre-occupations.

Panikkar of course was well aware of this. 'During its 5000 years of history,' he wrote,

> India, like China, has been conquered many times by invasions from the land side. But in the case of both, such conquests, though they led to temporary convulsions, only ended in the assimilation of the conqueror in the general pattern of the local civilization.

Sea-based threats to sovereignty were much more serious. 'Control from the side of the sea is different,' he pointed out.

> It operates as a stranglehold especially when, as in the case of India, as a result of geographical factors, the country's prosperity is dependent almost exclusively on

sea trade. The history of the last three centuries has shown that any power which has unquestioned mastery of the sea and strength to sustain a land campaign can hold the Empire of India, monopolize her trade and exploit her unlimited resources.[6]

India, he concluded accordingly, had to develop its maritime interests and the power to protect them. Without these capacities, India would never be prosperous or safe.

Indeed the sea was, and remains, important for almost any country's security and prosperity. It offered then and offers now vast marine resources – fish, oil, gas and who knows what else. It is by far the principal means by which most of the world's all-important trade is conducted. Not surprisingly these two basic attributes of the sea have resulted in the substantial 'blueing' of the world's economies, as more and more countries seek to take greater advantage of the opportunities it offers. Partly for such reasons, countries are increasingly aware of the implications of all this for their sovereignty, and in the case of archipelagic nations like the Philippines and Indonesia for their basic national integrity.

The extent of a country's maritime trade is usually closely related to the strength of a country's naval forces. Associated ships, seamen and ports can contribute directly to naval power, the social attitudes and the financial infrastructure that go with them doing so indirectly. Navies on the other hand help defend the conditions for trade and protect it at sea when necessary. As is explained in the next chapter, the result is a virtuous circle (Figure 1.1).

Trade needs and makes possible the maritime resources that help develop navies. Navies provide the condition in which trade can flourish thereby facilitating more advantageous trade – and so the circle continues – at least until interrupted from outside.

While trade requires the free use of the sea, the importance of exploiting its resources leads some to think of it in the same way as they do the land – to 'territorialise' it. Increasingly countries seem to regard their bits of the sea as part of the

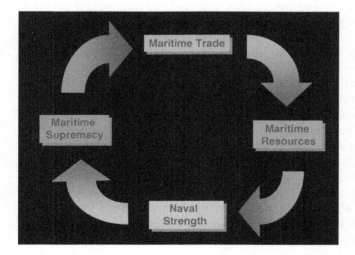

Figure 1.1 The Virtuous Circle of Maritime Power.

Source: Self-generated.

homeland.[7] Hence, the argument goes, the increased urge to monitor what goes on at sea and, if necessary, to control its malign aspects particularly in the varying shape of sea-based crime and marine pollution.[8] Hence also the tendency to set new boundaries, to fence in the previously unenclosed, to assert control over hitherto disregarded islets and other marine features. Potentially at least this could lead to substantial tensions with those who, instead, think of the ocean as free and open, owned by no one but as a common heritage available to all.

Over all these characteristics of maritime power, there also looms, as Maydman, Panikkar, Alfred Thayer Mahan, Sir Julian Corbett and many others have reminded us, its military consequence – 'hard' rather than 'soft' security. It is principally here that navies as a usually critical component of maritime power make their appearance. This explains why these earlier advocates of maritime power thought it so important to grow and nurture naval forces. The capacity to control the sea through the operation of effective navies can be, and frequently is, a major source of military power and strategic influence. Control of the sea, Mahan, Corbett and the rest proclaimed, allows your adversary's trade, homeland and territorial interests to be attacked and yours defended and expanded.

Accordingly what happens at sea can, and frequently does, have decisive consequences ashore. In *The Leverage of Sea Power* Colin Gray shows how this has repeatedly worked even against countries with fewer maritime interests and vulnerabilities. Countries with strong navies could seek to exhaust their more land-bound enemies financially, or blockade them from the supplies they needed. Being strong at sea meant they could engage in large scale operations on land and/or support allies in doing so. They could launch peripheral attacks from the sea, conquer their adversaries' overseas territory or forge continental alliances. '[S]uperior sea power,' he concludes in this classic formulation, 'has provided leverage critical for success in strategy and statecraft.'[9]

1.2 Developing Maritime Power: The Naval Revolution

Because maritime power is so advantageous, there are obvious incentives for countries to develop it as much as possible. In its naval form, the process can be slow and steady or, alternatively so rapid as to amount to the much-discussed concept of a 'naval revolution' that affected many navies in the 16th and 17th Centuries.[10] By no means was this restricted to the navies of Europe. For example, the Imjin war of 1592–1598, arguably the 'First Great East Asian War,' began with a massive Japanese invasion of Korea by an armada of 700 ships and a force of some 200,000 soldiers. The subsequent war between Ming China, Korea and Japan provides a spectacular case study of how the three navies responded to new technology in the shape of fire-arms, cannon and armoured ships, and how the associated complexities were handled and directed, financially, administratively, logistically and operationally.[11] Indeed, in its illustration of the way that the belligerents consciously sought to arrange detailed military costings, raise and train up their soldiers and sailors, equip their fleets with the latest technology, support their forces logistically and plan their campaigns while learning from the mistakes of the past, this ferocious war provides excellent examples of many of the ways of developing maritime and naval power addressed later in this book. Above all, perhaps, the war demonstrated the need to integrate maritime effort[12] – a major theme in what follows. This should be no surprise; the development of naval and maritime power, after all, is not an exclusively Western phenomenon and never has been.

In the classic case of the English and then British Royal Navy, however, it was a revolution, in that it radically and permanently changed the development and maintenance of the Navy, but it took place, in fits and starts, over the 150 years or so since the days of Henry VIII and 'the heroic years' of 1585–1594 under Queen Elizabeth.[13] Maydman's time – the 1690s – was certainly one of the periods of rapid advance, but so was the age of the Commonwealth, the 1650s, when the necessary reforms brought about before and during the English Civil War were consolidated. In his laments about the state of the navy in 1691, accordingly, Maydman may well have been over pessimistic about its real potential.

During this long period the Navy grew in the number, size and armament of the fleet, in its personnel and the professionalism of its officer-corps. It became a standing state-maintained fleet with a permanent body of officers and administrators, not one improvised for the occasion by the ruler of the time. Its building, supply and maintenance, though never perfect, became much more reliable and effective – so much so in fact that it was able to maintain a significant, long-term forward combat presence off the coast of Portugal and the Netherlands in the 1650s, for example.[14] Its procedures, both administrative and operational, became standardised, the latter in the form of the Royal Navy's 'Fighting Instructions.' Even by Maydman's day, all this resulted in England's having a major strategic advantage over its competitors – most of the time.

Probably the key element in the Royal Navy's coming of age was the slow and unsteady process by which the major elements of government in England came together to agree a sufficient and long-term scheme by which the Navy could be adequately financed over the years. In effect, this meant Parliament's accepting that one way or another it would have to own a responsibility which it had hitherto regarded as the King's business.[15] In short, the Royal Navy's future ultimately depended on a permissive, even constructive, domestic context. In this, at least, it was no different from any other navy.

Given the success and importance of the development of, in particular, European naval and maritime power at this time, the obvious question that arise are, how was this done, and to what extent is this experience applicable to the navies and countries of the 21st Century? To a large extent this is what this book attempts to explore.

1.3 Maritime Power: Its Propensity to Decline

Nonetheless, Colin Gray also shows that maritime power is far from unquenchable or even the only show in town. Strong navies fall as well as rise. Maritime power often seems cyclical. This helps explain why people like Maydman and Panikkar so often hark back to what they at least imagine to have been a better naval past. Only by following his recommendations, thought Maydman, could England, '... reassume her ancient Glory and prowess in her Naval Affairs, ... before it be past recovery.'[16] The problem seems to be that while, in the first instance, it may be easy for navalists and others of a maritime persuasion to urge the development of maritime power for the benefits just enumerated, it is also true that in some ways maritime power incorporates the seeds of its own decline.

Several things point in this direction. If, like most forms of military power, navies are regarded as a form of insurance, continued success may easily make the later payments of the premium seem less necessary. Worse, the premium is high because navies are expensive. They cannot 'live off the land' like armies were long able to. As capital-intensive organisations, their costs tend to be higher than usual rates of inflation; meeting those costs becomes increasingly burdensome. In more recent times, some of these higher costs come from the need to respond to new military-technical developments, such as airpower, that seem to challenge a navy's capacity to keep the sea; they may even offer cheaper non-naval ways of exerting control over it.

Exactly how burdensome all this naval effort actually feels depends in part on the degree of a society's general sea-mindedness. Here the problem is that many sea trades are dangerous, involve long periods away from home and are not particularly well paid. Accordingly, when they can, mariners seem often to defect to the more comfortable and remunerative occupations ashore that their original maritime enterprise made possible. The sea-mindedness of a country declines in consequence. If, as some historians argue, there is a connection between maritime power and liberal democracy that goes all the way back to ancient Athens,[17] then this decline in sea sympathy can have profound resource consequences (in money and people) for navies. Democratic governments will want instead to cater for their voters' competing preoccupations with the support of health and social care, education and local amenities.

At the higher level, the more successful a maritime country becomes on the world stage, the more likely it is to pick up commitments overseas, many of which though 'a mighty help to our Navigation'[18] come with expensive responsibilities ashore. Britain, so often said to be the quintessentially maritime country, in fact is a classic example of this, as will be seen later.[19]

The Athenians came across the same problem as they set up colonies, accepted the responsibilities that went with them, over-reached themselves strategically with an expedition against Sicily and ended up being roundly defeated at sea by Sparta at Aegospotami in 405 BCE.

The Vikings, or 'Northmen,' are another good example of this. Consummate mariners, explorers and adventurers, these sea-borne raiders came in search of plunder from richer, more settled lands in western and eastern Europe. They slaughtered priests and anyone else who got in their way, burnt and destroyed monasteries, churches and settlements, taking away everything worth stealing, including captives who they ransomed back or sold to Muslims in Spain and North Africa in exchange for silver. Later they developed over-wintering bases, often islands, convenient for more sustained local campaigns, rather than mere raids, of plunder. Their activities were so terrifying they were able to exact tribute from softer more advanced settlements and kingdoms in 'protection rackets' on a massive scale.[20]

And yet, despite this awesome reputation, Scandinavian Vikings increasingly looked for cheap and available land. The called it *landnam,* 'the taking of the land' through conquest. The fertile fields of England, southern Scotland, Ireland, France, even the Orkneys were a great temptation to people otherwise wedged inhospitably between mountains and the sea, or having to deal with the boggy ground of the Denmark of the time. With rents and produce, land would bring them much longer-term wealth than they could get from sporadic plundering. Before long, they settled down as farmers, assimilated with their victims, focussed more on trading, turned to urban life, began building kingdoms, states, even empires. Surprisingly early, they began converting into Christianity the religion they had once preyed upon.[21]

Their transition to a less sea-centred life was illustrated by changes in the Vikings' concept of the ship. Originally, ships were spiritual and secular symbols, illustrative of their owners' military power and privileged status, central to their burial routines and the ferocious poetry of their sagas.[22] Gradually, ships lost the characteristic and distinctive features that transmitted these not-so-subtle messages. They become more workmanlike, beamier, much more like the trading cogs of their southern neighbours. Ships were now a means of transport and trade, not the centre of Scandinavian life and culture.[23]

Vikings, though had always been a mixture of land and sea centric activity. Especially in areas of Scandinavia good for farming (such as Ostland in Norway where land was plentiful compared to Vestland where it wasn't[24]) agriculture was the main activity; raiding as 'warrior-farmers' was more of an occasional bonus for some.[25] Moreover, most of their fighting, whether as raids or as full-scale wars with others and amongst themselves, was done on land. Scandinavians also maintained normal sea-borne trading relations with their neighbours, and further afield, before and during the main raiding periods. This continued, even increased, especially with their exploitation of North Sea herrings and cod, from their role in the Hanse trading system and in more modern times from the carrying trade and the development of the offshore oil industry. The sea, in short, though less central than it was in the Viking hey-day, is still important to Scandinavia.

The Spanish were altogether much less maritime in outlook. Although they built up perhaps 16th Century Europe's biggest merchant marine,[26] it relied on Portuguese and Dutch shipping, and on Catalonia, the Basque Country and Genoa for navigation and skilled mariners. Getting the necessary crews was always difficult.[27] Recognising the problem, Spain set up the *Casa de la Contratación* to train its navigators but there were never enough of them. Spanish culture was based on sophisticated urban life not the coasts, nor the sea. When the Spanish heartland, Castile, prepared itself for maritime endeavour and succeeded in creating one of Europe's biggest overseas empires, its approach was naval rather than maritime.[28] Nonetheless, the Monarchy (as Spain and its empire referred to itself) did turn itself into a substantial maritime power of sorts, and one that could threaten, when need be, the more obviously maritime English and Dutch.

But again, Spain's maritime power showed that same tendency to dissipate, even in the narrower naval field. Operating in the Tropics meant exposing ships' crews to exotic disease, their wooden ships to rot, 'the rank growth of weed' and the depredations of the teredo worm. Accidents, disasters and hostile attacks were commonplace. The business case for most commercial enterprises was sketchy in the extreme, and fortunes were lost as well as won. Before the end of the 16th Century, the illusory wealth derived from bullion was largely swallowed up by the increasing expense of getting, protecting and distributing it. The acquisition of extensive territory overseas, required substantial investment in an extensive administration centralised on Seville and Madrid, plus significant legal and religious duties for the new overlords.

Investment in mining was needed and the cultural preference for living in large towns and cities generated a need for the production of the foodstuffs that would keep them supplied. In areas such as Chile's central valley, the Spanish settled into a farming life based on the *encomienda* system. Elsewhere, the limitations of domestic agriculture meant such supplies had to be shipped in from other parts of the empire or even from Europe. The empire was voracious in its demand for people, creating concerns about possible demographic problems in metropolitan Spain. All these were land-based preoccupations, not maritime ones. Worse, they were expensive, and strained a metropolitan treasury already distorted by excessive reliance on the import of bullion since this created inflation and reduced incentives for the state to support a balanced economy at home.

Of course, there was a two-way, sea-based link between Spain and its overseas empire. Food and manufacturers manufactured goods (many from France and the Low Countries) and, above all, slaves were sent to the Empire, bullion and other exotica returned. This all had to be defended by the creation of a substantial navy because Spain's policy in Europe, its apparent wealth and its vulnerability made it many enemies. The maritime interdependency of Spain and South America offered hostile naval forces and privateers the chance of inflicting real damage on their adversary's war economy while making a fortune on the side. And the Caribbean with its cloud of cays and islands was a particularly difficult place in which to try to defend maritime shipping. Spain found the task of trying to do so extremely onerous, and, again, very expensive.

Spain's maritime decline was marked not so much by the occasional disastrous loss of the bullion fleet and all the other perils of the sea which afflicted its maritime connections but more by the steady decline in the volume of that traffic across that sea. In turn this increased the independency of the Spanish of the Empire from the peninsular Spaniards of the Monarchy. This had been a factor from the start, given the venality of the administrative system and the inevitable practical problems of running a distant empire when an answer to a question asked of Madrid might take years to arrive. There naturally developed the tendency to go through Madrid's motions, to offer 'obedience without compliance.' As a result, there was literally a world of difference between what Madrid said, and what actually happened on the ground. In due course even protestations of obedience became increasingly rare, a trend culminating in the independence revolts of early 19th-Century South America.[29]

The Spanish example shows that the colonies which Alfred Thayer Mahan made so much of, as a foundation for maritime power can be at best a fairly short-term one. They can easily become a wasting asset as the expense of administering and protecting them grows and as the locals throw off what they increasingly see as the yoke of imperialism, whether as indigenous peoples anxious to recover lost freedoms (as in the Indian sub-continent and Africa) or colonial societies increasingly impatient with oppressive and uncomprehending rule from afar (North and South America) – or as a mixture of the two.

Spain's successors in South America had the same problem. In the War of the Pacific 1879–1884, Chile, largely by virtue of its naval strength, wrested the resource-rich Tarapaca and Atacama areas from Peru and Bolivia. These had to be defended by an expanded army, which grew to become a major factor. Paradoxically Chile's maritime success made it less maritime than it was before.

These illustrations of maritime 'decline' show it can be the consequence not of failure, but of maritime success in improving a country's prospects. It makes possible a better, less stressful, less maritime, life for the people. It can even lead to major naval reductions. Illustrating the point, Cnut, the Danish King of England had a standing naval force of 40 major warships at the combative start of his reign, but once it was secure, ended it having just 16.[30] His Anglo-Danish successors, in consequence, stood less chance of resisting the subsequent attacks that culminated in the final conquest of his realm by the Normans in 1066.

These sometimes gloomy prognostications for the long-term prospects of maritime power, help explain the anxious tone of many navalists and others of a maritime persuasion as, hoping to avert it, they rail against what they see as maritime neglect and decline. They know, all too well, that countries have often been unable or, worse, unwilling to take sustainable long-term advantage of the opportunities that the ocean presents. Sometimes this is simply the result of inattention, often the consequence of apparently even more pressing imperatives ashore and, occasionally, of strategic defeat and other geo-strategic convulsions beyond their control.

These anxieties are reinforced by their view that navies, far from being of less strategic significance in the future, as it was quite fashionable to argue some years ago, will in fact be more and important than ever. 'A naval century is upon us,' says Robert Kaplan, 'in keeping with an era of globalization that depends on safe and secure sea lines of communication for container shipping. But nobody should assume it will be peaceful.' If the future is indeed to be maritime and naval, missing the boat, or even deliberately deciding not to board it, will therefore have dire consequences.[31] This is likely to be as true for smaller maritime powers as it is for larger ones. Arguments for the enhancement of maritime power are by no means confined to countries with the potential for big navies.[32]

In recent years the United States, however, has seen something of a debate about the nature of maritime decline, elegant or otherwise, what causes it and what it might mean for the country and for the world. And, of course, what should be done about it.[33] Much depends on what is meant by the word 'decline.' It can simply mean a reducing capacity to provide the resources needed to protect existing interests; this can be aggravated by the rise of a potential adversary threatening those interests. Before 1941, this was Japan, and afterwards the Soviet Union.

More recently, anxieties have been expressed about the rise of the Chinese Navy,[34] relative to the US Navy and its capacity to meet its commitments. These anxieties are reinforced by the extent to which navies are seen as indicators of strategic weight as we proceed deeper into a probably more maritime future. 'The 21st Century is a Maritime Century,' says one Chinese author quoted by Geoffrey Gresh, 'Facing the Maritime Century's call, the Chinese nation's desire for resurgence has never been as strong, and its maritime connection has never been more inseparable.'[35] Other Chinese observers more cautiously emphasise that China's adverse circumstances mean that any such decline in US naval power will be relative rather than absolute.[36] China will share maritime power with the United States, rather than usurp it. Either way there can be little doubt that averting its possible naval decline has moved well up the American agenda.

In such circumstances sea power advocates take their task to be one of three. Either they advocate the development of maritime interests and power for the first time, or they seek to rescue them from a period of actual or prospective neglect. In many cases, however, they merely seek to persuade governments and societies to carry on in the relentless task of sustaining the maritime interests and power that they already have. In all three cases, the arguments and recommendations are broadly similar and will be reviewed in the following chapters.

1.4 Some Terms of the Debate

But, first of all, it seems advisable to outline a few of the terms that the advocates of maritime power constantly use and how in general they are understood. Writing about the sea is bedevilled by language, because people using the same words sometimes mean rather different things by them. Conversely, people writing about the same things use different words to describe them. Moreover, this leaves out the extra complexities brought about by the need to translate from one language to another. There is no right or wrong way to use sea-related words. All we can do is to lay out in advance how the words are going to be used in any particular piece of work – and to keep it as simple as possible.

In almost any debate about the development of 'maritime power,' three concepts and definitional challenges quickly surface. The first, most obviously, is what is meant by the word 'maritime,' when applied to a country. In this book at least, it will be used to cover any activity that is closely related to the sea. Thus it is most likely to include much more than the merely 'naval' since that term is usually limited to military rather than civilian concerns. A country's maritime interests can therefore range from the military-strategic to the economic and social, and everything in between. Non-naval maritime interests can, however, greatly contribute to naval strength as will be shown in the next chapter, and subsequently.

A country has not just maritime interests but maritime power if it can, to some degree at least, persuade others of the justice of its maritime interests or, if necessary defend them actively. This can be done by a variety of means, centred on a country's having the constabulary or military capability to enforce its views on the un-persuaded or unwilling. The latter might be competing countries or merely criminals with different views of the best way forward. In short, having maritime power means being able to protect your maritime interests.

Moreover, maritime power and sea power are synonymous; they mean the same thing. Broadly both relate to the capacity to affect the behaviour of other people by what is done at or from the sea. Making use of Corbett's approach,[37] a country for which the sea 'is…a substantial factor' and which can exercise sea power or maritime power strategically may be considered a 'sea power' (confusingly this can be either one or two words!) – or a maritime power. Generally, in this book, the simpler phraseology preferred by Sir Julian Corbett – maritime power – will be used.[38]

Being maritime and being a maritime power are therefore different except in that they are both related to the sea. Both are also matters of degree. They are relative concepts, not absolutes. Countries are more, or less, maritime in their interests, or more of less maritime in their power to defend those interests, than others. Mahan, Corbett and Henry Maydman too, were principally concerned with developing their country's maritime power *relative to others,* often arguing in fact that building up and protecting its maritime interests was obvious way of doing that.

The relativity of maritime power is also relevant to another perennial and frequently pointless debate – namely its juxtaposition against countries with principally non-maritime or 'continental' interests and power. All too often these are seen not as complements but as opposites. Countries should not be described in simple binary terms of being either 'maritime' or 'continental.' Such absolutes are purely notional 'ideals' (or theoretical possibilities) at opposite ends of the same spectrum. Normally, the two words are no more than crude shorthand labels for states that are individually more maritime than they are continental (or *vice versa*) and, in comparison, more or less maritime (or continental) than others. It is hard to conceive of a country anywhere in the world that has no maritime interests because it is totally unaffected by what happens at sea.

Some might point to the successive states in Mesoamerica, from the Olmecs to the Aztecs 'none of whom exploited its proximity to the sea to any significant degree' or maybe the Golden Hordes of Genghiz Khan who established a kind of globalisation based on horsepower rather sea power as examples of this.[39] Even if they partially justified this appellation they proved temporary exceptions to the rule. Under the Yuan dynasty, the latter rapidly morphed into a continental-maritime state that launched sea-based expeditions against Japan and Java, while the former eventually fell prey to someone else's maritime power.

It is even harder to imagine the contrary – an absolutely maritime state totally unaffected by what happens on land. It is all a matter of degree. Looking to its military dimension, Corbett goes on to maintain that what happens, or may happen, on land, is the ultimate decider of strategic outcomes, even for the most maritime of states – simply because that's where people live. 'Since men live upon the land and not upon the sea,' he famously pointed out,

> great issues between nations at war have always been decided – except in the rarest cases – either by what armies can do against your enemy's territory and national life, or else by fear of what the fleet makes it possible for your army to do.[40]

In short, sea power and land power go together since both can lead to the other. Maritime power can sustain land power, but the converse is equally true. Accordingly, countries have, and are, a relative mix of both.

'We commonly speak of Great Britain as the greatest sea-power' proclaimed Lord Curzon in 1908, 'forgetting that she is also the greatest land-power in the Universe.'[41]

Athens typifies the same thing. Although a *thalassocracy* – an empire based on the sea – it was far from being exclusively focussed on the more obviously maritime side of things. Trade and imported food and other supplies were crucial but they had to be protected not just by the navy but by the decidedly territorial Long Walls to Piraeus and by the deployment of the city's soldiers together with those of very necessary allies. 'We have to divide our attention,' reported Thucydides, 'between our navy and the many missions on which our troops are sent on land.'[42] Most Athenians made their living from the land, not the sea.[43] The 62,000 Athenians rowing the triremes at the battle of Salamis were mostly farmers.[44]

Countries are accordingly both maritime and continental; their preoccupations range across both dimensions. Many, naturally, will have more of the one than the other. So where phrases like 'the maritime powers' or 'land powers' are used the word 'principally' is generally to be understood as qualifying them, certainly when used as Colin Gray does, and also as in this book. The major aim of maritime advocacy is to increase the maritime component in a country's activity, but not to the point of exclusivity.

Another important issue is that a country's position on the maritime-continental spectrum is not fixed; instead its maritime interests and power vary over time and can be changed by design, argument and persuasive analysis as well as by long-term (in) attention or as a reaction to turbulent external circumstances. When discussing the development of maritime interests and power, it was just such analysis, argument and recommendation that Henry Maydman and his many successors were trying to provide.

Another concept sometimes encountered is that there are 'natural' or 'organic' sea powers, which operate under their own volition without the conscious direction from the top that characterises their opposite – the artificial sea power. The Vikings might be thought of as an example of this. Their 'maritimeness' welled up from below making them a proto state, in the classic formulation of Gerald Graham, 'whose security and very existence is rooted in the sea.'[45] In truth this is a dubious appellation despite its appeal to such luminaries as Admiral Herbert Richmond, and a dangerous one too if it is taken to mean that the development of maritime power doesn't need at least a degree of positive direction, or 'construction' as Andrew Lambert would put it.[46] Things generally go better when someone is in charge.

Finally, it seems worth emphasising that these issues do not arise solely in the case of the world's bigger navies. They apply with equal force to most of the smaller ones too, if often in very different ways because of the enormous diversity of 'small' and 'medium' navies through the ages. Small and medium navies are particularly amorphous categories[47] but one thing that both have in common is that their countries nearly all have maritime interests, incentives (if not the means) to develop more capacity to protect those interests and a continuing choice as to where they strike the balance between sea and land concerns. A glance at the published policy statements of smaller countries such as Albania or Sri Lanka demonstrate the width of their maritime interests.[48] The extent to which they can protect those interests will differ only in degree from that of the larger fry. Accordingly they will significantly feature in this book.

1.5 The Agenda: Profiting from the Past When Planning the Future

One of the things that drove Henry Maydman to write his book, was a strong sense that England's maritime interests, and its capacity to defend them, was in decline. The role of both in the country's past glories, especially in the age of Queen Elizabeth were in danger, he thought, of being forgotten. He made his recommendations with a view to helping the country recover from this, assuring its future prosperity and security. At the time, although Maydman had no way of knowing this, England, or Britain as it was soon to become, was teetering on the edge of maritime greatness. It was about to embark into a century in which it would rapidly become the dominating maritime power. Although severely challenged, particularly during the War of American Independence[49] and from the beginnings of the 20th Century, it only finally ceded this position to the United States halfway through the Second World War. Its naval dominance did much to shape today's world.

In large measure, Britain's maritime success was the result of the country following, if without realising it, the recommendations that Maydman delivered, or which can at least be inferred from his work. Most of the principles behind his recommendations would, however, seem to apply to any country and any navy at any time. Indeed, an unexpected conclusion that emerged in the course of preparing this review was their particular applicability to China since there seem to be so many apparently bizarre parallels between Britain as an emerging superpower of the 18th Century and China seeking to do likewise in the 21st. As will be shown, particularly in the last chapter of this book, China, too, seems to be becoming a thrusting, entrepreneurial country with a dynamic economy, a sense of threat and an increasing awareness of the maritime lessons of the past, particularly those that relate to the consequences of maritime neglect.

There are obvious differences too, of course. These parallels in fact will be one of the recurring themes of the book, although not its main preoccupation. Instead this is a book about the development of maritime power in general and, in particular, how navies are and have been grown and maintained.

As was admitted in the Preface, this is not, however, an attempt to design 'a strategy of means' of the sort to be discussed later, or to provide a detailed guide as to what should or should not be done. Given the huge variations in the conditions and circumstances that countries have faced and continue to face across the ages, and given also that the circumstances of each country at any particular time are unique, that would seem impossibly presumptuous. Instead it is an exploration of the issues involved, taking *Naval Speculations* as a rough guide of what to look out for. Experience, both historical and current, provides a rich quarry of ideas about this. It also delivers a huge number of possible illustrations for generic points that otherwise would seem unhelpfully abstruse and vague. In this, the book echoes Mahan, in believing that 'Historical instances, by their concrete force, are worth reams of dissertation.'[50] In their very substantial analysis of the maritime lessons of the past, the Chinese very evidently agree.[51]

What will hopefully emerge at the end of a process that might look to some as rather like a demented butterfly flitting through the ages from flower to flower, are some questions about recurring patterns in the maritime behaviour of states; the aim is more to uncover those questions rather than supply answers. Hopefully, that might offer points of helpful comparison if not guidance for those interested in the development of maritime interests and power, and the growth, maintenance and/or decline of navies.

The first such points of comparison are contextual and are addressed in the next chapter. This looks at the extent to which some countries have a natural predisposition towards the maritime through their geography, the nature of their society and government, the nature and shape of their economy and through their naval forces. It makes the point that much of this can be altered by changing circumstances or concrete action. It explores the extent to which the comparative 'maritimeness' of different countries can be measured.

Chapter 3, 'Henry Maydman, Maritime Power and a Strategy of Means,' takes the England of Henry Maydman's time and also his top-down, tiered, way of looking at maritime policy-making as a starting points. It addresses the role of a country's domestic and international context in shaping its need for, and views of, the sea. Navies both reflect and affect that context. In today's world, the drift into an era of enhanced great power competition seems at odds with the growing collective need for common action against such universal threats as climate change, pandemics and organised transnational crime. The resultant dilemmas of choice for maritime policy-makers and naval planners however, are far from new.

Chapter 4, 'The Vision Thing,' deals with attempts often at the highest level of government to make sense of all this by coming up with a maritime vision for the country. But the competing experience of Russia, Singapore, the Hanseatic league and Indonesia amongst others highlights the differences between top-down and bottom-up approaches to maritime development, suggesting a combination of both as the best way forwards. It underlines the point that navies need to be seen as part of the overall maritime package.

The next stage of the process, is moving from the wider definition of a country's maritime objectives down to the challenges of implementing them. In effect, this marks the transition from policy to strategy-making, from the definition of ends, to the consideration of ways and means. Chapter 5, 'Willing The Means: Establishing and Resourcing Priorities in National Strategy,' shows how in this process a country's maritime interests have to be integrated and resourced in a manner that fits all its other interests and responsibilities. Examples from ancient Greece, Britain and

20th-Century Germany show how difficult it is to set maritime development securely in a 'whole -of-nation' strategy. To prosper, the maritime case needs to be persuasively articulated.

Chapter 6, 'Going Joint,' narrows the field of enquiry down from the broadly maritime to the specifically military and so looks at the way in which the perspectives and needs of the naval service need to be balanced against those of the army, and these days, the airforce and still more recent forms of military power. Here the word 'maritime' embraces the contribution that such other services can make to a country's capacity to make use of the sea. The fact that maritime power is increasingly joint underlines the importance of getting the required 'unity of effort' from all the military services. A review of the experience of the early years of the Pacific War that started in 1941, and of the challenges faced by a variety of countries since, shows again how difficult this is. Various ways forward are identified.

Chapter 7, 'Establishing Naval Policy and Setting Strategy,' begins the specific re-view of the growth and maintenance of the naval service through the ages. It shows how prominent naval leaders such as Admirals Tirpitz of Germany, Gorshkov of Russia and Liu of China, approached the business of deciding objectives and im-plementing them – of deciding their objectives and setting the strategy to achieve them. The chapter makes the point that success usually requires success in advocacy too.

In their analysis of the Second World War some argue that the real battle was arguably less the grand encounters between each sides' deployed forces and more the production of military equipment and on the ability to move it to where it needed to be.[52] This un-derlines the point developed in Chapter 8, 'All of One Maritime Company,' that the growth of navies is largely dependent on the support of the rest of the maritime package, on the maritime defence industrial base, the merchant marine, the fishing community and so forth. Given this dependency, a holistic approach to what Maydman called the 'maritime affair' would seem to make sense, basically for the reasons he identified.

Chapter 9, 'Coastguards and the Assertion of Maritime Authority,' makes the point that maritime power depends on a country's ability to maintain order and assert its authority in its own waters and in areas where its vital maritime interests are involved. This will normally require Coastguard forces of various sorts operating alongside naval ones in that task. Usually neglected in the naval literature, their role especially in dealing with the lower reaches of maritime threat is crucial. Nor is this simply a modern preoccupation, despite the emphasis it is now given. Once again, a properly integrated maritime policy incorporating all these is called for.

Accounts of administrative procedures are often boring but that should not obscure their importance in the growth and maintenance of navies. This is dealt with in Chapter 10 'Naval Power: The Administrative Angle.' Ranging across almost the whole of naval experience, but with a particular focus on the British case, the chapter shows that it was essentially the existence of a permanent administrative system that allowed 'naval forces,' called up just for the duration of the latest emergency, to transition into standing 'navies.' In this chapter, a review of naval experience aims to tease out some of the ideal characteristics of effective naval administration. It singles out the ability to accommodate change and strategic uncertainty as being one of the most important measures of success.

Admirals nearly always say that people are their most important asset. Chapter 11, 'Delivering a Navy's People,' explores why this is so and, taking the post-war Royal Canadian Navy as an example, looks at some of the difficulties navies face in getting and retaining the people they need. A review of manpower policies in the galley-based navies of the Mediterranean perhaps unexpectedly throws up some of the ways in which navies have tried to solve this problem. The chapter ends with a review of the training requirements often identified as necessary for a navy's people.

The especially vexed and complicated issue of fleet design is explored in Chapter 12, 'Delivering a Balanced Fleet.' Fleet design is so challenging because it involves striking balances between different and often competing requirements. By definition, fleet design has to be future-orientated, but the long gestation period of modern warships makes it hard to deal with constant contextual change, not least when it comes in technological form. Although the chapter ranges widely over a long spread of naval experience, there is some focus on the approach of the modern-day US Navy, because they are more open about the process and its problems than most others. Nonetheless the problems they face usually generally challenge other navies too, and always have.

Historically, maintaining a fleet has often proved more demanding than building one in the first place. This is why the transition from temporary 'naval forces' to permanent 'navies' took so long. Chapter 13, 'Nothing is For Ever: Maintaining the Fleet,' shows why matching resources to commitments and sustaining readiness over time is so hard. In a way it exemplifies the natural tendency for maritime power to decay which was discussed earlier. The chapter explores the two ways that navies have sought to deal with this issue, firstly the conscious effort to sustain readiness over time, and, secondly, by making optimum use of the assets available. Over the ages, equivalent approaches have been necessary for the maintenance of ships and the navy's people.

Finally, Chapter 14, 'A Conclusion With Chinese Characteristics,' seeks to sum all this up by applying all the points made to the development of the modern Chinese navy. While Chinese spokespeople continually refer to the 'exceptionalism' of their approach to maritime power, this chapter shows that in large measure the Chinese have conformed very largely to the recurring patterns of behaviour exhibited by other navies of the time and before, although naturally with their own national twist. As such, the review seems generally to validate tentative conclusions arrived at in earlier chapters. Whether the new Chinese Navy will, in fact, be able to follow the same trajectory as Henry Maydman's Royal Navy, as seems quite possible, remains to be seen. Either way, the outcome will have profound consequences for the world's maritime future and so the answer to this question could turn out to be the most important of all.

If this is the book's agenda, then trying to locate recurring patterns is one of the main means of advancing it. Perhaps the most common pattern is the fact that for all countries maritime power declines as well as rises, either terminally in extreme cases or cyclically with alternating periods of growth and decay. In consequence, developing maritime power in the first place is one thing; maintaining it – or recovering it from a period of decline – is another, and in fact a far more common form of the phenomenon. Given the importance of the maritime dimension to a country's prosperity and security, its propensity to decline might well increase incentives for corrective action before it happens.

Success in the development of maritime power in the first place or in maintaining it afterwards, will depend on the ability to identify the factors helping or hindering it and to be able to do something about them. A British observer of the time, John Campbell, was fairly sure about what the real problem was for the Spanish. 'The weakness of the Spaniards is,' he wrote in 1747,

… the weakness of their government. There wants not people, there wants not a capacity of defence, if the governors and other royal officers were not so wanting in their duty, and did not thereby set so ill an example as corrupts and effeminates all who are subject to them.[53]

But gradually the rather more efficient French administrative procedures that Spain's new Bourbon rulers had brought with them, was a factor in a mild if temporary revival in the country's maritime fortunes in the 18th Century. In singling out such social and administrative issues, Campbell was pointing to just one explanation for a country's maritime success, or lack of it, but there are many others and these are all addressed in the next chapter on the constituents and elements of maritime power. All of them are important. All of them, to some degree, have shown themselves to be capable of improvement in the general cause of developing and maintaining maritime power.

Notes

1   Barrett, Barrett, Vice Admiral Tim, *The Navy and the Nation: Australia's Maritime Power in the 21st Century* (Melbourne: Melbourne University Press, 2017), 57–67.
2   Maydman, *Naval Speculations,* 52, 6.
3   Ibid, 233.
4   Panikkar, K.M., *India and the Indian Ocean: An Essay on the Influence of Sea Power on Indian History* (London: G. Allen & Co., 1945), 7.
5   For this see, Sharman, J.C., *Empires of the Weak* (Princeton: Princeton University Press, 2019) and for a specific example, Milton, Giles, *Big Chief Elizabeth* (London: Sceptre, 2000) and Clulow, Adam, *The Company. The Dutch Encounter with Tokugawa Japan* (New York: Columbia University Press, 2013).
6   Panikkar, *India and the Indian Ocean,* 84. I am grateful to Professor Patrick Bratton for these reminders. See his 'Pannikar, geography and Sea Power' in Sakhuja, Vijay and Pandey, Pragya, *K.M. Pannikar and the Growth of a Maritime Consciousness in India* (Delhi: IWCA, forthcoming).
7   Thus the 'Blue Homeland' thinking in Turkey's retired Admiral Lem Gurdenitz, of Koc University's Maritime Forum.
8   As laid out in Urbina, Ian, *The Outlaw Ocean: Journeys Across the Last Untamed Frontier,* (New York: Alfred A. Knopf, 2019).
9   Gray, Colin, *The Leverage of Sea Power* (New York: The Free Press, 1992), 56–91.
10 Wheeler, James Scott, *The Making of a World Power; War and the Military Revolution in Seventeenth Century England* (Stroud: Gloucs: Sutton Publishing, 1999), 43–65, 54–5, 202–5.
11 Swope, Kenneth M., *A Dragon's Head and a Serpent's Tail: Ming China and the First Great East Asian War 1592–1598* (Norman: University of Oklahoma Press, 2009), 67–79.
12 Swope, *A Dragon's Head*, op cit, 50, 131, 163.
13 Ibid, 46.
14 Ibid, 44, 47.
15 Ibid, 11, 25, 38–42, 49, 57 et seq. For an authoritative review of the whole period, Rodger, N.A.M., *The Command of the Ocean: A Naval History of Britain 1649–1815* (London: Penguin, 2006).
16 Maydman, *Naval Speculations,* op cit, preface, 5, also 325.
17 As. for example, Padfield, Peter, *Maritime Supremacy and the Opening of the Western Mind* (Woodstock and New York: The Overlook Press, 1999); Rodger, *The Command of the Ocean*. This is a major theme in Lambert, Andrew, *Sea Power States: Maritime Culture, Continental Empires, and the Conflict That Made the Modern World* (New Haven: Yale University Press, 2018).
18 Maydman, *Naval Speculations,* 267.
19 Lambert, *Sea Power States*, 264–310.

20 Sawyer, Peter, *The Oxford illustrated History of the Vikings* (Oxford: Oxford University Press, 1997), 1–18, 250–61.
21 Bartlett, W.B., *Vikings: A History of the Northmen* (Stroud, Gloucs: Amberely, 2019), 123–30, 205–25, 306–7.
22 Palssson, Hermann and Edwards, Paul (trans. and Introduction) *Orkneyinga Saga: The History of the Earls of Orkney* (London: Penguin Books, 1981), 52, 65–7, 93, 121–2.
23 Bill, Jan, 'Ships and Seamanship' in Sawyer, *The Oxford Illustrated History of the Vikings*, 182–3, 200–1.
24 Bartlett, *Vikings,* 10–15.
25 Ferguson, Robert, *The Hammer and the Cross: A New History of the Vikings* (London: Penguin, 2010), 10.
26 Parry, J.H., *The Spanish Seaborne Empire* (London: Hutchinson, 1971), 230.
27 Parry, *The Spanish Seaborne Empire,* 117–8, 234–6.
28 Ibid, 39–40.
29 Ibid, 327–60.
30 Bartlett, *Vikings,* 329.
31 Gray, Colin S., *The Navy in the Post-Cold War World: The Uses and Value of Strategic Sea Power* (University Park PA: University of Pennsylvania Press, 1994), 99, 179. For a contemporary example of the same message see Kaplan, Robert, 'The coming era of U.S. security policy will be dominated by the Navy,' *Washington Post Opinion,* 13 March 2021.
32 See, for example, Mecollari, Captain (Rtd) Artur, *Shaping the Future Albanian National Maritime Security Strategy* (2nd ed.) (Tirana: National Centre for Security and Defence, 2014).
33 Hendrix, Jerry, 'Sea Power Makes Great Powers,' *Foreign Policy,* Fall 2021. Also see his *To Provide and Maintain a Navy* (Annapolis: Focsle, 2021).
34 Gabriel Dominguez, 'China to have 'world's largest navy' by 2020, says report,' *Jane's Defence Weekly,* 28 July 2016.
35 Gresh, Geoffrey F., *To Rule Eurasia's Waves: The New Great Power Competition at Sea* (New Haven: Yale University Press, 2020), 16, 1–21, 29.
36 Hu Bo, *Chinese Maritime Power in the 21st Century: Strategic Planning, Policy and Predictions* (London: Routledge, 2019), 19, 238. Nonetheless, it is salutary to remember that navies do sometimes cease to exist altogether. For example, the Indian Navy of the East Indies Company (1863) the Austrian Navy (1919), the Yugoslav Navy (1992) and the Ethiopian Navy (1996). Both the American and the Canadian navies have come worryingly close on occasion.
37 Corbett, Sir Julian, *Some Principles of Maritime Strategy* (2nd ed.) (London: Longmans, Green, 1911) – reprinted with introduction by Eric Grove (Annapolis: Naval Institute Press, 1988), 1.
38 Except where the work of Mahan, is referenced.
39 Paine, Lincoln, *The Sea and Civilization: A Maritime History of the World* (New York: Alfred A. Knopf, 2013), 34; Weatherford, Jack, *Genghis Khan and the Making of the Modern World* (New York: Three Rivers Press, 2004).
40 Corbett, *Some Principles,* 67.
41 Curzon, George Nathaniel, *Frontiers* (2nd ed.) (Oxford: Clarendon, 1908), 8–9.
42 Thucydides, *The Peloponnesian War,* Bk 2, 38–41 (London: Penguin Classics, 1969), 18.
43 Roberts, Jennifer T., *The Plague of War: Athens, Sparta, and the Struggle for Ancient Greece* (Oxford: Oxford University Press, 2017), 294–5.
44 Strauss, Barry, *The Battle of Salamis: The Naval Encounter That Saved Greece–and Western Civilisation* (New York: Simon and Schuster, 2004), 145.
45 Graham, Gerald S., *The Politics of Naval Supremacy* (Cambridge: Cambridge University Press, 1965), 21.
46 Lambert, *Sea Power States,* 4–7, 330–1.
47 They are bravely explored in Speller, Ian, Mulqueen, M. and Sanders, Deborah (Eds), *Small Navies: Strategy and Policy for Small Navies in war and Peace* (Farnham: Ashgate, 2014) and McCabe, Robert, Sanders, Deborah and Speller, Ian (Eds), *Europe, Small Navies and Maritime Security* (Abingdon: Routledge, 2019). The forthcoming Goldrick, James and

Haines, Steven, (Eds), *Maritime Strategy for Medium Powers in the 21st Century* (Woodbridge, Suffolk UK: Boydell & Brewer, forthcoming) does the same for middle-sized navies.

48 For these evolving strategies see, Mecollari, *Shaping the Future Albanian National Maritime Security Strategy,* op cit, and Wijegunaratne, Vice Adm R.C., *Sri Lanka Navy's Maritime Strategy 2025* (Colombo: Ministry of Defence, 2016).

49 Willis, Sam, *The Struggle for Sea Power: The Royal Navy vs The World 1775–1782* (London: Atlantic Books, 2015).

50 Mahan, Capt. A.T., *Naval Strategy: Compared and Contrasted with the Principles and Practice of Military Operations on Land* (Boston: Little, Brown & Co., 1911), 161.

51 Erickson, Andrew S., Goldstein, Lyle J. and Lord, Carnes, *China Goes to Sea: Maritime Transformation in Comparative Historical Perspective* (Annapolis: Naval Institute Press, 2009), xiii–xxxii.

52 This apparently radical way of looking at the conflict, and one that emphasises the sea-air dimension to the war rather than its land component, is powerfully argued in O'Brien, Phillips Payson, *How the War Was Won* (Cambridge: Cambridge University Press, 2018).

53 Campbell, John, *The Spanish Empire in America* (London: 1747), quoted in Parry, *The Spanish Seaborne Empire,* 291.

2   A Predisposition towards the Maritime?

2.1 Introduction: Improving Mahan

Mahan came up with six 'elements' of what he called sea power, namely

Geographical position	Physical Conformations
Extent of Territory	Number of Population
National Character	Character of Government

Mahan made it clear that these were all intimately interconnected, and through them all he weaved the importance of a nation's economy, the availability of sufficient resources and the existence of effective naval forces. In his account of the period 1660–1783, Mahan also gave frequent examples of the various ways that his elements of sea power could change, either through shifting circumstances in the international and domestic context in which navies operated or by conscious policy and decision, but he did not articulate that point specifically. Perhaps he should have done, since the ability to improve, or at least maintain these constituents of maritime power as far as possible is central to its general development.

Accordingly for the sake of simplicity it seems possible to condense all this into just four re-brigaded and re-named 'constituents' of maritime power, namely[1]:

Maritime Geography	Governance, Society and Culture
The Maritime Economy	Naval Forces

These four constituents of maritime power are shaped by, but also have an effect on, the international and domestic environments, as shown in Figure 2.1. All four are so closely associated they are difficult to tease apart and the relationship between them is complex. We need to be particularly careful about inferring causality in that relationship. For example it is often claimed that liberal forms of government and maritime power seem to go together. As will be shown later this is a difficult issue, but any such association does not necessarily mean that the one 'causes' the other.

Probably more to the point for those interested in developing maritime power, is the extent to which these constituents can be changed. A government may wish to build up its maritime power by the construction of more naval forces or by improving its

DOI: 10.4324/9781003100553-2

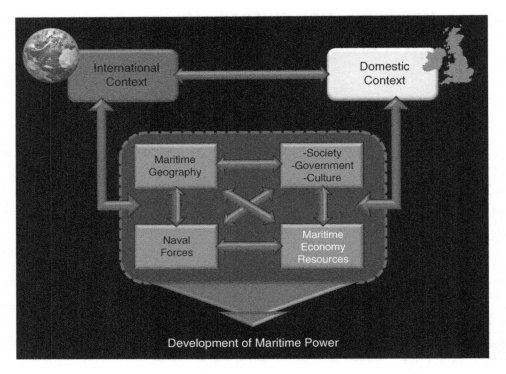

Figure 2.1 The Framework for Maritime Power.

Source: Self-generated.

maritime geography. The limiting effect of the domestic and international context means that this is much easier said than done.

2.2 Maritime Geography

Geography was the first 'element' of maritime power that Mahan explored. Proposing that sea-based trade is safer, quicker and easier than its land-based alternatives, he argued that it followed from this that countries with easy access to the sea and a coastline helpfully endowed with convenient harbours have a major advantage over those that don't.[2] In the days of sail a country's position in regard to the pattern of winds could be critical too. Strategically, the prevalence of south-westerly winds in the approaches to the English Channel helped the British fleet contain its French rival through the enforcement of blockade. Trading conditions could be shaped by the winds too. For Singapore and other Southeast Asian ports, the monsoons facilitated a lengthy but sustainable trading system in which their winds helped ships to the area and, as the seasons changed and the monsoons shifted direction, blew them back to the ports they had come from. Depending on its location, being an island could also help maritime access.

That Singapore enjoyed nearly all these advantages for both commercial and military activities was obvious to the British sailor William Hamilton at the start of the 18th Century:

In *Anno* 1703, I called at *Johore* in my way to *China* and he [the Sultan] treated me very kindly, and made me a Present of the island of *Sincapure*, but I told him it could be of no Use to a private Person, tho' a proper Place for a Company to settle a Colony on, lying in the Centre of Trade, and being accommodated with good Rivers and safe Harbours, so conveniently situated that all Winds served Shipping both to go out and come into those Rivers.[3]

Mahan also made the point that it was also very advantageous if a country's coastline was continuous rather than separated by territory held by other countries since this would make the 'concentration of its forces' much more difficult. France and Spain with their two or three distinct fleet areas were unfortunate in this respect.[4] Russia with its four separate fleets (or five counting the Caspian) was even more so, especially as its four access points were and largely remain, climatically challenging and subject to degrees of control by often unsympathetic neighbours. Such geographic features in the containing effect of the so-called First Island Chain makes the 'stepping out' of the Chinese navy difficult too (Figure 2.2).

Mahan acknowledged that outgoing states with maritime aspirations would increasingly also have such problems the further they went from home but the danger could be offset by the establishment of chains of bases and colonies able to support the operations

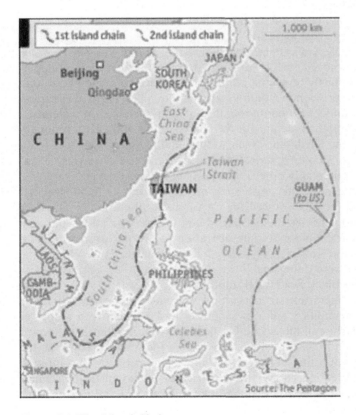

Figure 2.2 The Island Chains.

Source: US Gov.

of both the merchant fleet and the navy – provided that those bases or colonies were sufficiently well defended, and did not become strategic liabilities in themselves.

The nature and extent of the territory held could be a factor too, Mahan thought. He partly attributed the uneven development of French maritime power to its pleasant climate, ample resources and productive agriculture maintaining that such riches at home undermined the urge to seek them through alternative maritime endeavour. In fact, Mahan worried that this might apply to the United States too. If the Americans could satisfy all their needs like this, why should they bother to go to sea in any serious way?

Finally, Mahan was clear that a country's geographic situation could be changed – for better or worse – by specific state action. Spain's force concentration problems for example were greatly aggravated by the British seizure of Gibraltar in 1704, since it disconnected Spain's Mediterranean and Atlantic coasts.[5] Conversely, the building of the Panama canal on the other hand should, Mahan argued, ease the US Navy's two-coast, two-fleet problem. The Kiel canal would do much the same, the Kaiser thought, for Germany's High Sea Fleet. Accordingly, much depended on the extent to which the potential of a country's maritime geography was effectively exploited by state or perhaps private action. Unpreparedness, or not making the most of one's geographic circumstances, could transform a potential benefit into a dangerous vulnerability. Failing to defend important coastal areas like the Thames estuary or the Chesapeake Bay opened up equally undefended but key rivers to the decidedly unwelcome attentions of adversaries such as the Dutch burning the British fleet in the Medway in 1666 or the British destroying Washington in 1814.[6]

In this connection, one of Mahan's other more interesting books was *The Gulf and Inland Waters* in which he moved well away from the oceanic concepts and preoccupations for which he is chiefly remembered. In this, he tried to demonstrate that many of his observations and recommendations applied equally well to the narrow coastal seas, estuaries, rivers and lakes and that what went on in such narrow waters had made a material contribution to the outcome for the United States of the Revolutionary War, the War of 1812 and the Civil War. Such waters could equally well serve as a nursery for seapower, and so a country's endowment with and use of navigable waterways and big rivers were potentially other key aspects of its maritime geography.

There are countless examples of this, with such majestic rivers as the Tigris and Euphrates, the Amazon and the Nile. Indeed the Egyptians' exploitation of this river as a form of transport developed skills that sustained first trading operations and then arguably the first recorded amphibious/trading operation in history against Punt (in the Red Sea) as early as the 15th Century BC.[7] Two thousand years later, the Varangians (Russo-Swedes) were doing much the same thing on Russia's rivers, extending in due course to the Black Sea and Byzantium.[8]

The importance of river operations in peace and war and the intricate linkages between the commercial and military sides of seapower and also between seapower and landpower are particularly well illustrated by the way in which Chinese seapower first developed from rivers and coastal waters. Rivers like the Yangxi served as the fastest and safest highways for the transport of goods and people. This internal connectivity was also much enhanced by the construction of sophisticated canals particularly the north-south Grand Canal which linked the middle and north of the country with the enterprising and more sea-minded people of the south.

The commercial activity that these waterways generated provided the sailors, the ships and the financial resources for the creation of naval forces and a sequence of dynastic battles fought on rivers for the control of land. These started in 5–600 BC and involved the earliest dynasties; one of the most romanticised encounters being the Battle of the Red Cliffs fought in December 208 AD in the middle Yangzi between vast fleets and armies measured in the hundreds of thousands. These grew in scale and sophistication soon providing the means for the local sea-based battles of the Song dynasty (960–1279) with external adversaries such as Korea and the Champa and Annamites of modern-day Vietnam.

The fall of the trading city of Kaifeng in 1127 effectively closed land-based trade with the interior of Eurasia and increased the relative importance of sea-based trade still further. This again enhanced the quality and extent of Chinese seapower at that time. China's naval prowess was without equal anywhere in the world during the last period of the Song dynasty. As President of the Board of Revenue Chang I pushed the argument that,

> For today, the waves of the sea and the currents of the river are our Great Wall, the seamen, the fighting men and the shipwrights are the soldiers of the Great wall, and fire-ships, fire-rafts, the incendiary arrows and weapons are the equipments of the Great wall for repelling assaults. With this watery defence line of ten thousand *li* in length, there is not one inch of land which we cannot defend.[9]

This was probably still a counsel of perfection and the real apogee of Chinese maritime power was doubtless during the period of the iconic Indian Ocean voyages of Admiral Zheng He in the 15th Century. Not as peaceful as often made out, these voyages cowed the Majahapit empire into deference and '[a]t its height, the political sway of China extended from Japan to Ceylon and from Korea to Java.'[10] And it all started in China's rivers, showing how a country's maritime geography can be transformed by human action.

Shortly after Mahan wrote his seminal book, Halford Mackinder and the so-called geo-politics school addressed the impact of geography on seapower in a much more expansive way. In effect, Mackinder thought, geographical considerations were so important that they dominated all aspects of human history. Mackinder conceived of the Eurasian landmass as what he called the 'world island' and its central part (roughly greater Germany and Russia) the 'Heartland.' It commanded huge resources, human and material. It could generate great land or 'continental' power. Scattered around it were various other smaller less well-endowed islands, such as America, Britain and Japan which were the fount of maritime power. Mackinder thought 'Continental powers' would triumph because they could access enormous resources and develop overwhelming industrial power. They were increasingly impervious to sea-based attacks and could generate substantial naval forces well able to threaten the dependencies of the maritime powers, particularly their strategic reliance on shipping.

Mackinder argued that technology in the shape of internal combustion engines, railways, and arguably even airpower, was on the side of the exponents of land-power. Technological advances reduced the transportation advantages of the sea; land-based airpower threatened the relative invulnerability of countries like Britain and Japan which derived from their status as islands. The future, in short, would be more continental than maritime.

Later geo-politicians refined the basic argument in various ways. In 1944, Nicholas Spykman identified what he called the Rimland or an Inner Crescent of countries on the edge of the World Island. Their geographic position meant that they could be threatened by forces from within the Eurasian landmass, but at the same time, they could access the resources of the area and challenge the Sea Powers in their own domain by building big sea denial navies of their own and appropriating significant areas of the world ocean. First Germany, then Russia seemed to fit into that pattern of behaviour.

This reinforced Mahan's point about the importance, perhaps above all, of geographic position. This essential argument has led to an interesting debate about contemporary China, and indeed about its historic antecedents. On the face of it, China is a classic example of a Rimland country, with characteristics both of a land-power and a maritime power, and so one that could in a sense act as a bridge between Eurasia and the World Ocean.

This certainly seems to sit comfortably with China's extremely ambitious 'Belt and Road Initiative' (BRI) launched by President Xi in 2013, to be discussed later. The BRI aims to link one end of the Eurasian landmass with the other by a combination of long-distance rail and road ways and sea routes between critical and often newly developed ports. Nor is the scheme limited 'merely' to the World Island since it aims also to develop the connectivities between and inside all the other areas of the world as well.

Several points emerge from this. Firstly these aspirations and their successful implementation would confirm China as a Sea Power and a Land Power at the same time. This underlines the basic point made earlier that these attributes are not alternatives but positions on a common spectrum set by the domestic and international environment and the relationship between the four inter-connected constituents of maritime power discussed in this chapter. Consequently, countries are nearly always both sea and landpowers to some extent.

Secondly, the BRI is a good, if grandiose, example of a country seeking positively to make the most of its geographic potential and even radically to improve it. This reinforces Mahan's implicit argument that geography in many ways is much less fixed and more potentially adaptable than it appears.

Lastly, the ways in which the BRI is currently represented in maps often encapsulate many of the assumptions that people have at the time about their particular countries and, quite literally, their place in the world. At the time of the famous *Mappa Mundi* in Hereford Cathedral, England, Britain was shown as a small location on the very edge of the known world. With the discovery of America however, the focus shifted and the country now found itself, and indeed the whole of the North Atlantic seaboard, right in the apparent centre of the world. The details of maps often illustrate such unconscious attitudes, about their designers' sense of place, even their identity and these in turn can reinforce and help shape social and political behaviour – another example of the way in which the various constituents of maritime power interact with each other.

2.3 Governance and Society

Mahan argued that the nature of the population of a country was an important factor in its capacity to generate maritime power. For a start, the more people there were, the more smart people you would have. Equally obviously, the more people you have the greater your chance of being able to overwhelm commercial or military competitors by sheer weight of numbers. It is no coincidence that Britain's maritime ascendancy came at the same time as a relatively startling rise in the size of its population. Over the period 1550 to 1820, the general population of Europe grew by 80%, while Britain's rose by 280%.[11] By contrast, countries like contemporary Japan which face the prospect of losing between quarter and a third of its population by 2050 face a very serious demographic problem in economic development, the provision of services to a greying population and of course in the maintenance of its maritime power. During the Second World War, Britain became acutely aware of its relative disadvantages in this respect and sought refuge in technology, the efficient mobilisation of its human resources and the avoidance of a battle style centred on mass armies.[12] Contemporary Singapore does the same.

Visitors to Singapore in the 19th Century, however, used frequently to comment on the virtues of the industriousness and cosmopolitan nature of the city's mainly ethnic Chinese population. Alongside its geographic position, Singapore's people were a great asset. Now the country faces the same demographic challenge as Japan. To help offset the problem, it has quite deliberately chosen to seek labour-saving high technology solutions. More generally it encourages immigration of the required number and standard in order to bulk out the domestic population.

Making extensive use just of European experience over the past several centuries, Mahan also identified 'national character' and the 'character of the government' as critical elements in the development of sea power, and both of these were closely linked to trade and the shape of the economy. 'The tendency to trade,' he thought, was 'the national characteristic most important to the development of sea power.' But this meant having something to trade with. Accordingly, 'an aptitude for commercial pursuits' and the social sentiments that supported it were essential to the development of maritime power.

Henry Maydman's England certainly fits this description. While, like most other European states of the time, it was still basically agrarian there were many who believed that 'Commerce is the Fountain of Wealth, the true Foundation of all real Greatness.'[13] Trade's share in the national economy went up substantially in this period. It stimulated the domestic economy; it encouraged export industries, processing industries (such as sugar refineries) financial services, the national infrastructure and the extension of government. As night follows day, ship-building, the merchant shipping industry, marine insurance and the maritime community all grew accordingly. This was much less true of other European states and, Mahan thought, they suffered accordingly. He attributed their naval and political decline to the luke-warm attitudes of the Spanish and Portuguese to conventional patterns of sea-based trade.[14]

Even worse, some societies have exhibited a positive disdain for trade. Confucian China is the most familiar example with ancient Greece a rather more surprising one, even at the time of their great triumph over the Persians at Salamis. Both reflected social tensions between sailors and merchants on the one hand and the landed aristocracy on the other.[15] This contrasted strongly with the relationship between government, society and merchants characteristic of Venice and even more the Hanseatic league of trading city states around the Baltic which aimed 'to marry across land and sea.'[16]

Singapore might be considered a modern equivalent in demonstrating a close relationship between society and the maritime economy. The whole point of the place was to make money. 'The merchants who form by far the largest section of the community,' remarked Dr William Edwards, who visited in 1852, somewhat disparagingly, 'seem to look upon money-making as the chief end and object of their lives, and their topics of conversation rarely extend to any other subject than that of nutmegs or the latest price current ...'[17] What they were doing, in effect, was turning commerce into a civic virtue.[18]

From the start, Stamford Raffles, the city's modern day founder, was clear that success was most likely to come from the least possible government interference in the merchants' business. Singapore was to be a free port and latter day visitors, including Captain Captain Raphael Semmes, of the Confederate commerce raider *CSS Alabama* during the American civil war, was one of many who thought this explained why it had so conspicuously out-performed the over-regulated Dutch ports of Java.[19]

Most other visitors agreed, thinking that Singapore's immediate and sustained economic success was due to the combination of an industrious and cosmopolitan workforce and a liberal regime designed to encourage free trade. Those same visitors, all of whom in the 19th Century would have arrived by boat, will also have had little doubt that the city was thoroughly maritime simply from its geographic reliance on, and compliance with, shipping; it had, moreover, effected an entirely appropriate form of governance.

Further, Mahan tried to show that '...particular forms of government, with their accompanying institutions' were closely related to the degree of a country's sea-mindedness and the relative success of its maritime endeavours. What mattered was 'Whether it [the government] favors the natural growth of a peoples' industry and its tendency to seek adventure and gain by way of the sea.' In this vital task much depended on the nature, efficiency and strategic priorities of the government itself.[20]

Some have gone further still, pointing to a strong association between liberal, democratic forms of government and success in developing maritime power. They argue that transparency, accountability and faith in the independent rule of law characteristic of liberal forms of governance encourage enterprising societies and maritime power. In return the latter provides the ideal conditions for such forms of government.

Mahan was not so sure. 'Whether' he wondered

> a democratic government will have the foresight, the keen sensitiveness to national position and credit, the willingness to insure property by adequate outpouring of money in times of peace, all of which are necessary for military preparation is yet an open question.[21]

The absence of a politically influential 'commercial aristocracy' able to accept the necessary costs of preparing for war, still more of waging it, has often been a problem. It could slow things up or even put them into reverse for a time. Free and democratic peoples in representative political systems need to be persuaded to pay for the expensive prerequisites of war – it doesn't come naturally.[22] Democratic governments, on their fast-moving electoral cycles, it is often said, find long-term planning difficult, especially when 'jam tomorrow' requires pain today.

Against this, despotic government could, thought Mahan, sometimes produce brilliant if brief flowerings of maritime development, just as Colbert demonstrated in late 17th-Century France[23] but such successes were likely to have shallow roots and soon wither. Evidently, it is one thing to develop maritime power, but quite another to be able to maintain it. Despotic governments can get off to a good start but perhaps have less staying power. Since Mahan's time, the emergence of strong navies and maritime economies in countries not particularly noted for their liberal principles, such as Wilhelmine and Nazi Germany, the Soviet Union and contemporary China, would seem to cast further doubt on the strength of the association between maritime power and democratic governance. Had he been able to, Mahan would undoubtedly have pointed out, however, that the first three all failed in the end.

Sea-mindedness can however be associated with the *shape* as well as the extent and relative importance of the maritime economy. If a country's sea-dependence is a consequence of nothing more than the shipping out of commodities like coal or oil for other countries to process, awareness of that maritime dependency will tend not to go very deep, especially when that shipping is conducted by foreign-flagged vessels along sea lines of communication guarded essentially by other peoples' navies. In such cases, the social attitudes of the people towards the sea will likely be essentially transactional, valued only for its passing usefulness, if thought about at all. A more sophisticated national economy more centred on the two-way sea-based exchange of goods and services, satisfying both supply and demand could well result in greater sea mindedness since a larger proportion of the population is likely to become involved.

Recognising their vulnerability to future declines in commodity prices, oil-producing countries show every sign of seeking to diversify their supply economies. An enhanced reliance on sea transportation seems likely to make the Gulf States, for example, yet more maritime in the future which may help explain why they have been investing more in their navies over the past decade or so.[24]

Such pragmatic attitudes to the sea are quite different from the almost spiritual attitude towards it exhibited by many Polynesians. 'I was born a child of the ocean,' says the Greenpeace activist Victor Pickering,

> Growing up in Fiji, the ocean has influenced every part of me. From the food that nourished me, to how I spent my days swimming and diving. For us in the Pacific Islands, the ocean is our connection to one another. We recognize the ocean as part of our identity and wellbeing. We are the ocean, and the ocean is us.

Likewise the eloquence of Samoan, Brianne Fruean:

> A Samoan practice is that when we fish we always put the first fish back into the water and that is a sign of respect for the ocean. Because we treat the ocean like a living thing, a living, breathing thing within our culture. I've always believed that my elders knew how to live in harmony with the ocean and a lot of the times when we're talking about trying to save the ocean we miss a huge chunk of the narrative that comes from indigenous communities.[25]

Others such as the Egyptians and perhaps the Vikings too thought of boats as being vehicles of the Gods. The sea also figures importantly in the 'foundation mythologies' that underpin the cultures of some states as perhaps exemplified by the *sposalizia,* the Ascension Day marriage of the Doge of Venice and the sea at the *Bucintoro.*[26] A similar if much more intimate social relationship with the sea was a characteristic of early sea-going folk like the Bugis of Southeast Asia. China's Hokkien expressed similar sentiments in the identification of sea deities like the goddess Mazu who was, and is, worshipped because of her responsibilities for the safety of the Southern Seas. Across the Pacific, the beautiful La Pincoya, the sea princess of southern Chile who watches over the fish stocks and rescues distressed mariners clearly comes from the same mould.[27]

The modern, hard-working, hard-boiled commuters of Santiago or Beijing, though, will probably be much less conscious of such attachments. All this suggests that even amongst countries with an obvious maritime bent, there are shades of sea-mindedness. Some are pecuniary and transactional; others have a much deeper relationship with the sea, that is instead bound up with their identity and self-perception. It reinforces the point that being maritime is a matter of degree, and much shaped by one's circumstances.

This raises the issue of the extent to which a country's sea-mindedness and maritime culture are fixed and immutable or whether they can be amended, even constructed, by experience or governmental action. A convincing case certainly be made that the 'maritimeness' of a country's culture can certainly be encouraged directly by government support for support for maritime industries and indirectly by such things as private and public investment in the Arts, the control of public education and so forth.[28]

Chinese experience provides an example of the reverse of this. Governmental indifference and inaction can substantially limit a country's sea-mindedness. While the coastal peoples of southern China were familiar with and supportive of maritime endeavour there remained in most of China a residual agrarian pre-disposition towards a 'continental' mindset. Agricultural pursuits dominated the lives of the vast majority of the population and the product of their labours satisfied most of their needs. 'We possess all things,' the Qianlong Emperor told Lord Macartney who sought to persuade the Celestial Court to open up its markets in September 1793, 'I set no value on objects strange or ingenious, and have no use for your country's manufactures.'[29]

Stability, social harmony, status and dignity were the goal, not the pursuit of power and immoderate wealth with their tendencies to corrupt the potentially pure. This long-standing Confucian disdain for commercial activity reinforced the desire to protect the regime from the contaminating influence of outside barbarians. Such ideas were the complete opposite of allegedly 'Western' mercantilist views which 'conflated state power and commercial success' and elevated their importance.[30]

Even in the successful Tang period (618–906) such views led to a ban on Chinese people going abroad and on privately owned and operated shipping. Trade at sea was largely conducted by foreigners. However these restrictions were gradually relaxed and by the 1070s two-thirds of Chinese trade by sea was in private hands and this continued with regime encouragement through the Song dynasty (960–1279) and into the early years of the Ming dynasty (1368–1644), being closed down again after the famous voyages of Admiral Zheng He in the 15th Century. At that time overseas trade once more became a state monopoly which largely took the form of exchanging tributes from China's neighbours with gifts from a munificent and kindly Middle Kingdom. These were usually high-quality goods not produced for commercial gain. The bolder private merchants did what they could to circumvent these restrictions but it was only in 1684 that the Qing dynasty's Kangxi Emperor opened trade up again, thereby facilitating the exchange of large scale commercially produced manufactures (most obviously ceramics, silks and tea) and the import of commodities from abroad.[31]

These cyclical bouts of sea-mindedness in part reflected switches in the government's attitude to trade with foreigners which clearly affected the sea-mindedness of the Chinese people and/or on the extent to which the inhabitants, particularly of China's southern coastal provinces, could indulge in it. Restrictions also had depressing effects on the sea enterprises of the peoples of Southeast Asia but could also open up opportunities for others to try to fill the gaps, as the Japanese and Indians were sometimes able to do. To some extent, then, sea-mindedness could be exported as well as developed or depressed nationally by governmental action.

Governmental attitudes to the defence of the conditions in which trade could take place were also important to a society's sea-mindedness. From earliest days, making the sea safe for the passage of merchant shipping and, for the more aggressive, securing positions ashore in which one could, in Sir Walter Raleigh's words, 'trade with advantage' were both important requirements for success and essentially the responsibility of government. Failures here diminished the prospects for beneficial sea-based trade and this would inevitably reduce the population's contact with, and sympathy for, maritime endeavour.

Of course, the nature of government itself could be a problem. If the population thought it tyrannical, unfair or simply incompetent in the delivery of essential services (including maritime security) then social disaffection would tend to grow. This in turn could easily affect commercial maritime activities adversely, distract attention from the sea, even spill over into naval mutiny. The manifold inefficiencies of the Tsarist regime that sent an ill-assorted and ill-trained battle fleet from the Baltic to its doom at the hands of the Japanese at the battle of Tsushima in 1905 affected the morale, loyalty and confidence of the Russian navy very badly on the way[32] and contributed to its mutinous tendencies through the revolt at Odessa later than year and further on to its leading role in the revolutions of 1917. Since navies reflect the society they help defend, it's difficult for them to avoid reflecting its divisions too.

2.4 Resources, Power and the Economy

Mahan did not separate out a maritime economy as a distinct element of maritime power but instead interwove it with the other elements that he identified. Since all the elements are intricately inter-linked, both as causes and consequences of each other, this certainly makes sense. But there is also some merit in trying to tease out issues distinctively relating to the maritime economy of a country and the resources it may make available for maritime endeavour.

2.4.1 A Maritime Economy and Maritime Resources

Mahan and many others have emphasised the point that a maritime economy is ideally placed to deliver maritime resources that are of especial relevance to the development and maintenance of naval forces. What those resources were and are depends very much on time and place, as does the essential character of what would now be called the 'defence-industrial base.' In days of sail when it took 5000 oak trees to make the average ship-of-the-line, well maintained forestry resources to deliver the required ship-timber and effective dockyards were essential. With the technological changes made possible by the Industrial Revolution, it became more a question of access to iron and steel and of the manufacture of engines and naval machinery of various sorts. Today, perhaps, access to the latest things in Artificial Intelligence and Machine Learning and other such developments might have become the key requirement. But whatever the resources in question, the ability of the national economy to deliver them and the willingness of the government to make the necessary investments still seem critical.

Other such resources included the people, ships and practices of the maritime industries, most obviously merchant shipping and the fishing industry. Speaking of naval and commercial maritime power Mahan remarked, 'It was in the union of the two, carefully fostered, that England made the gain of sea power over and beyond all states.'[33] Not only were both industries a major source of revenue to the government, and hence their interests well worth fighting for, but they could help supply the Royal Navy with the ships, the people, the docks, the shore-side infrastructure and the political support it needed to defend those interests. These included everything from financial credit arrangements, the drafting of contracts, the establishment of a body of law, codes and protocols between trading entities. The more powerful and successful the navy, the more could the country trade with advantage, accumulating yet more maritime resources. Completing what was in effect a virtuous circle, (see Figure 1.1), it therefore made sense for the Government to do what it could to make sure this particular goose went on laying her golden eggs.

In consequence, the mercantile interest was taken seriously by successive British governments. This was reflected in the defence of the country's economic interests abroad, the passing of Navigation Acts to protect shipping and interventions to support the ship-building and related industries where necessary. The maritime industries were an element of seapower well worth nurturing. This also leads to the conclusion that a government's capacity to run the economy effectively is *a*, and arguably *the*, key element in the development of maritime power.

How well a particular country is placed in doing that is not simply a function of the size of its economy, an attribute often confused with its strength. The size of an economy is much shaped by the extent of a country's population and that population's buying power. Broadly, the more people, the bigger the potential economy. But of course with a larger population come greater requirements for the economy to deliver essential services in the form of healthcare, education, law and order, transportation and the like. Deficiencies here can transform potential strength into weakness, especially if dissatisfaction with government performance spills over into social disorder and threats to regime stability. For such reasons economic strength is much better measured by such metrics as gross domestic product (GDP) and income *per capita* and by the nation's capacity to balance the books, to invest in the future as well as the present and generally to do what it needs to do with the resources available. This again reflects a country's geography and the nature of its government and society.

But this is a two-way street for trade and maritime power help shape the international and domestic environment too.

2.4.2 Trade and Maritime Power

Because of its utility as the safest and cheapest way of transporting goods and people, the sea has always been a basis – and some would argue *the* basis – for trade. With success in trade, as just discussed, comes power – that is, the ability to influence, even determine, the behaviour of other people and other countries. Trade, maritime power and naval activity all involve the use of the sea. While the development of maritime power requires these three things to be properly integrated, the relationship between them is far from simple. In fact perhaps four different but related positions on this can be spotted on a spectrum where international cooperation characterises the relationship between trade and dominion at one end, while international competition so at the other. Those positions are important as they both shape and reflect how countries, governments and societies have approached the development of maritime power. The issue is not simply one of having a strong maritime economy – the attitudes that go with it are important too.

The first position on the spectrum was adopted by free traders such as the so-called Manchester School of 19th-Century Britain. For them, trading and fighting, or threatening to, were antithetical. Instead, the more countries cooperate in trading with each other, the less they would be inclined to fight, especially if as trading entities they became more liberal and democratic. As essentially free-marketeers, the trading activity they most had in mind was that conducted simply for reasons of commercial gain, by private individuals or companies, rather than by state companies. The less states interfere in the process, in fact, the more beneficial its consequences. If trade has any strategic consequences at all, they would good and peaceful ones, encouraging countries to cooperate in other ways as well. The 21st Century version of this is the view taken by the advocates of unimpeded globalisation who argue that free and open sea-based trade benefits everyone and should be the guiding principle for both economic and foreign policy-makers. Protecting globalisation should also guide the use of navies and coastguards.

The second position, though, recognises that the state is a economic player, whether it likes it or not because the requirement to govern means the employment of so many people. Moreover, it has often to intervene in trade. Trade was not, and is not, conducted in a strategic vacuum. The behaviour of the representatives of other states, competing companies or just plain criminals of various sorts (not least pirates) have often adversely affected the conditions for trade, at home, at sea and abroad. This has required state action to restore, regulate and eventually maintain a situation in which national trade could flourish. At home, the state did what was necessary to protect its commerce from unfair foreign competition. When Dutch shippers in the 17th Century threatened to monopolise the carrying trade, Britain introduced the first Navigation Act to nurture its own merchant marine. Today's free-trade deals between countries and sets of countries revolve around careful calculation by all concerned about how best to protect national economic interest.

In the past, when pirates or disorder ashore threatened the conditions for trade, the Navy was sent in to sort things out. The flag then followed trade. *Laissez-faire* British governments of the 19th Century were often reluctant to assume the burdens of empire but were grumblingly forced into it by the exhortations of their entrepreneurial citizens, when faced with such challenges. It is much the same now. The world's navies intervened in the Gulf War between Iraq and Iran in the 1980s mainly because of the threat it posed to the oil trade. All navies, moreover, take as sacrosanct the principle of the freedom of navigation because of its necessity for unencumbered trade, although their practical interpretations of what needs to be done to defend it significantly differ.

A third position on the spectrum was advanced by Mahan, and countless others of his persuasion; trade, and the economic power it generates, creates the resources for military and naval strength. In effect the relationship between maritime trade and maritime power forms a virtuous circle as shown in Figure 1.1. The more trade you have, the greater your maritime resources (finance, infrastructure, ports, ships, marine industry). These make your navies stronger and the better able to ensure that you 'trade with advantage' – and so on.

Once the Americans with their accumulated capital and industrial resources were able to build aircraft carriers faster than the Japanese navy could sink them, something that became apparent during the 1943 Guadalcanal campaign, thoughtful

Japanese began to realise that the Second World War was lost. It is not a great step from this for some to argue that trade advantages should be sought at least in part because they provide the means for greater security, even strategic dominion. In this case trade could well follow the flag as it did for the Portuguese when they first broke into the Indian Ocean in the later 15th Century.

The fourth and final position on the spectrum goes further still. It is associated with 'mercantilist' perspectives on the conduct of trade which emphasise its competitive nature. Trade can be seen as a zero-sum game; the more you had – the less they did. Because India currently lacks deep-water port infrastructure, much of its exports/ imports are transhipped in Sri Lanka. This is good for Sri Lanka, bad for India; but if India were able to improve its ports, the reverse would be true. For mercantilists, it was more a question of competition in cutting up an existing cake than of cooperation in baking a bigger one for everyone to share.

Success in sea-based trade can even usurp the role of military power at sea in shaping the way that other people behave. Economic strength can provide alternative levers in power politics, and is frequently used as such, not least because it seems much less incendiary than using military pressure.[34] That same military power, though, may quietly contribute to success by dissuading the victims from seeking non-economic counters to the economic pressure they are put under.

Indeed, some historians argue that until fairly recently the West (that is Europe, and by extension the United States) adopted different attitudes to this than did Asian countries. Westerners, the argument goes, tended to think of trade, less as something that facilitated the delivery of domestic services, and more as an attribute of power in its own right. An 18th Century British commentator who rejoiced in the name of Malachy Postlethwayt, nicely illustrates the point. 'The Balance of Trade' he said in 1757,' I cannot too often repeat it, is in Fact the Balance of Power.'[35] European countries and city states like Genoa and Venice wanted to control not territory, but trade for the manifest advantages it provided. These advantages were worth fighting for, and Western states habitually did so. The tendency to 'conflate state power and commercial success' led to a greater willingness to resort to 'organised maritime violence in pursuit of commercial ends.'[36] In turn this led to a greater willingness to invest in the resources and means by which that violence could be conducted against other peoples or countries through the construction of navies and a propensity to project maritime power ashore. The frequency of local conflicts over trade in the pre-European Middle East, South and Southeast Asia,[37] suggests, however, that there might be grounds for considerable scepticism about the extent to which this attitude to trade was a uniquely Western attribute. And with much contemporary concern about the general 'weaponisation of trade' in today's world it certainly isn't now.[38]

2.4.3 *The Maritime Economy and the Purpose and Nature of Naval Forces*

This reliance has often led to navies justifying their demands for support from their governments by referring to the extent that their country's economy depends on shipping and on secure sea lines of communication to other parts of the world. They take this as evidence of the extent to which their country's economy and fundamental interest is maritime. While there is much truth in this proposition, it is only a partial measure. It is not just a question of the extent of a maritime element in the economy but of the *shape* and nature of that economy that effects sea-mindedness as we saw earlier.

Mahan identified the unbalanced nature of the Spanish economy as a fatal flaw, making the case that their reliance in the 16th and 17th Centuries on basing their economy on extracting bullion from South America produced an unnatural, distorted and fragile economy which was susceptible to hostile attack at sea, especially from the Dutch and English, but which did not encourage the development of a merchant class. Indeed to the very end the Spanish empire was dependent on merchants and navigators from its Italian possessions – and the effects were serious when these were lost.[39]

To what extent the resultant economy can be termed a maritime one, however, is a different but equally complex matter. An obvious starting point for this would be to seek to measure the degree to which a country's GDP can be shown directly to derive from a clearly sea-related activity such as sea-based trade with other countries, shipping, ship-building, fishing and the offshore gas and oil industries. The intimate inter-connections between these businesses and the shore-side businesses that support them further complicate assessment.

These linkages in fact complicate the matter in another way too. Historically, successful sea-based trade has tended to lead to domestic entrepreneurs diversifying into other forms of economic activity that are not directly related to the sea. The apparently natural trajectory of a maritime economy paradoxically results in maritime activity being a smaller part of the whole. In this way too, as was shown in the last chapter, maritime power contains the seeds of its own decline.

That is especially true of those trades that are either dangerous and uncomfortable like fishing, or involve wholesale absence from homelife like merchant shipping; when profitable and more agreeable shore-side employment is available, people leave such industries. The result is a diminution in the maritime proportion of the population. The British fishing industry, once one of the staples of its economy, for example now contributes less than one-half of one percent of Britain's GDP, directly employing just 12,000 people out of a population of 66 million.[40] Much the same can be said of its merchant marine. If there is indeed such a tendency for the maritime component of an economy to dissipate like this, positive corrective reaction might be necessary for governments wishing to maintain the maritime nature of their societies and countries. Such action might be regarded more as a strategic investment in a country's maritime future rather than simply the provision of help for a currently struggling marine industry.

2.5 Naval Forces

'The history of Sea Power,' as Mahan put it in the first line of *The Influence of Sea Power*, 'is largely, though by no means solely, a narrative of contests between nations, of joint rivalries, of violence frequently culminating in war.'[41]

Accordingly, he thought, naval forces were important because they were the means by which the sea could be controlled for the conduct of trade and for moving military forces around. He did not specifically identify naval forces as a separate element in maritime power, no doubt because they were pervasive throughout it; while only a part of the overall maritime package they were and are indispensable. Naval forces were both an expression of maritime power and, at the same time, an obvious means of developing it.

Nearly everything Mahan wrote was about how naval forces should be developed and in particular used in order to defend national interests. His own historical studies of how this was done were largely confined to the previous several hundred years of European maritime endeavour, but he was certainly aware that naval activity had a much longer pedigree than that. Arguably one of the first fleets raised specifically for military purposes appeared about 2200 BC when one of the immediate successors of Sargon, a Mespotamian ruler, conducted operations against a hostile coalition around the Straits of Hormuz.[42] With the naval technology of the time and in fact until quite recently, perhaps the 15th or 16th Centuries, it was virtually impossible to intercept a hostile fleet on the high seas, although, with good fortune, individual ships could be chanced across and pounced upon, of course – especially in the narrow seas. This meant that most battles took place on rivers or in coastal waters, usually in conjunction with some raiding or amphibious enterprise.

The rarity of classic sea battles on the high seas, may help explain why the indirect and separate contribution that naval forces make to military operations, even ones intended to defend a country's maritime interests, has often been underrated. Mahan's primary intention was to correct this misapprehension, especially amongst his fellow Americans. Once the importance of the naval contribution was recognised, the next task, he thought, was to ensure that naval forces were used properly. Because it was so important as a characteristic of maritime power, the *operational* efficiency of naval forces was Mahan's major focus in all his many works.

The central aim of naval forces, he argued was to command on the high seas (or in minor key on rivers, lakes and in estuaries) because that conferred the capacity to protect your trade and project power ashore, while preventing the adversary from doing likewise. Mahan wanted to demonstrate how this was best achieved – what worked and what didn't. The quality of a navy's strategic direction at the highest strategic level and of its fighting efficiency at the operational (campaign) and tactical (battle) levels and the mix and quality of the battlefleet were all critically important. In sum, Mahan's main focus throughout his many books and articles was on discovering – and recommending – courses of action that would improve all this. Simply having a navy in the form of a gaggle of ships was not enough – it had to be militarily effective to make the investment worthwhile.

Not entirely convinced that his American predecessor had got all this right, Britain's Sir Julian Corbett in his celebrated *Some Principles of Maritime Strategy* refined and generally improved on all these ideas.[43] Corbett's observations about the kind of forces and strategies needed to exercise sea control rather than win it in the first place were especially valuable. The words of these two masters of maritime strategic thought have been tinkered with and refined to suit changing circumstances ever since by the legions of their successors.

Although they were perfectly aware that 'form follows function' and made their recommendations about how naval forces should be developed, their main interest was on how navies should be used, which is not the focus of this book. Nonetheless, it is worth underlining the crucial point, that consideration of the task that naval forces need to be able to perform is the essential starting point in any endeavour to develop the naval component of maritime power.

2.5.1 *Changes and Challenges*

Navies are always in a state of constant change, if at varying rates. This requires constant thought about what they are supposed to do and how they are supposed to do it.

For instance, Mahan and Corbett's conception of what constitutes maritime security might these days seem rather narrowly military, given that modern states have also to deal so much more with the consequences at sea of international crime, terrorism, environmental degradation and so forth. Accordingly, their 21st Century successors might also draw attention to their neglect of a country's capacity to defend its broader maritime interests by non-military maritime means, especially given the generally increased importance of the maritime element in a country's economy. In the main these difficult but low-level threats are handled less by navies than by coastguards and other Maritime Law Enforcement Agencies (MLEAs). Even though coastguards deal with the softer end of the maritime security spectrum, and their forces take different forms and operate in different ways than navies, they also have become an essential part of the overall maritime enforcement package and so their development needs to be taken seriously too.[44]

Technological change has had an equally profound effect on the nature of navies and the way they operate and need to be developed. With the introduction of the ram about 1000 years BC, the Greeks and Phoenicians began the long slow process of differentiation between the civilian cargo ship and the fighting warship. The successful development and exploitation of such technological possibilities could confer decisive tactical advantage in battle. The extent to which the Europeans when bursting into the Indo-Pacific in the 16th Century owed their success to technological superiority rather than to the locals not trying very hard to resist remains a highly contested point in the broad debate about the 'Naval and Military Revolutions' of the time. As the Dutch discovered when driven out of Taiwan by Koxinga in the 17th Century, superior capabilities on the high seas didn't always translate into victory[45] but there seems little reason to doubt that on the whole the more and the more powerfully equipped your naval forces are, the greater your prospects of success. This was certainly Mahan's view.

Mahan's most famous book came out in 1890, well over a hundred years ago. He was a creature of his time and we can only speculate about what he might have written if alive today, but it would certainly have included some observations about the various trends that have affected naval forces in the intervening 130 years or so. Technologically, today's situation is very different from his and although Mahan clearly thought the basic principles of naval strategy were permanently valid, technical change could certainly effect the way they were implemented. These days many commentators would argue that the advent of the air, space and cyber domains of war and the expanding reach of land-based forces, might be transforming the character if not the nature (to be Clausewitzian for a moment) of maritime operations and the naval forces required to conduct them. Some would argue, for example that with today's networked conceptions of modern operations at sea, conventional ships and submarines have become rather less important as constituents of the overall fleet, when compared, say, with offensive and defensive cyber capabilities.[46] Some go further still arguing that technological advance has seriously reduced the centrality of naval forces to maritime power.

This reinforces the point, made especially strongly by Sir Julian Corbett, that naval forces and their strategies of employment need to be treated as simply a subset of the overall military-maritime package, rather than as independent actors. Maybe the whole idea of naval strategy needs to be rethought or even abandoned altogether. 'Today...', argued Admiral Chernarvin, last Chief of the Soviet Navy, ... there is no purely specific realm of warfare. Victory is achieved by the combined efforts of [all branches of the armed forces] which brings about the need to integrate all knowledge of warfare within the framework of a united military science.'[47]

At the very least what is meant these days by 'naval forces' has become an interesting topic of debate, often questioning the certitudes of the past.

2.5.2 What Naval Forces Need

The actual or anticipated tactical and operational success of a country's naval forces in their battles and campaigns, and the strategic effect they could consequently deliver in support of a country's foreign policy, were the result of other maritime activities on land. These needed to be thought about as well. Even though they took place in the high councils of state or in Admiralty offices, warehouses, dockyards, factories and training institutions far from the smoke and fire of battle, naval forces critically needed the support of such secure foundations. Accordingly, a country wanting to increase of maintain its maritime power would also need to attend to those foundations.

This required what Mahan called a 'general line of policy.' Experience suggested that a government needed to be sufficiently aware of the advantages and requirements of maritime power in the domestic and international context of the time and able to devise national policy and a supporting strategy sufficiently resourced to make the most of them. Foreign policy and naval policy needed to be intimately linked. Although this was a point made more explicitly by Corbett, an effective maritime grand strategy meant striking an effective and mutually supporting balance between land and sea power (and these days he would probably have included all the other domains of warfare as well). The right relationship had also to be found between what Mahan called production, shipping, markets and colonies. None of this was trivial. Mahan pushed his point home by pointing to French experience and the examples it provided of all this being done well, and done badly.[48]

Developing a productive and mutually supporting relationship between navies and what would now be called the maritime industrial base and the overall national effort was especially important because only that would provide the means for the sustainment and the maintenance of the fleet. To this end Mahan approvingly quoted Jean-Baptiste Colbert, Finance and Naval Minister to France's Louis XIV whose intentions were,

> To organize producers and merchants as a powerful army, subjected to an intelligent and active guidance, so as to secure an industrial victory for France, by order and unity of efforts, and to obtain the best products by imposing on all workmen the processes recognized as best by competent men....To organize seamen and distant commerce in large bodies like the manufactures and internal commerce, and to give as a support to the commercial power of France, a navy established on a firm basis and of dimensions hitherto unknown.[49]

Clearly Mahan considered this an admirable summary by 'a great man' of what a government needed to do in order to make the most of its potential naval power. For France, the tragedy was that such a policy was not, and perhaps could not be, sustained.

For this reason, the French, thought Mahan, found it more difficult to develop and maintain a naval administrative system, the trained and experienced personnel and the balanced fleet their maritime needs and aspirations required. The production of naval forces needed to be seen as, in the words of Australia's Admiral Barrett, a 'national enterprise.'[50]

This feeds in to a major point made by many naval historians today. These challenges were so great that tackling them successfully made a major contribution to the development of the state as well. Naval administration, in short, was closely connected to, and even helped, the formation of the modern state. Near the start of this process, for example, since few Dutch individuals could afford to pay for a ship on their own construction costs had to be allocated between dozens of shareholders; in turn this increased the proportion of the population with significant maritime interests and encouraged the development of more sophisticated financial dealings in the private sector which leached through into state activities as well. This happened more and more with the shift from individual and primarily commercial preoccupations and on to matters of state policy and strategy. It resulted in a slow transition from navies raised from private sources when the occasion warranted, to permanent navies maintained by the state.[51]

All in all, this conferred a double benefit on the state; not only did effective navies provide strategic benefits, they could also make modern states more efficient and more sustainable – provided, of course, that naval spending was kept within reasonable bounds and the resultant forces used constructively. Moreover, the development of naval forces was, and is, an area arguably more susceptible to government control than the three other constituents discussed in this chapter, and so an obvious place to start the process of developing or maintaining maritime power.

Certainly that's what the great 18th Century French statesman, Choiseul, thought. 'Upon the navy,' he wrote, reflecting on the lessons of his country's defeat in the Seven Years war, 'depend the colonies, upon the colonies commerce, upon commerce the capacity of a state to maintain numerous armies, to increase its population, and to make possible the most glorious and most useful enterprises.'[52] In saying this he provided yet another illustration of the way in which the constituents of maritime power, if properly and consciously integrated, can be mutually supporting.

2.6 Putting It All Together: The Belt and Road Initiative

The two-way interconnections of these four constituents of maritime power and the way in which they can be made to come together to develop that power are also illustrated in the debate about one of the most remarkable maritime developments of the early 21st Century – China's 'Belt and Road Initiative' (BRI) launched by President Xi in 2013. Its basis is a massive Chinese investment in transportation infrastructure, both marine and terrestrial, across the Eurasian land mass, Africa and Central and South America. The idea has grown more ambitious, taking in more geographic areas (the 'polar silk road') and types (the 'digital silk road').[53]

The idea originated with President Xi, and his immediate political entourage. The BRI is a state-run exercise with a whole-of-nation, not just a whole-of-government approach. It illustrates the apparent advantages of a state-capitalist system which can approach an issue holistically through the close association of political, social, economic and maybe naval action in a manner which would decisively change the country's maritime geography. What China does, in fact, closely relates to what China is.

Many of these issues are a topic of considerable global debate. Much of this zooms in on the question of why China has developed the BRI and what its consequences

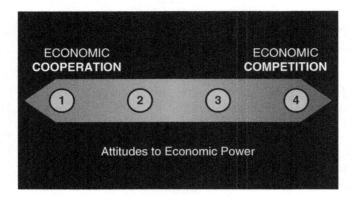

Figure 2.3 Power and Economics.
Source: Self-generated.

might be. The varying positions taken illustrate points on the economic cooperation-competition spectrum discussed earlier (see Figure 2.3). Chinese officials say that the BRI makes economic sense for China, offering a path to the development of its western regions, and new markets for its heavy industries. Overseas trade, both by land and sea, increases prosperity. 'To get rich,' the common Chinese saying goes (*yaoxiangfu, xianxiulu*), 'you start by building a road.' This would also be true for all peoples of the world not just for the Chinese. As a result of this Chinese 'dream,' the living standards of two-thirds of the world population would be radically raised. Accordingly, this is presented by the project's advocates in China and elsewhere, as a way of delivering that 'attractive' economic power associated with the first of the four spectrum positions identified earlier.[54] The BRI is a 'win-win opportunity,' not a threat.[55] It is a 'new blueprint for global growth' offering 'a ride on China's economic express train' open to its neighbours to the south, and west and indeed far beyond.[56] As a result, a new golden age for the world will emerge.

BRI narratives often refer back to the old silk roads, by which Chinese silks and ceramics used to reach Southeast Asia, India, the Middle East and later Europe from well before the Tang dynasty to the disruptive arrival of the Europeans in the Indian Ocean in the late 15th Century. These silk roads were both terrestrial and especially sea-based. This trading system between regions 'below the wind' and 'above the wind' was determined by the behaviour of the monsoons. Typically, ships would leave Guangzhou in October to December, pass through the Straits of Malacca to reach the Arabian peninsula in February or March and Muscat or Basra soon after. After a stay of three or four months they would leave Arabia in September or October, returning to Guangzhou in March of the following year.[57] This was part-and-parcel of a local trading system around Southeast Asia itself, operated by Arabs, Javanese and other Southeast Asians and Chinese vessels that exchanged forest and sea products for Chinese metals and manufactures.[58] The result of this settled wind-determined trading system, the Chinese claim, was an era of peaceful sea-based commerce benefitting everyone and threatening no-one. As such, it exemplifies what BRI would offer.

Still referring back to their own history, as the Chinese are wont to do, many commentators implicitly or explicitly link the old trading with the famous Indian

Ocean 15th Century voyages of the Chinese Admiral Zheng He, with his massive 'jewel' ships and huge armadas. They argue in terms reminiscent of the second of the four positions identified above that the Admiral's efforts demonstrated the benign and non-hegemonic role of China in its partial, episodic monitoring of the trading system in the Indian Ocean and the Southern seas.[59] Today they claim, the Chinese navy needs to perform the same protective function, partly to protect their own citizens and economic interests but partly also for the general good and for a harmonious future.

But this is not how the BRI is seen by everyone. Some historians for example take a rather different view of Admiral Zheng He's activities in the 15th Century, arguing that there were some decidedly hegemonic aspects to his various cruises. Kwa Chong Guan argues that it was a matter of 'prestige and the cosmographical centrality of China.'[60] Why else so many gigantic fighting ships and so many soldiers? It seems unlikely that either the King of what is now Sri Lanka (defeated in war taken back to China in chains) or the free-booting Chinese population of Java attacked for being where they were in defiance of the Emperor's command would have regarded this purely as a good-will cruise. To historians of this persuasion,[61] it all looks more like a display of power intended to support a China-centric political and economic system, characteristic of the third position identified above.

For less academic reasons, the United States, India, Japan and other countries seem increasingly wary of taking China's protestations of virtue at face value. They worry about the BRI being likely to end in China's securing considerable strategic advantage through political leverage over the countries receiving such Chinese largesse. They worry too about the particular advantage it seems to secure for Chinese shipping interests and for IT firms like Huawei. Might the Chinese navy not secure basing rights and strategic advantage at ports developed with Chinese money? In terms distinctly reminiscent of the fourth position on the spectrum, the resultant trading arrangements look to them like another form of dominion, somewhat reminiscent of the old European East India Companies, busily developing and defending their trading monopolies and political control. In short, to its sceptics, the BRI is nothing more than a covert bid by China for world power in an age where the overt threat of military force has become too costly and risky?[62]

Moreover, the result could well have material consequences for the future of the Chinese navy. Firstly and most obviously, it will in due course make China wealthier still and so provide revenue for the government and economic stimulus for its defence industrial base and its naval defence expenditure. Secondly it transforms geography, making China a global not just a regional power. It helps explain why that Navy is developing the capacity to 'step out' from local and regional seas to the wider world and set up the bases and port facilities it used once to condemn.

If China is indeed following such a policy, it would be no more than paying others back for what they had done to China in the past. It has often been subjected to this kind of military-commercial pressure. Referring to its Mongolian forebears who conquered China and established the Yuan dynasty (1279–1367), one Chinese historian was clear about the secret of their success. 'Although they accomplished this partly by the use of their strong and ruthless military power,' he wrote, 'yet it was commerce which they used as a weapon for the subjugation of peoples and nations... In their conquest of Song,' he concluded, 'commerce was their advance guard which they backed with armed might.'[63] From Beijing's perspective such a summary could equally be applied to the Opium Wars of the 19th Century, and potentially to China's exposure to American economic dominance at the end of the 20th Century.[64]

This is not the place for a discussion about who is right and who wrong in this on-going debate, or even if the BRI will deliver the promised goods; these issues are unlikely to become much clearer for some considerable time.[65] The project does however illustrate how geography, government, the economy and naval capability can come together to generate maritime power, whether or not that was the original intention. As such, it also demonstrates the advantage of the holistic approach towards maritime endeavour that is an important theme of this book.

2.7 Some Metrics of Maritime Power

This review of the inter-connections of geography, government, the economy and navies leads to some tentative observations about the distinctive nature of 'maritimeness' and maritime power. Accordingly, the next step in theory should be to try to come up with some generalisations, even working metrics, of 'maritimeness' and maritime power which determine where countries are on the maritime-continental spectrum discussed in the last chapter. These metrics are a combination of what countries are and what they do, the two being closely linked. Although these observations have largely been drawn from historical experience, they seem to have contemporary and future salience. They may also help identify what countries need to do in order to improve their maritimeness if they feel this necessary. Above all, these metrics of 'maritimeness' and its continental equivalent are essentially matters of complementary degree.

These generalisations (to which of course there are countless exceptions) are presented as they relate to the interlinked elements of maritime power originally identified by Mahan and amended in this chapter into four constituents as a framework for analysis.

Maritime Geography

- Maritime states enjoy a geographic position that provides easy access to, and potential control of, important sea lines of communication (SLOCS) and a coastline suitable for the construction and operation of ports. They often act to 'improve' their maritime geography.
- The national integrity of states with territories physically separated by seawater depends on their unimpeded control of those waters. Otherwise their integrity depends on the good will of others.
- Maritime states have sufficient resources in local seas to incentivise their exploitation and protection.

Governance and Society

- Maritime states 'naturally' develop liberal, transparent and orderly societal and governmental structures that facilitate the business of trade and politically empower those who conduct it.
- While encouraging the international acceptance of liberal trading values, maritime states are pragmatic and avoid ideological crusading.

- Maritime states will often consciously celebrate their relationship with the sea in forms of art that foster the sea-mindedness of their populations and the respect of other states.
- Maritime states develop a supporting narrative and remembered/invented past.

Economy and Resources

- Maritime states consider their land and sea-based resources insufficient for their material needs. They consequently have to import raw materials and to develop exports or services to pay for them.
- Sea-based trade rather than agriculture is therefore the recognized foundation of their economy.
- Concerned with their own strategic sovereignty and aware of its potential spill-over economic benefits, maritime states will want to develop a maritime defence industrial base.
- Maritime states are active participants in the global trading system and, because of the advantages of sea-based transportation, will often dominate it.
- Naturally active and competitive, maritime states can make ruthless use of their economic power against rivals but will often conclude that more benign and consensual approaches may be more sustainable in the long run.
- Wherever possible maritime states prefer to make use of economic sanctions and sea, rather than land- or air-based forces in peace and war.
- Having a strong sense of danger and aware of the costs of conflict, of the strategic vulnerability that derives from their dependence on sea-based trade and, some-times from the superior resources of large continental states, maritime states incline towards Corbettian limited and pragmatic policies that avoid antagonizing potential adversaries.
- Sea-based trade provides the infrastructure, financial and human resources for the construction and maintenance of navies to protect it, if necessary by acting offensively.

Naval Forces

- The direct and indirect protection of trade and of the country's maritime interests in peace and war becomes a major aim of state policy. Navies are seen as an important way of doing this.
- Maritime states will seek to establish trading stations and secure naval bases that help the conduct and defence of sea-based trade.
- Maritime states, however, will seek to avoid the costs and responsibilities that go with the political acquisition of overseas territory. Where this is unavoidable, such territory is expected to be as economically self-sustaining as possible. The more dependent territory they acquire, the less maritime they become.
- Conscious of the costs of continental interventions and the often superior human and physical resources of large continental states, maritime states incline wherever possible to offshore balancing strategies, involving the conduct of limited military expeditions and partnering with (and if necessary subsidizing) other maritime or continental states against potential adversaries.

- Maritime states prioritise naval over military land power, give serious thought to the composition, equipment and maintenance of their navies and require their armies and air-forces to be expeditionary in nature.

This series of generalisations about 'maritimeness' and about the interconnections of geography, governance, the economy and naval forces establishes a rough agenda for the development of naval power that nations have pursued or might intend to. Where people or agencies find themselves in the decision-making hierarchy will obviously shape their approach and the focus of their attention in this task. Clearly, Admiralties, navy departments and ministries of defence will be mostly preoccupied with the fourth of these constituents while the broader issues relating to the first three will be rather more associated with other governmental agencies. Their high-level strategic aspects will normally be handled by agencies higher up in the food chain.

As pointed out at the start of this chapter, the extent to which countries and their various agencies have either sought or been successful in developing their maritime power has very much depended, however, on the international and domestic context in which they operate and it is to that point that we now should turn.

Notes

1 To some *aficionados* of Mahan, this may seem to teeter on the edge of heresy, but there is some evidence that this first chapter of his book was an add-on requested by the Publisher and that the views were hastily expressed and owed much to other people. See McCranie, Kevin D. *Mahan, Corbett and the Foundations of Naval Strategic Thought* (Annapolis, MD: Naval Institute Press, 2021), 22–8 is an Executive Summary of Mahan's 'elements.'
2 Mahan, *The Influence of Sea Power*, 25.
3 Alexander Hamilton, *A New Account of the East Indies*, 1737, quoted in Wise, *Travellers Tales*, 13.
4 Mahan, *The Influence of Sea Power*, 27.
5 Ibid, 32.
6 Ibid, 36.
7 Gilbert Gregory P., *Ancient Egyptian Sea Power and the Origin of Maritime Forces* (Canberra: Sea Power Centre, 2008), 73–84.
8 Mitchell, Donald W., *A History of Russian and Soviet Sea Power* (London: Andre Deutsch, 1974), 3–4.
9 Lo Jung-Pang. *China as a Sea Power 1127–1368 (1957)* edited and with commentary by Bruce A. Elleman (Hong Kong: Hong Kong University Press, 2012), 142.
10 Ibid, 340.
11 Omrod, *The Rise of Commercial Empires*, 334.
12 O'Brien, *How the War Was Won*, 33–45.
13 *Angliae Tutamen: Or, the Safety of England* (1695), 3 quoted in Hoppit, Julian, *A Land of Liberty? England 1689–1727* (Oxford: Oxford University Press, 2010), 318. For more on this see ibid, 72, 193, 261–3, 318–22, 346–1, 344.
14 Mahan, *The Influence of Sea Power*, 44, 50–3.
15 Paine, *The Sea and Civilisation*, 105–6, 172, 215
16 Ibid, 317–20, 331–5; for Mahan's comparison of Britain and Germany before the First World War see Sumida, Jon Tetsuro, *Inventing Grand Strategy and Teaching Command: The Classic Worlds of Alfred Thayer Mahan Reconsidered* (Baltimore: Johns Hopkins University Press, 1997), 85–7.
17 Quoted, Wise, *Travellers' Tales*, 59.
18 Paine, *The Sea and Civilisation*, 226–8.
19 Comments quoted in Wise, *Travellers' Tales*, 81, 108, 120.
20 Mahan, *The Influence of Sea Power*, 58, 82, 87–8.

21 Ibid, 67.
22 Ibid, 48, 88. For his concerns about the possible consequences of democracy, see also *The Interest of America in Sea Power* (Boston: Little, Brown & Co., 1906), 175, *Lessons of the War with Spain* (Boston: Little, Bowen & Co., 1899), 20 and especially *Sea Power in Relation to the War of 1812,* vol. 1 (Boston: Little, Brown & Co., 1918), 310–11, 350; vol. 2, 27, 318. I am indebted to Professor John Hattendorf for these references.
23 Mahan, *The Influence of History,* 70–4.
24 Kate Tringham, 'Building new capabilities,' *Jane's Defence Weekly,* 14 March 2012; Charles Forrester, 'Gulf Challenges,' *Jane's Defence Weekly,* 1 February 2017.
25 Pickering's blog, accessed 15 June 2021 is https://www.greenpeace.org/international/story/47915/deep-sea-mining-disturbing-threat-home/. For Brianne Fruean, viw see https://www.greenpeace.org/aotearoa/story/pacific-voices-missing-from-seaspiracy/. Thanks to Christopher Till for these insights.
26 Paine, *The Sea and Civilisation,* 43–9, 135.
27 Thanks to Cdr Christopher Green of the Chilean Navy for this point.
28 This is a major theme in Lambert, *Seapower States,* op cit.
29 Edict 2 from J Mason Gentzler, *Changing China: Readings in the History of China from the Opium War to the Present* (New York: Prager 1977). The efinitive account is Peyrefitte, Alain, *The Collision of Two Civilisations: The British Expedition to China 1792–04* (London: Harvill, 1993).
30 Sharman, J.C., 'Power and Profit at Sea,' *International Security,* Vol. 43, No. 4 (Spring 2019), 163–96, 163.
31 Kwa Chong Guan, *Seven Hundred Years,* 22–4, 65.
32 Semenoff, Vladimir, *Rasplata (The Reckoning)* (London: John Murray, 1913), 10, 122.
33 Mahan, *The Influence of Sea Power,* 225.
34 Emre Peker, 'Russia levels Sanctions at Turkey,' *Wall Street Journal,* 1 December 2015. This was a particularly interesting example of economic pressure, in response to a military act – the shooting down by Turkey of a Russian aircraft.
35 Postlethwate, Malachy *Universal Dictionary of Trade and Commerce,* 1757.
36 For a succinct summary of this proposition and its consequences, see Sharman, J.C., 'Power and Profit at Sea,' *International Security,* Vol. 43, No. 4 (Spring 2019), 163–96; ibid, 167.
37 For some examples in the Middle East and Central Asia see Paine, *The Sea and Civilization,* 266–7, 273–8, 297, 362 and in East and Southeast Asia, 281–3, 295, 355–7.
38 Harding, Rebecca and Jack, *The Weaponization of Trade; The Great Unbalancing of Politics and Economics* (London: Publishing partnership, 2017). See also Paul Krugman, Paul, Obstfeld, Maurice, Melitz, Marc, *International Economics: Theory and Practice* (London: Pearson, 2017).
39 Mahan, *The Influence of Sea Power,* 41–2. See also Kamer, Henry, *Empire: How Spain Became a World Power 1492–1763* (London: HarperCollins, 2003).
40 Stephen Castle, 'An Emotional Fish Fight Could Snag Brexit Talks,' *New York Times,* 16 March 2020. (A).
41 Mahan, *The Influence of Sea Power,* 26, 1.
42 Paine, *The Sea and Civilization,* 64.
43 The similarities and differences of the two are compared in McCranie, *Mahan, Corbett and the Foundations.*
44 See Chapter 9.
45 Andrade, Tonio, *Lost Colony: The Untold Story of China's First Great Victory over the West* (Princeton, NJ: Princeton University Press, 2013); on the bigger issues, see Sharman, J.C., *Empires of the Weak* (Princeton: Princeton University Press, 2019).
46 Herbert Lin and Amy Zegart, *Bytes, Bombs and Spies: The Strategic Dimensions of Offensive Cyber Operations* (Washington, DC: Brookings Institute, 2019).
47 Chernarvin, Admiral V., 'On Naval Theory,' *Morskoi Sbornik.* No. 1, 1982.
48 Mahan, *The Influence of Sea Power,* 66, 60–7, 75.
49 Quoted, ibid, 70.
50 Barrett, *The Navy and the Nation,* op cit, 57–67.
51 Paine, Lincoln, *The Sea and Civilization: A Maritime History of the World* (New York: Alfred A. Knopf, 2013), 429–434.

52 Quoted in Graham, *The Politics of Naval Supremacy,* op cit, 67.
53 Friedberg, Aaron L., 'Globalisation and Chinese Grand Strategy,' *Survival,* Vol. 60 (2018), 7–40.
54 Hu, *Chinese Maritime Power,* 37–44.
55 Liu Xiaoming, (Chinese Ambassador to London) 'Take the new Silk Road as an opportunity not a threat,' *Financial Times,* 24 May 2015.
56 Li Kequiang, *Jakarta Post,* 16 September 2015; Alfred Romann, 'Initiative promises business bonanza,' *China Daily,* 2–26 November 2015.
57 Rong Xinjiang, 'A Study of Yang Liangyao's Embassy to the Abbasid Caliphate' (in 785 AD) in Victor H Mair and Liam C Kelley (Eds), *Imperial China and its Southern Neighbours* (Singapore: ISEAS, 2015), 256.
58 Anthony Reid, *Charting the Shape of Early Modern Southeast Asia* (Chiang Mai, Thailand: Silkworm Books, 1999), 43, 61, 70.
59 Miksic, John, *Singapore and the Silk Road of the Sea 1300–1800* (Singapore: National Museum, 2014), 93–6. 'Episodic' because the Emperor sometimes banned commercial trade with foreigners altogether.
60 Kwa Chongguan, 'East India Companies in the long cycles of Asian maritime trade,' in Yeo, Stephanie (Ed.), *Encounters and Connected Histories, The East Indies and Singapore before 1819* (Singapore: National Museum of Singapore, 2020). Ball, *The Water Kingdom,* Chapter 5 is a useful review of the competing positions.
61 For example, Wade, Geoff, 'The Zheng He Voyages: A Reassessment,' *Journal of the Malaysian Branch of the Royal Asiatic Society,* Vol. 78, No. 1 (June 2005), 37–58.
62 Frankopan, Peter, *The New Silk Roads: The Present and Future of the World* (London: Bloomsbury, 2018).
63 Wang Xiaotong, writing in 1937, and quoted in Lo, *China as a Sea Power,* 308.
64 Friedberg, *Globalisation.*
65 Keith Bradsher, 'China renews its Belt and Road Push for Global Sway,' *New York Times,* 15 January 2020.

3 Henry Maydman, His Context, Maritime Power and a Strategy of Means

3.1 Introduction

In 1691, Henry Maydman, a grizzled 30-year Warrant Officer in the Royal Navy, in the manner of a modern blogger, published his book, *Naval Speculations*. Deeply perturbed at the current state of his Navy and the potential peril in which this could place the country, his polemic analysed the problem and came up with a series of recommendations about what should be done about it. Maydman doubtless hoped that his book would attract attention from the political class. To that end, he dedicated it to Thomas Earl of Pembroke, the First Lord of the Admiralty, hoping for a 'favourable perusal' from an important and busy public figure.[1]

Stripped of its arcane, if often hilarious, language and its sometimes idiosyncratic approach, the result was what the French General Lucien Poirier would later call a 'strategy of means.'[2] This was a development of Admiral Raoul Castex's earlier emphasis on the need to take a strategic approach to the provision of the resources that a navy would need in order to operate properly in peace and war. What Maydman was providing was a deep dive into exactly this issue. Even though *Naval Speculations* related to a specific navy at a specific time, it helps illuminate and maybe solve the developmental problems of all navies and all times. Although sadly neglected for far too long, Maydman's book provides a logical framework for the review of the growing of navies conducted in the chapters that follow.

Naval Speculations, of course, is a book of its times. The context in which Maydman put pen to paper was important and needs to be borne in mind. This underlines the point made in the last chapter that the domestic and international context within which navies develop helps shape them. The reverse is equally true. Unless navies can influence their context, there would not be much point in having them.

Before launching into a review of Maydman's approach to the development of maritime and naval power, a short digression into just how important context can be seems justified. To do that, we will briefly turn to a world quite different from that of late 17th-Century England.

3.2 Singapore and the Importance of the Context

Mahan's 'elements' of seapower (translated into the four constituents used here) not only influence each other inducing change but they can all be much affected by, and indeed affect, the wider national and international environment. However wise and far-seeing they are, governments seeking to maintain or develop maritime power have

DOI: 10.4324/9781003100553-3

only a limited capacity to improve the context within which their nation operates. They generally do not have the initiative. They have to respond as best they can to what they see happening outside the country, and its possible effects for their country. Equally they can also find themselves at the mercy of internal and domestic events over which they may very well have only limited control.

The bewildering cycles of rise and fall in the development of Singapore as a maritime centre make the critical importance of the context very clear. Raffles in 'founding' modern Singapore was not writing on a blank slate and knew that perfectly well. As a trading port and under a variety of names Singapore had risen and fallen, again risen and fallen before he set foot in the place in 1819. Domestic changes in China in the 11th century had caused an explosion in Chinese trading and a trading boom into the 13th and 14th centuries when the misty city state known as Temasek on the island of Singapore flourished as an *entrepot*. It was where the marine and forest products of Southeast Asia were exchanged for Chinese manufactures, including ceramics.

However, with the malign effects on China of climate change and a sudden clamp down on trade by the Ming authorities in the 15th Century, Malacca (Melaka) rose and Temasek declined into merely a haunt of the *Orang Laut* nomadic sea-people. To an extent, Singapore (variously named) revived in part as a kind of naval base and port authority for the Sultanate of Johor, its changing fortunes reflecting domestic development in China, dynastic squabbles in Johor, local rivalries with Malacca, Aceh and Riau and before long the competing presence of the Dutch and Portuguese. In 1613 the small settlement on Singapore island seems to have been burnt to the ground, so that by 1703 when William Hamilton visited, and was offered it as a gift from the Sultan, the place hardly existed. A century later though, rivalry between the Dutch and the British created conditions in which Sir Stamford Raffles came, saw and set Singapore off on the next and as yet uncompleted round of trading success.

Significantly, a very recent and deeply authoritative survey of Singapore's changing fortunes as a maritime centre ends with a warning that in the long cycles of history, nothing can be taken for granted. 'Singapore could indeed falter, stumble and vanish, never to rise again' – perhaps, to give just one example of potentially transformative development in its context, if someone hacks a canal through Thailand's Kra isthmus – a project which might take away much of Singapore's trade and which people have been discussing for a hundred years and more. [3] For a while too there was concern that global warming would so open up the Northern Sea Route between Asia and Europe through the Arctic that this too might possibly have severe consequences for Singapore.

Whether the Northern Sea Route works as its advocates expect or not, the debate about it makes the first essential point. Context matters. But how a country reacts to its context is just as important. Singapore's survival and contemporary vibrancy are a testament to its success through the centuries in being able to respond to that environment effectively, by making the most of its overall maritime potential. Its example seems a good one for others to follow.

3.3 Henry Maydman's *Naval Speculations* of 1691: A Bleak Context

Henry Maydman published his polemic in the hope of inducing change. Certainly the context for his analysis and recommendations seemed quite bleak, both at home and internationally. His book appeared barely three years after England's so-called Glorious Revolution had transferred the throne from the Catholic James II to the Protestant William III and his consort Mary, one of James II's daughters. No one was entirely clear about the country's likely political future. A lot of prominent people were keeping their options open in case James II came back, including Lord Russell, the Navy Commander-in-Chief.

In any case, politics and government were fractured with the emergence of contending interest groups such as the Country landed interest *versus* the City merchant interest, the latter being much more maritime in its outlook. Compromise between these extremes was difficult and there was much lamenting of the absence of 'right management of public affairs.'[4] In short, the domestic environment was hardly conducive to the thoughtful development and effective use of maritime power.

Inevitably these domestic perspectives fed into and reflected some very basic ideas about what Britain was and about the role it should play internationally. As a Dutchman, William arrived with a whole set of continental and European ideas – and advisors – about how to deal with France. He revolutionised British policy, switching its previous pro-French stance to outright opposition. Many in England disagreed with these pre-conceptions, preferring a more maritime approach and less involvement in the difficult military-political affairs of the European continent. As Winston Churchill remarked, when writing of this period in his *History of the English-Speaking Peoples,* 'the Tories, ... resented the country being involved in Continental commitments and voiced the traditional isolationism of the people.'[5] The 'Country interest' resented the taxation required for war-fighting, especially if they had Jacobite sympathies. Nonetheless William had enough support in 1688 to initiate a new anti-French policy that was to last more or less continuously until 1815.

William's arrival in England, though, meant that war with France, on paper a much more powerful and populous country, indeed the strongest in Europe, would be hard to avoid, especially after the dispossessed James II sought French help. Britain's great strategic weakness was the general disaffection and Jacobite sympathies of most of Ireland. This opened up the prospect of James II reclaiming his realm through the back door. After the great work that Colbert had done in the 1660s and 1670s, the French Navy was still in sufficiently good shape to kick that door open.

In 1689, the French evaded a Royal Navy short of resources (because of all the administrative and fiscal confusions that followed the Revolution), and landed James and his supporters in Ireland. Although the Royal Navy only had a supporting role in the subsequent campaign against the Jacobites, particularly in relieving the siege of Londonderry in July of that year,[6] the Irish campaign which culminated in victory at the Battle of the Boyne owed more to the success of William and his Generals than to that of his Admirals.

While King William was occupied in Ireland, his wife, Queen Mary and her Counselors, were focused on the land fighting in the Low Countries and at sea between the British and the Dutch fleets on the one hand and the French on the other. There seemed every prospect of the initially superior French fleet being able to clear the way for a direct assault on an apparently divided England, particularly after it inflicted a potentially catastrophic tactical defeat on the British and their Dutch allies at the battle of Beachy Head in 1690. The French Admiral de Tourville frittered away what opportunities he had for mischief in some low-level raiding and sheep-rustling. British observers could hardly fail to note that their deliverance from something much worse owed more to French hesitation in exploiting their victory and the command of the English Channel that it gave them, rather than to the allies' efforts to deny them one. Withdrawing into the Thames, the Royal Navy abandoned the field of battle, although, arguably preserving itself as a deterrent. It was against this melancholy background that Henry Maydman wrote his book, and made his recommendations. The war wasn't over yet and the British needed to do a lot better.

3.4 Maydman on Britain's Maritime Potential

All was not lost. Britain had maritime potential. In his own idiosyncratic way, Maydman touched on the four main maritime characteristics of his country discussed in the last chapter. His observations about them and his recommendations about how some of them might be improved in order to recover the country's maritime power and fortunes are scattered, with heartless disregard for the modern reader, throughout his book.

3.4.1 Maritime Geography

Clearly Maydman thought the maritime nature of England's geography was so obvious to his readers that he only raised the issue in his summary at the end of the book, and then largely to lament the way in which its manifest advantages had been frittered away since the age of Queen Elizabeth. Providence had made the country an island and by ancient usage the narrow seas belonged to the British. If they lost control over them, all would be lost:

> *When England's Rule in Brittish seas doth cease*
>
> *Farewel their Wealth, their Glory and their Peace.*[7]

3.4.2 Governance and Society

Connectedly, the country and society was profoundly maritime too. Likening the command of the country with the command of a ship, Maydman concluded that 'Monarchy ... with moderate bounds and constitutions is the best of governments ever yet found out in the world, and therefore most to be desired and maintained.' It provided a governmental framework that should be 'unified and vigorous ..... (free from the) 'sulphorous vapours of that noisome weed of arbitrary, despotical and tyrannical power.' The King and his navy should stand in good credit with the 'maritime people ... for their welfare and the whole nation depends upon the prosperity of the Navy.' The Navy would only prosper if it was able 'to avoid divisions, party-makings ... trickings and designings ... instead of unity and concord.' And yet he warned things were not as they should be; 'not only the Navy, but the nation in general hath had a vein of debauchery running through it at a prodigious rate, not one vice only but all vices.'[8]

3.4.3 Trade, Economy and Resources

The nature of the state and the population reflected its economic activity and the importance of the country shipping, ship-building and fishing industries were a major focus of Maydman's recommendations. The importance of all this to England's glory and prosperity was obvious and so the government should do what it could to protect and advance the country's maritime/economic interests. For the same reason, the direct defence of trade should be a high priority for the Navy, rather than the pursuit of decisive battle against a 'dodging enemy' at a time when 'the seas swarm with privateers and small frigates' threatening England's merchant fleet.[9]

This battery of points nicely illustrates the close inter-connections of the four constituents of maritime power, remarked on earlier.

3.4.4 Naval Forces

Obviously this aspect of England's maritime power was Maydman's chief concern, no doubt reflecting the fact that successive English '... kings have always been very jealous of any competitor or rival as an Italian may be of his mistress.' Only a standing fleet could bring lasting peace and happiness to the country. 'The true splendour and glory of the navy lies in the good government thereof, the easiness of the expense to the nation, and the achievement of great actions, preserving the honour, safety and wealth of the nation.' But things had gone to pot in recent years and 'It is high time to lay our hands heartily to advance and promote the growth and strength of the navy, when our neighbours especially are so busie about the same thing.'

And so, wrote Maydman, 'I will address myself to a means, whereby we may assume our former prowess ... which we have lost to a great degree.'[10]

3.5 Maydman's Recommendations for the Developing Maritime Power, Tier by Tier

Maydman's approach was to offer a top-down review of what needed to be done in these four areas in order to develop British maritime power and strengthen its Navy. Implicitly, in the top-down way he structured his book, he identified both how this should be done and, sometimes in even broader terms, by whom and which authority. The result, represented in Figure 3.1, is a notional policy-making hierarchy associated with a broad indication of the main things that needed to be decided at each level.

- Tier 1 was the highest level responsible for setting national objectives. In Maydman's time, this was the task of the King and his Counselors.
- Tier 2, was responsible for the allocation of the necessary resources. This was also principally the job of the King and his counsellors, but other offices of state were also engaged. Parliament would both vote through the financial resources required and seek to ensure they would be available in the future by sustaining the national economy, and its maritime elements in particular.
- Tier 3 decided the required military mix and prospective use of sea and land forces. In Maydman's time, this level was the least developed. The task was performed informally by the King and his counsellors and validated by Parliament.
- Tier 4 got the most coverage in Maydman's book as it will in this one. It is the level of the Admiralty or navy department, where, in the development of the country's naval capacity, exactly the same top-down approach took place. This started at the top with the Board of Admiralty and went all the way down to the running of individual departments and dockyards, fleets and ships.

A closer look helps fill in the details about how he thought maritime power and naval

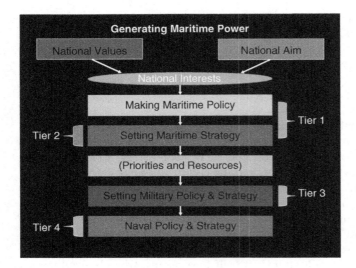

Figure 3.1 Generating Maritime Power.

Source: Self-generated.

strength could actually be developed in the England of his time, and arguably, by extension, in everyone else's too.

3.5.1 Tier 1: Deciding National Policy Objectives

It was at this rarified level of the King, his advisers in cabinet and when it came to high naval matters, his Lord High Admiral (or the Board of Admiralty in his place), that Britain's general policy objectives were decided. Essentially this was about ensuring regime survival and winning the war with France.

One of the central issues in establishing what Mahan called 'the general line of policy' was the balance Britain should strike between a sea-centred maritime war on the one hand or a land-centred continental one on the other – bearing in mind that it couldn't afford to lose either. This was the subject of much often highly politicised and contentious debate. The Earl of Nottingham, William's Secretary of State, effectively summarised the outcome arguing '... that we shall never have any decisive success, nor be able to hold out a war against France, but by making it a sea war,' but adding ' and such a sea war as accompanies and supports attempts on land.'[11] The last few words of this comment are significant. The recommended sea war would be justified mainly for its effects on the land.

Technically it was the King, William III, who had the final say on all this as, on all other matters of government policy, but Maydman was perfectly aware that other people and interests has significant input at this level too, especially as there were limits on the King's time, presence and sometimes state of health. Although he was perfectly aware of their crucial role, William's interest in maritime and naval matters was frankly limited, the Army being much more his thing. When Russia's Peter the Great visited him William very quickly tired of his huge guest's over-spilling enthusiasm for ships and carpentry.[12] This left the maritime policy-making field open to other influences.

To help him run the country while fighting a war with France, William created the beginnings of a 'departmental system' which represented all other aspects of governmental responsibility. This delegated authority provided those interests with a political voice and points of view that could be articulated, especially at cabinet meetings where both the sovereign and all other departments were represented. Finally, while the House of Commons represented a range of opinions on the central issue of the balance to be struck between a sea-based and a land-based campaign, it was united on the principle that the people who paid for it all should have a significant say in policy-making and in deciding what the desired outcomes should be.

A consensus on the way forward dropped out of the bottom of this noisy, untidy, often rumbustious but surprisingly effective policy-making system. When Maydman was writing, in 1690/1 it was by no means clear that it would be, however. Things had not settled down yet.

From this level of government downwards it was essential, he thought, that the more 'loyal, valiant, wise and just men … are put into the affaires of the navy, the better it will prosper and come into a regular government.' 'Controlling bribery and corruption was important because the very welfare of the politick body of this nation does hang upon it.' Maydman offered no comment on what we would call the country's grand strategic policy objectives should be, other than recovering its former glory as a maritime power.

3.5.2 *Tier 2: Allocating Resources*

This was the level where policy – the defining of objectives – turned into strategy – deciding the ways and means by which those objectives were to be achieved. In practice policy-making, strategy setting and the allocation of resources were all very closely linked because it's a very poor strategist who doesn't have some idea of his or her resources before setting the way forward.

The allocation of financial resources was obviously key. The costs of the War of Spanish Succession were high and have been variously estimated at between 60 and 90 million pounds sterling per year. The land-war and the Army got just over half of this.[13] Allocation priorities for William's government were in some ways less complicated than it was for today's governments since it bore far fewer responsibilitiesfor things like social welfare, health and education. Even in peacetime, spending on the Navy was twice that of public and private funding for social welfare.[14]

Nonetheless raising the necessary money through taxation was a real issue, partly because of divided opinions in the House of Commons about what it should be spent on. There were common and often sadly justified allegations about widespread corruption amongst ministers, and all government departments, including the Navy. For this reason, Parliamentary Commissioners were established to audit naval accounts for the first time.[15]

The country was 20% wealthier in 1701 than it had been in 1688, the year of the Glorious Revolution, but for all that, the economy still suffered from the occasional panicky convulsions as it did in 1696 over the coinage – and the infamous South Sea Bubble melt-down was just around the corner early in the next century. The result of this was a strong tendency for expenditure to outrun appropriations. There is absolutely nothing new about 'black holes' in defence expenditure plans.

Nonetheless the basic strength of the British economy pulled the country through all these difficulties, reinforcing Mahan's point that real maritime power lies in the combination of naval and commercial power at sea. What increasingly made the difference for successive British governments was their ability to establish a level of creditworthiness that meant they paid affordable levels of interest for the loans they received, mainly from domestic sources.

Maydman had lots of ideas about what should be done to preserve and develop the country's interests as a maritime nation on the one hand and to encourage the trade that would provide the necessary resources on the other. For the first of these two related tasks, he recommended establishing what he called a seminary 'for the breeding and maintaining of mariners and a Maritime People.' This would involve the country's parishes sending 'poor boys' to training schemes, as apprentices in all but name, and with tattoos to distinguish them. Afterwards they would be able to serve in the dock-yards, the merchant marine or the Navy. This would restore the maritime population and add 'to our naval strength many thousands of good and able mariners, and artificers, and would be an ever-living seminary thereof and for their constant employment both in war and peace.' Encouraging the fisheries would have the same effect.[16]

Relatedly it was incumbent on the government to support the fishing and merchant shipping industries since it was their profits that brought the necessary resources to the country. This called for a close partnership between the maritime services, such that at one point Maydman even suggested that some warships carried the necessary tackle for them to go fishing should the opportunity present itself. He also proposed that keeping a proper national register of seamen would '... avoid the great trouble, charges and abuses in the pressing of men.' Systematic collection of data about the country's seamen would provide 'a true and certain state of the Kingdom, as to maritime strength,' so offering evidence on which future action could be based.

Government should also attend to the health of the maritime economy as a whole, by doing all it could to defend and develop trade with the West Indies and other colonies and to ensure what he called 'evenness of trade' with France and other countries. Trade should 'balance' beneficially, both in size and type; the more the country exported of its manufactures and the less it relied on others for the essentials of life and power, the better. The extent to which the country upset the balance of trade by importing unnecessary frivolities, 'vanities, pleasures and luxuries' from France was therefore a real concern.[17] Better instead to focus attention, maybe through government subsidies, on encouraging domestic manufacture, even down to workhouse level.[18] In short, Maydman was advocating a very 'joined up' government policy towards society and the maritime economy and also what would now be called a public-private partnership for its development.

3.5.3 *Tier 3: Deciding the Military Mix*

At this level, policy and strategy-making was much more narrowly military – and much more operational in tone. The task was to decide where and how British strategy should focus on the maritime-continental spectrum. The chief players were all the main stake-holders, the King, the House of Commons, the Cabinet and the representatives of the Navy and the Army. The latter was not as well regarded by the political classes as the Navy, but William III's personal focus on the territorial defence of his Dutch homeland much reinforced its position – as did the role that success on land in the Battle of Namur in 1695 played in securing the first precarious peace with France two years later. The same strategic logic played out in the following War of Spanish Succession (1701–1714), a war in which the Navy had only limited direct strategic effect and for which the land victories of Winston Churchill's ancestor, the Duke of Marlborough, are chiefly remembered.[19]

In truth Maydman had little to say on this issue. Maybe he thought as a 30 year 'warranted officer' in the Navy that entering into strategic debate with Kings and Earls was above his pay-grade, or maybe it was fear of its being impolitic given how contentious the issue was. At all events, his own preferences for a focus on the maritime end of the spectrum were perfectly clear.

3.5.4 Tier 4: Deciding Naval Policy and Strategy

Although Maydman covered all the decision-making levels of his England at this time, most of his fire was unsurprisingly directed at the lowest one – where specifically naval policy, strategy and administration were dealt with. Clearly for nearly all this period, the international context meant that the Royal Navy was on a war rather than a peacetime footing. Its worst performances came in the 1688–1689 period when actually that was only partially true; instead all was political turmoil. The resulting degree of unpreparedness, when there was even talk about the fleet's being 'laid up,' in part explains the Navy's failure to stop William's original response to an invitation to 'invade' England with 500 ships, 20,000 military men and 5000 horses in 1688, and James II getting to Ireland in 1689. The Navy was only capable of limited interference with James' sea-based supply lines afterwards; worst of all, the Royal Navy effectively ceded sea control to the French fleet in and after the battle of Beachy Head. It was England's sheer good fortune that the French had such little idea about what they should do with their victory.

The Navy also suffered from a diffuse organisational structure which makes it difficult to identify who, if anyone, was actually in charge. Higher policy, that is the strategic and operational direction of the Navy's activities was principally conducted by the King in Council, which Flag Officers sometimes attended in order to receive their orders. Otherwise their orders and instructions were passed to them either directly from the Secretary of State, or via the Admiralty. The original Board of Commissioners, often representing the office of the Lord High Admiral (who himself represented the King) slowly morphed into a Board of Admiralty. Much depended on the quality of the people on this Board, on the extent of their sea experience, their probity and their political and personal contacts in other Government departments. Their relations with one another were important too, especially as there remained a fair degree of political disaffection even within the Navy. Personal relations could sometimes boil over as they did between Nottingham and Russell in 1692 and this too could paralyze the system. It was the job of senior 'civil servants' like the Secretary of the Navy to keep the show on the road and to maintain relations with the Treasury and the House of Commons with its commissioners and auditors.

Below and alongside at the same time, there were three other agencies responsible for lower-level naval administration – the Navy Board, the Commissioners of Victualling (who dealt with supply) and the Ordnance Board with a fourth looser set of Commissioners for the Sick and Wounded. Only the Navy Board was exclusively responsible for naval matters and usually half its members were naval professionals.

Appointees to the other organisations often had no naval experience at all. This did not necessarily mean they were bad people but too much depended on their individual approaches and characters. Crazily, the Ordnance Board was until 1887 also responsible for the supply of artillery to the Army and unsurprisingly 'enjoyed an unbroken record for procrastination and corruption.'[20]

Nor sadly was it alone in this. Following the money, the Treasury kept a very close eye on Commissioners of Victualling. But all the Navy's administrative systems at this time suffered from a defective auditing system which allowed but did not properly check the way in which subordinates spent the money that had been voted. This was a recipe for widespread corruption and a subject of continual complaint from the House of Commons.

Many of the same sorts of problems were evident lower down in the Navy's administrative system in dockyards and other shore-side establishments, fleets and ships. The dockyards were plagued with vague administrative procedures and regulations and age-old usage and customs, which were partly justified by the absence of a regular and reliable salary system. One such 'usage' was the right of dockyard employees to take away surplus wood chips and shavings to heat their houses; this often led to the large-scale embezzlement of wood. Running out of money, the dockyards were in a particularly bad state in 1689 and early 1690.

Fleet logistics was another area for legitimate complaints. Torrington's fleet was plagued with high levels of sickness even when loafing around in Torbay in early 1689. Long periods at sea had not helped. The basic problem though was the result of inadequately funding the Commissioners of Victualling, inefficient administration and crooked suppliers. The result could be disgusting, leading to well-merited complaints that:

> The beefe proves full of gaules ... and no longer ago than yesterday, in severall of the buts of beere, great heapes of stuff was found at the bottom of the buts not unlike to men's guts, which has alarmed the men to a strange degree.[21]

William III's Royal Navy like most others before and since, also had problems in getting enough people to serve and to stay. This was partly due to an official reluctance to accept the idea of continuous long-service commissions for officers and men, and of dockyard employees too, and of the reliable up-to-date system of payment that this would need. 'It is difficult,' concluded one historian, 'to overstress the human hardship caused by the irregularity of payment of wages to the yards and seamen.'[22] Conditions afloat on warships were often less than ideal, and as a result the health of the ship's company suffered and the ship itself became much less effective militarily.

Unsurprisingly Maydman had a very great deal to say about all of this, tracking current discontents from top to bottom and urging reform. At this level of specifically naval administration, as in the ones above, he emphasised the same need for men to behave '... as an honest, just and good servant' preferably 'not frequenting taverns, tipling-houses, gameings, nor use cursing, swearing nor any lewd living'; officers and officials should be content '... to wait in his station patiently for his advancement by his merit unto some higher degree,'[23] avoiding corruption in all its forms. As we shall also see in Chapter 10, Maydman thought an orderly system with clear instructions, regulations and responsibilities was necessary at every point. He discussed how they applied, or ought to be, at every specified level of naval officialdom.

He was particularly concerned about the state of the dockyards. While their function was the quick and cost-effective construction, refit and turn-around of warships, too often there were delays and cost over-runs through the 'purloining and embezzling (of) the King's goods,' advancing the interests of one ship against another purely on the time-dishonoured 'not-built-here' principle, and general laxness of enforcement of the rules so that a dockyard worker could break '… his instructions like cobwebs, with whole lies and denials of truth … as frequent as kisses at a wedding.'[24]

Maydman also had a lot to say about the running of ships and the treatment of the Navy's people afloat and ashore. He advocated much more sustained support of the sick, the wounded and veterans. When in port the people should be allowed to leave, rather than be subject to inhumane regulations which meant that 'I dare not lie a night with my wife, although come lately from the sea.'[25] He advocated continuous commissions and secure conditions of service for all. The degree of concern he showed for the care of the Navy's 'human capital' is impressive, and very modern sounding.

He likened a ship commander's task to running a well-conducted kingdom. Good examples had to be set by the officers who should ensure that ships were clean and commodious below decks. It was important 'that justice be plentifully administered on Board the ships that it might flow out at the scuppers, then will men's hearts be glad in the service.' The officers should avoid 'drunkeness, unclean and filthy talk of whoring boasted of openly before the Ship's company.' Feelingly, he singled out his own rank for better treatment as Warranted officers are 'pist upon by every body.'[26]

Maydman also had important things to say about fleet design, arguing in effect that 'form should follow function.' Because the most important permanent task of the Navy was the defence of trade, it followed that producing ships best able to do that should be a high priority. He was worried that, instead, too much effort was being devoted to the vainglorious pursuit of victory in decisive battles with the French Navy, a preoccupation that encouraged the building of expensive and ornately decorated great capital ships-of-the-line that were unsuitable for trade protection and convoy duty. The disastrous loss of the Smyrna convoy in 1693[27] and the continuing depredations of French privateers and of out-and-out pirates in the Caribbean underlined his point. In this, Maydman pointed up an issue about the balance to be struck between great ships and small ones that has divided opinion in naval fleet planning ever since, as we shall see in Chapter 12.

However what stands out, largely for its absence, from Maydman's review was any analysis about the extent to which naval personnel of every degree were prepared for their professional function – the conduct of battle and campaigns at sea. This was a period of great change, with the evolution of the concept of 'the line' (in which both fleets and indeed individual ships were positioned in line ahead formation best suited to firing broadsides, their principal weapon before boarding). Some strategic concepts such as 'Fleet-in-Being' were beginning to emerge but it was going to be another half-century before their codification finally appeared, in English, as major summary works on the conduct of amphibious operations like Thomas Molyneux's *Conjunct Expeditions,* 1759 or John Clerk's *Essay on Naval Tactics* of 1790. The nearest the Navy got to a written-down doctrine was in successive issues of the Fighting Instructions.[28]

This didn't mean there was no doctrine, merely that it was 'ambient' and understood rather than written down. Every now and again if there was uncertainty about a particular issue, an offending Admiral could be court-martialled, sacked or sometimes even shot for getting things wrong. The first and second of these happened to Lord

Torrington after Beachy Head. The general principle was that if you went for the enemy as offensively as you could reasonably do so, you wouldn't go far wrong. As for learning the tricks of doing that, you would pick it up through sea service, learning the necessary seamanship, navigational and war-fighting skills on the job. To modern day observers, this all seems disturbingly casual, but it occasioned no remark from Henry Maydman.

3.6 So How Did Things Turn Out?

Despite this depressing catalogue of British deficiencies, the situation in the French navy was certainly no better than in the Royal Navy and arguably significantly worse, especially by the mid-1690s when the effect of Colbert's reforms was wearing off. By contrast, in many ways things in Britain and the Royal Navy were beginning to move in the right direction.

During William III's reign, many of the most glaring deficiencies at the top decision-making level were corrected and, in particular the move to the division of responsibilities between nascent departments of government was a definite step forward in state formation and general efficiency. At least in part, it was a necessary response to the exigencies of conducting war, to the inevitable absence of the monarch in the case of King William and of the narrower visions of her role espoused by his successor Queen Anne. The result was a state better able to decide and advance its destiny, develop its maritime power and do so on the basis of a relatively secure and orderly financial position.[29]

In this, it was aided by the growing strength of the maritime economy. 'Our *Foreign Trade* is now become the Strength and Riches of the Kingdom,' one observer perceptively noted in 1718. '... and is the Fountain from when we draw all our Nourishment: It disperses that Blood and Spirits throughout all the Members by which the Body Politik subsists.'[30] With the encouragement of successive Navigation Acts which ordained that British goods should be carried in British ships, the shipping industry and sea-based trade grew throughout this period of turmoil and conflict. After their defeat at Beachy Head, the British built ships at three times the rate of the French. Overall British wealth was 20% higher at the end of 30 years of war against the French than it had been in 1688. This can indeed be attributed to the basic and growing strength of Britain's commercial maritime sector.[31] The issue was the extent to which the state could effectively tap into all this through a level of taxation that was both economically and practically sustainable and that provided for government credit on bearable terms. It was typical of a new level of governmental seriousness in this that the state invested essentially in the kind of naval forces and, effectively for the first time, in a revenue and customs service better, if still far from totally, able to defend its tax base against smuggling, piracy and other such forms of maritime malfeasance.[32]

For all its manifold faults, the Royal Navy of the time did sufficiently well to deliver the strategic effect required of it, and that was possible because the state's financial systems had been partially reformed and could support it. Even in the challenging field of logistics, significant improvements were taking place. For example, Admiral Russel's fleet, while overwintering in Cadiz in 1694, was kept supplied from a distance – a considerable achievement.[33] There were even thoughts about introducing training schemes into the dockyards and significantly more consideration was given to caring for the health of the sailors and the treatment of the wounded and disabled. This meant moving away from the antique and inadequate Chatham Chest system inherited from the Elizabethan age a century before. More surgeons were appointed, and hospitals and hospital ships were provided. Queen Mary too had a particular interest in this and was in large part responsible for the building of the magnificent Royal Naval Hospital at Greenwich, London in 1696.

This level of progress was all the more remarkable in that it was associated with a very substantial increase in the size of the fleet and the huge extra demands this made on the administrative support system. The fleet comprised just 173 ships in 1688 but had grown to 323 by 1697. In just a few years the Royal Navy had been turned from ineffective torpor in 1688–1689 to winning one of its most decisive victories for a generation over the French at Barfleur in 1692.[34] That the stain of Beachy Head was wiped out so very quickly in fact suggests that there was more residual strength in the Navy that Maydman was writing about than perhaps he recognised. Radical campaigns in the development or maintenance of maritime power usually take much longer than that.

Of course, it is quite impossible to assess the extent to which *Naval Speculations* was responsible for any of this, but at least it outlined a well-informed agenda, and an approach which perhaps fortuitously was broadly followed and which re-started a process that propelled Britain into two centuries of naval dominance and general good fortune.

3.7 Conclusion: Maydman's Applicability to Modern Times?

Maydman's interpretation of the elements of maritime power and the tiers of decision which could affect them were of course specific to the unique case of the England of 1691. Nonetheless, his way of looking at the development of maritime power can be broadened and extended beyond his time and place. Much of what he said has resonance for other countries in other periods that are intent on developing what Maydman described, rather nicely, as the 'maritime affair.'

Three points in the Maydman approach stand out, or can be inferred from the way he approached his subject. The first of these is the very obvious point that he did not choose, as did so many other people of his time, to focus on what England should be doing with its fleet, but rather on what he thought needed in the first place to be done to build up the fleet and, even more ambitiously, England's broader maritime power.

This approach is sufficiently difficult but sufficiently important to warrant closer attention than it normally gets. While there are libraries full of books and articles about the use of maritime power, there are surprisingly few general ones about how this is to be developed in the first place, that are not linked, as indeed was Maydman's, to a specific navy, time or place – or to a particular facet of maritime development. Fortunately, Lucien Poirier, a French General associated with his country's 20th Century nuclear programme came to the rescue in the 1980s. He proposed that alongside the more familiar conceptions of strategy relating to the conduct of military operations that are associated with the likes of Sun Tzu, Clausewitz, Mahan and Corbett, there is a need to develop what he called 'a strategy of means.' The effort is justified by the importance of the subject, for after all there would be no military operations if the means to conduct them had not been created in the first place. Moreover, the delivery of the means is in many ways just as complex as the conduct of operations – a point underlined by the old adage that 'while amateurs talk strategy, professionals talk logistics.'[35] Economic, financial and industrial strategies are part of the process. Such observations underline the point that developing maritime (or any other type of) power needs to be taken as seriously as the more familiar focus on using it.

Secondly, rather as Mahan was to do 200 years later, Maydman implicitly acknowledged the importance of the impact that the domestic and international context had on a country's perception of what its maritime interests were, and on the extent to which they were under threat – largely by his passing remarks on the domestic scene, which as a profoundly religious observer he thought often lamentable in so many ways and, of course, by what other countries were doing. He concluded that England *was* under serious threat and needed defending and so its maritime power should be built up, largely by improving the various constituents of maritime power, in the way he described. Many other observers have felt, and do feel, the same about their own countries and situations.

Thirdly, Maydman's methodical top-down analytical approach in his review of the problems facing the Royal Navy can be developed and adapted for much wider application. His four descending levels of responsibility and decision take different forms in different countries but nonetheless make sense as an exploration of the manner in which the concept of ends, ways and means should in theory work when developing maritime power and naval strength. First objectives are determined and a strategy is set and resourced as the way of achieving them. This will often be competitive as other interests jostle for attention. The same is true of decisions about the possible ways and means of acieving these objectives especially in the 20th Century as the sea and air domains of war were joined first by airpower and then by space and cyber space too. Finally here there is the same ends, ways and means debate about what the navy should be doing, what its priorities are and how it should go about achieving them. There will often be a focus on working out the Navy's relationship with other significant stakeholders in the 'maritime affair,' such as the merchant shipping industry or coastguards. Efficiency in the conduct of current operations and preparation for future ones will be a high priority.

But things were not in his day, and certainly are not in ours, as simple, neat and tidy as this figure suggests. Firstly, the divisions between the tiers can be very fuzzy and a great deal of bottom-up as well as top-down influence is to be expected. Indeed despite being a grizzled Warrant Officer, rather low in the food chain, Maydman was appealing in his book to the very top of the Naval hierarchy of decision to someone who as sometime Lord High Admiral also operated at the highest levels of state. And all the time pressures were coming in sideways from the domestic and international context as well. Maydman wanted to be one of those pressures.

This kind of decision-making is also a continuous iterative process; first comes the stage of identifying policy objectives (the ends) then setting strategy (identifying the ways and means); next comes the implementation stage; finally there's a process of evaluation, identifying what worked, and what went to rats and needs re-thinking – and off the cycle goes again. In practice, the process may look a good deal more like 'muddling through' than the cool and well-informed process that Myadman would plainly have preferred.

With that in mind, we should now turn to what would seem to be the obvious starting point for this exploration of the development or maintenance of maritime power, namely Tier 1, the top of the national decision-making hierarchy, where in the past and now, broad national policy objectives are decided and passed down the system for subsequent implementation.

Notes

1 The Earl's other preoccupations included three wives, seven sons and six daughters.
2 Poirier, General Lucien, *Strategie Theoretique II* (Paris: Economica, 1987), 124.
3 Kwa Chong Guan, Derek Heng, Peter Borschberg and Tan Tai Yong, *Seven Hundred Years: A History of Singapore* (Singapore: Marshall Cavendish, 2019), 287; Wise, *Travellers' Tales*, 229.
4 Baxter, Stephen B., *William III and the Defense of European Liberty 1650–1702* (New York: Harcourt, Brace & World Inc., 1966), 374.
5 Churchill, Winston S., *History of the English-Speaking Peoples, Vol III The Age of Revolution* (New York: Dodd, Mead & Company, 1957), 22.
6 Hoppit, Julian, *A Land of Liberty? England 1689–1727* (Oxford: Oxford University Press, 2010), 95.
7 Maydman, *Naval Speculations*, frontispiece, 322–3.
8 Ibid, 156, 166, 211, 220.
9 Ibid, 279–80.
10 Ibid, preface.
11 Quoted in Hattendorf, J.B., *England in the War of Spanish Succession* (New York: Garland Publishing, 1987), 68. I am grateful to Professor Hattendorf for his extensive help, especially with this chapter.
12 Baxter, *William III and the Defence of European Liberty*, 316.
13 Hattendorf, *England in the War of Spanish Succession*, 130; Hoppit, *A Land of Liberty?*, 102.
14 Ibid, 86.
15 Ibid, 295.
16 Maydman, *Naval Speculations*, 229, 251.
17 See also Hoppit, *A Land of Liberty?*, 316–7.
18 Maydman, *Naval Speculations*, 256–61, 315, 318.
19 Hoppit, *A Land of Liberty?*, 102.
20 Ehrman, John, *The Navy in the War of William III, 1689–1697* (Cambridge: UP, 1963), 176.
21 Russel report of 31 July 1689, quoted in Ehrman, *The Navy in the War*, 318.
22 Powley, Edward, *The Naval Side of King William's War* (Hamden, Conn: Archon Books, 1972), 349.
23 Maydman, *Naval Speculations*, 14.
24 Ibid, 66, 69.
25 Ibid, 101, 104–5.
26 Ibid, 208, 220, 227.
27 Hoppit, *A Land of Liberty?*, 100.
28 See Corbett, Julian S., Fighting Instructions, 1530–1816 (London: Navy Records Society) vol. 29; Tunstall, Brian, *Naval Warfare in the Age of Sail: The Evolution of Fighting Tactics* (London: Conway, 1936, repr. 1990), Chapter 2.
29 Hoppit, *A Land of Liberty?*, 42–3, 124–5, 278.
30 W. Wood, *A Survey of Trade*, 1718, quoted in Hoppit, *A Land of Liberty?*, 6.
31 Ehrman, *The Navy in the War*, 172; Hoppit, *A Land of Liberty?*, 101, 246, 320, 340–1, 344.
32 Ibid, 246–7, 269.
33 Ibid, 100–1.
34 Ehrman, *The Navy in the War*, 395–8; Rodger, *The Command of the Ocean*, 149–50.
35 Poirier, *Theories Strategique II*; also Wedin, Lars, *Maritime Strategies for the XXI Century: The Contribution of Admiral Castex* (Paris: Nuvis, 2016), 207–13.

4   The Vision Thing

4.1 The Need for a Vision?

Common sense suggests that it helps when planning a journey if someone has some idea of what the destination should be and roughly at least how best to get there. Applying this logic to the business of developing maritime power, it would seem to follow that the articulation of a vision of the importance of the task and about the purpose, extent and nature of that maritime power would be equally helpful, perhaps even essential, especially when starting from scratch. Ideally such a vision could include ideas about how the four constituents of maritime power, discussed before, might be improved.

But things do not always, or even usually, work out in that neat and logical way. Historically, some countries have become maritime powers organically – from the bottom up rather than from the top down. This was what Richmond and others meant when they distinguished between natural and artificial maritime powers. Sea-mindedness welled up naturally from the bottom in natural maritime powers, it wasn't commanded from the top. It was Richmond wrote, '… an expression of a national spirit, of the genius, character and activity of the people themselves.'[1]

4.1.1 The Hanseatic League

The Hanseatic League is a good example of this. The league was a loose assemblage of mainly German but also some Scandinavian cities and towns centred on Hamburg and Lubeck that banded together in a 'hansa' (a gathering, a convoy) of commercial co-operation in order to 'trade with advantage.' The aim was to secure and then defend trading and shipping monopolies. Particularly strong from the 13th to the 15th centuries, the League extended its reach into other parts of Europe, the Mediterranean and even the fringes of Asia. It developed its own commercial arrangements and laws that were applied in its trading centres in host countries. Capable of taking action against pirates, it undertook measures for navigational safety (such as building lighthouses and setting marker buoys) and even briefly went to war with Denmark in 1368 over access rights into and out of the Baltic.

But the league was loose, transient, held together only by commercial interest with no one actually in charge. Much depended on the personal relationships between the trading families in the constituent cities. It had no navy, no central administrative structure and from the 15th Century went into a slow decline as rising nations began to pull their cities and towns into different directions. It was finally wound up in 1862,

DOI: 10.4324/9781003100553-4

but at its peak the Hanseatic League was an extremely powerful commercial maritime organisation which had clearly developed from the bottom up.[2]

4.1.2 The Netherlands

In some ways, a similar situation developed in the Netherlands of the 15th or 16th century where no one was in a position consciously to decree that the country should become a maritime power; instead that power seemed to develop naturally out of the success of its herring fishing, and mercantile and financial strengths inherited in part from its own early Frisian experience and then from the Hanseatic League, admittedly helped along by facilitating governmental regulation and intermittent direction. Dutch policy-makers knew how important the maritime aspect of their economy and security was and did what they could to encourage it. No one had the authority to come out with, and still less implement, an overall vision of the kind of maritime power the Republic needed, with the brief and ultimately ill-fated exception of Johan de Witt and his brother in the 17th century. Instead, what resulted was a collective self-driven effort deriving from the circumstances in which most of the Dutch found themselves. For them, those circumstances were dominated by extensive fishing and sea trading interests and a manifestly watery geography.[3]

Their problem was that the Republic comprised three provinces that focused on the maritime side of things and four on the territorial, and so there was a serious political division between those who favoured a decentralised government focused on the former or a centralised one concentrated on the latter. The centralisers were associated with the House of Orange and they were much more immediately concerned about Spanish and/or French enemies on their land borders than they were about what might happen at sea. They argued for a focus on the army, not for a diffusely conducted and primarily maritime endeavor. The result was a permanent, highly politicised, institutionalised and sometimes deadly competition between the two sets of interests. Only for a brief while, perhaps 1653–1672 when the office of Stadholder was left vacant, was the maritime interest in total control. It was a series of land defeats on the borders that led to the grisly murder of Johan de Witt and the end of the primarily maritime era.

Until that happened, the direction of maritime affairs was left to the States General and the Admiralties of the three maritime provinces. Much of what might be considered the state's responsibility for maritime policy and naval defence was actually conducted by privateers (starting with the Dutch 'Sea Beggars' of the 16th Century), merchants and joint-stock companies like the *Vereenigde Oostindische Compagnie* (VoC) the East India Company. Inevitably founded on their massive herring industry of the 15th Century,[4] the Dutch diversified into wider trading in the Baltic, the Mediterranean, with Russia and into the East Indies and Japan. The sheer scale and sophistication of the Republic's burgeoning maritime base (The population of Amsterdam 'the greatest Trading city in Europe' quadrupled between 1600 and 1650[5]) provided the wherewithal for a thoroughly maritime power in every sense.

Perfectly willing to use force, Dutch private agencies attempted to capture the Cape Verde islands and Sao Tome in 1600, attacked and seized the rich Portuguese merchant ship the *Santa Catarina* near Singapore in 1603, blockaded Lisbon in 1606, and delivered a spectacular naval defeat of the Spanish off Gibraltar in 1607. The VoC was encouraged to patrol the sea, establish bases and ports abroad and exclude their rivals.

In 1623 they perpetrated the infamous Amboyna massacre against their erstwhile allies and present rivals, the English. Their jurist Hugo Grotius provided legal cover by arguing in effect that while Dutch waters were Dutch, everyone else's was were free, or at least negotiable. By the middle of the 17th Century they had a professional sea-going fleet and were able to engage in a series of iconic naval battles for command of the sea, their territorial vulnerabilities and political dissensions notwithstanding. Indeed in the Second Anglo-Dutch War, the Dutch won nearly all their battles, eventually humiliating the English by sailing up the River Medway to burn what was left of their sorely unfunded and neglected battle fleet.

4.1.3 Revolutionary America

The same kind of bottom-up push happened nearly 200 years later in the United States, most obviously at the start of the Revolutionary War when the Americans found themselves fighting for their independence from the British. George Washington had no personal experience of maritime power and very limited acquaintance with the sea, but as an American farmer, he was used to the transportation possibilities of rivers and boats. Under his broad direction, the Americans then went on to show that maritime power could exist without navies when an enthusiastic host of smugglers, rivermen and boats, shipbuilders, Marblehead fishermen, whalers, merchants and privateers and amateurs like David Bushnell of Connecticut (the world's first opera-tional submariner) spontaneously came together with 'all scows, schooners and boats of every kind' to fight an inshore campaign that the British initially found hard to deal with.[6] Paradoxically quite a few of the emerging Republic's sailors were able to draw on their sometimes enforced service in the Royal Navy.

Its geography and the shape of its economy predisposed the early United States towards the maritime. At its birth it was 'not much more than a narrow strip of sparsely populated beachfront real estate' between a sea of water to the East and a sea of inhospitable woods to the West. Its population of some 6 million people depended on sea trades. 'The genius, character and habits of the people,' said President John Adams in 1797,

> are highly commercial; their cities have been founded and exist upon commerce; our agriculture, fisheries, arts and manufactures are connected with, and must depend on it. In short commerce has made this country what it is, and it cannot be destroyed or neglected without involving the people in poverty and distress.[7]

As early as this, some thought the new republic should try to create a small but conventional fleet to take the war to the British, and particularly to their trade. Their privateers, most famously the renegade Scotsman John Paul Jones, had some largely symbolic success, but the early enthusiasm of 1775–1776 for a US Navy waned as the sheer difficulties of setting one up and keeping it going became apparent. Building '... any navy was always an immense struggle. It took endless time even for those with the requisite experience and skill honed through failure. Running a navy successfully also required political dexterity, financial ingenuity, administrative efficiency, logistical robustness and excellent leadership.'[8] A Navy Department with a Secretary of the Navy to preside over it was eventually established in 1798. Until then because so many of these requirements were in exceedingly short supply, the Americans had to rely on the conventional fleets of the French and the Spaniards and anyone else who could be cajoled into intervention against apparently overwhelming British maritime power.

Uncertainty remained about what kind of navy, if any, the Americans needed to survive their victory. Federalists like Alexander Hamilton and John Adams argued for a conventional, if modest navy of 'ships of the line' '... to give us a certain weight in relation to European nations.'[9] Adams indeed has a reasonable claim to be regarded as a naval visionary. 'The counsel which Themistocles gave to Athens, Pompey to Rome, Cromwell to England, De Witt to Holland, and Colbert to France,' he wrote in 1802, 'I have always given and shall continue to give to my countrymen – that the great questions of commerce and power must be determined by sea ... [and therefore] all reasonable encouragement should be given to a navy.'[10]

Their opponents argued this was unnecessary and would imperil American liberties and finance, instead proposing an affordable mini-fleet of sloops and brigs. Doing anything more than the bare minimum would give the Federal government too much power. One Senator, indeed, conjured up a nightmarish vision of the consequence of the United States becoming a conventional naval power:

> I tell you sir, naval victories in the end would prove fatal to the United States; the consequences which have uniformly followed in other countries must take place here. If the United States shall determine to augment their navy, so as to rival those of Europe, the public debt will become permanent; direct taxes will be perpetual; the paupers of the country will be increased; the nation will be bankrupt; and, I fear, the tragedy will end in a revolution.[11]

At issue was the substantial point about what kind of country the United States should strive to be – an engaged and significant power in the concert of nations, or one content in itself, purposefully abjuring entangling commitments abroad. Some like James Madison and Thomas Jefferson did not favor a heavy reliance on trade in the first place, instead wanting to develop an agrarian economy. On the whole they preferred an un-ambitious, politically acceptable gunboat navy, perhaps even locally raised.[12]

All this was at the heart of the continuing debate about the naval establishment, about the composition of the fleet, the stores to be held, the acquisition of timberlands and copper sheeting, about the construction of shipyards, even about whether there should be a Department of the Navy at all. The result was a complete lack of clarity about the way ahead.

In this situation there was a need for a little stimulus from above. A compromise was the result. Congress accepted that the country did need a navy, but one bespoke for two very definite and specific purposes, namely coastal defence and the protection of American merchant ships against the corsairs of North Africa. American assessments of what they needed were based on careful calculations about the strength of their adversary and the most cost-effective means of counteracting it.[13] The result was very curious, a fleet of six big, heavy, well-armed frigates and a number of smaller vessels for inshore work. These 'pocket battleships' of their time, were much more powerful than needed for Algerine pirates (and indeed too big for the necessary in-shore work) but operated with considerable effect in the War of 1812. In 1827, the debate concluded for the time being with the arguments of the anti-navalists more or less prevailing.

However, this unclear vision of the way ahead was specifically limited to the naval side of the maritime affair. No one (even the agrarian tendency) doubted the importance of sustaining the fishing and merchant fleets whose strategic needs were considered by all the disputants to be central to the debate, despite having radically different views about what those needs meant in terms of fleet composition. Indeed one reason why the 'Anti-navalists' were prepared to build warships but keep them 'in ordinary' or deep reserve, was an unspoken confidence that should the need arise, the necessary sailors and resources would naturally well up from the maritime base, just as they had for the Revolutionary War.

The US Navy was only jolted out of this complacence, and in effect out of a strategic reliance on the good offices of the Royal Navy, its erstwhile adversary, by the urgent exigencies of the Civil War in the 1860s. Even then it took another 20 years or so before a new and publicly articulated consensus about the nature and shape of the fleet began to emerge. This owed much to the efforts of another generation of visionaries such as Rear Admiral Stephen B. Luce and Captain Alfred Thayer Mahan and their coterie of the like-minded at the US Naval War College at Newport, and perhaps most of all to Theodore Roosevelt, historian of the U.S. Navy, its advocate and civilian head and ultimately President of the United States.[14] Roosevelt, something of a polymath, used both history and contemporary developments to show that to be prosperous and secure, the country needed a strong navy centred on a powerful battlefleet, his point being apparently underlined by the defeat of Spain in 1898 and the enormous success of the world cruise of the 'Great White Fleet' 1907–1909. This was advocacy by print, by oratory and by practical proof of concept. Roosevelt, a pugnacious soul, wasn't above re-constructing history, if that would help – thus the apotheosis of John Paul Jones at the Annapolis Naval Academy, but he understood the developing implications of modern technology too. Above all his achievements derived from energy. 'His forte,' said his Secretary of the Navy, John D. Long in not wholly admiring accents, 'is his push. He lacks serenity of discussion.'[15]

4.2 Top-Down Perspectives

The mixed results of the bottom-up approach in the American case suggest there is indeed something to be said for the top-down approach too. For centuries many states and their rulers had come to the reluctant conclusion that they could not afford simply to step aside, leaving their country's maritime development largely 'to the market.' Instead it needed to be, if not directed, then at least encouraged and fostered by the government, and that required action on the pitch, not merely nodding approvingly from the sidelines. Both the Dutch and the Americans in the end accepted that at the very least the State needed to contribute, invest in infrastructure and maintain a solid core of state ships and sailors that could be expanded if and when necessary. The American case suggests, also, that a few visionaries are also a necessary part of the mix, to help things along. Moreover, this was obviously not simply a matter of building a few ships. The approach had to be more broadly maritime and maybe broader even than that.

4.2.1 Russia

Eighteenth-Century Russia provides two related examples of a determined top-down approach to the development of maritime power, almost from scratch. Both Tsar

Peter the Great at the beginning of the 18th Century and later on, Prince Potemkin, the consort of Tsarina Catherine the Great, were quite clear that this task could not be left to others, and would instead need to be imposed from above. The outlook was not promising. When Peter the Great assumed power, Russia had very little access to the ocean, Archangel, founded 1693, being its only port. The country's merchant class was under-developed, the manufacturing base tiny and Russians had little experience of sea-faring. But this is not to say he was starting from a completely blank sheet of paper. There was some potential at least.

For a start there were the traditions of the Varangians; Russian-Swedes, their exploits on the country's mighty north/south rivers that ended with forays into the Black Sea where they left their own indelible mark on the region by sacking parts of Byzantium and leaving their *graffiti* on its monuments. These traditions were carried on by the famous Zaporogian Cossacks of the River Dnieper – maritime if largely in a riverine way – and operating their 60-foot reed-lined and oar-propelled boats – the *chaiki* or 'seagulls.' Said to be the first inventors of the submarine, they sported handlebar moustaches, shaven heads with a long pony-tail, Turkish pantaloons and turbans with ostrich feathers. Twice in the 17th Century armadas of 100 *chaiki* raided Constantinople. A formidable if unconventional fighting force, they were hired out to fight the Spanish at Dunkirk under the Prince of Conde and Potemkin built them into flotillas that fought their way down the rivers and out into the Azov and Black seas to take on the Turks.[16]

By the end of the 17th Century, moreover, Russian explorers had already reached the Pacific, lured immediately by the high price of fur, some hoping one day for access to Eastern spices and the gold of the Orient. Much depended on whether a Northern Sea Route to China and Japan could be found. But such adventurers were up against the climate, the conditions and the limitations of Siberian maritime endeavor at a time when the use of iron was unknown to the locals and when their ships were tied together with ropes, straps and wooden pegs, propelled by sails made of reindeer skin and held in place with wooden anchors.[17] But these indigenous peoples nevertheless had their maps of rivers and the coast on sealskins and wooden boards;[18] they knew their place and could find their way around. By Peter the Great's time, in short, the Russians had reached the Pacific, and knew the next stage was to get across it.

Despite such potential there was a clear need for a lot of top-down pressure to get things moving faster and Peter, the supreme autocrat, was in an ideal position to supply it. Enthusiastic to the point of fanaticism, Peter the Great could be appallingly ruthless when he needed to be, as his suppression of the Streltsy rebellion only too clearly showed;[19] he had no compunction about forcing people to do things they didn't want to. Guided by Fedor Stepanovch Saltykov, his maritime advisor, he had a uniquely 'hands-on' approach in his self-imposed task. He famously learned the trade of ship-building in the Netherlands and in England's Deptford shipyard and he bored the continentally-minded William III of Britain very much with his maritime chattering. 'He is mechanically turned,' thought England's Archbishop Burnet, 'and seems designed by nature rather to be a ship-carpenter than a great prince.'[20] Prince Potemkin, later in the century was significantly more humane, much more circumspect in his resort to autocratic power, but just as committed to the maritime cause.

Peter encouraged further expansion to the East and exploration of the Arctic. Also lured by the strategic promise of the south, he was responsible for a push down the rivers which for a while led to Russians reaching and using the Sea of Azov until forced by land defeats to retreat from this part of his maritime dream. Peter's main focus, though, was on the Baltic. Wanting a window to the West, he used his army to drive the Poles back and the Swedes from the southern Baltic shore. There he built his new capital, St Petersburg. Potemkin likewise completely transformed Russia's maritime geography by doing much the same to the South, finally consolidating Russia's hold on the Black Sea. Both of them left a locally built and powerful battlefleet as part of their legacy to remind everyone if need be, that Russia was a new and enduring player in those seas.

Both of them realised from the start that developing Russia's maritime power couldn't be done in isolation. It would need to be part of a much wider package of reforms developing the nature of the state, its society and its economy – the other constituents of maritime power. Unless such a policy was followed, any advances in building a navy would prove short-lived. Initially Peter focused his transformative energies on changing those aspects of Russia that were most needed to be able to wage successful war against his immediate enemies. After the defeat of Charles X at Poltava in 1709, however, his perspective widened to include everything from changing the calendar, persuading people to cut off their beards, wear Western-style clothes and be more welcoming to new ideas about national administration, the dispensation of justice and the role of the Orthodox Church.

Only with a much wider tax base could a modernised Russia survive so it was essential to build up the industries and the entrepreneurial classes that could provide that financial support. Potemkin absolutely agreed. Both wanted to encourage the development of a substantial shipping industry. Both encouraged the development of shipyards and supporting infrastructure and then diversified into unrelated civilian manufactures. Many such enterprises were state-owned from the start, state-subsidised or, especially in Peter's day, relied on forced contributions from individuals singled out for that honour. Economic policy was mercantilist and protectionist to defend Russian manufacturing and exports. High tariff barriers were imposed on foreign-made goods that competed, but none for anything that Russia needed but could not produce. The new hopeful ports they both created such as St Petersburg in the north and Kherson, Nikolayev and eventually Odessa in the south, were to charge the lowest of dues, or even operate as free ports to encourage foreigners to come. Wherever possible internal customs dues were to be reduced or abandoned.

The success of course was mixed. Both Peter and Potemkin got their battlefleets and both left more industry than they found. There were successes such as the fact that Russia outdid England in the production of pig iron by the end of Peter's reign, but failures too. Peter's scheme to advance Russia's silk industry did not prosper and neither did the attempt to establish a strong merchant marine, largely because of the opposition of Dutch and English shippers determined to defend their near-monopoly. As one of the few Russian decision-makers who really understood trade, Potemkin likewise did his utmost to encourage its development, particularly in his beloved south.[21]

Other caveats have to be noted. Both Peter and Potemkin were forced to rely heavily on foreigners, not just to command their fleets and ships, or to build their cities and ports, but also as the principal means for a massive project of all-round 'technology transfer.' Indeed that was the aim, successfully achieved, of Peter's 'Great Embassy' to Western Europe. It was also the reason for Potemkin's welcome of so many experts, adventurers, entrepreneurs, fortune-seekers, scoundrels and the merely curious from all around the western world who flocked to his side in St Petersburg and down south and who became intimately involved in his great projects.

The problem was that that reliance on foreigners continued; it did not result in an indigenous trade and manufacturing base of a strength that the size of the Russian empire required. In 1839, 50 years after Potemkin died, that acute if the opinionated observer of the Russian scene, the Marquis de Custine was convinced the experiment had failed. 'The trades-people who ought to form a middle class are too few in number, 'he concluded, 'to possess any influence in the state; besides, they are almost all foreigners.'[22]

Part of the reason for that was the innate conservatism of the ruling classes and the disdain that many of them affected towards sordid matters of business. But as Custine and many other contemporary Western observers concluded, the real problem was Russia's societal resistance to change of any kind. Bypassed by the Reformation and the Renaissance there was an often resigned absence of free-thinking in Russia. Indeed the Old Believers, religious fanatics who wanted to turn back the little progress that had been made, were still a powerful force. Peter himself had no illusions on the matter. 'You know yourselves,' he said 'that anything that is new, even if it is good and necessary, our people will not do without being compelled,' but as both he and Potemkin found, this was exceedingly difficult. Peter's contemporary admirer Ivan Pososhkov concluded, 'The great monarch works hard and accomplishes nothing. The Tsar pulls uphill alone with the strength of ten, but millions pull downhill.'[23] As Custine noted a century later even the prohibition of beards had not reached into the countryside where clean-shaven men were regarded with deep suspicion as traitors to Russia's traditions.[24]

Because they were unable to exploit an impetus for change welling up from the bottom, both Peter and Potemkin tried to use their autocratic power to force the necessary change downwards on a reluctant people.[25] It was indeed 'commerce by decree.' The autocratic nature of the Russian regime mandated close supervision of every aspect of this all-round maritime endeavor, even down to fine detail such as Potemkin's designing the shape of the bells in the new monastery in Nikolayev.[26] Given the continuing limitations of the Russian maritime base, the success of its navy and the broader maritime 'affair' depended too much on the passing enthusiasms of the current Tsar – and there were always a host of other, often more immediate, territorial and domestic preoccupations to be considered. Russia's continuing maritime limitations reflected the broader constraints on the country itself as a society and a political system, most obviously as it manifested itself in a failure to provide a sufficiently responsive and supportive maritime base for naval endeavor.

The admittedly jaundiced Maquis de Custine visiting Russia in 1839 saw the problem from another angle. He plainly thought what he called 'despotism without pity and without precedent' was the problem, not a solution, even a partial one, to the challenges that Russia faced.[27] For him, autocracy destroyed initiative, resulting in a passive and guarded society yearning for an imagined past, clinging on to the present in case the future was worse. This inhibited the free exchange of ideas and resulted in a wealth of 'useless formalities.'[28] Worse still the Russian people had grown to love their servitude. 'Despotism still exists in Russia,' the then Tsar, Nicholas I, told Custine personally, 'it is the essence of my government, but it accords with the genius of the nation.'[29] Much later still Admiral Gorshkov successful Commander-in-Chief of the Soviet Navy from 1956–1985 was inclined to agree with some of this: the real problem underlying all Russia's maritime problems, Gorshkov argued, was the nature of the Tsarist regime itself.[30] With the Revolution, things changed but observers may wonder by how much.

Peter the Great and Potemkin between them had unarguably revolutionised their country's maritime geography by expanding its access to the world ocean from a thin sliver of frozen territory opening to the White Sea at Archangel to the Black and Baltic seas. They had also set up an irresistible surge to the East that would soon open up the Pacific too. Such access was by no means perfect since these were four widely separated areas making the concentration of naval power difficult; they were restricted by choke points held by potentially unsympathetic powers and the weather conditions were challenging. Although the geographic position was much better than it had been, progress in the next two constituents of maritime power, namely Government and Society and the Maritime Economy, over time, was much less marked. As a result, neither top-down nor bottom-up impulses could work properly.

All this certainly had its inevitable impact for the efforts of both Peter the Great and Prince Potemkin's efforts to develop the fourth of the constituents of maritime power – the navy. The navy had its victories and its home-grown heroes such as Admiral Ushakov. Russia's navy was of a sufficient size and quality for the British, scrabbling around for an ally, to try to persuade Potemkin and Catherine II to send a battlefleet – a 'Great Armament' to join them in the war against the revolting Americans and maybe an expeditionary army to fight alongside them as well (with who knows what consequence?).[31]

There were signs, too, that the Russian navy might yet push out beyond the narrow seas onto the open world ocean and it was certainly something that both Peter and Potemkin yearned for. In the south, the navy did indeed pass through the Golden Horn (or come down from the Baltic) and break into the Mediterranean to occupy Greek islands and, later, Malta.[32] In the Pacific, Russia's historic surge to the East would not stop at the water's edge once the ocean was reached. Recognising this, Peter the Great encouraged the development of a group of Japanese linguists to facilitate further expansions overseas, leading to significant encounters with Imperial Japan that eventually led to the establishment of bases and ports in California in 1812 and Fort Elizabeth on the Hawai'ian island of Kaua'i in 1817.[33]

But all the same, the Navy was a fragile construction with shallow foundations. Even by Catherine II's time, many of its command decisions were still being made by foreigners. The Navy's role as a strategic enabler was limited. Instead of that, the acquisition of a real, sea-going Navy was more a reward for the success of the Army and its supporting riverine flotillas than an agency for great strategic advantage in its own right. Much was owed to successful generals and diplomats particularly down south where four competing empires intersected – the Russian, Polish, Austrian and Ottoman. Fifty years later, Custine, as he sailed into Kronstadt echoed other Western commentators of the time by dismissing what he saw of the Russian marine, namely the Baltic Fleet, liberated from its seasonal ice blockade and busily exercising, as '... a recreation of the present emperor's ... a mere parade,' noting 'that one of the noble vessels we had seen manoeuvering around us had just been lost on a sandbank.'[34] To the extent this was a true reflection, it all underlined the point that in Russia's context, the flowering of maritime power that both Peter and Potemkin sought would prove difficult to achieve and harder still to maintain.

4.2.2 Singapore

The story of Singapore provides another example of a top-down approach – but one that had much more bottom-up support than was available in Russia. At more or less the time the Americans were agonising about what kind of navy they wanted, across the world Sir Stamford Raffles was putting forward his ideas about this for what was long after to be another new country. A long-time employee of the British East India Company, he was definitely a man with a vision. When he arrived in Southeast Asia in 1805, the Company was not doing too well financially and its Dutch rival seemed to be making all the running. Raffles thought the British could recover the position and even dominate the area, provided they exerted themselves, won over the locals and developed a few ports and strongholds.[35] Singapore, now a neglected steamy little island off the southern tip of the Malay peninsula with perhaps 150 residents, had centuries before been a significant regional port. It could become one again, as lynchpin of the whole enterprise. In January 1819, Raffles stepped ashore at Singapore.

As his biographer says, 'Raffles had a coherent vision of exactly how the settlement must be developed and administered and left [his then colleague, William] Farquar fully briefed with detailed instructions on absolutely everything.'[36] Although the two men quarreled bitterly over details, then and afterwards, they cooperated enough to secure the approval of the local ruler, and together energetically laid the foundations of a port, and eventually a maritime country, that became a success at lightning speed.

It clearly wasn't going to be easy. The combination of limited medical knowledge and a challenging climate killed colleagues, wives and children with frightening speed and Raffles was never particularly healthy in the first place. The Company was beset with its own tensions, jealousies and turf battles and parsimoniously wedded to the doctrine of 'trade not places,' and so inclined more to bring resources back to London than to invest them out in the area of operations. To get a return, Raffles said, the Company had to invest: 'the maintenance of a marine establishment similar to that of the Dutch will probably be found absolutely necessary.'[37] The local rulers with whom imperialists had to work had their own quarrels and jealousies with each other and sometimes with the British and Dutch too.

But Raffles had amazing energy and knew what he was doing. As one of the 'word-processors' in Company headquarters, India House, Leadenhall Street, London he had already read and indeed copied much of the avalanche of reports and suggestions coming in from men on the spot. He knew the Company's style and protocols. Arriving in Penang in 1805, with a passion for learning, he made himself proficient in the local languages and culture, and it would not have taken him long to realise the illustrious past and the future potential value of that fecund little island away to the south of the Asian landmass – 'the site of the ancient city of Singhaphura ... once the great emporium of these seas, whose history is lost in the mists of antiquity .... (where) ... [t]he lines of the old city, and its defences, are still to be traced.'[38]

With the encouragement of the Company and other like-minded imperialists, Raffles immersed himself in the area's zoology and botany, and set himself to know everything there was to know about this new theatre of operations. As Abdullah Bin Abdul Kadir, his sometime secretary, remarked, 'It was Mr Raffles' nature to study with great enjoyment the history of countries and their ancient customs, and to make enquiries and ask questions about unusual things.'[39] He had a burning desire to make a difference, to 'do good' (by abolishing slavery and introducing smallpox vaccination for example) – as well as to make money, and spread British influence.

Within 14 months, Singapore could claim to be a 'considerable commercial port.'[40] Raffles did not achieve all this himself of course. He had a host of collaborators including William Farquar who deserves more credit than he is usually given. Success in Singapore's rebirth and in the area generally came from efficient administration, from the enlightened encouragement of traders of all nationalities and types to come, settle and do their business with a minimum of interference, and from the free trade that resulted from a refusal to exact port duties from visiting vessels.[41] 'One free port in the seas,' Raffles said, 'must eventually destroy the spell of Dutch monopoly.'[42]

Raffles' attention to detail was remarkable. When the American William Hornaday visited Singapore in 1878, he thought it

> the handiest city I ever saw, as well planned and carefully executed as though built entirely by one man. It is like a big desk, full of drawers and pigeon holes. where everything has its place and can always be found in it.[43]

Occasionally, of course, the capacity to determine outcomes and to maintain order by the force of arms was useful, not least against pirates.

Personally, Raffles was not so successful, dying early and in penury, but his maritime legacy was, and is, extraordinary. It derived from great clarity of purpose, boundless energy, a willingness to take risks and to anticipate approval from others that wasn't always forthcoming; above all he had a total determination to lead from the top.

The aptitude for business and the sheer industriousness of Singapore's inhabitants, however, was another key ingredient of Raffles' success. Given the opportunity, they came to trade, entirely sharing his vision of the future and ultimately provided much of the resources needed to sustain it. The geography was right, the culture and political systems were right and the economy blossomed. In due course, the new city-state of the 20th Century was able to support a small but highly professional navy, well-equipped and trained and able to punch above its weight.

This review of the 'Vision thing' will end with a glance at two contemporary examples of people and countries trying to develop their maritime power. Both of them are unusual in that they have explicitly laid out their intentions and approach in some detail. Both of them are decidedly top-down but since they are contemporary, and, at the time of writing, still engaged in the process, their degree of success remains conjectural.

4.2.3 Modern China

China's President Xi offers the first of these contemporary examples of such a top-down approach to the generation of maritime power, although more detailed discussion of this is held over to the last chapter. Building on the ideas of his immediate predecessors, Xi publicly stated his determination at the Third Plenum of the 18th Party Congress in November 2013 not just to recognize the importance of the country's maritime interests but to turn China into a maritime power. The difference is significant. China's subsequent *2015 Military Strategy* is unequivocal about this 'maritime power dream':

The traditional mentality that land outweighs sea must be abandoned, and great importance has to be attached to managing the seas and oceans and protecting maritime rights and interests. It is necessary for China to develop a modern maritime military force structure commensurate with its national security and development interests, safeguard its national sovereignty and maritime rights and interests, protect the security of strategic SLOCs [Sea Lines of Communication] and overseas interests, and participate in international maritime cooperation as to provide support for building itself into a maritime power.[44]

Commonly said to be China's most powerful leader since Chairman Mao, Xi is in an excellent position to push such ideas through and fully to exploit the country's burgeoning economic, industrial and human resources across the whole range of maritime enterprises from the delivery of fishing boats and shipping lines to aircraft carriers and nuclear submarines. Plainly this has already required significant procedural and institutional reform,[45] and great turbulence but, as by far the biggest tiger on the mountain, President Xi has shown he can get things done.

Nonetheless, China's maritime 'stepping out' will take time, because there are many obstacles in the way, ranging from much of China's agrarian and continental traditions and marine-geographic constraints discussed earlier, to its need still further to generate its scientific and industrial base. Additionally, it faces the urgent and immediate problems of any country in the throes of rapid economic development.[46] The process of developing maritime power, in short both predates and will post-date President Xi's political career. Even in his case, the key role of the supreme leader or maritime champion can be exaggerated. Articulating the vision is not the whole story; much will depend on the subsequent ability to get it done, and typically that will take much more time. It reminds us that having a vision is all very well, but to have much chance of getting implemented, it needs to be shared with subordinates and almost certainly with successors as well.

Under President Xi's guidance, China has however evolved a broad approach, apparently designed to improve all four constituents of maritime power. The country's policies in the South China Sea when combined with its own interpretations of international maritime law seem set to effect radical although not total improvement in the nature of its maritime geography. Although improvements in governance remain obscure to outsiders, the decision to amalgamate and rationalise the country's five maritime law enforcement agencies into a China Coast Guard provides evidence of such an administrative drive. The success of the country's maritime economy hardly needs labouring, other than noting that its success casts considerable doubt on the long-held Western proposition, advanced as we have seen by de Custine during his trip to Russia and by countless scholars since, that a free, transparent and incorrupt political system is a prerequisite for a vibrant economy. Finally, improvements in the fourth constituent of maritime power, the Chinese Navy, have already been substantial; its order of battle and capacity to operate effectively both regionally and globally is such as to cause some concern to its neighbours and anxiety from the United States.

The *scale* of China's maritime aspirations moreover, is still unclear because there remains much, perhaps necessary and deliberate, ambiguity in the country's current policies, not least its intentions towards the South and East China Seas.[47] This plus the intrinsic problems of predicting a future beyond the next 20 years mean that while we can be pretty sure that the country will be a maritime power by its 2049 centennial, it is far from certain that it will be *the* maritime power.   •

4.2.4 Indonesia

Indonesia provides another example of a contemporary top-down approach. In 2013 President Joko Widodo (popularly known as Jokowi) also launched a campaign specifically to make the most of his country's maritime potentialities. He and his team, especially Dr Rizal Sukma, were concerned that while Indonesia was indisputably maritime in that it comprised some 18,000 islands and sat squarely on the crossing point of east-west and north-south shipping lanes between the Indian, Pacific and Southern Oceans, it hadn't really exploited all the opportunities this provided. Instead other people were stealing Indonesia's fish, making free use of its waters and there was a startling lack of economic interconnectivity between one end of its island chain and the other such that a bag of cement cost four times as much in Papua as it did in Java. Accordingly, the ever-present possibility of absolute or partial secession of its very diverse island communities could not be entirely ruled out and in general the country wasn't making the economic progress that its resources and population suggested it could, and should.

Jokowi put forwards the idea during his first election campaign, was duly elected in 2014 and to some people's surprise then set about doing what he had promised. First of all, more flesh was put on the bones of the initial idea. Jokowi's team then came up with a title for the project which is usually, if somewhat mysteriously, rendered in English as the 'Global Maritime Fulcrum.'[48] It comprised five so-called pillars, or areas of proposed advance. Inevitably interconnected, they represent something of a remix of the four basic constituents of maritime power identified earlier. Unusually their development was specifically and publicly identified as the new government's policy targets. They were, and so far remain:

- The development of a maritime culture
- The effective management of maritime resources
- The development of a maritime infrastructure as a means of increasing the country's economic connectivity
- Maritime diplomacy to create the political conditions for this
- Maritime defence in order to protect the country's interests at sea.

Broadly, the first pillar was about correcting the sea-blindness of many Indonesians, to remind them of their past maritime greatness in the days of the Sumatra-based Srivijayan and the Java-based Majahapit 'empires' (or at least maritime conglomerates) of the 9th–13th and 14th and 15th centuries, respectively[49] and to emphasise the potential benefits of making the most of Indonesia's maritime assets. In effect it aimed to give a new much broader twist to the narrow operational phrase 'Maritime Domain Awareness.' It was a modern-day revisiting of Peter the Great's determination to marinise the largely territorial culture of 18th-Century Russia.

By 2030, Indonesia is likely to have some 300 million people and so the second pillar was all about ensuring that the country could properly and sustainably exploit the oil, gas and fish to be found in its waters because otherwise there was the danger that the country could become an expensive net food and energy importer. This required major investment in the extractive and processing industries. Effective management also implies ambitious reform of the administrative systems and bureaucracy charged with looking after the country's maritime interests.

The third pillar of the project was designed to tackle the gross inequalities in the spread of Indonesia's shipping and their malign economic consequences. No less than 70% of the country's shipping was going in and out of the port of Tanjung Priok in Java; as a consequence, the system was vulnerable to disruption and the economic benefits were spread unevenly between the islands. Clearly there was a need for a major investment programme in ports and shipping to improve archipelagic connectivity and maybe to cater for traffic passing through the archipelago from one ocean to another. This would strengthen the country's geographic integrity and turn its maritime geography into a positive advantage.

The fourth pillar, maritime diplomacy, was thought to be about securing the levels of practical cooperation with other countries that would make all these projects possible. Since the area is plagued with a number of local disputes about who owns what areas of sea, Indonesia would need to continue its work to find some way of managing, if not solving, the problems these disputes cause. Relations with China were and remain a major issue.

Finally, the Indonesian Navy, BAKAMLA (the nearest Indonesia has to a coast-guard) and other Indonesian maritime law enforcement agencies needed to be able to monitor and respond to unauthorized intrusions and illegal activities in the country's waters, to preserve good order at sea and if necessary defend Indonesia's maritime interests further afield. Implementing these tasks would shape the size and composition of these various sea-related forces and especially a Minimum Effective Force (MEF) for the Navy. This would require added resources for all these agencies and a definite programme to encourage the closer integration of their work.

So far, so good. During Present Widodo's first term, efforts were made to move from the articulation of the vision towards its practical implementation. A Coordinating Ministry was set up to help integrate the efforts of all the various ministries and governmental levels of involvement, all of whom were given sets of targets to be achieved. Clearly, the intrinsic institutional complexities of Indonesian governance, the huge geographic area to be covered, existing deficiencies in infrastructure, turf battles and resource limitations all meant all this could not be achieved overnight. The implementation phase commanded far fewer headlines and perhaps in consequence the Global Maritime Fulcrum was hardly mentioned in the 2019 elections for Jokowi's second term.

Some worried that without this visibility and push from the top, there was a danger that the whole project would run into the sand as the government got embroiled in more urgent and dramatic issues, of which there is no shortage in Indonesia. Others concluded that by the end of Jokowi's first term, perhaps one-third of the project's objectives had been met wholly or in part. In terms of port construction a start had been made but much more remained to be done. If this was reasonable progress, it still underlines the point that developing maritime power is a long-term process and that continued political visibility and top-down pressure would be needed to maintain progress. The requirement to reform governance and Indonesian culture has also proved to be a daunting prerequisite.

Paradoxically the Chinese might help out in less obvious ways than providing investment in Indonesia's ports and infrastructure, which they do. In December 2019 and January 2020 an armada of 50–60 Chinese fishing boats accompanied by four powerful China Coast Guard vessels and one China Marine Surveillance ship operated and fished in what Indonesia considered its waters near the Natuna islands for over two weeks despite protests from Indonesian authorities. Another bout of intrusions in March 2020 reinforced the outrage of the Indonesian population.[50] The vehemence of the normally low-key Indonesia diplomatic reaction, its sending three civilian patrol ships and six warships into the area, building up its force on Natuna island itself and finally a well-publicised Presidential visit underlined the point. External pressure on the country's valued marine resources could well re-inject more energy into the implementation of the GMF programme as a whole.

One undoubted difficulty faced by President Jokowi, especially when compared to the very strong position of President Xi in China must be residual doubts about his relative ability to get things done given the complex domestic political circumstances that he faces, particularly in the wake of the ravages of the Covid epidemic. Jokowi's articulation of a vision seemed clear enough, but Indonesia's capacity fully to implement it remains uncertain.

The implementation of a whole-of-government project like developing maritime power is a particular problem in that it requires implementation by multiple agencies. This is difficult in Indonesia, a country where responsibility for sea-related matters is divided between a dozen or more authorities. Because it is difficult, maybe impossible for the top decision-makers to maintain tight control over all these agencies at the same time, there is a danger that each will interpret and implement the directive in different and possibly self-serving ways. The overall coherence of the project may well suffer in consequence. One obvious indication of this is the failure so far to identify which agency should assume overall charge for responding to China's Natuna intrusions. In Indonesia's case, frustration with the slow and cumbersome mechanisms of government appears to have led President Jokowi to conclude that real progress must depend on wholesale reform of the government's administrative and bureaucratic structures *before* serious implementation of the maritime project can take place.[51] In this too, his experience echoes that of Peter the Great

In both China and Indonesia, while we may not be able to assess the probable degree of success in the two campaigns to develop maritime power we do at least know they are being seriously tried

4.3   Conclusions and Modern-Day Approaches

4.3.1   A Mixed Approach

Several things emerge from this survey. The first is that in all the historic cases mentioned is not a matter of either a top-down or a bottom-up approach, but instead of a mixture of the two. Inspirations, advances and retreats bounce continuously between the two perspectives. But both seem to be necessary for sustained success since where either the one or the other is significantly defective, progress commonly seems limited. Inadequate direction from above leads to strategies of drift. If inadequately supported from the bottom the most perfectly expressed aspirations for maritime power will evaporate into nothingness and join the great coterie of articulated ideas which should have made a difference but didn't.

The contrasting fortunes of the French and British in the decade after the American War of Independence underline the importance of mutual support between the top-down directed state-based approach and a socio-economic push up from the bottom. It has been well said that Britain lost that war but won the peace that followed.[52] In large part this was because under Prime Minister William Pitt and guided by such driven men as Admiral Sir Charles Middleton and the Duke of Richmond, the British adopted proactive rather than reactive strategies for reforming and making more cost-effective all aspects of government, and of naval administration, and the dockyards in particular. Britain was consciously preparing for war. In this, though, it was hugely helped by its bounding economy, with growth rates between 1783 and 1802 of 6% per annum, an expanding population, the ownership of a quarter of European merchant shipping, extensive international trade and in the young Prime Minister himself stable leadership for the next 18 years. In short, Pitt had the vision and the means. This provided, he thought, '[t] hat great foundation of our strength, of our glory and of our characteristic superiority over the rest of the nations of Europe.'[53] Progress was made through a series of public-private partnerships providing access to a vibrant maritime industrial base through innumerable generally well-regulated contracts.

By contrast in the last decade before the Revolution, the French state went through very difficult times. In the American war, the French with the initial success of a well built and trained navy showed they also had the right ideas (showing the British sometimes disagreeably proficient gunnery and sailing skills[54]) but by the end of it and into the subsequent peace demonstrated that they did not have the fiscal and often industrial means to sustain their advances. The confusion that derived from the Revolution made things even worse. The same disconnect between top-down vision and bottom-up reality was likewise evident with the Swedes and the Russians of the 1780s; both advanced ringingly ambitious plans for their dockyards at Karlskrona and Kronstadt respectively; neither had the slightest chance of actually building them.[55]

4.3.2　Countries Articulating the Vision

A second conclusion that emerges from this review when seeking to develop a country's maritime power is the common need to engage with its lack of sea-consciousness. Some would term this a cultural phenomenon, which can often take institutionalised form. Often labelled by affronted navies as 'sea blindness,' this is a very common condition. Both a cause and a consequence of policy failures at the top, it leads sufferers either vastly to under-rate the relative importance of the maritime domain or to acknowledge this in theory but to delay or postpone measures to protect maritime interests to some later and unspecified date after more apparently urgent national requirements are met. Either way, clear and prioritised maritime objectives are not provided for those lower in the policy and strategy-making hierarchy to seek to achieve.

One way of engaging with this ailment is publicly to justify and articulate a maritime policy and a vision of what needs to be done. Once historically rare, this approach has now become commonplace. Presidents Xi and Jokowi have provided recent examples.

Portugal's attractive and well-argued *National Ocean Strategy 2013–2020* (NOS 2013–2020) and renewed in March 2021 for the next decade is another.[56] Counting the country's extended continental shelf, it claims that at some 4 million km^2, Portugal's coastal estate is 40 times the size of its territory. In striking contrast to the dismissive verdict of Andrew Lambert that Portugal was 'profoundly continental,'[57] NOS 2013–2020 claims that Portugal is 'one of the great maritime countries of the world,' its maritime character being 'expressed in historical and cultural values.' It admits that the country's maritime identity was weakened through the last quarter of the 20th Century by the need to focus on the development of the European Union. The sea-related share of the country's GDP is only some 2%–3%. Because Portugal's future remains linked to the sea, its true maritime identity needs to be rebuilt. Other countries, it says, are doing likewise.[58]

NOS 2013–2020 identifies areas for improvement in the development of marine knowledge both in the sense of scientific data and general awareness of the importance of the sea to Portugal, the protection and sustainable exploitation of marine resources (fish, oil, gas methane hydrates) and leisure potential, plus the construction of the necessary infrastructure of ports, and wide-ranging merchant shipping industries. Restricted to the commercial and civilian side of the maritime affair, it makes no reference to military or political considerations other than passing references to the importance of freedom of navigation and the need for international cooperation.

These objectives are to be secured through the *Mar-Portugal Strategy*, effectively an Action Plan mobilising human, financial, material and information resources with everything subject to monitoring, evaluation and review processes. In short, *NOS 2013–2020* is a good example of a bid first to articulate a maritime policy that establishes the reasons for one and identifies the objectives before moving to set a strategy that will deliver them. The strategy is to be dynamic with constant review and updating. Its aim is to 'add value' and ensure that 'the overall result [is] more than just the sum of the sectoral values.' Covering administration and governance, 'blue growth' requires reform administration reform to reduce bureaucracy and integrates overlapping responsibilities. A new 'Base Law' will set a legal framework. The emphasis is on this being an integrated national effort. 'Only with everyone's commitment' it says can we make the sea a national goal and thus renew Portugal's maritime identity.'[59]

Countries now seem to articulate their visions for the development of maritime power for two separate but related reasons. Seen as a means of winning further acceptance and political support, it also could demonstrate that progress in the development of maritime power is underway, assuming that it is. Varied though these statements might be in the level of detail they provide, in the degree of their public availability and in who issued them, they at least show that the subject warrants significant attention.

The second perceived advantage of such publicly stated visions is that detailed promulgations of policy objectives are seen as a way of maintaining top-down push in that they provide something of a headmark – or guidance – for those lower in the food chain. In the absence of sufficiently precisely articulated objectives, subordinate policy and strategy makers may maintain options rather than establish priorities with talk of 'balanced' approaches towards the future. All too often, these offer very little real practical guidance to decision-takers even lower down in the system. When this happens, those lower in the hierarchy either do the same thing, or, more insidiously, decide their own way forward in the light of decisions which they think the policy-makers above them should have made but didn't. Sectoral responses of this kind tend to be much harder to integrate into coherent national responses. Ideally everyone should be singing from the same hymn sheet.[60]

The Portuguese emphasis on a stated 'Action Plan' shows a lively awareness of the fact that there is a world of difference between stating a policy and actually getting anything much done. Practical problems and the pressure of daily distractions abound. This, for example, is manifest in India. Although having nothing like the scope and historical depth of K.M. Panikkar's work that was mentioned earlier, the Indian equivalent of NOS 2011–2020 was Prime Minister Modi's 'Maritime Agenda, 2010–2020,' a policy specifically focused on developing the kind of maritime infrastructure in shipping, ports and related industrial capacity) that historically has been associated with naval growth. This has morphed into the 'Sagarmala' (ocean-centred) project announced at the 2016 Maritime India Summit. This aims to extend India's national oceans thinking throughout the Indian ocean region. Both approaches are based on India's burgeoning population, economic growth, maritime trade and reliance on external energy sources. Taken together, they represent '… a paradigmatic shift away from a more continental strategic outlook.' It is also associated with a more 'navalism' independently sparked to a degree by the growing presence of the Chinese navy in the Indian ocean.[61] Sceptics, pointing to such problems as an inefficient national bureaucracy, continuing infrastructure limitations, financial constraints and the distracting effect of more immediate concerns – such as those revealed by the Covid pandemic – worry that turning these lofty ambitions into reality will be hard.

The same problems arise elewhere. Colombia also developed and promulgated an 'oceans policy' intended to integrate and advance all aspects of the maritime cause, at the highest level. Its *Politica Nacional del Oceano y de los Espacios Costeros*, which, though concise and less glossy than NOS 2011-20, is more than a 'vision' in that, while covering everything, treatment of each maritime dimension comprises a statement of requirements followed by specified 'lines of action.' The policy was produced in October 2013 by the Ocean Commission of Colombia, chaired by the Vice President of the Republic, which continues to act as a focal point for future development.[62] The problem of course, is that Colombia also has enormous distractions, a frail economy, continued domestic upheavals and a backwash from its much more troubled neighbour, Venezuela.

In Malaysia, the equivalent public statement of a maritime vision was *Malaysia Ocean Policy* 2011–2020, issued in 2010.[63] Associated with ambitious plans to upgrade the country's maritime economic infrastructure, it specifically excluded defence- and security-related issues and its public availability was limited. The document was issued by the National Oceans Directorate of just one of the stake-holders – the Ministry of Science, Technology and Innovation – perhaps in search of support and resources from above, and sideways from other stakeholders. Since then little progress has been made. There has been a change in government with leaders, 'mired in the politics of survival,' not giving it the priority it deserves. The situation has not been helped by the abolition in 2019 of the NOD, the organisation that produced the plan.[64]

Something rather similar has happened in Australia. In the absence of an overarching coordinating ministry, or even a special task force reporting to the Prime Minister, responsibility for the production of a national oceans policy was assumed by the Environment Ministry, which, in 1998, set up the National Ocean Office to produce one. The result was *Australia's Oceans Policy* which appeared in May 1999. Other stakeholders,(particularly the maritime industries and their associated Ministries) felt neither sufficiently engaged in the policy nor that their interests were properly represented. Unprotected by any legislative or statutory safeguard, the policy languished until a new and less concerned government, came in, abandoned it and, again, closed down the originating agency. In both the Australian and Malaysian cases, the lack of integration in the maritime sector meant there was no shared ownership of a policy that was bound to be challenging because it covered so much.[65] Sectoral maritime governance only works if all stakeholders are closely and mutually supportive and have a sense of ownership. Coordinating Ministries, such as the one President Jokowi set up in theory should help here.

These examples illustrate political and/or institutional limitations on the visionary's capacity actually to get things done. This is particularly difficult because success in the development of maritime power requires a broad multi-dimensional approach designed to increase the synergies between the four constituents of maritime power discussed earlier. A whole-of-nation rather than just a whole-of-government approach is needed. Organising that takes a lot of political capital. The visionary may not be in a strong political position to push such a comprehensive and all-embracing agenda. Here again, President Xi, who, although by no means untrammelled, is in a position of great authority in the Chinese system, may well prove better able to advance the maritime cause than President Jokowi for example.[13]

Another problem is that developing maritime power (rather than just building a navy) takes time. Very evidently, the development of maritime power is a long-term business well beyond the political life of any individual however able, willing and commanding. The short-lived nature of brilliant achievements by the likes of France's Jean-Baptiste Colbert or the Ottoman Empire's Mehmet II[66] suggests that unless a vision is shared with successors as well as subordinates its prospects of overall success remain limited. Here, the short-term democratic horizons of most politicians in Western-style democracies are often said to be a problem. Having to respond to a host of other apparently more urgent and immediate distractions, the argument goes, limits their capacity to plan for the long term. Maybe the Chinese who have over the centuries hoisted in the need for strategic patience have an advantage here and; eschewing the need for the 'quick fix,' they have made 2049 – the centennial of the founding of the Peoples Republic of China – their headmark.

Not only does developing maritime power take time; it demands foresight. Deciding policy objectives requires having at least some degree of confidence about the nature of the longer-term future that one is preparing for. Having to 'see through a glass darkly' and to decide the line to take, is intrinsically very difficult, maybe now more than ever. Things change all the time, often in ways that cannot be predicted. The extent of this problem is such that it may seem naively optimistic to expect much in the way of a *guiding* national policy in the first place. Wide consultation with competing sources of expertise may help develop future-proofed policy objectives but this depends on the existence of a free and informed 'commentariat' (derived essentially from academia, industry and national think-tanks) and a willingness for policy-makers to engage with those who disagree. For a variety of different reasons, this might not be possible for many countries.

Nonetheless, despite the very real problems in turning theory into practice, such visions, to the extent they are successful, seem likely to provide a comparative advantage over countries that do not have them at all.

Henry Maydman certainly had the necessary maritime vision but of course, was not in a position to implement it, so targeted the people who were. Implicitly this identifies the key difference between policy–making, the defining of overall objectives and the next step down, strategy, setting the ways and means by which those objectives might best be achieved. It is to a deeper look at putting maritime objectives into practical effect that we should now turn.

Notes

1 Richmond, H.W., *Sea Power in the Modern World* (London: Bell, 1934), 17.
2 Abulafia, *The Boundless Sea*, 415–46; d'Hanens, Albert, *Europe of the North Sea and the Baltic; The World of the Hanse* (Antwerp: Fonds Mercator, 1984).
3 Lambert, *Seapower States*, 156–203.
4 Abulafia, *The Boundless Sea*, 668, 674–5 et seq.
5 Ibid, 674; Lambert, *Seapower States*, 165.
6 Willis, Sam, *The Struggle for Sea Power: The Royal Navy vs the World, 1775–1782* (London: Atlantic Books, 2018), 56, 75, 78, 82. The paradox was that it was exactly these people who suffered most from the British reaction to their defeat. Toll, Ian W., *Six Frigates* (London: Michael Joseph, 2006).
7 Adams quoted in Toll, *Six Frigates*, 88.
8 Willis, *The Struggle for Sea Power*, 90–1.
9 Symonds, Craig, *Navalists and Antinavalists: The Naval Policy Debate in the United States, 1785–1827* (Newark: University of Delaware Press, 1980), 11 et seq.
10 Adams, quoted in Toll, *Six Frigates*, 143.
11 Senator Adam Seybert, quoted in Symonds, *Navalists and Antinavalists*, 155.
12 Toll, *Six Frigates*, 285–7.
13 Toll, *Six Frigates*, 33–43.
14 Hattendorf, John B. and Leeman, William P. (Eds), *Forging the Trident: Theodore Roosevelt and the United States Navy* (Annapolis, MD: Naval Institute Press, 2020).
15 Quoted by Marolda, Edward J., 'A Tempest in the Navy Department,' in Hattendorf and Leeman, *Forging the Trident*, op cit, 57.
16 Montefiore, Simon Sebag, *Potemkin: Catherine the Great's Imperial Partner* (New York: Vintage Books, 2005), 265.
17 Abulafia, *The Boundless Sea*, 800–1.
18 Short, John Rennie, *The World Through Maps: A History of Cartography* (National Library of Canada: Firefly Books, 2003), 32–3.
19 Massie, *Peter the Great*, 244–61.
20 Ibid, 210.
21 Montefiore, *Potemkin*, 233, 269.
22 De Custine, the Marquis, *Empire of the Czar: A Journey through Eternal Russia* (New York: Doubleday, 1971), 236.
23 Massie, *Peter the Great*, 773, 769.
24 De Custine, *Empire of the Czar*, 547.
25 Lambert, *Seapower States*, 227–65.
26 Montefiore, *Potemkin*, 227–8.
27 De Custine, *Empire of the Czar*, 365.
28 Ibid, 82–5, 128–32.
29 De Custine, *Empire of the Czar*, 228, 233, 195.
30 Gorshkov, *The Sea Power of the State*, 68–70, 79.
31 Montefiore, *Potemkin*, 206–7.
32 Ibid, 231.
33 James R. Gibson, 'Russian Expansion in Siberia and America,' *Geographical Review*, Vol.70, No. 2 (April 1980), 132.
34 De Custine, *The Empire of the Czars*, 76–7.
35 Glendinning, Victoria, *Raffles and the Golden Opportunity* (London: Profile, 2018), 83–4.
36 Ibid, xiv.
37 Ibid, 72.
38 Ibid, 210, 229, 218.
39 Ibid, 70.
40 Ibid, 232.
41 Ibid, 255.
42 Abulafia, *The Boundless Sea*, 822.
43 Quoted in Wise, *Travellers' Tales*, 127.

44 *China's Military Strategy* (Beijing: State Council Information Office of the People's Republic of China, May 2015), 4, available at http://eng.mod.gov.cn/Database/WhitePapers/index.htm (accessed 2 March 2018).
45 Hu, *Chinese Maritime Power*, 243–4.
46 Ibid, 226–35, 243–4.
47 Hu Bo, *Chinese Maritime Power*, 238–40.
48 Octavian, Amurulla, *Indonesian Navy, Global Maritime Fulcrum and ASEAN* (Jakarta: SESKOAL Press, 2019), 64–87.
49 Abulafia, *The Boundless Ocean*, 148–65, 279–81.
50 'Gone Fishing', AMTI on-line publication, 30 January 2020.
51 For this see Dr Evan Laksmana, CSIS Jakarta, 'No Time for Maritime,' Podcast interview, *Indonesiaindepth*, 29 March 2020 at http://hyperurl.co/notimeformaritime (accessed 30 March 2020) and 'Here's why Jakarta doesn't push back when China barges into Indonesian waters,' *Washington Post*, 28 March 2020.
52 Knight, Roger, *Britain Against Napoleon: The Organisation of Victory 1793–1815* (London: Penguin Books, 2013), 56.
53 William Pitt, speech of 6 October 1796. Reprinted in *The Speeches of the Right Honourable William Pitt in the House of Commons* (London, 1806).
54 Willis, *The Struggle for Sea Power*, 206–9, 273, 288.
55 Knight, *Britain Against Napoleon*, 35.
56 *National Ocean Strategy 2013–2020* (Lisbon: Directorate General of the Sea, 2013), available at https://www.msp-platform.eu/practices/national-ocean-strategy-2013-2020.
57 Lambert, *Seapower States*, 219.
58 *NOS*, 27, 36, 50.
59 Ibid, 66, 43–5 and 7.
60 This important issue is further discussed in Chapters 9 and 10.
61 Gresh, *To Rule Eurasia's Waves*, op cit, 145, 132–56. 'Sagar' is 'Ocean' in Hindi, and 'mala' is 'necklace'; Padmaja, G., 'Modi's Maritime Diplomacy: A Strategic Opportunity,' *Maritime Affairs*, Vol. II, No. 2 (2015).
62 *Politica Nacional de Oceano y de los Espacios Costeros* (Bogota: Colombian Ocean Commission, 2013).
63 While this is not publicly available, its outlines were usefully discussed in 2009 presentations of 2009 by Mohd Nizam Basiron and Cheryl Rita Kaur available at http://www.pemsea.org›sites›default›files›aiDan
64 I owe the insights and the phrase to Mohd Nizam Basiron. See also Vu Hai Dang and Cheryl Rita Kaur, 'Comparing Ocean Policy Developing Processes in Vietnam and Malaysia: Lessons Learned and Way Forward,' *MIMA Bulletin*, Vol. 26, No. 1 (2019).
65 *Australia's Ocean Policy*, May 1999 available at https://library.dbca.wa.gov.au/static/FullTextFiles/018882.pdf). I am indebted to Steve Raamaker for his insights here. See also Vinson, Joanna, 'Australia's Ocean Policy: Past, Present and Future,' *Marine Policy*, Vol. 57 (July 2015).
66 Paine, *The Sea and Civilisation*, 414–8.

5 Willing the Means: Establishing and Resourcing Strategic Priorities

It should be written in letters of fire before every War Cabinet and before every General Staff:

HE WHO WILLS THE END MUST WILL THE MEANS

Lt General Sir George MacMunn, 1915, Gallipoli campaign

5.1 Introduction

Time, energy and resources are finite. Accordingly, choices between the courses of action that require them have to be made, consciously or unconsciously. In 1492, Christopher Columbus and his companions sailed across the Atlantic from Spain to the West Indies, inaugurating the European age of exploration. He went at the behest of, and was subsidised by, King Ferdinand of Aragon and Queen Isabella of Castile. Columbus and his generation of ocean explorers – and indeed those who came afterwards – were only able to transform the world because of such financial backing, and because of technical progress in developing three or four-masted sailing ships and the use of the navigational instruments such as the astrolabe, the sextant, the magnetic compass and so on. But these advances had not happened of their own accord. They represented an investment in time, effort and money made by kings, ship designers and amateur scientists. Their investments in maritime endeavour were necessarily at the expense of other non-maritime things they could have done. These positive choices about what to spend their money on reflected the priorities they had arrived at, consciously or unconsciously.

This experience illustrates the point that once broad national policy objectives (or 'ends') have either emerged or been established, the logical sequence of events is to proceed to their implementation through the setting of a strategy that is aimed at identifying the ways and the means by which these objectives can be met. This requires making choices and allocating resources – thereby achieving the task of 'willing the means,' as recommended by General MacMunn. At this level the treatment is broad and general; it is essentially an exercise in what is usually thought of as Grand Strategy, concisely described by the political scientist Richard Betts, as 'a practical plan to use military, economic, and diplomatic means to achieve national interests (or political ends) over time, with the least feasible cost in blood and treasure.'[1]

Historical experience suggests responsibility for progress will tend to require dropping down from the level of the leader and his or her entourage to Tier 2 where they may be

DOI: 10.4324/9781003100553-5

joined by the top representatives of all major areas of government business. It is at this Cabinet level that the implementation of national policy priorities tends to be hammered out. This sounds right in theory but in practice, it may not be that simple; the dividing line between the top tiers varies greatly between countries, and can anyway be very fuzzy. It also isn't a simple top-down process either. William III's advisors, or cabinet members and main officers of state operating at this level expected, for example, to be able to influence the King's decisions about national priorities even though he was at the top of the hierarchy of decisions and they were not. Moreover shaping information about the resources available usually comes from below.

At this level, what Maydman called 'the Maritime Affair' comprises its commercial side (shipping, the fisheries and so forth) and the military/naval side; the first of these is part of a country's economic strategy, while the second is an aspect of its defence strategy, not of course that people at the time would have recognised either of these labels. Though generally mutually supportive, these two elements of the maritime affair can easily compete. While the Government wishes to invest in its domestic ship-building industry as part of a general industrial strategy, a navy may want to acquire the cheapest ships quickly from whatever source. Instead, it may be required to take ships built at home that are be less good, cost more and arrive later.

The Defence element in a country's grand strategy, moreover, is just one of the major responsibilities of the state and as such has to compete for attention, and for the national resources it requires, with all the others. At a time when governments are finding it more difficult to access the wealth of their countries equitably and sustainably, and most depend on credit, this puts even more pressure on them. Moreover, Defence is growing intrinsically more expensive and is often associated with waste. Outside periods of war or high levels of strategic competition with other countries, getting resources for defence is likely to become harder.

5.2 A British Illustration of the Resources-Commitments Problem

Although as we shall see Themistocles was fortunate to have access to the revenues of the Laureium silver mines,[2] strategic priority choices still had to be made. The money could have been spent on other things. Like all governments at all times and everywhere, Athens could not do everything it might wish with the resources available. A gap between those resources and possibly desirable commitments was inevitable. Arguably the basic function of government is constantly to manage that gap while providing for the security and sufficient well-being of its citizens and the survival of the regime. The campaign to ensure that the maritime cause gets the resources it needs in order to provide General MacMunn's 'means' to secure the desired 'ends' has to be fought against this basic reality.

At first glance this task would seem to be much simpler for a country as impeccably maritime as Britain is often said to be.[3] Its range of choices should be narrower, the level of sympathy and the revenues from sea-based trade higher. This would seem to make the task easier. But there were a number of reasons why things often did not look that way for the Royal Navy.

Firstly, successive British governments felt, above all, that the economy had to be nurtured. This remained true even in the age of *laissez-faire* with its preference for the least interference in the market as possible. The consensus was that the economy had to be protected from undue interference, foreign or domestic, and undue stress from excessive government spending. Maintaining a working economy was the essential task of government since success or failure would shape all other policy choices.

The challenge for the Navy tended to be more difficult in peace time and worse still when economic tribulations made it difficult for the government to balance its books. The extent of chronic underfunding varied but tended to be worse in times of economic trouble, such as the coinage crisis of 1696–1697 or the 'South Sea Bubble' affair of 1720 or when Henry Pelham, the well respected First Lord of the Treasury of 1743–1754 was grappling with a terrifying level of the national debt,[4] or the crisis of 1797 which led to the mutinies at Spithead and the Nore, all the way through to the Depression of the 1930s, another mutiny at Invergordon in 1931 and the Great Recession of 2008–2009. It could be worse still if the government was in the hands of those less than totally sympathetic to the maritime cause, or if Parliament came to believe skulduggery or institutional incompetence was wasting the resources that had been granted to the Navy.[5]

In the interwar period, the British Treasury made the point, and subsequent events were to show that there was much in what they said, that the economy should be regarded as 'the fourth arm of defence.'[6] As a result, British defence spending in 1935 and 1936, was the lowest of all the major powers and had to soar to 5.5% of GNP in 1937, 8.5% in 1938 and 12.5% 1939 in an effort to catch up. In the meantime, however, much of Britain's heavy war industries had atrophied beyond the hope of rapid recovery through reduced demand. The armour for the Royal Navy's new carriers could only be obtained from Czechoslovakia, for example.

How the government responded to such economic challenges also reflected the values of the particular time, and, as discussed in Chapter 2, the relative political power of the main economic stake-holders. For much of the time in Britain, as for many other countries too, the debate about government maritime priorities reflected unceasing competition between agricultural/land and city/industrial/trading interests. The City of London was a particularly important maritime contender and could be relied on to support the kind of naval activity that it thought supported British trade in peace and war. Politically it could still be check-mated by the continuing influence of the country squires and great landowners who drove the policies of the Tory party through the 18th and 19th Centuries and into the 20th. Even in maritime Britain things could be difficult.

Secondly, bidding for government support was unavoidably competitive since the demands of the maritime cause, always had to be compared with those of all other branches of government responsibility. Moreover, Britain like other countries from Henry Maydman's time onwards, has been faced with the need to accept increasing governmental responsibility for the provision of such public goods as health, social welfare and education grew, together with their associated costs. William III had some but much less requirements to deliver these than do modern governments all; the indications are that this trajectory is more likely to intensify than diminish in the future. In the 17th Century European states spent about half of government revenue on defence, rising to 75% or more if they were at war – and servicing the accumulated national debt would take up much of the remainder.[7] By the 1840s successive British governments were spending about 30% on defence while servicing the debt took nearly twice as much; moreover the calls for more social spending were growing ever louder.[8] Nowadays, taxation has to be justified by much more than keeping the people safe from enemies, foreign and domestic; the voters increasingly expect their growing, essential life-needs to be catered for as well. The inevitable implication of these other expanding commitments could easily mean fewer resources available for maritime defence unless the country was at war. And maybe not even then.

Thirdly, there was the pull of other domains of defence. The extent to which the country's domestic, continental or imperial defence commitments demanded investment in land rather than sea forces varied over time, but was always there. In the War of Spanish Succession and the period of the Revolutionary and Napoleonic wars, it was high and again in the First and Second World Wars. The same was true during the Cold War and parts of the post-Cold Cold war periods. As capital-intensive services, navies always seem expensive in comparison with armies. Their equipment takes longer to produce, so peacetime neglect is harder to correct in more dangerous times. The arrival of the newer domains of war – air, space and cyberspace have aggravated the problem still further.

Finally, under-funding sometimes reflected convulsions in the international context and could be acute in form. Such were the massive demobilisations that followed the successful conclusion of the Napoleonic wars, the First and Second World Wars and to some extent the pursuit of a 'peace dividend' after the fall of the Berlin Wall. In all these cases there followed a massive shift in governmental priorities from the waging of war to national recovery. Inspired by the urgency of the need to re-build the peacetime economy and maintain the social fabric in a time of great strain, these reductions were pursued with more speed than caution. Domestic circumstances and the maintenance of the social order provided additional incentives for hasty demobilisation particularly after the end of the Napoleonic and First World War when revolution did not seem totally inconceivable. In 1918–1919, moreover, Britain was effectively bankrupt and saddled with huge debts partly deriving from iredeemable loans to allies. The situation in Britain after the Second World War was hardly any better. In such circumstances, there could be little disputing that defence and naval spending must lose priority.

Singly, or more usually in combination, these issues posed real challenges for the 'maritime affair' even in maritime Britain. This produced chronic under-funding of the Navy nearly all the time but sometimes periods of exceptional challenge. The resultant almost cyclical periods of waxing and waning tend, however, to be much worse for countries less blessed with a maritime predisposition.

5.3 An Athenian Example of Success

All the same, Ancient Greece provides an early example of how this problem of securing sufficient priority and resources for the development of maritime power was, and perhaps can be, overcome. After losing the Battle of Marathon in 490 BC, the Persians pulled back from their campaign against Greece. Themistocles, one of the battle's veterans and a consummate politician of Athens, was sure, however, that they would be back.[9] He knew, as Thucydides records, that 'navies … brought in revenue and … were the foundations of empire.'[10] But he also knew that navies were just part of the overall maritime package which was necessary. He urged investment in the port of Piraeus for economic as well as strategic reasons, the building of the 'Long Walls' between it and Athens for the protection of both and a great expansion of the Athenian fleet to 200 triremes. Themistocles, says Plutarch, had noticed the favourable shape of its harbours, and wished to attach the whole city to the sea; thus in a certain manner counteracting the policies of the ancient Athenian kings. For they, as it is said, in their efforts to draw the citizens away from the sea had accustomed them to live not by navigation but by agriculture.[11]

Themistocles was particularly ambitious; knowing that Greek culture with its landed interests was against him, he wanted not just more ships for the navy, his aim was to change society too. This was a prerequisite for making Athens more maritime. Above all, 'war is not so much a matter of armaments,' as Thucydides remarked, 'as of the money which makes armaments effective; particularly is this true in a war fought between a land power and a sea power. So let us first of all see to our finances ...'[12]

It was an uphill struggle. Themistocles had to deal with political rivals within the City, fractious and unreliable semi-allies outside it who 'still cherished a frivolous and unreasonable jealousy of each other.' Worst of all he had to deal with the entrenched disdain that many Athenians had for anything that smacked of 'the rowing pad and the oar.' Rather than be degraded as 'sea-tossed marines' his fellow-citizens preferred the 'spear and the shield.' In any case, after losing at Marathon the Persians seemed a less immediate strategic threat than some of Athens' Greek neighbours.

Developing maritime power requires investment in the future. That takes money. Fortunately, revenue from the new silver mines at Laureium came on-stream, providing potential capital for Themistocles's maritime project. Accordingly, the necessary resources were available, the issue was what to spend them on – enriching the citizens of Athens, building up the army or the navy. Themistocles managed to out-manoeuvre his political opponents in a skilful, arguably unscrupulous, campaign that attacked their credibility and honour; he got on 'good terms with the common folk' according to Plutarch, rallied the patriotism of the otherwise disputatious Greeks against the barbarians while justifying naval spending to the Athenians as being necessary against their local rival Aegina rather than the Persians. His last stroke was to make imaginative use of the mystic sayings of the Oracle of Delphi. Having duly 'brought to bear the signs from heaven and oracles, 'perhaps through some judicious bribery, Themistocles' campaign was successful. He got his 200 trireme fleet.

Better still, he then moved from developing Athenian maritime power to actually using it, when the Persians did indeed come back. Acutely sensitive to the political realities of the time, he left the command of the combined Greek fleet to Eurybiades, from Sparta, the 'master state of the Peloponnesus' but he was the inspiration behind the decisive victory that was achieved over the much bigger Persian fleet in the narrow waters off Salamis in 480 BC.

Of course, some caveats have to be entered against this tale of maritime success. Luck was undoubtedly with the Athenians, particularly in the 'tempestuous and heavy sea' following a bad storm off Aphetae which sank many of the Persian ships before the main battle. Moreover, the land campaign, including the battles of Marathon and Thermopylae, and the efforts especially of the Spartans were vital too. It was indeed fortunate that the Spartans were on the same side, for once.

If this was the ultimate 'proof of concept' that consolidated support and resources for the rapid development of maritime power, success depended on initially winning positions of authority from which maritime representations could be effectively made. It needed high levels of political skill, the availability of sufficient resources, a context of credible strategic threat, an all-round narrative for all levels of Athenian society and the ability to enlist sufficient allies from 'abroad.' Victory at the battle of Salamis demonstrated the validity of the case in practice, thereby sustaining maritime fortunes for the longer term. This meant that in the future it would be easier for Themistocles' successors, particularly Pericles and Alcibiades, to argue the maritime case. The ultimate decline of Athenian maritime and naval power, however, showed there would always be difficulties and resistance, and that sometimes these would prevail. Occasionally of course, battles were lost, such as the catastrophe at Aegospotami in 405, when under Lysander, the Spartans beat the Athenians at their own game. After that, the Athenians had to go into recovery mode. This underlines the point that in the process of developing maritime power setbacks as well as successes, have to be expected.

Many of the issues that appear in this Athenian example of the development of maritime and naval power have also appeared in later attempts by other countries to do the same thing. The 'coping mechanisms' that Themistocles' resorted to have likewise been tried on countless occasions since sometimes with success and sometimes not. Delivering sufficient priority and resource for maritime power has rarely been an easy sell.

5.4 Managing the Resources-Commitment Problem: Seven Coping Mechanisms

Essentially, Themistocles and other proponents of maritime power had to come up with an effective approach and a narrative that convinced sceptics. Typically, this has involved some or all of perhaps seven coping mechanisms.

5.4.1 A Case That Sells the Sea

Themistocles was successful because he was able to identify the choices that he thought Athens needed to make, to persuade his fellow citizens that he was right and to secure the necessary funding for his project. He was prioritising the maritime affair over other things that the money could have been spent on. Subsequent events consolidated his success and validated his choices. Plutarch doesn't tell us the detail of Themistocles' advocacy of the case for the Athenians to seek their prosperity as well as their security at sea, but we can fairly safely assume that his argument was based on trade and the revenues it would generate. This would not be dissimilar to the arguments of later navalists, and other people of a maritime persuasion.

As far as the commercial side of the maritime case is concerned, the narrative in fact is fairly simple and largely economic in form. These days its advocates push the idea of the 'blue economy' arguing that the resources of the sea (fish, oil, gas, manganese nodules, energy and who knows what else) are so vast that if properly exploited they would transform national economies. Relatedly in many countries, other sea-related industries, such as ship-building, shipping companies, and marine insurance can be shown as good investments for all-round economic prosperity and the provision of a wider and more sustainable tax base when compared to other competing areas of economic industrial activity. After their Revolution in 1949, the Chinese, for example, set about developing their ports, their ship-building industry and their national fleets as soon as they possibly could. It was one of their top priorities. Subsequent developments have shown how right they were to do so.[13]

The military-naval side of the maritime case was probably more difficult for Themistocles because of the largely territorial preoccupations of the Athenians before this time. He had no Athenian precedent to refer back to. The Royal Navy, on the other hand, often benefitted from the fact that its song was a familiar and traditionally accepted one. This was certainly the case in Henry Maydman's time. The first plank of the argument tended to be the number and variety of military strategic options that a maritime approach can confer, both defensive and offensive. Its essential elements were summed up in the theories most obviously associated with Sir Julian Corbett at the beginning of the 20th Century but much of which had been less formally articulated by others well before then. This isn't the place to delve too deeply into what this narrative actually was, but its bare bones are familiar enough. Broadly the proposition was that Britain's strategic circumstances demanded investment in the Navy for the conduct of a maritime strategy that centred on four related things.

Firstly and most obviously, there was the need to defend the country from invasion by nearby powers that usually had much bigger armies than Britain could ever hope or wish to produce. Invaders could be intercepted at sea, or deterred from even coming before they set foot on land. This would also ensure regime survival, an important consideration for William III. Two such invasions had just taken place after all; nor, despite legend, were they the last.[14] Ireland and Scotland were strategic vulnerabilities, and the Jacobite rebellion of 1715 was just around the corner.

Secondly there was the need to defend Britain's all-important sea-based trade, its merchant shipping and its overseas interests which combined into a major source of national revenue. Successive wars showed only too clearly that unless properly defended this dependency could be a major source of strategic vulnerability. The City of London and the Parliamentary interest in general thought these hard-nosed commercial imperatives vital to the future glory and prosperity of the country. The synergy of the commercial and the naval sides of the maritime case was a constant refrain. Maritime power in short was a virtuous circle, as shown in Chapter 1.

Thirdly, in peace and war, naval action could not merely defend but actually improve the present and future conditions for British trade. By action overseas in setting up and then defending markets and colonies abroad, Britain could multiply its trade relative to its opponents, especially if it could attack their war economies by seizing other peoples' markets and damaging their war economies.

Fourthly, a happy combination of geographic isolation (being an island) and maritime supremacy meant that Britain could play the role of being an offshore-balancer in Europe. With a powerful navy, the British could exploit the ubiquity of the sea to worry and distract their more land-bound adversaries with threats, raids and limited interventions while providing the funding for continental allies to do their land-fighting for them. For William III, a Dutchman, anxious to defend his homeland from the French, this argument had obvious appeal. It was neither the first nor the last time, that maritime Britain assumed a major continental commitment; but even when it did not, limited sea-based interventions could prove strategically cost-effective.

These arguments were not necessarily totally convincing, and some maritime advocates harked-back to a nostalgic re-imagining of the great days of the first Elizabeth. The Royal Navy's capacity actually to deliver these strategic benefits was significantly less than perfect. But this was not necessarily fatal to its cause, because that was what the 'political nation' actually *thought* to be true. Whether it was, or not, was a secondary matter. In its basic strategic narrative, then, the Royal Navy was pushing on an open door.

Its difficulty lay in explaining why sometimes these things did not work, and the concept wasn't proved, as everyone expected them to. Very often the Navy's critics would ascribe this to the corruption, villainy or stupidity of those charged with carrying out the Navy's tasks. Equally often the Navy's defenders would counter with the claim it had been given insufficient resources, but the point was that both sides in these sporadic tumults were at least broadly agreed on what the tasks actually should be.

Few navies of other countries have found or do find themselves in quite this happy position, and in fact it has become increasingly less true for Britain too. One reason why Sir Julian Corbett wrote his most famous book, *Some Principles of Maritime Strategy* in the transformational period just before the First World War was that he feared that this broad consensus was dissipating and that the pendulum was moving away from the maritime and towards a more continental style of grand strategy. The experience of the Royal Navy, particularly through the last part of the 20th Century, suggests that he was right to worry.[15]

More broadly, a natural focus on the immediate threat of territorial neighbours and internal insurgency often makes it difficult to sell the relative importance of the sea. As Pannikar was all too aware, much of India's experience had this effect and in consequence, the army tended to dominate the decision-making process. Much the same happened in Indonesia, and indeed further elsewhere in Southeast Asia and Africa, where internal security and simply holding the country together demanded a primary focus on land-centric defence.

5.4.2 *A Case That Conforms to Strategic Reality*

For an argument to be convincing it has to be credible strategically. Faced with widespread scepticism that the defeated Persians actually were still a threat, Themistocles had to resort to the tendentious proposition that he was aiming at Athens' immediate Greek neighbours, but the Persian Empire looming over Ancient Greece was the real priority. And to be totally effective they would have to come at least in part by the sea. Simple geography in fact has often shaped the atmospherics for priority decisions in ways that have helped the maritime cause.

As a collection of islands, Britain was critically dependent on the sea lines of communication that kept its war economy going, maintained its links with the United States and the Empire and was the means by which it could transport its military forces abroad. From the end of the 19th Century, it was the same for the United States; the ability to project power against its enemies required it to dominate and to get its military power across vast oceans.

The relative availability of maritime resources in maritime states could also ease the problem of ensuring future support for the maritime case. After the US had begun to recover from the devastating reverses of December 1941, President Roosevelt was confronted by the urgent but competing demands of his two Pacific warlords. While General MacArthur urged an advance on Japan via the Dutch East Indies and the Philippines, the Navy in the shape of Admirals King and Nimitz favoured a thrust directly at Japan across the Central Pacific. Both would be island-hopping campaigns requiring naval support. Fortunately, by that time American superiority in material was such that Roosevelt could avoid making such a difficult decision by authorising both avenues of approach, operating in parallel.

Sometimes, this broadly applied to modern Japan too. In this case, it was just a a question of going with the flow – following the natural logic of strategic geography, but it also needed to reflect the strategic predispositions of its rulers. For many centuries,

Japan neglected its naval forces because there was little appetite for military engagement abroad. Instead the Japanese were content to fight each other. But as we have seen Hideyoshi changed all this in the 16th Century with his ambitious plan to re-order the strategic architecture of East Asia. He even had plans for operations against the Spanish Philippines.[16] After his defeat it took the arrival of Commodore Perry's 'black ships' in 1853 to jerk the Japanese out of their Continentalist torpor, with dramatic and tragic consequences later that culminated in the Second World War in the Pacific.

In the Autumn of 1941, as President Roosevelt was to do the following year, the Japanese also backed all the horses in the race. Unable to prioritise between attacking the British in Malaya, the Americans in the Philippines and at Pearl Harbor and the Dutch in the East Indies (while fighting a war in China and maintaining options against the Russians), the Japanese decided to do everything simultaneously. Given the limits of the forces available, this was a level of operational boldness that apparently bordered on insanity but through surprise and *kirimomi sakusen* (their 'driving force') they succeeded – for the time being at any rate.[17]

The Japanese plan can be seen, likewise, as a consciously desperate response to circumstances – an occasion, as quite often happens, when the strategic context effectively *makes* the priority decision for national leaders. With the continuing American embargo on steel and oil, Japanese leaders knew that their only other choice was caving in to US pressure and abandoning their plans for empire, and that was unthinkable.[18] The simultaneity of these attacks could only be sanctioned if the Japanese were prepared to accept high levels of operational risk and low levels of material support. The Japanese forces that landed in Thailand and Malaya for example had very little by way of logistic support. Instead they relied on what they called the 'Churchill supplies' which the British obligingly left for them as they retreated south. It was much the same in the Philippines. Curiously, their wafer-thin supply base turned out to be an advantage for the Japanese. The British expected an operational pause of several weeks after the Japanese landed in Thailand as the invaders got their supplies sorted out. Not having much to sort out, the Japanese instead started surging south immediately, catching the British by surprise; moreover the pressure of their possibly running out of supplies in the future reinforced the relentless push to Singapore. Paradoxically, a shortage of resources can sometimes have its benefits in the development and use of maritime power. Once again, circumstances set strategy.

It was the same for the Russians. For them the shortage of resources and the requirement to prioritise was crucial – but simple strategic geography, plus the operational context effectively made the key decisions for Stalin. After the catastrophic consequences for the Soviet Union of the stunning German advances in *Operation Barbarossa* in 1941, there could hardly be any doubt about the need to shift the war industries that could be moved behind the Urals and to destroy the rest before it fell into German hands. Likewise, the obvious focus for that newly re-located industry would have to be the material needs of the land/air war not on what might need to be done at sea, because the land battle was the most obviously pressing concern. In this case the only realistic option for the maritime interest was to argue the case for, and wherever possible to demonstrate, the extent to which it could support the land campaign. This the Soviet Navy did in critical lake and river campaigns on the Stalingrad and Leningrad fronts, in the supply of beleaguered Soviet garrison forces, as in the Crimea, and in the conduct of more than a hundred largely small scale amphibious or *desant* operations on the flanks of the Soviet Army as it advanced westwards. As will be seen later, only in more propitious times after the Second World War period could the maritime cause be more ambitiously advanced in the Soviet Union.

5.4.3 *A Case That Makes the Most of What's Available*

An important plank in Themistocles's argument was the need for action on land as well as on sea and this meant getting alongside Sparta, the land-power of the time. Moreover, all aspects of Athenian power, including the ability to move the people out of the capital and to engage in huge building projects needed to be factored in.

Likewise, Nicholas Rodger in his majestic survey of British maritime experience makes an important point about the way that 18th Century decision-makers approached the problem of setting strategy. First of all, they had neither the word – nor the concept. Instead,

> British policy towards the outside world was a single, large subject, which embraced diplomacy, commerce and war. Each of these aspects of national policy had naval implications, and could be seen to influence the employment of British fleets and squadrons, but contemporaries were not in the habit of isolating the naval implications of policy. It was in many ways, the strength of their approach ... it encouraged a unified approach to foreign policy.[19]

In effect, this kind of approach turns the prioritisation process up-side down. Instead of competing, the priorities are made to cooperate, support each other and act synergistically. It was a way of finding a way through the problem by seeking unity in opposites. In large measure this is no more than a straightforward recognition of what power actually is. In his magisterial account of the decline of British power, Corelli Barnet usefully summarised what he thought it was,

> The power of a nation-state by no means consists only in its armed forces, but also in its economic and technological resources; in the dexterity, foresight and resolution with which its foreign policy is conducted; in the efficiency of its social and political organisation. It consists most of all in the nation itself, in the people, their skills, energy, ambition, discipline, initiative, their beliefs, myths and illusions. And it consists further in the way that all these factors are related to one another. Moreover national power has to be considered not only in itself, in its absolute extent, but relative to the state's foreign or imperial obligations; it has to be considered relative to the power of other states.[20]

This reinforces firstly the point that there is far more to maritime power than the accumulation of great numbers of ships and naval weaponry and secondly that the successful development of that power is likely to depend on the effective marshalling of all these elements and all the options they provide so that they work with, and not against, each other. In a way that is what the Japanese did in 1941. Their strategy, mad as it seemed to the Allies at the time,[21] seemed to do everything the Japanese wanted. Attacking the fleet at Pearl Harbor would prevent the US Navy from interfering with their plans in the South while hopefully persuading an apparently reluctant American people to throw in the towel after they lost the first decisive round. At the very least it would gain the Japanese time to prepare against an eventual counter-attack. The seizure of Malaya, Singapore and Burma would do the same to the British, deprive them of vital strategic supplies and prevent their assisting the Dutch in the East Indies, and by blocking off supplies via the Burma Road make the campaign in China more winnable. Taking the oil of the Dutch East Indies would support Japan in a defensive war against all its current adversaries and even put the Empire into the best position for a possible future war against Russia. Moreover, given the weakness and strategic distractions of all their adversaries at the time, the Autumn of 1941 seemed the obvious time to strike. For the Japanese everything could be made to hang together.

Another way of doing this is to follow Themistocles in gaining access to and making use of other peoples' power, in his case Sparta and Athens' other Greek allies. The British as part of their 'offshore-balancing' role tried to do this all the time, fighting wars in Europe to the last drop of Prussian, Russian, Austrian or Spanish blood as the case may be. Moreover they sought to defray the increasing costs of maritime power and of acquiring and running their empire as much as possible. Initially, the British aimed at no more than the establishment of trading centres agreed with the initial consent of local potentates. Rivalry with other European powers, and sometimes the turbulence of local politics, led to such centres having to be garrisoned; over time they generated significant administrative responsibilities which the home government was reluctant to pay for.

The hope was that much of this could be delegated to the grateful recipients of Britain's imperial favours on the one hand and, on the other, to semi-private agencies like the East India Company, stiffened and supported if and when necessary, by elements of a British army that were decidedly expeditionary in outlook. In economic terms, neither option worked well. In America, the War of Independence came about largely because the Government tried to persuade the Americans to pay for the heavy costs of their own defence; the Americans were not, however, persuaded. Later, the Indian Mutiny of 1857 showed that the East India Company was incapable of defending the country's interests; only then did the government reluctantly assume full responsibility for the administration and defence of much of the country. Even in the 19th Century era of *Pax Britannica,* naval status declined, and more had to be spent on the army than on the Navy.[22] Afterwards, all too aware of the probable costs, the British government's reluctance to accept yet more colonies, was only overshadowed by an even greater reluctance to allow other countries to get them instead. Nor were these concerns unique to Britain; most of the other European empires followed suit to some degree but it was the British (and the Dutch) who led the way.[23]

The experience underlined the point touched on in Chapter 1 that the greater the level of a country's maritime success, the higher the risk of it picking up commitments that diverted effort into non-maritime directions. As also remarked earlier, technological development could make the situation worse. The Indian Mutiny occurred shortly after the Crimean war with Russia 1853–1856, which had already demonstrated the deficiencies of the British Army, even in expeditionary mode, when up against a major industrial-age European adversary, rather than minor colonial ones out in the Empire. Even though the war was arguably won by naval rather than land power,[24] it provided an early warning of the increasing challenges that Britain would face in trying to balance its land and sea commitments in an adjustable maritime grand strategy as it moved into the 20th Century.

The much narrower field of armaments production in the Second World War provides further evidence of the advantages of synergistic integration that is becoming a significant theme in this book. Although given the circumstances it was agreed in principle that the production of war *materiel* was an urgent priority, much depended on how that policy was implemented. And here, according to Richard Overy, the Allies had a decisive advantage over their Axis adversaries:

> Italian war production was riddled with corruption and administrative incompetence; Japan's economic effort was stifled by tensions between her soldiers and her businessmen, and a debilitating rivalry between the navy and the army; German industry and technology were the victims of ceaseless rivalry between the Nazi satraps and a military establishment whose technological fastidiousness made mass production almost impossible.[25]

In Germany, until Speer improved things somewhat from 1942, the military dictated the selection and development of anything that promised immediate dividends on the battlefield. 'It produced a situation where a proper sense of priority and evaluation was replaced with a chaos of demands and programmes.'[26] There was a level of 'polycratic chaos' in the way that Germany ran all aspects of the war – rivalling ministries and sub-empires (Army, SS, the Gauleiter the Economics Ministry) that prevented any coherent assessment and allocation of resources, let alone the hammering out of what elsewhere would be termed a 'grand strategy.' 'This' says Paul Kennedy, 'was not a serious way to run a war,'[27] or for that matter to develop maritime power.

By contrast, the British, under Lord Beaverbrook, rapidly expanded their war industries and, despite the Battle of Britain and the Blitz by the end of 1940 produced more aircraft than Germany, a lead it retained until also able to latch onto American production. It was also well ahead in new technologies such as radar and atomic energy, with the significant help of many refugees from Germany and occupied Europe.[28] The Americans only started serious planning for economic mobilisation in the summer of 1941, and the administration was curiously slow to set up an agency to coordinate its efforts.[29] But their bottom-up, more decentralised, entrepreneurial production system based on a national culture of enterprise indeed proved highly efficient in meeting the administration's enormous aircraft and ship-building targets. The ruthless top-down autocratic and pragmatic system in the Soviet Union, based on a 'regime of emergency measures,' quite different in nature was equally effective if less ambitious in the exploitation of new technologies. Both the United States and the Soviet Union though had the significant advantage of much greater starting capacity. The antagonists' experience in the production of war *materiel* differed widely during the Second World War but they all underlined the basic point that much depends on the way in which ideas about policy and strategy were actually implemented and integrated.

Today, China's controversial maritime Belt and Road Initiative (BRI), discussed in Chapter 2, illustrates the same point. Both its admirers and its critics see it as an example of strategic synergy. The BRI project is intended, by President Xi at least, to satisfy a wealth of different Chinese objectives. It provides employment possibilities for domestic industries now struggling to find them internally; it will help the economic development of western rather than coastal China; it will secure safe access to markets and necessary commodities; new ports and overseas facilities will facilitate the 'stepping out' of the Chinese navy; it will raise the living standards of recipient countries; it will increase Chinese influence and so make world governance seem fairer from Beijing's point of view; finally in the aftermath of the Coronavirus pandemic it should help revive world trade.

Not only do the policy objectives seem to be mutually supportive, so are the strategic ways and means by which these objectives are supposed to be achieved. One critic points to the development of the Greek port of Piraeus as an example of this. The Marseilles-based merchant shipping company CMA CGM, is heavily financed by Chinese banks and is a member of the Ocean Alliance, one of three consortia set up to manage excess capacity in times of economic downturn through load-sharing and other such arrangements. CMA CGM's attempts to link up with the Danish shipping company A.P.Moeller/Maersk were blocked by the Chinese Ministry of Commerce on the grounds that it would give foreigners too big a share of crucial Asia-Europe shipping routes. As a result these routes are virtually monopolised by Ocean Alliance. The Chinese company COSCO is a major player in the Ocean Alliance. Both COSCO and CMA CGM are heavily engaged in the Piraeus project. So is the Chinese company Huawei which has redesigned and replaced the port's IT network and communications infrastructure, a matter of some concern for the US Navy. COSCO is also the main supplier of shore-side support for the Chinese navy and is busily engaging in developing a global logistics network that will sustain Chinese naval operations around the world.[30]

Whether this kind of integration of the military and commercial sides of the maritime affair actually works will only emerge in due course, but its doing so will depend very much on a high level of coordination between the ministries and government agencies that share responsibility for the development of maritime power. In China, as elsewhere, the civilian maritime community is very diverse in covering shipbuilding the shipping industry, the fisheries, the Coast Guard and other maritime law enforcement agencies and they may well report to different ministries. Each of these then identifies their policy 'ends' or objectives, deduces their strategy, decides their 'ways' and allocates their 'means.' Integrating all this is no easy task.

Critics of such an apparently integrated approach in the BRI project, perhaps reflecting in part the assumptions of the Manchester school discussed in Chapter 2 that trade and dominion were antithetical and should be kept carefully apart, are inclined to see such linkages as illegitimate, devious and sinister. Instead national interests in trade and foreign relations should both be judged on their own merits, separately but with scant attention paid to their potential for mutual support.

Admirers of the Chinese approach to the BRI, on the other hand, argue that is nothing more than a pragmatic and level-headed acceptance of the close and inevitable linkages between industrial, economic, financial, diplomatic and military activity in an age of globalisation. Instead of complaining about what the Chinese seem to be doing, other countries would be better advised literally to get their act together and follow the Chinese example in the development and indeed the use of all aspects of maritime power. While coming to conclusions about the ultimate intentions and likely consequence of the BRI is well outside the scope of this book, the practical advantages of an integrated comprehensive maritime approach in which all the elements support each other seem indisputable as an especially good way of advancing it.

5.4.4 A Case That Deals with Uncertainty

With the advantages of hindsight, we know that Themistocles was right in thinking that the Persians would be back. Nonetheless he illustrated the point that making decisions about the balances to be struck between competing courses of action requires those responsible to take a view on what the future holds. From Cassandra onwards, our inability to predict or to recognise the evolving shape of the future and to respond to it effectively has been a universal lament. Themistocles, however, got it right.

The requirement was to establish balances of probability about what might happen in the future and how this might impact national interest. Determining this and the relative importance of those interests is intensely difficult.[31] Nonetheless, Cabinets, foreign and defence ministries and treasuries have to do the best they can to 'future-proof' their decisions.

One entirely natural and very common response of governments to the unpredict-ability of the future is to try to maintain their options and to come up with generalised and balanced strategies for 'dealing with contingency' that provide them with lots of alternatives. In other words, expecting that there is every chance that their anticipa-tions about the future will be wrong has encouraged governments to focus on their ability to deal with strategic surprise. The problem here is that the more they do this, the less guidance they provide for people lower down in the decision hierarchy as to what their priorities should be, and the greater the prospect of those lower in the echelons of power, deciding their own futures on the basis of sectoral interest. As already discussed, there are those who would argue that the residual ambiguities in President Jokowi of Indonesia's vision of the 'Global Maritime Fulcrum' allow the various Ministries and agencies involved to chart their own courses of action. This can be a problem when responding to such challenges as the presence of Chinese fishing boats in the waters around Natuna island since such situations require a coherent and integrated approach between all government agencies and levers of national power.[32]

Another approach is to concede the unknowability of distant possibilities and to focus instead on the nearer term probabilities of the more immediate future, even though investing in that may diminish the prospect of responding effectively to longer-term challenges. This is clearly a matter of weighing the relative risk between these two courses of action. Focussing on the more knowable parts of the future, however, is very common, and fits in with Churchill's advice when dealing with 'the' usual clash between short-term and long-term projects. War is a constant struggle' he wrote, 'and must be waged from day to day. It is only with some difficulty and within limits that provision can be made for the future. Experience shows that forecasts are usually falsified and preparations are always in arrear. Nevertheless,' he concluded, 'there must be a design and theme ...' for a 'reasonable' future.[33]

Admiral Doenitz, initially commander of the German U-boat force and subse-quently of the German Navy as a whole, was confronted by just such an early di-lemma. The U-boat force he had developed was not ideal for the conduct of the Battle of the Atlantic. The Type VII U-boat was more of a submersible than a true sub-marine when compared to the Types XXI and XXIII that came after it. Because the Type VII was a more familiar technology, it would be much easier and faster to use it as a basis for an expansion of the undersea fleet than its less certain more futuristic successors, even though a fleet based on the latter was likely to be much more effective in the end. The requirement to have the necessary effect *now* rather than at some indeterminate date in an uncertain future was overwhelming and more or less forced Donitz into the easier option for the time being of backing the Type VII.[34]

In the same way, Germany 'decided' on the development of the V1 'flying bomb' and the V2 rocket rather than develop its atomic bomb programme, not because of any assessment of their relative military effectiveness but more about whether they would be available in time. Whether the VI and V2 were worth the unavoidable opportunity cost of perhaps 24,000 lost aircraft which could have been built instead but weren't, however, remains debatable.[35] The real point was that Hitler liked the idea of these rockets but was dubious about the feasibility of the alternative of Germany's developing atomic weapons in time and indeed about their operational consequence.

Likewise the British Admiralty halted the production of battleships not because of emerging doubts about their military utility but more because they would not be ready soon enough given the accepted urgency of the need to invest in anti-submarine, amphibious warfare vessels and merchant ships, that were needed immediately, and which could be produced at speed. If these urgent requirements (particularly for the battle of the Atlantic) were not met, the war was unlikely to last long enough for the Admiralty's battleship production programme anyway.[36]

Another response to uncertainty, and in theory a more logical one, is less to accommodate policy to uncertainty and more to do as much as possible to reduce uncertainty by institutionalised reflection on alternative futures and ways ahead. Having a more accurate vision of the road ahead obviously makes planning less of a gamble.

Here a very practical problem in preparing for the future for many countries might be the absence, or at least the under-developed state, of the kind of governmental institutions needed to frame long-term policies and strategies. Around the world nations are developing some sort of National Security Council (NSC) system that represents all the major stakeholders in governmental policy and strategy-making as an increasingly common way of tackling this issue. Introducing such institutions and engaging in the kind of high-level bureaucratic reform that will make it work is no light task, however. Indeed the problems that India has faced in radically reforming its bureaucracy in order to provide a range of institutions better able to coordinate a national security strategy is often said to explain why India so often has seemed to be punching below its weight.[37] For this reason, countries as varied as Singapore, Malaysia, the UK and now India have fairly recently introduced and are developing their versions of an NSC system, having reflected on the advantages it gives to countries that have it in prioritising resource allocation, compared to those that do not.[38]

Whatever the particular institutional remedy sought, a willingness to listen to the competing views of a range of informed outsiders usually seems to clarify options. In the past, it was the habit of great rulers, aware of the need for diversified advice to gather around them a no doubt disputatious *coterie* of advisors about their best courses of action. Peter the Great and Prince Potemkin, for example both deliberately enveloped themselves with foreign experts more than willing to suggest possible policy ways ahead. Many Chinese emperors did the same, despite generations of scholars 'striving to keep their heritage intact by guarding against Western intrusion.' Even the notoriously self-absorbed court of the Qianlong Emperor found room for Catholic priests who were astrologers/astronomers, interpreters, architects, painters, portraitists and clock-makers.[39] Much depended on the quality of those advisors and on the extent to which they were acting in their own interest rather than in the interest of the state.

Accordingly, there seems to be an advantage in producing an informed 'commentariat' (from think tanks, academia and the Press) able to make suggestions but with less stake in the game, and perhaps therefore, more objectivity. Developing such centres of possible advice, and even paying for it, also seems to be a developing trend.

Certainly, the fate of regimes and countries that deliberately seal themselves off from alternative points of view such as (sometimes) early modern Japan, 19th-Century China under the Qing dynasty or Nazi Germany in the 20th is not encouraging. The latter for example wilfully disposed of, to its own detriment, many key scientists who were Jews or who did not otherwise conform to the regime's values. The initial successes and extraordinary advances that Japan made after the dramatic stimulus provided by Commodore Perry and his 'black ships' would seem to reinforce the value of being open to this kind of challenge.

5.4.5 A Case That Derives from Sufficient Representation

For the maritime case to be effective, it needs to be heard. Themistocles won for himself a position of authority. His first battle required considerable political skill and a degree of ruthlessness. His aim was to manoeuvre himself into such a position that people would be more inclined to listen to what he had to say in what was an intensely competitive process. This allowed him to participate in, and even dominate, the process of preparing for the future. For his successors this has also meant helping shape strategic reflection and general opinion, both inside and outside government, and engaging in the discourse with the defence industry, the commentariat and advisory industries as well, firstly to refine the narrative itself and secondly to convince others. Sometimes, navalists have been accused of complacency in assuming that the validity of their narrative is so self-evident that 'it goes without saying'; to their chagrin, this can easily prove to be literally true. Without the saying, the narrative goes.

In modern times many have argued for some kind of Maritime Ministry should be set up, on a par with other ministries for education health and so on. Would this not ensure that the maritime case is properly represented and so gets the spending priority it deserves? This is a big and deceptively complex topic requiring much more discussion than space allows here. Advocates of such a move argue that only this will be able to pull all aspects of the distinctive maritime case together and represent them at the highest level.

In most countries, however, maritime interests are currently distributed around, and an intrinsic part of, the business of many other departments and agencies, which in many ways seems as it should be for fully integrated governance. Those agencies will resist the loss of this aspect of their responsibilities, while if successful the resultant ministry for all maritime affairs might end up with more responsibilities than it can handle. At the time of writing, President Jokowi's Indonesia is going through precisely this exercise in bureaucratic reform and institutional engineering, and in particular is exploring whether the idea of a 'Coordinating' Maritime Ministry will square this circle by providing an institutional focus for the expression of the overall maritime case on the one hand while preserving the maritime element in all aspects of government business on the other.[40] However this compromise experiment turns out, it at least shows awareness of the issue. This is a difficult area in which to generalise since every country's system of governance is unique and so requires a distinctive solution. The issue, though, is evidently an important one.

5.4.6 A Case That Ensures Follow-up

So far as we know, the processes of Athenian governance did not require Themistocles to issue a 5th century BC version of a Defence White Paper (or if they did they haven't survived). The last chapter covered the issue of whether a government's policy aims should be publicly stated in this way, and much the same applies to the formal and public articulation of the strategic ways and means of achieving them. A common criticism of some public policy declarations about the development of maritime power or even as we shall see about ringing statements of naval doctrine is that they don't move on to that critical next implementation stage and the whole thing runs into the sand for that reason.

The publication of documents that explicitly link stated objectives (policy) with an outline of the intended way of achieving them (strategy), is one way of getting around that problem. As already mentioned Colombia's *Politica Nacional del Oceano y de los Espacios Costeros* does do that by identifying the 'lines of action' that will be needed. Another example is the European Commission's Maritime Security Strategy,[41] first published in December 2014 and linked to an Action Plan which was formally revised in June 2018. In its recommendations for implementation, the Commission emphasised the need for what it calls a 'cross-sectoral approach', which it defines as requiring the cooperation of all,

> .... partners from civilian and military authorities and actors (law enforcement, border control, customs and fisheries inspection, environmental authorities, maritime administration, research and innovation, navies or other maritime forces, coast guards, intelligence agencies), as well as EU agencies, to industry (shipping, security, communication, capability support) need to cooperate better, respecting each other's internal organisation.[42]

Whatever the likelihood of real practical progress in the development of the maritime power in both Colombia and the European Union, at least the headmark and the required courses of action of all key stakeholders have been identified.

5.4.7 *A Case That Provides Proof of Concept*

For Themistocles victory at the battle of Salamis and the subsequent retreat of the Persians provided proof of concept and seemed to justify all his arguments. It also set up a precedent and established a set of expectations that made it easier for his successors to make the same case. There followed a period of Athenian maritime dominance which only ended when it was frittered away in the over-ambitious assault on Sicily in the Peloponnesian War (431–404 BC). Obviously, being able to demonstrate that the maritime case actually works in the circumstances of the time, is a major aid to credibility – at least until those circumstances change.

These seven coping mechanisms only go so far of course. They do not really provide a solution to one of the fundamental problems in deciding resource priorities because in comparing the demands of Defence with those of Health and Education, it is more of a case of apples and oranges than of like with like. But at least this approach has helped ensure that the maritime case is represented as well as it can be.

Much the same can be said of the next level down when the requirements of specifically naval power are set against those of other forms of defence – the subject of the next chapter.

Notes

1 Richard K. Betts, 'The Grandiosity of Grand Strategy,' *Washington Quarterly,* Vol. 42, No. 4 (Winter 2020), 8.

2 This device of permanently associating certain parts of the economy with funding for the navy is not unique, such as oil (in the case of Malaysia and the Gulf States) or copper (as in the Chilean 'Copper law.') The latter was introduced partly to insulate naval spending from political controversy and fluctuations in government allocations. But all these devices introduce the budgetary vulnerabilities that come from oscillations in commodity prices. Drops in the price of oil have sometimes meant fewer ships for the Royal Malaysian Navy.

3 Lambert, *Seapower States,* 267–310.

4 Rodger, *The Command of the Ocean,* 260–2.

5 Disraeli, for example, was constantly concerned about the 'bloated armaments' being sought by the Admiralty in the 19th Century. Blake, *Disraeli,* 393–5, 428, 454, 484–5. Also he was by no means averse to quarrelling with their Lordships about what kind of warships they should build.

6 Peden, G.C., *British Rearmament and the Treasury* (Edinburgh: Scottish Academic Press, 1979).

7 Paquette, Gabriel, *The European Seaborne Empires* (New Haven: Yale University Press, 2019), 61–2.

8 Blake, Robert, *Disraeli* (New York: St Martin's Press, 1967), 329.

9 The following account leans heavily on Strauss, Barry, *The Battle of Salamis: The Naval Encounter That Saved Greece–and Western Civilisation* (New York: Simon and Schuster, 2004), Roberts, Jennifer T., *The Plague of War: Athens, Sparta, and the Struggle for Ancient Greece* (Oxford: Oxford University Press, 2017) and Smith Jeffrey A., *Themistocles: The Powerbroker of Athens* (Barnsley: Pen and Sword Books Ltd., 2021). Plutarch's *Parallel Lives* (Loeb Classical Library, 1914), 55–65 and Thucydides, *The Peloponnesian War* (London: Penguin, 1969), Diodorus Siculus, *Library of History,* vol. 11 , *Fragments of Books,* 21–32– originally Loeb Classical Library but reprinted (Cambridge: Harvard University Press, 1957) and Lytton, Sir Edward Bulwer, *Athens: Its Rise and Fall* (Leipzig: Bernhard Tauchnitz, 1843), 71–109, provide the classical foundation.

10 Thucydides, *The Peloponnesian War,* Bk 1, 12–16, 25.

11 Plutarch, *Parallel Lives,* 55.

12 Thucydides, *The Peloponnesian War, op cit.* Bk 1, 80–4, 59.

13 Muller, *China as a Maritime Power,* 73–88, 151–63, 232–62.

14 William's arrival in England in 1688 was an invasion as was James II's reappearance in Ireland shortly afterwards. Both Jacobite rebellions of 1715 and 1745 involved descents on Scotland. In 1797 the French invaded Wales. The common claim that the Royal Navy's superiority has always secured the country against invasion is less than wholly true.

15 Kennedy, Paul, *The Rise and Fall of British Naval Mastery* (London: Penguin, 4th ed, 2017) remains the best account of this.

16 Turnbull, Stephen, 'Wars and Rumors of Wars: Japanese Plans to Invade the Philippines, 1593–1637 (US),' *Naval War College Review,* Autumn 2016.

17 Mawdsley, Evan, *December 1941: Twelve Days that Began a World War* (New Haven: University of Yale Press, 2011), 13.

18 Haruro Tohmatsu and H.P. Willmott, *A Gathering Darkness: The Coming of War to the Far East and the Pacific, 1921–42* (Lanham: SR Books, 2004), 93–4. The industrial, economic and military deficiencies of Japan at this time are explored, 59–60, 84–7. The Japanese argument for initiating the war in December 1941 seemed to reflect a view that the correlation of military and forces would only get worse from the Japanese point of view. And that was almost certainly true.

19 Rodger, *The Command of the Ocean,* 260.

20 Quoted in Kennedy, *The Rise and Fall of Great Powers,* 202.

21 One of the basic preoccupations that so confused Allied intelligence efforts at this time, was the issue of deciding which of the known options the Japanese would go for. An assumption that the Japanese would attempt them all, on the other hand, would have simplified their task.

22 Graham, *The Politics of Naval Supremacy,* 106–10.

23 Paquette, *The European Seaborne Empires*, 97–114.
24 Lambert,*The Crimean War,* 1990.
25 Overy, Richard, *Why the Allies Won* (New York: W.W. Norton and Company, 1995), 5.
26 Overy, *Why the Allies Won,* 201.
27 Kennedy, *The Rise and Fall of the Great Powers,* 350.
28 Ketchum, *The Borrowed Years,* 265–75, 386.
29 Ibid, 213, 619, 651, 655–6.
30 O'Dea, Christopher R., 'China Has Landed,' *National Interest,* 31 October 2018.
31 Air Vice Marshal Andy Turner, 'The United Kingdom's National Interest: A Framework and Definition,' *Airpower Review,* Vol. 18, No. 1 (Spring 2018).
32 Basten, Gokkon, 'To deter Chinese sea claims, Indonesia puts its fishers on the front line,' *Mongabay,* 14 January 2020.
33 Churchill, Winston S., *The Second World War; Vol III, The Grand Alliance* (Boston: Houghton, Mifflin Company, 1950), 657.
34 Murfett, Malcolm, *Naval Warfare 1919–1945: An Operational History of the Volatile War at Sea* (London: Routledge, 2009), 462–3.
35 Overy, *Why the Allies Won,* 238–41.
36 Compare Murfett, *Naval Warfare 1919–1945,* 28–34, 468–9, and Barnett, Correlli, *Engage the Enemy More Closely* (London: Penguin, 1991), 380–1.
37 Rory Medcalf, 'Imagining an Indian National Security Strategy; the Sum of Its Parts,' *Journal of International Affairs,* Vol. 171, No. 5 (July 2017).
38 Official discussions in Singapore and Malaysia in 2016; Kaura, Vinay, 'India's National Security Coordination and Policymaking,' *RUSI Journal,* Vol. 165, No. 7 (November 2020).
39 Peyrefitte, Alain, *The Collision of Two Civilisations: The British Expedition to China 1792–04* (London: Harvill, 1993), 132–40, 145.
40 Compare Paraeswaran, Prashanti, 'Indonesia's Maritime Ambition: Can Jokowi Realise It?' and Arifianto, Alexander, 'Jokowi's Sixth Reshuffle: Securing His Legacy?,' *RSIS Commentaries* of 4 March 2015 and 30 April 2021, respectively.
41 Available at http://register.consilium.europa.eu/doc/srv?l=EN&f=ST%2011205%202014%20INIT
42 European Union Maritime Security Strategy (Brussels, 24 June 2014), 4, available at https://data.consilium.europa.eu/doc/document/ST%2011205%202014%20INIT/EN/pdf

6 Going Joint: The Maritime Mix

6.1 Introduction

Even when maritime power is considered just from the military point of view, and more at the operational than the strategic level, its diversity is evident. As discussed earlier, there is much more to maritime power than grey painted ships with numbers on the side. Maritime power by definition is multi-dimensional. Alongside the contribution of its civilian and commercial side, landpower, airpower and, these days, the space and cyber dimensions of military power also have very significant roles to play in the development of maritime power. With this diversity of in-put, comes, once again, a need for effective integration so that all these elements work with, rather than against each other. The aim is to secure a 'unity of opposites,' or as near that ideal state as feasible.

Failure to do so can have dire consequences, not least when it comes to the actual conduct of operations, which, after all, provides the best measure of effectiveness in developing maritime or any other form of power.

6.2 Malaya, Pearl Harbor and the Philippines, 1941: An Operational Case Study of Failure and Success in Jointness

Illustrating the point, another look at that fateful Autumn of 1941 shows just how difficult achieving this operational unity of effort can be; it also pitilessly reveals both the operational consequences of failure in preparation and the rewards of success. Defeat in Malaya, Pearl Harbor and the Philippines showed the consequences of poorly integrated inter-service relations clearly enough; its causes, though, were complex.

Had there been the post mortem of the Malaya campaign that many expected and some demanded, it is likely to have come to the conclusion that clearer command structures, more resolute leadership and a greater willingness to think about all these possibilities before they happened rather than at the time would have resolved at least some of these difficulties in the provision of an effectively integrated military effort. That was also effectively the conclusion of the 1946 Congressional enquiry into the Pearl Harbor disaster.[1] The unhappy events of that December in all three cases suggest perhaps five key factors impeded the effective collaboration of the various dimensions of conflict required for the development of effective maritime power – and still do.

DOI: 10.4324/9781003100553-6

6.2.1 Competing Service Agendas

In the two Philippines and Hawaii campaigns, the US Army and the Navy had different agendas. Apart from building up Philippine forces, the Army's task was territorial defence and by virtue of their larger aircraft an important role in the provision of long-range reconnaissance capabilities to warn of any approaching threat. In both the Philippines and Hawaii much faith was pinned on the ability of newly arrived B17 bombers to keep any seaborne invader at bay.[2] One preoccupation there and in Hawaii was to protect aircraft from sabotage or attack from elements in the local population. This followed on naturally from the Army's concern with internal security. For that reason aircraft were clustered together on the ground, with their ammunition safely under lock and key. This made them lucrative targets for Japanese air attacks when it came, and delayed a possible response.

If, as was assumed to be likely, the Japanese got ashore in the Philippines, the army, in accordance with the standing plan, would retreat to the Bataan peninsula and island of Corregidor and try to hold out until a relief force arrived. The Navy also had responsibility for long-range reconnaissance but in the Philippines their low strength levels precluded any real prospect of sea control operations. Instead their task was to support land operations to the extent possible. The effectiveness of this depended on closer relations with the Army than proved to be the case.

Contesting sea control was the main role of the fleet at Pearl Harbor; much less thought was devoted to the protection of the base itself. Although representatives of both services combined to produce some shared analyses of the threat to Pearl Harbor, such as the Martin-Bellinger report of November 1941 (which warned of the possibility of a surprise dawn air attack and recommended all-round distant air patrols,[3]) these were largely discounted by higher authorities who assumed the main Japanese attack would be elsewhere. Probably for that reason neither Admiral Kimmel nor General Short, his Army equivalent, increased air patrols; nor did they even agree to a common alert system.[4]

The situation for the British in Malaya was more complicated still in that there were two more service equivalents that needed to be folded into any integrated effort, an independent Royal Air Force and the British civil authority, in the shape of the Governor, Sir Shenton Thomas. The Governor's task was to liaise in effect with local representatives of five ministries back in London (The Foreign, Colonial, Dominion Offices, the Ministries of Information and Economic Warfare) and multiple Malay political authorities; above all he was to keep up the economic contribution that the country could make to the war effort through the continued and vital supply of rubber, oil and tin. This required the least interference possible from the military who wanted and needed much more cooperation from the civil authorities than they got.[5] This clash between military and civil-economic imperatives led to constant argument and stress.

The same contentions and tensions could be seen at work at the operational level in the relations between the three services in Singapore. Before the war, the Royal Navy and the Royal Air Force had sharply differing conceptions about how Malaya in general and Singapore in particular should be defended. These were entirely in keeping with their broader visions of the relative importance of the strategic role that their service should play in national and Imperial Defence.

For the Royal Navy, the issue initially seemed simple. One First Sea Lord used a rugby football analogy in 1937: 'In a war with Japan, the Navy would constitute, as it were, the forward line and the other two Services would form the backs.'[6] Any Japanese attack on the peninsula would have to come by sea. Dealing with such sea-borne threats was the Navy's essential task; an effective naval base at Singapore and sufficient and timely reinforcement from the main fleet in European waters would defeat any such effort it could not deter. There were two problems with this. Firstly, having occupied French Indo-China in the summer of 1941, the Japanese were much closer than any pre-war planner had envisaged and so the warning time would be much less and the correlation of naval and air forces much worse. Secondly, the over-riding demands of the European theatre meant there were far fewer forces available for the relief of a threatened Singapore than had been assumed and the 'period before relief' would be longer.

The Royal Air Force argued that cost-effective air reinforcements from the European theatre could arrive much sooner and that experience elsewhere had shown the effectiveness of land-based air in defence against sea-borne attack. This reflected its pre-war claims and expectations. 'It is the power to strike at shipping that matters most here,' said the C-in-C, Air Chief Marshall Sir Brooke-Popham,

> I have no doubt what our first requirement here is. We want to increase our hitting power against ships and our capacity to go on hitting. In this way we shall make it difficult for the enemy to land and equally difficult for him to nourish any initial successes.[7]

The RAF hoped that they would be able to knock out 40% of the Japanese fleet in repeat attacks before it hit the beaches and this required its strike aircraft to be deployed from forward air bases.[8]

In the event of a Japanese landing, the Army was responsible for the territorial defence of the Malay peninsula against Japanese forces heading for Singapore. Successive Army commanders concluded that the best use of inadequate resources required focussing defences in southern Malaya. For the final defence of Singapore island, the Army pinned its faith on the provision of long-range 15″ guns to keep invading forces at bay.[9] Once the Japanese landed, the Army bore the brunt of the defence of Malaya, but lacking sufficient air support and continuously vulnerable to sea-borne outflanking attacks, their capacity for effective resistance proved weak. In the year before Brooke-Pophams's arrival local Army-RAF relations were particularly bad.

Worse, the operational needs of the three services conflicted. Seeking to maintain warning reconnaissance patrols and air attacks against an incoming invader as far out into the Gulf of Siam and China seas as possible, the RAF wanted to base its airfields in the far north of Malaya. These rather primitive sites were hastily constructed close to the coast and the Siamese border apparently without consultation with the Army. The Army, though, would have to defend them, and this extra commitment conflicted with their initial preferences for a defence of Singapore lower down the peninsula. This unlooked for commitment also added to uncertainties about the possible launch of *Operation Matador,* a pre-emptive advance into Siam. Brooke-Popham's focus on the air defence of Singapore city meant, fatally, no fighters were deployed to the north of the country, and none were available to Force Z when Admiral Phillips sailed north to contest the Japanese landings in Siam.

This lack of operational coherence contrasted strongly with the Japanese performance. Although it is perfectly true that the Japanese Navy and Army fought different wars up to 1945 and that relations between them were generally very bad,[10] in this case, they were excellent. The urgency and the extraordinarily ambitious scale of Japan's opening attack on their adversaries in December 1941, seems to have driven the two services into very effective, if temporary, levels of cooperation. In the Central Pacific the Japanese navy was to conduct an independent naval/air campaign designed to destroy the US Pacific Fleet that would protect Japan's three-dimensional air/land/sea operations against Southeast Asia from American naval intervention. In the Japanese Navy's other campaign in Southeast Asia, however it was acting in support of an Army-led operation to secure what it quite frankly called the 'Southern Resources Area.'[11] The Navy's task was to secure local command of the sea largely against British forces, to deliver landing forces to the operational area and then to support their operations ashore to the extent necessary. Before and after the destruction of the British *Force Z* (the battleship *Prince of Wales* and the battle-cruiser *Repulse)*, all naval ships and aircraft were at the disposal of the Army's General Yamashita, who had overall theatre command.

From 1939 it had been the Japanese Army that had stressed the criticality of securing oil supplies from the Dutch East Indies for their war in China and in due course a possible 'resolution of the Soviet question.'[12] Accordingly the southern campaign was essentially an Army operation. Amphibious operations were conducted by specially trained Army units. The Navy went along with the Army's insistence on the landings taking place at night even though it would increase their own vulnerability before and afterwards. The Navy also accepted that its 27 available Zero naval fighters would deploy in support of the landings and the break-out; they would not be available to protect the fleet nor would they provide cover for the naval aircraft that attacked and sank Force Z. This unity of effort contrasted strongly with that of their adversaries in the Philippines, Hawaii and Malaya.

6.2.2 The Disuniting Effect of Insufficient Resources

In the Philippines, day-to-day liaison between the Army and the Navy was limited. The two theatre commanders, Admiral Hart and General MacArthur, rarely met, even though before and during the campaign they often stayed in the same hotel in Manila. That Hart actively disliked MacArthur did not help. Relations remained poor throughout the subsequent Bataan and Corregidor campaigns.[13] There was, though, some bitter truth in a diary entry by Hart at this time: 'Anyhow, it matters little now whether we cooperate or not for there seems not so much for us to cooperate *with.*'[14] His comment illustrates the extent to which resource shortages helps explain and can certainly exacerbate inter-service rivalry. After the Japanese landed and established themselves in the Philippines, the resistance became a land-centric affair, but at the tactical level, the Navy's Inshore Squadron did what it could to support the beleaguered forces ashore.[15]

There was no doubt, moreover, that resources were very short, in all three cases; in Malaya this meant that none of the three service agendas could be confidently achieved. As the Service Chiefs gloomily noted in July 1940, the Royal Navy could not currently dispatch a substantial fleet to Southeast Asia and,

> In the absence of a Fleet our policy should be to rely primarily on air power. The air forces required to implement that policy, however, cannot be provided for

some time to come. Until they can be made available we shall require substantial additional land forces in Malaya, which cannot in present circumstances be found from British or Indian resources.[16]

A year later, after countless local appeals to London for more support, things were little better. The Commander-in-Chief Far East Air Vice Marshal Sir Brooke-Popham made his feelings on this perfectly clear. 'Primarily of course the defence of Singapore depends upon the Navy,' he said,

> but as we haven't got any ships, it's been laid down quite rightly that we must rely mainly upon the air. But as we are so short of aeroplanes we have to face the fact that landings are at least possible and so we come back to dependence largely upon the Army.[17]

This problem reflected the fact that Churchill's strategic focus in the Autumn of 1941 was elsewhere, perhaps unsurprisingly even given the probable approach of war with Japan. It was an example of the operational consequences of an unavoidable dilemma in the allocation of resources between competing higher-level strategic priorities of the sort discussed in the last chapter.

The future attitude of the United States remained uncertain. The Germans seemed triumphant in Russia and Britain's hold on the Mediterranean appeared tenuous indeed. Churchill had only had a finite number of ships, new tanks and aircraft at his disposal; the issue was where should they go? There were three overseas options:

- The Far East. This might deter Japan's probable attack or at least delay it until a more propitious time. It would add very significantly to the strength of Singapore, satisfy the Australians and New Zealanders, maintain options for future reinforcement, secure access to Malaya's rubber and tin supplies and show the Americans that the British Empire was taking the situation seriously and so deserved support. There was the possibility, though, that the prospects of reinforcement would precipitate the conflict it was supposed to deter.
- The Mediterranean theatre. Much was hoped of *Operation Crusader* a major advance across North Africa. Success here would offer access to oil, secure links to India and the rest of the Empire and provide a means of supporting Russia through the Caucasus should that prove necessary.
- Russia. By early December 1941, the Germans had reached the small town of Khimki just over 10 miles from Stalin's Headquarters in Moscow. This underlined the importance of supporting Britain's only ally – or at least companion in adversity – at the time. By then, about a quarter of the tanks defending Moscow had been sent from Britain.

The last two options would help secure British security in Europe which nearly everyone agreed was the main theatre of operations. Both would also hopefully deter Japan, for as Churchill had concluded, 'Japan is unlikely to attack us unless and until she is sure we are going to be defeated [in the European theatre].'[18] So while all three options made eminent strategic sense, there was little doubt in the circumstances that the priority selected was the right one, distressing for the defenders of Malaya and Singapore though that was. The result was what Churchill called 'the worst defeat and largest capitulation in British history'[19] and the beginning of the end of the British Empire. More immediately, the diversion of forces from the Middle East to the last-ditch defence of Singapore proved unable to save it but did contribute to a substantial and near-fatal retreat in North Africa from the temporary strategic gains of *Operation Crusader*.

Britain survived the loss of Singapore, but it is extremely debatable whether it would have pulled through without the support of Russia or if it had lost the Mediterranean or the Indian Ocean. In the end, the Empire even struck back inflicting perhaps the biggest defeat of the Japanese army at Kohima/Imphal in the Summer of 1944 during the victorious Burma campaign and as the war ended was hurrying to re-take Singapore. Churchill was quite unrepentant about his choice. 'If the Malay Peninsula has been starved for the sake of Libya and Russia,' he said, 'no-one is more responsible than I, and I would do exactly the same again.'[20] As a result, despite their larger numbers, the British defenders only had a small, unbalanced naval force, few modern aircraft available, a high proportion of inexperienced personnel, no tanks at all and shortages even in such basics as telephone wire which made communications very difficult.

The only real issue, then, is whether a compromise could have been found whereby enough aircraft and tanks could have been diverted to Singapore to have made a difference to the conduct of the campaign of defence without imperilling sufficient support for Russia or North Africa. To judge by General Yamashita's palpable relief at the British surrender, Japan's margins of victory by February 1942 were narrow enough to make that an interesting if basically unanswerable question.

But the Japanese were short of resources too. They were up against an enemy larger in number, who was fighting on its home ground. General Yamashita was well aware of his logistic deficiencies, particularly in artillery shells, which became obvious in the last stages of the battle on Singapore island. But since such shortages underlined the need for ruthless driving momentum they became, paradoxically, a source of strength. In any case, it could be argued, the obligation in such an unfortunate situation is to do the best one can in the circumstances. Resource shortages undoubtedly had very bad results for inter-service cooperation in the British case, but are not a sufficient explanation for the catastrophe in Malaya.

6.2.3 Uncertainty of Purpose

Uncertainty as to the nature of the precise task they were supposed to be performing was another major factor in explaining deficiencies in the multi-dimensional operations of the three military services in Malaya. Although by December 1941 a Japanese attack was increasingly anticipated somewhere, neither the Americans nor the British knew where. Detailed and accurate American intelligence on Japanese intentions and capabilities was inadequate partly because of the fragmentation of effort between the intelligence organisations that both US services operated. The Army and the US Navy and indeed four other departments had their own Signals Intelligence organisations; especially at the start of the Pacific War cooperation between them was low, suspicion and rivalry high. 'It took a long time for them to make the fullest use of their massive resources by eliminating these corrosive inter-service rivalries.'[21]

The distribution of intelligence was defective too. Local commanders were not fully briefed on key developments since they were not shown the details of MAGIC interceptions of Japanese diplomatic cables. Washington certainly supplied sufficient urgent war warnings, but none that pointed specifically at Pearl Harbor. Admiral Kimmel was unaware of intercepts that showed close Japanese interest in the presence and position of ships in Pearl Harbor that the Japanese had evidently separated into what later was shown to be 'bomb zones.' Nor was Kimmel told specifically of one message from Tokyo, that suggested the Japanese would attack Pearl Harbor at 7:30 a.m. on Sunday, 8 December.[22] Regardless, the real problem was that the interpretation and dissemination of intelligence was not strong enough to challenge American *a priori* assumptions that the Japanese could not possibly be coming to attack Pearl Harbor but were instead going against the Philippines and/or Malaya. Suggestions that they might have Pearl Harbor in their sights were accordingly dismissed.[23]

After two years of war, the British had resolved some of these liaison problems, but even their best local organisation, the Far Eastern Combined Bureau, which united the efforts of the three services was short of people and equipment; although the British were much less surprised about the date and place of the attack on them, these shortages undoubtedly contributed to the air intelligence agencies grossly under-estimating the scale and quality of the coming onslaught and to a failure to tell Phillips specifically of the presence of the Japanese Navy's all important 22nd Air Flotilla, for example.

Consequently, the British and the Americans were uncertain about Japanese intentions; worse still, the British were confused about what they were authorised to do in response to those intentions. This became a major problem first in the political hesitations about whether or not actively to seek and attack the incoming Japanese invasion force when still on the high seas, either by naval or air action. 'There was always the danger,' thought Major General Playfair, Chief of Staff, Far East 'that HM government would not have given prior permission for ships to be attacked.'[24] Strategic anxieties about what might be the American response to such apparently aggressive pre-emptive defence reinforced the problem.[25] An inability effectively to clarify these issues in advance meant that nothing effective could be done in time. It is hard for the services to cooperate effectively if they do not know what they are supposed to be doing.

The same applied to the possible launch of *Operation Matador.* The aim would be to move premptively into neutral Siam in order to seize possible landing sites before the arrival of the remnants of any invasion fleet which had survived British air or naval efforts at interception on the high seas. Unfortunately this meant the Army had to move forwards and out of their rather improvised defensive lines in northern Malaya. With the combination of landings at Singora and Patani in Siam and another at Khota Bharu in Malaya, the Japanese seized the operational initiative. They immediately destroyed the RAF base near Khota Bharu and opened improvised air bases in Siam. Worse, the British expected an operational pause after the landings, as Yamashita consolidated his logistic supplies in the ponderous way the British expected; instead Yamashita broke out of the bridgehead immediately and surged southwards many days before the British thought it possible and were able to catch local defenders before they could get back to and organise their defences on the Jitra line across northern Malaya.

The resultant dithering demoralised the forces at least half prepared for *Operation Matador,* not least the unfortunate elements of the 11th Indian Division leaving their defences and tramping backwards and forwards in the rain near the Siamese border, doubtless wondering if higher command knew what it was doing. As another result of this muddle, Admiral Tom Phillips, in the absence of clear direction from London, felt he had no choice but to embark on his bold, risky and ill-fated foray to the north. Further confusion at Kuantan down to the south, led to his investigating the area while on his way back to the greater safety of Singapore and being caught by Japanese aircraft. These reverses proved terminal. The British never recovered from these uncertainties in their pell-mell retreat to the south and opportunities for effective inter-service cooperation were few, although there were more brave improvised attempts at this than generally realised.

6.2.4 Leadership Problems

Noel Coward's unkind quip (years before) that Singapore was 'a first class place for second-class people' has nurtured a general view in some quarters that local leaders were woolly-headed fools, steeped in Singapore Slings and colonial langour.[26] With the advantage of hind-sight, local leaders could have done more to clarify residual ambiguities in British policies in advance than they did. They also certainly lacked the charisma, ruthlessness and the drive of General Yamashita. The acerbic and perceptive diary comments of Margaret Spooner, the wife of the Admiral Superintending the Dockyard, showed they certainly had their foibles: the Governor, Sir Shenton Thomas, ('nice' but 'with an aged insensitive brain, not a leader … a poor reed') nor Air Marshal Sir Robert Brooke Popham ('unusual' but 'first class mind … I think he is a little shy … improves on acquaintance'), nor General Percival ('very nice and a sense of humour but not showy and not very quick … may have brains but certainly is short of guts and decisions').[27] None of them had the stature of Yamashita, who could bang heads together and get things done with the speed they needed doing.[28]

The conduct of British leaders in Malaya and of General MacArthur in the Philippines remains a subject of controversy; after the war the Congressional investigation found the leadership of Admiral Kimmel and General Short's leadership in Hawaii to be defective, although here too there are many opinions about the nature of those deficiencies and to what extent they should be blamed for what happened. There is though, little doubt that in none of these three cases, was local leadership able to overcome the obstacles in the way of close inter-service cooperation.

6.2.5 Defective Coordination Machinery

All three services had important and distinctive capacities to offer in the development of maritime power in Southeast Asia and these were indeed argued before and during hostilities by people proud of their service and professionally able to articulate the operational options potentially available. These claims could then be dispassionately compared, prioritised and resourced accordingly. Inevitably, then, there was an element of competition between the services. This was no bad thing; advocating the special contribution that one's own service could make might even be thought essential. Through this kind of discourse, constructively conducted, compromises could be made and an optimum 'unity of opposites' achieved.

The problem in Malaya was that the machinery for sorting these issues out was inherently ineffective. Overall command of the effort in Malaya was complicated and contentious and meant that the outcome of the effort was significantly less than a sum of its parts. Instead of enforcing more effective integration between the services, the command structure in Singapore simply reflected the gaps and overlaps between them.

Sir Shenton Thomas, the Governor, shared command responsibility and indeed chaired the Defence Council that in theory made all the strategic decisions. There was no single in-theatre commander for although Air Chief Marshal Sir Robert Brooke-Popham, the Commander-in-Chief Far East in theory 'directed' military operations, Admiral Phillips was not under his command, nor for that matter under that of the experienced Admiral Sir Geoffrey Layton (C-in-C China) who was two ranks senior to him. Neither was Layton under the Command of C-in-C Far East. In consequence, even after the disastrous start of the campaign, there was no clear cut decision as to where the British should make their main stand. As a result the situation constantly unravelled and confusion reigned.[29]

Command relationships between Singapore and London were not clear either, particularly over the extent to which local commanders had the final authority to make key decisions, about when and where first to engage and later where to fight – or in the end when to surrender. All these issues were evident in advance but were not resolved in time. Churchill uneasy about the complex situation in Singapore, effectively sacked Brooke-Popham on 1 November 1941 long before the Japanese attack; this was known and much weakened his command authority. He was only relieved by General Sir Henry Pownall on 27 December. In the meantime Churchill sent out Alfred Duff Cooper to report on the situation and make recommendations. Duff Cooper was principally concerned with the civil side of things, took a very low view of Brooke-Popham's state of mind and capacity to command, and for a few days headed a new 'Far East War Council' whose terms of reference he very vaguely designed, but he too departed Singapore shortly afterwards.[30] For such reasons, the British campaign lacked clear and sustained operational direction.

This was not the case at the higher level in London, however. While there remained strong inter-service disagreements – such as over the extent to which the RAF should divert its bombers from their main strategic bombing mission to assist in the battle of the Atlantic or provide close support for land operations, there was nonetheless no doubt who ultimately was in charge – namely the Prime Minister, Winston Churchill. While the relations between him and the service chiefs were often extremely acrimonious, there was no doubt about Britain's overall strategic priorities and about what contribution the Prime Minister expected the various services to make. Force Z was in Singapore to deter the Japanese ,persuade the Americans to be more forthcoming and to act as the first line of defence of the all important Indian Ocean until a new Eastern fleet was built up. Those priorities might not have been right, but they were at least, eventually, definitively made and clear.[31]

It was the same in the United States. President Roosevelt appeared to welcome the expression of competing views because it provided him with a variety of options and meant he remained in charge. Accordingly the services were able to work together through the Joint Board to agree on a set of contingency plans, which as the situation unfolded, resolved into 'Plan Dog' – that Europe would be the main focus in the coming war, if necessary at the price of remaining on the defensive in the Pacific. On matters of detail Roosevelt asserted his authority. In 1941, he repeatedly overrode the objections of General Arnold, the Chief of Air Corps to despatching new aircraft to France and Britain and threatened to send him to Guam if he didn't obey. When in 1941, Admiral James O. Richardson, a popular and experienced 'Pacific hand,' and in effect Commander-in-Chief Pacific Fleet (CinCPAC) wanted his fleet to return to the West Coast for training and expansion as it normally did after annual exercises conducted from Pearl Harbor, Roosevelt over-ruled him. The President thought the fleet's departure would send the wrong message to the Japanese. When Richardson objected to both the policy and the manner in which it changed – and then was unwise enough to say the fleet had no confidence in the President, Roosevelt had him sacked.[32]

The same was true of Japan. Although relations between the Japanese Army and Navy services were generally bad, the strategic direction of the 1941 campaign was good both in the defining of objectives and in the arrangements made for their achievement. If anything, it was too good, in that it made little allowance for constructive dissent.

6.2.6 December 1941: Conclusion

For the allies, these campaigns demonstrate the adverse operational consequences of failures and deficiencies in providing the integration of effort required for the delivery of effective maritime power. For the Japanese, success demonstrates the reverse. Amongst the many reasons for all this, five factors have been shown to stand out. A much wider survey of past and present military experience suggests that these factors have general application to the modern delivery of this aspect of the delivery of maritime power.

6.3 Modern Day Equivalents

6.3.1 Introduction

In 1714 Louis XIV of France, no doubt aware of the problems of coordinating the various aspects of his country's defence effort was amongst the first to create a Ministry of War. Then and since such Ministries have brought together the army and the navy, and now the air force, and have been charged with the task of implementing, within the constraints of the resources allocated, broader grand strategic decisions taken higher up. Nowadays other sections of the maritime community, the industrial, fisheries and the coastguard, report to other ministries which also need to identify their policy 'ends' or objectives, deduce their strategy, decide their 'ways' and allocate their 'means' in the same way. Today's Ministries of Defence focus on the defence aspects of national security, including its maritime dimension and it is their task to co-ordinate those aspects into a hopefully cohesive whole.

In seeking to do so they often run up against, and deal with, exactly the same five problems in developing maritime power as were encountered in Hawaii and Southeast Asia, in December 1941. For a variety of reasons, the issues they may face can seem even more challenging. The delivery of maritime power can suffer accordingly.

6.3.2 Competing Service Agendas

The most obvious example of the problem that differing service agendas can create in both Britain and the United States, has been the often rancorous relationship between the air force and the navy, which was evident in the 1949 'Revolt of the Admirals' in the United States and in Britain especially through the 1950s and 1960s.[33] These both echoed the disputes that had plagued their relations in the interwar period and through the Second World War.[34] Such problems have affected many other navies too, the Canadians and Italians as two examples.[35]

The British and American examples, centred on the aircraft carrier programme and the future of the nuclear deterrent. Significantly, these were both areas of overlapping interest for the two services. Another American example is the continuous tensions between the US Army and Marine Corps. Instead of becoming an opportunity for cooperation, these overlaps in activity became subjects of truly venomous competition. What was really at issue, however, were different interpretations of the threat facing the country and the validity of the roles, missions and functions that each service aspired to in an age when new technology (especially in nuclear form) was posing everyone some very unsettling challenges.

Elsewhere the problem has tended to be more acute between the navy and the army. For very many countries the historic centrality of the concern for internal security and immediate threats from territorial neighbours has given effective primacy to an army whose greater size and larger representation in the MOD has therefore meant it tends to dominate the defence decision-making process and the allocation of defence resources. One of the constraints, for example on Indonesia's development of maritime power as described earlier is the much greater visibility and political influence of the country's army, at 350,000 compared to its navy at 75,000. Numerical imbalances can easily lead to conceptual ones. For the same reason, ensuring sufficient 'jointery' has also long been a major problem for India.

Given the demands of the sea, land and air environments in which the three military services operate, a level of competition, especially in areas of overlap, is doubtless inevitable. Since proficiency in all three is usually strategically important, workarounds if not solutions to the tensions that inevitably derive from competing service agendas have to be found. A common response is to make a conscious effort to increase awareness of the outlook of the other military services and the help they can offer to each other. This effort for improved understanding is typically done through the establishment of joint rather than single service doctrine centres (such as the UK's Development, Concepts and Doctrine Centre), the establishment of joint command and staff courses, and an even more liberal policy of detaching personnel to posts in and with the other services (such as is mandated by the US Goldwater-Nichols Act of 1986).

These devices are tricky and often controversial. Sceptics are concerned lest this process of homogenisation threatens the distinctiveness of the contribution that each service can make. In effect, they say, it can level down, not up.[36] Better, they suggest, to seek synthesis through a Hegelian clash of thesis and antithesis. Very evidently, the debate about the best way to handle this problem continues.

6.3.3 The Disuniting Effect of Insufficient Resources

Resources, especially money, play a key role in determining the way forward. 'I equate planning and budgeting,' Robert McNamara once remarked, 'and consider the terms almost synonymous, the budget being simply a quantitative expression of the operating plan.'[37] Many embittered military people would say the reverse. Excessively tight budgeting and insufficient resources often exacerbate inter-service rivalry, or lead to one, or indeed all, of the services backing off from a particular joint task in the hope that it will be performed by someone else. Nowadays the allocation of resources between the services is usually decided at the Ministry or Department of Defence level, rather than in a straight fight between service ministries as used to be the case before the Second World War. Because the Ministry now becomes the arena where these important matters are decided, inter-service relationships tend to be much worse there than out in the field, where their representatives often tend to feel they are less rivals and more companions in common adversity doing the best they can with what they've got. The Ministry will also usually have the extra task of persuading the government to invest in defence as a whole, before its apportioning out between the services and experience has shown that divisions between them may well be exploited by the money men only too willing to play one service off against the other.

In the Britain of the 1960s, rivalry between the Royal Navy and the RAF over 'ownership' of the national nuclear deterrent and the future carrier programme resulted in the Navy losing its carriers and the RAF its TSR-2 strike-reconnaissance aircraft. That experience did not, however, result in much of an improvement in the relationship between the two. Grudgingly accepting the principle of 'equal misery' for all has at least moderated, if not resolved such poisonous and often destructive inter-service disputes. In the same way the Canadian Navy and Air Force, plus the army, despite their differences, have managed to ensure their differences do the least damage: '... although harmony was never complete, ' their historian has concluded, 'it was in the interests of the Service Chiefs to get along.'[38] The Australians too had similar problems between their air and naval services over everything from operations to acquisitions, but likewise sought refuge in sufficient if sometimes difficult compromise.[39]

In the United States as well, while the public argument in the late 1940s and the 1950s might have been about what new technology might mean for the roles, missions and functions of the US Navy and Air Force, the real issue was over how the defence budget was to be divided between them, both now and in the future. In the United States, the services have, however, managed to evolve a similarly pragmatic solution to the problem which is in effect to agree to a default position of 'constant shares' in which normally the USAF gets about 35%, the US Navy and Marine Corps, 31% and the US Army 28% of the budget.[40]

These informal arrangements to tamp down inter-service disputes, however have remained vulnerable to the changing strategic context and events, such as 9/11 and the American involvement in the Iraq and Afghanistan wars. These real-world events have a disconcerting habit of upending the arrangements the services come to in peacetime in order to moderate their inevitable rivalries. For both the United States and Britain, the land-air centric nature of the strategic preoccupations of the early 21st Century had adverse consequences for the navy and the marines. Moreover the impact of the space and cyber dimensions of war may exacerbate service rivalries.

The problem has also been aggravated by the widening of defence commitments and the increasing costs of personnel and military equipment. The resultant and continuous inability to control costs has generated 'black holes' or unsustainable overspends, that would have been perfectly familiar to Henry Maydman over 300 years before. In response to these difficulties, the UK government has had to respond with savage cuts and/or programme delays which are usually described as value-for-money 'efficiency measures' by their advocates or derided as strategically senseless by their adversaries. Such was the case in the cancellation of the country's nearly completed Nimrod MRA4 maritime patrol aircraft programme, at a time when Russian submarines were reportedly operating in British waters.[41]

Malaysian critics have likewise worried that allocated resources are inadequate for identified tasks. Defence, they say, only accounts for 6.09% of government expenditure and a declining percentage of GDP; as a result programme delays (such as the replacement of Malaysia's Mig-29s) and budgetary cuts have made the strategy of deterrence and forward defence aspired to in its 2010 Defence White Paper problematic. However, the October 2014 budget envisaged a year-on-year increase of 10%,[42] with the Navy's being given a larger allocation than was previously the case.[43]

This increase reflected the shock of the Sabah incident of 2014 (when Philippine-based insurgents suddenly invaded Malaysia) and perhaps growing concerns about what some see as increasing Chinese assertiveness in the South China Sea.[44] Both of these demonstrate the impact of the external environment on the availability of resources, and in both cases pointed to the need for closer cooperation between the Malaysian services. However what that extra 10% will actually allow, depends on the state of the economy and particularly on the future price of the oil that Malaysia exports. Defence planning in countries whose economies depend on particular commodity prices is acutely vulnerable to their price fluctuation, and inter-service cooperation can indirectly suffer in consequence.

In all these cases the ability to strike a sustainable balance between the demands of commitments and the total level of resources available indirectly aids interservice cooperation.

6.3.4 Uncertainty of Purpose

Most commentators would agree that strategic and operational uncertainty is as great now as it was in the Autumn of 1941, if not more so. As for most countries, 'security' for the UK has widened from a pre-occupation with threats to national territory and vital interests to incorporate all manner of new challenges, such as counter-terrorism, serious organised crime, cyber threats, and environmental threats. Defence is, accordingly, no longer preoccupied simply by the task of identifying where and from whom conventional future threats might emanate, complicated enough as that is. Now it has to deal with a much wider range of types of conflict that will also fold into such new areas of concern as cyber-attack, space and a whole range of asymmetric 'grey zone' operations.

To deal with this, the UK like many other countries has explored the idea of setting up a regular rather than emergency review process. The British envisage a series of now five-yearly reviews of all aspects of national security and defence policy, which would take account of, and hopefully anticipate, major changes in the security and fiscal environments. In principle a National Security Strategy established at Cabinet level (Tier2) should define objectives and requirements followed by a narrower Defence Review to decide the military contribution to their achievement. In the UK, the first of these two-phase operations took place in 2010 but was widely criticised as being time-and-resource rather than strategy led, with little real connection between the objectives laid out in the first phase and the decisions announced in the second.[45] The second review, of 2015, was closer to the 'strategy-led, resource disciplined' ideal.[46] The Integrated Review of 2020 went one step further in considering Defence as just one part of the overall package.

Such processes usually comprise, firstly the production of an all-round holistic statement of the country's security challenges and needs and secondly (after allowing sufficient time for informed discussion) a formulation of how exactly the military are expected to contribute to their resolution. From this, spending priorities for, and within, Defence should hopefully emerge. Ideally this orderly and apparently logical process serves to encourage an integrated approach to the challenges facing Defence forces and, often, the development or maintenance of maritime power.

Sadly and perhaps inevitably, the surge of unexpected events, such as financial crises, in Britain's case BREXIT, the Covid-19 pandemic, Russia's invasion of Ukraine and so on continue to play havoc with such neat and tidy plans. Continuing uncertainty has meant continuing review. This is a very common problem and is one that makes a stable base-line for the kind defence planning that all three services would appreciate as a foundation for their cooperation, extremely difficult.[47]

6.3.5 Leadership Problems

The drive, assumptions, experience and personalities of key decision-makers in ministries of defence can still make a significant difference. Indeed the importance of individual personalities and the associated web of inter-personal contacts that they weave continues to be a significant factor in decision-making, for better or worse depending on the circumstances. Second World War experience in Malaya, the Philippines and Pearl Harbor at the operational level and, at the strategic, the key roles of Churchill, Roosevelt and Stalin (and of Hitler too come to that) show that personalities and leadership styles matter, whether they are consensual or autocratic, right or wrong. This human element accordingly still helps explain why things happen the way they do. For instance, the personal attitudes of the then Secretary of Defence, Denis Healey, through the carrier controversy of the 1960s were important because, politically he was particularly astute, highly respected and very influential within government.[48] Likewise the British Nott review of 1981, which adversely affected the Navy far more than it did the other services appears to have been influenced by senior civil servants in the new 'purple centre' who happened to have been in the Air Ministry in the earlier parts of their careers. A year later, there is general agreement that much of Mrs Thatcher's response to the Falklands crisis of 1982, at a time of uncharacteristic uncertainty, was determined by the personal and persuasive intervention of Admiral Sir Henry Leach in full dress uniform at the House of Commons one critical evening.[49]

It follows, therefore, that the leadership quality of key individuals and of the line they take may well continue to shape inter-service relations. But alongside personal influence, increasingly institutional processes of decision have been developed that also partly determine the campaign to integrate all the elements of defence into a cohesive whole. These include the review process just mentioned. Relatedly, another, common example is the MOD process, in Britain and elsewhere, of agreeing periodic statements of aim and intention that are usually articulated in some kind of Defence White Paper (DWP). Increasingly this follows on from a higher declaration of some sort about national security objectives. Typically the DWP establishes identified ends for the individual services and provides the context within which those lower in the hierarchy need to deliver the required capabilities by various ways and means. In effect, the DWP process is intended to provide some of the functions of peacetime leadership.

The DWP process does not preclude the expression of differing service views, not least in the vexed business of forecasting the shape of the strategic environment of the future. These differences of approach are hammered out then and in subsequent spending reviews – the intense and iterative negotiations between the MOD and the

Treasury set up to balance commitments and tasks (as provided by the strategy review) and the budget available (as agreed by Cabinet and delivered by the MOD as a spending review).

The Strategic Review/DWP/spending review process is supposed to provide the necessary comprehensive context for defence planning, full consultation with relevant domestic interests and with key allies and partners and plenty of opportunity for informed debate and criticism. Thus, in the UK, policy is continually held to account by, amongst others the House of Commons Select Committee system, particularly the all-party Defence Committee whose reports and the official responses to them provide a mine of detailed information.[50] The result of all this provides specific guidance for the short- and medium-term. It also sets the tone for a family of other such review processes in narrower fields of interest. The 2010 review process for example at least had the benefit of providing the context for *The UK National Strategy for Maritime Security*, UK's issuing, in May 2014, its very first and long overdue thinking on maritime security.[51]

Broadly, most other countries have their own versions of this DWP process, similarly hoping that it will explain their defence policy and strategy to outsiders and provide decision and guidance for those who have to implement it. Malaysia for example produced its first comprehensive DWP a 'National Defence Policy' in 2010,[52] but in other respects does things differently. There have been no further DWPs and at the time of writing, no general reviews seem in prospect. The process did not involve foreign and domestic consultation and was neither as transparent nor as specific in its recommendations when compared to the British version.[53]

It is commonly assumed in Europe and the US that external analysis and conceptual challenge provide a means of rigorously testing this way of formulating national defence policy, but that depends on how transparent and available it is. In common with most other countries in the region, this process in Malaysia appears relatively opaque; although defence white papers are at least published, their level of detail is not high. The same is true of important budgetary statements. The Defence Budget of October 2014 for example announced the establishment of a new base and a Marine Corps but there has been no indication of any specific budgetary allocation towards these two purposes.[54] Likewise parliamentary analysis of government defence policy through the Parliamentary Defence Committee does not appear to be as searching as it is in, say, the United States.[55]

The process varies from country to country in accordance with their way of doing things and, particularly with their perception of the strategic context and what it requires of them, given the level of resources available. While countries vary in the rigour with which they engage in this process, they at least have the same aim, namely to provide the kind of leadership that will encourage team-work between the services. It is hard to resist the conclusion that the more rigorously they do all this, the better is the consequence.

In some countries, difficulties in civil-military relations further complicate the provision of leadership in the process of service integration, although the problems this causes are fortunately nothing like as acute as they were in Germany or Japan in the interwar period.[56] Such issues may of course lead to anxious politicians buying the military off through generous budgetary allocations or to give them inordinate influence over the determination of security policy. In such cases the Army tends to represent potentially the worst threat to civilian control and so may benefit most from this situation; this situation probably exacerbates inter-service tensions rather than ameliorates them.

Some analysts think this may apply to China where, for example, where compliance may seem 'conditional.'[57] Conversely from the earliest days of the Peoples' Republic avoiding excessive military influence has been a high priority. This explains the constant balancing between ensuring that the military is 'Red' while allowing it to be 'Expert' as well which is discussed later. In such a case personalities still matter but they are more likely to be those of civilian and party people rather than military.[58]

Under President Xi, the Chinese have been engaged in a major reform programme designed to consolidate the political direction of the military, rationalise the country's command and control system and encourage the country's military services to work together more effectively.[59] The manner in which this has been implemented in fact seems likely to support the maritime case in that the Army is likely to feel most of the pain from the 300,000 man reduction in military personnel that is envisaged; the Navy should benefit from greater access to joint positions, and the need for the Navy and Air Force to work together in the protection of China's interests in its 'near seas' is now clearly recognised. Moreover a navy's capacity to operate effectively in the new space and cyber domains will also depend critically on the efficiency of its operational integration with the other services, something of which the Chinese with their preoccupation with 'informationised' warfare seem particularly well aware.[60] Nowadays, more than ever, 'maritime' means much more than 'naval.'

In India there has long been resistance to the creation of a Chief of the Defence Staff post lest it weaken civilian control over military policy and strategy. Uneasy civil-military relations make it more difficult for the Navy to get its case heard at this Ministerial level. In any case this, in such a vibrant democracy, is likely to be constrained by the perceived illegitimacy of the military questioning, still less opposing, the decisions made by their elected political masters. Instead, they rely on 'the Minister' to advance the case. In India, there is an additional problem. For a variety of reasons, not least residual concerns about the politicians 'meddling' in operational matters widely held to have contributed to the deficiencies of the 1962 campaign against China, the political class have tended to steer clear of involvement of major defence issues in India, being content, it would seem, to leave such matters to the professional judgement of the individual services. The result is something of a lack of political 'ownership' of defence and insufficient dialogue between the political class and the military. As a result, there is little pressure from on high to maintain oversight over the military's day to day activities or to provide much in the way of political direction.[61] The result, as acidly remarked by K. Subrahmanyam, can be that 'politicians enjoy power without any responsibility, bureaucrats wield power without any accountability, and the military assumes responsibility without any direction.'[62]

It follows from this that providing sustainable leadership, whether it be personal or institutional, civilian or military, is both critical to the defence coordination of the services but can be very difficult to deliver.

6.3.6 Defective Coordination Machinery

In India inter-service competition has contributed to the long failure to produce a 'Chief of the Defence Staff' partly also because the navy and air force worry that the army would dominate such a position and have accordingly resisted the idea, even though it was presented as a way of improving inter-service relations and effectiveness. Historically the very idea of a centralised 'purple' Ministry of Defence notion has often sparked resistance from the services in many other countries too, chiefly because they fear the consequences of a loss in identity and autonomy. The creation of other joint or 'purple' institutions like a Central Staff, Joint Commands, Joint Doctrine Centres and training establishments have led to the same reactions.

As in many other countries, major measures to promote better inter-service relations have constantly been proposed in India over the years and are now in train,[63] including turning its 19 separate Commands into joint ones, but progress has been slow, occasionally even seeming to go into reverse.[64] At the time of writing, India now has its first Chief of the General Staff who has been charged with encouraging more inter-service cooperation. But his 'Department of Military Affairs' remains small, his task is defined as coordinating rather than commanding the three services whose heads retain direct access to the Prime Minister.[65] This reform effort is nonetheless intended to discourage institutional 'stove-piping' in which each service essentially goes its own way, rather than contribute to a defence team effort.

The fact that it has taken India 70 years to get this far, confirms historical experience that shows that defence coordination is a long, contentious and arduous process, but one critical for the development of maritime power. British policy-makers likewise began addressing the issue shortly after similar deficiencies emerged in the First World War but only began to bear fruit in the 1960s, when Admiral Lord Mountbatten, especially, worked to integrate the services by creating a central defence administration for all three.[66] Guided by the British experience, the Americans began taking the same path after the Second World War, initially setting up a Department of Defence in the late 1940s, but giving its first Secretary, James Forrestal, a small staff and a co-ordinating role, while specifically limiting his capacity to interfere in the affairs of what were then three independent but notably discordant military services.[67] The general direction of travel since then has universally been evident in two ways.

Firstly it is revealed in the establishment of machinery that is intended to help the effective operational *use* of military power. The formation of joint strategic and operational commands is the most obvious example of this, and the need for it made manifest in the wars and conflicts of the late 20th Century. British experience in the Falklands campaign, where there was no in-Theatre operational commander, led to a process of reform that lead to the establishment of the Permanent Joint Headquarters in 1996 and a whole series of subordinate joint commands. Much the same has happened in the United States, where the conduct of *Desert Storm* in 1991 raised questions about, in particular, coordination between the US Navy and Air Force as a matter of concern.[68] Many other countries have done the same.

Secondly, there have been major institutional changes in the *delivery* of military capability, rather than in its use. This is characterised by higher levels of joint rather than single service policy-making, strategy-setting and procurement via a more 'executive' department of defence, secretary/minister of defence and chief of the defence staff. In some cases the Ministry, and divisions within it, may be the problem. It is often said to apply to India for example, and has led to countless attempts at reform, revived in July 2021 by the Naresh Chanra committee.[69] Excessive service independence in the decision and the policy-making system means in the Chief of the Navy like his colleagues in the other two services, wearing two hats. In the old style, he is both an operational commander and a capability deliverer. In today's circumstances, these probably amount to too onerous a task. The problem is aggravated by the tendency to regard the 'Service Headquarters as 'attached offices' to the Ministry of Defence as a result of which, besides innumerable delays, the services are kept out of the decision-making loop.'[70] Delays derived from the fact that once a procurement policy has worked its way all the way up, say, the Navy hierarchy before being passed on to the MOD by the Navy Chief, it then plunged to the bottom of the MOD hierarchy in order to go through the same process all over again. Instead, reformers argued that time, money and energy would be saved were the two processes to be united through a closer association between Service department and the Ministry, with the latter assuming many of the historic higher administrative functions of the former.

This has become a global trend. With their talk of the 'joint force' transitioning to a 'seamless' one' the Americans may push still further, provided, of course, that practice matches the rhetoric.

6.3.7 Conclusion

In effect there appears to be a global trend that takes the services from effective autonomy, to being separate but coordinated, then into supporting and supported commands, joint commands and even propels them into joint training and equipment acquisition systems. The result arguably has generally been a diminution of inter-service rivalry and higher levels of cooperation.

Service nervousness about this process of homogenisation is understandable, however. When such organisations submerge the individual distinctiveness of the services and obscure or even reduce the special capabilities each has to offer, these reactions seem not entirely unwarranted. However the more the services cooperate the more likely their efforts will be greater than the sum of their parts in the delivery of multi-dimensional maritime power; the trick is to achieve synergy without losing service pride and distinctiveness. For many countries this process has proved to be extremely contentious and difficult – and still is.

Experience suggests both that effective inter-service relations do not come naturally and have instead to be worked at, and that success in this makes a material contribution to a country's power. They require effective and sustainable institutions and procedures, constant practice, and thorough preparation in professional military education and training throughout an officer's career. The resultant personal attitudes seem likely to be at least as important as the details in the machinery of coordination that individual countries may think best for them.

Some countries are further along this road of better coordinating the three services, than others, but all exhibit the same direction of travel.[71] Its consequence for the development of maritime power remains to be seen, but since maritime power is inherently joint, potentially it would seem critically important. Accordingly, lessening the factors likely to impede service teamwork will be a priority for the rest of the 21st Century.

Obviously, the navy's standing within these often relatively new political, institutional and the joint arenas is important for its ability to help shape the maritime consciousness of the nation and to advance the maritime case, and deficiencies in those institutions or in the navy's representation within them may make that more difficult. This is reviewed in the next chapter.

Notes

1 Morgenstern, George, *Pearl Harbor: The Secret War* (New York: Devlin & Adair, 1947). One of the first books also to scent conspiracy in the confusions. By contrast see Wohlstetter, Roberta, Pearl Harbor: *Warning and Decision* (Redwood City, CA: Stanford University Press, 1966).

2 Morris, E., *Corregidor: The End of the Line* (New York: Stein and Day, 1981), 29, 159–61.

3 Prange, Gordon, *At Dawn We Slept* (London: Harmonsdworth, 1991) is the classic account; Ketchum, Richard M., *The Borrowed Years* (New York: Random House, 1989), 719–21;

4 Ibid, 730–1.

5 Farrell, Brian P., *The Defence and Fall of Singapore* (Stroud, Gloucs: Tempus, 2005), 70. Brooke-Popham, letter to General Ismay, 5 December 1940, BP 6/2, Brooke-Popham papers, Liddell Hart Centre, KCL, London.The best trecent account is Boyd, Andrew , The Royal navy in Eastern Waters: Lynchpin of Victory, 1935-42 (Barnsley: Seaforth Publishing, 2017).

6 Quoted, Marder, Arthur, *Old Friends New Enemies: The Royal Navy and the Imperial Japanese Navy* (Oxford: Clarendon Press, 1981), 35.

7 Quoted Farrell (2005), 87–8.

8 Farrell (2005), 88. The origin and indeed existence of the 40% claim is discussed in reactions to a letter by General Percival 4 August 1946 in Brooke-Popham papers 6/8, Liddell Hart Centre, King's College, London.

9 The common idea that these guns could only fire out to sea is a myth, but their position and anti-armour ammunition supplies made many of them unsuitable for counter-battery fire.

10 Ketchum, *The Borrowed Years,* 674–5.

11 Swinson, A., *Four Samurai* (London: Hutchinson, 1968), 94–5; Yamamto, Fumihito thesis, *The Japanese Road to Singapore: Japanese Perceptions of the Singapore Naval base 1921–1941* (PhD Thesis) National University of Singapore, 2009, 153. https://scholarbank. nus.edu.sg/handle/10635/17361v

12 Yamamoto, Fumihito, *The Japanese Road to Singapore.*

13 Morris, *Corregidor,* 368.

14 Quoted Mawdsley, *December 1941,* 137, also 180, 257–8.

15 Morris, *Corregidor,* 304–5.

16 Report by Chiefs of Staff Committee, 31 July 1940, COS(40)592 and WP(40)302, Cab 66/10 TNA. This assessment fell into the hands of the Japanese after the SS *Automedon* was captured by the Germans.

17 Brooke-Popham, Letter to General Ismay, 26 March 1941, BPP 6/2/8.

18 Quoted Gordon, Andrew, 'The Admiralty and Imperial Overstretch,' in Till, Geoffrey (Ed), *Seapower: Theory and Practice* (London: Frank Cass, 1994), 80.

19 Churchill, Winston S., *The Second World War: Vol III, The Grand Alliance* (Boston: Houghton, Mifflin Company, 1950), 94.

20 Churchill to Clement Attlee, 30 December 1941, quoted Baxter, Christopher J., 'A Question of Blame?,' *Journal of the RUSI,* Vol. 142, No. 4 (August 1997), 72.

21 Stripp, Alan, *Code Breaker in the Far East* (Oxford: University Press, 1995), 116–7.

22 Mawdsley, *December 1941,* 179–81, 315. See also Morgenstern, *Pearl Harbor,* 197. This still contentious subject is well covered in Prange, *At Dawn We Slept.* Ketchum, *The Borrowed Years,* 728–9.

23 Ibid, 710–1 and 718 for an example in January 1941.

24 Personal observations of Major General I.S.O. Playfair, Chief of Staff Far East July 1941–January 1942 of April 1943, BPP 6/9/2.

25 These concerns were probably unfounded, but Roosevelt's assurances of support in the event of a Japanese attack on Siam, were disturbingly informal. Mawdsley, *December 1941,* 130, 144.

26 See, for instance, Lyman, Robert, *The Generals from Defeat to Victory* (London: Constable, 2008) on Percival, 59–97; but see also Elphick, Peter, *Singapore: The Pregnable Fortress* (London: Hodder & Stoughton, 1995), 145–80.

27 Diary comments by Mrs Spooner, wife of Rear Admiral E.J. Spooner, Admiral Superintendant Naval Dockyard, then Flag Officer Malaya. Spooner MSS 1/1–3, Liddell Hart Archive, KCL. Diary entries for 8, 11 September, and 3 December 1941. These comments are very much in line with those of Cecil Brown, Chief Correspondent in Singapore for NBC. who

also interacted with them all. Brown, Cecil, *Suez to Singapore* (New York: Random House, 1942), 149, 213.Thomas he wrote scathingly in September 1941 'lives in a dream world where reality seldom enters and where the main effort is to restrict the entrance of anything disturbing' 210.

28 Much of this has also been inadvertently confirmed by a recent defensive biography of Brooke-Popham: Dye, Peter, *The Man Who Took the Rap: Sir Robert Brooke-Popham and the Fall of Singapore* (Annapolis, MD: Naval Institute Press, 2018), 162–76.

29 Till, Geoffrey, *Understanding Victory* (Santa Barbara: Praeger, 2014), 117–20.

30 Cooper, Duff, *Old Men Forget* (New York: E.P. Dutton & Co., 1954), 289–305; Mawdsley, *December 1941*, 141.

31 Boyd, *The Royal Navy in Eastern waters* argues that this was perfectly sensible and the result of close collboation between the Admiralty and Churchill

32 Coffey Thomas M., *HAP: The Story of the US Air Force and the Man Who Built It* (New York: The Viking Press, 1982), 206–7; Ketchum, *The Borrowed Years*, 552–4.

33 Barlow Jeffrey G., *The Revolt of the Admirals: The Fight for Naval Aviation 1945–1950* (Washington: Naval Historical Center, 1994).

34 Coffey, *HAP*, 172–4 for the bomb v the battleship debate and 243–4, 254–5 for the dispute over the use of heavy bombers for strategic bombing or ASW patrols.

35 Haydon, Peter, 'Sailors, Admirals and Politicians: The Search for Identity After the War,' in Hadley, *A Nation's Navy*, 211–2.

36 Wills, Steven, 'The Effect of the Goldwater-Nichols Act of 1986 on Naval Strategy, 1987–1994,' US *Naval War College Review*, Vol. 63, No. 2 (Spring 2016).

37 Quoted in Toprani, A., 'Budgets and Strategy: The Enduring Legacy of the Revolt of the Admirals,' *Political Science Quarterly*, March 2019, 2.

38 Bland, Douglas, *The Administration of Defence Policy in Canada 1947–85* (KIngston: Ronald P Frye, 1987), 150.

39 Cooper, Alastair, 'The Korean War Era,' in Stevens, David (Ed), *The Royal Australian Navy* (Oxford: Oxford University Press, 2001), 164–6. For the Air Force view see Stephens, Alan, 'From Ostfriesland to the air-sea gap: He RAAD and maritime air interdiction' in Stevens, David, *Maritime Power in the 20th Century: The Australian Experience* (St Leonards, Australia: Allen & Unwin, 1998).

40 Toprani, Budgets and Strategy.

41 House of Commons Defence Committee, *Future Maritime Surveillance*, HC 110 (London: The Stationery Office, 2014); B. Farmer 'Britain forced to ask NATO to track 'Russian Submarine' in Scottish waters,' *Daily Telegraph*, 9 December 2014.

42 Jon Grevatt and Dzirhan Mahadzir, 'Malaysia Increases 2015 Defence Budget by 10%,' *Jane's Defence Weekly*, 14 October 2014.

43 Ibid.

44 Jon Grevatt, 'Striking a balance,' *Jane's Defence Weekly*, 23 March 2016.

45 *A Strong Britain in An Age of Uncertainty: The National Security Strategy* Cabinet Office (London: The Stationery Office, October 2010) and *The Work of the Joint Committee on the National Security Strategy in 2012* (London: The Stationery Office, 28 February 2012.

46 Chuter, Andrew 'Fallon: Expect UK Defense Review late 2015,' *Defense News*, 8 June 2015.

47 James William D., 'Between a Pandemc and a Hard Brexit,' *RUSI Journal*, Vol. 165, No. 7 (November 2020) summarises the result.

48 Healey, Denis, *The Time of My Life* (London: Penguin, 1989), 249–87.

49 Hampshire, Edward, 'Strategic necessity, or decision-making 'along the grain'? The Royal Navy and the 1981 Defence Review,' *Journal of Strategic Studies*, Vol. 39, No. 7 (December 2016).

50 See, for example, *Rethinking defence to meet new threats: Government response to the Committee's tenth Report of Session 2014–15*. HC 366 published by the House of Commons July 2015, or Ewen MacAskill, 'MPs fear £5.2bn shortfall in MoD spending on equipment,' *The Guardian*, 20 March 2015.

51 *The UK National Strategy for Maritime Security CM 8829* (London: The Stationery Office, 2014).

52 See Ministry of Defence (Malaysia), 'Malaysia's National Defence Policy,' 2010, accessed 17 July 2015 at http://www.mod.gov.my/phocadownload/DASAR-PERTAHANAN/ndp.pdf

53 Some speculate that a more detailed classified edition exists that is not open to public scrutiny. Thus Marhalim Abas, 'The National Defence Policy; Dasar Pertahanan Malaysia,' *Malaysian Defence*, 12 November 2010, accessed on 30 October 2013 at www.malaysiandefence.com/?p= 1279

54 See also Ministry of Defence (Malaysia), *Annual Report 2013*, 2013, accessed 17 July 2015 at http://www.mod.gov.my/en/publication/category/81-annual-reports.html?download= 724:year-2013

55 For further details on some of these issues, see Jitkai Chin, Chin-Tong Liew and Nur Jazlan Mohammad, "Role of Parliament in Defence Budgeting in Malaysia," paper presented during the 4th Workshop of the ASEAN Inter-Parliamentary Forum on Security Sector Governance, Phuket, Thailand, 23–24 May 2008, accessed 17 July 2015 at http://ipf-ssg-sea. net/4th_WS/Chin_et_al.pdf. This paper states, for example, that "According to the Malaysian government's policy, defence procurement details are protected by the 'Official Secret Acts' (OSA) and may not be discussed publicly," 5. It also makes the following observation: "The classification of defence documents resulted in MPs lacking sufficient information to engage actively in debate, or, in the rejection of MPs questions by the House on different grounds," 6.

56 Ketchum, *The Borrowed Years,* 671–3.

57 James Mulvenon, 'China: Conditional Compliance,' in Muthiah Alagappa (Ed), *Coercion and Governance: The Declining Political Role of the Military in Asia* (Stanford, CA: Stanford UP, 2001).

58 Muller, *China as a Maritime Power,* Chapters 4, 9 and 14.

59 Dennis J. Blasko, 'Integrating the Services and Harnessing the Military Area Commands,' *Journal of Strategic Studies,* Vol. 39, Nos. 5–6 (2016), 685–708.

60 Kevin Pollpeter, 'Space the New Domain: Space Operations and Chinese Military Reforms,' *Journal of Strategic Studies,* Vol. 39, Nos. 5–6 (2016), 709–27.

61 Phillips and Mukherjee, op cit, 4. Also Mukherjee, *The Absent Dialogue.*

62 Interview, New Delhi, March 2008 cited in Anit Mukherjee.

63 Admiral Sureesh Mehta, 'India's National Security Challenges- An Armed Forces Overview,' address at the India Habitat Centre, 10 August 2009, 7, available at http:// maritimeindia.org/pdfs/CNS_Lec_atHabitat.pdf

64 At the time of writing this is true only of Strategic Forces Command and The Andamans and Nicobar Islands Command.

65 'A Major Modern General,' *The Economist,* 18 January 2020. My thanks to Anit Mukherjee, 'The Indian Chief of Defence Staff and Civil Military Relations' Interview, *The Diplomat,* 25 February 2020. See also his 'The Absent Dialogue: Politicians, Bureaucrats and the Military in India' (Delhi: Brookings, 2020). Kaura, *India's National Security.*

66 Healey, *The Time of My Life, op cit,* 255–9.

67 Millis, Walter (Ed), *The Forrestal Diaries* (New York: The Viking Press, 1951), 145–7, 153, 164, 167, 206.

68 Cordesman, Anthony H. and Wagner, Abraham E., *The Lessons of Modern War: The Gulf War* (Boulder: Westview Press, 1996), 249–52.

69 Mark Phillips and Anit Mukherjee, 'British and Indian Perspectives on the Higher Management of Defence,' *RUSI Occasional Paper,* July 2012.

70 Wg-Cdr R. Venkataraman, 'Integration of MOD and Defence Planning,' *Air Power,* Vol. 5, No. 2 (April–June 2010), 25–51.

71 For Malaysia's efforts in this direction see "Malaysia's National Defence Policy," 1–2; "Organisation" (Organisational Chart in Malay), Malaysian Armed Forces Headquarters website, last updated 16 July 2015 at http://www.mafhq.mil.my/index.php/en/about-us/ organization. "Ahmad Kamarulzaman takes over as Navy deputy chief," *Sun Daily,* 15 November 2013, accessed 17 July 2015, http://www.thesundaily.my/news/882260

7 Establishing Naval Policy and Setting Strategy

This chapter and the next six deal with Tier 4 the last level in the hierarchy of decisions discussed earlier. Broadly, the major tasks that the navy is expected to perform are set by the government, but it is up to the navy to decide how it performs those tasks with the resources allocated. With this, the focus narrows from the broadly maritime to the merely naval part of the maritime package. The ends, ways and means approach identified earlier apply just as much here as it does before. The Admiralty or the Navy department, reflecting the policies and strategic needs of the state and adjusting to the resources with which it has been allocated, decides its objectives and what is needed for its achievement, so that it can do what the government requires of it. It becomes a 'capability deliverer.' With a nod to General Poirier, it goes on to develop a 'naval strategy of means.'

7.1 Introduction

Very often though, things are more complicated than this. The navy can expect the government to take a close interest in, and possibly influence, how the navy performs its allotted duties, not least because it is spending government money. Furthermore, and especially in cases where the country's military has become more joint along the lines explored in the last chapter, one can expect the other services to monitor and perhaps help shape the way the navy does its business.

Moreover, the navy is not, usually, a merely passive and reactive recipient of general orders from above. It is 'on transmit', as well as 'receive.' Most navies already have a conception of what they can offer and seek to persuade the decision-makers above them of its validity. If successful, they can hope to influence governmental thinking on the tasks they will be asked to perform and, critically, be rewarded with more resources.

In order to do this, navies usually develop a vision of their strategic potential – a narrative hopefully effective as a means of advocacy, which seeks to change expectations of their worth or at least defends them against challenges. This kind of vision-based naval advocacy is aimed upwards in the hierarchy, also sideways at the navy's sister services, the 'political nation' and the wider general public. This will be easier in a country already of a more maritime persuasion.

There also will be a second version of this vision that is aimed downwards at the navy itself. This is less advocacy, more of a means providing guidance for those decision-makers lower down in the naval hierarchy so that they can best perform their tasks. Commonly this will help mediate between the different interest groups within the navy (surface sailors, submariners, naval aviation, the support services, educators

DOI: 10.4324/9781003100553-7

and trainers and so on). Because resources are always finite and nearly always inadequate there will be legitimate competition between these interest groups over the contribution they can make to the navy's overall performance. Where navies also include the marines (as applies to the Indonesian, Malay, Russian and most Western navies) or the Coastguard (Chile, Norway), guidance will need to shape the place of these sectoral interests in the overall naval scheme of things as well.

These two kinds of visions, as advocacy and as guidance, will normally need to be closely aligned. The targets are different but the message, broadly similar. Gaps, inconsistencies and contradictions between them will surely be exploited by sceptics and external competitors on the one hand and on the other will tend to undermine confidence in their leadership amongst the navy's own people. The vision in short needs to be believable to outsiders and insiders at the same time.

Clearly, then, establishing a naval policy and setting a naval strategy of ways and means to achieve the necessary objectives is critically important. Navies are individual and unique and they perform this central task in different ways, but two approaches on a common spectrum stand out. One is the corporate, collective, routine approach, of which more later. The other is the approach of some commanding naval personality who champions the naval cause, wins governmental approval and resources and sets the navy on its course. Here the approach of just three such champions will be reviewed, to see how they did it.

7.2 Three Naval Champions: Tirpitz, Gorshkov and Liu

In the 20th Century, Admiral Tirpitz of the Imperial German Navy and Admiral Sergei Gorshkov of the Soviet Navy clearly emerge as exemplars of people with visions of what their country's navy needed to be and who managed to communicate such dual-purpose visions so successfully that mighty navies emerged in surprisingly short order. Less well known, 'China's Mahan' Admiral Liu Huaqing was important too, for setting the People's Liberation Army Navy (PLAN) on its way by the end of the century. All three of them were faced with initially quite challenging circumstances, for at the time their countries were of a more land-centric, continental persuasion and they faced formidable challengers at sea. Their success depended on four main groups of factors that bore distinct echoes of the approach adopted by Themistocles 2000 years before.

7.2.1 Developing a Narrative

First they all came up with a narrative that changed the terms of strategic debate within the country and, at the same time enthused their own navy people. This is not the place to go into their arguments in detail but broadly, Tirpitz emphasised the naval part of maritime development arguing that this underpinned Germany's future growth and security. This reflected a very different vision of his country's destiny from Bismarck's. Bismarck had overseen the unification of Germany in the heart of Europe, a change essentially delivered by the success of its army. Bismarck was very aware that unification could be seen as a threat by Germany's neighbours, so, wanting his country to be seen as a satisfied power he pursued modest policies principally intended to prevent hostile combinations against it.

However, Germany was changing, shifting from an agrarian economy to an industrial one and to go on growing, it needed more markets and resources which were already largely taken by the other great European powers, moreover ones inclined to wariness of the powerful newcomer in their midst. Slowly, and despite Bismarck's efforts to control events, the strategic context was moving in a new direction. Germany was turning into a revisionist power, seeking radical change. Tirpitz catered for this new spirit by arguing for the development of a great navy that would give the country influence and global reach.

Because the scale of his naval ambition would have alarmed Germany's main naval rival, Britain, and probably provoked a damaging response, Tirpitz was careful to conceal its full extent as long as he could. The British and sceptics within Germany were assured that all he was planning was a navy big enough to deter the British by posing them the real risk that after incurring the losses required for defeating it they would be inferior to a combination of the French and Russian fleets. But this *Risikogedanke* cover story seemed increasingly suspect from the publication of the second Naval Law of June 1900, which exposed the true extent of Tirpitiz's ambition. This suggested he was really after a navy that if not 'second-to-none' was at least of equal stature to the Royal Navy.[1]

The result was predictable. The British, under the guidance of Admiral Jacky Fisher (another such champion) and his colleagues, did not behave as the 'cooperative enemy' that Tirpitz's plan required. Instead they befriended France and Russia and, being better able to concentrate on naval expenditure than Germany with its two vulnerable land borders, they won the naval arms race that followed. But each of the British responses in this race, was used, reactively, to justify further German building. Tirpitz's vision was strategically senseless. It added to, rather than limited, Germany's enemies. The country ended up encircling itself strategically. While Tirpitz did indeed produce a powerful navy, it was clearly inferior to the Royal Navy; its only hope of strategic success depended on the British making a whole series of egregious operational mistakes, such as attempting a close blockade of German ports on the other side of the North Sea.[2] As things turned out, the British did indeed make some operational mistakes, but not enough.

Another fatal weakness of the Tirpitz plan was that it explicitly pitted the Navy against the Army, the inherent strength of whose position was the currently unavoidable fact that Germany had potentially vulnerable land borders with two major military powers (France and Russia) generally opposed to its policies. The Army was hardly consulted in Tirpitz's campaign and could not but notice that a direct consequence of his success would be a substantial reduction in its share of Germany's defence spending. There was no joint defence budget as such, but the implications for the Army were clear. By 1911 in fact the Navy, swallowed up 55% of the country's defence spending; the Army found this insupportable. The Generals were joined in opposition by those worried about the domestic and economic consequences of this kind of naval programme and who could point to the furious and damaging reaction from the British. Reductions were irresistible; by 1914 German naval spending had fallen away to 32% and Tirpitz's long-term plans were fading into pipe-dreams.[3]

Given the logical flaws and general tendentiousness of his naval vision, at least for Germany's immediate future, and certainly in comparison with the much more effective response of the Royal Navy under Admiral Jacky Fisher, it seems all the more remarkable that Tirpitz was able to communicate it so convincingly to the Kaiser, to politicians and the general public. Moreover, Germany was unaccustomed to a maritime way of looking at things. Despite the success of the Hanseatic League, the land-centric continental approach to the maritime endeavour was a much stronger strain in German history.

The same challenge confronted Admirals Gorshkov and Liu too, both of whom were also seeking to respond to initially much stronger foreign naval forces. Gorshkov, upon his appointment as Commander-in-Chief of the Soviet Navy in 1956 faced an additional problem as well – in the mercurial nature and assumptions of the Soviet leader, Nikita Khruschev. Khruschev was a great believer in what became known as 'the Revolution in Military Affairs': technological advance, particularly in nuclear weapons and missiles would reduce the value of conventional military forces. The future of naval warfare, Khruschev thought, would revolve around submarines, missiles and land-based aviation, not carriers and large surface warships. These should be scrapped; any money saved could be diverted into other ways by which the Soviet Union could advance its interests at home and abroad.

Gorshkov's response was, firstly not to mount any overt challenge to this line of thought. Military officers who seriously questioned Party policy all too often ended up getting shot or uncomfortably exiled. Instead, he dutifully accommodated it with the scrapping of a large proportion of the Russian surface fleet and the disbanding of the Naval Infantry in 1956. He accepted the loss of much naval aviation to PVO-Strany (Khruschev's new air defence force) and agreed that running the nuclear deterrent was the responsibility of the largely land-based Strategic Rocket Force (SRF). But, alongside that, he invested heavily in the development of submarines, and, without too much fanfare, advanced the production of new generation surface ships starting with the *Kynda* class cruisers of 1961. Essentially, Gorshkov was able to argue that with its heavy concentration on naval missiles and submarine development, his navy was actually acknowledging and responding to the military-technical challenge of the 'Revolution in Military Affairs.'

Preparing the way for the great expansion of the Soviet Navy from the late 1960s he advanced three arguments. Firstly he worked with the other services (the Army, the Air Force, PVO-Strany and the SRF) not against them. He made no bid for primacy or for the Navy to have independent missions. He accepted that command in each Theatre of Military Operations would be joint and usually under the Army, but made clever and credible use of recent history, especially of the Great Patriotic War (1941–1945) to prove how essential the naval contribution had been, and would be, for the Army to succeed in its tasks. Secondly, he demonstrated again through the clever use of history that a submarine-centric navy would fail unless it had the support of significant surface forces and organic, sea-based air.[4]

Thirdly, he capitalised on the Revolution in Military Affairs to argue that basing some of the Soviet Union's nuclear deterrent in ballistic-missile firing submarines (SSBNs) would contribute greatly to the security and credibility of the SRF. This would face adversaries with new angles of attack and reduce the danger of those adversaries being able to make decisive pre-emptive counter-force attacks.[5] This also reinforced the supportive role of surface forces because the 'bastions' in which Soviet SSBNs operated would need to be protected against Western attempts to attack them. This mission even ushered in a role for carrier-based aviation.

Finally, Gorshkov was eventually able to capitalise on the growing realisation in the Soviet Union as elsewhere, that 'nuclear-weapons had negated themselves' and that even in Europe excessive reliance on their early strategic use was not such a good idea after all. Instead, longer periods of pre-nuclear conflict needed to be catered for, alongside the possibility of the Soviet Union finding itself engaged in sub-strategic conflicts further afield. Both of these scenarios required increased conventional naval forces, including aircraft carriers. Gorshkov was able to develop this last argument surprisingly early, even during Khruschev's time because the latter's promise of 'burying' the West was based on the idea that by enlisting the aid of the Third World (an international mission if ever there was one) the Soviet economic system was bound to prevail over the struggling Western capitalist one. For this reason, Gorshkov was able in the early 1960s to command his navy to sail the waters of the world ocean, not simply mooch about off the coasts of the Soviet Union. This promised to turn the Soviet Union into a global superpower, not just a regional one and for that, a strong navy eventually with carriers for fleet air defence was essential.

This was a coherent, informed and persuasive set of arguments that went down sufficiently well with successive Soviet regimes for a navy to be created which the United States and its allies considered a very serious challenge. Gorshkov's argument was buttressed by the explicit and skilful use of historical experience, in a body of published work far in excess of the writings of any other naval figure of the period. But there was one fatal flaw in his overall argument. Like Tirpitz, Admiral Gorshkov under-played the likely reaction of the more maritime West. President Reagan's 600-ship navy and robust *The Maritime Strategy* (published in 1986, but extant years before that) and the determined responses of US allies posed greater and greater challenges. Worse still, this maritime response combined with others, such as the 'Star Wars' Strategic Defence Initiative, and put an intolerable strain on an already suffering Soviet economy that was in any case markedly inferior to that of the West.

The Chinese have also shown themselves alive to the contentious 'lessons of history' and well aware of the consequences of these two previous experiments in the development of maritime power. Admiral Liu Huaqing, sometimes colourfully referred to in the West as 'China's Mahan,' was Commander-in Chief of the PLAN from 1982 to 1988 and after that was awarded an influential position in the Central Military Committee (CMC) as Deputy Secretary General (1989–1989) and from 1989 to 1997 in the Politbureau Standing Committee, a rare honour. To some extent, he followed Gorshkov's lead in publishing his thoughts, although rather more of the detail remains opaque to outsiders. Again the 'message' was carefully adapted to the political and strategic realities of the time. As ever, the international and domestic contexts framed the debate.

Admiral Liu had one advantage over Tirpitz and Gorshkov. His ideas were not so new. Indeed Chairman Mao himself had publicly confirmed the need for China to build a major fleet back in 1975. This plan, indeed something of a crash programme, was set in motion with Mao's death and the purge of the Gang of Four in 1976.[6] Nonetheless, the international background for Liu's campaign to develop Chinese maritime power was much less conflictual than that of Tirpitz or Gorshkov. Accordingly, domestic reform of China's economy not building a navy was President Deng Xiaoping's top priority in the 1980s. In general, this required the country to maintain a low profile and avoid trouble wherever possible. The threat posed by the Soviet Union was thought to be lessening and that of the United States not yet clear. China had had its fingers burnt in 1979 when seeking to teach the Vietnamese to be more accommodating by temporarily invading them; this had underlined the need to modernise the military and for China indeed to 'bide its time.' South China Sea disputes were to be shelved for the time being and 'joint development' was offered. The main effort was to be on economic reconstruction, in which the PLAN had only a minor direct role to play. As a proportion of the total government budget, the military share dropped to less than 9%.

Against this unpromising background, Liu and his entourage were able to show that the increasing range of modern weaponry meant that the defence of the coastal cities that were to be China's economic powerhouse and sustaining the seaward flank of any land-air campaign required a strategy of 'near sea active defence.' This represented a significant advance on the humble Maoist conceptions of coastal defence that was based on the shallow-water operations of a cloud of fast patrol boats, mines, and land-based air and artillery. The immediate programme focused on research and development, and on laying the foundations for future development. What constituted 'near seas' was left vague, understandably so since it was shaped by the range of sea-based threats (and that in turn depended on who you were talking about and when). But Western and other analysts generally interpreted 'near seas' as being within what was to become known as the first island chain. Liu left open the prospect, in the more distant future, of a more developed PLAN 'following the threat' out to the Second Island Chain and eventually out into the world ocean beyond, in time perhaps for the centennial of the People's Republic in 2049.[7]

In China too there were worries about whether diverting Chinese energies, even to this extent, away from economic reconstruction and China's more familiar land-air preoccupations might spark a counter-reaction from an apparently more maritime United States (and also amongst its closer neighbours, Japan and South Korea) which could prove counter-productive in the end. The long-term and conditional nature of the Liu programme however evidently assuaged those fears for the time being. Moreover, China's growing economic strength meant that the Chinese navy would be in a much better position to respond to the reactions of the United States, should that prove necessary, than the Soviet Navy had ever been.

Summarising the importance of the narrative, Tirpitz's failure shows that its long-term success depends on that narrative being sufficiently credible and realistic. Its flaws became so evident, even within the Navy, that the Kaiser was forced to intervene in 1910 and try to ban the public discussion of maritime strategy, at least by Admirals who were presumed to know most about it.[8] Both Gorshkov, and perhaps Liu, on the other hand developed a vision for their navies which made sense and which led on naturally to a set of achievable ways and means through which that vision could be realised. In all three cases, naval technology and construction followed policy and strategy, not the other way around. Tirpitz got his battleships and battle-cruisers, specifically designed to fight in the North Sea, rather than submarines. Gorshkov and Liu both set in train a general-purpose navy intended incrementally to advance from the near seas to the open ocean. Liu did not get the carriers he wanted because Deng and his successor Jiang Zemin, considered them unnecessary for the Taiwan issue and were content to put the South China Sea on hold for the time being.

Both the last two admirals were able to define and get accepted, a set of realistic and achievable naval purposes which seemed to fit national needs that were generally agreed upon. This experience suggests the more such narratives are actually 'true,' or at least make sense, the more effective and convincing they become. One of the best metrics for this is the subsequent operational success of the fleet that the vision produced. The best tribute of effectiveness that all three admirals could have wished for was how seriously their maritime opponents were concerned about the apparent threat their product posed, and in that at least, they all succeeded.

7.2.2 Achieving Representation

Back in 1691, Henry Maydman was wise enough to know that the opinions of a long-service Warrant officer in the Royal Navy wouldn't cut much ice with the decision-makers of the England of his time and so dedicated his book to the Lord High Admiral knowing that his opinions would count much more. In this he was recognising the importance of a 'champion' – someone who was either in, or had the political skill to acquire, a position of authority. Only then would his views be listened to with attention and respect. However convincing a narrative might be, it needs re-presentation in order to make a difference. For that, naval visionaries, need to manoeuvre themselves into positions where they would be really listened to.

Tirpitz certainly managed to do this. After a successful naval career, he secured the support of the Kaiser himself. Wilhelm II, quite independently, had succumbed to the general spirit of navalism of the time and so was highly receptive to what Tirpitz had to say. Moreover, his support guaranteed a position of authority for Tirpitz not only for him to spread his views with great effect but also the bureaucratic clout to neutralise objectors. Tirpitz profited from what some have called 'the polycratic chaos of the German constitution.' Germany had no equivalent to Britain's Committee of Imperial Defence or France's *Conseil Superiere de la Guerre* where national policy and strategy could be discussed and decided, at least, in theory. There was no policy-making Cabinet, no 'defence budget' as such, no Chief of the Defence Staff; the Army and the Navy prepared for different wars and avoided talking to each other. Even the naval professionals in the Admiralty Staff were specifically excluded from the strategy-making, such as it was, that emanated from the Tirpitz's own Imperial Navy Office (*Reichsmarineamt*). But even that organisation had no associated think tank to challenge or even give substance to Tirpitz's views.[9]

In many ways all this merely reflected the basic weaknesses of the German state. All the stakeholders had different world objectives and produced a policy, complained the exasperated Chancellor Bethmann Hollweg in July 1914, that apparently seemed designed to '… challenge everybody, get in everyone's way and actually, in the course of all this, weaken nobody.'[10] In such a situation, it was easy for the craziest ideas to prevail.

Gorshkov's task was much harder, and his success as a bureaucratic in-fighter all the more impressive. He did however have one big advantage and that was the web of personal contacts he had developed during his service, largely in the Black Sea theatre during the Great Patriotic War, 1941–1945 and his membership of the so-called Stalingrad Group. In the early days of his appointment as Commander-in-Chief of the Navy, he was well supported by two other members of this group, namely Marshals R.Y. Malinovsky and A.A. Gretchko who in 1957 were Minister of Defence and First Deputy Minister of Defence, respectively. In 1964, Khruschev was replaced as Party Secretary by Leonid Brezhnev who, as a political officer had served alongside Gorshkov in the amphibious landings at Novorossik on the Black Sea in September 1943.[11] This happy combination of circumstances meant that Gorshkov was reasonably assured of a fair hearing by the two agencies – the Army and the Party – who might otherwise have proved his biggest obstacles.

Even so, his narrative needed to make sense, and the challenges he faced were considerable. His skill in arguing the naval case was attested by his appointment in 1961 to the Central Committee of the Party, essentially as the political as well as the military head of the Navy (and so acting as though he were Navy Minister), his ultimate promotion to the rank of Fleet Admiral and his recognition as 'Hero of the Soviet Union' for his war service. He assembled around him an able command team of close associates, young ambitious officers, some of whom became, at least to some extent, his 'ghost writers,' and of course a coterie of reliable retirees.

It was necessary to consolidate and build up an institutional base for the naval message because the problem with the personality-based approach is that one's senior contacts have a disagreeable habit of dying or retiring. Later, when new men like Marshall Ogarkov took over as Chief of the General Staff or when Dimitry Ustinov became Minister of Defence, such personal contacts were not so effective.[12] Marshal Zhukov's unceremonious replacement as Minister of Defence in 1957, however, shows that not everyone can make sufficient political capital out of their military success and general popularity.

Because the Chinese system is so much more opaque to outsiders even than the Soviet equivalent, we know much less about Admiral Liu's road to success and a position of authority. The more ambitious parts of his narrative were 'acknowledged' rather than accepted by Deng Xiaoping but his unprecedented appointment from 1992 to 1997 to membership of the Central Military Committee (CMC) and the Politburo Standing Committee indicates that he had won himself a position of authority before that. It may have helped that firstly Liu actually started life in the Army and was often referred to as a 'General.' Allegedly, he was also personally friendly with Deng Xiaoping which doubtless helped consolidate effective good civil-military relations with the Party.

Nor was there any doubt about his professional competence. Starting in 1961 when Liu was appointed as head of the new Seventh (Warship) Research Academy (an agency specifically set up to monitor and respond to foreign naval technological development) he developed real expertise in this aspect of naval development and maintained strong links with the Chinese ship-building industry.[13] His inclusion and promotion within the august ranks of the CMC was very important since its chair had the final say on all major military decisions, senior promotions, budgetary allocations, troop deployments and nuclear weapons.[14] This was where the 'former naval person' and Chief of the Navy needed to be for naval plans to prosper.

7.2.3 Developing Support and Winning Allies

Enlisting potential allies is an important part of anyone's campaign for the development of naval power and other members and stakeholders in the maritime community are an obvious target. With his close connections to Chinese ship-building and naval engineering, Admiral Liu was in an ideal position to do this, and in turn helping to develop those industries. This would materially assist Deng Xiaoping's emphasis on economic construction in the country as a whole.

Much the same was true of Admiral Gorshkov too, although his background was more operational than technological. Moreover, once enlisted in the campaign and having invested in the plant and skills required, the resultant maritime defence industry became another stakeholder in the general maritime campaign, although their interests were not exactly the same as the navy's.

Admiral Tirpitz's position here was different, in that his naval advocacy was rather more of a *response* to pressures welling up from below than was the case with either of the other two. To an extent, these were fuelled by the astonishing rise of Germany's industrial base, which had started well before Tirpitz attained his position of

authority. Coal and steel output had grown enormously along with newer speciali-
sations in electronics, optics and chemicals. Giant German firms like Siemens and
AEG dominated the European scene. Between 1890 and 1913, exports tripled, following close behind those of Britain. By 1914 Germany's share of world industrial
output at 14.8% higher was higher than Britain's at 13.6%, and over twice as much as
France's at 6.1%.[15] Accordingly there was an appetite in Germany for new markets,
new commodities from distant places and new maritime horizons. Ambitions for
empire and 'a place in the sun' and a navy to make it possible seemed in the spirit of
the times to follow naturally.

This industrial strength in fact had before his time had already leached through into
the maritime world. Although its ships were still generally British-built, the Hamburg-
Amerika line (HAPAG), under the energetic and far-sighted Albert Ballinn, became
the biggest shipping line in the world by 1914, with 442 ships and 1.4 million tons, 8
times its 1885 size. Its *Deutschland* won the Blue Riband for the fastest crossing of the
Atlantic in 1900. Thereafter HAPAG chiefly contested the prize with the world's
second biggest liner fleet Nord-Deutscher-Lloyd, which was also German.[16]

The building, launching and operation of glamorous ocean liners attracted huge
levels of public interest. In 1906, publicists famously arranged for the Duchess of
Roxburghe to be photographed being driven in her car through sections of the three
funnels of the *Mauretania* laid end-to-end.[17] All over Europe children were routinely
photographed in 'naval' costumes. In Germany as elsewhere, yachting had taken off in
a big way and there was a huge following for events such as the races for the America's
Cup. As a result, there had already developed in Germany a public appetite which
Tirpitz could easily tap into, encourage and exploit. The Navy League, *Flottenverein,*
was founded in 1898 and by 1906 had a million members, vastly outperforming its
British equivalent with its modest 40,000 members,[18] and equally significantly the
membership of the Pan German League.

Not a technologist, and operating in a strictly controlled political system in which
there was no general public to appeal to, Gorshkov needed to be both tough and
clever in order to get his message across to the country's policy-making elite. He stuck
to his guns through successive regime and strategic policy changes, without engaging
in futile and dangerous polemics that might challenge the Navy's relations with the
Party. When he had to be ruthless and determined, such as when sending submarines
to sea with known safety deficiencies, he was.[19] No one prospering in the Soviet
system, after all, was likely to be a pussycat. Gorshkov exemplified the Leninist
principle of 'correct and purposeful leadership ... by one person, centralism, and unity
of will from top to bottom.'[20] He was able to develop a power base within the Navy
and clearly attracted respect and fierce loyalty. The 'Gorshkovschina' that resulted
was a cause of some resentment in some senior naval circles and, no doubt, in the
General Staff too.[21]

Gorshkov is practically unique amongst 20th Century sailors, especially chiefs of
navy, for the sheer volume of his published work – but this was publication for a
purpose, as already mentioned. His books and articles turgid in translation and
wrapped in Marxist-Leninist jargon do not make for easy reading. But they were
cleverly modulated and made intelligent use of history to develop potentially challenging points elliptically. His writings were clearly critically important and led to the
establishment of a major cottage industry, especially in the United States, devoted to
identifying from minute textual examination exactly what the Commander-in-Chief

of the Soviet Navy was really advocating. His output was appropriate for the system he had to deal with and an essential part of a brilliantly successful political campaign for the Navy to win the support and the resources from the Party and Soviet state he knew it needed.[22]

Although Russians were, and remain,[23] proud of their navy and its achievements, in the Soviet Union there was nothing like the navalism of Germany before the First World War. Commentators have, however, seen the development in China of a kind of 21st Century navalism which takes the form of mountains of glossy naval magazines, thrilling action DVDs, an enthusiastic presence on the social media – even, apparently, some popular disco dance steps, modelled on the gyrations of aircraft handlers on US carriers.

The extent to which this 'social currency' is spontaneous or created remains a matter of debate, as are questions about its effect and durability. But it certainly helps the cause, and always has. Note that 2500 years ago, in the theatre-crazy Athens of the time, plays like Phrynichus' *The Phoenician Women* and Aeschylus' *The Persians* supported sea-mindedness by harking back to the lauded Themistocles and his era of naval greatness. The techniques may change, but the principles don't.

7.2.4 *Delivering the Goods*

A narrative becomes justified and sustainable when it is seen to deliver the goods, or proof of concept, and, on the face of it, Tirpitz did indeed do so. By 1914 the German Navy had risen from being sixth in the world to second. It comprised 13 first-class Dreadnoughts, five Battle-cruisers and 16 high quality older battleships. The Battlefleet was well trained for operations, specifically in the North Sea. In many ways their ships were better than their British opponents in internal construction, compartmentalisation, shells, optics, gunnery control and night training.[24] At the Battle of Jutland in 1916 they gave a good account of themselves but accepted they had no chance of decisively defeating the much larger British fleet. Having to spend so much on the Army, Germany could not provide the resources necessary for that. Tirpitz may indeed have provided his country with an impressive battlefleet, but whether its strategic effect (which is really the point of the exercise) justified the money spent on it is much more debatable. It certainly did not improve Germany's prospects before the war; if anything, Tirpitz's project can be said to have worsened them, because it sparked such a reaction from Britain.

The same argument could be, and indeed was, applied to Gorshkov's programme of course. In the end, however good the Soviet Navy was, it could not compensate for, or avoid suffering from, the political and economic deficiencies of the Soviet Union; indeed by representing such a drain on national resources it may be said indirectly to have contributed to those deficiencies. But in the meantime, Gorshkov certainly delivered a large and high-quality fleet. Even the Soviet Navy's failures were used to good account: thus the Cuban missile crisis of 1962 was shown to confirm the already established need for high-quality conventional surface forces, and longer range sea-based missiles, to support the submarine effort. The resultant fleet was also able to achieve far more sea-days, conduct some of the biggest naval exercises ever seen, visit much more widely and operate on the world ocean effectively for nearly 30 years. All this forced the United States and its allies to respond with heavy naval expenditure of their own and constantly adapt their naval strategies in order to cope with a succession of naval challenges posed by the Soviet fleet. Its naval power undoubtedly did help turn the Soviet Union, despite all its short-comings, into a global superpower – at least for a while. Perhaps it is nostalgia for that achievement that now drives Mr Putin's very evident continuing support for its descendant, the Russian Federation Navy.[25]

There seems much less reason to qualify the apparently modest and preparatory achievements of Admiral Liu, although their result became clearly apparent only some time after his departure. But even by that time, the PLAN had made its presence felt. It had already started conducting exercises and commissioning ceremonies in the far south of the South China Sea at James Shoal deep inside the Malaysian Exclusive Economic Zone and in 1988 took on and decisively defeated the Vietnamese navy in the vicinity of Fiery Cross reef. The PLAN is now a major navy that the United States and its allies, especially in the Indo-Pacific region have to take very seriously. Enough of the credit for that can be traced back Liu for him to be not undeserving of the title bestowed on him by some Western observers – the 'father of the Chinese navy.' So far at least, there seems no reason to doubt that China's enthusiasm for the development of the PLAN as a part its maritime power will continue.

7.2.5 *Champions of a Smaller Scale*

Just as naval champions such as Tirpitz, Gorshkov and Liu operated in a smaller arena than the broader, more maritime one of Themistocles, so can champions of a lesser scale be found within the ranks of the navies they led. These smaller champions can be found inspiring and leading sectors of navies rather than whole ones. In the nature of things, there are a lot more of them. In the US Navy, for example, there were great pioneering leaders such as Admirals William A. Moffett who developed naval aviation or Hyman Rockover so instrumental in developing nuclear propulsion in the fleet. If on a smaller scale, their success required the same qualities and influence techniques as those of their rarer and still more illustrious seniors.

7.3 The Normal Pattern of Naval Advance

The serious objection to this portrayal of the way in which navies are developed of course is that recognised and effective champions like Themistocles, Tirpitz, Fisher, Gorshkov and Liu are relatively rare; most navies do not begin or develop in this clear-cut way. Instead, their approach is more corporate and cumulative. They advance incrementally, responding to shifts in their domestic and international contexts and in line with their implications for naval development. Instead of controlling their environment, they float down the river, while doing their best to steer.

The Canadian navy is a good example of this. It grew, in fits and starts, from a Fishing Protection Service; though rarely welcome to successive politicians, it was finally created in 1910 but only played a modest role in the First World War compared to the Amy. Suffering from a classic, chronic case of being out-of-sight and so out of mind, and having little to offer the Army or the Air Force in return for their support, it hovered on the brink of extinction through much of the interwar period. The circumstances of the time created much resistance to its becoming much more than a coastal defence force.

In the Second World War, though, it grew fantastically from a force of just under 4000 to 100,000 people, playing a leading role in the Battle of the Atlantic and becoming the world's fourth biggest navy. But by 1 April 1946, it had shrunk back again to just 6600 sailors. Its later recovery and expansion especially though the 1950s owed much more to changing perceptions of the Soviet threat than it did to anyone's long-term vision of what kind of navy a country like Canada needed.[26] Shortly after the resultant expansion, however, it was formally abolished in 1968 as the Royal Canadian Navy and became instead The Maritime Command of the country's unified military. Changes continued after the Cold War with a prolonged period of 'rust out' and governmental neglect until the experience of the complexities of the post-Cold War world started to reshape thinking about the kind of navy Canada now needed; in 2011 it even emerged once more as the Royal Canadian Navy.

In short, this roller-coaster ride suggests there was no long-term and enduring vision for the Canadian navy, enunciated by a commanding person of authority. Instead, the Canadian navy stumbled from one urgent challenge to another, apparently having to make it all up as it went along. The result was a whole series of reactive decisions made (or sometimes not made) in response to changing external or domestic challenges. These often had to be taken in a hurry and were more tactical than strategic, more immediate than long-term. Further, it might well be argued that in this, the Canadian model of naval development actually applies to most other navies as well, in a world where commanding figures like Tirpitz, Fisher or Gorshkov are rarities.

Instead, naval leadership is a more collective affair in which personalities still matter but are not so dominant. It is hard to pin the great explosion of naval effort that characterised the Royal Navy of Henry Maydman's day for example down to any particular individual. Instead it happened corporately in the deliberations of the Navy Board and the Board of Admiralty, often in response to initiatives from below, from above and sometimes from outside the government-naval chain altogether. This indeed is the more usual pattern. The Navy Executive Committee of today's French Navy, togther with its Navy Steeering Committee, systematically examines the budgetary technological, legal and Human Resources aspects of each major issue that comes before them - and provides a good example of this pattern.

In the expanding Canadian navy of the late 1950s, the equivalent was its Naval Board, centred on the Chief of the Naval Staff, comprising a handful of senior naval officers, representing sectoral naval interests, who were responsible for establishing naval policy. They were supported in their work by various subordinate naval committees and a naval staff. Their recommendations were passed to the joint Chiefs of Staff Committee for endorsement (or not) and then on to the Cabinet via the Minister of Defence, and with due reference to the Department of External Affairs, Treasury Board, the Department of Defence Production and ultimately the Prime Minister. This was often a disagreeable lengthy and iterative process bouncing around between all the stakeholders until finally resolved – or not.[27] After the war, observed one historian, 'There had been no real effort ... at the cabinet level to define the overall mission of the armed forces; through the service chiefs proposing, and the government disposing, a policy of sorts emerged almost by accident.'[28] Over time, of course, these institutional procedures varied, generally becoming more joint, and more centralised in defence as a whole; their workings were of course affected by the personalities of the key place-holders.

There could also be substantial inputs to the implementation process from allies and partners, provided this was consistent with the country's foreign policy and had the political approval of the government. In the Canadian, Australian and New Zealand cases, their continued membership of the British Empire and Commonwealth was an important factor shaping their naval policy, as was the case for many other former members of the various European colonial empires. All three shifted much of their attention after the Second World war to the United States as their ultimate security guarantor, and in Canada's case policy was in large part shaped by the requirements and preferences of NATO.

A closer look at Canadian naval development, though, suggests that even in such cases there *are* lurking visions or at least unspoken assumptions to be found that shape policy decision. In Canada's case, the first discernible vision, and one that long commanded considerable domestic support, was of a naval force restricted to fishery protection and coastal defence. This persisted deep into the 20th Century, with McKenzie King, Canada's Prime Minister 1935–1948, for example saying: ' The Navy had no need for aircraft carriers. I had always opposed this from the start as un-necessary. We should have a purely coast defence.'[29] Others at the time, and after-wards, thought of the Canadian Navy being a part of a British imperial fleet, or of a 'general purpose fleet-in-being,' a specialist anti-submarine organisation, a 'good workable little fleet' as a contribution to NATO or a modest expeditionary navy supporting humanitarian and peace-keeping operations. All these competing visions related to Canada's developing identity and to how the country thought of itself and its role in the world. It was as one historian put it 'a thread imbedded in the broader story of Canada.'[30] Even if not dramatically articulated, these visions existed and they shaped policy and strategy decisions. Moreover the resultant decisions reflected the effect of the broad approaches and techniques displayed in the campaigns of Admirals Tirpitz, Gorshkov and Liu that were uncovered above. These techniques apply just as much in the more corporate and incremental efforts of less obvious decision-makers in navies, big and small, around the world.

7.3.1 Techniques of Universal Applicability?

As a common pattern, this applies to small and medium navies as well as large ones. Some would argue that smaller navies like the Belgian typically 'don't do grand strategy.' They may not be able to access sufficient geo-political guidance at home, and so find it difficult to come up with a valid strategic vision for themselves. For them, working together with others in organisations like NATO and the EU certainly has advantages in that it helps provide a justifying conceptual framework for their aspirations. The Belgian Navy's ambitious 'Strategic Vision' of 2016 is a case in point; its intrinsic chances of success may not be high but by linking in with wider thinking it can at least credibly articulate what it believes to be necessary. For its part, the rather larger Royal Netherlands Navy knows its vision of itself has at least to fit into and at best exploit the opportunities offered by *Netherlands Defence Doctrine.*[31] Other countries like Israel or Singapore, perhaps because of their strategic situations, also seem able to develop a credible rationale for their navies, even if they are not particularly transparent about what it actually is. No doubt their doctrine is much more for guidance than advocacy.

7.3.2 What Navies Need: South Asian Examples

The 'new' small and large navies of South Asia (that is the Indian, Pakistani, Sri Lankan and later Bangladeshi navies) that were established in the wake of independence from

Britain in the late 1940s show what the successful development of naval power typically entails. A brief review of this experience recapitulates earlier chapters by showing how the domestic and international environment shaped naval development in South Asia and also reinforces the need for a coherent vision of the navy's place in a country's overall defence strategy. To a greater or lesser extent, all four navies failed to do this for some time, in part because of the reluctance or inability of their governments to provide the necessary seed-corn funding. Their experience shows what's needed for abstract aspirations to be turned into practical reality. Effective policies were needed in four crucial areas,

- the establishment of a maritime community,
- appropriate exploitation of naval technology,
- the development of the navy's people and
- the delivery of an effective fleet.

Not, of course, that the navies of India, Pakistan, Sri Lanka and Bangladesh were entirely 'new.' All four countries had always had their fishing, trading and ship-building communities. The sea-based Chola empire of the 9th–11th Centuries was based on Sri Lanka and southern India. The Mahratta navy of northern India provided stout resistance to the increasing power of the Portuguese and British in the 17th and 18th Centuries. The success of the Anglo-Indian 'Bombay Marine' showed that much of that power could also be replicated in India. Above all, all four of these new navies strongly reflected their more recent imperial antecedents, to the extent, particularly in their early days, that they were initially commanded and partly manned by British officers and ratings on loan, gratefully accepted British ships and weapons and absorbed British assumptions about what they were for. At first, they reflected vague ideas that they were not just national forces but at the same time constituents of the naval power of the British Commonwealth, united in a need above all to protect sea communications, possibly from the Soviet Union.[32]

Later the naval planners of all four navies were influenced by the changing international and domestic context in which they had to operate. The initial separation and then mutual antipathy between India and Pakistan delayed serious preparations for naval independence but afterwards dominated the operational priorities of both their navies; it resulted in three wars which also underlined the centrality of the army in their country's military affairs – something that severely limited the national resources available to both navies. They were caught in a vicious circle. They failed to get the resources required for achieving strategic effect; because therefore they could not achieve strategic effect, they did not get the resources they needed. Cooperating with them was a low priority for the army and the air force. In the third Indo-Pakistan War of 1971, the Pakistan Navy was considered so marginal to the outcome, that it was not even made aware of the Army's plans.

That war led to the emergence of Bangladesh – and of yet another navy which had to plot its future course, virtually from scratch; this fourth South Asia country simplified Pakistan's strategic thinking while complicating India's. As for the Sri Lankan Navy, its thinking was much more focused on the domestic environment, especially on the complexities arising from its restive Tamil community. As their British inheritance declined, all four navies found themselves influenced by wider global events, especially in that the Cold War helped shape their relationship with the United States, the Soviet Union and China as possible mentors and arms-suppliers.

For all their differences though, all four navies of South Asia faced similar problems in developing their naval power as their ideas of what their navies were for slowly crystallised in the light of changing circumstances. The first common issue was to establish the place of the navy in their country's wider maritime community. All four governments had to decide on the desirability and the feasibility of setting up a national defence maritime industrial base as an offset to their heavy reliance on foreign arms suppliers. They were aware that this dependency could easily threaten their newly won strategic autonomy. India's non-alignment policies reinforced aspirations for a sound maritime defence industrial base, from the early 1960s, although the obstacles were to prove formidable.[33] These difficulties were even greater for the other three South Asian navies since they had far less industrial potential.

Changes in the international law of the sea, especially the 1982 UN Convention on the Law of the Sea reflected the growing economic importance of the offshore estates of all four countries. This inevitably led to the issue of whether monitoring and protecting these more extensive maritime interests should remain the responsibility of the navy or be handed over to new coastguard agencies and what the relationship between them should be.[34]

The second issue faced by these four navies was the impact on their thinking of the naval technology which was developing even faster than the law of the sea.[35] The importance of getting this as right as their resources would allow was hammered home by the three Indo-Pakistan wars and their intermediary crises, by India's 1962 conflict with China war and by Sri Lankan Navy's campaign against the Tamil Sea Tigers. At the same time, South Asia's naval planners could hardly be unaware of the speed and decisiveness of military-technical developments in the wider world and how this might influence them. But how to reconcile the higher and higher costs of this new technology with their limited access to national resources? Buying foreign-made platforms and systems 'off the shelf' was one partial solution to this problem but brought with it problems of strategic dependency and vulnerability to embargoes and other such potential pressures. It also led to the challenge of integrating systems from different manufacturers and nations. The most extreme response, perhaps, was provided by the Indians who found that splitting their Navy between a West coast fleet that had largely European and American equipment and an East coast fleet that was principally Soviet in origin. This led to both halves of the fleet having little to do with one another, and so was a far from ideal response to the problem.[36]

Thirdly, like all navies everywhere, past and present, all four navies found getting the people in the number and of the quality they needed was a challenge. The Indian and Pakistan navies had filled the gap in senior commanders with Royal Navy loan officers until their indigenous replacements had been nurtured and developed by the early/mid-1950s. While these British officers often turned out to be *plus royalist que le Roi* in terms of developing local naval operational independence, they inevitably consolidated British assumptions and perceptions. The Indians found the traditional aversion of high-caste Hindus to the sea a continuing problem,[37] although this was in part compensated for by their access to Muslims from the Punjab. The Pakistan navy started with just 200 officers, led by an Acting Captain with 14 years of service and 3000 sailors[38] likewise including Muslims from the Punjab (now India) in engineering and other technical posts. The Bangladesh navy was based on East Pakistani officers and men, some 3000 of whom left the Pakistan navy before the war of 1971 began, but these professional 'repatriates' and the irregular Mukti Bahini who actually did most of the fighting in the war proved hard to combine after the conflict. In early 1972 the Bangladesh Navy's first temporary Chief of the Naval Staff was Nurul Huq, merely an engineering Lieutenant Commander, who had come over from the Pakistan Navy.[39]

There was then the question of the quality rather than just the number of their people. This depended in large measure on the quality of the national education system. For all four navies, the establishment of a sound training regime for their people became an urgent requirement. Until this was accomplished, much of the necessary training was accomplished in the UK.

Fourthly and finally, all four navies found that stitching these three concerns into a coherent fleet design process that made sense, when set against the demands of their domestic and international contexts, was a real challenge. In all four cases assembling the constituents of a fleet that would serve their strategic purposes was made more difficult by the continual shortage of resources and foreign exchange that resulted from limitations in their national economies, from the natural dominance of their armies and in both India and Pakistan from a significant lack of sea-mindedness in the government. For the Indians this unhappy combination of circumstances killed off early aspirations for light fleet carriers, a naval air arm and a powerful submarine service.[40]

If anything, resources became still tighter in the aftermath of the first two of the Indo-Pakistan wars and the 1962 conflict with China, in none of which navies had played a major part.[41] Ambitious naval plans to narrow the gap between resources and presumed commitments were inadequately funded and indefinitely delayed.[42] Worse still in some ways, over-lengthy and complex acquisition procedures resulted in the Navy sometimes being unable to spend all of its inadequate funding.

Responding to each other's naval preparations nonetheless provided the obvious agenda for fleet designers in both India and Pakistan. They decided their navy's main missions and sought to acquire the appropriate platforms and weaponry. Pakistan focussed on sea denial off Western Pakistan, but resource shortages led to their neglecting the defence of sea communications to, or the direct defence of, the geographically separated eastern part of their country. Their particular interest was on the acquisition of submarines, essentially as weapons of sea denial. This was eventually achieved in 1964. The success of their first elderly submarine, *Ghazi,* in constraining superior Indian naval forces in the war of 1965 underlined the point.

With their greater resources, the Indians sought a more balanced mission portfolio and despite a constrained budget acquired a range of surface ships, submarines and eventually a naval air arm and carrier force. Their aspirations for a properly 'balanced' fleet seemed confirmed by the experience of the 1971 war, but so was the need for substantial modernisation of their existing assets.[43] In India's case, perceived success in that war seemed to justify the subsequent development of a much more formidable fleet.[44]

Sri Lankan fleet designers, on the other hand, had first to focus on coastguard-type activities in regard to illegal immigration and smuggling across the Palk Strait. They found it difficult to man their bigger ships, and about 1964, resigned themselves to becoming a small ship navy with very local preoccupations. This was reinforced by the need to respond to the growing Tamil insurgency. Eventually this led to a long-drawn out but ultimately successful and innovative small boat campaign against the initially highly effective asymmetric tactics of the Tamil Sea Tigers. Clear-sightedly they designed a fleet specifically intended to beat the insurgents at their own asymmetric game.[45] Once the war was over however, the Sri Lankan navy also exhibited a developing interest in more familiar naval missions and platforms, though inevitably limited by the national need to recover from a long and debilitating struggle.

Starting in 1971–1972, much later than the other three South Asian navies, and with very limited resources indeed, the new Bangladesh Navy had perforce to engage in a strategy of improvisation and 'making do,' but in due course it too followed more or less the same trajectory gradually expanding its mission aspirations from an initial focus on coastguard-type activities in Bangladeshi waters. The dispute with India over the island of South Talpatty in 1981 was something of a turning point however, and the Bangladesh Navy set about the acquisition of capabilities that would provide a more credible defence of their wider maritime interests, given severe resource limitations.[46]

Initially, the UK was the main source of the first generation of modest and second-hand warships for the Indian, Pakistan and Sri Lankan navies but over time they diversified into other European sources of supply, the United States, Russia for India[47] and China for Pakistan and, later, Bangladesh. Inevitably this opened them up to greater engagement in the wider global maritime world, bringing with it risks, challenges and commitments as well as opportunities for a wider role and further naval development. All the same, they remain especially interested in capabilities of special value against stronger forces. As evidence of all this, Bangladesh has now achieved its early goal of developing a submarine capability, with Chinese help.[48] In all these cases, developing a vision was a gradual corportae matter, there were no latterday K.M. Pannikars really to speed things along - underlining the point that such people are rare.

7.4 Ways and Means: Turning Vision into Reality

This review of the experience all these navies suggests that whether they are big or small, they all have, at least to some degree visions, preferences or assumptions about what kind of navies they think their countries need to have. There do seem to be some broad commonalities They usually want their fleet to have more ships, that are better equipped with sensors and weapons, resting on a larger and better-trained complement of people and a vibrant maritime economy. Only in this way can they aspire to more challenging tasks in the world ocean or at least their country's maritime are of interest. Accordingly it seems to be an iron law of naval development that naval officers around the world nearly all want to expand their fleets.

But if the aspirations are similar, so are the problems. Taken together, the experience of all these navies suggests there are four inter-connected requirements for them to meet their aspirations.

7.4.1 Winning Sufficient Resources

First must come the winning of sufficient resources, the subject of the last chapter. This depends on whether their country has the necessary resources in the first place, and secondly on the relative priority attached to meeting naval, rather than alternative demands on these resources. The problem they face is that their narrative is all too often dismissed by the money people as no more than the kind of thing you would expect sailors to say, and so much of it can be dismissed as self-serving.

In order to counter that entirely understandable and sometimes justified reaction, those naval people need to know what their visions are and to ensure that they are credible, convincing and really do serve the best interests of the country they serve.

7.4.2 *Having Clarity of Purpose*

An effective and convincing narrative depends on the clarity of purpose. This may well be advanced by a conscious decision to develop the doctrine that was briefly raised earlier. As guidance, doctrine identifies and prioritises the navy's roles; as advocacy, it helps justify them. Accordingly, and provided they are not too safely bland these vision statements should help in making clear the navy's purposes, capabilities and intents to the political establishment, the media and the population, to the other services and most importantly to its own people. Increasingly the world's navies have participated in a major proliferation of doctrine that is written down and made available in both classified and unclassified form, rather than merely 'ambient' as it was in Nelson's day.[49] Examples include those of India, the US, Russia, and Sri Lanka amongst others.[50] One of the most interesting, and at 390 pages, probably the longest, is *Fundamentals of Maritime Operations: Netherlands Maritime Military Doctrine* of 2014.[51] Written within a framework set by earlier versions of *Netherlands Defence Doctrine*, it is periodically reviewed and re-issued in accordance with changing circumstances. It is admirably comprehensive and leaves little excuse for any Dutch naval personnel not being clear about their purpose! The latest version of *Netherlands Defence Doctrine* is interesting, moreover, in that it is noticeably more joint than its predecessors. Differing in form though they may be, these doctrinal publications from around the world, and perhaps above all the collective effort required to produce them, clarifies and articulates what their navy is for both as guidance for its own people and as explanation and advocacy for everyone else.[52]

Historically, this often does not come naturally to navies where scepticism about the on-shore bookworms commonly held to produce it, is contrasted with the fighting sailors at sea who have no time and little patience for such things. More substantially, the huge variety of possibilities offered by activity at sea encourages resistance to the very idea of having to do things 'by the book.' The requirements of being joint, may also lead to the navy having to soft-peddle its distinctiveness. These hesitations may lead to under-investment in the more cerebral strategy-making aspects of the naval profession. In the United States at least, this is sometimes held, rightly or wrongly, to lead to a situation where the navy is unable fully to explain itself to the wider world or perhaps even to its own people, and so less effective strategically than it should be.[53]

Not surprisingly, this charge leads to widespread and often acrimonious debate, that indirectly attests to the perceived and fundamental importance of clarity of purpose. For this reason alone, the creation of 'thinking' groups of people within the naval or general staff, such as the US Navy's N7 branch or the Russian Main Operations Directorate in the General Staff, seems a good idea. Often the processes and habits of strategic reflection are more valuable in the long run, than the probably temporary nature of their conclusions.

7.4.3 *Winning a Sympathetic Audience*

The issue of clarity of purpose is also closely bound up with the importance of se-curing a sympathetic audience. To be effective, naval visions have to be commu-nicated. When doing so Tirpitz, Gorshkov and Liu, like Themistocles at the higher maritime level, found it necessary to lobby for their case. They had also to come up with arguments and take actions that over-came the sea blindness of their nations. This distressing ailment is a common one. Sufferers either vastly under-rate the re-lative importance of the maritime domain or, if they are in positions of authority, acknowledge this in theory but delay actions to protect maritime interests to some later and usually unspecified date after other and apparently more urgent national requirements as already remarked. It is a classic illustration of the sad fact that what happens at sea, can easily be out of sight and so out of mind. 'It is the usual fate of sea power,' Gwythian Prins has put it, 'not to be noticed; except when it fails.'[54] Even the US Navy in successive Gallup poll surveys in the *Washington Times* has found itself regarded as the least important section of the military services by the American public, barring only the US Coast Guard.

Other causes may be deep-rooted indeed. One former head of the Indian Navy, Admiral S.M. Nanda, blamed his country's sea-blindness on the arrival of the Mughals in 622. For them 'the security of the plains of Hindustan' were all that mattered.'[55] Indonesians tend to blame the Dutch who came, saw, conquered and appropriated much of the locals maritime enterprise.'[56] Digging out such deep-rooted conditions is no easy task.

To an extent, though, this may be the navy's own fault. For many years the Royal Navy was proud of its long tradition of being the 'silent service.' In an era of instant news, maintaining a modest and knowing silence is not a sensible option. Navies these days have to be 'media-savvy.' Perhaps aspiring navies should follow the example, particularly, of air forces which being 'new' and in many quarters unwelcome have from the start typically developed a lively sense of self-preservation and mounted sophisticated campaigns of word and deed in order to ensure it. In 1921, in order to advance the creation of an independent air force, Colonel Billy Mitchell deliberately disobeyed the rules of a naval experiment in order to dramatically and publicly bomb and sink the old German battleship *Ostfriesland.* It proved nothing whatsoever, but as a publicity stunt it made his point much better than any number of sober papers speculating about the respective futures of air and naval power. From that day on, air forces have been especially concerned about their public image and shown willingness to invest in its protection. Not for nothing did cynical British sailors sometimes refer to the RAF as the 'Royal Advertising Force.'[57]

Instead of simply complaining about it, navies now generally accept the need to follow suit, and have done so to varying degrees, in varying ways and with varying success. Often this is accepted with some reluctance on the premise that if they don't do it, who will? Their campaigns usually have two objectives. Effective public relations narratives are based on all forms of engagement (twitter broadsides, fleet and ship visits and reviews etc) and are anchored in issues that the attentive public already cares about (economic prosperity and the sanctity of national territory). Experience suggests even in the most avowedly un-military of countries, there is latent pride in the pos-session of a sea-going fleet, to be exploited. '[I]t will be a proud day for this country' said Canada's navy minister, illustrating the point,' when our Canadian naval effort will be directed by naval men, trained in Canada and operating ships built in this country.'[58] The rest is about winning over senior government officials and elected representatives, by showing how supportive they are of the aims and interests, that a government has, or sometimes perhaps, should have. In both democracies and autocracies, this last perspective needs to be handled with great care, however.

With this as a brief introduction to the task of turning naval aspirations into concrete reality, we should now turn to a deeper look into the first of the four critical policy areas identified earlier, namely that of establishing the place of the navy in the wider maritime community.

Notes

1 This is a much studied and sometimes highly contentious area of study. For a useful historiographical review see the introduction to Seligmann, Matthew, Nagler, Frank and Epkenhans, Michael (Eds), *The Naval Route to the Abyss: The Anglo-German Naval Race, 1985–1914* (Farnham: Ashgate for the Naval Records Society, 2015). The book provides a meticulous documentation of the process. Seligmann, Mathew (Ed), *Naval Intelligence from Germany: The Reports of the British Naval Attaches in Berlin, 1906–1914* (Farnham: Ashgate for the Naval Records Society, 2007) tends to support the orthodox view, presented here.
2 The British indeed did make some mistakes, most notably in responding to the U-boat threat to commerce, but avoided the close blockade and operational recklessness that were the Germans' best hope for the necessary whittling away the Royal Navy's otherwise decisive numerical superiority.
3 Herwig, Holger H., 'Imperial Germany: Continental Titan, Global Aspirant,' in Erickson, Andrews S., Goldstein, Lyle J. and Lord, Carnes (Eds), *China Goes to Sea: Maritime Transformation in Comparative Historical Perspective* (Annapolis, MD: Naval Institute Press, 2009), 177–83, 186.
4 Gorshkov considered this a lesson from the ultimate failure of the German U-boat campaign of the Second World War. *The Sea Power of the State,* 100, 188, 197.
5 Ibid, 221.
6 Muller, *China as a Maritime Power,* 200–9.
7 Cole, Bernard D., *The Great Wall at Sea: China's Navy in the Twenty-First Century,* 2nd edition (Annapolis, MD: Naval Institute Press, 2010), 174–8. Goldman, U.S. Naval Lieutenant Commander Jeffrey B., Naval Reserve, 'China's Mahan,' *Proceedings of the Naval Institute,* March 1996.
8 Herwig, *Imperial Germany,* op cit.
9 Holweg, *Imperial Germany: Continental Titan, Global Aspirant,* 179–81.
10 Kennedy, *The Rise and Fall of the Great Powers,* 214.
11 Polmar, Norman, Brooks, Thomas A., Federoff, George, *Admiral Gorshkov: The Man Who Challenged the U.S. Navy* (Annapolis: Naval Institute Press, 2019), 101–6.
12 Polmar, *Admiral Gorshkov,* 123–5, 178.
13 Hartnett, Daniel, 'The Father of the Modern Chinese Navy – Liu Huaqing,' *CIMSEC,* 8 October 2014; Liu Huaqing, *Liu Huaqing Huiyilu [Memoirs of Liu Huaqing]* (Beijing: PLA Publishing House, 2004).
14 Nan Li, *Chinese Civil-Military Relations in the Post-Deng Era* (Newport, RI: USNWC China Maritime Studies, 2010), 6.
15 Kennedy, *The Rise and Fall of the Great Powers,* 210–11.
16 Paine, *The Sea and Civilisation,* 533–4; Lavery, *The Conquest of the Oceans,* 279; Maxtone-Graham, John, *The North Atlantic Run* (London: Cassell, 1972), 83–118.
17 John Maxtone-Graham, *The North Atlantic Run* (London: Cassell, 1972), 27.
18 Lavery, *The Conquest of the Oceans,* 285.
19 Weir, Gary E. and Boyne Walter J. Boyne, *Rising Tide: The Untold Story of the Russian Submarines that Fought the Cold War* (New York: Perseus Books, 2003), 3, 5, 129–30, 202.
20 Gorshkov, *The Sea Power of the State,* 132.

21 Mawdsley, Evan 'The Russian Navy in the Gorshkov Era,' in O'Brien, Phillips Payson (Ed), *Technology and Naval Combat in the Twentieth Century and Beyond* (London: Frank Cass, 2001), 174–5; particularly Rear-Admiral N.P. V'yunenko. See Robert Weinland, 'Developments in Soviet Naval strategy,' in Pay, John and Till, Geoffrey, *East-West Relations in the 1990s: The Naval Dimension* (London: Pinter Publishers, 1990), 139–46.

22 Polmar, *Admiral Gorshkov,* 142–51. Gorshkov, *The Seapower of the State* (London: Brasseys, 1979). James McConnell then of the Center for Naval Analyses, Washington was the leading exponent of this arcane art.

23 Gorshkov, *The Sea Power of the State,* op cit,70.

24 Kennedy, *The Rise and Fall of the Great Powers,* 212.

25 Glanz, James and Nilsen, Thomas, 'A Deep-Diving Sub, a deadly Fire and Russia's Secret Undersa Agenda,' *New York Times,* 21 April 2020.

26 Hennessy, Michael, 'Fleet Replacement and the Crisis of Identity,' in Hadley, Michael L., Huebert, Rob and Crickard Fred W. (Eds), *A Nation's Navy: In Quest of Canadian Naval Identity* (Montreal: McGill-Queen's University Press, 1996), 133.

27 Hennessey, Michael A., 'Fleet replacement and the Crisis of Identity,' in Hadley (Ed), *A Nation's Navy,* 134, 145–7.

28 David Bercuson, quoted in Drent, Jan, '"A Good, Workable Little Fleet": Canadian Naval Policy 1945, 1950,' in Hadley (Ed), *A Nation's Navy,* 206.

29 Quoted in Haydon, Peter, 'Sailors, Admirals and Politicians: The Search for Identity After the War,' in ibid, 224.

30 Hadley, *A Nation's Navy,* 7.

31 See below. *Netherlands Defence Doctrine* (Den Haag: Defensie Staf, 2005).

32 This is a consistent theme in Goldrick, James, *No Easy Answers* (New Delhi: Lancer Publishers, 1997), 8, 16.

33 Goldrick, *No Easy Answers,* 30–1.

34 Sakhuja, *Asian Maritime Power,* 35–64.

35 These were explored in ibid, 215–50, Roy, *War in the Indian Ocean,* 124–33, and Menon, Rear-Adm, *Maritime Strategy and Continental Wars* (London: Frank Cass, 1998), 171–207.

36 Goldrick, *No Easy Answers,*111–13.

37 Roy, *War in the Indian Ocean,* 5.

38 Goldrick, *No Easy Answers,* 47.

39 Goldrick, *No Easy Answers,* 157.

40 Ibid, 20.

41 Ibid, 29; Roy, *War in the Indian Ocean,* 81–9.

42 Roy-Chaudhury, Rahul, *India's Maritime Security* (New Delhi: Knowledge World for IDSA, 2000), 144–5.

43 Roy, *War in the Indian Ocean,* 114–23.

44 Roy-Chaudbury, Rahul, *Sea Power and Indian Security* (London: Brasseys, 1995), 87–133.

45 Colombage, Jayanath, *Asymmetric Warfare at Sea: The Case of Sri Lanka* (Saarbrucken, Germany: Lambert Academic Publishing, 2015); Goldrick, *No Easy Answers,* 178–92. I am grateful to Captain Rohan Joseph, SLN, for his help on this point.

46 Cole, Bernard D., *Asian Maritime Strategies: Navigating Troubled Waters* (Annapolis, MD: Naval Institute Press, 2013), 156–7.

47 Roy, *War in the Indian Ocean,* op cit, 114–23.

48 Rahmat, Ridzwan, 'Bangladesh receives two refurbished Type 035 submarines from China,' *Jane's Defence Weekly,* 15 November 2016.

49 This useful distinction is in Gordon (1996), 580.

50 Dhowan, R.K., Admiral (approving authority); Chief of Naval Staff, "Ensuring Secure Seas: Indian Maritime Security Strategy, Indian Navy: National Security Publication (NSP 12), Ministry of Defence, 10 October 2015: Joseph F. Dunford, General, US Marine Corps, Commandant of the Marine Corps, Jonathan W. Greenert, Admiral, Chief of Naval Operations, Paul F. Zukunft, Admiral US Coast Guard, Commandant of the US Coast Guard, *A Cooperative Strategy for 21st Century Seapower: Forward, Engaged Ready,* March 2015; 'Russian Federation Marine Doctrine' Press Release, Office of the President of the Russian Federation, 26 July 2015 on amendments to the 2001 Doctrine; Vice Admiral R.C. Wijegunaratne, *Sri Lanka Navy's Maritime Strategy 2025,* Colombo, 2016.

51 *Fundamentals of Maritime Operations: Netherlands Maritime Military Doctrine* (The Hague: Defence Staff, 2014).
52 Sebastian Sprenger, 'The Pros of a National Military Strategy "For Everyone to see",' *Defense News,* 10 October 2016.
53 See Wills, Steve, *Strategy Shelved: The Collapse of Cold War Naval Strategic Planning* (Annapolis, MD: Naval Institute Press, 2021).
54 Prins, Gwynthian, 'Si Vis Pacem, Para Bellum? The Royal Navy's next date with destiny is coming,' *Naval Review,* November 2019. I would like to thank the author and the Editor of the *Naval Review* for permission to use this quotation.
55 Roy, *War in the Indian Ocean,* op cit, vii.
56 Marsetio, Adm (Ret) Prof Dr, *Archipelago Leadership* (Citereup, Indnesia: Defence University, 2019).
57 For the airpower perspective of the US Air Force on this, see Alan J. Vick, *Proclaiming Airpower: Air Force Narratives and American Public Opinion from 1917 to 2014* (Santa Monica, CA: RAND Corporation, 2015).
58 Quoted in March, William A., 'A Canadian Departure: The Evolution of HMCS Royal Roads, 1854–1948,' in Hadley (Ed), *A Nation's Navy,* 301.

8 All of One Maritime Company: The Search for Synergy

Merchant and Fishing Fleets-Constituent Parts of the Sea Power of the State.
—Admiral Sergei Gorshkov[1]

8.1 Introduction: The Concept of Maritime Synergy

'The very nature of our operating environment,' said the then US Chief of Naval Operations in 2020, 'requires shared common values and a collective approach ...' The occasion, the Regional Seapower Symposium, was a gathering of 34 Chiefs of Navy and other senior representatives from 58 different navies meeting in Venice as they had done for the past 24 years. At the meeting there was a strong sense of fraternity and a recognition that common interests and common problems in providing for good order at sea made 'steady, enduring relationships more important than ever.'[2] But the Admiral was talking just about navies and about delivering multinational naval co-operation needed in one common task – Maritime Security.

Navies may be the most visible – and the most expensive – members of the maritime community, but there are others too, and the value of achieving synergy between them and navies is obvious and always has been. This has not proved easy however. A true synergy between the elements in the package depends on effective integration and that in turn requires understanding of, and compromising on, agendas, priorities and procedures that inevitably differ. In the next chapter, how this relates to coastguards and other agencies and instruments of law enforcement will be considered. This one, though, will review the other three chief components of the maritime community, namely the merchant shipping industry, the fishing industry but first the ship-building industry and the role of the Maritime Defence Industrial Base (MDIB).

Not for nothing did Henry Maydman extend his naval speculations to what he called the 'oeconomy,' incorporating the manufacturing, fishing and shipping ('navigation') industries. Noting the tensions between state and private yards, Maydman was well aware that these maritime interests could conflict.[3] He insisted they be 'brought under one Interest...like a well-twisted cord, made up of many threads, although some thereof were not of any strength themselves, yet by their near conjunction...acquireth a considerable strength.'[4] The same call has been made many times over the centuries. Underlining its critical importance, for example, the first of the four chapters in Admiral Gorshkov's book about the navy he commanded, a sizeable proportion of the whole, is devoted to the non-naval parts of the overall Soviet maritime package.

DOI: 10.4324/9781003100553-8

8.2 The Ship-Building Industry, the Wider MDIB and the Development of Maritime Power

There is these days a near-universal desire to set up ship-building and a wider set of defence industrial capabilities – or to maintain them if they already exist. This is certainly true in South America and India, respectively, where efforts to do so illustrate both the perceived importance of the task and some of the methods employed. The problems are equally clear.

8.2.1 South American and Indian Case Studies

Brazil sees an MDIB as an essential part of its wider maritime economy, the so-called Blue Amazon project.[5] Like many other countries, Brazil's strategy for developing its MDIB comprises cooperation with foreign suppliers (such as through its recent acquisition of the Royal Navy's HMS *Ocean* helicopter carrier[6]), guided domestic building and maintenance and indigenous construction both public and private. PROSUB the project to build four of Brazil's version of the Scorpene French diesel submarine and eventually a nuclear-propelled submarine is central to this aspiration.[7] Based at the new Itagui Naval Complex near Rio de Janeiro, this very ambitious project involves massive investment in infrastructure. The programme is also designed to have 'a multiplier effect' for all sectors thereby contributing to social development of the economy. The production of hundreds of high-value technologists and increased collaboration between national companies will stimulate the MDIB and the whole economy with the training of hundreds of engineers and technicians, in addition to the collaboration of national companies, high-value-added technology and trained professionals that stimulate the Defense Industrial Base and contribute to social and economic development.[8] The Complex is a subsidiary of the French 'Naval Group' and the Brazilian conglomerate Odebrecht. Alongside this, the Naval Arsenal in Rio de Janeiro maintains and modifies foreign supplied platforms and independently builds its own naval platforms, currently the *Tamandare* corvettes. Sadly, this effort has long been plagued by the less than stellar performance of the Brazilian economy and by factionalised politics which all too often combine to produce the infamous *cointingenciamento* – sudden major withdrawals of governmental financial support resulting in substantial 'black holes' in budgets already too dominated by personnel expenses.[9]

The *Armada de Chile* faces a wider range of requirements than do many others. Its constituent coastguard service is wholly responsible for the maintenance of good order at sea over an area four times its land territory and which includes Easter Island. Moreover it has to cope with a wide range of weather conditions including those of the fjord waters of the South, the potentially ferocious seas around Cape Horn and Antarctica and the open Pacific ocean. Clearly wanting to avoid being relegated to a coastal navy centred on OPVs, the Navy's top priority is the maintenance of its eight strong war-fighting frigate force and its submarine and amphibious forces which provide Chile with global options to contribute to the sea-based trading system on which the country depends. Able more than most to define its needs independently, it has long enjoyed some financial security through its institutional access to the proceeds of the sale, through the state-owned CODELCO company, of the country's copper – the *Ley del Cobre* – or 'Copper law.' All the same at the start of the 21st Century its fleet was badly in need of renewal at a time when conflict with its neighbours seemed much less of an urgent concern.[10]

The solution was seen to be a combination of developing further Chile's MDIB and the judicious acquisition of second hand but good quality warships from like-minded countries, including three Type 23 frigates from the UK and two Oliver Hazard Perry based frigates from Australia. Although there was originally a clear preference for Chile being able to build its own frigates this easier alternative enabled closer and beneficial cooperation with high-quality naval partners. The Chilean Navy's 200-year history amply confirmed the dangers of letting the fleet decay; from the start in 1817 it was recognised that Chile needed to be able to overhaul, maintain and adapt its own fleet. Still that reason, in 1960 the navy reorganised its support facilities into *Astilleros y Maeanstranzaa de la Armada* (Navy Shipyards and Workshops – ASMAR). Wholly state-owned and run under an Engineering Rear-Admiral, ASMAR has three main shipyards at Valparaiso, Talcahuano and Punta Arenas and, enlisting the cooperation of the Catholic University of Santiago Engineering School, has steadily increased its capacity to handle complex over-hauls and mid-life extensions. It has also built some 50 vessels for the Navy, mostly patrol craft and auxiliaries. ASMAR's business case also rests on its export and maintenance of civilian vessels for foreign countries, the delivery of a few OPVs to Mauritius and Iceland and the maintenance of foreign warships, especially from the region. Talcahuano's ability to recover from a devastating tsunami in 2010 attests to the resilience of the Navy's solution to the task of delivering a balanced and medium-sized fleet of sufficient quality. Whether it will be able to sustain that capability with prospective changes in the price of copper and the distribution of its proceeds in a post-Covid age is more problematic, however.[11]

In striking contrast to South American experience, India has a long ship-building tradition. A shipyard in Surat was commissioned to build warships for the East India Company as early as 1635, and the current Mazagon dockyard (one of the country's big four) in 1774. All the same, in more recent times India's ship-building industry has encountered many problems. Perhaps because its biggest operators are run by a state that many would consider over-bureaucratised, India's ship-building industry has long suffered from a stultifying defence acquisition system. The Navy still relies heavily on uncompetitive State Owned Enterprises (SOEs) with low productivity and a poor record in delivering quality products on time.[12] The result is that both the Navy and the ship-builders have frequently been unable actually to spend the inadequate resources they have been provided with. This is both vexatious and uncommon elsewhere.

These institutional, supply chain and industrial weaknesses mean that the government's stress on 'Made in India' has been problematic for Navy. The recently completed Kamorta class ASW corvette programme for example resulted in too many defects, long delays and cost over-runs and a final product that has not cmpletely met the original specification.[13] Nonetheless, lessons have been learned and the overall effort will doubtless help the country develop an economically viable MDIB. Successive governments have sought. to reform a failing system, but the emphasis on 'Made in India' in recent years is showing signs of some success.[14] The government has set up its own Research and Development (R&D) bodies and tapped more effectively into the Indian University system. High levels of growth in the national economy have helped a good deal, but being in a position fully to exploit the country's vibrant IT industry remains a challenge. Nonetheless it could yield a decisive advantage for the Navy.

Successive governments have sought to compensate for indigenous weaknesses by productive reliance on foreign sources, initially the British and then the Russians.

Over-bureaucratisation has proved a problem here too but much has been gained through technological transfer and other such off-sets; foreign suppliers have long complained of the need for still more reform in this area. The Navy has nonetheless acquired many ships, weapons and sensors at 'friendship prices,' and been able to enter into joint projects such as the Brahmos hypersonic missile. It also hedges its bets by cooperation with other suppliers too, such as Israel and Italy over the Oto-Melara, France with its submarines and so on. Traditionally, India has developed real expertise in systems integration, making sure that systems bought from different suppliers work together effectively. Most commentators, however, stress that there is still room for improvement.[15]

These three national campaigns to develop a maritime defence industrial base show common levels of aspiration but also reveal some common problems. Trying to develop 'sovereign capacity' is technologically challenging and doesn't necessarily save money in the short term. So the question arises – why not buy 'off the shelf' instead? Why set up an MDIB?

8.2.2 Why Set up a Maritime Defence Industrial Base (MDIB)?

Nations have invested in an MDIB for four basic reasons. Firstly because they build and sustain the fleet, the ship-building and associated industries are and have always been central to naval development, at least since warships reached a level of sophistication and size that meant that individual groups of mariners could not build their own vessels. Since then most countries, such as those just looked at, have sought to define the kind of maritime capabilities they need and then investigated how those capabilities (ships, sensors and weapons) might be either bought off-the-shelf or built, partly or wholly at home. The latter route is often associated with the conscious creation of some kind of national ship- building plan and strategy. Sometimes these are produced with much fanfare and public consultation; sometimes quietly and behind closed doors. Sometimes, though, not at all.

India's critics have long claimed that successive governments have lacked any kind of broad maritime vision of the sort discussed in Chapters 4 and 5. Instead of deriving from the ability to think and plan strategically, they say, it has been shocked into sometimes temporary existence by sudden escalations of threat. It may be that the appearance of the Chinese Navy into the Indian Ocean has had just that effect and concentrated minds wonderfully.[16] If so, this weakness is by no means confined to India.

A nation's capacity to build and sustain the fleet by the efforts of its own MDIB reduces its vulnerability to military pressure from foreign suppliers, especially in times of crisis and war. Hence the desire of so many contemporary nations to develop and maintain a 'sovereign' ship-building capacity. The more self-sufficient it is, moreover, the less likely it is to be subject to commercial interruptions in the supply chain or to outside political pressure in the form of arms embargoes and sanctions. However a reliance on others for essential components, such as micro-processors these days, can still prove a major vulnerability. This encourages more expanded concepts of what a MDIB requires.

Thirdly, a secure domestic ship-building capacity provides a country with resilience against sudden, unexpected shocks and needs in the future. Accordingly, the Australian *Naval Shipbuilding and Repair Sector Strategic Plan* of 2002 summarised the aim like this:

Our self-reliant defence cannot be assured unless the capabilities exist in Australian industry to maintain, modify, upgrade and repair our warships. As the facilities, equipment and skills needed to build new warships could be vitally important if our strategic circumstances were to deteriorate, these are important long-term strategic assets.[17]

Such sudden unanticipated demands are common, especially in times of war. After the disaster at the Battle of Coronel on the 1st November 1914, the British Admiralty had to send two of its battlecruisers, HM Ships, *Invincible* and *Inflexible* out to the South Atlantic to deal with Admiral von Spee's Asiatic squadron. Just four days were allowed for refit and supply and the two ships duly left Devonport dockyard on schedule, even with bricklayers still on board repairing the boilers. Similarly prodigious efforts were required to fit out the British Task force when also proceeding to the Falklands in 1982. An American example was the repair of the battered carrier USS *Yorktown* in 48 hours after the battle of the Coral Sea and before that of Midway.[18] A strong MDIB helps develop such resilience.

Finally a domestic MDIB is often thought as we have seen to benefit the national economy, through the prospects for employment that it offers, through its beneficial spin-off into other sectors of the economy, through saving the foreign exchange costs of buying equipment from abroad, and, indeed, through the possible profits of arms exports. Since the government, and sometimes regime survival, depend on economic prosperity and high levels of gainful employment these are powerful incentives to support a MDIB, especially in political systems based on voter satisfaction. Late 19th Century Britain is a good example of this economic spill-over showing that the MDIB could play a substantial and constructive role in the national economy. It is suggested that by 1897 one worker in six depended on some form of naval contracting.[19]

Whether, economically this is a good thing remains however, a matter of some controversy amongst economists. The dispute arises through differing calculations about the relative benefits of investing effort and money into defence as opposed to civilian manufacturing. Sceptics point to a possibly increasing divergence between military and civilian needs and wonder how valid the concept of 'dual use technology' really is. They argue that advocates of investing in defence seem often to assume that everyone else in the economy is 'living up trees and eating nuts,' as one Australian group described it. That is, everyone else was engaging in much less ambitious manufacturing enterprise. Instead, they say, purely civilian advanced industry could well produce more spin-off benefits than defence related enterprises. Supporters counter that it is precisely the challenge of having to deal with increasingly complex technological challenges in the production of 21st Century platforms, sensors and weapons that makes them so valuable; you are much more likely to produce advanced and possibly unexpected technical spin-offs from a factory making modern anti-ship missiles than from one producing washing machines.[20] And so on. Nothing in economics, it seems, is simple.

Developing and maintaining an MDIB however, is difficult and tends to become more so as the sophistication and intrinsic costs of its product rise. Two main problems arise.

The first is the problem of developing a knowledge base sufficient to develop and maintain sovereign ship-building and related industrial capacity. A common contemporary though partial solution to this is to seek some form of technology transfer as part of any arms deal with foreign manufacturers. Historically, this could be done simply by importing large numbers of skilled workmen from abroad. In the 17th and 18th Centuries, France, Russia, Sweden and Prussia all brought in artisans and managers from the Low Countries to help set up and develop national arms industries. Sometimes this kind of support was extended for strategic reasons. Before the First World War, Britain and France provided such aid to Russia as a means of defending all three against Germany.[21]

These days foreign suppliers from abroad are typically expected to train the locals in how to operate the equipment they have bought, how to maintain it and in the longer term to develop its replacement requirements. In effect the foreign supplier may be helping the recipient start on a journey to much greater level of industrial self-reliance. Typically, this moves on from buying a foreign warship, to maintaining it, to assembling it domestically from foreign-made parts, to building it domestically with help, and finally to designing its replacement, constructing it and eventually upgrading it themselves – all to varying and hopefully increasing degree. The process can be helped by tapping into the expertise of the wider national economy, including the university research sector. Limited strengths in these areas and excessive security concerns about opening the military up to outside scrutiny can be a real disadvantage here.

Finally, the necessary expertise can simply be stolen, either through a process of reverse engineering foreign products already obtained by various means or through outright industrial espionage. The problem with this method of catching-up is that it tends to antagonise the more advanced supplier who may respond punitively. The Russians, stung by previous Chinese success in reverse engineering and then selling cheaper versions of Russian designs abroad, have now become noticeably wary of helping the Chinese solve their continuing aero-engine problem for example.

A second source of difficulty in developing an MDIB is the inevitably less than complete convergence of interest between the arms supplier and the customer. At one level different building standards apply to military and civilian ship-building and manufacturers may find it difficult to handle both.[22] Manufacturers will also want a steady drumbeat so that they can avoid the 'valleys of death' in which a temporary absence of orders means they have to lay off their trained and skilled work-people and cut back on their plant, before (possibly) starting all over again at some later date. 'Without consistent and continuing commitment to steady and predictable acquisition profiles,' warned the US Senate Armed Services Committee in 2020,' the industrial base will struggle and some elements will not survive.'[23] Recovering neglected infrastructure and workforce skills takes time and money, especially when dockyards or shipbuilders have closed altogether. The same goes for the vendor base providing supplies to the shipyards, moreover.

On the other hand, the customer may think all that is properly the manufacturer's problem not the government's; instead the government may want to preserve its budgetary flexibility and focus on alternate uses of government finance (perhaps for health or social welfare). More basically still, private manufacturers will want to make a profit while governments will want to reduce costs. This explains why some would advocate bringing back formerly closed public shipyards. 'If the Navy and the nation want a stronger shipbuilding base,' warned Captain Sam Tangredi in 2020, 'we need to bring back the construction capabilities of public (Navy) shipyards.'[24] Relying on private investment for specialist manufacturing from the market when so much more profit could be made through backing real estate or software companies would not work.

These problems are particularly acute for the world's smaller and medium navies. Their more limited means and inability to exploit economies of scale mean they cannot hope to maintain the kind of MDIB that can cover the full range of possibilities that the bigger fry are coping with. The more energetic of them respond in various ways. Some like Israel[25] focus on the much narrower range of strategic requirements they face and are well aware of the market appeal of their specialised products to other small and medium navies. While relying on extensive help from Germany for its Sa'ar corvettes and Dolphin and Dakar class submarines, Israel for example builds its own advanced Reshef class OPVs and has developed sufficient missile expertise in its Gabriel missile programme to be able to sell its products to other countries. Their quality is impressive enough to warrant complaints from Russia when sold to its neighbour, Finland.[26]

Others also look to invest in niche projects that could also appeal to the bigger and better-endowed navies too, such as the Norwegian *Penguin* anti-ship missile. Still others focus on simpler less ambitious projects as a starting point for more ambitious aspirations later on. Colombia's COTECMAR shipbuilding enterprise is a good example of this, using its long experience in riverine patrol vessels as a basis for future endeavours.[27]

Fast becoming very capable, the South Korean Navy has based its advance on the experience and resources gained from what has developed into an impressively capable commercial ship-building sector. It is now a significant exporter, building supply ships for the Royal Navy, submarines for Indonesia, and LPDs for Myanmar and Peru.

The converse of all this is that countries without such a productive MDIB find their acquisition choices constrained and their autonomy limited.

8.2.3 Setting Up a Maritime Defence Industrial Base

Aware of both the attraction and the problems of setting up an MDIB, governments can approach the task it in two ways, and usually oscillate uneasily between them, as both approaches have advantages and disadvantages. Firstly they can invest in the MDIB directly by setting up state owned enterprises, (SOEs). SOEs tend to be slower, less innovative and productive, as in India where it commonly takes five years rather than three to build a frigate. On the other hand, if there's an acceptable drumbeat the longer build time may not be critical. SOEs are safe and reliable and their often larger if perhaps less productive workforces bring wider benefits to the economy. Less inhibited by commercial sensitivities, they also allow closer relations between customer and supplier. For such reasons, the British were one of the last to abandon the idea of protecting a state monopoly in the design and manufacture of guns and shells, principally at London's Woolwich arsenal.[28] The temptation to protect sovereign capability in this way, moreover remains strong, in part strengthened by a rise in economic nationalism and concern about supply-side reliability in the wake of the Covid pandemic.

Alternatively, governments can stand clear of industry and leave as much as possible to the free market. A vigorous navy construction programme will hopefully incentivise private industrial entrepreneurs to supply its needs, compete with each other and engage in constructive technological innovation. This market-driven approach tends to appeal to governments who want to have more capable navies but either don't have the resources to invest directly in a MDIB or who, ideologically don't think they should intervene in the economy more than they have to.

The advantage of this latter approach is that, shaped by the necessity to compete in the domestic and international markets, private entrepreneurs are often thought to be more agile and innovative and so able to offer a bottom-up and more cost-effective product. London's Woolwich arsenal for example was constrained in its ability to export and so depended on the Royal Navy as its single naval customer. In part because of this, it could not cope with gunnery innovations, such as the use of steel pioneered by private concerns like Armstrong and, in Germany, Krupps.[29] Thereafter, Woolwich largely developed and put into practice other peoples' ideas. This kind of thing has led to the widespread idea, right or wrong, that 'command innovation' is an oxymoron.

On the other hand, private enterprises need to make a profit for their shareholders, and this may create tensions with the customer and skew the project, certainly as far as cost is concerned. The experience of Imperial Spain illustrates some of the standard problems of relying on private contractors. Going out to charter, rather than simply relying on royal shipyards, offered the unscrupulous opportunities for fraud, made planning difficult and led to disputes over ship dimensions, and the quality of nails and other materials. It was even sometimes quicker, easier and cheaper to buy things from the enemy.[30] Mutual suspicions of this kind help explain why in the early 19th Century, '[c]ordial dislike prevailed between private arms makers and their official customers in every country of Europe.'[31]

Moreover simply passing the risk down to private contractors may produce short and maybe long-term savings but is likely to imply diminished control and increases the adversarial component in the relationship between customer and supplier. If the rising costs of new technology mean both market and the MDIB are getting smaller, Monopsony can result, where there is essentially one customer (the government) and one supplier.[32] Clinging to each other for the illusion of safety in turbulent waters, this can be the worst of all worlds. All too often they both drown.

Success in the constructor-customer relationship seems to depend on the government and maritime defence industry treating each other as allies rather than adversaries and developing enough technically literate naval people to act as a bridge over the chasm between the navy and the business world of the manufacturer.[33] The ideal result would seem to be effective partnering between, industry, the navy customer and defence science. Either way, the development of maritime synergy depends on an effective reconciliation of divergent interests and positions.

Given the complexities, most governments adopt a third, mixed approach that compromises between the state-based or market-driven alternative approaches. One is to encourage the defence industry institutionally rather than in monetary terms. This might be by establishing bodies that are designed to facilitate cooperation between all the stakeholders such as Australian defence science organisations like the Weapons Systems Research Laboratory which is designed to partner the Navy, industry and defence science in research and development. The US DARPA organisation has similar aims and there are many other such agencies, world-wide. Another obvious approach is the provision of direct subsidies to selected parts of private industry, often for the specified capabilities the customer wants. This is more in the historic tradition. Because Research and Development can be extremely expensive, manufacturers have often proved reluctant to invest in it without cast-iron guarantees of state support. In this way, hopefully, subsidised and otherwise supported manufacturers will gain financial security for the longer term while retaining their competitive and innovative edge as entrepreneurs.

There is little new about this. Between 1000 and 1600 says William McNeill, '... despite differences in degree, in every instance, European ventures on the oceans were sustained by a combination of public, quasi public, and relentlessly private enterprise.'[34]

Extreme positions in striking the balance between state-operated and private enterprises seem generally best avoided. Probably a happy median needs to be struck between the wild-eyed adherence to the free market of Thatcherite Britain in the 1980s on the one hand and the earlier era when China and India poured public money into their unresponsive and uncompetitive SOEs of the time

8.2.4 Problems with the Solutions

Getting the Money. These approaches all cost money and require government effort. The extent of both directly relates to the quality and nature of the platform or system. The approximate relative expense of, say, submarines to patrol craft is shown in Figure 8.1 but there are enormous quality variations in each category.

Navies are inherently expensive and the required resources may be difficult for cash-strapped countries and hard-pressed regimes to provide. The navies of even wealthy countries such as Canada have consistently suffered the consequence of governmental reluctance to invest in sustainable long-term construction projects, as the fate of the country's General Purpose Frigate programme of the 1960s pointedly illustrated.[35] Various solutions have been sought. One is for countries to restrict major investments to times of great need or when the national economy is in good shape. This may be combined with the hope that national industries can keep going in the meantime by

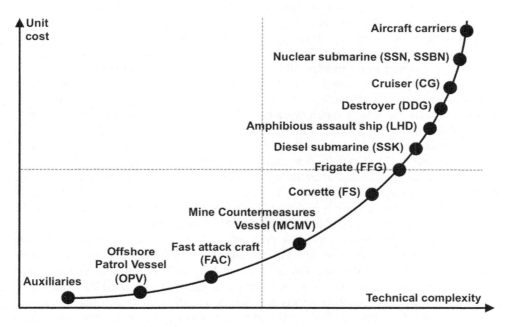

Figure 8.1 Unit Cost and Complexity.

Source: Kirchberger, Sarah, *Assessing China's Naval Power: Technological Innovation, Economic Constraints and Strategic Implications* (Heidelberg: Springer, 2015).

selling their product to other countries. Historically, this off-and-on model increases the problem of maintaining a standing navy which in turn could have unfortunate operational consequences when confronted by unexpected situations or an imaginative adversary.

Another apparent solution is for the authorities to borrow the necessary money to finance SOEs or subsidise particular firms; this assumes it is available at home or abroad and the money people consider you a good bet. In 1694, the English realised the advantages of an efficient mechanism for the management of credit and a set of sympathetic money-people and so set up the Bank of England, a notable step forwards in the financing of war. This gave King William and his successors what turned out to be a permanent strategic advantage over France, and greatly facilitated the subsequent development of British maritime power.[36]

All too often though, financial support from the government varies over time in consequence of domestic or international change and so does not provide the long-term support that manufacturers crave. Australian experience illustrates this well. The Australian Government recognised that in trying to wean the Navy from excessive reliance on British equipment, heavy investment in its fledgling national MDIB of up to 45% of total cost in 1972 would be necessary – running down to 25% after five years.[37] But the Government soon started backing off from this level of support and by 1988, with a much improving strategic outlook, decided that 'there is no priority for using Defence funds to sustain non-Defence capacity for ship-building and ship-repair in excess of that capable of existing on a commercial basis.'[38] The return of great power competition over the past two decades however, has prompted another reversal of course with much higher levels of government commitment now assured. Coping with the consequences of this kind of contextual change is not easy for manufacturers, but never has been.

The problem for navies and their governments on the other hand is the fact that resources are finite and the simple fact is that individual platforms are getting more expensive. In consequence and for all the talk of 21st Century navalism, the world's navies are getting smaller than they were – and this applies to the Chinese navy as much as it does to the navies of Europe.[39] Paradoxically, at the same time, their numerically diminished fleets are getting much more capable and perhaps much more important.

Compromising on Sovereignty. Finally, with the best will in the world, most countries facing the remorseless increase in the technological sophistication and cost of naval platforms, weapons and systems are unlikely ever to achieve the dizzying heights of complete sovereign manufacturing independence. Nor, for that matter, are even the biggest of manufacturing enterprises. This, therefore, requires degrees of multinational collaboration between countries and manufacturers, whether this takes the form of the mergers and acquisitions that characterised the British MDIB in the late 19th Century[40] or cooperation in particular technical projects. The bigger and more ambitious the project, the bigger the requirement. The British *Queen Elizabeth* project for example required the establishment of the Aircraft Carrier Alliance between three giants – BAE Systems, Babcock and Thales along with heavy engagement by the UK Ministry of Defence. In their Type 31 Frigate programme, the British have also discovered the benefits, in cost, time and quality, on the imaginative use of the well-established characteristics of foreign-built ships, such as the Danish *Ivor Huitfelt* on which it is based.[41] These days this kind of collaboration is particularly marked when the hull is outfitted with systems, weapons and sensors which can come from a multitude of sources.

Inevitably, these multinational solutions bring their own problems with them. The particularity of individual countries and their navies makes a compromise between their differing requirements demanding even between those with long habits of co-operation such as the Scandinavians.[42] The history of multinational naval construction is littered with projects that have foundered on the uniqueness of the participants.

Complexities, complications and dilemmas accordingly follow as night succeeds day, because, inevitably and however skilfully arranged, these arrangements limit the independence of all the stakeholders. Four sometimes long-standing problems stand out.

The first is the extent to which foreign concerns should be allowed to invest in the commanding heights of the defence economy. Generally their money and often their special expertise is welcomed but their operational control isn't, since this could limit the government's future freedom of action in times of trial.

Secondly, special protection for key MDIB enterprises might prove hard to reconcile with the demand for 'a level playing field' that is characteristic of international free-trade deals since these often assume an absence of 'unfair' state subsidy. Such deals might nevertheless be very good for the general economy. This therefore once more raises the issue of just how important the MDIB is when compared to the rest of the economy.

This is not an easy calculation to make and is often quite scenario dependent. For example, when the Cold War ended and a substantial 'peace dividend' was expected, new orders dried up and European warship-building capacity significantly exceeded likely domestic demand. Exports took up some of the slack but there was much discussion about how best the defence industry both nationally and across Europe could be rationalised and in effect made smaller but sustainable. Now, with the return of great power competition, such rationalisation tends to mean smarter rather than smaller, better able to take on large scale US, Russian and Chinese competition. Illustrating the point, there is now a much more energetic desire to rescue Defence Research and Development (R&D) from the lamentably low rate of investment characteristic of more optimistic times.

Thirdly, and this is a point hammered home by the Covid-19 pandemic, relying on other manufacturers in other countries for such essentials as semiconductors and other widgets in microelectronics means accepting risk in supply chain resilience, leaving governments open to exactly the kind of exposure to adverse circumstances or to malign intent that their whole objective is to avoid.

All this assumes that statesmen-like and business-like people are more in control of events than often proves to be the case. Very often, unyielding political considerations intrude and make ideal solutions impractical.

Technological change, even more, can prove a policy driver, changing relationships and priorities between people, governments, navies designers and manufacturers, even determining outcomes. Technical developments in Europe's middle ages that increased a ship's capacity to operate in rough and even winter weather, for example, meant that there was no off-season and so changed the way that navies operated and had to be maintained and funded by the government. Technology has also played a key role in differentiating between warships and merchant ships and that has profoundly altered the relationship between navies and merchant fleets as will be discussed shortly.

This process accelerated with the 'Gunpowder revolution' from the 14th Century, starting a process which began with the expectation that weapons should be fitted to, and so shaped by, ships and ended with the reverse – that ships should be shaped around the weapons and sensors they were to carry.[43] Indeed nowadays with the growth of technological networking, cyber-operations, space power and so on, the platform itself is becoming much less central a concern in the design of fleets than it once was. These days, perhaps even more than in the past, it is more a question of the MDIB responding to technological change than of being in charge of it.

The question that follows on from that, is which aspects of technological change were, are or should be prioritised? Much depends on the circumstances of the time. In Maydman's day, the areas of particular interest were ship design and naval gunnery. These days, as we move into what is often referred to as the 'Fourth Industrial Revolution,'[44] the Chinese and Americans seem increasingly preoccupied by Artificial Intelligence and Quantum Computing and the huge military advantages they offer through data connectivity and utilisation. But there are other related candidates too, including space, cyber, biotech, robotics, automated systems, hypersonics and directed energy; the list is endless, and many of them, on their own or in combination, are said to represent such a transformational change as to amount to yet another 'Revolution in Military Affairs.'[45] Plainly the successful development of maritime power will always depend on getting the technology right.

Several conclusions emerge. Firstly and most obviously, countries with a strong and innovative MDIB are best placed to take advantage of these opportunities; countries without one will either remain stuck in some previous and now vulnerable 'metal-bashing' era or compromise their sovereignty by relying on others. Secondly, the fact that there is so much uncertainty about which technological opportunities are best followed and integrated[46] suggests the importance of investing in some kind of 'technological horizon scanning' institutions to provide policy guidance. Thirdly, the free-wheeling nature of the 4IR would seem to highlight the need to accommodate agile, high-tech companies that tend to be impatient with the red tape and tedious procedures all too characteristic of government business.[47] Finally, all this seems to underline the reducing centrality of straight forwards ship-building industry and the need to take a more holistic view of the MDIB of the 21st Century.[48]

8.2.5 *Need for an Industrial Strategy*

For all these reasons, developing a wider MDIB is important. 'Industrial capacity' remarks Sarah Kirchberger, 'must indeed be considered the decisive factor in conventional wars.'[49] It is also a complex issue. It needs conscious consideration, active decision and a strategic approach. This lies behind the increasing calls for, and acceptance of, the need for an industrial strategy for the creation, development or maintenance of an MDIB even in the most fundamentalist of free-market economies. The issue also demonstrates the extent to which such decisions both depend on, and help shape, the nature of its government and society. Navies, and their industrial appurtenances, really do reflect the nature of the state and society; developing navies requires developing them too.

8.3 The Merchant Shipping Industry

8.3.1 *Introduction*

Henry Maydman had no doubt that the merchant shipping industry was an essential part of the maritime affair for the reasons outlined in Chapter 2. Merchant shipping enriched the country and, through taxation, the government. It built up sea-mindedness amongst the population. It provided an obvious incentive to develop a navy to defend shipping but also supplied many of the resources (sailors, ports, hulls, shipyards, financial structures) that would help the Navy do so. Accordingly, he wanted the government to support so essential a part of the maritime company. The requirement to 'maintain a great navigation' should be factored into the country's economic and foreign policies, in peace time as in war.[50]

8.3.2 *The Traditional Narrative*

In this, Maydman was reflecting the traditional narrative about the importance of the merchant shipping industry in the development of maritime power. In the case of his own country, it helped change Britain from a gaggle of off-shore islands into a global superpower, a process that began perhaps with the arrival there of the Genoese in the 1270s.[51] Thereafter, in peace and war, the navy and the merchant navy were locked into mutual dependence, a relationship made crystal clear by the experience of the First and Second World Wars. The Falklands war of 1982 underlined the point.

In that conflict, the Royal Navy task force was supported by 52 merchant ships from 33 different companies, all 'ships taken up from trade' (STUFT); 22 Royal Fleet Auxiliary (RFA) ships and two Royal Maritime Auxiliary ships supported the operation as well. The STUFT ships included tankers, repair ships, tugs, auxiliary aircraft and helicopter carrying ships (one of which, the *Atlantic Conveyor* was lost), stores ships, ferries and cruise liners. Many of them had to be very rapidly modified for military use in what was both a triumph of effort and improvisation and a speaking demonstration of the strategic value of a sufficiently vibrant shipyard industry.

The conversion of the ferry *St Edmund* was typical. In Devonport, two helicopter flight decks were fitted, her four diesel engines were modified to take marine diesel rather than her normal heavy fuel oil and her bow doors were welded shut against the rough weather to be expected in the South Atlantic. These were only the more obvious changes. 'She appeared,' wrote her Second Officer, Louis Roskell, 'as though she was being rebuilt.' New wiring, cabin conversions, heavy duty windscreen wipers – everything needed to be adapted.[52] Not everything was foreseen; on some ships, naval lighting plugs would not fit merchant navy sockets, so replenishment at sea after dark had sometimes to be done by torchlight, which was not ideal.

The crews and their procedures had to adapt too. Merchant ship complements were generally lower and had to be supplemented by Royal Navy and Royal Fleet Auxiliary (RFA) personnel; larger complements meant less room for everyone but also required more cooks. Inevitably there were frictions over different service conditions and expectations.[53] Both sides had to learn each other's ways, when exercising helicopter operations, darkening ships, anti-submarine zig-zagging and so forth. The RFA, used to working with the Navy, was especially useful in bridging the gap between the military and civilian worlds, and of course were more immediately available when the Task Force first sailed south. For all the problems, though, the experience showed that indeed the operation could not have been successfully concluded without the use of (semi) civilian shipping. 'My contention is,' concluded one Member of Parliament (from a port city, admittedly), 'that the merchant navy should be regarded as an essential part of Britain's defence strategy.'[54]

To the extent that accessible civilian shipping is either unavailable or unsuited to military requirements, the world's maritime communities increasingly lament that the logistical side of the naval business will might prove much harder to deliver unless extraordinary efforts are made.

8.3.3 *Challenges to the Traditional View*

Nonetheless, the difficulties encountered also underlined emerging challenges to traditional thinking about the relationship between navies and the merchant shipping industry. In the first place, over the years the widening technical divergence between warships and merchant ships has reduced the cross-over between them, especially in their hull construction.[55] Moreover, much of the fleet had switched from conventional break-bulk cargo ships to less militarily useful container ships that require specialised loading/unloading facilities.

Such developments made it seem more cost-effective for navies to maintain an expandable fleet train of supply and transport ships specifically designed to support naval operations, such as those of the RFA or the US Sealift Command, rather than rely on the conversion of commercially operated shipping.

In any case, by 1982, market developments had already drastically reduced the extent to which some of the traditional naval powers (such as the US and the UK) commanded sizeable merchant fleets. Instead, shipping companies were 'flagging out' to much cheaper and often laxer supervising states and operators. While not impossible, chartering foreign-owned and operated vessels was, and remains, more complicated and more expensive. The particularly drastic 40% reduction in the British merchant fleet from 1975 also led to a reduction in the number of national personnel available to crew the ships in 1982.[56] Merchant service people in the Falklands Task Force were all volunteers. Paradoxically, the decline in the British merchant fleet up to then was helpful, since many of these volunteers evidently decided that service in the Falklands operation was better than being unemployed, if only marginally in some cases.[57] This decline in the national flag fleet did not necessarily mean a corresponding lack of maritime interest since much of this had shifted into the maritime service industries (insurance, brokerage, maritime law etc) such that London has remained the centre of the global shipping world. But while still offering indirect support for Maydman's 'maritime affair,' this was in 1982, and would be today, of limited direct value for the actual conduct of naval operations.

8.3.4 *Differing Conclusions*

The continued relevance of the capacity to transport large numbers of people, and more significantly their equipment and supplies by sea was subsequently reinforced by the experience of the Balkan, Iraq and Afghan wars. Moreover, the temporary blockage of the Suez canal in March 2021 reminded the world of the continued strategic importance of the capacity to transport goods and people safely and expeditiously by sea.[58] To a degree, there has also been a slight reduction in the rate of decline of Western merchant shipping fleets, which in the British case resulted from the introduction of a 'tonnage tax' introduced in 2000. But complexities in the requisitioning/chartering of British-flagged but foreign-owned ships, or those flagged to British dependencies remain; moreover, the steep decline in the number of British seafarers has continued, despite much political protestation of countervailing effort. Taken together these points do not mean that the shipping industry has completely lost its military value, merely that it is increasingly in different hands.

Nor does it mean that, even in its diminished state in some Western countries, the merchant shipping interest has altogether lost its capacity to influence society and government/naval policy. For the general population the mantra 'no shipping, no shopping' still has some resonance while the influence of companies such as Maersk on Danish (naval) policy remains significant. 21st Century outbreaks of piracy in the Straits of Malacca, off Somalia, in the Gulf of Guinea, and the occasional terror-related incident have reminded many that the protection of shipping is basically a role for navies, whether they like it or not.[59] The Chinese navy certainly seems to appreciate this and has done so from the very start in 1949, one of the earliest signs, incidentally, that China would eventually become much more maritime.[60]

China now operates the world's second-largest merchant fleet, much of it state owned. Moreover the country's recent policy document *Technical Standards for New Civilian Ships To Implement National Requirement* directs design requirements that comply with naval needs.[61] The Chinese have evidently concluded that despite modern developments, the merchant shipping industry retains sufficient strategic value to demand its effective integration into the national effort.[62] Many would argue that this is in strong contrast to the policy adopted in the United States and have lamented its possible consequences.[63] Moreover, the advent of miniaturised and modularised sensor and weapons systems means that, merchant ship hulls may well actually regain strategic value in an age when there is growing interest in the idea of 'distributed lethality' and the diffusion of naval power among much larger numbers of smaller and/or more dispensable platforms.

Nor is this a concern just for the greater maritime powers. In their differing ways the smallest of states like Singapore and Djibouti have very deep interests in maritime shipping and in its successful and innovative use auxiliary ship *Bunga Mas Lima* in its counter-piracy role off Somalia, the Royal Malaysian Navy showed smaller and medium navies may even have extra incentives to exploit the wider opportunities that civilian shipping can offer.

All the same, making the best use of merchant shipping poses real challenges for there are significant differences between the two types of sea service. Reconciling these again will demand an exercise in effective integration.

8.4 The Fishing Industry

8.4.1 Introduction

'Encouraging the trade of Fishing,' Maydman thought, was essential, because it would 'advance the Naval Strength,' enrich the country and increase 'Maritime People.'[64] More than 300 years later, much of this still holds. The fishing industry can indeed be a critically important component of a country's maritime character and its economy. Moreover, it plays a significant role in the international maritime order. The challenges and changes the industry faces are, however, considerable and so are likely to have both national and global consequences. In the first place, fishing is a dangerous and demanding profession, often hovering on the brink of financial unviability despite the rising market for its products. This is especially true in Asia. Its contribution to the

GDPs of advanced industrialised economies is fast declining though increasing elsewhere. The fishing industry's potential for developing countries is particularly significant.[65] The vast majority of the world's overall fishing fleet is now in Asian, and especially Chinese, hands. Although less than it was at its peak in 2013, the Chinese fishing fleet, at some 864,000 vessels, comprises nearly a third of Asia's overall fishing fleet but also rivals the rest of the world's fishing fleet put together.[66] 85% of the world's fishers are Asian.

But even here there are substantial doubts about the industry's long-term sustainability, certainly at the current level of fish-take. A third of the world ocean, not least the northern part of the South China Sea is effectively 'fished-out.' This forces fishers to operate further afield. Hence the particular rise of large distant water fishing fleets, where once again China has taken a commanding lead. The result is flotillas sometimes of several hundred vessels operating in distant waters on an industrial scale with accompanying processing, refrigerating, refuelling/supply ships; this is an especially notable sign of increased competition for fast declining stocks nearer home. These fleets threaten the livelihoods of local fishers, raise international tensions and threaten the marine environment. Generally, though they serve very little, if any, direct military purpose.[67]

The effects of unsustainable levels of fish-take are further aggravated by the effects of climate change and rising levels of marine pollution. Paradoxically, the consequences of all this force desperate fishermen to resort to operational methods such as the taking of protected species making the situation still worse. Scientists now argue, for example, that bottom-trawling disturbs the marine sediments which are the world's largest pool of carbon storage and so releases more carbon dioxide than the global aviation industry.[68] The fishing industry, in short, is both a victim and a source of environmental damage. For that reason alone its needs taking seriously, but there are many other reasons for doing so as well.

8.4.2 Why the Fishing Industry Matters

The world's fishing interests are important for perhaps ten reasons and are indeed part of the maritime power of the state, as Admiral Gorshkov said.

Political resonance. Despite the insignificant contribution it makes to British prosperity, the fishing community still commands cultural and political significance even if only as an element in historic memory. Successive governments in Britain have been acutely sensitive to the charge that they are neglecting the fishing interest, as for example in the Brexit negotiation of 2020.[69] In Asia especially, an attentive public, empowered by the social media and sometimes animated by a resentful localism follow fishing disputes closely. For this reason and whatever their political persuasion, governments take the fishing interest seriously, and their foreign policies reflect that fact.

Fishing is a Source of Wealth. Historically, the fishing industry has made, and in some parts of the world is still making a major contribution to a country's prosperity, and indirectly to the provision of financial resources that increased its maritime power. The rise of the Hanseatic League and of the great trading regimes of the Low Countries initially owed much to wealth derived from North Sea fishing. Globally this was a common pattern, which only became less sustainable when the demands of a rising human population were set against a stable or declining fish population. This contributed to growing levels of competition between different fishing communities within countries, and between them, to declining stocks. The Icelandic-British 'cod wars' of the 20th Century and the current jurisdictional disputes in the South China Sea, are modern examples.

Delivering Food Security. The pressure of increased populations combined with reductions in the agricultural value of land through the impact of industrialisation, urban sprawl and climate change raise concern about food security in many parts of the world. Increased access to the apparently abundant resources of the world ocean can be seen as a partial solution to this problem and a means of providing food security, one of the most basic responsibilities that governments have to their people. Spurred by the social unrest over this that occurred in 2007–2008, China, for example, has accelerated the development and modernisation of its national fishing fleet that had already hugely expanded since the country's opening up in 1978.[70] Marine resources, however, are finite. The more one country takes, the less there is for everyone else, and the greater the long-term threat to sustainability.

A Community to Be Managed. Because the fishing industry can be so important economically, it represents a community of interest that has to be catered for and managed by the government whatever its political hue. Governmental responses have varied. Some, as in Britain, have largely stood aside leaving the 'market to decide' and so have presided over a process of decline in the fishing industry its advocates feel was far from graceful. Other countries do more to manage the process. China, for example, claims to be reducing the overall size of its fishing fleet whilst subsidising its more sustainable or important components.[71] Around the South China Sea, it is generally accepted that fishing capacity needs to be reduced more than it is at present and better supervised against malpractice.

A Source of Disorder at Sea. Struggling fishermen are inevitably tempted into a host of unsustainable and environmentally damaging operational practices, such as dynamite bombing, the illicit killing of protected species and the gross abuse of their own personnel. Moreover they can be complicit in various forms of serious often transnational, crime, such as arms, drugs and people smuggling, piracy (as off Somalia) and international terrorism (the attack on Mumbai in 2008). In all these ways an unsustainable fishing industry represents a significant threat to national stability and the international order. This in turn increases the need for navies and coastguards to monitor what is going on and where it is necessary to intervene in defence of national and international interests. Day to day defence of international stability against such varied threats has become a major commitment for the world's navies and coastguards.

A Possible Cause of International Tensions. Inevitably, increased competition for scarce resources leads to peacetime rivalries, tensions and potentially dangerous incidents at sea, especially when fishing boats from elsewhere are thought to be stealing the locals' fish. It is now commonplace and by no means confined to Asian waters, for fishing boats to be sunk or physically destroyed by navies and coastguards in incidents that seem likely to escalate into a real 'fish war' sooner or later. Argentina's destruction of a Chinese fishing boat in 2016 shows just how global this issue is.[72] There is little new in this, however.

A Nursery for Seamen. Historically, much of the esteem with which fishermen were often held (if usually at a considerable distance) was the common idea that they provided a 'nursery for seaman.' Henry Maydman certainly thought so and was amongst those advocating that a register of them should be kept so they could be 'called up' into the Navy if necessary. How justified this view was has been debated by historians (some believing for example that the coal and other coastal trades was much more important source of sailors for the Navy in the British case), but the real point is that it was widely thought to be true.[73] In the conduct of his North American operations in the 1740s, for example, Vice Admiral Sir Peter Warren, one of the most thoughtful sailors of his time had no doubts about the matter. He was determined to secure the '[t]he whole cod fishery, a glorious nursery for seamen upon whom the security and prosperity of Great Britain does very much depend.'[74] Certainly, an active and prosperous fishing industry made a country more maritime in its outlook, and so, indirectly at least, contributed to the naval cause. In the American War of Independence fishermen were significant in manning the small coastal craft that so annoyed the Royal Navy and in the longer term contributed to the establishment and early development of the US Navy. There is, of course, rather more doubt about the modern salience of this point. Many would argue that in today's navies the computer game industry might provide a more useful 'nursery for seamen.'

A subject for capture and attack in war. 'The number of ships,' Lord Admiral Lisle reported in November 1543, no doubt with some satisfaction, 'is...sufficient for to disturb their fishing considering that the Frenchmen neither hath nor dare set forth for the wafting [escort] of their herring fishing.'[75] This projected attack on French herring fishers was just one of countless such attacks in naval history. They were conducted because the fisheries, and such other marine industries as whaling, were seen to contribute so much to an adversary's war economy. Admiral Warren was just as keen on 'distressing' and 'annoying' the French fishing fleet in Canadian waters 200 years later.[76] Nor was he alone in such thoughts. Seizing the French fishing interest (and the fur trade as well for that matter) would, thought the Duke of Bedford, First Lord of the Admiralty, deprive the French of 'vast sums besides the means of training up of great numbers of seamen and thereby gaining a prodigious additional strength to their naval forces.' Just in case, intelligence on foreign fisheries was eagerly sought and the issue of their future disposal could be a keenly debated in subsequent peace negotiations.[77] Conversely the protection of one's own fishing fleet had high priority. For the British the defence of its Icelandic distant water fleet was always important, right up to the 1970s.

Direct Military Value. The fishing fleet could however make a much more direct and immediate military contribution at sea, however. In both world wars, trawlers acted as auxiliary mine-sweepers (as in the 1915 Dardanelles campaign) or anti-submarine surveillance vessels, or merely provided a covert means of transporting people and military material around operational theatres.

Contemporary Paramilitary Value. The increasing costs of conventional war have led in the 21st Century to a growth in interest in hybrid/grey-zone operations in the shadowlands between peace and war. Paramilitary forces pose difficult assessment and response problems for conventional naval forces and so may prove an effective means of securing national objectives short of the use of lethal force, especially when deployed in large numbers. Hence the establishment by countries like China and Vietnam of 'People's Fishing Militias.' These comprise hundreds of fishing boats especially equipped for tactical advantage in such situations, which nonetheless stop just short of imperilling their allegedly civilian status. Extra signals equipment means they can be marshalled with advantage; steel hulls help them shoulder aside less robust wooden vessels. The combination of increased competition at sea with a reluctance to engage in armed conflict is likely to increase the perceived attractions of such sneaky options.[78]

8.4.3 Managing and Integrating the Fishing Industry

The importance in so many ways of the fishing industry in maritime development is generally accepted as justifying a greater effort to manage it effectively at the national, regional and global levels. Space precludes going into what these management measures are and they are likely to take different forms in different countries. But they would seem to require systematic governmental understanding and oversight and a willingness to support the industry both financially and through legislation.

This, however, is more complicated than might at first appear. Taking China as an example, a range of issues are at stake as has been shown. (See Figure 8.2) These may compete and need to be reconciled. Moreover, China is no more a unitary actor than any other country. Accordingly, the differing combinations of interests of a number of different stakeholders have also to be reconciled. These include Party and Government institutions, the Ministry of Foreign Affairs, the Navy, the China Coast Guard and so on. Local authorities also have their particular agendas, especially in the main fishing provinces of Zhejiang, Shandong, Fukien and Guangxi. Finally, the interests of the main fishing companies and the fishermen themselves have to be considered.

Nor of course, is the issue a purely national matter. The recent appearance of a large and mainly Chinese distant water fishing fleet in the purely international but environmentally fragile waters between the Galapagos marine reserve and the Ecuadorian Exclusive Economic Zone has raised world-wide concerns. These operations require delicate handling and are likely to have considerable ramifications. Proposals to turn those waters into another protected area, for example, will raise questions of supervision and enforcement and over time could have implications for the freedom of navigation for civilian and naval vessels as well as significant economic and resource consequences for all the parties concerned.

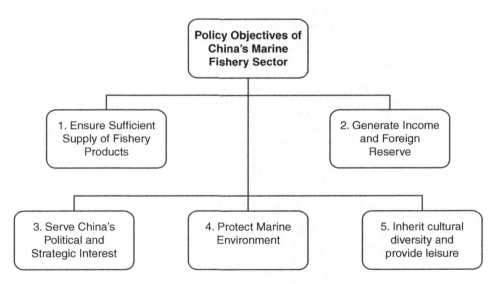

Figure 8.2 Chinese Fishing Objectives.

Source: Zhang, Hongzhou, *Securing the 'Rice Bowl': China and Global Food Security* (Singapore: Palgrave, 2019).

This underlines the need for the fishing interest to be taken seriously, for it to be considered holistically and integrated into wider policies concerning the maritime community as a whole. Maydman was very clear about this, closely linking the encouragement of fishing to the promotion of '…Navigation and the more large exportation of our manufacts to our great enrichment and security from our Enemys abroad.'[79] Countries with aspirations for maritime power clearly need to take a strategic approach to these matters and invest constructively in all aspects of their management and further development.

There is however often a large gap between theory and practice; what governments and international institutions say about the need to manage these aspects of the maritime affair and what they actually seem able to do can be very different. This problem will be considered in the next chapter.

Notes

1 Gorshkov, The Sea Power of the State, 27.
2 Toremans, Guy, 'Maintaining Peace on the Oceans is a Matter of Trust,' *Warship IFR,* January 2020, 8–9.
3 Maydman, *Naval Speculations*, 72.
4 Ibid, 267.
5 Brazilian Navy, *Bue Amazon: The Last Frontier* (Brasilia: Navy Media Center, 2013
6 Felipe Salles, 'New Era for the Brazilian Navy Off to a Flying Start,' *Warships IFR.* September 2019.
7 Scott, Richard, 'PROSUB: Building Brazil's Future Submarine Capability,' in Waters, Conrad (Ed), *World Naval Review 2020* (Barnsley, Seaforth Publishing, 2019), 184–92.
8 Navy Chief, Admiral Eduardo Leal Ferreira quoted in 'Brazilian Navy begins Final Assembly of Riachuelo S-40 Submarine in Rio,' *Naval Technology,* 22 February 2018.
9 Juliano da Silva Cortinhas, 'Brazil and the Construction of Its Power to Defend the South Atlantic,' in Duarte, Erico and Correira de Barros, Manuel (Eds), *Navies and Maritime Policies in the South Atlantic* (London, Palgrave, 2019); Tom Phillips, 'Three military chiefs quit after Bolsonaro fires defence minister,' *The Guardian,* 31 March 2021.
10 I am grateful for the Insights in discussion of Cdr Christopher Green Vaccarezza, Chilean Navy.
11 Kouyoumdjian, thesis of 2018; ASMAR website; interviews and discussions with Chilean naval officers especially Cdr Christopher Green; Toro, Juan Pabla, 'Chile-Australia: Two Frigates, Prospects for a Strategic Alliance,' *Athena Lab,* 7 April 2020.
12 Roy-Chaudhury, *Sea Power and Indian Security*, 114, 154.
13 Mazumdar, Mrityunjoy, 'Project 28 Kamorta Class,' in *Waters*, 2019, 105–19.
14 Sakhuja, *Asian Maritime Power*, 145–9.
15 Holmes, James R., Winner Andrew C. and Yoshihara, Toshi, *Indian Naval Strategy in the Twenty-First Century* (London: Routledge, 2009), 90–1.
16 Ibid, 9–13, 67.
17 Quoted in Jeremy, John C., 'Australian shipbuilding and the impact of the Second World War,' in Stevens (Ed), *The Navy and the Nation,* 209.
18 Michael Duffy, 'William James's Record of the Work Done at Devonport Yard,' *British Dockyards in the First World War,* Transactions of the Naval Dockyards Society, Vol. 12, August 2019, 125.
19 McNeill, *The Pursuit of Power*, 270, 285.
20 Ergas, Henry, Thomsdon, Mark and Davies, Andrew, 'Australian Navy Shipbuilding,' in Forbes (Ed), *The Naval Contribution,* 276–304.
21 McNeill, *The Pursuit of Power,* 176–7, 300–2.
22 Jeremy, 'Australian Shipbuilding,' 199, 262.
23 US Senate Armed Services Committee Report, 116–236, 24 July 2020, S 4049.
24 Quoted in Dimitry Filipoff, *Force Structures Perspectives Series* (Washington: CSIS, 2020), 5–7.

25 McCabe et al., Europe, Small Navies and Maritime Security, 61, 64.
26 Chris Parry, As Hypersonic era dawns, West's Navies Must Sharpen Their War-Fighting Game,' *Warship IFR* Nov 2019, 18–20; 'Israeli Fleet's major uplift in surface force,' *Warship IFR,* January 2020, 16.
27 Santiago Rivas, 'Brown water War in Colombia,' *Warship IFR,* November 2019, 21–3.
28 McNeill, *The Pursuit of Power*, 285.
29 Ibid, 271.
30 Goodman, *Spanish Naval Power,* 124–6, 144.
31 McNeill, *The Pursuit of Power*, 255.
32 Kirchberger, Sarah, *Assessing China's Naval Power: Technological Innovation, Economic Constraints and Strategic Implications* (Heidelberg: Springer, 2015), 78.
33 McNeill, *The Pursuit of Power*, 275.
34 McNeill, *The Pursuit of Power,* op cit, 103.
35 Hennessy, 'Fleet replacement,' in Hadley (Ed), *A Nation's Navy,* 150–1.
36 McNeill, *The Pursuit of Power*, 178–80.
37 Jeremy, 'Australian shipbuilding,' 203.
38 Quoted from 1988 Industries Assistance Commission Enquiry, ibid, 208.
39 For excellent reviews of this see, respectively, Kirchberger, Assessing China's Naval Power and Stohs, Jeremy, *The Decline of European Naval Forces: Challenges to Sea Power in an Age of Fiscal Austerity and Political Uncertainty* (Annapolis, MD: Naval Institute Press, 2018).
40 McNeill, *The Pursuit of Power,* 290.
41 Steve Grant, 'Design for UK Future T31 Frigate Selected,'*Warship IFR,* November 2019, 16 and 'Contract for Future Warship Signed,' *Warship IFR,* January 2020, 29–31.
42 McCabe 83.
43 McNeill, *The Pursuit of Power,* 79–102, 278.
44 The usual narrative has the first industrial revolution as the steam and iron era of the late 18th/early 19th Centuries, the second that of steel, oil and electricity from the late 19th Century and the third starting in the 1950s, information technology and the internet. Each is associated with a 'Revolution in Military Affairs.'
45 Michael Raska, 'The Sixth RMA Wave,' *Journal of Strategic Studies,* November 2020.
46 Ian Bowers and Sarah Kirchberger, 'Not So Disruptive after All: The 4IR, Navies and the Search for Sea Control,'*Journal of Strategic Studies*, 2020; William J. Broad, 'Analysis Raises Doubts about the Capabilities of Hypersonic Weapons, *New York Times,* 16 January 2021.
47 David C. Gompert, 'Spin-on: How the US Can Meet China's Technological Challenge,' *Survival*, Vol. 62, No. 3 (May 2020), 115–30.
48 Liza Lin, 'China Targets AI, Chips among Seven Battlefronts in Tech Race with US,' *Wall Street Journal,* 7 March 2021 and Gompert, 'Spin-on,' 115–30.
49 Kirchberger, *Assessing China's Naval Power*, 110.
50 Maydman, *Naval Speculations,* 268–72, 300–15.
51 Salonia, *Genoa's Freedom,* 18–19.
52 Johnson-Allen, John, *They Couldn't Have Done It without Us: The Merchant Navy in the Falklands War* (Woodgridge, Suffolk: Seafarer Books, 2011), 155–6.
53 Ibid, 201.
54 Ibid, xvii. The Right Honourable Bob Mitchell was MP for Southampton.
55 Kirchberger, *Assessing China's Naval Power*, 139–42.
56 Johnson-Allen, *They Couldn't Have Done It*, xvi–xvii.
57 Johnson-Allen, *They Couldn't Have Done It,* op cit, 236.
58 Gwyn Topham, 'Industry Warns of Huge Cost to World Trade,' *The Guardian,* 27 March 2021; Elisabeth Braw, *Without Shipping the World Economy Sinks* (London: National Preparedness Commission, 31 March 2021.
59 Lt Cmd (RNL Navy) W. Matthijs Ooms, 'It's a Navy's Job, Only No Navy Can Do It: Understanding and Addressing Western Neglect of Maritime Trade Protection,' *International Journal of Naval History*, forthcoming; Henry Nichols, 'UK 'SBS' Special Forces Storm Tanker and Detain Stowaways in Channel,' *Reuters,* 25 October 2020.
60 Muller, *China as a Maritime Power*, 58, 73–84.

61 Gresh, Geoffrey *To Rule Eurasia's Waves: The New Great Power Competition at Sea* (New Haven: Yale University Press, 2020), 153.

62 Shannon Tiezzi, 'China Wants Its Civilian Ships to Be Ready for War,' *The Diplomatm* 12 June 2015; Franz-Stefan Gady, 'China Prepares Its 172,000 Civilian Ships for War,' *The Diplomat,* 23 June 2015.

63 Elee Wakim, 'Sealift Is America's Achilles Heel in the Age of Great Power Competition,' *War on the Rocks* (2019); Salvatore R. Mercogliano, 'Suppose There Was a War and the Merchant Marine Didn't Come?,' *United States Naval Institute Proceedings,* Vol. 146, No. 1 (2020).

64 Maydman, *Naval Speculations,* 264–7.

65 *The State of World Fisheries and Aquaculture 2020: Sustainability in Action* (Rome: Food and Agriculture Organization of the United Nations, 2020), 137–8.

66 Ibid, 10–1, 41–2; Zhang Honzhou, *Securing the 'Rice Bowl': China and Global Food Security* (London: Palgrave, 2019), Chapter 5.

67 Sharon Johnson, 'Leadership on the High Seas: Sink or Swim?,' *Galapagos Matters,* Spring/ Summer 2021; Shuxian Luo and Jonathan G Panter, 'China's Maritime Militia and Fishing Fleets: A Primer for Operational Staff and Tactical Leaders,' *Military Review,* January– February 2021.

68 Karen McVeigh, 'Fishing Boats that Trawl Sea Floor Release as much CO_2 as Aviation Sector,' *The Guardian,* 18 March 2021.

69 Steven Morris, 'Angry Fishers Say Industry Will Suffer Lasting Harm,' *The Guardian,* 20 December 2020.

70 Zhang, *Securing the 'Rice Bowl.'*

71 Ibid.

72 Wang Qingyun, 'Argentina Sinks a Chinese Fishing Boat,' *China Daily,* 17 March 2016.

73 Maydman, *Naval Speculations*, 251–6; Ralph Davis, *The Rise of the English Shipping Industry*, 1962, 114–15. Bromley, John, 'The Manning of the Royal Navy: Selected Public Pamphlets 1693–1873,' *Navy Records Society,* Vol. 119 (1974), 54, 93.

74 Warren to Commodore Charles Knowles, 2 June 1746 in Gwyn, Julian, *The Royal Navy and North America: The Warren Papers 1736-52* (London: Navy Records Society, Vol. 118, 1973), 255.

75 Lisle to Secretary Paget, 7 November 1543 in Rose, Susan (Ed), *Naval Miscellany Vol VII,* (Aldershot: Ashgate for the Navy Records Society, 2008), 8.

76 Warren to Corbett Superbe, 4 July 1745 in Gwyn, *The Royal Navy and North America,* 133.

77 Bedford to Newcastle (Secretary of State, southern) 24 March 1745 in ibid 223 and Warren's report on the State of the French fishery at Cape Breton of June 1739 in ibid 10–13; Baugh, Daniel A., *The Global Seven Years War 1754–1763: Britain and France in a Great Power Contest* (London: Routledge, 2014), 617.

78 The extent and significance of such militias remains a hotly debated issue. Compare Shuxian and Panter, 'China's Maritime Militia' op cit and Brad Lendon, 'Beijing Has a Navy it Doesn't Even Admit Exists,' *CNN,* 12 April 2021.

79 Maydman, *Naval Speculations,* op cit, 256.

9 Coastguards and the Assertion of Maritime Authority

9.1 Introduction

Henry Maydman's focus on what he called the 'Brittish seas' indicates the importance he attached to maintaining order, from England's perspective at least, in very local seas. Otherwise, the country's fishing and trade interests, as discussed in the last chapter, and even its security would be at risk from pirates, smugglers and foreign powers and the Government deprived of desperately needed tax revenues. Partly because of the confusions inevitably associated with the 'Glorious Revolution,' smuggling and all these other threats were on the rise. To deal with this, the new government recognised the need to impose its authority on local waters, where it really mattered. '(T)o prevent the bringing over of Prohibited Goods and carrying out of Wool and Stop Intelligence between England and France,' it re-invigorated the old Customs service and set the Army and Royal Navy to help.[1] At sea, warships and Revenue cutters patrolled to deal with foreign and Jacobite agents, smugglers, pirates and privateers. Army units on 'coastal watch' were posted along the shore to back up the 'Riding Officers' of the Customs service. Authority would be imposed, and good order maintained.[2]

Although everyone agreed this would be a good idea, things didn't work out ideally. The Navy was less than enthusiastic about this extra task, thinking it a distraction from their main job; the Army and the Riding Officers squabbled about who was in charge, about what needed to be done and about dividing up the 'seizure money.' Military people tended to be impatient with the complicated legal procedures often involved. Some officials were open to 'persuasion'; all too often smugglers had the initiative, not the good guys. But the principle at least was reinforced, and things did improve.

If this was the 'home game' there was an 'away game' too; British trade, government revenue and maritime development all depended on the security of distant seas as well. Customs officials were sent to British possessions abroad and army and naval forces enjoined to help them in their duties. Indeed, the customs revenues it generated helped pay for their presence overseas. This was part of a general European tendency visible from the late 15th Century onwards, to impose their varying ideas on what good order at sea should be on everyone else. Inevitably, there were disputes between them, and with the locals, about the nature of that order and on how it was best maintained. In particular, whose law should prevail? Uneasy compromises sometimes resulted.[3]

All these difficulties have been commonplace ever since. Experience has confirmed the basic point that a country's capacity to grow its economy, develop its maritime interests and expand or maintain its maritime power, depends on its ability to impose its authority and ensure good order at sea, especially in home waters, but more

DOI: 10.4324/9781003100553-9

broadly too. That 'good order at sea.' (something frequently and confusingly called Maritime Security with capital letters, or reduced to MARSEC) is the foundation of the sea-based trading system on which everyone's maritime fortunes and the world's peace and prosperity depend.

'Bad order at sea' on the other hand, does the reverse. It undermines the capacity to make use of the sea, and so to take legitimate advantage of the opportunities that it offers. It covers challenges to national security (such as pressure from hostile states or terrorist attacks), threats to personal and human security (such as drugs and people trafficking and piracy), or environmental security, (through activities that pollute or degrade the maritime environment.) Through their effect ashore, these threats also circle back to undermine a country's maritime power, if only indirectly. Nor are these different types of security threats discrete; they vary, merge and diverge, shape-shifting all the time. Accordingly their ambiguous nature poses real challenges for countries trying to grapple with such threats. Maritime disorder is the consequence of an inability to assert authority at sea.

There is nothing new in this. In Europe awareness of the need for security at sea long preceded Henry Maydman's time. Starting with the Greek maritime commercial code of 320 BC, the Atlantic maritime powers, unlike others such as China, or the Omani and Ottoman empires, recognised that establishing authority over the sea and control by regulation was not only a measure of sovereignty but also essential in creating optimum conditions for its use. 'The Law, 'declared the Byzantine Emperor, Justinian in 533 AD, 'is the Lord of the Sea.'[4] Maybe, but the problem is enforcing it, and always has been. The campaign to assert authority and to gather the forces and procedures needed remains key to maritime development.

9.2 What's at Stake?

Perhaps the best way to define and measure the significance of Good Order at Sea is by its results, by what it makes possible. Essentially this is the ability safely to enjoy the six leading and largely beneficial peacetime attributes of the sea safely, sustainably and to the general advantage. Taken together, these attributes combine to help shape, if not determine, a country's capacity to develop its maritime interests and power. All six attributes are under threat. Protecting them sets challenges and tasks for a country's navy, coastguard and agencies of law enforcement.

9.2.1 The Sea as Sovereign Jurisdiction

In recent years perceptions of its economic value have encouraged an increase in land-based jurisdiction over the sea. What was a 3-mile territorial sea has quadrupled in size to 12 miles, and limited forms of jurisdiction have been extended beyond that. The ownership of marine features with maritime entitlement has become more important, and more disputed. Claims to sovereignty are bolstered by the perceived capacity to assert authority and exercise jurisdiction. Conversely, an inability to do this often has a reverse effect; in practice, a country's inability or failure to assert its authority in contested areas weakens any sovereignty claims it might have. There is some truth in the old adage: 'Possession is nine tenths of the law.'

The UN Convention of the Law of the Sea (UNCLOS) is seen as a means of establishing, and if necessary contesting, claims of maritime entitlement that derive from sovereign territory. This is challenging for everyone. Archipelagic countries like the Philippines and Indonesia have a special problem. A lack of authority over the waters that separate their many islands tends to undermine their integrity as states. With other countries, an inability to assert their authority at sea may simply imperil their offshore interests. Amongst the worst placed are the Pacific mini-states of Kiribati, with 690 km^2 of land but 3.5 million km^2 of sea and the Marshall islands with 181 and 2.1 million km^2, respectively. Both have few resources with which to exercise their authority. They are extreme examples of a common problem. Aware of the dangers, claimants to different parts of the Western Pacific have substantially increased their naval and coastguard capabilities and made robust use of them for this purpose.[5]

Disputed sovereignty not only aggravates the relations between states but also makes the maintenance of good order at sea much more difficult. Although there are instances of joint development where sovereignty claims have been set aside, more usually, disputed borders are a real impediment to progress in resolving all the threats to maritime security in disputed areas such as the South China Sea and around the coasts of Africa.[6] The equitable distribution of marine resources and the protection of the marine environment suffer accordingly.[7]

9.2.2 Marine Resources

Oil and Gas: One-third of the world's petroleum reserves are at sea. Before their replacement by clean energy resources, these are likely to be of increasing commercial interest as land sources become depleted. Moreover, exploitation of these resources is steadily being conducted in deeper and deeper waters, currently reaching 10,000 ft in some cases. Because they make such a material contribution to the wealth of coastal states, their damage can have such catastrophic economic and environmental effects as the *Deepwater* disaster of 2010 showed, Accordingly, those oil and gas resources have to be located, developed, managed and if necessary defended against all manner of intentional and unintentional harm. In cases such as oil exploration in the Arctic, this can raise all kinds of extremely difficult dilemmas to resolve.

As was discussed in the last chapter, managing the fisheries is also extremely important to the prosperity of very many countries, most especially in Asia. Sustainable fishing depends on the maintenance of good order at sea. Excessive levels of demand, lawlessness, jurisdictional disputes and marine pollution, however, all threaten it. When and where sustainability is in doubt,[8] the world's fishers either leave a profession noted for its discomforts and dangers (as in Western Europe) or resort to alternative and often criminal employment (as off Somalia and around Southeast Asia). Domestic stability and international peace can suffer as a consequence.

Pollution of course further aggravates the problem and by 2050 there is likely to be more plastic than fish (by weight) in the world ocean.[9] In the Gulf of Thailand, climate change, the destruction of spawning grounds and habitats through coastal development, and land- and sea-based pollution have all increased the already extreme vulnerability of local fishing stocks. Irresponsible fishing methods and the construction of military bases in the South China Sea resulting in the destruction of coral reefs will have similar effects since they serve as fish spawning grounds.[10]

Illegal, Unregulated and Unreported Fishing (IUU Fishing) is also linked to other criminal threats to good order at sea. In some fishing fleets, there is extensive use of illegal migrants and crews are subject to systemic abuse amounting in effect to slavery.

The linkages between under-regulated fishing fleets with piracy, smuggling and general criminality are lamentably clear.[11]

Declining fish stocks also lead to higher levels of competition between fishermen from different areas and countries and so contribute to growing international tensions. Even in regions (such as the European Union) where there are high degrees of political consensus, agreeing a way out of these problems can be extremely difficult,[12] but when political enmity is added to the mixture, resolution of the fishing problem becomes next to impossible. Examples of this include the regular fishing clashes between India and Pakistan, in Northeast Asian waters and the East and South China Seas. In the so-called Cod Wars between Britain and Iceland, rivalry was limited to some aggressive seamanship, and of British fishermen broadcasting spirited renditions of 'Rule Britannia' and throwing potatoes at the Icelandic vessels seeking to drive them off.[13] Nowadays sinking fishing boats and the threat or use of lethal force have become regular options, especially in the Western Pacific.

9.2.3 Safe Transportation

The sea's value as a means of transportation is a particularly complicated and wide-ranging topic. Because the economies of all countries benefit to a greater or lesser extent from the free flow of world trade, global and national security and prosperity depend on safe maritime transportation. Some states are more directly integrated into the system than others and so have higher stakes in the game.

Disorder at sea poses many varied risks to sea-based trade and so can threaten the international order which depends on it. The most obvious set of threats relates to the secure operation of the shipping itself, through the threat of piracy for example. But, a little less obviously, merchant ships themselves can represent a threat to good order at sea and to the sea-based trading system more generally, if the cargoes they carry are dangerous and represent an illegitimate use of the sea as a means of transportation.

Some of the threats that ships face are intentional, some are not. Intentional threats may include cyber attacks on the electronic communication systems that increasingly lubricate the shipping system and land-bound disruption of ports of despatch and receipt. Restrictive legislation (for environmental or jurisdictional reasons) on rights of passage through straits and narrow seas, is represented by the traditional maritime powers as a worrying constraint on the freedom of navigation. Moreover, the prevalence today of a 'just-enough-just-in-time' operating philosophy makes the modern shipping system much more fragile, and less resilient than once it was. Higher value cargoes are also now concentrated in fewer hulls.

Shipping also needs protection from involvement in the quarrels of others. In the so-called tanker war of 1981–1988, both Iraq and Iran chose to attack and harass international shipping as a means of influencing the policies of the great powers. Some 450 merchant ships belonging to 32 countries ships were attacked and 471 merchant seamen were killed.[14] Although the tanker war of the 1980s is the most obvious example of this type of intended threat – it is far from being the only one. So far, though, most others have occurred in the Eastern Mediterranean, the Gulf and its approaches and the Red Sea. Many are concerned about its possible further spread to the Western Pacific.

Piracy is another traditional threat to shipping. In the conventional view, piracy has a long and dishonourable history,[15] but is a much more complex subject than most people realise. It has greatly varied in form over time and in different places. Unsurprisingly, even defining it can be a real problem, politically, culturally and legally.[16] UNCLOS considers it as only taking place in international waters; such attacks within territorial seas are more properly described as 'sea robberies,' so dealing with them is the responsibility of the coastal state. Most attacks on ships take place in or near ports. The main focus of such attacks has shifted from the Straits of Malacca, to the Arabian Sea off the coasts of Somalia and Aden and more recently to the Gulf of Guinea. What happens at sea often very much depends on what happens ashore.[17] Piracy threatens the orderly conduct of maritime commerce, raises insurance costs, increases local tensions and puts peoples' lives at risk. In addition to the economic consequences of piracy, which are generally reckoned to cost, all-in, some US\$ 7–12 billion per year,[18] the potential for environmental catastrophe is also immense.

By contrast the threat posed by terrorism is relatively new and still more potential than actual. It was brought into high relief by the attack on the French tanker the *Limburg* off Aden in October 2002,[19] and more recently by several attacks on ships by the Houthi rebels in the Yemen. The apparent vulnerability of tankers given the nature of their cargoes is a matter of concern. The same applies to large cruise ships; the large numbers of potential victims on board make them lucrative targets and their routes and schedules are well known in advance.

Threatening and illegitimate cargoes are an issue too. Maintaining the legitimate use of the sea as a means of transportation is not just a matter of ensuring the safety of shipping however. What the ships carry can itself represent a threat to national, regional or global security, in a variety of ways. Most obviously this applies to the enormous trade in illicit drugs, the trafficking of human beings and the transport of illegal arms and terrorists. Although the first two of these are by far the most serious threats to domestic and international order, the terrorist attack on Mumbai in November 2008 was a tragic reminder of the need to pay attention to the fact that these enemies of mankind use the sea as a form of transport just like anyone else.[20]

9.2.4 The Sea as an Environment

For centuries the marine environment has been taken for granted if thought about at all, but through the 20th century, its perceived importance grew dramatically. And yet much is still mysterious about the way in which the ocean system actually works. But one thing we do know is that it is under increasing threat. In 1998, Mario Soares, Portugal's leading elder statesman, released the report of the 'Independent Commission on the World Oceans.' It made sombre reading. It argued that there was a 'crisis of the oceans' caused by pollution, jurisdictional disputes, over-exploitation and widespread ignorance. What takes hundreds, even thousands of years to develop can be unknowingly destroyed in days, and all too often is. Already two-thirds of the world's population lives within 100 km of the coast, and the pressure this puts on the fragile environment of the ocean is tremendous and bound to get worse, as the total population increases over the next several decades.[21] The trajectory of concern has increased still further as the 21st Century unfolds.

The consequences of continued environmental degradation at sea for mankind's future are likely to be dire indeed. They include a worsening of climate change, a rise in sea levels with potentially catastrophic consequences in many parts of the world, and drastic cuts in fish-stock.

Much of this may be regarded as 'soft security' (distinct from the 'hard' security of alliances and wars) but it is 'security' all the same because such concerns amount to an indirect attack on the prosperity and stability of international society and its constituents. Indeed, in the case of small island countries like the Maldives, Kiribati and Tuvalu facing the prospect of extinction or massive damage through rising sea levels it is hard to imagine a security issue that deserves to be taken more seriously.[22]

9.2.5 *The Sea as a Data Set*

In some ways, of course, the historic function of the sea as a means of acquiring and exchanging information and ideas has been lost to the internet, apart from the critical importance of the under-sea fibre-optic cables which carry over 90% of the world's electronic data. All the same, the sea remains a hugely important source of knowledge about the planet we live on and about human history. Because it is increasingly recognised that the sea helps us understand our past, there is growing acceptance that the sea should be seen as a repository of mankind's maritime heritage. As such it needs to be positively protected from neglect and destructive plundering, difficult though that frequently is.

Moreover the sea is crucial to our understanding of the future as well. It also perfectly illustrates the paradox that we do not know what we do not know, and the more we know the more we realise how true that is. Most obviously, as the Australians have pointed out, marine biotechnology is a developing field and since marine biological diversity is so much greater than its terrestrial equivalent it '...represents a vast, relatively untapped source of potential new materials, compounds, and organisms.'[23] The need to protect this invaluable storehouse of future knowledge from present, unknowing damage reinforces the drive towards more regulation and environmental protection of the world ocean. The more we know about the sea the better able we are to exploit its benefits sustainably – hence the burgeoning growth of interest in oceanographic research.

9.2.6 *A Leisure Resource*

Finally, because of the key role of the tourism industry in the economy of many countries, the sea is important to very many countries as a leisure resource. For this, once again, its sustainability needs management and protection. Ensuring that sustainability requires complex balances to be struck between the rate and nature of development on the one hand and, on the other, the protection of the environment that attracts the tourists in the first place. In the same way, the needs of the leisure industry have to be reconciled perhaps with those of the with those of the oil, cruise or fishing industries. To most people, leaving the management of such things to market forces would not seem a sensible option.

9.3 Asserting Authority: The Problems

The assertion of legitimate authority has been difficult and remains so, for many reasons. The first is that the resources committed to the task have often proved to be significantly less than its nature and scale demand. In many cases, the resources are insufficient for the authorities even to know what is going on, let alone be able to do anything about it. Secondly, the capacity to assert authority over the high seas (which belong to no one and everyone at the same time) is contentious and inherently difficult. The danger is that if no one owns it, no one will look after it. Thirdly and worse still, many of the interwoven strands in this complex maritime tapestry of opportunities and threats are themselves ambiguous. To defend themselves against future uncertainties, for example, criminals like all other business-people, diversify their activities. Experience in and off Somalia showed that piracy, illegal fishing and domestic disorder can be hard to disentangle.[24] Moreover, piracy or terrorism, are in any case slippery concepts, subject to a great many different interpretations and responses.[25]

9.4 The Penalties of Failure

'The unity of the Ocean,' wrote Halford Mackinder, 'is the simple physical fact underlying the dominant value of sea-power in the modern globe-wide world.'[26] This essential unity is also expressed in the way that the sea is used, or misused when conditions of maritime disorder prevail. Because the sea is all joined up, the bad consequences that follow are all globally linked and demand consideration as a whole. They break down, though, into three overarching and usually inter-related categories of consequence that are all malign for the development of the maritime interests and power of all countries to a greater or lesser degree.

9.4.1 Pollution, Environmental Degradation and the Loss of Marine Resources

Concern about the state of the ocean has been growing steadily, especially from the beginning of this century. Authoritative surveys such as the massive United Nations *Second World Ocean Assessment* (WOA II) which came out early in 2021 have confirmed the alarming conclusions of earlier reports such as the Intergovernmental Panel on Climate Change (IPCC) *Special Report on the Ocean and Cryosphere in a Changing Climate* and Greenpeace's well regarded *30 × 30 Blueprint for Ocean Protection.* They all make the points that unrestrained human activities have seriously imperilled the health of the world ocean, which unless corrected, will have tragic consequences for biodiversity, all marine resources and the human race; accordingly a sensible response requires integrated action across the spectrum of social, economic and scientific policy. Greenpeace is particularly clear that a major source of the problem is firstly a lack of sufficient regulation and secondly a reluctance fully to enforce the regulation that does exist. Its *High Stakes: The Environmental and Social Impacts of Destructive Fishing on the High Seas of the Indian Ocean* is a good exploration of the problem and its consequences.

9.4.2 Loss of Income for Coastal States

Maritime disorder means that local countries cannot fully exploit the marine resources that could otherwise supply the revenues needed to tackle domestic challenges on land. Tanzania's offshore oil and gas industry for example seems likely to increase the country's GDP by some 30%–40% if properly defended. The McKinsey Report of 2010 suggests this is broadly true for Africa as a whole – and to this figure needs to be the added value of the fishing industry, participation in world shipping development and so forth.[27] Being able to exploit such opportunities would produce the investment capacity and the youth employment that Tanzania and indeed all the economies of Africa urgently require.[28] Much the same can be said of many other countries too.

But much of this potential value is lost. According to one estimate, the Nigerian economy alone loses about US$ 7 billion annually to oil theft.[29] The economy of coastal states may also suffer indirectly from the damage that piracy and other forms of maritime disorder inflict on international sea-based trade. When local seas degenerate into wild ungoverned spaces, sea traffic diverts elsewhere, limiting the capacity of local states to participate and benefit.

9.4.3 *Instability and Increased Disorder*

Not only does maritime disorder deprive countries of their rightful income, but it also tends to undermine their stability and their capacity to govern. Individuals pay taxes to the state in the expectation that the state will look after them and provide other essential services. When it cannot do so, the entire legitimacy of the regime is imperilled. A failure to deal with maritime/transnational crime and attendant corruption therefore undercuts the social contract that binds the individual and the state together, destabilises government, further weakens good governance and creates the conditions for still more disorder and crime in a never-ending vicious circle.

To take just as one example, the illicit trade in drugs when facilitated by maritime disorder rewards domestic drugs smugglers and other criminals, such that exactly the wrong kind of people are seen by everyone else to prosper. State authority is corroded by the rise of powerful people who not only break but subvert the law, who do not pay taxes, whose richness encourages other desperate people to follow their example. They may well maintain their own armed militias, operating independently of the state. They probably diversify their business into other forms of crime which spread through the economy like cancer. They also seek cover in legitimate business, subverting parts of that as well. Funding their habits drive drugs addicts into crime, with consequences that often feed back into diminished human security for the population as a whole. The involvement of criminal organisations in the illicit trade in drugs, has threatened the domestic stability of countries like Colombia and parts of northern Mexico by suborning the instruments of state – the police, the judiciary and the administration. Much the same effect seems threatened in parts of West Africa where fragile state authority is likewise put at increased risk of their spiralling down into becoming simply 'narco-states.' Local instabilities of this sort, moreover, can often have serious consequences for neighbours and for regional and possibly global consequences too.

Much the same can be said for the other main types of maritime crime, with which the drugs trade is often closely associated, arms and people smuggling, piracy and terrorism. Moreover at sea, which is indeed 'all joined up,' everything is connected to everything else. For this reason, countries eager to develop their maritime opportunities need to view the interconnected elements in this complex maritime tapestry, and the threats that they face, as a single malign whole. The maintenance of good order at sea, and the international maritime collaboration it requires, demands a holistic approach.

The US Navy's Admiral Kurt Tidd (then heading US Southern Command) summed it up like this:

> These illicit networks operate unrestrained by laws, unimpeded by morality, and fuelled by enormous profits. They prey on weak institutions, transcend national borders, and exploit the interconnected nature of our modern financial transportation and technological systems .... [We need] a shared way of seeing and acting on these problems.[30]

9.5 Asserting Authority: The Requirements

9.5.1 Maritime Horses for Maritime Courses

Countries seeking to defend their maritime interests need to secure all their access to the different attributes of the sea sustainably. Although their inter-relationships always need to be borne in mind, securing each of these sustainable uses of the sea requires distinctive responses, equipment and procedures. Meeting the challenge is the task of a wide variety of government departments, agencies of law enforcement, coastguards and navies. There are three critical requirements for this.

9.5.2 Securing Multinational Cooperation

Agreed jurisdiction. Firstly, and as already said, a vicious circle is at work. The less national authority is asserted over particular areas of sea, the greater the likelihood of maritime disorder; the greater the maritime disorder, the harder it becomes to assert authority. The task may be rendered more difficult still if a country's right to assert authority in a particular sea area is contested especially by its neighbours. UNCLOS left, maybe even created, many disputed jurisdictions, the most notorious being in the South China Sea. Generally, it is much easier for a country to assert authority in a particular sea area if its sovereign right to do so is generally recognised. In short, winning acceptance of sovereign rights over local seas, where that is in dispute, may well prove both an essential first step in the assertion of authority and, at the same time, an indication of success. Where an area remains in dispute, the right to assert authority needs to be established by a rigorous legal and political campaign and then sustained and exercised by effective operational patrolling against all possible threats. An inability to do the second, compromises the first.

The Recognition of Shared Interest. Even so, most threats to good order at sea are transnational. Fish, pirates, drug smugglers and the causes of environmental degradation all show a heartless disregard for national jurisdictional boundaries especially when those boundaries are ill-defined or poorly enforced. In these circumstances, no single country can defend its maritime interests against the threat of disorder, possibly even in its own waters. Accordingly, most problems of disorder require multinational cooperation. Acceptance of this results in increasing levels of maritime cooperation institutionally around the world (through collective agreement on aims and the establishment of mechanisms by which they might be achieved, such as those regulatory arrangements discussed a little later) and operationally (by coordinated patrolling, agreements on the prosecution of offenders and the provision of technical support). Paradoxically, since the aims are common, a country's capacity to defend its own maritime interests rests on its political, legal and technical capacity to operate alongside others doing the same thing for theirs.

9.5.3 Situational Awareness

It has been well said that before crimes can be countered, they have to be counted.[31] Knowing what has gone on and probably still is, acts as the first step in correcting the problem. In the fishing industry, for example, the costs of IUU Fishing are variously estimated to be between US$ 10 and 23 billion annually. IUU Fishing boats typically hide by switching off navigational transponders if they have them, flout laws and regulations, abuse their crews and engage in irresponsible fishing methods. They take fish before they reach the age of reproduction, violate agreed limits by landing illegal 'black' fish, destroy protected species and are unwilling to switch to alternate and less vulnerable species. Knowing the real 'price of fish' and detecting such practices and their costs requires the accumulation of sufficient information through close monitoring. Hence Canada's new 'Dark Vessel Detection Programme.'[32] It is equally important to track the transnational on-shore processing and trafficking infrastructure that markets the fish.[33]

Maritime Domain Awareness. The necessary Maritime Domain Awareness (MDA) comes in two forms. The first is more oceanographic than operational although it certainly has operational consequences. General scientific understanding is needed about how the ocean works, about what it provides now and may do in the future and, perhaps above all given current concerns about climate change, how to mitigate the many dangers it faces. It is generally accepted that we know far less about the deep ocean than we do about the surface of the moon; barely 5% of it has been properly 'imaged.' Discoveries in the huge mid-Ocean ridge (which comprises some 23% of the world's surface and contains the highest mountain ranges we have) are recent and often accidental, or incidental. One new marine species is discovered every two weeks. The more we discover about the deep ocean, the more we realise how much we don't know.[34] Increasing oceanographic awareness is plainly key to the long-term protection of maritime interests.

Operationally, sufficient surveillance and awareness across particular sea areas is crucial to the effective management of the oceans.[35] The International Maritime Organisation defines MDA as '... the effective understanding of any activity within the maritime environment that could impact upon the ... [world's] ... security, safety, economy or environment.'[36] Improved MDA is gradually making possible a slow transition in the monitoring of merchant shipping such that the ships themselves begin to be treated like airliners, handed on from one sea-traffic monitor to another. One such scheme is the European Union's Blue Belt project, a pilot for which began in May 2011.[37] Others are the Information Fusion Centre that operates in Singapore, India and the Combined Maritime Forces' Shared Awareness and Deconfliction Centre (SHADE) Centre in Bahrain. The overall aim of such data conflation is to help identify normal maritime activity of all sorts so that the abnormal can be more easily spotted.

Raw data on ships both depends on, and facilitates, regulation, but in many areas – such as the world's 4 million fishing boats – it is decidedly imperfect. The shipping world is also bedevilled by obfuscation and deception with ships choosing to 'go dark' by switching off their AIS or entering false data in pursuit of commercial or operational advantage. Dealing with this requires real administrative effort and that costs money.[38] Nonetheless more and more agencies are being set up to collect and process such data deriving from a whole range of both open and confidential sources including everything from human intelligence through maritime patrol aircraft, submarines, patrol craft and UAVs. Singapore's Information Fusion Centre and the 'Windward' organisation recently established in Israel, are a couple of the many endeavours to rise to this challenge.[39]

Information Sharing. The huge advantages of a Common Operational Picture (COP) between participating units call for a culture of information sharing between government agencies and foreign partners. The better this is, the more likely is it that ocean management will succeed.

Providing and sharing the information needed for a COP is difficult, however. In many cases, firstly, the agencies collecting and processing such data may have sensitivities that inhibit information sharing, either in an attempt to protect its source or their own (in)capabilities. Secondly, their capacity to gather and process information between participating navies may differ in method, aim and technical sophistication; this too inhibits information-sharing. The data collected by risk management companies is proprietorial so sharing it for free does not come naturally. In any case, sometimes, governments would rather not know.

This is especially true when it comes to turning data into actionable intelligence before passing its results on to forces that need it, when they need it. Smaller navies, and those with least interest in this kind of maritime security operation may find it difficult to generate the necessary specialised equipment and personnel.

9.5.4 The Apprehension of Wrongdoers

The effective and timely implementation of good order at sea depends on having sufficient units in the required area to provide a deterrent presence against wrong-doers and the prospect of their likely interception and prosecution, should they nonetheless proceed. The apprehension of perpetrators can be difficult and dangerous, frequently involving the risk of collision, accident and potentially lethal force in cases of non-compliance. Worst still it can involve stand-offs with foreign law-enforcement vessels, apparently protecting their own conceptions of the law. It can involve long periods of patrol sometimes requiring ventures far into the high seas.[40] Few protecting navies have the equipment, time, resources, professionalism and maybe inclination to do this kind of thing to the extent it needs doing.

This accounts for the global trend to set up Coastguard forces and other such Maritime Law Enforcement Agencies. The way in which this is done varies from country to country, in accordance with their geographic position, perception of threat and socio-political culture. What they all have in common is a focus on the lower reaches of Maritime Security. Instead of focussing on the security threats posed by other states, as most navies mainly do, they concentrate on dealing with safety issues (where the threats come from inanimate sources such as pollution, climate change and pandemics) and the challenge of dealing with non-state actors who deliberately engage in harmful activities (maritime criminals of every persuasion and terrorists). The lines between these responsibilities are fuzzy and overlap; many navies have responsibilities in this area too.[41]

Whether from navies or coastguards, the ships themselves need to be fast and sufficiently armed, guns generally being more useful than missiles. Armed soldiers or sailors skilled in rapid-roping and other boarding and search techniques will often also be needed. Warships on such duties also need appropriately robust rules of engagement.[42] The same applies to Coastguard ships. It's not just China Coast Guard vessels that are getting bigger and more capable.[43]

Securing sufficient numbers of law enforcement assets is another problem. The world ocean, as the Russians call it, is a very big place and the number of assets devoted to the task of maintaining good order at sea is relatively small. This particularly applies to the seas around Africa, where few countries have the necessary level of GDP (about US$ 10 billion) to operate effective coastguards/navies. The result is a vast area of 7 to 8 million km^2 of sea policed by too few assets, many of which are barely serviceable, although the growing economic power of the African continent will hopefully generate more law-enforcement resources in the future. Moreover, while the volume and extent of world trade is expected to increase over the next 20 years, the number of Western naval assets will decline by about 30%. The resultant shortfall will need to be filled by a mixture of local forces, MLEAs, the newer naval powers of the Asia Pacific and elsewhere and *properly regulated* private security companies.[44]

To some extent technology in the shape of long-range and discriminating shore-based radars, UAVs, light aircraft and Artificial Intelligence/Big Data may come partially to the rescue since by effectively 'cueing' patrol craft onto targets, they make the best use if limited numbers. But all this costs money.

9.5.5 The Prosecution of Wrongdoers

Legal and regulatory foundations. Once caught, terrorists and criminals of all persuasions have to be prosecuted and punished as a means of removing them as continuing threats to good order and hopefully deterring others. This, however is far from easy. 'For all its breathtaking beauty,' says Ian Urbina powerfully,

> the ocean is also a dystopian place, home to dark inhumanities. The rule of law often so solid on land, bolstered and clarified by centuries of careful word-smithing, hard fought jurisdictional lines and robust enforcement regimes – is fluid at sea, if it's to be found at all.[45]

The absence of the necessary legislation, 'chaotic, desultory nature of maritime regulation' and what Urbina calls 'the half-hearted policing of laws on the high seas' makes the prosecution of elusive offenders very difficult.[46]

The level of evidence required for a successful prosecution is the same as it would be for a crime on land. Getting such evidence is often much harder, not least because the sheer size of the world ocean still offers offenders so many places to hide their activities. For naval personnel, the gathering of admissable evidence requires special training. Sometimes the legalities hinder rather than help the defence of good order. Attempts to rescue migrants from drowning in Libyan territorial waters, for example, are constrained by EU warships having first to know that the incident is occurring without being there and, second, to be assured that local authorities are willing to admit they are not capable of dealing with that particular incident. The consequent delays can prove disastrous.[47] These kinds of impediments have also led to the pragmatic 'catch-and-release' anti-piracy methods employed by some navies off Somalia. This is as an alternative to legal prosecution. Instead, sinking the pirates' boats and destroying their engines and weaponry is seen as an economic attack on the pirates' business plan. Differences of view as to what is legally possible also complicate cooperation, and can be deeply frustrating for the forces concerned.[48]

The perpetrators' standard defence mechanism against prosecution is a restless search for such weaknesses in the law enforcement process relating to their area of interest. The gaps at the global, regional and national levels that they are able to find are their opportunities for concealment and protection from apprehension and prosecution. Bureaucratic inertia and the sheer size of modern state administration however often mean that the response-time of forces of law enforcement to new moves by the perpetrators tends to be slower than *vice-versa*.

Globally, the fact that the high seas are by definition beyond national jurisdiction provides many other areas of deficiency that the malign can exploit, in order to conceal and protect their activity. This is 'the tragedy of the commons' – the tendency to neglect what you do not own, and the temptation to stand aside in the expectation that someone else will fix the problem.[49]

Discontinuities of response also derive from differences between the legislation of neighbouring countries. In the *Tampa* incident of August 2001, for example people smugglers benefitted from marked differences between Indonesia and Australia in how their activity was regarded and treated.[50] More recently differences in national legislation about the protection of sea cucumbers, a lucrative object of trade, has caused major problems for India and Sri Lanka.[51] Even determining what is, or is not, a crime can be difficult given the 'confounding knot of jurisdictions, treaties and national laws litigated over centuries of sea-faring travel and commerce.'[52]

Nationally, exploitable loopholes might be a country's inability to enforce its own laws that can be traced back to the resource and operational deficiencies discussed earlier. They can, however, equally well reflect the absence of enforceable domestic laws in the first place, and/or a tottering domestic legal system unable to cope with the responsibility for administering them. The rules and regulations applying to shipping for example are both lamentably lax in themselves and in any case unenforceable by the weaker states operating 'flags of convenience.' Shippers looking for economies naturally gravitate in their direction.[53] From this it follows that countries seeking to extend and protect the good order at sea on which their maritime interests and power in part depend have strong incentives for legislative action at all three levels, globally, regionally and nationally. But this is easier said than done; it takes time and effort that could be devoted to other apparently more important things.

When one country's maritime interests may be threatened by the actions of another on the high seas, countries may act to protect them either unilaterally or collectively. The 'Turbot war' of 1995 between Spain and Canada on the Grand Banks off Newfoundland is an example of the first. Even though this was beyond Canada's EEZ, the Canadian Navy felt that marine conservation justified its seizing a Spanish trawler, the *Estai*, fishing there in defiance of local agreement that the area should be allowed to recover from former depredations. A sense that unacceptable advantage was being taken of the high seas as an ungoverned space was seen by the Canadians at least as justifying the unilateral extension of their jurisdiction if for a good cause.[54]

However, countries have strong incentives to agree international regulations and laws that nonetheless suit their national interests and then to act collectively to enforce them. As was shown above, since so much of the problem is transnational it makes sense for such threats to be handled at the regional if not global level. Hence, as responses to the threat of terrorism, the introduction of the International Ship and Port Facility Security Code (ISPS Code) in 2004 made sense; as did the international effort which led to important amendments to the Safety of Life at Sea (SOLAS) and Suppression of Unlawful Acts (SUA) conventions.[55] Other such regulations include the UN International Maritime Organisation (IMO)'s International Convention for the Prevention of Pollution by Ships (1973 MARPOL Treaty, and its 1978 Protocol designating special areas for such protection, part of its bid for 'making shipping safer, cleaner and more efficient.'[56]

The UN Convention on the Law of the Sea (UNCLOS) is the most obvious example of such a global and transnational approach. A significant addition to the customary law that has been built up over the centuries, UNCLOS as treaty law, was a compromise between different groups of countries with different maritime interests. The result was a degree of ambiguous wording that papered over the cracks; this provides cover for differing interpretations over the detail of the resultant law. Some states accept UNCLOS in its entirety, some with reservations, and some have not ratified it at all. More insidiously, the manner in which they apply UNCLOS to their own circumstance, for example over the drawing of the base lines from which jurisdictional entitlement is calculated, is regarded by others as dubious in the extreme. While such legal sleight of hand may prove of immediate tactical benefit, it weakens the international legal order, to everyone's loss, in the longer run.

For this reason, countries seem increasingly willing to agree to local compromise deals which include the regulation of all sorts of activity at sea, difficult to arrange though this might be. While this approach is perhaps most evident in Europe, the same processes of maritime community-building are evident elsewhere too. The Malacca Strait Patrol of Singapore, Indonesia, Thailand and Malaysia is a case in point.

Finally the rules and regulations agreed at the global and regional levels can usually only be enforced at the national level. Accordingly, individual countries have to enact supporting domestic legislation that hopefully accords with that of their neighbours while investing in the people and legal infrastructure needed to prosecute and punish offenders. This all takes time, effort and resources, that may be beyond the capacity of some states to deliver. There is a tendency for countries to sign up to such conventions in principle while failing to take the practical steps needed for their implementation. In 2014, the initial Search and Rescue operation search for the missing airliner MH 370 was bedevilled by such problems.[57]

Even where the law and the legal machinery exists, however, countries and their agencies may still be unwilling to take action. Naval vessels have a right, and, most would argue, duty to arrest and punish pirates on the high seas – but in practice many do not.[58] The expectation that prosecution of pirates caught at sea becomes the responsibility of the warship that seized them is a major disincentive to decisive action since this could ruin an exercise or visits programme. Likewise, the capacity to prosecute pirates may be constrained by inadequate legislation in the warship's home country or, in the case of European warships, by the putative effect of the European Convention on Human Rights which may in effect turn punished pirates into asylum seekers.

Finally, if all this is needed to defeat maritime disorder and protect a country's wider maritime interests, the next step is to enquire how they set about creating the capabilities required for the purpose. Essentially this is another exercise in the identification and conduct of ends, ways and means. The process of delivering the necessary ships, aircraft, equipment and people is much the same as for their purely naval equivalents to be discussed later, but some are peculiar to the task of ensuring good order at sea. Most of this requires cooperative effort.

9.6 Delivering Cooperative Effort

9.6.1 Cooperation at the National Level

The first step at the national level, obviously, is to establish and maintain effective navies and coastguards and the organisations to run them. They also need to be able to work together as seamlessly as possible, given the propensity of the forces of disorder to search out and exploit weaknesses and to wriggle through gaps. In 1995, India's Admiral Mihir Roy, lamented that his country had '...nearly sixteen different ministries ...dealing with ocean activities but with hardly any coordination either for overall for overall planning or rationalising, funding and budgeting.'[59] Though speaking for his own country, the Admiral was identifying a very common problem.

Nor is there any single, far less 'right,' way of resolving it. Much depends on the challenges individual countries face, their geography, their social and political culture and their resources. Some like Japan and China and the US do aim at creating a powerful and distinctive coastguard. Britain and Australia have a hopefully co-ordinated model in which all the agencies are networked together. The French Secretariat General for the Sea (SGMer) which has a strong naval component is a particularly sophisticated coordinating agency that reports directly to the Prime Minister. Others like Norway, Denmark or Chile have coastguards as semi-autonomous elements of their navies. Many countries without the resources to operate both, have navies that effectively act as coastguards. In many cases, coastguards also have a reserve military function especially in times of war.

For the enforcement of good order at sea, establishing separate coastguard forces has both advantages and disadvantages, the balance depending on their national circumstances.[60] Some would argue that navies are less suited to dealing with soft security issues, that they are not trained for it and that its conduct takes them away from their real deterrence and war-fighting job. They can also seem too escalatory. On the other hand, they are often much better resourced technically and operationally and can perform such duties as a useful sideline to their substantial purpose.

Coastguards may be thought less provocative and so can feel free to act more recklessly – and that has its dangers too, as the various water cannon fights in the East China Sea make clear. The appearance of increasingly powerful and better armed and even more determined coastguard vessels more prepared in every sense to use force if necessary[61] narrows the gap between grey and white hulls and blurs the difference still more. An example of this must be the China Coast Guard vessel *Haixun* which is not just a massive 10,000 tons but also built in such a deliberately robust style as to be able to 'shoulder aside' other smaller vessels with impunity, including if necessary major combatants of the US and other navies.

Such 'grey zone' possibilities illustrate the fundamental problem for coastguards, MLEAs and navies, operating along the amorphous spectrum of maritime defence, security and safety. The shape-shifting contingencies they consequently have to deal with are ambiguous, constantly changing and overlap in ways that make clear-cut distinctions between their complementary roles exceedingly difficult. This tends to aggravate existing institutional rivalries and budgetary turf battles.

Against such challenges effective navy-coastguard cooperation in the maintenance of good order at sea depends on the development of a comprehensive framework for maritime security cooperation between the various national authorities for the home game and international ones for the away game. For this, navies, coastguards and other maritime law enforcement agencies, need to agree their objectives, assure the free flow of information, integrate their MDA capacities and command and control systems and their operational procedures. Shared training and exercises also help. The ultimate aim might be to aim at an ideal of 'One National Fleet' as in the US and South Korea.[62] The travails and complexities faced by countries as varied as Italy and Argentina, show how just how ambitious this can be.[63] Equally obviously both the areas of responsibility and the operational capabilities of individual countries vary enormously.

9.6.2 Capacity Building

The defence of good order at sea requires multinational cooperation, and the more effective forces there are that can help, the better. Since maintaining maritime order is in the interests of the maritime community as a whole and given the propensity of bad people to exploit gaps and seams in its defence, it makes sense for the better endowed generally to help their more challenged colleagues and to help build their capacity. Hence the programmes to help other countries develop aspects of their maritime power that can be seen at every turn. These are now so common that they seldom secure the recognition that they deserve. Because they are now almost taken for granted, it is easy to miss the fact that they are basically a quite novel activity and one of the few cases where it is hard to find convincing historical precedent.

9.6.3 Multinational Cooperation for Multinational Problems

The same can be said for the very necessary operational multinational cooperation at sea required to maintain maritime order. The extent to which this has become a commonplace of the late 20th and early 21st Centuries also tends to conceal how historically novel this actvity is. There were of course instances of *ad hoc* multinational naval cooperation in the past, usually in response to a humanitarian disaster like the end of the Russian civil war, or the Smyrna crisis of 1922 but these days maritime cooperation in defence of good order at sea has become routine business, certainly in Europe, in Southeast Asia (such as the Malacca Straits Patrol, and the cooperation between the navies of Indonesia, Malaysia and the Philippines in the Sulu sea) and so forth. It has become routine, because it is widely recognised as an essential element in the development and use of maritime power. Creating, servicing and improving such cooperative efforts is a critical element in the defence of good order at sea.

9.6.4 The Requirement for Integrated Governance

This review suggests that the protection of a country's maritime interests depends on its capacity to assert authority in its own waters and to contribute to good order at sea more widely. In turn, the capacity to do this depends on international cooperation, on effective maritime domain awareness in every sense of that phrase, on the capacity to apprehend offenders, on sufficient investment in effective naval/coastguard forces of law enforcement and a body of enforceable maritime law that can be administered successfully.

   This requirement covers so much that the adoption of a national, holistic and integrated maritime policy and system of governance is increasingly thought necessary.

Singapore provides something of a model in its 'National Maritime Security System' which indeed builds inter-agency cooperation and helps develop an effective national approach to the challenge of assuring maritime security. Indonesia, facing much more serious challenges, has to struggle more.[64] Without at least moderate success in this enterprise the assertion of maritime authority becomes much harder. Even the United States encountered major problems in deciding who was responsible for dealing with the 2010 *Deepwater* disaster; after that, the US Federal government sought to ratio-nalise responsibility for the management of its coastal interests but with only moderate success.[65]

This leads to the next necessary step in integrated maritime governance which is to fold such a maritime security framework into the tapestry of differing national mar-itime economic interests discussed in the previous chapter. Ideally, countries have to think through their requirements in ocean management strategically and arrive at a properly balanced policy that is comprehensive – not captured by any particular sectional maritime interest but representing all of them with sense and equity. Everything maritime is connected, one way or another, to everything else. A nation-wide oceans policy helps identify overall objectives and sets an agenda for consequent operational implementation. High-minded aspiration, accordingly, is turned into ef-fective practice. Only with that can the country's maritime interests be developed, extended and defended, and order maintained at sea. Hence the development around the world of formal declarations of broad state policies towards the sea, such as Russia's *The Maritime Doctrine of the Russian Federation* adopted in 2015.[66]

This is easy to say but much harder to effect, both at the national and the regional level. Nationally, Maydman's 'maritime affair' will typically involve many different government departments whose sectoral interests have to be balanced. All countries have this problem in integration no matter how developed they may be. For example, both Indonesia and India have over a dozen interested departments of central gov-ernment and legions of local interests. They both clearly want to reduce the overlaps and confusions that result by producing a useful oceans policy that integrates every-thing. 'Siloed sector-based governance systems,' says one expert however, 'are the norm.'[67] But, should all the maritime interests be gathered under one Ministry or department of state, or systematically distributed and linked together between the main stake-holders? Should such an agency direct maritime policy or coordinate it? To what extent does this require, first of all, the wholesale reform of the civil service and adjustments to the balance between central and local government? What role should the navy and the ministry of defence play in all this? Such key questions are numerous and may seem common to all, but the answers will be distinctive to each country and to its particular and unique circumstances. There is no 'right' and 'wrong' way of resolving such issues.

At the same time, India and Indonesia, have both shown that they are also fully aware that integrated and effective maritime governance cannot be achieved in isolation from the policies of regional neighbours and external countries. Accepting this, India's Prime Minister Narendra Modi has outlined a holistic oceans policy that called for a regional approach to balanced multidimensional economic development at sea, not least in his SAGAR (Security and Growth for All in the Region) project as first outlined in Mauritius in March 2015.[68] For the same reason maritime outreach was one of the five pillars in President Jokowi's development agenda for Indonesia. Such aspirations de-monstrate rising awareness of the advantages of a regional maritime security community aiming collectively to assert, establish and maintain maritime order.[69] Given the universal threat of climate change this is equally true of the global level.

This multilevel approach to the collective control of the various forms of maritime disorder and the sustainable use of the ocean reinforces the need for countries intent on the longer-term development and protection of their maritime interests to act positively on the regional and global levels as well as domestically.

9.7 Conclusion

This chapter has focussed on the concept of, the need for, and the requirements of, the assertion of authority over what happens at sea. The world's peace and prosperity and each country's capacity to extend and defend its maritime interests depend on this to a significant degree.

Naval forces have been shown to have an important role in this complex maritime campaign and it is to their specific development that we will now turn in the last section of this book.

Notes

1 Quoted in Ziegler, Hannes, 'Very Prejudicial to the Service of the Revenue; The British Army on Coastal Duty in Eighteenth Century East Anglia,' *British Journal for Military History*, Vol. 7, No. 1 (March 2021).
2 Hoppit, *Land of Liberty?*, 246–8. The most comprehensive review of the Revenue service is still Elizabeth Hoon, *The Organisation of the English Customs System*, reprinted, (Newton Abbot: David and Charles, 1968).
3 Rafferty, Mathew Taylor, '"The Law is the Lord of the Sea": Maritime Law as Global Maritime History,' in Benton, Lauren and Perl-Rosenthal, Nathan (Eds), *A World at Sea: Maritime Practices and Global History*, Ibid, 62.
4 Quoted in ibid.
5 AFP 'S Korea shoots at Chinese boats for the first time.' *Straits Times*, 3 November 2016; Gabriel Dominguez, 'Duterte orders military to secure unoccupied islands and reefs in the SCS,' *Jane's Defence Weekly*, 19 April 2017.
6 Timothy Walker, 'Why African States Must Resolve their Maritime Boundary Disputes,' *Institute for Strategic Studies, Policy Brief no 80*, October 2015. Sam Bateman, 'Sovereignty as an Obstacle to Effective Oceans Governance and Maritime Boundary-Making – The case of the South China Sea,' in Clive Schofield, Seokwoo Lee and Moon-sang Kwon (Eds), *Limits of Maritime Jurisdiction* (Leiden: Brill Academic Publishers, 2013), 201–24.
7 'Outlook for China's maritime environment 'not optimistic': top oceanic officer,' *Xinhua*, 13 March 2012.
8 Graham Readfearn, 'Scientists say fish species now vanishing from seas around equator on a huge scale,' *The Guardian*, 8 April 2021.
9 Ellen MacArthur Foundation, *New Plastics Economy Background to Key Statistics*, February 2016.
10 Tabitha Grace Mallory, 'Preserving Diversity and Diversity: Challenges to Managing the Marine Environment in the South China Sea' Unpublished Paper, November 2016.
11 Don Liddick, 'Illegal Fishing and Organized Crime: A Threat to Maritime Security?, Penn State-Fayette in Piracy- Studies.Org.'
12 'Sustainable fishing reforms to be blocked by EU states,' 16 March 2012.
13 For an Icelandic account see Valur Ingimundarson, 'Fighting the Cold Wars in the Cold War,' *Journal of the RUSI*, June 2003.
14 Politakis, George P., *Modern Aspects of the Law of Naval warfare and Armed Neutrality* (London: Kegan Paul, 1998), 627.

15 Elleman. B., and Paine S.C.M. (Eds), *Commerce Raiding: Historical Case Studies* (Lmdon: Routledge, 2010) is a good survey. Some argue that Western concepts of piracy have not always applied in places like Southeast Asia with its concept of maritime tribute and pre-modern state-craft. Robert J. Antony 'Turbulent Waters: Sea Raiding in Early Modern SEA,' *Mariner's Mirror* 99:1 (February 2013), 23–38 and N.A.M. Rodger, 'The Law and Language of Private Naval Warfare,' *Mariner's Mirror,* Vol. 100, No. 1 (February 2014), 1–16.

16 Liss, Caroline and Biggs Ted, *Piracy in Southeast Asia: Trends, Hotspots and Responses* (London: Routledge, 2017), 1–31.

17 'Somalia's ever arduous transition,' *IISS Strategic Comments* Vol. 23, Comment 6 March 2017.

18 This figure includes the costs of ransoms, re-routing, excess insurance, increased merchant ship protective measures, naval costs and the cost of prosecutions. Large though it is, this total barely dents the US$ 337 billion dollar value of annual sea-borne trade. See Anna Bowden The Economic Costs of Piracy' accessed at www.rusi.org/downloads/assets/Anna_Bowden.pdf 16 May 2012; Stephen M. Carmel, 'A Contrarian Perspective on Piracy,' Unpublished paper, 4 April 2011.

19 *The Guardian,* 'Al-Qaida suspected in tanker explosion,' 7 October 2002. 'Seafarers Want Navy Escort,' 12 October 2002. Murphy, Martin, *Contemporary Piracy and Maritime Terrorism* (London: ISS Adelphi paper no. 388, 2007) is a useful study of piracy and sea-based terrorism and the alleged links between them.

20 'Terror Boat was almost nabbed off Mumbai,' *The Times of India,* 10 December 2008.

21 'Sewage and fertilisers 'are killing the seas,' *The Guardian,* 30 March 2004; 'Time is running out to curb effects of deep sea pollution,' *The Guardian,* June 2006. For the background see Van Dyke (1993). For IWCO Report see Herr (2000), 44–51.

22 'Climate refugees can't weather the rising seas,' *The Straits Times,* 5 December 2011; 'Pacific isle may move entire populace,' *The Straits Times,* 11 March 2012.

23 Australia's Oceans Policy (1998) (vol. 2), 7.

24 Liss, Carolin and Biggs Ted, *Piracy in Southeast Asia: Trends, Hotspots and Responses* (London: Routledge, 2017), 160. Arguably the 1982 UN Convention on the Law of the Sea can be seen in this light.

25 Liss and Biggs, *Piracy in Southeast Asa,* op cit, 130.

26 Mackinder, *Britain and the British Seas,* op cit, 12.

27 Roxburg, C. et al., *Lions on the move: The progress and potential of African economies',* McKinsey Global Institute Report, June 2010, McKinsey & Company.

28 Okonjo-Iweala, N., 'Securing Development: Challenges of Economic Inclusion'; Swaniker, F., 'Africa's Rising Economies,' *Survival,* August–September 2013, 121–8 and 129–42, respectively.

29 Defence IQ, Interview with Rear Admiral Emmanuel Ogbor, Nigerian Navy, 8 January 2013.

30 Cited in Charles Strathdee, 'Multiple Threats in a Multipolar World,' *Warships International Fleet Review,* March 2017.

31 Urbina, Ian, *The Outlaw Ocean* (New York: Alfred A. Knopf, 2019).

32 Rafferty Baker, 'Canada launching $7 M project to track international 'dark vessels at sea,' *CBC News,* 24 February 2021.

33 Mary Utermolen and Phil Kittock, 'Beyond Illegal Fishing: Tracing IUU Fishing to their On-shore Beneficiaries,' *C4ADS,* 15 February 2017.

34 Australia's Oceans Policy (1998) (vol. 2), 34; *Sydney Morning Herald,* 23 February 2002.

35 'Maritime Awareness: Briefing,' *Jane's Defence Weekly,* 4 April 2007; George Galdorisi, 'Empowering the Global Maritime Partnership with Effective Maritime Domain Awareness,' *RUSI Defence Systems 2010.*

36 London: IMO, 2016 *Amendments to the International Aeronautical and Maritime Search and Rescue IAMSAR Manual,* 2016, 1.

37 See www.emsa.europa.eu for further information.

38 Sarah Percy, 'Maritime Crime and Naval Response,' *Survival,* Vol. 58 No. 3 (June–July 2016), 155–86,175–6.

39 Barnara Opall-Rome, 'Israeli Startup Scours the Seas for Threats,' *Defense News,* 9 November 2015; Buger, Christian and Chan, Jane (Eds), *Paving the Way for Regional Maritime Domain Awareness* (Singapore: RSIS, 2019).

40 The epic pursuit of the Togo-registered fishing boat *South Tomi* detected illegally fishing for Patagonian Toothfish in Australian waters and followed all the way across the Indian Ocean to South Africa where it was finally apprehended by the Royal Australian Naval personnel with the cooperation of the South Africans. It was indeed the 'one that didn't get away.' Lt Cdr Trevor Gibson 'The One that Didn't Get Away,' *Journal of the Australian Naval Institute,* Autumn–Winter, 2001.

41 Palerie, Prabhakaran, *Role of the Coast Guard in the Maritime Security of India* (New Delhi: Knowledge World, 2004) is a comprehensive study of the issues involved. See also Bowers, Ian and Koh, Swee Lean Collin (Eds), *Grey and White Hulls: An International Analysis of the Navy-Coastguard Nexus* (London: Palgrave, 2019).

42 'Fighting the Hydra; Multinational piracy operations move inshore,' *Jane's International Defence Review,* September 2010.

43 Canada's Arctic patrol ship of 2018, the *Harry de Wolf* is 6600 tons and helicopter capable.

44 On this see interview with Peter Cook of SAMI (Security Association for the Maritime Industry) in *Warship International* August 2012; also Segun Adeyemi, 'Nigerian move to outsource naval tasks sparks row,' *Jane's Defence Weekly,* 8 February 2012.

45 Urbina, *The Outlaw Ocean,* op cit, xi.

46 Urbina, *The Outlaw Ocean,* op cit, 4, 47, 107.

47 Interview with Italian naval officers, October 2016; Lorenzo Tondo, 'It's a day off': Wiretaps show Mediterranean immigrants left to die,' *The Guardian,* 16 April 2021.

48 'Captain Kidd: Human Rights Victim,' *New York Times,* 20 April 2008.

49 Urbina, *The Outlaw Ocean,* 199.

50 *The Guardian,* 30 August 2001.

51 Richa Syal, 'They take the sea cucumbers. We're losing our riches,' *The Guardian,* 12 April 2021.

52 Urbina, *The Outlaw Ocean,* op cit, 114.

53 Rosen, Mark E., 'Challenges to Public Order and the Law of the Sea,' in Bekkevold, Jo Inge, and Till, Geoffrey (Eds), *International Order at Sea* (London: Palgrave Macmillan, 2016), 22–6.

54 Choi, Timothy, 'Ready to Secure: A Sea Control Perspective on Canadian Fisheries Management,' in Bowers and Swee (Eds), 234–9.

55 Cited by James Pelkofski, 'Before the Storm: Al Qaida's Coming Maritime Campaign,' *Proceedings of the USNI* December 2005; The background to the crafting of the ISPS Code is usefully summarised in 'IMO 2004: Focus on maritime security' in *IMO News,* No. 3, 2004. Nazery Khalid, *Fear at the Harbour: Securing Ports from Threats in the post 9/11 World* (Risk Intelligence, Strategic Insights No. 17, March 2009).

56 'All Hands on Deck to curb ship emissions,' *The StraitsTimes,* 7 December 2010; For a more detailed review of this see *IMO News,* Editions 3 and 4, 2008, Edition 3, 2009.

57 Carlyle A Thayer, 'Revamping Regional SAR Cooperation,' *Diplomatist,* Vol. 2, No. 5 (May 2014).

58 'Anti-Pirate patrols 'Not really producing': Clinton, *Defense News,* 4 March 2011.

59 Roy, *War in the Indian Ocean,* 262.

60 Bateman, Sam, 'Managing Maritime Security,' in Bekkevold, *International Order at Sea,* op cit and Bowers and Swee, *Grey and White Hulls* are good introductions to the range of possibilities.

61 Yew Lun Tian, 'China authorises coastguard to fire on foreign vessels if needed,' *Reuters,* 27 January 2021; Caitlin Doornbos and Hana Kusumoto, 'Japan Coast Guard may fire on foreign vessels attempting to land on Senkakus, Government says,' *Stars and Stripes On line,* 26 February 2021.

62 Sukjoon Yoon, 'Establishing a Maritime Security Joint-Force Partnership Between the Republic of Korea Navy and the Korean Coast Guard,' in Bowers, *Grey and White Hulls,* op cit.

63 For the poor relations between the *Armada Argentina* and the *Prefectura Naval Argentina* see Nicole Jenne and Maria Lourdes Punte Olivera 'The Navy-Coastguard Nexus in Argentina: Lost in Democratisation?' and for equivalent issues in Italy, Alessandra Giada Dibenedetto, 'Ensuring Security in the Mediterranean Sea: The Italian Navy and the Coast Guard,' both in Bowers, *Grey and White Hulls,* op cit.

64 Swee Lean Collin Koh, 'Singapore's Maritime Security Approach' and Muhammad Arif, 'The Navy Coast Guard Nexus and the Nature of Indonesian Maritime Security Governance,' in Bowers, *Grey and White Hulls*.
65 Urbina, *The Outlaw Ocean,* 204–5.
66 Approved by Presidential Decree, 26 July 2015 (http://docs.ctnd.ru/document/555631869).
67 I am grateful to Steve Raamaker for this comment.
68 G Padmaja 'Modi's Maritime Diplomacy: A Strategic Opportunity,' *Maritime Affairs,* Vol. II, No. 2 (2015).
69 Christian Bueger & Jan Stockbruegger, 'Pirates, Drugs and Navies,' *Journal of the RUSI,* Vol. 161, No. 5 (2016).

10 Naval Power: The Administrative Angle

The best and safest thing of all is when a large force is so well disciplined that it seems to be acting like one man.[1]

The true splendour and glory of the Navy lies in the good Government thereof.[2]

10.1 Introduction

Navies are complicated and expensive organisations and, even from the earliest days, always have been. As the following chapters will show, getting the necessary people, their ships, equipment and supplies and maintaining them, even over short periods of time, has always been difficult and remains so.

Firstly, the people necessary to, sail, operate and maybe fight the fleet had to be hired or conscripted. Since time immemorial that was a permanent challenge for all navies. Sometimes worse than others, but always a challenge. On top of that, there were the countless people necessary to build and maintain the ships. In England until 1715, dockyard workers could be 'impressed' if necessary, just like sailors were to remain for well over a century afterwards. And the task of keeping them all supplied and, not least, paid, required considerable administrative effort too. Since many of these tasks required specialist skills and there were other and often more congenial ways for people to make use of them, it was, and usually is, hard to find, train and retain the necessary personnel in all these areas.

Then the fleet had to be designed and built. The first issue was deciding what it needed to do. In the early Medieval European period this was largely a matter of carrying military forces overseas and supplying them once they landed. Occasionally enemy forces could be attacked in harbour or during the landing operation but such engagements were fought as land battles that just happened to take place on the water. Only later when there was a better chance of intercepting enemy forces on the open sea, and naval gunnery became available were battles that were distinctively 'naval' really possible. The form of individual ships within the fleet would be closely linked with their particular function. The result was a growing variety of much more sophisticated ships and that made their acquisition increasingly complicated and demanding in terms of required resources, building time and, nearly always, money. Accordingly, ship and fleet design and maintenance required a whole host of difficult choices, balancing between alternatives: a few 'great ships' *v.* rather more smaller ones? Which mix of warship characteristics worked best? What proportion of ships should be held 'in Ordinary' – or reserve? How were wooden ships subject to rot and the depredations of the Toredo worm best preserved?

DOI: 10.4324/9781003100553-10

Then, where were the King's ships to come from? They could either be built to order in the state or private shipyards or bought 'off the shelf.' Existing naval ships might need to be reconditioned. Most likely ships would also need to be hired or requisitioned too, but that was a much more temporary state of affairs. The King (or the state) would often maintain a core squadron of vessels that could be augmented when necessary by hiring or by new build if the war lasted long enough.

The fleet would also require bases, dockyards and shore-side establishments from which to operate. Were they to be temporary or permanent – and on what scale? Both the position and permanence of naval bases and their supporting infrastructure depended very much on the operational scenario as well as the availability of the necessary finance.[3] It all meant developing and maintaining the navy's real estate in a manner that was fit for the purpose of the day. Welding all this into an effective maritime organisation demanded a challenging range of varied, specialist skills and procedures. England's navy in the reign of the first Elizabeth comprised just some 30–45 ships but depended on dockyards that developed into 'the largest industrial organisation in the land and needed a huge and relentless intake of materials' like wood, cordage, iron, glass, coal-tar, hemp, canvas and much else bedsides.[4]

Supplies for the fleet and its people needed to be found from somewhere as well. These were copious and amazingly varied. In addition to marine supplies for the ships, foodstuffs and other provisions for the ship's people had to be supplied. Given the extreme perishability of most foodstuffs at this time, this was a major challenge requiring specialist expertise. The ship's military equipment, especially its all-important cannon (from the time in the early 16th Century when fighting *at sea* became the preoccupation), had to be ordered, manufactured, paid for and supplied. This required the customer to understand, and be able to exploit, current and future technological development, and maybe steer it in the appropriate directions. Some of this could be supplied from state-run enterprises; more often the navy would rely on the services of private contractors, so their special procedures and needs had to be understood and catered for as well. This could mean having to appoint agents and contractors to go out into the market at home or abroad to find and buy what was needed.[5] In both cases, manufacturing enterprises had to be located or set up in order to provide the fleet with the ships and supplies it needed.

Running through all of this was the issue of cost, dependence on the availability of the necessary money, and its judicious expenditure. Raising the necessary revenue, allocating it and supervising its spending were all important, and in many ways key, parts of the naval enterprise.[6] How this was done both in establishing a navy fleet or in sustaining it over a period of time depended very much on the nature of the state in question. While the management of money matters varied enormously between countries and over the years, a common element was the need for credit, because navies were, and remain, extremely expensive. Their budgetary requirements often exceeded the finance immediately available.

Maintaining the fleet over time was the real challenge. Then as now, it was a question of the management of risk, of balancing these naval perceptions and requirements against what the economy and state resources could sustainably support. Whatever the result, how the money was spent remained critical; the recording and accountability of expenditure was needed to ensure that one got the 'best bang for the buck,' which is perhaps the final justification for taking naval administration seriously.

After his long career in the Royal Navy, Henry Maydman was well aware of this, and in particular of the role of the Navy Board, the Victualling Board and the Ordnance Board[7] in supplying what was needed. But if he was a man with a mission, that mission in his *Naval Speculations* was to encourage reform in all this. By the end of the 17th Century, he thought, the Navy had got into such a state of decay that a re-launch was needed. The Navy had to be re-invented. Maydman's wholesale re-commendations were a bid to do just that. They covered a whole range of things but underneath the particular topics he addressed, he spotted a need to reform what he often called the 'Method' – the broad manner in which the Navy was being run, and which affected everything it did. Only with such a reform would it be possible to return the Navy to what he rather mistakenly imagined to have been its regular, previous 'well-ordered and well governed' state. The Navy needed, in short, a 'true Method of Government.'[8]

Maydman was really talking about administrative efficiency and what Jeremy Black has called a navy's 'organisational sophistication' – the ability to make the most of what it has.[9] The need for this is universal across time and place. 'One is struck' says Kenneth Swope of Ming China's preparations for the Great East Asian War of 1592–1598, 'by the emphasis placed upon logistics and the acumen of Chinese and Korean bureaucrats in estimating such things as transport times and wastage rates.' They needed to take account of regional variations in their capacity to supply what was needed, and given the decentralised nature of the Ming accounting system were well aware of the crucial importance of putting everything together.[10] Today, Australia's Admiral Tim Barrett argues that 'it is critically important that the Navy visualises itself as a fighting system' and shows how important it is that all the elements of the system are managed and made to work together. Delivering capability is what naval administration should be all about and is the subject of this chapter.[11]

Although obviously critically important to their development and maintenance, this quality of navies is very difficult to talk about in the abstract. Because the proof of the pudding lies in the eating – the result being the best indicator of success – it is all too easy to get seduced into the detail of what was done, and how it was done, in a way that obscures the basic importance of over-all organisational efficiency. Moreover, because each navy is unique in the way it reacts to its particular circumstances, greater detail risks undermining the general applicability of the basic points to other navies. Maydman himself was half aware of the problem, acknowledging the dangers of departing from his broad review by going into too much detail; 'if I proceed,' he said, 'I should be too tedious in this work.'[12] Even his most ardent admirers can hardly deny his less than perfect success in avoiding the temptation to obscure his own argument by too often disappearing down the nearest rabbit hole. Fortunately, he usually re-appears a few pages later, resuming normal service.

But when exploring the general concept of organisational and administrative efficiency, another major rabbit hole opens up. Many navies are large complex organisations and so share characteristics with other large complex organisations. Consequently, some would say, the navy is a business – so run it like one. Others would be appalled by the very idea. Navies, they point out, are not set up to make a profit; instead they are infused with ideas of public service. Few naval outputs can be quantified. Treating navies as a business is not just inappropriate – it may in fact do harm. The issue of the value and applicability of general organisational theory to the understanding of the development or navies accordingly depends on which of these views is taken. Here the line adopted is that 'business studies' and 'organisation theory' do apply, but that distinctively naval considerations will often serve to constrain their relevance. Accordingly, this chapter will acknowledge but not peer too deeply down this necessary but worryingly seductive rabbit hole.

10.2 Navies, Administration and Permanency

The first and obvious question is what do we mean a 'navy' anyway? A '… permanently established squadron of …vessels,' says medieval historian Susan Rose, 'supported by an administrative system and dockyards for maintenance and ship-building.'[13] As understood today, navies, says Nicholas Rodger, are '… instruments of the state; permanent fleets of warships, manned by professional officers and men, supported by an elaborate infrastructure and maintained by the revenues of central government.'[14] They are, he concludes, a comparatively modern invention. They came later than standing armies and were intimately associated with the rise of the modern, bureaucratic state, capable of raising the necessary resources on a sustainable basis. In this respect at least, navies, administration and bureaucracy go together.

The emphasis here is not just on the creation of a force capable of operating at sea, but on its maintenance over time – on relative permanency. This distinguishes 'a navy' from 'royal fleets' or naval forces raised for a specific purpose at a specific time – here today and gone tomorrow. It is only when its administrators start to prepare for tomorrow, and even the day after tomorrow, rather than simply focus on today, that 'naval forces' or 'fleets' start to become 'navies.' Accordingly, issues of administration are not just about the tedious requirements of getting things done; instead they are at the very heart of what navies are.

Both Susan Rose and Nicholas Rodger were investigating the vexed and long-running question of when the Royal Navy 'started' as a permanent force. As with many other navies, it was all a matter of degree, leaving plenty of room for different opinions. Permanent or standing navies evolved slowly, often in fits and starts, going through various intermediate stages, developing administrative support as needed.

Standing navies were and remain very expensive, and so only developed in response to perceived need. This could only be done to the extent that the king, city or country had the economy, the population base, the dockyards and the financial resources to pay for them. The way in which this happened varied from one country to another, but there was enough in common for something of a historic pattern to emerge.

In medieval England, as elsewhere, there was a widespread initial preference for a bespoke fleet raised only when events showed it to be necessary. Thus in 1338 when Edward III planned to invade the Low Countries, he managed to raise 371 ships and 12,263 mariners carrying 8770 military personnel and 4614 horses.[15] Eight years later, in 1346, his invasion of France needed over 700 ships, including 38 foreign 'hires.'[16] In such cases, there was a heavy reliance on ships provided by the king's subjects either levied in some way, hired on a commercial basis or simply requisitioned. Because the ships existed already and the mariners did not need training, this process did not usually take very long. Nonetheless, creating a fleet more or less from scratch called for an efficient administrative system. Detailed records had to be kept and monitored, contracts drawn up and so forth. The deeper the king's purse and the more bureaucratic the state, the easier this was to provide. But, delivering the necessary administrative support cost money too.

Edward's fleets were impermanent, raised for a particular purpose, thereby limiting, if not completely avoiding, defence expenditure when naval forces seemed strategically unnecessary. This was the normal practice of the time, but its extent depended on the strategic situation; the more warlike the times, the more these temporary fleets approached permanent status. Edward's two fleets were raised separately but within a decade; there was doubtless an overlap between the two, with some of the same people and vessels being involved. It was the same in the Mediterranean. Incessant squabbles over trade, ports and colonies between Aragon and the competing city states of Italy in the 14th and 15th Centuries, also meant that war fleets as proto-navies existed in the Mediterranean most of the time.

The prospect of a surprise attack was another incentive that pointed in the same direction of longer periods of existence if not permanency. Even though there was little prospect of intercepting such an attack on the high seas, a standing force might well deter it or, failing that, help in immediate local defence. Thus the Viking attack on the Muslim Caliphate of Cordoba in 844, provided a strong incentive for the victim afterwards to develop a sophisticated and centralised naval system with standing forces, to try to prevent a repeat of this disaster. Although this system did not survive the subsequent collapse of the Caliphate, it was a very early example of a major move towards the creation of a standing fleet, or navy.[17]

Normally, the king would often own a few ships himself and so be able to use them as the basis for expanding the fleet when needed. When not needed for this, they could be used for other non-military purposes such as trading to raise revenue. The reign of England's Henry V (1386–1422) marked a mid-way point in the drift towards a standing Royal Navy. Henry maintained two -to six royal ships, hiring or requisitioning the rest when he needed to. He was the first English King to try to keep his royal shipmasters together as a single body – the beginnings of an officer corps. He gave them innovative if not unprecedented annual salaries, although they were not generous; to make ends meet, some of them had recourse to a bit of piracy on the side. Organising all this called for 'the hard and detailed work of the sober, serious people who kept the royal fleet in being.' When Henry V died in 1422, though, most of his fleet was sold off to help pay his debts; his bureaucrats turned to other things and his body of semi-professional royal mariners dispersed.[18]

Through the 14th and 15th Centuries, the same slow and often fitful, drift towards more of a standing naval force was also evident in France and elsewhere.[19] In fact, with their impressive state shipyards at Rouen, the French were rather in advance of the English in this respect. The model varied. Both Venice and its rival Genoa maintained substantial fleets. Venice was an example of a centralised state-run navy based on galleys. Its tight regulation of sea-based trade and the maintenance of a superlative dockyard in the famous *Arsenale* showed that it was indeed a *stato da mar,* a state wedded to the sea. For the 14th Century, it was 'a real laboratory to modernity.'[20]

But if Venice was a state that had a navy, Genoa was the reverse. It was a web of private fleets that had a state, and a notably disputatious one at that. The entrepreneurial instincts of its ruling families and the sheer maritime professionalism of people like Andrea Doria guaranteed its success and ultimately its critical role in the support of Spain and the Hapsburg empire. The difference was that Genoa did not bear the burden of a state bureaucracy for the sea affaire, but delegated this to its leading citizens. Suffering its consequences, Genoa eventually followed the Venetian lead to state control by the middle of the 16th Century.[21]

Another feature that tended to push states in the direction of setting up navies rather than fleets only raised when necessary was the extent to which evolving technology and the different fighting styles that it led to increasingly distinguished the merchant ship from the fighting warship. This made simply relying on 'ships taken up from trade' (STUFT) more challenging. To a certain extent, the distinction between the warship and the merchant ship was evident from the very start, since the latter needed enhanced cargo space, very possibly at the expense of speed, handiness and military utility. The increasing dilemma was demonstrated by the appearance in the late 15th Century of the Portuguese fleet caravel, regarded by some as the first dedicated ocean-going sailing warship of the modern European era. At some 150–180 tons, the needs of its crew, artillery and military supplies accounted for so much of its carrying capacity as to make it 'almost completely useless for cargo.' But it was ideal in fleet escort and expeditionary operations.[22] Cargo-carrying was better left to the larger *nau*.

In the kind of infantry fighting at sea characteristic of the earlier period, the advantages of height led to the addition of possibly temporary fighting platforms (or castles) fore and aft, and sometimes on mast-tops too. If the temporary 'warship' was only going to be used as a troop or supply transport, much less militarisation was required. Even so, higher levels of costly conversion of merchant-ships would be needed if the strength of the prospective victim of raiding operations or invasions demanded the carriage of heavy cavalry, catapults and other heavy ordnance and equipment. When sea fighting required serious naval artillery intended to smash ships rather than just kill people, conversion would be more demanding still.

This new technology was costly, increasingly pushing investment in it beyond the reach of all but the biggest of private fleet operators. Again, the more such capabilities seemed to be a lasting requirement, the greater the incentive to explore the cost-effectiveness of specialised ships for war instead. These military-technological developments undoubtedly accelerated the shift to professional and permanent navies, although how and when this happened remains a matter of lively debate.

Summarising, it is generally agreed that a recognisable standing Royal Navy had certainly emerged by the early years of the reign of Henry VIII, perhaps more specifically in the reforms of 1512–1514. Elsewhere in Europe the trajectory was much the same. This meant there was a naval future to be catered for, alongside the naval present. This in turn meant there was a need for a standing bureaucracy. Front office bureaucrats, alongside their rulers and political masters, defined the need for, and tasks of, the fleet and shaped its size and shape. The backroom bureaucrats, in every area, did the necessary veering and hauling to ensure that the fleet remained on course to deliver what was expected of it – either for the present or for the future or for both. Upon the success of their multifarious administrative activities depended on the success of the fleet. 'The powers best able to wage war,' says Jeremy Black, 'were those who got close to a synthesis of military organisation and political/administrative capacity.'[23]

The key questions, then, were the administrators' level of experience and expertise, their relative success and how that success might be measured. As we shall see, even at the time of its golden Nelsonian era, the administrative efficiency of the Royal Navy, left a lot to be desired, but it was much better than that of its main adversaries – and this was the main point. Administrative efficiency is a not an absolute, but a characteristic relative to others as well as to the challenges of the task.

All too often, those at the receiving end of any less-than-perfect product of the administrative process were apt to focus on its deficiencies and failings rather than its strengths and successes. The reputation of most aspects of naval administration was often worse than it deserved. This may help explain the low regard with which these administrators, uniformed or not, were often held.[24] Perhaps, to some degree, it also shaped the extent to which the focus of naval literature has been on naval biographies, ship design, fleet operations and the guns, smoke and dramas of battle, rather than on the, generally speaking, less appealing supporting work going on (or not!) behind the scenes.[25] Nonetheless, 'it was the thinking, organisation and administrative ability of the bureaucracy at the heart of the state, founded on an expanding maritime economy and financial capability' claims Roger Morriss, 'which made Britain the dominant power at sea between 1755 and 1815.'[26]

More generally, an effective and professional naval bureaucracy is key to the successful setting up of a navy, (or rescuing it from a period of neglect) and to its maintenance over time. It deserves more attention than it often gets. The question then arises, what does experience suggest leads to administrative success?

10.3 The Qualities of Successful Naval Administration

At the strategic, operational and tactical levels, navies have to identify and prioritise their tasks, allocate resources accordingly and finally 'deliver the goods.' Their ability to do so effectively depends in large measure on their administrative efficiency. That in turn depends on the quality of their procedures and their administrators. This chapter identifies nine closely related and generally mutually supportive indicators of administrative success that seem to have paid off in the past.

A look not just at the experience of the Royal Navy in Henry Maydman's time but also at that of the founding of four new navies, those of Chile, Peru, Brazil and Greece will help illustrate some of the important points. All four of these new navies owed at least something to the redoubtable if controversial Admiral Lord Cochrane at the beginning of the 19th Century, even if, in some cases, more in the negative than the positive. Setting up a navy in the first place is of course a particularly demanding aspiration and so provides a good test of what in naval administration seems to work, and what doesn't. The following have often proved necessary.

10.3.1 An Orientation towards the Future

This flows naturally from the notion of the permanence of navies, and the consequent assumption that there is a naval future to plan and prepare for. Maydman was clearly in the business of establishing the Navy on a more secure footing to be able to deal with an unpredictable future and anything that it or the French could throw against England. This could mean building up the future supply of mariners, or providing dockyard apprenticeships, roughly on the basis of one per eight dockyard workers, so the Navy would never run out of joiners, caulkers, sail-makers, or hammermen 'for anchors and large iron-work.'[27] It could mean building new dockyards and bases better to support future naval deployments. It could mean striking a balance, perhaps in a war, between modest ships that could be built quickly and more sophisticated ones that would take longer. It could mean the conscious pursuit of 'readiness' against future threats. It was Philip II of Spain, of all people, who acknowledged in September 1555'...that the chief defence of the realm of England consists in this, that her ships are always ready and in good order so that they can defend the realm against all invasion ... always prepared and in readiness." Thirty-three years later, Philip discovered that his advice had indeed been followed.[28]

Preparing for the future could also mean defending the navy's institutional resilience against domestic turmoil, and in the England of Maydman's day there was plenty of that. The new navies of South America, though, faced a much bigger challenge. Like the US of the Revolutionary era, or the South Asian navies addressed in the last chapter, the task was not to maintain or hopefully improve what was already there but to create something new. In this case, it is hard not to focus on the immediate imperatives of the present rather than on the needs of the longer term. The same goes for naval administrators having to cope with the urgencies of war.

This calls for a bureaucracy not only capable of striking an effective balance between the present and the future but also of developing a clear idea about what the demands of the future are likely to be. In times of change, this is extremely demanding. Admiral Collingwood, Nelson's right-hand man, had the habit of planting acorns wherever he went on the basis that the oak they produced would be of value to his successors. This was preparing for a future that resembled the present. The naval industrial revolution, though, made a nonsense of his expectations, but basically his approach was surely correct. Successful naval administrators have to do their best to lay the foundations for a successful future. They need the procedures and bureaucratic skills to prepare for tomorrow's problems as well as today's. This is by no means as easy as it sounds.

10.3.2 A Sense of Mission and Duty

When reading *Naval Speculations*, it doesn't take long to realise that Henry Maydman was motivated by a professional love of the Royal Navy, at least as it ought to be, and straightforward all-round patriotism, tinged with religious conviction. Nor does it take long to see that he expected the Navy's officers and men and their officials and supporters ashore to be animated and driven by these same convictions. The resultant sense of mission and duty would inspire professionalism and a determination on everyone's part to do their best for the 'naval affair.' In the later words of the Navy Board, '... we are by the nature of our office responsible to the public for the due execution of the trust reposed in us...'[29]

That sense of mission might well be inspired by the kind of exemplary naval leadership of the kind touched on in Chapter 7, supported maybe by the punishment of transgressors. Without question, Admiral Lord Cochrane aspired to be a leader of this kind. He considered there to be few limits to the benefits that an active, motivated and well-founded navy could bestow on a nation's fortunes, and that in theory at least these would justify the expense of setting them up and running them efficiently. For this reason he was often exasperated by the operational consequences of the inefficiency of much of the Chilean naval administration in 1818–1823. Inevitably at the start, it was rough and ready, plagued with personal and institutional discord, corruption, theft, indolence and always seriously underfunded.' Away with Siestas, and Godsfeast and fastdays,' he declared. 'Let all attend to their duty without the monstrous interruptions and delays that take place, especially in the public departments.'[30] Even when preparing fopr the ultimaely triumphant Chilean liberation of Peru, everything need for the fleet was regarded as top priority so in effect nothing was. Not surprisingly relations between the fleet and its people and institutions was bad.

Sometimes Cocrane's assumptions about permanency were in marked contrast to the rather more caveatted view of at least some of his South American hosts. There were many in Chile, for example, who doubted, given the great expense involved, whether it was worth retaining a navy at all, once its main purpose, the interdiction of Spanish reinforcement and supply shipping, the support of the Army – and the war of independence itself was over.[31] Clearly a much greater sense of mission was required for a navy as a permanent force for national good rather than a temporary 'hostilities-only' expedient.

The Brazilian navy had a bumpy start occasioned in part by the fact that the commitment to the cause of many of so many of its Portuguese sailors was at best conditional, particularly on the arrival of their pay. The Brazilian Navy's long-term survival and prosperity, however owed much to the vision of its second Minister of Marine Francisco Villela Barbosa and to his cold, calculating and ruthless administrative efficiency. Much the same was true of his Chilean equivalent, Jose Ignatio Zenteno, likewise no charmer, but organisationally astute and dedicated to the long-term success of the navy.

Both were all too aware of the fact that the culture of their countries, so far, was basically continental, and that there was a chance their previous colonial masters might stage a later sea-based counter-offensive. Likewise in the turbulent South American world other more local threats might emerge, at sea as elsewhere. Both of these contingencies required an effective and functioning navy.[32] For all his success as a frigate commander and his operational brilliance, Cochrane personally was no administrator; but his reputation and his repeated successes at sea provided the driving inspiration that both Villela Barbosa and Zenteno profited from in their administrative campaigns.

10.3.3 A Sufficiency of Administrators

Finding, keeping and deploying enough effective administrators, whether in uniform or not, is the third of these necessary qualities. Maydman only refers to it elliptically when talking about what he called the 'Architecture' of people below the dockyard Master Builder who all '...in their distinct stations, execute his orders and are material instruments under him.'[33] Whoever they were, such people had to be lured away from other tasks and occupations (in this case often private shipyards). Many of these alternative sources of employment could prove more lucrative and, given the waxing and waning of navies in an ever-changing economic and international context, very possibly more permanent. The key was getting the numbers of such people commensurate with the task.

This balance has often proved hard to calculate. Sometimes the numbers seemed surprisingly low. In 1760, at the height of the Seven Years' War, the Admiralty comprised just 7 commissioners, 2 secretaries and 7 clerks with another 12 for hostilities only.[34] On the other hand, the complexity of running a navy seemed to many outsiders to require suspiciously high numbers in comparison with other aspects of government. By the early 1790s, the Admiralty Office had grown to 45 at a time when the Treasury had 17 people, and the Home and Foreign Offices 19 each. This impression of apparent prolificacy in human capital was reinforced by the fact that the Admiralty Office at the time was by no means the largest element in naval administration: the Navy Office had 108 people all told, the Victualling Office comprised 65 in 1787, and this leaves out the 15,000 or so employed in the Royal dockyards by 1815.[35]

Unsurprisingly, this very common and widespread tendency has often led to complaints that the administrative' tail' was growing at the expense of the operational 'teeth.' In 1955, Cecil Northcote Parkinson based his famous law that 'work expands so as to fill the time available for its completion' on his review of the British Civil Service that started with a comparison of Admiralty statistics in 1914 and 1928.[36] These showed that while the number of ships and officers and men in the service had significantly declined, that of the officials had substantially increased. Parkinson added that the 8118 Admiralty staff of 1935 came to number 33,788 by 1954. Related observations that the uniformed part of the service had become top-heavy with more admirals than ships, too many chiefs and too few indians, were, and remain, equally common.

Against such a background of accumulated scepticism it has proved all too easy for reformers to take a scythe to naval officialdom, sometimes with lamentable results. In sum, the effective matching of numbers of people to the demands of the task has contributed greatly to administrative efficiency, and still does.

All the same, it has often proved very difficult to provide. In the Royal Navy's records, complaints of inadequacy especially in times of '… a great increase in business,' are common. In 1727/1728 the Navy Board complained that after a reduction in the number of clerks, '… the numbers retained in these offices are but barely sufficient to carry on the current business with any tolerable despatch.'[37] The problem is especially acute for nations with little in the way of a maritime background and so a limited pool of maritime people from which to draw when trying to set up a navy from scratch.

Of course, these observations about the number of administrators available have to be qualified by others about their quality and the manner in which they are used. Observers both uniformed and not, who comment on India's naval bureaucracy do so on the basis of their inefficiency, not their inadequate number.[38]

10.3.4 Loyalty to the Naval, Governmental and National Interest

Loyalty to the Government and the national cause amongst the navy's administrators was a particular problem for the Royal Navy of Maydman's time as it had to pick its course between adherence to the old regime and the new one that emerged after the Glorious Revolution of 1688. Many at this time were uncertain about which cause it was worth being loyal to. To an extent, similar issues continued well into the 18th Century, as party politics and different conceptions of what the national interest was plagued professional relationships within the Navy and between its leaders and the politicians of the day. The execution of Admiral Byng on his quarter-deck, 'in order to encourage the others,' is just the most obvious example of this. The special danger in such cases is the tendency to appoint people for their perceived loyalty rather than their administrative and operational ability.

The related problem that Cochrane claimed to have encountered in South America was that in those volatile times, with the emergence of the new nations of Chile, Peru and Brazil and perhaps still more that of Greece as it struggled out from under Ottoman rule, visions of the desired future varied enormously. Cochrane's own social and political ideas were liberal to the point of being radical. In their initial appeal for him to come to their help, the Brazilians hoped that he would bring to the job the values and procedures, 'the marvellous order and incomparable discipline of the mighty Albion.'[39] But they wanted him to bring those qualities to the navy not necessarily to the state, for the new Brazil in the main was a conservative and monarchical country. His ideas and those of his new and very varied South American political masters did not always coincide.[40] This may help explain the extent to which he sometimes was seen as putting his own personal interest (in his case principally over money) above the interests of the state. However varied their own visions of the desired future, the locals were often sceptical about the extent to which the British.

This went for many others in the naval service. It underlines the point that the efficiency and loyalty of navies will reflect and be in part shaped by the order and efficiency of the state they serve. Unsurprisingly, in such volatile times in South America and Greece, an extreme shortage of money, corruption, political dissension and the shameless pursuit of personal advantage were all commonplace, and much naval practice, Cochrane's included, simply reflected that reality. Inevitably this was detrimental to administrative efficiency.

Less obviously, there is a balance to be struck, especially amongst senior administrators, between loyalty to one's political masters and one's professional knowledge and judgement. The continuous tensions between being 'red' or 'expert' characteristic of Soviet Russia or China showed the dangers for naval effectiveness in exhorting the first at the expense of the second. The willingness to speak truth to power, in such cases, might be the real loyalty. It might, on the other hand, also mean an abrupt and perhaps particularly unpleasant end to one's career.

10.3.5 *Individual and Corporate Honesty*

'Corruption, bribery and private interest' were Maydman's particular collective target.[41] The problem with corruption is that it so easily results in decisions being made for the wrong reasons. The apparent success of those corrupted can also chip away at the probity of the whole administrative system. Both can easily undermine naval effectiveness.

The high costs of navies, however, mean large amounts of money need to float around and so can be illicitly siphoned off in corrupt practices. Accordingly this combination of enhanced opportunity plus some of the less admirable traits of human nature means that naval corruption seems as old as time. Back in China's Song dynasty, around 1051 AD, the Academician-in-waiting Xu Yuan in the beginning of his career was Intendant of Exchange which meant he was responsible for checking up standards. 'He was greatly distressed by the fact that most official boats had proved unseaworthy, perhaps because the contractors had used fewer nails than they charged for. Since all the badly constructed boats had sunk, there was no means for checking the number of nails actually used so the suspected perpetrators were getting away with it.

> One day Xu Yuan gave orders that a newly constructed boat be burned. (After having raked the ashes) the nails were weighed and found to represent but one tenth of the amount paid for. He then fixed the amount to be used.[42]

This example shows how often fraud and corruption have been associated with naval development; the 'Fat Leonard' tribulations of the US Navy from 2015 and President Xi's campaign against corruption in the present-day Chinese military show that they still are.

The fact that Xu Yuan simply fixed things rather than punished the perpetrators probably reflected his doubt about whether it was the contractors or the dockyard officials who were responsible. It shows that corruption is difficult to identify, punish and eliminate, especially when it is associated with cultures of gift-giving and is widespread throughout society. Certainly even in one of its golden ages, the Napoleonic wars, the Royal Navy could be legitimately criticised for its patronage, corruption and sloppy procedures by reformers as varied as the First Lord, Earl St Vincent and, at the same time, by one of his most infuriating critics, Thomas, Admiral Lord Cochrane when launching his 'frontal assault on that jungle of corruption which his friend Cobbett used to call "the THING."'[43] Their quarrel, though, was in part about methods of reform, rather than its necessity. Interestingly, although Cochrane railed against both corruption and patronage he himself benefited from both and practised them too, quite extensively in all five of the navies he served in.[44]

Although by this second decade of the 19th Century the performance of an over-tired Royal Navy was beginning to tail off,[45] its experience shows that a degree of corruption and of institutionalised patronage are by no means incompatible with operational success, but they can hardly be said to help it.

Accordingly, effective navies have tried to contain corruption to manageable proportions. One approach has been to ensure that all in the naval service are paid enough and paid regularly. Paying people enough reduces the need for additional sources of income. By any account, the Royal Navy was slow to do this. 'Prize money' was seen as a completely acceptable way of incentivising operational and tactical performance. The novels of Jane Austen show that this was seen as a perfectly honourable way of amassing a personal fortune. 'Ah, those were pleasant days when I had the *Laconia!*' says Captain Frederick Wentworth, the wholly admirable hero of *Persuasion*, 'How fast I made money in her!'[46]

The problem was that prize money blurred the difference between personal interest and the good of the service and also yielded endless divisive arguments and resentments about the amount and allocation of the money in question. Even the great Nelson was not immune to this. Cochrane's career certainly showed exactly the same financial preoccupations, if to an extreme and remorseless degree that shocked many of his contemporaries.[47] Since enormous sums of money could be made by people in the front line like this, it is also hardly surprising that those who supported them ashore should also look around for equivalent perquisites of the trade. For Dockyard workers it was the right to take away 'chips' (wood off-cuts) which led to the wholesale stealing of timber. For officials it could be coming to dubious deals with contractors.

Paying people regularly was important too. In 1754, the British Admiralty made the essential point that some were tempted into taking advantage of opportunities for gain which could be 'imputed to no other cause than that necessity which the insufficient pay of the officer imposes on him of either ruining himself in the discharge of his duty or of increasing his profits by imposition on the public.'[48] Cash-strapped governments in South America and Greece meant that Cochrane had endless difficulty getting his men paid, although he was more successful in securing his own emoluments. The results were both predictable and unhappy, especially in Greece, where disaffected sailors either deserted, turned instead to out-and-out piracy and other forms of brigandage or simply fought amongst themselves.

Navies have always faced tensions between the need to run themselves in a business-like way, without their simply degenerating into becoming a commercial concern where concepts of duty and national service could be eclipsed by pecuniary considerations.

10.3.6 *Effective Monitoring, Regulation and Reward*

Another approach has been, and remains, to regulate performance procedures such that corrupt practices at every level were and are weeded out to the extent possible and efficiencies added. Hence in 1785 after its less than perfect performance in the War of American Independence the Royal Navy was included in a national Commission on fees, gratuities, perquisites and emoluments in the public offices.[49] The public expression of a determination to root out corruption and to provide a fair day's pay for a fair day's work has been a feature of political election campaigns ever since.

The same regulatory approach was taken towards the general efficiency of administrative procedures and working practices. For instance, in the early 18th Century, not long after Maydman produced his polemic, the Commissioners of the Victualling Board were enjoined 'to sign all certificates and other papers at your office, and not at taverns and coffee houses as has been heretofore practiced.'[50]

To improve performance, it needed first to be monitored. Records needed keeping and supervising. Maydman himself proposed the idea of 'Riding Surveyors' who would go round checking up that everyone was doing what they were supposed to. He also discussed the idea of establishing an 'Intendant' (evidently distressed by having to use a French word for this post, he wondered whether 'Censor' would be better) to correct errors, hear complaints and suspend the negligent and disloyal.[51] In much the same spirit, Admiral, Lord St Vincent's personal 1802 visits to dockyards, hospitals and a series of other such establishments, yielded official reports which provided ample evidence of shocking abuses and of the need both to monitor and regulate administrative process. The advantages of regularly checking on what was actually being done were recognised by the end of the 18th Century as warranting the establishment of Inspectorates to report on aspects of naval business such as artillery, gunpowder manufacture, and naval works.

Monitoring and regulating performance had its dangers, though, as well as its benefits since it could lead to a level of bureaucracy that hindered advance rather than supported it. One member of Admiral Sir John Fisher's Naval Establishments Enquiry Committee was shocked by what he found at Devonport Dockyard in 1905. 'I found it a huge bureaucracy,' he said,

> in consequence almost nerveless, real energy, initiative or true responsibility had been obliterated; and the object of everyone was to save their face by compliance with the Regulations...each [department] struggling for its own, the efficiency of the yard as a whole was lost sight of.[52]

Like everything else, bureaucracy has to be taken in moderation, and with due regard for the required outcome.

It was obviously of benefit if those who transgressed in the monitored performance of their tasks suffered in consequence, while those who did well, benefitted. Rewarding those who delivered the goods through merit-based advances was the other side of the coin. One recurring problem in the Royal Navy was the pernicious system of promotion by seniority rather than on merit since this quite often recognised experience rather than expertise as the basis for advance. Cochrane's successive appointments to head the navies of Chile, Peru, Brazil and then Greece, sometimes at the expense of local commanders, was based on the inspirational value of a generally well-deserved reputation for operational success such that people sometimes surrendered simply because he had turned up in his ship or squadron. Given the aim of the exercise, this made sense, despite Cochrane's lack of administrative skill.

10.3.7 Individual and Corporate Expertise

Naval expertise, another major and obvious contribution to administrative efficiency, was to be encouraged too. This was difficult to find in the fledgling navies of South America in the naval sphere but the administrative successes of Zenteno in Chile and of Villela Barbosa in Brazil show that administrative efficiency in other spheres could be carried over into the navy. This raises the broader issue of the extent to which successful administration in fact depends more on general administrative skills, rather than navy-specific ones.

The choice affects the balance to be struck between generalist administrators who come from elsewhere with their own distinctive things to offer and then depart rather than long-serving specialist administrators such as Samuel Pepys in the 17th century and Admiral Hiram Rickover in the 20th who, instead, come, develop their expertise in service, and stay. Maydman clearly favoured this last approach; he said 'Clerks ought to be permanent, settled and steady in their employments, with a prospect of advancement.' That way they were more likely to generate the kind of expertise in their area of interest that would avoid '…filling the Service full of Confusion and Discontent. 'It was wrong, therefore, 'to put a stranger who never served, nor knew the Practice of the Navy over the heads of able men who have spent their whole days in the said service.'[53]

Daniel Baugh makes the additional point that subject expertise increases the administrator's capacity to influence policy. By the mid-18th century, the Commissioners of the Navy Board had become '… counsellors whose advice was normally to be accepted rather than as servants whose duty was quiet obedience.'[54] Expertise, in short, matters; but perhaps accumulated assumptions also need to be tested by periodic exposure to other ways of seeing and doing things.

Navies are particularly demanding technologically and so expertise in the technical domain was especially valuable. Here Cochrane's restless fascination with steam-power and many other areas of technological innovation, including his advanced mosquito fleet ideas and even his 'secret war plan' for the reduction of fortresses by smoke, bombardment and poison gas all indicated a level of interest and technical expertise likely to be conducive to administrative success.[55] The ability to be what would now be called a 'smart customer,' should help when evaluating competitive tenders for ships, cannon or other military equipment. Sadly Cochrane was not always succesful at this himself, to judge by the delays and failures in actually getting his steam-ships, such as the pretty useless *Rising Star,* delivered in time – and by the lamentable financial consequences of so many of his technical projects.

10.3.8 Openness

Providing the free flow of information around the system, upwards and downwards, that is needed for planning based on processed evidence has proven critical to administrative and indeed operational success.[56] The administrative system, needed to be thoroughly aware of what was actually being done by its various constituents. All too often it wasn't.

Seeking, recording and keeping information about this is the first step in the process. Obvious though this may seem these habits took time to accumulate. When Samuel Pepys arrived at the Navy Board in 1660, he found it hard to believe that there was no list of the ships in the Royal Navy; he had to compile one himself. For years it was the custom of senior administrators to keep their papers at home and casually to regard them as a private property to be handed down to later generations of their own families.

Gradually, though, the advantage of centrally recording and holding the information that was needed for decision making was recognised. Based on the proposition that you can't manage what you cannot measure, central administrators depended on an upwards flow of data. The system needed regular surveys of the fleet, its state and current and future expenditure. With this came the corresponding need to chase up subordinates who were lax in their paperwork and failed to passing the necessary information upwards. 'Captains,' complained the Navy Board in 1729,' are sometimes very remiss or backward in returning their muster books to the office.' As a result too many dead men were still being paid. Nor was their sufficient information 'whence the men came and whether they are prest or not.'[57] Keeping track of the fiendishly complicated business of financing a navy has always been difficult especially when the people at the top didn't quite know what was going on.

Passing the necessary information downwards was also important, so that subordinates knew their place in the scheme of things, what they were expected to do and told what they needed to know in order to do it.

The reluctance of fighting men and others to attend to their paperwork, tedious though it might be, no doubt helps account for the widespread antipathy there was and still is to mindless bureaucracy and the stultifying effect of too much 'red-tape.' This response is increased if the point of collecting such information is not clear, perhaps when the data suppliers are unconvinced that the data consumers are either willing or able to take the requisite action afterwards. It is not a great step from there to conclude that large bureaucracies, creaking under their own administrative processes, are prone to be closed to challenging ideas from elsewhere, or even from within. Receptivity to innovative and uncomfortable information has after all often proved important too.

The Royal Navy of the Victorian era had, and still has, a reputation for representing just the kind of mindless conservatism that a closed attitude towards new information can easily generate. Its success in developing the *Dreadnought* battleship in 1905–1906 suggests that this is probably undeserved. The largest, fastest most heavily armed battleship in the world that was produced, with an eye to public effect, in a year and a day was revolutionary in many ways. It was also risky. Designing its propulsion system was especially so since the Navy's experience of the benefits of steam turbines was limited to its destroyers and the expectation of their introduction to civilian ocean liners. The frantic speed with which *Dreadnought* was built meant age old customs in the dockyard went out of the window. Building work was done in two 12 hour shifts, at night conducted by searchlight. Dockyard workers had a 6-day, 69-hour week, with just 30 minutes every day off for lunch. They worked through the Christmas/New Year break without pause.[58] The same precedent breaking approach carried on to the First World War. The great reforming influence of Admiral 'Jacky' Fisher notwithstanding, the success with which all these innovations were so quickly absorbed suggests that the Victorian Navy was more open to innovative ideas than sometimes claimed.

Subsequent experience also underlined the general importance of navies, and for everyone administering them, of being receptive to disconcerting information, challenging ideas and innovation. War games and exercises need to *test* assumptions not just protect them.

Given the extent to which it is so critical to the naval function, making the best use of available and future technology is particularly important from this point of view. There is much to be said for the widespread view – sometimes known as 'Martec's Law' – that technology is changing much faster than an organisation's capacity to respond to it. Hence the growing interest in developing a 'culture of innovation' and adaptive organisations that can cope with continuous technological, and other, challenges. As to how that might be done, there is also a widespread view, perhaps dating back to the 1930s writings of Joseph Schumpeter, that innovation comes more normally bottom-up than top-down. The task of (business) organisations is therefore to drive the changes that well up from inspired individuals, lower in, or even outside, the system. To do this, organisations have to be open to challenge, even 'creative destruction.' For hierarchical organisations like navies, this is as difficult as it is important. For that reason, countries often set up horizon-scanning organisations like the US Defense Advanced Research Projects Agency (DARPA) to monitor possibilities, especially technological ones, and encourage their exploration.[59]

10.3.9 Collegiality

It was to be more than 250 years after Maydman's time before the literature on 'bureaucratic politics' appeared[60] and scholars began to expose the extent to which administrative behaviour, decision-taking and policy-making depended on perceptions of sectoral and institutional interest – that 'where you stood depended on where you sat.' Even so, Maydman was perfectly aware of the extent to which running the Navy could easily be de-railed by its officials being so concerned to protect their local institutions, and the resources they commanded, and to compete with those in other institutions, that the interests of the Navy as a whole were lost sight of. He picked out the dockyards of his day as being particularly prone to this kind of nest-feathering. One example of the 'not-invented-here syndrome' he identified was the attitude dockyards too often took towards the maintenance and refitting of ships built elsewhere. In contrast with the 'beloved or favourite ship as they call it' such a ship was likely to be left to shameful rotting and decay, 'for want of careful preventions.' This was 'one great evil in the Navy.'[61]

Such attitudes and petty jealousies, quarrels and rivalries are probably inevitable, people being what they are. From this perspective the notoriously prickly Cochrane appears quintessentially human! The lack of cooperation and 'silo mentality' they produce is certainly universal. They may of course encourage local performance against perceived competitors, and ensure that a greater range of possible options is considered. Even so, they can also disrupt the over-all interest of the navy itself and so need to be kept in check.

10.4 Conclusion

This chapter on naval administration began with the observation that administrative and organisational efficiency is hard to discuss in the abstract, and so to an extent it has proved. Given this problem, it is all too easy for such analyses to degenerate into the provision of motherhood statements that are little more than blinding glimpses of the obvious. Experience nonetheless perhaps allows at least some generalised observations about what constitutes effective administration. With these in mind, the next three chapters will explore some of the key areas in the business of growing a navy in which these administrative approaches were actually applied.

Notes

1 Archidamus, quoted by Thucydides, *The Peloponnesian War,* op cit, Bk II, 11–13, 104.
2 Maydman, *Naval Speculations,* 99.
3 In this light, Susan Rose interestingly discusses the establishment of Portsmouth on the south coast of England as a naval base and dockyard, now one of the Royal Navy's main bases. The town received its royal charter in 1194 in the reign of Richard I and its naval facilities were further expanded by his successor King John, but there is a real question about how permanent all this was. See Rose, Susan, 'A Re-appraisal of the King's Ships in the Reigns of Richard I and John, 1189–1216,' *The Mariner's Mirror,* Vol. 106, No. 1 (February 2020), 12–13.
4 Knighton, C.S. and Loades, David, *Elizabethan Naval Administration,* xxvii.
5 Morriss, *The Foundations of British Maritime Ascendancy,* 172–3.
6 Ibid, 78–130.
7 The classic work on the Ordnance Board is Tomlinson, H.C., *Guns and Government: The Ordnance Office under the later Stuarts.* (London: Royal Historical Society, 1979). See also Morriss, *The Foundations of British Maritime Ascendancy,* 190–2. For naval administration in Maydman's time, see Rodger, *The Command of the Ocean,* Chapters 3, 7 and 12.
8 Maydman, *Naval Speculations,* 33. This basic point is referred to throughout his book. For other examples, see the Preface and 11, 35, 99, 106.
9 Black, Jeremy, *Naval Warfare: A Global History Since 1860* (Lanham: Roman and Littlefield, 2017), 3, 118.
10 Swope, *A Dragon's Head and a Serpent's Tail,* 130–2.
11 Barrett, *The Navy and the Nation,* 49–56.
12 Maydman, *Naval Speculations,* 116.
13 Rose, *A Reappraisal of the King's Ships,* 6.
14 Rodger, Nicholas, 'The New Atlantic: Naval Warfare in the 16th Century,' in Hattendorf, John B. and Unger, Richard W. (Eds), *War at Sea in the Middle Ages and the Renaissance* (Woodbridge: The Boydell Press, 2003), 233.
15 Runyan, Timothy J., 'Naval Power and Maritime Technology During the Hundred Years War,' in Hattendorf and Unger (Eds), *War at Sea,* 59.
16 Friel, Ian, *Henry V's Navy: The Sea-road to Agincourt and Conquest 1413–22* (Stroud: The History Press, 2015), 35.
17 Mott, Lawrence V., 'Iberian Naval power, 1000–1650,' in Hattendorf and Unger (Eds), *War at Sea,* 105.
18 Friel, *Henry V's Navy,* 21–2, 15, 50, 53, 43, 150.
19 Runyan in Hattendorf and Unger, *War at Sea,* 63–4.
20 Doumerc, Bernard, 'An Exemplary Maritime Republic: Venice at the End of the Middle Ages,' in Hattendorf and Unger (Eds), *War at Sea,* 143–5, 153–88.
21 Balard, Michel, 'Genoese Naval Forces in the Mediterranean in the Fifteenth and Sixteenth Centuries,' in ibid, 128, 135; Salonia, Matteo, *Genoa's Freedom: Entrepreneurship, Republicanism and the Spanish Atlantic* (Lanham: Lexington Books, 2017).
22 Domingues, Francisco Contente, 'The State of Portuguese Naval Forces in the 16th Century,' in Hattendorf and Unger, *War at Sea,* 195.
23 Black, Jeremy, *Rethinking Military History* (London: Rowan and Littlefield, 2004), 163–4.
24 Morriss, *The Foundations of British Maritime Ascendancy,* 1.
25 This is not, however, to deny existence of the many detailed and authoritative studies of all these behind-the-scenes topics, many of which will be referred to in this book. For the UK, the various publications of the Navy Records Society are pre-eminent for this.

26 Morriss, *The Foundations of British Maritime Ascendancy, op cit,* 6.
27 Commissioner Richard Hughes to the Navy Board, 11 July 1744, printed in Baugh, *Naval Administration 1715–1750,* 309.
28 Minute on matters before the Privy Council, September 1555, printed in Knighton, C.S. and Loades, David (Eds), *The Navy of Edward VI and Mary I* (Franham, Surrey: Ashgate for the Navy Records Society, 2011), 306.
29 Navy Board to the Admiralty Secretary, 23 May 1746, printed in Baugh, *Naval Administration,* 32.
30 Cubitt David, *Lord Cochrane and the Chilean Navy, 1818–1823* (Santiago, Chile: Museo Maritimo, 2018). 229–53.
31 Vale, Brian, *The Audacious Admiral Cochrane* (London: Conway Maritime Press, 2004), 130.
32 Vale, *The Audacious Admiral,* 155, 99.
33 Maydman, *Naval Speculations,* 70.
34 Morriss, *The Foundations of British Maritime Ascendancy,* 42.
35 Ibid, 9.
36 Parkinson, C. Northcote, 'Parkinson's Law,' *The Economist,* 19 November 1955.
37 Navy Board to Admiralty Secretary, 1 March 1727/1728 in Baugh, *Naval Administration,* op cit.
38 Gresh, *To Rule Eurasia's Waves,* op cit, 150–1.
39 Lloyd, Christopher, *Lord Cochrane- Seaman-Radical-Liberator* (London: Longmans, Green and Co, 1947), 163–5.
40 Twitchett, E.G., *Life of a Seaman: Thomas Cochrane, 10th Earl of Dundolald 1775–1860.* (London: Wishart & Co, Ltd. 19310.21).
41 Maydman, *Naval Speculations,* 144.
42 Cited in van Gulik, R.H. *Crime and Punishment in Ancient China: T'ang-Yin-Pi-Shih* (Bangkok: Orchid Press, 2007), 90–1. I am grateful to Jon Welch for pointing this example out to me.
43 Lloyd, *Lord Cochrane,* op cit, 82.
44 Ibid, 9–10; Vale, *The Audacious Admiral,* 216.
45 Wilson, E., 'The Limits of Naval Power: Britain after 1815,' in P. Kennedy and E. Wilson (Eds), *Navies in Multipolar Worlds: From the Age of Sail to the Present* (London: Routledge, 2020).
46 Austen, Jane, *Persuasion,* (1818), Chapter 8. It is worth remembering that two of Jane's brothers were successful Admirals.
47 Lloyd, *Lord Cochrane,* op cit, 100–2; Vale, *The Audacious Admiral,* 151–9.
48 Quoted in Baugh, *Naval Administration,* 41.
49 Morriss, *The Foundations of British Maritime Ascendancy,* 15.
50 Quoted, Morriss, *The Foundations of British Maritime Ascendancy,* op cit, 280.
51 Maydman, *Naval Speculations,* op cit, 119, 330–1.
52 Quoted in Haas, J.M., *A Management Odyssey; The Royal Dockyards 1714–1914* (Lanham, MD: University Press of America, 1994), 170–1.
53 Maydman, *Naval Speculations,* 48, 84, 114.
54 Baugh, *Naval Administration,* 3.
55 Lloyd, *Lord Cochrane,* 6, 203; Vale, *The Audacious Admiral,* 191, 19.
56 Morriss, *The Foundations of British Maritime Ascendancy,* 44.
57 Knighton and Loades, *The Navy of Edward VI,* 105; Knighton and Loades, *Elizabethan Naval Administration,* 21; Baugh, *Naval Administration,* 56.
58 Brown, Paul, 'Docking the Dreadnoughts,' in MacDougall, Philip (Ed), *British Dockyards in the First World War,* (Transactions of the Naval Dockyards Society), vol. 12, August 2019, 43–4.
59 Stewart, Heather, 'US-style agency for innovation to get go-ahead,' *The Guardian,* 18 February 2021. I am grateful to David Max Jones for pointing Martec's Law out to me.
60 Allison, Graham T., 'Conceptual Models and the Cuban Missile Crisis,' *The American Political Science Review,* 1969 was an early leader in this field.
61 Maydman, *Naval Speculations,*72–4.

11 Delivering a Navy's People

All areas required significant strengthening, but I believed the key was developing capable personnel.[1]

—Admiral Liu Huaqing, 2004

While our ships are made of steel, our Sailors and their families are the lifeblood of our force.

—Admiral Mike Gilday, Chief of Naval Operations, US Navy, October 2021[2]

11.1 Introduction: Navies Need People

As both the US and Chinese Chiefs of Navy remind us, a navy's people are crucial to its operational success. Numbers matter because there needs to be enough of them to build, support, direct and operate the fleet. They need, also to be sufficiently good at their jobs compared to the demands of the task and to the quality of the opposition and therefore provided with the education and training to be so. Their degree of motivation matters too so a strong sense of being 'all of one company' is important.

None of this is easy. Partly because their people were less able to 'live off the land' than soldiers, people costs mean that navies, from the start, tended to be more expensive than armies. For all these reasons, when tackling personnel issues, a navy especially needs sufficient resources and support from the government and society. Above all, perhaps, a navy also needs to develop a settled and considered policy and strategy to handle what is clearly one of the most serious of challenges it has to overcome, namely getting, keeping and training its people. This has very often been a major problem for navies and probably always will be.

The up-and-down experience of the Royal Canadian Navy (RCN) in tackling this challenge provides salutary evidence of the importance of all of these points. In its comparatively short existence, it has been through many tribulations. Originally built as a tiny fishery protection service, it was founded in a small and rather unenthusiastic way in 1910. After a modest role in the First World War, it was very nearly extinguished at the end of it. The RCN staggered on through the interwar period and shortly after the beginning of the Second World War was massively expanded and became one of the leading players in the Battle of the Atlantic. As that wound down, the RCN was also reconfigured into becoming an expeditionary navy for a prospective role in the war in the Pacific.

At the end of that conflict, the RCN was massively cut back very nearly to its interwar level. Initially focussing once again on its anti-submarine role for the Cold

DOI: 10.4324/9781003100553-11

War, it later refocused on a more global but still limited role afterwards. The RCN was formally abolished in 1968, becoming simply 'Maritime Command.' This ushered in an unhappy and uncertain period that combined quite a high and varied level of operational activity with a long period of what its officers termed a 'rust out' of the fleet. Since then, things have improved. It was reconstituted as the RCN in 2011 to the relief of all concerned and has since embarked on a rather ambitious naval modernisation programme.

These convulsions are hardly an ideal backdrop for a settled manpower programme. They make the RCN's successes all the more impressive, but they also help identify, sometimes by their absence, what a navy's people policy has nearly always had to deliver, sufficient numbers and sufficient quality.

11.1.1 People in Sufficient Number

For the Second World War the RCN expanded massively and very quickly from 5000 to 100,000, the great majority being volunteers for hostilities only. It soon became the world's third biggest navy, contributing very significantly to allied success. Its demobilisation, however, was equally massive. It recovered afterwards, surviving the Government's torpedoing of its post-war plans. Since then it has managed to keep up the overall numbers, though like all navies everywhere has sometimes found it difficult to meet the demands of particular trades, especially when there are more lucrative alternatives ashore.

Wars increase the need for people. In Maydman's days the navy would need roughly three times as many people as in peacetime and the same was true of the dockyards.[3] Not getting them constrains operational performance and always has. Illustrating the point, when in 1756 Admiral Byng departed on his ill-fated campaign to save Minorca from the French, his already inadequate ten ship squadron was 772 men short of complement, and this in part resulted in his abandoning the mission and falling back on Gibraltar. This was an eminently understandable decision but for him a fatal one.

Manpower problems can arise, as in this case, if sufficient volunteers cannot be found. In such cases, ships perfectly capable of earning their keep at sea are forced to stay alongside for want of people to operate them, even in wartime. This was even true for the Royal Navy from the early months of 1944. The reasons for the failure of the right people to come forward or 'get volunteered,' of course varies from navy to navy. The life style which involves long periods away from home seems unattractive to very many civilians, especially in days of sail when ratings all too frequently found their pay sometimes years in arrears and their families often falling into acute financial distress while they were away. This had been a point that Henry Maydman had tried to hammer home, while also complaining about the practice of transferring crew members to a departing ship immediately on their arrival back in port after a long deployment.

The gap between living conditions and food on board between sailors at sea and their civilian counterparts is now not considered by historians to have been as great as it once was, but it was still a tough life, with the extra disadvantages of the sometimes ferocious discipline, plus the prospect of drowning, dismemberment or death at the hands of the enemy. These days, prospective recruits for navies around the world will often be lured away by the higher salaries and better conditions available in the civilian economy.

In the early postwar period, something less tangible seems to have plagued the RCN, a worrying dissonance between the social values and general *mores* of the Navy and the population they sought to protect, especially amongst the young. It was a time of restlessness, uncertainty and change, and there were many who thought that this conflicted with the traditional upper/lower deck proclivities thought characteristic of the Royal Navy. This and poor pay and conditions were held to be responsible for a spate of mutinies in 1949. Whether that was true or not, it underlined the point that a navy that allows itself to get too far from the values of the population and government it is defending tends to increase its personnel problems, while reducing its level of general sympathy and support from the government and the population.[4] Unsurprisingly the RCN at this time found it impossible to get the recruits it needed even from maritime areas like Newfoundland, which in fact had often proved quite hard even before.[5]

Sometimes though, there are different explanations for the problem. In the case of both Canada and Australia, it was less a question of the general availability of manpower, more of governmental willingness to allocate it to the fleet.[6] Again, sometimes the country simply doesn't have enough people for its strategic needs. The gross manpower shortages which became evident in Britain from 1943 had a strategic effect in shaping policy regarding its major entry into the sea war against Japan later that year, for example. For many countries, manpower shortages, resulting from adverse demographic trends, have become a major problem.

11.1.2 People of Sufficient Quality

Equally clearly, the quality of the people is critical too. The rapid expansion of the RCN had led to the neglect of some parts of the training effort. Historians attribute to this many of the early failings in the RCN's performance in the Battle of the Atlantic especially in the tough year of 1942, and to its consequent need to take time out for the early part of 1943.[7] Though ultimately successful, the learning process was a painful one. In 1944, the RCN had to re-train from being an ASW escort navy in the Atlantic to the very different demands of an expeditionary campaign against Japan. The unexpectedly early end of the war made this unnecessary but paid off in Canada's useful contribution to the naval side of the Korean war 1950–1953. Thereafter the RCN had simultaneously to train for its coastal roles, a continuing focus on ASW and convoy/task force operations and increasingly with the end of the Cold War a global and expeditionary role. All three required keeping up with the challenges of developing technology.

11.1.3 People Sufficiently Motivated

Ideally, a navy like a warship or indeed any large organisation should be 'all of one company,' operating as a team committed to, and well trained for, the achievement of the mission. Its absence can lead to indifferent performance, lack of cooperation even insurrection and mutiny.[8] Like any large organisation, the RCN has had its problems in this regard, and arguably more than most other navies. Human beings being what they are, tensions, divisiveness and inadequacies are bound to emerge, but to be successful navies as organisations need to be able to accommodate and manage these realities. The RCN's fragile morale in 1942 probably owed something to the fact that the urgent training pipeline left too little room for such niceties. The all-important

Divisional system by which officers were specifically tasked to look after the interests of the men whose work they supervised, suffered in consequence.[9]

Nor was the situation in the lower deck much better as the Second World War drew to a close. Governmental policies then made things worse. On the basis of an edict that participation in the Pacific war should be 'voluntary' the crew of the cruiser HMCS *Uganda* on the way out to join the British Pacific Fleet, voted not to participate, wanting instead to turn back for home.[10] There were also naval riots in Halifax on VE day. Rapid demobilisation of the fleet immediately after the war appears not to have eased the problem for those who remained, but a series of proposals for reform of pay and working conditions were rejected by the Government for reasons of economy.[11] Finally a number of 'incidents' culminated in three ship mutinies in 1949.

The Government insisted on a public enquiry, chaired by Admiral Mainguy. Fairly typically the commissioners quarrelled amongst themselves with one ex-naval but then civilian member, Louis Audette producing a minority report.[12] Broadly, the enquiry recommended a series of reforms placing particular emphasis on the need to 'Canadianise' the fleet and to wean it away from the people-management practices that many officers had picked up, rather like the measles, from their 'big ship time' in the Royal Navy. This reflected the view that the, admittedly successful, democratic feudalism characteristic of the British naval people system was unsuited to the more egalitarian North Americans. Nonetheless, as late as 1946, the Royal Navy's institution of Welfare Committees for the lower deck was regarded as 'too progressive' even for the Canadian Navy.[13]

These personnel problems were doubtless aggravated by the fact that from its earliest days the evolving RCN's officer corps appears to have been a disputatious lot. For example, a notorious tension arose between two officers who went on to the highest positions in the Second World War, namely Rear-Admiral Leonard Warren Murray and Vice Admiral George C. Jones, both very able members of the class of 1912.[14] Apparently taking an instant dislike to each other on their first acquaintance, circumstances (and not least the loss of many of their classmates in the 1914 battle of Coronel) led to heightened competition between them throughout their careers. That by the late 1930s, Jones had one day's seniority over Murray made things worse. It culminated in the latter's eventual sacking by the former as the Navy's senior operational commander in May 1945[15] and his seeking exile and refuge in Britain. Camps of followers formed around both protagonists. While this may have contributed to the success of their individual policies it split the officer corps too.

Worse still, this animosity was played out against a background in which, according to one admittedly embittered British victim of the more general furore,

> No two senior officers trust each other, they have less loyalty among themselves than they have from us [the British] if only they could see that…how can the service function smoothly and efficiently with…[such]…intriguing and jockeying for their own suds…Most of the pully-hauley work is even now being done by RN (ret) [retired] officers.[16]

At this time, Jones who was widely regarded as a 'careerist' who put his own interests above that of the service was also suspected of intriguing with the naval minister Angus L. Macdonald against the easy-going Vice Admiral Percy W. Nelles who had been Chief of the Naval Staff since 1934 but who was quietly put aside for alleged mismanagement of the modernisation of the Canadian Navy after its indifferent performance in the 1942 phase of the battle of the Atlantic.

This was an officer corps characterised by general antipathies between its most senior Canadian figures, between them and the British and between the pre-war professional generation and the swarms of hostilities-only reservists needed for the Canadian Navy's massive expansion. The only reason why the French Canadians weren't adding to the mix, one suspects, is that there were so few of them in a position to be so.

These experiences underline a navy's need to take care of its people and to do its utmost to support the cohesion of its officer corps. Canadian experience suggests first the need to provide the silent majority with the opportunity, the education and the training to get on with their careers and do the best they can, and secondly to find flexible and pragmatic work-arounds to ease and accommodate emerging frictions. As an example of the latter, which goes back to the Murray-Jones feud, a temporary commander of HMCS *Assiniboine* was appointed, in 1940, so that Murray would not have to take over from Jones personally, when unpleasantness would probably have ensued.[17]

11.1.4 Sufficient People Planning

The predictable need to secure sufficient people, and to train and manage them all underline a navy's need for a sustainable people plan. The ups and downs of the RCN's fortunes made this especially difficult. One former RCN officer who turned to the dark side and became a historian, is severely critical of his old service. 'It is sufficient to say,' he wrote, 'that the development and execution of personnel policy in the post-war RCN was an abject failure and represented muddling through at its worst.'[18] Another ex RCN officer reinforced the point suggesting that his navy had neither enough people nor a policy. For example, the so-called Brock Report appeared in 1961. This was an important investigation headed by a prospective Vice Chief of the Naval Staff of the role, tasks and composition of the fleet for the next ten years. Although, as one historian has concluded, 'It was a thorough examination of the role of the RCN in the nuclear age and made far-reaching recommendations for the future posture of the Navy,' it completely left out any reference to the fleet's 'manning.'[19] Canadian experience underlines the need to have a personnel policy and to take it seriously.

11.1.5 Having Sufficient Support

In mitigation of the RCN's performance in this area, there is some evidence that successive Canadian governments sought to control what it thought the Navy's wilder aspirations by imposing excessively tight manpower restrictions.[20] As already mentioned, successive governments have refused to accept the people plans the RCN did occasionally produce. Aside from saving money, one apparent justification for this was Canada's apparent ability to shelter behind the superior resources of first Britain and then the United States, and the absence of a nearby threat. Generally, the Navy was a small blip on the Government's radar;[21] its budget was seriously constrained, its plans were continually thwarted. Much of the population had little conception of the importance of the sea, so there was little pressure for improvement.

Given this background, the RCN's leaders did well to stave off its near-extinction after the First World War and after the Second, also, to see off the 'good, workable little fleet' devoted to coastal defence that the famously sceptical Prime Minister,

McKenzie King, had wanted to see. Its recovery in the early part of this century is just the latest stage of what has been a roller-coaster ride, which has shown just how hard people plans can be, especially in such circumstances. Nonetheless getting, training and managing the people they need is a challenge that navies cannot avoid.

11.2 Solving the People Problem

11.2.1 Getting the People You Need: The Lessons of the Galleys

How the problem of manning the galleys of the Mediterranean in the 16th–18th centuries was solved, while far removed from the experience of the RCN, nonetheless provides some intriguing insights into how the people problem can be solved.

The typical Spanish galley of that era was about 40 m long and 5 to 6 m wide, making for a length to beam ratio of roughly 8:1. Accordingly, with sails raised such a galley could reach a respectable 10 to 12 knots. More normally though, a galley's cruising speed was about three knots, when without a helpful wind and powered only by oars. On those occasions when speed was essential this could be raised to about six knots, but only for short periods. At 26 strokes a minute the oarsmen could not keep this speed up for much more than about 20 minutes. The oarsmen worked below the raised deck. The rowing deck would have about 25 benches on each side each bench seating five oarsmen. A well-trained rowing crew could turn the galley rapidly in narrow spaces. Potentially the galley was a very agile weapon of war.

When underway, conditions below decks were squalid in the extreme. Oarsmen had to relieve themselves where they were, sleep and feed there too, as best they could. It was usually very hot so oarsmen worked near-naked; in the broiling heat of the Mediterranean, trapped below deck and with very little access to the open air, they were often critically dehydrated.[22] They needed eight litres of water a day. Galleys could only carry water for about three days. Their consequent reliance on water supplies ashore, limited them to coastal operations.

But even in this brutal world, common sense and expediency dictated that manpower policies paid at least some regard to practicalities and the interests of the oarsmen, as well as those of the *gente de cabo* (people in command).[23] A fit and trained oarsman, even if a slave and chained to the spot, was a valuable resource that justified some consideration. Also, teamwork was essential for tight manoeuvring and bursts of speed; men on the same oar had to pull equally and at the same time (one reason why freemen and slaves were intermingled so the former could keep an eye on the latter). Shirkers, the weak and the sick could all hazard the ship and everyone aboard. Everyone had literally to 'pull together.'

Accordingly, the authorities and the galley commander, provided he had an ounce of sense, had to develop a working strategy comprising arguably five elements which in other circumstances have proved common to all navies facing the challenge of getting the manpower they need. The first of these was accepting the need to widen the net from which possible recruits could be found and accepting the consequential management complexities and requirements that would inevitably follow. A galley's oarsmen were a mixture of volunteer free-men, conscripts and slaves.

Themistocles' Greek triremes were rowed mostly by the *thetes* farmers and free citizens who saw this as their way of defending Athens and the 'democratic values' they profited from.[24] (Indeed there was a strong link between the city's need for rowers and the 'democratic' enfranchisement of the lower classes.) Even in the 16th century, quite a few rowers of the time were volunteers, hard though it might be to believe this. Many others though were conscripts. The Ottoman regime expected every 20 to 30 households in its empire to provide and pay for one oarsman for the fleet. Venice had its *Milizia da Mar* which from 1545 delivered the oarsman to the fleet from the 10,000 registered names on its books, the unlucky ones usually chosen by lot.

The third category was slaves (often prisoners of war); unlike those in the other two categories, they were chained to the spot. Should the galley sink, their prospects were bleak. This accounts for the appalling loss of life in the cataclysmic battle of Lepanto of 1571, many of the victims of which were Christian slaves on sinking Ottoman galleys. Each category of rower had to be dealt with differently even though seated next to one another on the same bench. Treating volunteers as slaves would simply dry up that source of future recruits.

Secondly, there was the measured resort to force, both in securing manpower resources and in ensuring that once on the rowing benches everyone did what was required whether freemen, slaves or conscripts. Prisoners of war and captured enemy personnel were simply forced to the rowing benches, as slaves. Conscripts and criminals also had little choice. In other European navies, the press-gang similarly produced forced recruits. Once the rowers were aboard they were subjected to the harshest discipline, especially the slaves. Volunteers could expect more consideration. Discipline in the running of the ships of more conventional sailing navies of the time was also hard, but usually less so.

Thirdly, a sensible galley commander would pay some attention to the working conditions of his rowers, including the slaves. Their physical condition was important. Even in a harsh regime of iron and unforgiving discipline, common-sense determined that the oarsmen's living and working conditions were made as palatable as possible. A sensible rowing master would try to keep his men as well-fed as the rations allowed. In Spain's galleys from Sicily, the rations comprised 26 ounces of ship's biscuit each day, with four ounces of meat every other day alternating with vegetable stew. To allow the rowers to eat, the galley would need to stop, or at least slow down.

It would also make sense for the rowing master to get the muck below the benches washed out whenever he could. The rowers' collective energy was a finite resource that needed to be husbanded carefully; if possible a shift system was operated in order to provide periods of recovery. Longer time off was available ashore in the galley-fleet quarters, the *bagni*, (with their own markets and shops) where most oarsmen spent most of their time, especially in the winter. Living conditions in the *bagni* could be deplorable but were usually better than those afloat.

Fourthly, some attention had to be paid to the individual's career prospects. The system allowed for some prospects of reward in terms of career progression. Some of the oarsman, after all, were volunteers. Freemen and conscripts were paid, and for the cooperative and skilled, there was the chance of promotion to the much more wholesome upper deck. Slaves could always recant (perhaps temporarily) on their religion and also progress upwards. Quite a few Barbary galleys were commanded by ex-Christians. Once ashore, even slaves had the opportunity to make money in the *bagni,* or outside it, working to pay for their freedom.

Fifthly, while it would be absurd to imagine there was much 'job satisfaction' in being an enslaved oarsman, there might have been an element of this for the others, even afloat. There needed to be at least some team spirit, even if it only derived from the inescapable fact that everyone on board had the same basic incentive to do what they could to help avoid being sunk. It would probably have helped if volunteers and perhaps some of the conscripts had had a sense of their own worth since the state of an individual's morale no doubt helped shape the level of his contribution to the common effort.

At the time and since, there were huge variations between navies in both competence and success in implementing these various aspects of what might be rather grandly called their manpower policy. Moreover, as societies developed, and values changed, there was a general move away from the harsher aspects of seaboard life and towards the more tolerable. Nonetheless, the same six characteristics of the naval approach to the eternal problem of getting the people a fleet needs, still seem to apply in more recent times and today, even if their mix these days is radically different from what it was in the Mediterranean galleys of the 16th Century. Those six characteristics are:

- Attracting Volunteers
- Widening the net
- Resorting to Force
- Establishing Sufficiently Good Working Conditions
- Establishing Acceptable Career prospects
- Ensuring Sufficient Job Satisfaction.

Generally acknowledged as necessary for the acquisition and retention of sufficient sailors by navies through time and around the world, these six approaches repay a slightly closer look.

11.2.2 *Attracting Volunteers*

Around the world there has been a slow but definite trend towards relying less on 'pressed men' and reluctant conscripts and much more on volunteers. But for the reasons discussed above these have often not seen to be available in sufficient number or sufficient quality, depending on the state of the civilian economy. It is hard for navies to compete with the pay and conditions that the newer industries can offer.

One approach recommended by Henry Maydman was for the Royal Navy to grow its own people in seminaries and to encourage the keeping of a registration system for seamen.[25] France and Spain did much the same. The approach was Jesuitical: get them young, treat them well, and you would have them for life.[26]

Accordingly, the need to attract volunteers encouraged navies to be concerned about their public image. 18th Century recruitment posters appealed to the pride and patriotism of the potential volunteer, and offered an adventurous and rewarding life, in which the prospect of prize money often figured. These days too, navies clearly feel they need to be attentive to how they are seen by the public and the political establishment. Making the general population believe what they ought to believe has therefore become a major preoccupation. The result is a campaign in public relations characterised by supporting media stories, the issue of commissioned postage stamps, navy days and staged events ranging from impressive marching ceremonial of the Chinese navy in Tianamen Square (in which everyone looks to be smart, young, good-looking and exactly the same height) to the Royal Navy's 'Procedure Alpha' when the crew in their best kit line the ship arriving and departing port.[27] These concerns also explain the much greater attention now given to 'media training' and the importance now assigned to the 'information campaign.' Traditionalists may find investment in such things an unnecessary distraction, even distasteful but, all the same, social trends require navies to participate.

If one of the aims of such displays is portraying an image that should attract support and recruits, then the more specific message might be an opportunity to serve the country, to confound the enemy, to 'see the world,' to be made into a better, more qualified person. In effect these are a navy's promises to deliver future job satisfaction to potential volunteers. If those promises are unfulfilled, and pay, conditions and job satisfaction spiral downwards, the reverse tends to happen, and people desert or leave when they can.

More narrowly, navies set up reserves or naval militias of various kinds comprising personnel who may have served in the navy previously or who like the idea but not full time. The innovative Royal Canadian Naval Volunteer Reserve founded in 1923 not only provided some limited manpower and kept the naval profile going in very difficult times, but when war came provided the means by which the Canadian Navy was able to expand to 100,000 people by 1945, of whom only 5000 were regulars.[28] Reservists can be drafted into the navy, individually, trained up and then generally absorbed within its professional structures. In some cases, their civil occupations will determine their role – as naval doctors, engineers or lawyers for example. Alternatively, reservists may be collectively assigned to, and hopefully equipped for, particular war-time responsibilities such as coastal defence, inshore mine-sweeping or handling the media. Either way, reservists are also often seen as a good way, in peacetime, of connecting the navy to society, provided there are enough of them.[29]

11.2.3 Widening the Net

Potentially skilled recruits are distributed throughout the community. Navies that cannot, for social or political reasons, access all sections of the population will clearly be disadvantaged in their bid to get the people they need in comparison with those that can. Nonetheless for a whole variety of practical and social reasons, this has proved difficult to manage. The RCN for example has had to confront the issue of how best to access a population for whom either French or English is the first, preferred or possibly only language. In the late 1960s attempts to cater for this by setting up specifically francophone ships foundered not least because that community could not generate the numbers of specialists needed to keep such ships in continuous commission.[30] Since then, the government policy of developing a bi-lingual approach has alleviated matters. But in fact the international composition of Admiral Nelson's HMS *Victory* and most other warships of the period suggests different language problems need not be insuperable.[31]

The recruitment and employment of women in the navy has proved a more intractable problem. Most navies, realising that by not doing so, they arbitrarily cut themselves off from the skills of half the population and effectively double their recruitment problems, have moved in this direction. The Royal Navy was the first to create the Women's Royal Naval Service in 1917. Numbering some 5000 by the end of the First World War it was disbanded but recreated in 1939. Other Commonwealth navies followed suit.[32] The RCN was one of the earliest navies to grasp the nettle of not only recruiting women but integrating them fully and in every respect to treat them in the same way as men, rather than keep them in a separate section of the service. This included eventually giving them operational roles at sea. Only in that manner, the argument went, could their skills be properly utilised.[33] 'Ironically,' concludes one historian, 'military service, with all its regulations, limitations, and restrictions on personal freedom, may have been a liberating experience for women.'[34]

The problem is that this approach is much easier in some societies than it is for others, and so some of the world's navies while generally all moving the same way are further along than others. The biggest dividing issue is how women in the navy are treated once enlisted in practice, rather than in theory, and whether they really get the advertised equal opportunities. Ensuring gender equality, in practice, continues to be a real if usually declining challenge.

The same goes for the employment of ethnic minorities, an issue which again illustrates the issue of the broader relationship that navies need with the nations they serve. American experience with the recruitment and treatment of Afro-Americans underlines the point. As early as 1943, the pragmatic and tough-minded Admiral Ernest J. King found it necessary to remind the US Navy of the need to treat Afro-Americans within the service equally. He directed '.... rigid and impartial adherence to Naval regulations, in which no distinction is made between the color of individuals wearing the uniform.' He did so because such a policy was 'right.' We say that we are a 'democracy,' he said on one occasion, 'and a democracy ought to have a democratic navy.' Equal treatment was also sensible: the 'Navy accepts no theories of racial differences in inborn ability,' ... and so, 'Restriction, because of racial theories, of the contribution of any individual to the war effort is a serious waste of human resources,' he wrote pragmatically.[35]

These days, theoretically, there is no ethnic bar to career advancement, as the appointment of General Charles Q. Brown as Chief of Staff of the US Air Force demonstrated in 2020. That officer's unprecedentedly open and powerful testimony of the discrimination he had suffered earlier in his career, however, revealed a more disturbing reality. The troubled summer of 2020 showed all too clearly, that there is a world of difference between declaratory regulation and social acceptance; the US Navy, like most other institutions, has still to combat racial prejudice, spoken or unspoken, within its ranks – for its own sake as an effective service as well as for general principles of equity and human rights.[36] This also applies to many other navies.

Against all this, though, the more varied the sources of a navy's people, the harder it may be, to weld them into a coherent force. This was certainly a problem that Cochrane faced in South America. The new navy of Chile for example had to rely on foreigners, prisoners, local volunteers, conscripts, even slaves. Their successful operation depended on the quality of their commanding officers and of Cochrane's own inspiring leadership and record of success; proper treatment and being paid helped too. Even so, getting sufficient numbers remained a problem. Chilean warships were typically 17 to 25 per cent below complement. One problem, Cochrane felt, was that potential recruits spent too much time in the drinking dens of Valparaiso. Accordingly, he proposed such dens be taxed either to drive them out of business or force them to raise their prices such that their customers would more quickly run out of money and so be encouraged to re-enlist.[37] Attending to the problem of getting enough people often calls for such imaginative solutions.

11.2.4 Resorting to Force

In 1589, anxious to get enough people for another operation against England, Philip II issued orders that demonstrated a desire to get volunteers if possible but forced men if need be. Admiral Guipuzcoa was ordered to recruit

> the greatest number of seaman possible…using gentleness. But, in the event of this not succeeding, you are to use whatever means and severity you think necessary, forcing them to serve without accepting any excuses, so that the armada's departure is not prevented by lack of seamen

and Philip's necessary parsimony breaking through, 'ensure the agreed pay is the lowest possible.'[38]

Today's navies have moved a long way from the use of force that characterised those of the 16th and 17th centuries first to get seamen and, then to discipline them once aboard. During the 19th century corporal and capital punishment were much reduced as they slowly became less acceptable in civilian society, for all but the severest of crimes. Nonetheless there remained echoes of the old ways well into the 20th century. On Japanese warships of the Second World War for example ratings were told to avoid eye contact with their superiors and could routinely expect to be 'started' by punches and slaps to encourage them on their way, in a manner distinctly reminiscent of practices, with a rope's end, of 18th-century navies in the age of sail.[39]

In most other navies, increasing attention was given to the need for good relations and two-way respect between the officers and their people. Where this was conspicuously lacking, as it was all too often in the Russian Tsarist fleet of the earliest 20th Century, trouble followed. This was especially likely when political-economic conditions ashore did not encourage support for the regime and when the officer corps itself was riddled with factionalism, 'careerism' and tensions between real sailors afloat and naval bureaucrats ashore. Even then, though, good man-management could make a difference at the individual ship level.[40] In the Revolution, not all Tsarist officers got shot.

11.2.5 Establishing Sufficiently Good Working Conditions

Maydman was clear that ensuring sufficient creature comforts on board and that living conditions are as good as they can be, helps morale.[41] As conditions ashore improve, so must those afloat, to the extent physically possible. The incentives to keep a ship's people well-fed and fit are obvious. After a disastrous series of collisions in 2017, for example, the US Navy urgently reviewed its operational and training expectations, not least for their effect on how much sleep its people were getting.[42]

Even in Maydman's day, the more advanced navies accepted that caring for their people extended outside the ship, particularly in regard to the crew's families ashore. Often, though this obligation was more honoured in the breach than in the undertaking. Nowadays there is much more recognition that the fighting efficiency of a ship can well depend on such things. The view that sailors confident that their families back home are looked after will be happier and perform better justified the establishment in the RCN of 'Family Support Centres' for ships participating in the *Desert Shield/Storm* in 1990–1991.[43] Such arrangements supplement or, (given the trend to working wives/partners) replace the informal arrangements made (often by the wife of the Commanding Officer) so that the families of a ship's crew could keep in touch with each other during long deployments. Therefore, 'a recent US Chief of Naval operations has remarked, '... we must take care for them and their families and providing stable and predictable deployment cycles because at the end of the day, it's not high technology that will win a fight – it's going to be the individual sailors.'[44] Accepting that such family concerns should be a significant element in fleet deployment planning, at least in peacetime, is a clearly significant development.

11.2.6 Acceptable Career Prospects

If a sense of recognised individual self-worth is accepted as the topmost aid to people's recruitment and retention, then pay, conditions and terms of service must support it. Experience, rank and post need to be equitably balanced and promotion based on merit not simple seniority, ethnic identity, gender, religious or sexual orientation. When these standards fall grievously short, and are seen as evidence of the system not recognising the worth of the individual's contribution, then disenchantment, even mutiny, quickly sets in. Conditions that were poor, particularly since they were seen as intrinsically 'unfair,' led in the Royal Navy to the Invergordon mutiny of 1931. This shook the British to the core and in effect helped force the country's economy off the gold standard. It was more a 'down tools' than a full-blown mutiny in which officers feared for their lives or there was much prospect of the mutineers turning their guns on their oppressors, but it reflected extreme dissatisfaction with what looks in hindsight like a crassly stupid decision to cut the pay of sailors, some more than others, and most of them in comparison with their equivalents ashore.[45] In addition to practical concerns about whether they would be able to pay their family's bills ashore, there was the vaguer but arguably more important point that the authorities did not, from this evidence, seem to the unhappy sailors to value their contribution as much as they should.

Navies may well have to accept the need to adapt long-standing career structures to cater for modern market conditions. The Danish Navy, for example, has accepted the modern preference for 'job-hopping' and so intends 'to make it easier to swap between navy and civilian jobs, and vice versa' accepting that this 'will require a change of mindset in the Danish armed forces' in that full-time continuous professional engagement will need to be complemented by other patterns of employment.[46] Australia's Admiral Barrett, advocates the same constant two-way flow between a navy's people and the society they protect, adding that this can also have the benefit of adding to society's sea-mindedness.[47]

Finally, modern navies accept that keeping a contented workforce increasingly requires the care of personnel who are sick or injured in the course of their duties, and whose interests and prospects after their period of service need to be protected. Once again this was in theory recognised certainly from the 16th Century, but the practice was far short of the ideal. In Maydman's England, the foundation of a grand and deservedly famous naval hospital at Greenwich in 1692, was a decided step in the right direction, but all too many sick and wounded failed to benefit from it.

11.2.7 *Job Satisfaction*

A major and, according to some recruitment experts arguably the major, requirement in attracting and retaining volunteers is the sense that the job is intrinsically worth doing, at the individual, ship, fleet and service levels.

A sense of success breeds success in the attraction and retention of volunteers and failure has the reverse effect. In times of war, and remembered war, battle honours can conveniently be paraded, 'scoreboards' of 'kills' posted. Enhanced survival prospects usually provided an incentive for maximum effort and and acted as its own reward. In today's circumstances, though, demonstrating value and proficiency at every level is rather more tricky and probably needs more attention. This also applies, if in minor key, to the individual ship or submarine. Today's ship commanders will often provide their crews with a set of measurable targets in their future programme, the achievement of which fosters ship-team spirit, (the importance of which is hard to exaggerate), individual engagement in the service and of course adds to the proficiency of the ship as a military unit. Targets give people things to aim at and serve as 'performance indicators'; they need to be appropriate, demanding but achievable. The world's warships when passing through the Royal Navy's legendary and rigorous now renamed Fleet Operations Sea Training (FOST) processes find their targets set for them and their achievement during the 'Thursday wars' stressful at the time but immensely satisfying afterwards. Often, though targets have to be self-generated. In the Gulf, HMS *Duncan* was tasked with escorting British-flagged vessels in 2019. 'It was rewarding,' *Duncan's* Commanding Officer concluded, 'because we could measure what we achieved: 29 transits of the Strait, 26 ships accompanied (comprising 1.28 million tons of ship) and not one ship was taken on our watch.'[48]

With the best will in the world, all these admirable personnel policies can still fail to attract and retain sufficient people for the navy to be able to do its job as fully as it might wish. In such cases, other solutions tend to be looked for, such as trying to reduce the need for people and/or making more effective use of the ones you have. One option is the 'lean-manning' of ships and a greater reliance on technology and automation. Difficulty in getting the helicopter pilots it needed for its *Braunschweiger* frigates, reinforced the German navy's interest in drones, for example. In countless such ways, and at every level, the search for people is at the very heart of naval policy.

11.3 Training and Educating a Navy's People

> A strong, modern navy not only needs modern weapons and equipment; it also needs a cadre of personnel well versed in naval theory, strategy and tactics; and capable of skilfully commanding and deploying modern weapons and equipment. An organic fusion of capable people and modern equipment is the only means to create a powerful fighting force.
>
> —Admiral Liu Huaqing[49]

Once a navy has the numbers of people it needs, the next task is to train and educate them for the tasks that lie ahead, so that the navy in turn can achieve its purposes. The extent and subjects of the necessary training and education, and when it should be provided and for whom, however, remains a huge topic well beyond the capacity of one part of a single chapter to cover in any depth. Some basic points predominate however.

11.3.1 Training and Education Matter

The subject is perhaps the most important factor of all in the development of maritime power because it so directly supports a navy's performance in peace and war. If anything, most navies would agree that this is even more true as they progress into the 21st Century reinforced by the ever-increasing demands of new technology. This is one of the main reasons why the requirements in educational attainment in naval recruits seem constantly to be going up, but the trend in this direction is long-established. As navies became more professional, the requirement for specialists increased. Doctors and, in the Royal Navy from 1864, Engineers were needed and required specialist training. This led to their often being much better educated than officers of the Executive branch. This long evolutionary process continues with ever-higher educational standards required of entrants. The necessary attainments could be acquired either before they joined or 'on the job.'

The increased importance of training and Professional Military Education (PME) also follows from the fact that the concept of national security has widened so much from the relatively simple requirement to protect a country's territory, citizens and broader interests, characteristic of earlier times. Now alongside traditional warfighting preoccupations, navies have to deal with so-called 'grey zone' operations in the uneasy twilight between peace and war, humanitarian operations, law enforcement at sea, environmental protection, pandemics, and so on. For navies, the future has never been so challenging. Accordingly, generally navies accept the heightened need to train and educate their people to deal with it.

11.3.2 Training and PME Compared

Although the differences between training and education are fuzzy and often made more so by the casual way words are used – such as saying 'staff training' when Professional Military Education (PME) is meant. Both are clearly important. Training tends to be practical and empirical in approach and these days much concerned with getting the best out of military technology. Usually it aims at delivering effective and standardised responses to known and anticipated challenges. PME on the other hand is more conceptual in approach, concerned with faculties more than facts, and aims to develop intellectual agility and the capacity to think strategically so that sound judgements can be made even in totally unexpected situations.

As Darwin reminds us, the species that won out in the evolutionary race were not necessarily the strongest but those who could best adapt to change. PME develops logic, the ability to analyse and the habits of continuous reflection that should turn its graduates into independent learners long after their current bout of PME ends. It is not about facts and data, which are perishable but developing the habits of thought and analysis which, hopefully, are not.

11.3.3 Training Matters

The advisability of good and thorough training is non-controversial and widely accepted because of the warfighting advantage it confers. That at the battle of Trafalgar a British gun crew could fire three broadsides in three and a half minutes, which was two or three times faster than their French and Spanish opponents, was a tremendous tactical advantage. Moreover, the knowledge that they were so much better than their adversaries greatly contributed to their morale and commitment.

The relative performance of HMS *Shannon* and the USS *Chesapeake* in the war of 1812 is instructive. To that point in the war, the worrying success of the super frigates of the fledgling US Navy had been a disagreeable shock to a Royal Navy which had grown accustomed to its mastery of the seas. The training standards on both sides were generally about the same (not least because quite a few American sailors had been trained by the Royal Navy whether they liked it or not) and so previous American victories can be attributed to the fact that their ships were more heavily armed and with the extra-dense 'live oak' sandwiched in their sides much more resilient. The USS *Constitution* wasn't called 'Old Ironsides' for nothing. But things were different on June 1 1813, off Boston. The *Chesapeake* was a little larger and better armed than the *Shannon* but went into battle with a half-trained crew. Capt Phillip Broke, on the other hand, was a gunnery expert and had trained his men in *Shannon* to perfection. This bloody battle (one of the most relatively sanguinary in the history of sail) was over in 10 to 15 minutes and its outcome supports the widespread contention that high training and professional preparation are key to military success and are often more important than the numbers involved or the quality of the weaponry employed.

11.3.4 PME: Differences of View

There has always been much less unanimity of opinion about the need for PME, particularly for officers and much scepticism about whether it was necessary at all for anyone else, who had, after all, just to do what they were told. This aversion to anything that smacks of book-learning and preference for reliance instead on natural and innate qualities of leadership has ancient roots. The Spanish and most other Europeans of the 16th and 17th Centuries considered noble blood a sufficient qualification for command – the hum drum business of sailing being left to the ship's Master. Nobility '… infused courage, a talent for facing danger and death without fear. The social precedence of nobility induced deference and obedience. Nobles also possessed huge estates, whose wealth might be employed in subsidizing the military forces of princes.'[50] It was easy to slip from this into the proposition that natural leadership was what really mattered and that couldn't be taught.

Olivares tried to change this in his *Gran Memorial* of 1624 recommending that the second rank of nobles, the *cabaleros,* be given command instead; being more modest in their outlook they were likely to pay more attention to the wishes of the force commander. But, as Samuel Pepys and other reformers found, top-line bluebloods had a barnacle-like tenacity and they were hard to scrape off. They were often quite uninterested in learning about seamanship; '[M]any are offended even by discussing it, as if the seaman's art were a mechanical thing unworthy of any man of status and *reputacion.*'[51] This may well explain Spain's early inability to cope with the new-fangled stand-off gunnery tactics of its adversaries.

Later, navies had a general tendency to think that the essentials of their profession indeed had to be learned but the best place to do it was at sea. The more time that was devoted to PME in shore establishments the less there was available at sea for developing the practical aspects of their profession upon which success and often lives depended. More time spent in educational pursuits meant less sea-time and training 'on the job.' The Royal Navy is often said, with some justification to have exhibited considerable ambivalence on the matter. Its undoubted operational success, moreover, seemed to provide apparent support for this sceptical approach. For many, education was best and most narrowly regarded as 'pre-job training,' the minimum necessary for the effective performance of the next appointment rather than broadening a person's intellectual skills and horizons. These minimalist attitudes towards education were passed on to the RN's daughter navies in the Dominions,[52] and proved long-lived indeed.

It is frequently claimed that this was one of the main reasons why the British, the Canadians and the Australians all lost their arguments against their Air Force colleagues on the retention of a future strike carrier capacity. 'Lacking an intellectual tradition and a cadre of officers schooled in strategic thought, it [the RAN] never succeeded in articulating a convincing position.' The airmen argued a poor case well; the sailors did the reverse.[53] The RCN, for example, is frequently charged with taking professional military education less seriously than it should have, especially when compared to service at sea. Too many senior officers thought that an 'Upper Deck Watch Keeping Certificate' was all you really needed.[54]

On the other hand, there has been, and remains, acceptance of the argument that PME is especially beneficial for those destined for staff (and policy-making jobs) as well as for those with higher command appointments. Here, the US Navy was able to establish something of a lead towards the end of the 19th Century. 'The Navy faced challenges common to most organisations: limited budgets, rapidly advancing technology, and constant pressure to keep ahead of – or at least even up with – determined competitors'[55] Under the guiding spirit of senior officers like Admiral Stephen Luce and Alfred Thayer Mahan the US Navy became proficient in PME, primarily at the US Naval War College at Newport, Rhode Island (NWC). From then and to the eve of its entry into the Second World War, the US Navy '…demonstrated an ability to learn, innovate and evolve that places it at the forefront of modern ideas regarding management, organizational structure, and innovation.'[56] The phrase wasn't used, but it was clear that Luce accepted that the Navy needed to be a 'learning organisation.' If it wasn't, it would probably lose unless dealing with another navy that was even worse. By the end of the 1930s, the product of all this was a level of sophistication in campaign planning and operations that far exceeded that of the Japanese navy, its main adversary in the Pacific.

None of this happened by accident. It depended on the acceptance that there was a need to think through the novel problems set by developing technology and the international scene, rather than confidence that established ways of doing things could still cope. Sufficient 'thinking space' was needed. Above all, it needed enough people of the right intellectual calibre, to do the thinking. Josephus Daniels, the Navy Secretary made attendance at the NWC a requirement for promotion to high command.[57] This encouraged the Navy to develop into a complex learning organisation for it depended not on a single guiding spirit issuing a series of edicts but on continuous tinkering with the process by a whole lot of bright, motivated and informed people continuously refining existing ideas while introducing new ones.

Before the First World War, the same principles were applied potentially to everyone else in the US Navy as well. The result was an effective educational system that developed the skills of sailors, increased their professional knowledge and helped the Navy retain them. 'It is my ambition', said Secretary Daniels, to make the navy a great university, with college extensions ashore and afloat. Every ship should be a school, and every enlisted man, and petty and warrant officer should be given an opportunity to improve his mind, better his position and fit himself for promotion...Training produces skill, and skill not only produces efficiency but enhances self-respect.

These prospects proved so attractive that by 1914, the US Navy had more applicants than it had billets for, so it could pick and choose and established a waiting list. Even better, more than 85% of the sailors re-enlisted when they could.[58]

Of course, this was not a guarantee of operational success and there were still those who in effect disputed the link between this and PME. It did not prevent a series of early war disasters (such as the Japanese attack on Pearl Harbor), but these can be attributed to the Navy's rapid and huge expansion, which absorbed much of its corporate energy.[59] The same was to happen to the RCN as we have seen. Those reverses however reinforced the need to learn and innovate that had been temporarily submerged by the urgent requirements of expansion.

Neither was the debate about the relative importance and optimum form of PME silenced by this apparent success. Since the Second World war, the debate about the relative importance of PME and its optimum format has continually raged and constantly been tinkered with. As far as PME is concerned, in most navies it seems, nothing is for ever – but perhaps given the rate of global change that is as it should be.

Time at Staff and Command Colleges has other, largely incidental, benefits as well. Getting to know a much wider circle of people than one would otherwise normally expect to encounter encourages the creation of networks and contacts that have often proved of great value later on. They can also be a means by which less well-resourced navies can tap into the expertise of the more fortunate. In other ways too, the provision of places on staff courses can be internationally significant in building beneficial relationships between different countries. More prosaically, staff courses provide convenient options to Appointers in managing people for whom nothing more useful or suitable can be found in a particular year.

11.3.5 Balancing Training and PME

For all these reasons, navies accept the importance of both training and PME. They generally aim at providing an optimum balance of the two, that best caters for the needs of the individual as a means of benefitting the service. Commonly they recognise the need to raise the intellectual standards of PME increasingly by explicitly linking it with growing demands for post-graduate level university accreditation.

Moreover, there is broad recognition that what is true for officers is also true for ratings. Many of the advantages of developing the intellectual skills and education of officers apply to everyone else in the navy as well. In sum, far more than lip service is now paid to the idea that modern navies need to be real 'learning organisations' for everyone in them.

11.3.6 What Should Be Taught, When, How and to Whom?

Finally, there is a large and continuing debate about what should be learned by whom, when and how it is best administered. The topics addressed range widely. The continuing discourse about what should be taught tends to reflect underlying assumptions about the exact purpose of PME. Some pointing to the continuing difficulty that navies have in balancing their books argue the need for an emphasis on fiscal and business acumen and project management.[60] Others reflecting on problems between navies and defence manufacturers prefer a focus on developing the 'smart customer.' The 'latest thing' in defence technology also produces enthusiasm for any number of 'topics *du jour*' for harassed course designers to accommodate. Obviously, current events have their influence too. The 'Fat Leonard' scandal in the United States, for example, led to an explosion in demand for coverage of ethics and leadership and it's a fairly safe bet that dealing with pandemics and climate change will be emerging issues from the experiences of 2020–2021. Anything new demands special effort. It was the same in the 17th Century when the Dutch started going East for the first time and had little relevant experience to go on. Sufficient expertise had to be generated and distributed.

In the debate about how PME should be conducted, the question of the balance to be struck between residential and on-line learning became a topic much highlighted by the Covid-19 pandemic. Another leading issue is the extent to which staff courses should be joint rather than single-service. A joint approach may seem cheaper and more likely to encourage inter-service cooperation; a single service approach is likely to go deeper into issues of particular interest to the service in question. After all its advocates argue, naval people need to know more about the law of the sea and the merchant shipping industry, the ideas of Mahan and Corbett and naval history than would their equivalents in the other services.

Then there is the question of who should get PME and when. Navies generally seek to distinguish between differing levels of PME linking them to individuals if and when they are thought to need it. As Figure 11.1 shows, the result is a people pyramid sliced horizontally between three or sometimes four PME levels, entry, initial, intermediate and advanced flag-level courses. The higher the level, the fewer the people who need it.

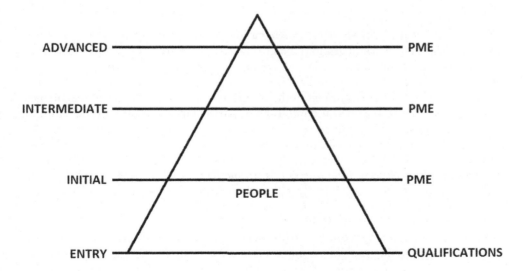

Figure 11.1 The Levels of PME.

Source: Self-generated.

This calls for an elaborate exercise in matching the capability and availability of the individual, the requirements of their likely next job and the most appropriate level of PME. It is an imprecise art, however.

For smaller navies, there is the hard-nosed issue of at what stage it makes sense for them to invest seriously in their own advanced PME systems rather than rely on attachment to foreign courses, or simply doing without. Many make use of schemes such as the US-led International Military Education and Training Programme (IMET). This saves their having to invest in the infrastructure required to deliver it at home, which, given the low number of students involved is often unlikely to be cost-effective. One problem with this is that it may prove difficult to reconcile the career interests of graduates of foreign staff colleges of differing character, levels and attainment. For such reasons, other small navies, such as that of Ireland, choose instead to accept the cost set up their own national PME arrangements.[61]

11.3.7 Alternate Sources of Expertise

For many navies, cooperation with others provides countless opportunities for tactical and operational training. The Canadian, Australian, Indian and other Imperial navies all benefitted from loans or exchange officers from the Royal Navy. This fast-tracked the acquisition of expertise and much reduced the resources that small, developing and overstretched navies initially needed to devote to institutions providing it. But those same foreign officers brought not just expertise but British attitudes and ways of doing things. As the local sense of national identity grew, this increasingly jarred local sensitivities, and incentivised home-grown programmes where cost-effectiveness can be a challenge.[62]

In a narrower way, the training packages that these days come with the acquisition of platforms, weapons and sensors from abroad, usually offer more than just the ability to operate the system in question and are another significant way of acquiring expertise. That needs to be taken into account when seeking, instead, to encourage the local production of equipment.

The same benefits derive from participation in exercises with other countries, especially when those countries may be considered more advanced in particular disciplines. Above all multinational naval exercises are key learning experiences; this is why so many navies devote so much effort into participating in them. NATO's naval exercises form a major commitment in the programmes of all the navies of the alliance. Some exercises are in the special conditions of particular areas, such as the Baltic or the Mediterranean. Many others seek to explore the problems of and potential for interoperability in particular disciplines. The Canadian Navy's *Cutlass Fury* is a good example of a NATO exercise primarily dedicated to ASW[63] but there are many more. The US-led two week long *International Maritime Exercise 2019* (IMX 19) held in the Gulf on the other hand was largely devoted to Mine Counter-Measures (MCM)[64] while the German/Danish led *Northern Coasts 2019* was intended to rehearse a newly established German Maritime Forces Staff.[65]

Other ways of learning from and with allies and partners include exchanging personnel and/or attaching individual ships, submarines or aircraft to an ally's maritime formations, such as European navies providing escorts to ride shotgun for the US Navy's carrier groups.

Navies such as the Russian or Chinese operating with few or even no allies and partners have limited opportunities for such synergies but can always set up 'red teams' in order to explore possibilities by 'attacking' each other. Hence the relatively unusual practice of two Russian submarines attempting to torpedo each other with practice weapons.[66] In such circumstances, there is a special need for home-grown and innovative thought and for the kind of PME/training regimes likely to encourage it. Whether that kind of free-thinking can be reconciled with the autocratic nature of such regimes, remains to be seen.

In the Cold War, recognising that the more realistic the exercises, the more valuable they were, both sides engaged each other (especially covertly and underwater) in ways that sought to elicit information about the other's procedures and weaponry and to practice their own. The same apparently confrontational ethos lies behind the success of the Royal Navy's 'Thursday Wars' run by Fleet Operations Sea Training (FOST), already mentioned, and indeed the 'Perisher' course for aspirants for submarine command. Such is the reputation of these realistic and sometimes exceedingly stressful training activities that many other navies seek to profit from them, including the US Navy.[67] All navies that can afford them also invest in the technology that simulates demanding, even alarming, situations in which a ship's company might find itself, such as is found at the Swedish Naval Warfare Centre.[68] But for all the efforts to create such tensions and stress, it's not the same as doing such things for real. While the Royal Navy had for decades prided itself on the realism of its peacetime training it was still very jolted by 'the real thing' in 1982 during the Falklands campaign, when the grim lesson was re-learned that the best-handled ships can still take destructive hits at the hands of a determined adversary.[69]

11.3.8 *Teaching Leadership?*

Finally, another Training/PME-related topic of apparently continuing fascination is the extent to which 'leadership' can be taught or, failing that, best developed and managed. Whole libraries have been devoted to the subject. The questions are deceptively simple, but the answers are complex and vary according to circumstances. Most obviously the qualities of leadership required may well be different for an operational commander at sea than for a 'capability deliverer' on shore. How, and even if, those qualities can be inculcated continues to be widely debated. Some would argue that such qualities are innate. All that navies need to do is create a career monitoring and reporting system that is principally designed to identify and encourage the people that have such qualities by appointing them to the appropriate positions. Others suggest a more proactive stance – and provide courses intended to foster the qualities needed for particular posts as a kind of 'pre-job training.' Most navies follow both tracks to some degree.

In wartime, or situations of strain, monitoring and responding to perceived performance tends to be rather more operationally focussed and decisive, even brutal, in effect, with the apparently incompetent, or merely unlucky, 'relieved' for failures to deliver what the service requires. Anyone getting something like the probably apocryphal leadership report that their men would always follow them '... if only out of simple curiosity' would undoubtedly get the message. In peacetime things tend to be more relaxed, rather more administratively focussed, with a greater stress on fostering leadership potential that individuals might have. In British and Commonwealth navies the means for this is still the S206 annual reporting form – or some derivative of it. The reporting officer assesses the individual's performance in the previous year, identifies weaknesses that need to be addressed and may make recommendations to the individual's 'appointer/detailer.' Most other navies play variations of this theme. Usually, if to differing degree, this will reflect not just what the navy needs but also the values and the expectations of the wider society from which the navy has sprung; accordingly, people management in most navies has got more solicitous than it used to be.

Some of these desired qualities can be evaluated relatively easily – such as 'ship handling' but many are more difficult. In their assessment, much depends on personalities of the reporter and reportee. This is an amorphous area, but one playing an important part in the workings of the navy as an organisation, simply because naval people are, after all, people and need to be treated as such. As an organisation, a navy, has to be flexible enough to accommodate the implications of this simple fact, especially since to some extent its success will depend on its drivers and thrusters who don't necessarily fit into the standard expectations.

Moreover, throughout history, navies have often seen the formation of groups, retinues, cliques that seem to form around those individuals whose intellectual calibre and personality traits marks them out as 'rising stars.' Sometimes as in the case of the poisonous relationship between Admirals Fisher and Beresford in the Royal Navy before the First World War, this phenomenon destroys a navy's 'all of one company' ethos. It can also undermine a Navy's image in those cases where the cliques collide in public, as they often do. Sometimes though these collisions can be positively helpful in delivering just what the navy needs. Admiral Hyman Rickover may have antagonised half the US Navy in the process, but he certainly energised the other half and its nuclear development. Such dynamics may well produce a kind of dialectic in which the fittest survive, the service prospers while the unfit fall away but do what they can. It appears, as ever, to be all a matter of balance.

11.4 The Unavoidable Issues of Cost

None of the personnel policies identified above are either easy or cheap. They all require the investment of large sums of money and human resource. And if to them is added pay and pensions, it is easy to see why direct and indirect people costs gobble up so much of the naval budget that other forms of expenditure (particularly capital expenditure for new platforms, weapons and sensors and Research and Development) seem dangerously squeezed. In the case of the RCN, personnel costs have hovered around the 50% mark, sometimes more sometimes less, in a way that had reduced the overall capital budget for new acquisition well below the 'ideal' 23%–27% range, once Operations and Maintenance (O&M) are also factored in.[70] The result was a 'rust-out' of the fleet, deteriorating standards, a lowering of operational ambition and a dishearteningly heavy 'tail' in relation to its 'teeth.'

This is a common problem and always has been; arguably with a growing need for higher levels of training and PME, it is getting worse. Navies have to work around it. One response is to challenge the starting assumptions by arguing that the navy should have a bigger share of the overall defence budget, or that the defence budget should be greater, or both. This doesn't often work. A less ambitious way round the problem is to resort to accrual accounting, in effect buying-on-credit, and putting the payments off to a later time. This delays the pain but does not make it to go away.

Instead the navy is enjoined to find the necessary 'efficiency savings' by 'trimming its own fat.' This can be by finding compensating cuts perhaps in reduced R&D, in its acquisition of new equipment or through the closure and sale of real estate and other crown jewels. Cuts in the O&M budget such as planned reductions in ship days at sea, or reduced fuel allowances, naturally have a direct operational impact, and can also adversely affect morale.

More narrow targets can be found within an apparently excessive Personnel budget itself. Such devices have included out-sourcing of naval jobs to cheaper civilians. This saves money but also reduces the number of shoreside billets (and family time) available to older, experienced serving personnel. Reducing overall numbers may alleviate the recruitment problem but reduces capability. The lean-manning of ships may do the same, and compensating technology can be expensive. Reduced pay and conditions increase the recruitment and retention problem. Direct cuts in the PME/Training budget, perhaps by the transfer of some of these activities to sea (as in the Royal Navy's SLIMTRAIN exercise) is another option. Many of these are in effect exercises in a-bit-jam-more-jam-today-but-less-in-the-future. While none of these choices are attractive, generally navies accept that tolerating excessive cut-backs in its personnel or suspensions in its training and PME programmes in the name of short-term economies are likely to prove expensive in the long run, simply because a navy's people are, or at least should be, its greatest asset. But all too often they have to do it anyway, because saving money seems to be a more urgent requirement.

11.5 People Issues 'with Chinese Characteristics'

A preliminary look at Chinese naval experience underlines the point that these issues in the provision of a sufficiently trained and educated naval workforce are a universal naval preoccupation and that the methods adopted to deliver it show great similarities. For their 'great war' of the 16th Century the same preoccupation for the raising and training of naval personnel required a sophisticated mobilisation system – and the same was true of their Korean allies.[71]

From the earliest days of the People's Republic, the Chinese recognised that service at sea was particularly demanding and required longer periods of service. In the 1950s enlistments in the army was three years, the air force, four and the navy, five.[72] Politics, especially the never-ending red-v-expert tensions often got in the way of the need for professionalism.[73] By the early 1980s, the Chinese navy was in serious need of a major overhaul, in particular of the way in which it trained and educated its people as the opening comment in this chapter shows.

Like any other country, China brought its own assumptions, concepts and indeed terminology to this task as the PLAN slowly shifted from being a largely conscript to a more volunteer force. Even so, in broad terms, its campaign to professionalise its people resembled those of many other navies, only on a much bigger scale. The Navy wanted to widen the pool from which it fished its officers so that more came from other than military colleges. It planned a 'cradle-to-grave' training and educational system that would support officers, NCOs and enlisted personnel through every stage of their careers. It invested in specialist Academies that catered for the various branches of the service. But like other navies it wanted to increase the proportion of its people that had university degrees, or the equivalent, at both graduate and post-graduate levels. It also acknowledged an urgent need for well-qualified NCOs/Petty Officers to bridge the gap between officers and enlisted personnel.

Even the problems encountered seem similar. A review of the system in 2008 fretted about poor coordination between the various tracks in the supposedly seamless 'cradle-to-grave system,' about the low quality and poor motivation of too many students and the high drop-out rate, and about the inevitable tensions between shore side training and education time and sea-time where one could learn the fundamentals of command 'on the job.'[74] There were worries about the command qualities about too many of the PLAN's people specifically the notorious 'five cannots' of an earlier generation of leaders who:

- cannot judge the situation
- cannot understand the intention of higher authorities
- cannot make operational decisions
- cannot deploy troops
- cannot deal with unexpected situations.[75]

The last of these 'cannots' takes us back to Clausewitz who famously warned that, 'war is the realm of uncertainty; three quarters of the factors on which action in war is based are wrapped in a fog of greater or lesser uncertainty.'[76] Dealing better with the 'black swans' and 'pink flamingos'[77] of an unpredictable future is very evidently a universal requirement.

At that time, too, few PLAN officers engaged with their equivalents in the other services in joint command-and-staff colleges until reaching flag rank as Commodores or Rear Admirals, by which time it was arguably too late. There was also debate about the comparative benefits of residential rather than on-line, distance, professional military education. Given all these concerns, it is hardly surprising that as the Chinese navy evolves into a traditional blue-water force that it finds itself confronting the same personnel issues faced by all the others.

The same is true in the business of designing the fleet that people operate, the subject of the next chapter.

Notes

1 Liu Huaqing, *Memoirs* (Beijing: PLA Press, 2004), 440.
2 Birthday message to the Fleet, 12 October 2021.
3 Hoppitt, *A Land of Liberty,* op. cit, 129, 330. The Navy had 13,000 people in 1715, but had been voted 40,000 for the period's wars.
4 Boutilier, James A. (Ed), *RCN in Retrospect 1910–1968.* (Vancouver: University of British Columbia Press, 1982), xxv and Audette, L.C., 'The Lower Deck and the Mainguy Report of 1949,' in ibid, 243–7.
5 Ransom, Bernard, 'A Nursery of Fighting Seamen? The Newfoundland Royal Naval Reserve 1901–1920,' in Hadley (Ed), *A Nation's Navy,* 239–55.
6 Goldrick, James, 'Carriers for the Commonwealth,' in Frame, T.R., Goldrick, J.V.P. and Jones, P.D. (Eds), *Reflections on the Royal Australian Navy* (Kenthurst, NSW: Kangaroo Press, 1991), 220–4.
7 Milner, Marc, 'Royal Canadian Participation in the Battle of the Atlantic Crisis of 1943,' in Boutilier (Ed), *RCN in Retrospect,* 158–74. For fuller treatment see also his *North Atlantic Run: The Royal Canadian Navy and the battle for the Convoys* (Toronto: University of Toronto Press, 1985) and *The U-Boat Hunters* (Annapolis: US Naval Institute Press, 1994) and Douglas, *No Higher Purpose.*

8 Mutiny at sea is a fascinating and important subject. See Guttridge Leonard F., *Mutiny: A History of Naval Insurrection* (New York: Berkeley Books, 1992).

9 Lund, Wilfred G.D. and Vice-Admiral E. Rollo, 'Mainguy: Sailors' Admiral,' in Whitby (Ed), *The Admirals*, 193.

10 Ibid, 192–3.

11 Lund, Wilfred G.D., 'Vice-Admiral Howard Emmerson Reid; Vice Admiral Harold Taylor Wood Grant: Forging the New "Canadian Navy",' in Whitby (Ed), *The Admirals*, 172–3.

12 Ibid, 173.

13 Ibid; 'Vice Admiral Harold Taylor Wood Grant,' in Whitby (Ed), *The Admirals*, 164.

14 This section owes much to Milner, Marc, 'Rear-Admiral Leonard Warren Murray: Canada's Most Important Operational Commander,' and Mayne, Richard Oliver, 'Vice Admiral George C. Jones: The Political career of a Naval Officer,' both in Whitby (Ed), *The Admirals*.

15 Milner, 'Rear Admiral … Murray,' in ibid, 118.

16 Captain Massey Goolden, RN quoted in Mayne, 'Vice Admiral … Jones,' in Whitby (Ed), *The Admirals*, 138.

17 Milner, Rear Admiral … Murray, 103.

18 Lund, Wilfred G.D. Lund, 'Vice-Admiral … Mainguy,' in Whitby (Ed), *The Admirals*, 199.

19 Haydon, Peter, 'Vice-Admiral Herbert S. Rayner: The Last Chief of the Canadian Naval Staff,' in Whitby (Ed), *The Admirals*, 258. To be fair the so-called 'Brock Report' also paid little attention to either technological possibilities or political and economic realities. It was completely invalidated by the Trudeau administration's focus on sovereignty and peace keeping functions rather than on NATO support. Sokolosky, Joel, 'A Question of Balance: Canada and the Cold war at Sea, 1945–1968,' in Frame (Ed), *Reflections on the Royal Australian Navy*, 361–4.

20 Haydon, *Vice-Admiral Rayner*, 254–5.

21 Whitby, *The Admirals*, 23.

22 Abulafia, *The Great Sea*, 424–7; Pryor, John H., 'Byzantium and the Sea,' in Hattendorf and Unger (Eds), *War at Sea*, 93.

23 Phillips, Carla Rahn, 'Why Did Anyone Go to Sea?,' in Benton and Perl-Rosenthal (Eds), *A World at Sea*, 26.

24 Roberts, Jennifer T., *The Plague of War: Athens, Sparta, and the Struggle for Ancient Greece* (Oxford: Oxford University Press, 2017), 15.

25 Maydman, *Naval Speculations*, 241, 257–62, 264.

26 Phillips, 'Why Did Anyone Go to Sea?,' in Benton and Perl-Rosenthal (Eds), *A World at Sea*, 30–1.

27 Michael L. Hadley, 'The Popular Image of the Canadian Navy,' in Hadley (Ed), *A Nation's Navy*, 35–8.

28 Hadley, *A Nation's Navy*, 4.

29 Pullen, Hugh Francis, 'The Royal Canadian Navy Between the Wars,' in Boutilier (Ed), *RCN in Retrospect*, 63–4; Glover, William, 'Commodore Walter Hose: Ordinary Officer, Extraordinary Endeavour,' in Whitby (Ed), *The Admirals*, 60.

30 Bernier, Serge, 'HMCS *Ottawa* III: The Navy's First French Language Unit, 1968–1973,' Hadley (Ed), *A Nation's Navy*, 310–22.

31 As will be shown in the next chapter, the *Armada* of 16th and 17th-century Spain was in fact a cosmopolitan mix of Spanish, Basque, Catalan, Flemish and Italian personnel and ships, with a fair sprinkling of other European nationalities as well.

32 Mason, Ursula Stuart, *Britannia's Daughters; The Story of the WRNS* (London: Leo Cooper, 1992).

33 Winters, Barbara, 'The Wrens of the Second world War: Their Place in the History of Canadian Servicewomen,' Hadley (Ed), *A Nation's Navy*, 280–96.

34 Winters, Barbara, 'The Wrens of the Second world War: Their Place in the History of Canadian Servicewomen,' Hadley (Ed), *A Nation's Navy*, 280–96, 295.

35 US Naval War College archive, King Papers, Box 9, Whitehill notes, "Race Relations;" Box 19, Navy Department, Bureau of Naval Personnel, "Guide to Command of Negro Naval Personnel – NAVPERS-15092" (February, 1945). I am grateful to Dr David Kohnen for this material from his forthcoming book on Admiral King.

228 *Delivering a Navy's People*

36 Luke Broadwater, 'New First for Air Force: Black General Becomes Chief,' *New York Times,* 1 June 2020. The General's testimony may be seen on https://www.youtube.com/watch?v=brQLhb_4fqs. Accessed 30 June 2020. The Navy responded in July 2020 by Establishing 'Task Force One Navy' to ensure equality of treatment.

37 Cubitt, Lord Cochrane, 268.

38 Quoted Goodman, *Spanish Naval Power,* 202.

39 Yoshida, Mitsuru, *Requiem for a Battleship* (Seattle: University of Washington Press, 1985), 20–1.

40 Timirev, Adm S.N., *The Russian Baltic Fleet in the Time of War and Revolution, 1914–1818* (Barnsley: Seaforth Publishing, 2020), 22–7, 38–43, 61–3 et seq. Also Aselius, Gunnar, *The Rise and Fall of the Soviet Navy in the Baltic, 1921–1941* (London: Frank Cass, 2005), 29–54.

41 Maydman, *Naval Speculations,* 60.

42 Correll, Diana Stancy, 'After McCain, Fitzgerald Collision Reports, Navy Says It's Focused on 'Fundamentals' of Warfighting,' *Navy Times,* 1 July 2021.

43 George, Vice-Adm. Robert E., in Whitby *The Admirals,* 342–3.

44 Admiral Mike Gilday, CNO US Navy quoted in Guy Toremans interview, *Warship IFR,* February 2020, 18.

45 The Admiralty did its best to make things worse by blaming and hunting for non-existent political political agitators amongst the disaffected crews.

46 Rear Adm Torben Mikkelsen, quoted in Guy Toremans, 'Danes Devise a Fleet…,' *Warship IFR,* December 2019, 27.

47 Barrett, *The Navy and the Nation,* 72–4.

48 Cdr Tom Trent, quoted in 'Gulf Escort's Joyous Return,' *Warship IFR,* November 2019, 44.

49 Quoted in Allen, Kenneth and Clemens, Morgan, *The Recruitment, Education and Training of PLA Navy Personnel* (US Naval War College: China Maritime Studies No. 12, 2014), 27–8.

50 Goldman, *Spanish Naval Power,* 221–3.

51 Ibid.

52 March, William A., 'A Canadian Departure: The Evolution of HMCS Royal Roads, 1942–1948,' In Hadley (Ed), *A Nation's Navy.*

53 Boutilier, James A., 'Get Big or Get Out: The Canadian and Australian Decisions to Abandon Aircraft Carriers,' in Frame, *Reflections on the Royal Australian Navy* 382–408, 403. See also Healey, Denis, *The Time of My Life* (London: Penguin, 1990), 275–7.

54 Douglas, *No Higher Purpose,* 33–4; Lund, *Admiral…Mainguy,* in Whitby, *The Admirals,* 197.

55 Hone, *Learning War,* 14.

56 Ibid.

57 Ibid, 46.

58 Ibid, 50–1.

59 Ibid, 302–15. Compare, Moretz,Joseph, *Thinking Wisely, Planning Boldly: The Higher education and Training of Royal Navy Officers, 1919–1939* (Solihull: Helion, 2015).

60 Whitby, Michael, 'Vice-Admiral Harry G. DeWolf: Pragmatic Navalist,' in Whitby (Ed), *The Admirals,* 220–3.

61 Ciaran Lowe, 'A Comparative Analysis of Three Small Navies,' in McCabe (Ed), *Europe, Small Navies and Maritime Security,* 188, 192.

62 James Goldrick, 'Strangers in their Own Sea? A Comparison of the Australian and Canadian naval experience, 1910–1982' and Winters, Barbara, 'The Wrens of the Second world War: Their Place in the History of Canadian Servicewomen,' in Hadley (Ed), *A Nation's Navy,* 328, 331.

63 'Cutting Edge Combat Lessons,' *Warship IFR,* November 2019, 26–7.

64 'Massive Exercise Staged in Middle East to Tackle Mine Menace,' *Warship IFR,* January 2020, 12–13.

65 'Northern Coasts tests German Command Team for NATO,' '*Warship IFR,* November 2019, 32–4.

66 'Russian subs in torpedo "duel",' *Warship IFR,* December 2019, 12.

67 'Full menu of training for forward-based [USS Donald] Cook,' *Warship IFR,* November 2019, 42.

68 Oliver, David, 'Exploiting the Virtual naval Universe to Liberate Front Line Units for Ops,' *Warship IFR,* 20–2.
69 See review of *British Cruiser Warfare: The Lessons of the Early War* by Capt Gerry Northwood (rtd) in *Warship IFR,* January 2020, 46–8.
70 'Getting the Personnel and Capital Mix Right,' in Griffiths, Ann and Lerhe, Eric (Eds), *Naval Gazing: The Candian Navy Contemplates Its Future* (Halifax: Dalhousie University, 2010), 55–6.
71 Swope, *A Dragon's Head and a Serpent's Tail,* 69–70.
72 Muller, *China as a Maritime Power,* 54.
73 Ibid, 265.
74 Allen, The Recruitment, Education and Training of PLA Personnel, 9–10.
75 'One Extraordinary Examination,' *PLA Daily,* 22 January 2015, cited in Dennis J. Blasko, 'Integrating the Services and Harnessing the Military Area Commands,' *Journal of Strategic Studies,* 2016, Vol. 39, Nos. 5–6, 704.
76 Carl von Clausewitz, *On War* (trans. Michael Howard and Peter Paret) (Princeton: Princeton University Press, 1984), 101.
77 Frank Hoffman, 'Black Swans and Pink Flamingoes: Five Principles for Force Design,' *War on the Rocks,* 19 August 2015.

12 Designing the Fleet

> My focus is towards maintaining a combat-ready and agile force, capable of dealing
> with the entire spectrum of challenges stretching from the non-traditional and sub-
> conventional realms to high end conventional threats.
> —Admiral Muhammad Amjad Khan Niazi, Pakistan Navy[1]

A fully equipped and effective fleet available to defend the nation's interests at the
right place at the right time is the ultimate expression of maritime power. Delivering it
though, has always been difficult. Its essence in peace, war and everything in between,
is to strike the right balance between commitments, resources, time, capabilities – and
degrees of acceptable risk. All this has to be done within a framework shaped by a
country's unique domestic and international context since this framed the process.

Very few, if any, fleet designers start with a blank sheet of paper. Instead they precede
from a 'legacy' force of vessels and equipment acquired in an earlier period when conditions and demands might have been very different. This means that new acquisitions
have to be worked into the demands of maintaining and operating an older force. In
itself, this can introduce significant planning complexities and problems of integration.

12.1 Fleet Design and Acquisition: Why So Difficult?

A British group with formidable experience in the field has recently described defence
acquisition, as one of the most demanding forms of human activity.[2] This is in part
because it is about preparing for the future and so tends to suffer from the unpredictability of the economic, budgetary and strategic environment during the platform or the fleet's gestation period and service life.

This raises the important issue of whether a navy's fleet planning needs to be
generic, against all eventualities, or focused on particular perceived threats, usually the
fleets of potentially opposing countries. The planners may have a definite adversary in
mind or simply pick some convenient nation as a 'pacing threat' – a means of exploring issues. In the 1920s, for example, the Royal Navy used the United States as a
potential enemy for planning purposes. This approach tends to have shorter time
frames. It has the advantage of offering greater specificity about military-technological
and operational requirements but this can be unfortunate if the adversary turns out to
be someone else. Moreover, treating another state as an enemy has sometimes proved
worryingly self-confirmatory.

DOI: 10.4324/9781003100553-12

The generic approach, on the other hand, is based on an inability to identify enemies or operational areas but is intended to deliver capabilities that hopefully will come in handy for almost any situation. Ship requirements in theory can be measured 'objectively' when set against the area to be covered in the cases of the patrol boats needed for MARSEC or, in the case of the Royal Navy's cruiser numbers in the interwar period by the length of Imperial sea lines ofcommunication. The problem is that even this approach tends to be inherently technology-heavy and often largely ignores how such faceless adversaries might react operationally. 'No matter how absorbed a commander is in the elaboration of his own thoughts,' Churchill warns us, 'it is sometimes necessary to take the enemy into consideration.'[3] Both approaches have their advantages and their disadvantages; a judicious mix of the two is therefore often adopted.

Either way, planners have to cope with the fact that a platform's service life can be surprisingly long, maybe when filling gaps left by the failure of other prgrammes. Often it may become involved – in roles, missions and functions that were quite unexpected during the design phase. The longer the gestation period and service life, the greater the degree of unpredictability.

The highly varied and operationally effective career of the UK's *Invincible* class of light carrier – ordered in 1973 essentially as ASW platforms in the North Atlantic but used for virtually everything else as well and only phased out in 2015, suggests that large naval platforms are specially useful for the inherent flexibility they offer.[4] At the same time though, longevity comes at a price; arguably it makes the design of big ships more complicated and potentially hazardous than is the case with their land and air equivalents. While some of these equivalents have also been around for a long time too (and so also need to be able to deal with changing technological challenges), their range of activities tends to be much narrower and more predictable.

The length of the design and gestation phase in the procurement process can be a problem too. The longer this lasts, the greater the temptation to tinker around with the original specification in order to keep it more in line with emerging strategic challenges and technological possibilities. As the manufacturer adjusts the production programme to cope, the result is delay and, very often, extra cost. At the same time, spending large amounts of public money on long-term projects provides ample opportunity and plenty of reason for the money people, politicians, defence industry itself, and not infrequently, the other services to get involved as well.

Complex and ambitious projects such as the UK's *Queen Elizabeth* carrier (ordered 1993 and initial commissioning 2020) make them particularly vulnerable to this kind of iterative delay, As a result, they arrive later and cost much more than they should have. All too often, they do not arrive at all. Although some of the experience gained in failed projects can be used in support of other later ones, this is wasteful and tends to undermine the case for defence expenditure as a whole. Everyone involved in such problems of course blames everyone else

The real price though may be paid much later if and when the platform is called upon to perform its tasks for real. In the middle 1960s, Britain's Defence Secretary Denis Healey insisted, in order to make them more affordable, that some of the Royal Navy's Type 42 guided missile destroyers be 'shortened.' Fifteen or so years later, that decision materially contributed to the loss of British lives and ships in the Falklands War because it adversely affected the efficiency of the Sea Dart air defence missile, the Type 42's *raison d'etre*. At the time, it was a calculated risk and one that seemed better than not being able to afford those Type 42s at all. The experience shows that naval procurement is a process of painful compromise between assessments of the required capability, when it is needed, its cost and the degree of acceptable risk. None of these things is at all easy to calculate.

The other major problem is, inevitably, money. Defence inflation has continuously and significantly outstripped conventional inflation – annually by about 10% since 1945 according to some. This poses a particularly vexatious problem.[5] Nor, in many cases can the money people themselves predict the future performance of the national economy which is the main yardstick against which 'what will be affordable' can be calculated.

Into that complex issue come all sorts of other considerations, such as the politicians' own views about the relative importance of the naval case when set against the other things that public money could be spent on. Variations in the world economy, such as the recession that hit Asia in the 1990s, the Great Recession of 2008–2009 and the aftermath of the Covid-19 crisis may make nonsense of all the carefully crafted compromises of naval planners in previous years. Arbitary rulings sich as 'there won't be a war for ten years' have a poor track record.

Where national economies are heavily dependent on the sale of particular commodities (oil in the case of Malaysia, East Timor and the Gulf States, or copper for Chile) market price variations can play havoc with previous planning. For this reason, Chile is in the process of moving away from this method of financing its naval procurement programmes.[6]

The result of this sad litany of problems is that a navy may well tend to acquire new *materiel* in a piecemeal, opportunistic way rather than as part of any overall cohesive plan that, ideally, it might have derived from careful thinking about its projected roles, missions and functions. This risks producing capability gaps and short-falls likely to limit the navy's capacity to perform its present roles, let alone its future ones.

Generally the extent to which this is true is directly linked to the level of sophistication of the naval *materiel* in question. The more 'high tech' naval weapons, sensors and platforms are, the longer their gestation period and the higher the degree of their technological or budgetary risk. All too often the result, when the extent of this becomes clearer in the gestation process, is the savage reduction or even complete cancellation of the programme such as occurred for the US Navy's Zumwalt class destroyer or the UK Royal Air Force's Nimrod Maritime Patrol aircraft in 2010.

In most cases, the first of class will anyway reveal unexpected 'teething problems' which delay the overall programme and result in increased costs to fix. Hence the Royal Australian Navy's very advanced Collins class submarines went through a troubled period in which they were often dismissed, especially by their opponents, as 'duds' before finally emerging as amongst the most capable submarines in the Indo-Pacific. Exactly the same happened to the Royal Navy's Astute class diesel submarines. The indirect consequences of such difficulties may include the extra expense of keeping their less cost-effective predecessors longer than budgeted for.[7] In all such cases such 'unexpected' teething problems and their consequences should be an 'expected' element in realistic planning.

One compensation for all this is that follow-on platforms in the programme usually come through the process faster and at less cost and controversy. Thus, profiting from the experience of the design experience and sea trials of the Royal Navy's *Queen Elizabeth* carrier, the second in class, the *Prince of Wales* had a significantly easier time.[8] In the same way, combining the acquisition of two Ford class carriers (CVN 80 and 81) provided a massive saving for the US Navy of US$ 4 billion dollars over what they would have cost under separate contracts. Likewise, while the procurement cost of the first Columbia class SSBN was estimated by the Congressional Budget Office at US$ 8.2 billion, the remaining 11 would be a steal at US$ 6.5 billion each.[9]

The more units there are in the programme the more of an advantage this is. Here smaller and medium navies encounter special problems in that they find it more difficult to generate the economies of scale that help make such procurement problems more manageable.[10] All too often they have to get their ships in penny packets which make each unit excessively expensive to acquire, crew and maintain while the uncertain manner of their acquisition makes it hard for defence industry to plan for the future. Such was the case for New Zealand Navy's two frigates or Malaysia's two *Scorpene* submarines. Moreover, the iron law of necessary refits will mean that it will be extremely difficult to extract a *continuous* and cost-effective capability out of such small numbers and this complicates any overall mission planning based on such availability. Larger navies, though, are by no means immune to such problems.

Putting it all together, designing a fleet requires planners to choose the threats they need to meet and how best to do it. This involves speculation about an uncertain future. The technological feasibility and likely cost-effectiveness of various options over time have to be estimated. This is true of decisions about both the best mix of the fleet and the characteristics of the individual ships within it. Both sets of decisions and choices are framed by general technological and operational trends in war at and from the sea. Very possibly this is exemplified by possibly inaccurate perceptions of what other countries and fleets are doing.

These are complex issues which take time to sort out. Moreover designing fleets and their individual components is never simply a discrete time-limited event. Instead it is a continuous process that never stops because everything changes all the time. A glance at some examples of the way in which some of these problems and choices have been tackled in the past and are being tackled now shows that they are far from new, although they have almost certainly got worse.

12.2 Fleet Design and the Search for Balance: Insights from Past and Present

It is difficult to be certain about what the fleet may actually be called upon to do, and what that may require. There are unending options in choosing the mix of the fleet as a whole and deciding the balance in the competing capabilities of the individual ships which comprise it. Almost inevitably, planners end up with some kind of 'balanced fleet,' which is designed to cover as many options as resources will allow.

The naval fondness for the notion of a 'balanced fleet' is often derided by their adversaries as demonstrating no more than the world's navies inability to predict their present or future tasks and their general desire to have their cake and eat it too. This easy criticism is unfounded. The alternative usually offered is a 'focussed' fleet but that tends to mean one with a deliberately limited range of tasks. In any case, 'focussed' fleets have to balance too. Henry Maydman himself was by no means immune to this affliction. He thought investing in great ships (by which he meant ships of more than 70 guns) '...is vast expence and...only serves to gratify the itch of grandeur.' But that was because he thought the Navy should be more focussed on the protection of commerce than on trying to force battle on a 'dodging enemy.'[11] In effect he was simply balancing between a reduced range of options.

The evolving notion of a balanced fleet in fact is a naval requirement that reflects firstly the fact that even the smallest of navies have a multitude of different tasks and secondly that technological advance requires ships and other platforms to specialise in some of these tasks more than they do in others. The idea of a ship that can do everything, everywhere is no more feasible now than it was in the 17th Century.

12.2.1 Medieval England and the Search for Balance

The more specialised 'warships' became and the greater the variety of tasks the fleet had to perform, the greater the level of choice confronted the fleet designer. Increasingly they had to strike balances between adapted civilian ships and warships on the one hand and between different kinds of warships on the other. These two sets of choices were separate but related. Both were shaped by the different tasks that their ships of war needed to perform. In the 15th Century, England's Henry V personally invested in four 'Great Ships,' the biggest, the *Grace Dieu*, built between 1416 and 1420, was of 1400 tons, 'the greatest ship England had ever seen.'[12] Like the rest of the royal fleet it was fully operational for well over half of its service life, not too bad by modern standards, conducting war patrols, expeditionary/amphibious operations and being used for such high profile activities as the transport of VIPs. Like most large ships of every age it was also thought of value 'for general purposes of greatness.'

Henry's eight double-masted carracks varying between 400 and 600 tons likewise mainly engaged in war patrols but also protected ports and in some sea areas were useful for convoy protection.[13] He also had 16 single-masted 'ships' varying between 50 and 330 tons intended for war patrols, expeditionary operations and convoy protection, but also for the transport of supplies and less well-favoured VIPs. Henry's fleet also comprised 19 oar-propelled barges or 'balingers' ranging from 24 to 120 tons that were used in small ways for virtually everything. Finally there was the *Jesus Maria* a galley of 252 oars for which no use whatsoever could be found.[14] Its acquisition is a case study in how not to do things.

But the *Jesus Maria* does raise one of the big choices that navies of that period had to think about – what type of main propulsion – the oar or the sail? Much depended on the particular sea conditions to be faced. Ships intended for operations in coastal or estuarine waters would probably need to be shallow-draft, smaller and handier. Those having to 'keep' rougher and higher seas on the other hand tended towards the reverse. Unsurprisingly, the need to cater for the military needs of different areas was hard to satisfy. Medieval Castile for example, with one coast on the Mediterranean and another on the Atlantic, had to deal with the hostile war galleys of North Africa in the former and the sailing ships of its English adversaries in the latter.

Geographic considerations affected choices in galleys as well as in sailing ships. Some were designed and chosen for operation in the Mediterranean, others for the shallow coastal fringes of the Baltic and others still for the choppier, deeper Atlantic seaboard. Weather conditions were a real constraint for galleys; even in the Mediterranean, military operations were generally suspended in the winter.

When conditions were right, galleys' independence from the wind could prove a decisive tactical advantage when dealing with slow or becalmed sailing ships in coastal waters, a point demonstrated as late as 1714 by the Russians in their victories over the Swedes as in the battle of Hango Head. Moreover, their capacity to mount forwards firing heavy guns in the prow (if at some cost to their seaworthiness) gave them a considerable tactical advantage over slow-moving sailing ships, not least because the low trajectory of their shot was especially dangerous.[15] In short oar-propelled ships long remained an important option for fleet designers, especially in riverine and estuarine operations and in enclosed seas like the Baltic and the Mediterranean.

Galleys also came in all shapes and sizes, so offering further choices for fleet designers, as measured by their length and beam and by the numbers – and, indeed, decks – of oars and by their carrying capacity of fighting men and/or cargo. Smaller more manouevrable galleys made for quicker and easier loading and unloading in port or on the beach; they were also obviously better suited for riverine operations. Larger ones, for instance bi- or triremes with two or three banks of oars were better for coastal operations, but usually couldn't keep the sea for more than three days.

The same problem of deciding size and role specialisation applied to sailing ships as well. As naval engagements became more common there was something of a move away from smaller vessels to 'Great ships' and larger fighting carracks. As always, striking balances between these alternative types of warships meant reconciling assessments of military needs, with what was practically available and what could be afforded. All too often, it was really a question of making do with whatever you could get hold of.

12.2.2 The Spanish Tackle the Problem

Just a few decades before Maydman uncovered many of the same issues in England's Royal Navy of 1691, the Spanish had also to grapple with all the complex problems of fleet design. For them it was less a question of building a new fleet, more of trying to lay down the foundations of a long recovery after a period of neglect and failure. Their relative success should give partial comfort to naval planners.

The Spanish period of naval recovery was book-ended by two catastrophic defeats, the disaster of the first Armada against England in 1588 and the Battle of the Downs against the Dutch in 1639. In this period the country's maritime power was successfully recovered but then lost again. In the process many of the issues discussed above dutifully make their appearance.

Spain, though, was less a country and more a varied and multinational empire – its ruling elite indeed referring to it as 'The Monarchy.' For that reason, the King and his advisors had some extra complications to deal with. The Spanish empire included most of Latin America, the Philippines, much of Italy and the Spanish Netherlands. Its extent certainly brought extra maritime resources, but extra strategic commitments too. The Genoese influence could be seen everywhere. Additionally, there were domestic political considerations to be born in mind. Old Castile, Spain's heartland, had an essentially land-centric outlook; Catalonia and the Basque country, on the other hand were much more maritime but had a certain independence of mind that needed to catered for. Flanders was distinctly maritime too, as were parts of Spanish Italy.

So the King, the *Junta de Armadas* (Naval Committee/Board) and its various supporting boards and committees, especially the *Junta de Ejecución* (Committee of Ways and Means) needed a 17th Century version of an 'Estimate of the Situation,' followed by something resembling what we might call a 'mission analysis.' This would have identified a naval need to secure sea communications with South America and the safe passage of the annual silver fleets, which were critical to the whole Imperial enterprise. The Mediterranean coast and northern Italy had to be protected against the still powerful galley fleets of the Ottoman empire. Any hope of success in the apparently endless war against the heretical Dutch over Flanders and the Spanish Netherlands would depend on getting supplies and reinforcements through the English Channel to the Army at the front,[16] and preferably finding some means of inflicting damage on the Dutch war economy. There were also the opportunistic and potentially predatory French and English to worry about.

Such was the complexity of the situation, planners sometimes almost gave up. In 1591 for instance the Council of War trying to prepare for the renewed Armada enterprise, threw up their hands in resignation admitting it 'does not know what forces will be needed, because that depends on what arises.'[17] In this, they spoke for many other naval planners in similar plight throughout history.

There were some things they could be certain of, however. The first was how important the maritime dimension of the conflict was to the Monarchy's success, even survival, since its possessions were all 'joined by the sea' and its wealth arrived by that means as well. 'Quite simply, maritime thinking came to dominate Madrid's overall conception of war.'[18] Philip III's Navy Secretary Martin de Aroztegui and Philip IV's powerful First Minister, Gaspar de Guzman, Count-Duke of Olivares were absolutely clear about this, reminding all that needed it that, in the terms of the very influential Piedmontese theorist Giovanni Botero, 'whoever is master of the sea is also master of the land.'[19]

Secondly, the Monarchy's competing strategic requirements needed very different kinds of fleets. The Mediterranean theatre demanded galleys. The safe Atlantic passage of the silver fleets relied on the *Armada de la Guardia de la Carrera de las Indias*'s large well-armed galleons, with substantial carrying capacity together with medium galleons and supply vessels. The Monarchy's two permanent and forward-based squadrons protecting the Caribbean and Spanish settlements in South America needed a mix of small, medium and a few large galleons. A successful war against the Dutch in the treacherous English channel depended on clouds of privateers and small and medium-sized galleons, lean, fast and innovative 'frigates.' These specially designed frigates represented a bold and carefully thought-out response to the need to attack Dutch sea-based trade and their all-important fishing fleet. They were 'a major technological breakthrough,' and very successful too – as indeed were the variegated privateers.[20]

Such judgements about required ship-types were often based on hard experience. The catastrophic defeat of the 1588 Armada, for example was carefully analysed in Spain. The conclusion seemed to be that the English had prevailed by building fast ships which could seize the weather gauge and so determine the terms, and probably also the outcome of the engagement. Broadly, it was felt, that the Spanish needed to follow suit.[21]

Resources were decidedly finite, however, and so the *Junta de Armadas* had to make careful choices and compromises to deliver a fleet mix which could cater for as wide a range of contingencies as possible within the bounds of reality. As ever, limits on what was possible were set by the availability of the necessary finance. Ocean-going navies were very expensive indeed, and irregular, intermittent Royal funding was a continual problem. Once the *Junta de Armadas* had decided what ships were needed that year, these estimates were passed up for approval to the Council of Finance, (the *Consejo de Hacienda*). In 1621, as the King pointedly reminded the Marquis de Montesclaros, the

Council's President,' only so long as these provisions are punctual can we rely on my navy to bring us success.'[22] Once approved, the plans were then set in motion by the *Junta de Armadas* or one of its side- and sub-committees.

But actually getting and being able to spend the money was another matter; providing the royal ship-builders and suppliers along with private contractors with the finance when they actually needed it was particularly difficult. The problem arose because there were limits as to what taxes could be squeezed out of Castile, and the more maritime parts of Spain, hence the importance of the timely and safe arrival of the silver fleet. Hence also the comparative attraction of privateering which largely paid for itself.[23] Yet another problem the planners faced was the fact that prices were rising all the time and it was difficult accurately to assess what they would be in the future.

Getting the necessary manpower was always another challenge, especially from Spain. Fortunately, much of the Flanders squadron could be manned by the locals, although generally commanded by Spaniards, and towards the end of the period some of these Flemish ships could be redeployed to the *Armada del Mar Oceano* (the Atlantic Fleet) based in Spain. The use of privateers alleviated the problem of course and the new Frigates were helpfully much less manpower-intensive. Nonetheless, it remained extremely difficult for the King, Olivares and their subordinates to find- and keep – the people they needed.[24] The same went for the supplies the fleet required, victuals, guns, powder and so forth. These could only be sourced from often inadequate Spanish suppliers,[25] from elsewhere in the empire and not infrequently from potential adversaries too. Famously, a lot of the guns in the 1588 Armada were made in England.

Olivares and the officials of the *Junta de Armadas* of course knew about all these practical limitations in advance and since there was clearly no point in asking for the impossible, their estimates hovered somewhere in the grey area between what was desirable strategically and what they thought was actually possible. They reflected not just the objective demands of the strategic situation they faced but also the practical world in which they lived. As do all naval planners. In recognition of this unavoidable reality the Committee of Ways and Means, the *Junta de Ejecucion,* comprised a necessarily comprehensive mix of expertise – political leaders, civil servants, sailors, businessmen and technocrats and would, when necessary, consult outside experts and Flemish ex-pats as well.[26]

One much-discussed possibility was the extent to which the tension between the competing roles, missions and functions required of the Monarchy's fleet could be ameliorated not just by juggling the overall fleet mix of various types of ships, but also by the building of ships that were capable of more than one function. The chimera of the general-purpose warship that could do anything, anywhere was as alluring then as it is now. But of course,

> The all purpose ship is an impossibility. The various characteristics that the Spanish were seeking to combine in one and the same vessel – speed, capacity, manoeuvrability and stability – cannot be simultaneously optimized. All ship design is a matter of compromise .... Altering one dimension to maximise one desirable characteristic will be at the expense of another[27]

Juggling the dimensions of beam, length, depth of hold and weight was an exceptionally complex matter and its science was imperfectly understood, as to a certain extent it still is. However, the appearance of the new-fangled Flanders Frigate, the general trend to longer, less beamy ships with higher speed potential and the demonstrated value of ships like the Mediterranean galleass which was capable of being rowed and sailed while mounting more artillery, demonstrated real attempts, and some success, in exploring compromising possibilities.

Alongside this, the large, heavy galleon that sacrificed speed for stability and so was able to mount banks of guns, was increasingly, seen as the ultimate and indispensible arbiter of sea power, both in Spain and internationally. Big ships were essential, especially on the open ocean, for their fighting power, range, sea-keeping, endurance and the *reputacion* their possession conferred.[28]

Clear-cut decisions about such things were made more complex by the fact that theoreticians disagreed amongst themselves. The practical men of the shipyards often dismissed such theories in favour of experience and 'skill craft.' The notional dimensions of ships often meant rather different things from one shipyard to another. What other nations were doing, or at least were thought to be doing, had to be borne in mind as well.

Despite all these uncertainties, bravely specific estimates of what was required for the Monarchy's various fleets sometimes emerged. In 1631, for example, it was agreed that the Atlantic fleet required 12 new galleons one of 700 tons, another of 650, three galleons of 500 tons, three more of 400 tons, two of 350, one of 300 and one of 250 tons. Illustrating the basic point that 'function determines form' the lighter faster galleons would be good for pursuit, the medium ones for engagements and the heaviest for 'subduing the enemy and gaining victory.' Collectively such an armada would 'be suitable for all eventualities.'[29] Six years later, it was urged that some of the lighter ships could also be provided in the form of Frigates of Dunkirk construction, 'which are suitable for almost any emergency.'[30]

Sadly for the Spanish it all ended in decisive defeat at the hands of the Dutch at the Battle of the Downs in October 1639, but more because of the operational mistakes of Antonio de Oquendo, the Spanish Admiral commanding, than any fault in the composition of the fleet. And at least, despite this disaster, his fast frigates got vital supplies and reinforcements through to Spanish forces in the Low Countries.

12.2.3 France 1789–1794: An Exercise in Rapid Regeneration

Another example of the issues involved in a fleet design for recovery, but this time a much more rapid one, is provided by the French Navy of 1789–1794. This also underlines the important point that there is a lot more to a successful fleet than the number of its ships and guns.

The French Navy of 1789 had been the world's second most powerful fleet and had absorbed many of the improvements pioneered by the British, including the 'coppering' of hulls and to a limited extent the employment of 'carronades,' short-range man-killing cannon. Operating under a well organised Ministry of the Marine, the French had 64 ships-of-the-line in three categories based on the number of guns they carried, the 118s, 80s or 74s; their design was considered superior to that of their British adversaries – and the same went for their 64 frigates.

Money, manpower and maritime supplies were all problems, however – as were frictions between officers and administrators (the 'pen *v* the sword') and indeed amongst the officer corps between the high nobility and the rest.[31] They also lacked the level of operational control delivered by the British Admiralty.

The programme of gradual improvement of the late 1780s as the French Navy absorbed some of the lessons of the American war, came to a halt, and then went into brutal reverse, with the onset and immediate impact of the Revolution of 1789. Widespread political and social unrest had a devastating impact on the Navy and especially so in its major base-ports, Brest and Toulon. In both places there was descent into bitter factionalism, officers were purged or left voluntarily, ships mutinied, and the logistics infrastructure collapsed. The French Navy's low point was the wholesale surrender of the Mediterranean fleet in Toulon to the British in 1793.[32]

The turn-around from this desperate situation was master-minded by the Committee of Public Safety's naval expert Jeanbon Saint-Andre who was sent to Brest to ensure that the Atlantic Fleet did not disintegrate or even think about following the example of the Mediterranean Fleet. Saint-Andre did much to recover France's Atlantic fleet, in a tremendous eight-month burst of energy.

The first requirement was to see to the Fleet's ships-of-the-line and its supporting vessels. Aided by France's most talented and energetic naval architect, Jacques-Noel Sane, Saint-Andre ensured that existing ships in the dockyards were finished off, refitted, maintained and supplied, all in record time. A new construction programme was laid down. Anything that stood in the way of success in this great effort was removed. The supply chain for all naval materials and rations for the crews were improved; fraud and other long-standing dockyard customs were controlled.

The apparently unreliable and less competent officers were ruthlessly weeded out, 'Schools of seamanship' were set up in every ship to turn novices into sailors. Saint-Andre was able to make order out of incipient chaos by the threat, and sometimes implementation, of the 'Terror' unleashed by the Committee of Public Safety back in Paris. 'All movements [of the fleet],' he ordered in March 1794, 'must be uniform, simultaneously executed with as much precision as speed; and the divisions which in the navy of despotism dishonoured the French flag must be known no longer in the regenerated navy of the Republic.'[33] Earlier, Saint-Andre had driven the essential point home with a decree which made it clear that ship commanders who failed to execute a signalled order, pass them on or who surrendered their ships would be guillotined. This concentrated minds. Finally command of the rejuvenated Atlantic Fleet was given to the talented and professional Admiral Villaret-Joyeuse.

Shortly afterwards, Villaret-Joyeuse took his fleet to sea. The aim was to defend an all important grain fleet coming in from America that seemed essential for the survival of a Republic then reeling from widespread food shortages. Villaret-Joyeux managed to intercept, distract and engage the British Fleet under Admiral Howe in the battle, far from land, which the British called the 'Glorious First of June.' The Atlantic Fleet paid a heavy price losing 5000 sailors and 7 ships of the line but the critical grain convoy slipped past and arrived at Brest 12 days later. Subsequent analysis of the battle made it clear that there was more work to be done; French gunnery, and seamanship were clearly inferior when set against the standards of the Royal Navy. Moreover, despite the threat of the guillotine hanging over them, some ship-commanders had proved insufficiently resolute. Nonetheless, this strategic success for Saint-Andre was a tribute to a remarkable achievement in rejuvenating a fleet (in the widest sense of that word) in a very short period of time. Saint-Andre also worked his magic in Toulon helping turn France's decayed Mediterranean fleet into a worthy fighting force – although it was ultimately likewise overwhelmed by Nelson at Aboukir in 1799.[34]

While Henry V, the Count-Duke Olivares and Jeanbon Saint-Andre would obviously have had absolutely no conception of the intricacies of 21st Century naval planning, the procedures that they must have followed in their calculations about what needed to be done when, seem roughly to have conformed to them. The problems their modern successors now face often seem identical, but if anything, with added complications, and so worse. These added complications derive from the widening of the roles, missions and functions of the navies of the 21st Century and a pace of technological change that is much faster now than it was then.

12.2.4 The Search for Balance: Modern Approaches

The 'balanced fleet' even by the early 20th Century, had already absorbed a great variety of such special ships for distinctive functions, as a glance at Figure 12.1 reveals. This conception of part of the British fleet in cruising disposition in the early 1920s illustrates the Royal Navy's expectations of battle and the numerous functions that that would require. On the assumption that any prudent adversary would naturally be seeking to run away from the Royal Navy, the first requirement was to locate the victim. Hence the land- and carrier-based reconnaissance aircraft and the advanced light cruiser screen. Submarines, carrier strike aircraft and destroyers would slow down or 'fix' the located but fleeing enemy and disrupt him as he reluctantly sought to move into line of battle. The heavy mob in the shape first of battlecruisers and then the main battle force – its battleships – would then engage their opposite numbers, protected by fighters, and their gunnery aided by spotter aircraft. Submarines and destroyers would then finish off enemy survivors. Everything had its place in the scheme of things. The essential unit was the fleet as a whole and not its individual components.

But this, of course, was just a balanced *battlefleet*. On top of this, the navy as a whole would have a variety of tasks other than securing command of the sea. It would accordingly need ships and other platforms suited to the attack and defence of merchant shipping and sea lines of communication (SLOCSs) and a variety of specialised forces for the conduct of amphibious, riverine and coastal operations, fishery protection and so on.

Naval procurement planning then is about assembling a kaleidoscopic mixture of platforms able collectively to perform the roles, missions and functions that the nation and the strategic situation require of its fleet. The same principle also be applied to the 'Fleet Unit' Admiral Jacky Fisher's conception of how the Dominions could best contribute to the naval defence of the British empire. A 'Fleet Unit' would comprise '… a number of smaller cruisers and destroyers, operating around the citadel provided by a fast, heavily gunned armoured cruiser (later battle cruiser) of the *Indomitable* type.' This would be an effective deterrent, a commerce raiding force and the basis for later growth into a balanced navy.[35] The modern concept of a Task Force is a further development of this line of thinking. Provided that the fleet had the necessary range of options, a task force can be tailored to fit the particular contingency it was needed for.

Technological possibility and its cost have a major role in shaping the modern planners' search for operational balance in ship and fleet design. Often the real complexities and hazards only become specially apparent when the hull is 'fitted out' with weapons, sensors and systems which need to be integrated with one another for speedy intercommunication, resilience and to avoid mutual interference. The need to integrate the 'new' cyber and space domains of today's military operations adds to the difficulty.

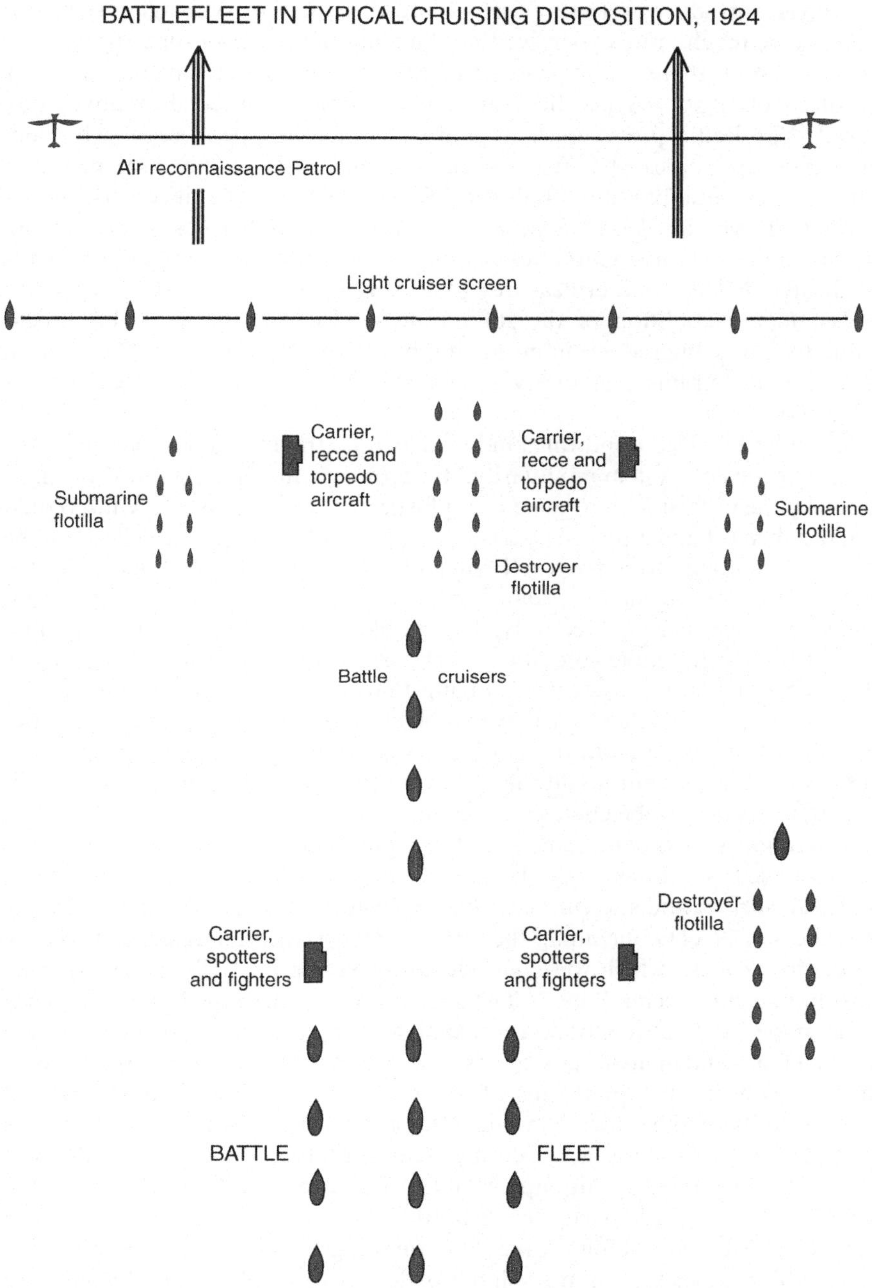

BATTLEFLEET IN TYPICAL CRUISING DISPOSITION, 1924

Air reconnaissance Patrol

Light cruiser screen

Carrier, recce and torpedo aircraft

Carrier, recce and torpedo aircraft

Submarine flotilla

Submarine flotilla

Destroyer flotilla

Battle   cruisers

Carrier, spotters and fighters

Carrier, spotters and fighters

Destroyer flotilla

BATTLE   FLEET

Figure 12.1 The Battlefleet 1924.

Source: Self-generated.

Maintaining interoperability with the other services and maritime agencies and allied and partner navies introduces yet more factors into the equation. Managing such systems will usually be much more expensive than building the hull and superstructure.

Budgets being finite, these issues produce painful dilemmas in balancing quality *v* quantity for fleets of all sizes. When the Danish Navy decided it needed to move away from its Cold War Baltic preoccupations and out onto the open ocean, while deploying high-end capabilities, it had to accept that the costs of the three new *Iver Huitfeldt* frigates, eventually with a Ballistic Missile Defence capability and longer-range missiles and two *Absalon* combat support ships/flexible frigates would require the de-commissioning of three Corvettes, 13 out of 14 fast attack craft, the replacement of dedicated Mine Countermeasures platforms by modular systems fitted to other vessels and the abolition of the submarine service. The price of this much-improved quality was a big reduction in the number of the Navy's ships.[36] A reduced number inevitably constrains availability, since a ship can only be in one place at one time, however good it is.

In their bid to find ways around this kind of dilemma, the Danes were amongst the first to explore the idea of 'system modularity.' Each of their major ships could be made more versatile by the provision of a range of sophisticated weapon systems which could be bolted on or taken off and replaced by something else and the ship 're-roled' when the need arose. The resultant *Flyvefisken* ('Flying Fish') programme introduced by the Danish Navy 1985–1995 seemed a promising way of increasing the flexibility of individual ships and/or fleets cost-effectively. The problem here is that the ship's permanent crew can't be re-roled quite so easily and at least some specialists will need to be attached to each modularised system; arranging that cost-effectively can be difficult since it is not obvious to imagine how they can be used in their 'down-time,' when not allotted to a ship. For that reason, the US Navy's Littoral Combat Ship' programme explored a somewhat less ambitious alternative in which the modules allotted to ships of this class are not expected to be changed as frequently, if at all.

The latest iteration of this continuing search for ship (and therefore fleet) versatility through technological solutions is the large scale deployment of a whole variety of unmanned aerial, surface and sub-surface vehicles on ships of every description. In late 2018, 13 members of NATO, including the United States signed an agreement to pool their resources in 'drones,' which were considered to be a 'potentially game-changing leap forward in maritime technology.'[37] The application of unmanned underwater vehicles to the mine-hunting function, for example, has become popular with the Americans, the Danes and many others, and is a harbinger for many other naval tasks.[38]

Investing in much cheaper platforms of moderate but still useful capability and providing more hulls in the water is another approach. The British T31 Frigate is thought to represent just such a 'general purpose/multi-mission frigate, ' although at 6000 tons it looks very much at the upper end of the 'cheap and cheerful' range of vessels – not least because it is partly based on the Danish *Iver Huitfeldt* class.[39] The US concept of 'distributed lethality' takes this thinking one step further by bolting higher-end capabilities (such as ship to ship missiles) onto auxiliaries or amphibious support vessels. This approach is echoed around the world by navies intent on increasing their overall versatility by the provision of more ambitious capabilities to their 'lesser vessels.' The new 27,000 ton HMNoS, *Maud* of the Norwegian navy exemplifies this way of pursuing versatility. In addition to its impressive basic capacity to replenish warships, it can operate every kind of helicopter in the NATO fleet, has extensive medical facilities, can act as a 'mother ship' for submarines, MCM vessels, engage in Humanitarian and Disaster Response (HADR) operations, and act as a command ship.[40]

Other navies seek to complement this approach by the unabashed pursuit of excellence, where a ship or submarine's particular capability is buttressed either by a deep specialisation and/or by its great size. The large ballistic missile firing nuclear propelled submarine (SSBN) is a good example of this first alternative but complementary approach. The high expense and opportunity cost (for the rest of the fleet) of the SSBN, which by some reports will account for 40% of the global submarine market by 2029 is thought by an evidently increasing number of navies to be justified by the strategic effect such submarines deliver.[41] At the other end of the scale of specialist vessels, Colombia's fleet of 50 LPR-40 'heavy fast patrol boats' are specifically designed and locally built for the riverine operations so important for the internal security of that country. The demanding conditions in which such vessels have to operate requires them to be specialist and their collective cost (together with all the other parts of what is in effect a 'balanced fleet for internal waters') necessarily comes at a cost for the more conventional parts of the Colombian navy. The same goes for the riverine elements of many other navies in South America,[42] and for that matter to smaller vessels specialising in amphibious operations, fishery protection, intelligence-collection and so on.

This emphasis on excellence in the particular conditions or in the functions they are specifically designed for, of course limits their utility for other roles. By extension, fleets that are specifically and solely designed for operations in their own geographical area may well encounter difficulties if any of their constituents are deployed for operations elsewhere where the conditions are different. When, as discussed in Chapter 6, Force Z, HM Ships *Prince of Wales* and *Repulse* were deployed to Singapore in 1941, the crew of *Repulse* suffered from the fact that their ship had not been 'tropicalised'. Today's Singapore navy accordingly has insisted that its Swedish built submarines are fitted with air conditioning, marine growth protection systems and corrosion-resistant piping.[43] The Russian-built Kilo submarines that are now such a feature of the Indo-Pacific region were originally designed for cold-water operations and are likely to require such adaptations. Navies that have to cater for a variety of such local conditions are at a disadvantage, compared to ones that do not; this is one of the issues that tends to narrow the difference between small navies and large ones since the latter usually have much bigger areas of responsibility and therefore a wider range of physical conditions to contend with.

The second alternative but complementary approach to the problem of maintaining fleet flexibility is to invest in (inevitably expensive) vessels of a size that allows for the widest range of offensive and defensive weapons, sensors and systems, while providing a greater degree of resilience in the case of damage. This kind of thinking is most obviously exemplified in the continuing aspiration around the world for large aircraft carriers. Defying the continuous criticism that carriers have always had, more and more navies are investing in them for the first time (China, South Korea), or in some cases (such as Japan, Australia, and the UK) re-investing in them after a pause.[44] Aircraft carriers come in all shapes and sizes, but one of their common characteristics is that they absorb a large part of a navy's procurement and operational budget. Their individual flexibility is thought to add a great deal to the mix of capabilities required of a balanced fleet and so justifies the effort.

12.3 Fleet Design: The Process

Naval professionals around the world are of course perfectly aware of the difficulties of procurement and mostly take its planning and conduct very seriously. They think that while by no means 'solving' all the problems, good planning helps mitigate them. Hence General Poirier recommended planning for procurement is taken as strategically as planning for operations. Accordingly, they follow procedures broadly comparable with those of the 'Estimate Process' in operational planning. In the US Navy these latter procedures are laid down as the Naval Planning Process (NPP);[45] although dealing with the conduct of operations, they nonetheless make perfect sense when applied to the procurement of ships, submarines, weapons and sensors.

This process goes through four phases that quite often adds up to 20 years, or more. The expected acquisition timeline of the 12 strong Australian/French *Attack* 'Shortfin Barracuda' diesel submarine that was intended to replace the *Collins* class in the 2030 s was to have been designed and built provides a good example. Rowan Moffitt identified four main phases in the process: two-to-four years to define the project, another seven-to-eight to design it, the same to build it and two years for operational testing and evaluation – up to 22 years in all.[46] As a very ambitious procurement project, the programme generated a huge amount of consultation, discussion, decision and industrial investment. Of course, the dividing lines between the phases can be decidedly fuzzy, and projects sometimes bounce backwards as well as forwards between them. Indeed in the Summer of 2021, the whole project was blown out of the water by the AUKUS announcement when the Australian government finally decided its submarines needed nuclear propulsion.[47] Nonetheless the principles that drove the Attack class submarine project remain valid.

Step one in the 'Define' phase is 'mission analysis,' which, in this procurement case, involves identifying the requirement that needs to be achieved as exactly as possible, in the light of inputs received from the various naval stakeholders, other government departments, all hopefully framed by a shared understanding of the country's strategic purposes. (This is where the Australian-French submarine replacement project reportedly went off the rails, by taking insufficient account of the need for the submarine's forward deployment). The resultant 'estimate of the situation' will usually lead to some provisional conclusions about the tasks that need to be performed (Commander's intent) against the current and future operational environment, ('Intelligence Preparation of the Operational Environment' (IPOE), derived in part from 'Staff Estimates' of the nature of current and future operations.[48] Critical capabilities, requirements and vulnerabilities need to be identified.

The next steps that take the project into the 'Design' phase are to identify possible 'courses of action' or in this case competing ways of performing those tasks, perhaps with different kinds and numbers of platforms or assets. These then need to be measured against the challenge, which may of course include comparisons with the future characteristics of the platforms etc they may be up against. ('Analyse relative combat power'). Budgetary limitations, other naval options, other service options, manufacturer's limitations and needs may well be part of this, and their views and interests seriously considered. Stakeholders will be briefed and consulted.

These alternative possibilities will need to be compared, and their relative advantages and disadvantages assessed. NPP has stern warnings that people should not 'admire the problem' continually polishing their conceptual models rather than getting on with things. Some have called this tendency 'paralysis through analysis.' They should be as objective as possible about this and avoid being swayed by any personal associations that these possibilities might have.[49] The feasibility, acceptability and suitability (or in this case cost-effectiveness) of each have to be realistically and continuously assessed.

Once the best option is decided, its development has to be meticulously planned, and key targets identified, action points synchronised and its risks identified, together with measures to mitigate them. This tends to involve what is sometimes called 'red teaming' – in other words deliberately trying to pick holes in the recommendation (and indeed in all the procurement procedures that have been followed to get to this stage) in order to uncover hidden weaknesses and deal with them. 'Regularly scheduled meetings to share information among participants are critical.'[50]

After maybe eight-to-ten years, if all has gone well so far, the project can transition into the 'Build' phase when those charged with executing the mission (manufacturers building the submarine) assume their responsibilities. This will usually begin with the preparation of a specification for the required characteristics of the ship in question before it is offered to the industry for expressions of interest and then invitations to tender. A preferred bidder may be identified and after further discussions to iron out the remaining differences between the customer's requirements and the manufacturer's offer, a contract is agreed and then signed. In fact it can make sense to bring the prospective builder in earlier than this, perhaps with a contract to assist in design, as was indeed done in Australia's Attack submarine project.[51]

Obviously the manufacture's actions need constantly to be monitored and assessed against the decisive points identified in the campaign to get the ship(s) actually built on time and within budget. Are the costs under control? Is the process on schedule? Often, as the project develops, the customer may seek to amend the specification and/or the manufacturer may discover unexpected snags. Adjusting the plan to accommodate either usually costs time and money because it involves going backwards in the process to some extent. Reports suggest there soon developed concerns in Australia about this. The project seemed to be running behind schedule and costs were rising. People began to worry about whether the submarines would arrive in time, and whether the Collins class could be run on long enough to accommodate the delay.

One this has been sorted out, the project goes into the final phase of Operational Testing and Evaluation (OT&E) as the unit (whether ship, submarine or weapon system) is delivered, inspected, accepted, subjected to trials at sea, certificated and then accepted into service. Here too snags that develop (and in complex platforms they nearly always will), will require going back into the development process to correct things. Whether the project concerns a submarine, a warship, a weapon or a sensor, the procurement process is long and complicated and a million things can go wrong, especially when the technology concerned is complex.

Finally, the procurement system itself needs to be assessed. The experience gained in this whole process needs to thought about, its 'measures of effectiveness' assessed, its revealed weaknesses identified, together with suggestions for their correction – for the next round and the next project in what is an endless cycle.

Stripped of its sometimes arcane language and mystifying acronyms, this application of NPP to the general problem of force design and procurement would be recognisable to navies past and present when reflecting on their experience in the development, recovery or maintenance of both individual platforms and the mix of their fleets as a whole. At most, the process is intended to reduce some of the obvious risks.

By no means do these broad principles guarantee success in a task that remains hard because of the unavoidable challenges noted earlier. The problems addressed by Henry Maydman back in the late 17th Century, the collapse of Canada's 'wish fleet' proposals in the 1960s, and 2020 suggestions of reductions in China's plans for a six carrier fleet together with countless other examples, suggest that all navies have had, do and will have to, address these issues and problems, whatever their period, size and aspirations; because of that they all need to resort to procedures of this kind, knowingly or not.[52] They apply not just to the fleet and its components but to its infrastructure as well.

The through-life costs of a ship are likely to be much greater than those of initial acquisition. Accordingly experienced naval professionals tend to be at the heart of the design process, as they are the most likely to be familiar with operational realities – and their costs. That same naval experience suggests that particularly big projects within the fleet design process (whether in terms of the number or platforms or its complexity) probably need to be developed by a special organisation set up for the purpose, like the KSS-III Program Group of the South Korean Defence Acquisition Programme Administration. An earlier example of this was the Royal Navy's 'Polaris Executive' established to develop Britain's first nuclear submarine programme, mentioned earlier. Famously, when its first leader Rear Admiral Sir Hugh McKenzie arrived on Day One, it was to a small office empty of all but a desk, a chair and an unconnected telephone, with no staff and no paperwork. Its success was arguably due to its operation outside the normal administrative system. He was the recognised champion of the project, with access to anyone he needed and the capacity to fight and win his own financial battles.[53] To some extent this principle has been followed in subsequent programmes to renew or replace the Polaris system, such as the Trident Group of 1980 and the current Director General Nuclear organisation tasked to manage the UK's 'Successor' programme. As almost certainly the biggest and most technologically complex developmental programme in Europe, Successor, like its predecessors, is subject to intense political interest (both for and against) and the shifting economic vagaries of the time. Keeping the programme running against these varying pressures from above has been and will be the biggest challenge facing those responsible for delivering the product.[54]

12.4 Battle Force 2045: Applying Theory to Practice

All these issues featured in the US naval force structure discussions that took place occurred between 2016 and 2020, culminating in the final months of the Trump administration, with a plan called *Battle Force 2045*. The process began when the Navy, anxious to break away from the tyranny of the immediate commitment, sought to engage in some long-range thinking about the fleet that it needed. This was inspired first by a realisation that the Navy was facing new levels of high-level war-fighting challenge in the Chinese and Russian fleets, a number of novel naval approaches by 'rogue states' like Iran and North Korea while all the time having to maintain demanding levels of presence apparently everywhere. Secondly, It had already proved impossible to maintain late Cold War levels of capability, not least in the numbers of operational carriers and there were a host of new technological challenges to be considered as well.

In close collaboration with the US Marine Corps and with the aid of outside civilian analysts it eventually put forward a proposal labelled the *Integrated Naval Force Structure Assessment* (INFSA) which aimed at delivering a 355 strong fleet by 2035, with an option for more later. It was rejected evidently as too traditional by the then Secretary of Defense, Mark Esper, whose Office led a replacement study with the aid of the Cost Assessment and Evaluation Office (CAPE) and the civilian Hudson Institute think tank. *Battle Force 2045* was the result. Needless to say, this plan was, in its turn subjected to a great deal of analysis and public comment.[55]

The aim was to produce 'a comprehensive, cost-constrained and threat informed assessment of the fleet that the US needed, aligned with the U.S. *National Defense Strategy* of 2018. 'Survivability in a high-intensity' conflict' was essential, along with 'adaptability for a complex world' and a capacity for 'precision at very long ranges.' Hopefully the resultant fleet would be more agile, less predictable while able to operate on the 'forward edge of America's interests,' and '…retain our decisive overmatch for decades to come.' The end product was a 500 ship fleet design that was to comprise, 8–11 fleet carriers, up to 6 light carriers of various sorts, 70–80 submarines, 50–60 amphibious ships, 60–70 smaller surface ships 79–90 combat logistics ships and 140–240 unmanned or lean manned units. This 'once-in-a generation change in fleet architecture'[56] was the biggest proposed increase in fleet size for 30 years.

This is not the place to go into the complex detail of either the manner by which *Battle Force 2045* evolved, or of the competing proposals that emerged in the process. Instead, a brief review of the issues discussed reveals remarkable similarities with the same processes conducted by the French and Spanish several centuries before, despite the very different circumstances the American planners were facing. The world's other navies have encountered, and continue to encounter, these issues as well. Perhaps eight leading issues emerge.

12.4.1 Agreeing the Fleet's Missions and Tasks

First they had to agree on the fleet's tasks through a process of mission analysis. Broadly the debate here focussed on the balance to be struck between deterrence and high-intensity war fighting, secondly much lower intensity operations intended to monitor and protect the worldwide trading system and thirdly stabilisation operations somewhere between the two. These might require operations on the high seas, the intermediate zone and coastal waters. All three missions required agreement on the capabilities necessary for narrower operational and tactical tasks such as anti-submarine warfare or logistical support. Each mission and each task should have the capabilities it needed.

Because it was important that such plans could be seen as supporting national policy objectives and the strategy for achieving them, the planners took the objectives of the *National Defense Strategy* as a guide. This still left open the question of the balance to be struck between those objectives. More fundamentally, there remained the unavoidable unpredictability of the future and uncertainties about whether planning should be based on notional situations or (semi)-identified adversaries, on expectations of long or short conflicts, and so forth. This underlined the risks of being too prescriptive and the need to build in flexibility.[57]

12.4.2 Identifying and Prioritising Task Requirements

Since the three missions (high-intensity war-fighting, medium intensity stabilisation and low-intensity protection operations) and the areas in which they were most likely to be exercised could well require different sorts of ships and capabilities, balances between them were required. The need to think of all three missions in terms of a sequence of chronological stages complicated this process. The tactical and operational requirements of each mission might well vary over time depending on the sequential stage of each operation. Planners had therefore to think in terms of a matrix of choice with the two axes, intensity and time (Figure 12.2). What kind of operation were you thinking about, and at what phase?

Taking carrier operations as an example, operating a fleet super-carrier forwards in the Western Pacific, might be thought appropriate for general deterrence, but too vulnerable for the initial stage of a serious conflict, the battle for access, because of the power of a possible adversary's sea denial capabilities (submarines, 'carrier-killing missiles' etc) but well-suited to the subsequent campaign to exploit access gained by other means. At the same time, a forward carrier presence could be thought 'overkill,' for humanitarian operations and other forms of low-level stabilisation, even if highly effective. There again carriers could be necessary and decisive for more demanding versions of these tasks. Opinions on all this were shown to differ and materially affected the balance recommended between large surface combatants on the one hand and smaller, cheaper lean- or un-manned vessels and submarines on the other.

However, some analysts worried that thinking about the kind of fleet that was needed rested in part on three concepts of operation which were immature. One of them, *Distributed Maritime Operations*, advocated the defensive physical and temporal diffusion of concentrated maritime power to complicate, divide and confuse the enemy's attack, while maintaining offensive capability; the second *Expeditionary Advanced Base*

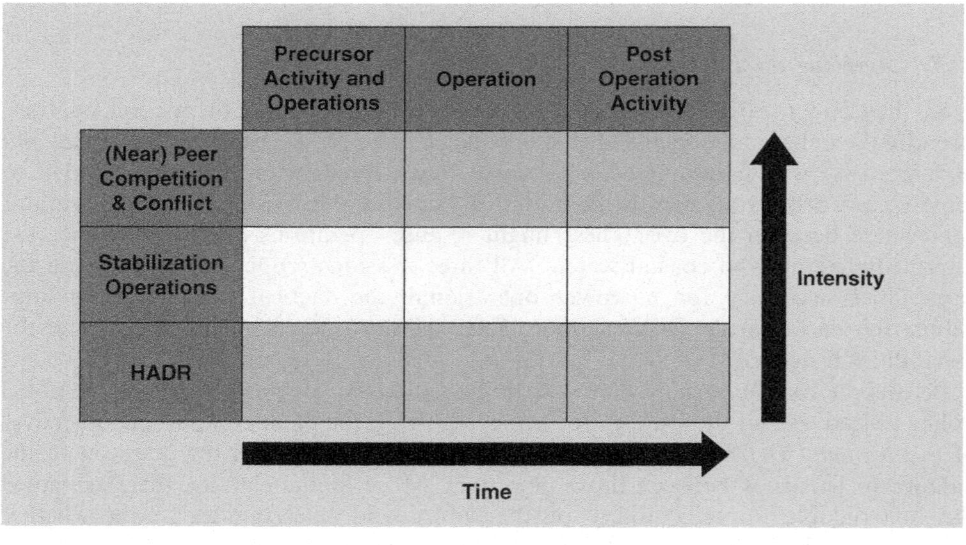

Figure 12.2 A Matrix of Time and Mission.

Source: Self-generated.

Operations envisaged the use of mobile forward island positions against the enemy's fleet. The third concept, *Electronic Maneuver Warfare* was designed to conceal your intentions and movements while exposing the adversary's. However potentially interesting they might seem, all were broad brush ideas that left to one side detailed consideration of such requirements as command and control, logistic support and so forth.[58] However, they all provided a doctrinal foundation for the subsequent decisions.

12.4.3 Exploring Technological Possibilities

There was a lot of debate about the extent to which technology could come to the rescue in narrowing the yawning gap between the resource-constrained numbers of units available and the capabilities that America's likely commitments would require. One approach was to recommend that particular platforms or weapon systems be designed for multipurpose use. Another angle was the push to diffuse firepower, or 'distribute lethality' by putting missiles on smaller combatants or support vessels as the Russians had convincingly shown during the Syrian civil war when firing Kalibr missiles from *Steregushchiy* corvettes. Generally, there was much interest in apparently novel ship types such as light carriers and smaller amphibious ships, rather than the 'established shipbuilding program of record.' Particular attention was devoted to the vexed issue of the extent to which small, cheap unmanned systems could reliably perform a whole variety of tactical tasks that would otherwise use up the resources of larger, fewer because more expensive, platforms. To what extent could you 'trust the algorithms' in the performance of really crucial tasks?

If naval power was to be diffused in this way, all the units would need to be networked to provide the necessary concentration of force in defensive or offensive 'distributed maritime operations.' Some analysts argued that the network was so important that it had become the 21st Century's version of the 'capital ship.' Given its technical complexity and the likelihood of hostile attack, how safe would that crucial connectivity be? Many concluded that the importance of such technological possibilities made fixations on the number of platforms in this or that desirable fleet seem pretty pointless. The focus should be on systems and capabilities not the number of platforms. Others accepted this but had the nagging suspicion that there might still be some connection between the two. Fortune seemed to favour the side with the big battalions. Didn't numbers have a quality all of their own?

Concerns were also expressed that the fleet structure plans relied too much on unproven technology; instead, some advocated a more cautious policy of investing incrementally in experimental 'technology demonstrators' before committing to major programmes. Instead of backing risky projects such as the troubled Littoral Combat Ship or the ultra-expensive *Zumwalt* destroyer, the Navy should follow the philosophy of the father' of the Aegis programme RAdm Wayne E. Meyer: 'Build a little, test a little, learn a lot.'[59] At some stage, though, you had to go firm, lest you got to war with an uncoordinated 'fleet of experiments' like the unfortunate Admiral Rozhestvensky on his way to perdition at the hands of the Japanese in 1905.

12.4.4 Resourcing the Programme

Throughout history, planners have had to be disciplined by resource constraints, whether these were money, people or industrial capacity. These also had a crucial temporal dimension. What would be reliably available when? One of the major differences between INFSA and *Battle Force 2045* was that the latter pushed the completion date back ten years to 2045. Its critics thought this cloud-cuckoo land where anything might happen, rendering detailed planning nugatory. The further forwards it went, the less and less credible the planners' assumptions. For example, how could they possibly predict such basic things as the rate of inflation, so far ahead? Nor was the Navy's recent record encouraging. Apparently, the growth of cost over the initial estimate for the lead ship ranged from 155% for one version of the Littoral Combat Ship, 84% on the San Antonio-class amphibious warfare vessel, 44% for the DDG-1000 Zumwalt destroyer and 25% on the Gerald R. Ford aircraft carrier, the costliest warship ever.[60]

Vice Adm. William Merz Deputy Chief Of Naval Operations For Warfare Systems showed that the Navy was all too aware that such problems posed the daunting task of taking the feet from under 300 to at least 355 ships. 'We're also coming to realize what that is going to cost, and how you're going to sustain today's fleet while continuing to grow,' he was quoted as saying in 2019. The planning process was 'much more challenging than anyone realized, but we're much smarter about our business' than just a few years ago. ... We don't have the complex modeling to even understand what all of these costs are going to materialize to over the next 20 years,' but the Navy was '... working hard to converge on a model' to sustain the programme.[61] Other navies, especially perhaps those with less experience, are likely to encounter the same problems.

Sceptics also worried that the lack of detail both in the prospective mix of capabilities and in the technical design of many of the units involved, added to the problem of assessing risk and cost-effectively. Moreover, since initial construction typically accounts for only about a third of the through-life cost of an individual platform – the rest being operations and maintenance- there were bound to be huge uncertainties here too. The large slice of the future acquisition budget already taken up by agreed programmes like the expensive *Columbia* SSBN project, further aggravated the problem.

Nor was it just a question of meeting the 'through life cost' of the platforms, sensors, weapons and systems. The tail needed to be funded as well as the teeth. Resourcing the programme also meant having and costing the industrial requirements to build the fleet in the first place and the personnel and equipment needed to operate and maintain it at sea and ashore. Reversing the decline in industrial capacity and its supply base that followed the end of the Cold War would take some 'reconfiguring,' but was essential if this expanded fleet was ever to be constructed.

Lest naval planners get too depressed by all this, they could perhaps remember that their difficulties may be at least partially offset by identifying ways in which the other military services, together with allies and partners could reasonably pitch in and help. *Air-Sea Battle* was just one example of this.

Even so, the general consensus was that it would be necessary to 'impose cost discipline up front' and the greatest criticism of *Battle Force 2045* was that it hadn't done this. The danger was not merely that its recommendations would be ignored, but that the failure to realise such a public declaration of the country's needs would damage morale at home and encourage that of possible adversaries abroad. Accordingly it was essential that participants in the design process avoid engaging in the conspiracies of optimism that made all of this more likely. The budgeteers of CAPE, in other words, for all their unpopularity, had a crucial role to play.

12.4.5 Ensuring Readiness – But When?

Fifthly, over much of the debate loomed the fact that both the immediate and the long-term future were inevitably unpredictable to a degree and that the fleet had to be flexible and ready for both. But how should the necessary adaptability be built into the process? There were two angles to this, the first concerned practical ship design and building issues. The very long lead times needed to design and deliver complex platforms, weapons and sensors make future-proofing an especially difficult aspiration for today's fleet planners. In contrast, their predecessors in the days of oar and sail could create or reconstitute a fleet much faster, as the Ottomans showed when recovering from the disaster of the Battle of Lepanto or Napoleon after Trafalgar. This is more difficult now. Possible expedients included filling gaps in the programme by extending the life of existing platforms or weapons (usually an expensive option) or by the constructive use of rapid turn-over, cheaper short-life substitutes, or, again sticking with the bigger hulls that experience showed were easier to convert to cope with the unexpected.

The second angle, the temporal element, was trickier. How should today's readiness be balanced against tomorrow's? One school argued for taking the risks now in order to secure the future. At one stage, the Secretary of Defence, Mark Esper, made the apparently counter-intuitive point that. 'You can spend too much money and be too ready,' he said, ' particularly if you know the trade-off for that one extra dollar may be modernization, which we call future readiness, and that's one of the things that I'm constantly balancing and juggling, is today's readiness versus future readiness.'[62]

This was the kind of thinking that led the British to take the risk in 2010 of a deliberate 'capability holiday' in order to finance their carrier programme. Inevitably this meant the Royal Navy would be less ready than desirable in the short term. This was shown in the Libyan operation of 2011 when it was reduced to operating army helicopters off HMS *Ocean*, the lightest of light carriers. But the risk paid off and HMS *Queen Elizabeth* commissioned ten years later.

The US Navy though had already had another complication to deal with in that the two futures (the immediate and the long-term) might demand different sorts of fleets). Such was the focus on the 'war on terror,' in the high operational tempo of the decade after 9/11, that the Navy made little effort to re-tool for operations against a first-class adversary later. Even if they had tried harder, success would probably not have attended their efforts, politically. Hence their current problem.

A second school of thought though made a different but equally sensible-sounding point. It was important not to take too much risk with the demands of the present and the immediate future. 'Present preparedness must not be sacrificed to an illusory future readiness' said the Navy's General Board in January 1933.'national emergencies cannot be foreseen and must be met by existing forces.'[63] A few years later as was shown in Chapter 8, Admiral Doenitz thought the same, feeling he had to stick with his current type VII U-boats for the current Atlantic campaign at the expense of higher investment on the next generation Type XXIs. Planning had to ensure that the fleet would therefore need to be sufficiently ready, responsive and fit-for-purpose in every year of its interim development. Readiness, in short needed to be sustained.

All navies face these problems and in the management of risk in maintaining readiness, there are no easy solutions.

12.4.6 Agreeing the Mix

These sometimes conflicting possibilities had to be resolved, choices made and a balanced fleet produced. The general consensus seemed to be that a modest shift in relative balance from high-performance units like fleet super-carriers and large amphibious vessels to smaller combatants and unmanned systems would make sense. Pretty much everyone engaged in the process of designing a new transformative fleet for the US Navy agreed on this principle, despite differences in detail. Most of the world's other navies appear to have come to much the same conclusions about their need to deliver a mix of high, medium and low intensity units, although their definitions of what these units are and the form they take varied according to their circumstances.

12.4.7 Planning Delivery

The country's capacity to build and deliver what, and when it was required, also generated much discussion. This took planners into the uncomfortable territory of having to deduce the future performance of the US economy and the likelihood of successor administrations being content to support the details as well as the overall cost of the recapitalisation project over time. Produced when the Covid pandemic was turning all such assumptions upside-down, this seemed especially challenging.

A lot of emphasis was placed on the advantages of 'demand predictability' over time for ship-builders in public and private yards and for their suppliers, discussed in Chapter 8. 'Our shipbuilding industrial base and supporting vendor base,' said the Senate Armed Service Committee, 'constitute a national security imperative that is unique and that must be properly managed and protected.'[64]

Maintaining the reliable predictability thought to be so important for this was likely to be very difficult. The Japanese submarine programme, which for years operated on the principle of building and replacing one submarine a year in its 16 strong fleet, showed it could be done however. Expanding that fleet though has much complicated the model.

12.4.8 Allocating Responsibilities

In a break with tradition, INFSA was rejected by the then Secretary of Defense Mark Esper who replaced it with one of his initiation. Both designs were produced in consultation with industry, a wide range of think tanks and external sources of expertise. In addition, Congress constantly reviewed all these proposals and, often apparently unimpressed, made its own detailed points, and required further analysis.[65] The Navy, Defense Department and Congress, themselves webs of smaller interests, were all major stakeholders in the fleet design process. They shared in the articulation of policy; they also expected to be able to monitor and strategically influence the way in which the resultant policy objectives were delivered. Around them hovered clouds of analysts, retired officers and contractors, frequently solicited for their advice.

This and the continuous nature of the process was likely to make a direction from above a real challenge. One CIMSEC participant in the debate, Captain Jeff Kline justly concluded that '...great changes in fleet capabilities are normally associated with a strong visionary and leader who had the longevity to realize the introduction.' He went on to recommend that 'A flag officer should be appointed with the authority and tenure in office to transform the fleet ...'[66] The problem is that key decision-makers rarely have the kind of length of tenure enjoyed by Admirals 'Jacky' Fisher (1886–1910) and Sergei Gorshkov (1956–1985) in supervising the mix of the whole British and Soviet fleets respectively or by America's Admiral Rickover in his personal crusade for a nuclear navy for the United States (1949–1982).

The application of continuous pressure over a long period, for example, helped Rickover achieve his objectives. Asked once how he solved problems and got things done, he replied: " You just outlive them." The designation SSN is a nice case in point. Initially the US Navy wanted it to be SS(N). Rickover thought this could be seen as implying that nuclear propulsion was just an add-on rather than the determining characteristic of nuclear submarine design, but he did not waste his energy in a fight. He simply told his people to drop the parentheses, or brackets, in all their reports. 'The other people rotate, we endure,' he said. 'Before long, the parentheses will be gone.' And, of course, he was right.[67]

The rapid turnover of senior staff and constant institutional turbulence also militates against sustained thinking. Admiral Richardson established the 'Office of Future Strategy' to start the ball rolling in force design in 2016, but it was disbanded shortly after its report was delivered and all its key figures departed.[68] Instead the re-establishment of some sort of the 'Future Plans Division' comprising 'dangerous' people specially trained to think strategically about fleet structures and oversee their delivery would seem sensible. The advantages of continuity can be demonstrated by the success of shorter-term 'champions' appointed for just parts of the overall enterprise, such as Admiral Wayne Meyer's ownership of the campaign to deliver the *Aegis* destroyer. Generally, though, fleet design is more of a collective effort over time and perhaps suffers for it., Moreover, in this case, the fleet design project's manifest uncertainties reinforced Congress's determination to have its say in the matter alongside the Navy and the Defense Department. The longer the process continued the more cooks seem likely to appear in the kitchen. Paradoxically, hardly had *Battleforce 2045* appeared at the end of 2019, than a new Administration took over the White House. Instead of being 'a plan,' it therefore merely set the agenda for continuing discussion. Even so for all those deeply involved in its preparation, there was the consolation that their efforts are un-likely to have been wasted, as the process rolls on.

12.5 The Smaller Navies Angle

Looking at major projects like this may inadvertently give the impression that these considerations only apply to the world's grander navies with large numbers of so-phisticated platforms, weapons and sensors to worry about. Such an impression would be untrue. Leaving aside the vexed issue of what a smaller navy is,[69] they are likely to entertain a narrower range of operational aspirations, and so fewer complexities of choice. On the other hand, they have fewer people to handle the problem. In many cases, limited and uncertain budgets often compel the opportunistic acquisition of vessels from a range of different providers that bring with them significant problems of integration. Malaysia's 15-to-5 project, which involves a cost-effective reduction in platform types while maintaining and even extending the Royal Malaysian Navy's capabilities is an important but demanding exercise which in its way is just as de-manding as the larger projects of larger navies.

Malaysia has a more local but still very varied set of missions that range from the defence of its territory from external threats (most recently demonstrated by the invasion of Sabah by insurgents in 2013), to the defence of its interests in the South China Sea and of its shipping interests off Somalia and elsewhere. Its requirement to match commitments and resources within finite budgets is the same as that of any of the larger navies, and its solutions may well be too. Its imaginative use of a converted merchant ship the *Bunga Mas Lima* with modularised weapons and special forces to protect Malaysian shipping off Somalia was a good example of the US Navy's concept of 'distributed lethality,' for example. One other thing that smaller and greater navies have in common, of course, is that they all think they need to be bigger.

Smaller navies (and especially those set on substantial growth) are likely to have a limited maritime defence industrial base. This raises the issue of the extent to which they should invest and build their own (accepting the likely extra delays and costs) or buy off the shelf from foreign suppliers. The usual compromise is to pursue both options simultaneously in the hope that the offsets and technological transfer associated with the second will nourish the growth of the first. The resultant complexities can, however, lead to delays, confusion and bitter argument, as it certainly did in China in the 1970s.[70] These final prospective 'building issues' will often circle back and help shape (even dominate) a navy's starting assumptions in the fleet design process.

Nonetheless, the success of the American super-frigates in the war of 1812 shows that small navies can build first class ships when sufficiently motivated and perhaps endure fewer inhibitions as far as innovation is concerned as well. 'The rapidity with which the Americans build and fit out their Ships,' warned Admiral Warren in 1813, 'is scarcely credible, and I am very apprehensive of the mischief their Cruizers will do to our Trade.'[71] Today's activities of the Iranian Revolutionary Guard Navy suggest, as then, that there is little room for complacency in the fleet design processes of the bigger fry when responding to those of the smaller ones.

12.6 Summarising Fleet Design, Acquisition and Development

> Strategy should govern the types of ships to be designed. Ship design, as dictated by strategy, should govern tactics. Tactics should govern principles of armament.
> —Admiral Sir John Fisher[72]

Just as earlier Spanish and French experiences had shown, the American example confirmed many of the basic issues in the process of fleet design, not least that it's a never-ending process, a race without a finishing tape. Policy objectives have to be established and what is required to meet them. What technological, constructional and financial support is required? While the future fleet evolves, the current one has to be sufficiently ready all the time. Adaptability has specifically to be built into the process. Responsibilities for delivery have to be allocated and continuously monitored. Identifying these issues is not the hard part. They have been known for ages. The hard part is living up to them.

To help, Frank Hoffman has provided an interesting set of five principles for fleet planners/designers to bear in mind. Although he is plainly talking about much more than just fleet design he addresses most of the salient issues:[73]

- Force design and posture must embrace uncertainty – we have to plan in the expectation of surprise.

- Force design must be strategically driven – we need to define priorities for the long term.
- Force design must be risk-informed – we need to insure against unknown but intelligent adversaries.
- Force design must emphasize versatility over adaptability – our fleet needs to be able to do everything all the time, not simply shift from one task to another.
- Force design must ensure a degree of balance as a hedge against uncertainty – we need a fleet without major capability gaps, including in research, PME and training.

Of course, these are observations more about general principles than specific recommendations.

Hoffman's use of the word 'force' not 'fleet' is a timely if fortuitous reminder that the platform centric approach which tends to be the default setting for fleet design discussions (and so is the focus here too), is only part of the story. It does, though reflect Admiral Jacky Fisher's down-to-earth observation that appears at the start of this section. During the course of the discussion over *Battleforce 2045,* some wondered whether this strategy-led top-down approach was not too simple. Perhaps the transformational potential of things like Artificial Intelligence was such that there needed to be more bottom-up circularity in force design. In response, this sparked concern about the dangers of technological determinism and the prospect of military technical-tactics driving strategy. These are big and complex issues, beyond the scope of this chapter, but force designers clearly need to be aware of them.

Regardless, the same design and acquisition process approach can be applied not just to platforms but to weapons and sensors too. Moreover, the inter-relationship between platforms and weapons underlines the point that the overall force design has to incorporate capability-based planning as well. The consequences of the possible widespread introduction of the rail gun illustrate the point nicely.

Its advocates argued that since the magazines of ships so equipped need only store 'warheads' (not missiles) they could carry with them and deliver roughly three times the offensive punch. The project was cancelled in 2021, but since its inception in 2005, it had accordingly affected deliberations about how many ships would be required. The replacement of the 40 year old Harpoon anti-ship missile project with the hugely more effective Long Range Anti Ship Missile (LRASM) could have the same implications.[74] In short, these examples show that although platforms, weapons and sensors ships are developed in parallel, coherent fleet design demands that everything has to be to be put together at some stage. The question is, when?

Today's fleet design issues are evidently as complicated as they are important. This should not, however, obscure the fact that in their travails to make sense of it all today's fleet designers are grappling with broadly the same issues as their predecessors in the days of galley, galleons and dreadnoughts. Moreover, the same goes for the closely connected problems of fleet maintenance that is the subject of the next chapter.

Notes

1 Interview, *Jane's Defence Weekly,* 13 October 2021.
2 Ken Hambleton, Ian Holder and David Kirkpatrick, 'Ten chronic challenges in UK Defence acquisition,' *Defence Studies,* 2013 Vol. 13, No. 3, 361–71.

3 Churchill, W.S., *The World Crisis Vol III 1916–1918* (London: Thornton Butterworth, 1927), 258. My thanks to Dr. Richard Longworth for tracking this quotation down.
4 Childs, Nick, *The Age of Invincible* (Barnsley: Pen and Sword, 2009).
5 David Kirkpatrick, 'Rising Costs, Falling Budgets and their implications for Defence Policy,' *Economic Affairs,* Vol. 17, No. 4 (1997), 11.
6 Hitherto, 10% of the sales of copper by the state-owned mining company Codelco was devoted to military procurement. 'Jane's Defence Report 2019,' *Jane's Defence Weekly,* 11 December 2018, 44.
7 Usman Ansari, 'UK SSN Programme Slows to a Crawl' and 'Enduring Worth of Sub Force Explained,' *Warships IFR,* December 2019, 35, 39.
8 'Milestone Moment as UK Strike Carrier Number Two makes Debut,' *Warships IFR,* November 2019.
9 'Annual Defence Report 2019', *Jane's Defence Weekly,* 11 December 2019, 10.
10 Sanders, Speller & Mulqueen (2014), op cit.
11 Maydman, *Naval Speculations,* 289, 294–6. For a modern example see White, Hugh, *How to Defend Australia* (Melbourne: La Trobe University Press, 2019) and Davies, Andrew, *Defence 'Balance' is Lazy Thinking,* Australian Strategic Policy Institute, July 2019.
12 Friel, *Henry V's Navy,* 45.
13 Ibid, 102.
14 Ibid, 164–87.
15 Rodger, Nicholas, 'The Development of Broadside Gunnery 1450–1650,' *Mariner's Mirror,* Vol. 83, No. 2 (August 1996). Ship designers came up with a series of responses mixing the qualities of galley and sailing ship, emphasising bow and stern-chasers, before eventually settling on the broadside solution.
16 The alternative land-route, the 'Spanish Road,' was slower, more expensive, potentially dangerous and meant that the *tercios* were tired when they finally arrived.
17 Quoted in Goodman, *Spanish Naval Power,* 43.
18 Stradling, R.A., *The Armada of Flanders: Spanish Maritime Policy and European War 1568–1668* (Cambridge: Cambridge University Press, 2003), 52.
19 Goodman, *Spanish Naval Power,* 9–11.
20 Stradling, *The Armada of Flanders,* 32–3.
21 Goodman, Spanish Naval Power, 6–7.
22 Stradling, *The Armada of Flanders,* 53.
23 Goodman, *Spanish Naval Power,* 40–60.
24 Ibid, 181–220.
25 Stradling, *The Armada of Flanders,* 115–16.
26 Stradling, *The Armada of Flanders,* 96–7.
27 Goodman, *Spanish Naval Power,* 115–16.
28 Goodman, *Spanish naval power,* 123.
29 Ibid, 124.
30 Stradling, *The Armada of Flanders,* 171.
31 Cormack, *Revolution and the French Navy,* 22–5.
32 Crook, Malcolm, *Toulon in War and Revolution*(Manchester: Manchester University Press, 1991), 138–48.
33 Decree of 21 March 1794, quoted in Cormack, *Revolution…in the French Navy,* 213.
34 Crook, *Toulon in War and Revolution,* op cit, 158–70.
35 Stevens, David, 'HMAS Australia: A Ship for a Nation,' in Stevens, David and Reeve, John (Eds), *The Navy and the Nation: The Influence of the Navy on Modern Australia* (Crows Nest, NSW: Allen & Unwin, 2005), 169.
36 Guy Toremans, 'Danes devise a fleet to meet the challenges of a 'diverse, complex and unpredictable' world' – interview with Navy Chief Rear Adm Torben Mikkelsen, *Warships IFR,* December 2020, 26–9.
37 'Pushing the Envelope of Naval Drone Ops,' *Warship IFR,* December 2019, 33.
38 David Axe, 'The US Navy has a plan to beat mines: Make Every ship a mine-hunter,' *Warship IFR,* February 2020, 28; Guy Toremans, 'Royal Danish navy sets New Course in Conducting Mine Warfare Operations,' *Warships IFR,* January 2020, 36–7.

39 Usman Ansari, 'After a Home Win How Will the T31 Frigate Fare in the Away Match?,' *Warship IFR,* January 2020, 30–1.

40 Guy Toremans, 'Norwegian Navy's 'One-Stop Support Ship,' *Warship IFR,* November 2019, 28–31.

41 'Nuclear Arms Race Under the Sea Heats Up,' *Warship IFR,* November 2019, 8, quoting a Global Data report; Usman Ansari, 'North Korean SLBM Test Demonstrates Deterrent Resolve,' *Warship IFR,* December 2019, 18–19.

42 Santiago Rivas, 'Brown water War in Colombia,' *Warship IFR,* Nov 2019, 21–3.

43 Andy Wong Ming Jun, 'Lions Beneath the Waves,' *Warship IFR,* February 2020, 31.

44 'Milestone Moment as UK Strike Carrier Number Two Makes Debut,' *Warship IFR,* 10–15.

45 This unclassified document is available in its 2013 guise as Naval Warfare Publication, NWP 5-01.

46 Moffitt, Rowan, 'Australia's Future Submarine,' in Forbes, Andrew (Ed), *The Naval Contribution to National Security and Prosperity* (Canberra: The Seapower Centre, 2012).

47 Kerr, Julian, 'Australian sub decision driven by technology, Chinese assertiveness,' *Jane's Defence Weekly,* 22 September 2021.

48 NWP 5-01, K-1–2.

49 NWP 5-01, D-11.

50 NWP 5-01, 6–9.

51 'Annual Defence Report 2019,' *Jane's Defence Weekly,* 11 December 2019, 37.

52 Hennessey, *Fleet Replacement,* 150–1; David Axe, 'China's Carrier Ambition Cools,' *Warship IFR,* February 2020, 9.

53 Hennessey, Peter and Jinks, James, *The Silent Deep: The Royal Navy Submarine Service Since 1945* (London: Penguin, 2015), 217–27.

54 Ibid, 510, 660, 683–4.

55 This section draws on the following sources: Congressional Research Service, Navy Force Structure and Shipbuilding Plans: Background and Issues for Congress, 1 October, 2020. https://fas.org/sgp/crs/weapons/RL32665.pdf; Bryan Clark, Peter Haynes, Bryan McGrath, et al., *Restoring American Seapower,* Center for Strategic and Budgetary Assessments, 9 February 2017; In Dmitry Filipoff, CIMSEC **Force Structure Perspectives Series,** 2020, the views of a number of luminaries were sought, including retired Captains Robert C. Rubel, Jeff Cline, Sam Tangredi, Trip Barber, Cdr Phillip Pournelle, Col T.X. Hammes, Dr John T. Kuehn and Congresswoman Elaine Luria; Transcript of Secretary Esper's talk on 'Readiness and Modernisation' at the Heritage Foundation, 15 October 2020; Bryan Clark, Timothy A. Walton and Seth Cropsey, *American Sea Power at a Crossroads: A Plan to Restore the US Navy's Maritime Advantage,* Hudson Institute, September 2020.

56 CRO, *Navy Force Structure and Shipbuilding Plans* 2.

57 Hoffman, Frank, 'Designing Tomorrow's Marine Corps,' *Proceedings* of USNI, November 2020; Pournelle, Phillip, 'A Fleet to Do What?,' *War on the Rocks,* 14 September 2017.

58 Capt Sam J, Tangredi, CIMSEC Force Structure Perspectives Series, op cit.

59 Ibid. Tangredi, CIMSEC.

60 Anthony Capaccio, 'Navy's Frigate Seen Busting Goal By 40% At $1.2 Billion Each,' *Bloomberg News,* 13 October 2020.

61 Quoted, CRO, *Navy Force Structure,* 47.

62 Esper, Transcript of Speech to Heritage Foundation, 15 October 2020.

63 Cited in Kuehn, John T., *Agents of Innovation; the General Board and the Design of the Fleet that Defeated the Japanese Navy* (Annapolis: US Naval Institute, 2008), 58.

64 Senate Armed Services Committee Report 116–236, 24 June 2020. Quoted in CRO RL 32665, 60.

65 These are usefully summarised in CRO RL 32665.

66 Kline, 'On Bringing the Fleet into the Robotics Age,' CIMSEC, 4.

67 Theodore Rockwell, *The Rickover Effect: How One Man Made a Difference* (Annapolis, MD: Naval Institute Press, 1992) (AuthorsGuild backinprint.com edition), 320.

68 Frank T. Goertner, 'The Navy Should stop talking about the Future and start building it,' *Proceedings* of the USNI, 2 November 2020.

69 An issue taken up in McCabe, Sanders and Speller, *Europe, Small Navies and Maritime Security,* op cit.

70 Muller, *China as a Maritime Power,* 200–5.
71 Toll, *Six Frigates,* 431.
72 Fisher to the Committee of Seven 7 May 1940. P. Kemp (Ed), *The Papers of Sir John Fisher* (London; NRS, 1960), 40.
73 Frank Hoffman, 'Black Swans and Pink Flamingoes: Five Principles for Force Design,' *War on the Rocks,* 19 August 2015.
74 Hanley, Capt John, 'An Alternative History for US Navy Force Structure Development,' *CIMSEC,* 14 July 2021.

13 Nothing Is for Ever: Maintaining the Fleet

England must resolve to be at the constant charge of keeping a great Fleet in continual action, if ever the Nation hopes to have and Peace or Tranquillity.

—Henry Maydman[1]

The only sure way to deploy a first class navy in wartime is to maintain a first class navy in peacetime.

—Geoffrey Parker[2]

13.1 Maintenance: Its Nature and Scale

Maintaining maritime power is difficult and demanding because it has a natural tendency to decay. Mahan generally took a more sanguine view. He envisaged the virtuous circle referred to in Chapter 1 in which the conduct of trade provided the resources and the incentives to develop naval power, while naval power created the conditions for yet more advantageous trade. Assuming they attended properly to their own needs, maritime powers should therefore sail into an ever more beneficent future. In fact, though, history suggests a maritime horizon more dominated by a setting than a rising sun.

There are many reasons for this. At the tactical level, the wear and tear of naval operations degrades ships, weapons and sensors and tires out its people. Consequently the fleet needs constant replenishment, but this costs time and money. The 'maritimeness' of a country can, and often does, wear out too, for the reasons partly introduced in Chapter 1. A recent article on the fisherfolk of the Canary islands reminds us of one of them. 'The tasks of fisherman were also very hazardous,' it says. ' [...T]hey often suffered poverty and ... many were delighted to leave their work at sea for other employments stemming from the growth of the industrial sector throughout Europe in the 19th Century.'[3] The same goes for much of the European merchant shipping industry. People preferred more comfortable, home-based and often better-paid lives in the commercial sector ashore which, paradoxically, the maritime enterprise had done so much to make possible in the first place. Countries became somewhat less maritime as a consequence.

Another perhaps less common explanation is the slow atrophy of the maritime outlook that seems to afflict countries that have in the course of their business unavoidably acquired colonies and bases from which to carry out and then defend their maritime trade. With this comes a creeping and often reluctant acceptance of the need to assume their territorial not just their naval defence. The British Empire is a classic example of this. With the acquisition of more and more real estate overseas, came

DOI: 10.4324/9781003100553-13

expenditure on land forces, on administration, on all sorts government responsibility for their new subjects (if sometimes only to stop them from questioning their changed status) and on an endless and often self-defeating search for other people to pay for it. One of the reasons why Sir Julian Corbett put pen to paper just before the First World War was that he could see the way things were going, not least in the diminution of the maritime component of the country's strategic thinking, and wanted to do what he could to correct it. But even he had only limited success in turning back the tide.

More narrowly, technology poses fleets with a continuing challenge. Surveillance and sea-denial systems often seem cheaper than their sea control equivalents. Over 170 large-size unmanned underwater vehicles, for example, could be acquired for the cost of a modern Arleigh Burke-class destroyer.[4] Across the board, traditional forms of naval power are getting more costly. With the appearance of coastguard vessels like Canada's 6600-ton helicopter *Harry de Wolff* Arctic Offshore Patrol Vessel and the monster vessels of the China Coast Guard, it seems to be an iron law of maritime development that, left unchecked, ships get bigger, certainly more capable, but less affordable and fewer in number. As the annual surveys of the world's Chief of Navies conducted by the US Naval Institute seems regularly to demonstrate, most navies, grappling with budgetary constraint are having to do more and more with less and less.[5]

For many, the task is to fend off maritime decline, or at least to manage it as gracefully as possible until changes in the international or domestic context allow much-needed exercises in recapitalisation. This cyclical tendency, in which it is not so much a question of developing maritime power in the first place, as recovering it from a period of decline, is commonplace. At the end of the first quarter of the 21st Century both patterns are evident. China is rapidly developing first class naval capabilities for the first time for a long time; the United States, Russia, most European countries, Australia and Canada are amongst those in recovery mode. Others are somewhere between the two. But this should not obscure the fact that decline can prove terminal, or virtually so. Henry Maydman was most bothered by a fear that it might be getting too late to 'restore lost capability' (in Admiral Barrett's words). '[I]t is high time,' Maydman said, 'to awake out of this lethargy, to recover our Dominion, Honour and Prowess, before it is past recovery.' In this he spoke for countless other naval enthusiasts through time.[6]

Even in recovery mode navies have to make the most of what they've got in terms of both fleet assets and people. 'We all use the phrase 'Economy of Force,' has admitted Admiral Radakin, then First Sea Lord of the Royal Navy,

> that wonderful military euphemism for not quite having the laydown that an Operational Commander would prefer to have – but economy of force operations abound across the world ... The Royal Navy is operationally very busy and in demand. We are being invested in but we have to do more to reflect the changing strategic context.[7]

Ideally the strategic context and the operational requirements it produces should drive a navy's programme, rather than its maintenance schedules or people pressures but things are rarely that simple. There are two theoretical answers to the universal naval dilemma of matching resources to commitments over time, and because the problem is far from new, always has been. The first is to generate and maintain fleet readiness. The second is to make the most cost-effective use of the assets available. In both cases, success and cost-effectiveness are measured by being able to do what is needed with the least expenditure of readiness. Both answers are inter-twined and complement each other. Both cost serious money. It is no use building a first class fleet which cannot be sustained because of inadequate investment in its maintenance and sustainable use. 'We must build sustainment,' says Admiral Barret, ' into both the design and operation of our fleet.'[8]

13.2 Generating Readiness over Time

Maintaining a fleet over time has usually proved more expensive and more of an effort than building it in the first place. It requires the same kind of effort in planning, heavy financial investment, industrial power and personnel training discussed earlier but spread over a longer and often indefinite period. There are extra requirements as well. The consequences of operational wear and tear and possibly even battle damage have to be made good. Personnel have to be rotated to keep them fresh. Each unit in the fleet has to be kept as near up to the challenge of constantly evolving technological developments as the budget and the available scientific and industrial capacity available will allow. Design and deployment plans have to be adapted to suit changing circumstances.

Above all, perhaps, it requires the ability to respond to the temporal dimension of military policy through the maintenance of 'readiness.' 'Readiness' means assured availability for effective use in possible immediate- and longer-term future commitments. It applies to ships, systems, the fleet, to a navy's people and to its infrastructure ashore. It is best understood as a finite consumable, something that evaporates over time as the navy goes about its business, and performs its tasks. Simultaneously a navy has to generate and maintain readiness for tomorrow's tasks. Every operation tires people and wears out platforms, weapons and systems. Every aspect of a fleet's activity has accordingly to be constantly replenished. Ensuring that there is enough readiness when required is the chief objective of a navy's maintenance effort and first proof of its success or failure.

This means being clear (and realistic!) about readiness to do what, when and with what. As far as the 'what' is concerned it is, in part, a matter of deciding on the degree to which particular tasks need to be performed. In an age of increased great power competition, there appears to a general ratcheting up to higher 'war-fighting' standards, as the strategic context worsens.[9] As to 'when,' the trick is striking the right balance between today's readiness and tomorrow's and indeed preparedness for the day after that as well. The focus on responding to the tyranny of the immediate commitment can be at the expense of being able to do so with future ones; being 'too ready' today may indeed mean being unready tomorrow as was shown in the last chapter. Nonetheless, there may well be a general tendency to over-focus on short-term readiness. Finally there is the issue of whether the readiness of some parts of the fleet is more worthy of investment than others.

Measuring 'readiness' can be tricky too. Because 'performance' is so much more difficult to quantify, there is a natural tendency to assess this by what you put into readiness rather than on what you get out of it – to focus on inputs rather than outputs. Concentrating on the hours devoted to the acquisition of skills rather than the quality of the skills produced can be, to say the least, misleading.

How successfully one country's navy grapples with such difficult issues and manages to sustain the fleet and maintain readiness over a period of time is often considered to be an important indicator of the extent to which it is more or less maritime than another. Typically the less maritime find this more difficult as the necessary resources are sucked away by other competing preoccupations. Equally typically, the more maritime countries tend more easily to find the resources over time to refresh the characteristics that allow them to enjoy the benefits and opportunities that maritime power provides.

There are generally considered to be two major areas of naval business where readiness has to be maintained. The first is material readiness, ensuring that the fleet's platforms, sensors, weapons and systems are technically capable of enabling it to perform its operational tasks effectively at all times. The second closely related area is the quality of its people and the extent to which they can get the best out of the *materiel* available. Shore-side infrastructure support is necessary for both of these areas. Taken together, all three are the foundation for readiness and operational performance over time.

13.3 Programmatics: The Art of Making the Best Use of What's Available

On paper, one obvious way of improving the ratio between the demands of the operational task and the number and quality of the assets available is to get other people and their navies to do things for you, or, more ambitiously, with you. Both devices involve programming other people's assets into the tasks that confront you. Both reduce your operational wear-and-tear and so make it easier to maintain overall readiness. Of course such cooperation comes at a cost, particularly if the second of these options is selected. There has to be sufficient agreement with allies and partners as to what the operational task is and how it should be performed. Close cooperation with other navies demands high levels of tactical and technical inter-operability and achieving this also takes sufficient investment in time and effort. It requires the devotion of substantial sea-time to rehearse and exercise interoperability at sea. In making sure that the whole is at least a sum of its parts, nothing comes for free.

The difficulties are such that many a combined force commander, wistfully thinking of the comparative simplicities of national command, will have perhaps reluctantly concluded that the only thing worse than having to rely on allies and partners is not being able to. This really explains the quite extraordinary extent of multinational naval cooperation in today's world. This phenomenon is now almost taken for granted but in historical terms is unprecedented, certainly in times of peace. Sometimes, and especially in NATO, this can reach a peak of operational seamlessness where the particular nationality of the cooperating ship often does not seem to matter very much. Since this is the whole aim of the organisation, it is hardly surprising after 70 years that there is a multiplicity of such linkages amongst NATO navies.

Greater pressure on budgets has accelerated the drive in this direction. In 2008, for example, the defence ministers of nine European countries signed a declaration of intent to set up the European Carrier Group Interoperability Initiative with the instantly forgettable acronym of ECGII. The aim is to establish a multinational Carrier Strike Group complete with escorts and logistical support capable of deploying in support of NATO or European Union operations.[10] Similar, if less deep and far-reaching, arrangements are made in other parts of the world as well.

From this point of view, navies that can operate effectively with a shoal of reliable allies and partners have a tremendous operational advantage over those that cannot.

Because of what is widely considered to be their often loutish foreign policy behaviour, China and Russia are seriously disadvantaged in this regard. Apart from each other, they only have clients, not allies.

The same philosophy of aiming at synergy through operational burden-sharing is applied at the national level too. This is often done by grouping platforms together in bespoke task forces of mutually supporting ships, submarines and aircraft (and these days all the other components of multi-domain operations as well – land, cyber and space). This is never easy.

In the days of sail the performance of individual ships depended on their condition and age. Freshly careened and recently coppered 18th Century ships-of-the-line sailed much better and faster so were difficult to operate to their true potential in the company of their less fortunate brethren. It was difficult to operate a battlefleet comprising ships of different sailing qualities as a cohesive unit. Integrating HMS *Prince,* which was unkindly described as having the sailing qualities of 'floating haystack,' into the line was just one of Nelson and Collingwood's preoccupations before the battle of Trafalgar. Almost exactly a century later, for that same reason, Captain Wladimir Semenoff of the Imperial Russian Navy called the Baltic Fleet on its way to perdition at the hands of the Japanese in 1905, not a fleet but just a 'chance concourse of vessels' of different types, hastily assembled.[11] Improving the capacity of groups of ships to work together effectively helps make the most of available resources.

The requirement to cope with operational wear-and-tear can also be managed and kept to a minimum by cost-effective deployments – or what the Americans sometimes call 'programmatics.' This means the adoption of patterns of use which serve strategic purposes but at the least cost in fleet readiness. It requires an effective balance between commitments, resources and time.

The introduction during the early stages of the Cold War of the US Planning, Programming, Budgeting, and Execution process was intended as a through-life way of managing such problems. It has been constantly refined ever since, with some success, but faces constant challenges. The US Chief of Naval Operations in 2014 released some interesting figures showing that the US Navy of the time had 104 ships operational, out of a fleet total of 285. This is about the same number of ships actively deployed as it used to maintain 20 years before when the US Navy comprised around 400 ships.[12] Through its 'Optimised Fleet Response Plan,' (OFRP) of 2014, the US Navy, still anxious about the gap between resources and commitments, sought to refine the balance between deployment and maintenance cycles to ensure as much sustainable time-at-sea from each platform as possible.[13] Since then, US Fleet Commanders have pushed for the OFRP philosophy to be applied to their fleets as a whole rather than just to individual ships or groups of ships. In their own ways and with varying degrees of success, other navies have been trying their own such experiments.

Getting the most out of what already exists also involves properly exploiting the balance between forces designed to deal with high- and low-end threats which the fleet designers have hopefully already provided. The Danes provide a good example. 'We are pushed to our limits,' reported its naval chief Rear Admiral Torben Mikkelsen in 2019. 'Although we are still capable of performing all the tasks set by the Danish government, hard choices and focussed prioritisation have become the order of the day. I have to be selective in drawing up the ships' programmes.'[14] Accordingly the Danish Navy's new higher-end frigates are deployed in support of its more ambitious missions for NATO and in the wider world, while the older patrol frigates are more often assigned to the constabulary tasks around Greenland and the North Atlantic, for which they were designed.

Effective use may also mean making the right decisions about which forces should be maintained forwards and which kept back in home waters or reserve. Resource constraints will encourage the search to improve the current 2/3:1 ratio between support and forward forces to make the most cost-effective use of existing platforms. One way of doing this is to save on the sea days 'wasted' in transitions out to and back from a ship's operating area by basing it forwards and flying out relief crews as needed. This can apply as well to naval auxiliaries like the Norwegian Navy's new HNoMS *Maud*.[15]

Good programming not only reduces wear-and-tear but also adds operational effectiveness. The analogy of making the best use of carrier aircraft illustrates the point. Generating the most sorties requires flight controllers to launch their aircraft as fast as possible in order to avoid the first aircraft up using too much fuel before the last joins them. Landing them, one by one, has to be equally fast and efficient, making due allowance for maintenance, re-arming and refuelling. Landing and launching aircraft at the same time adds still further complexities. For the Japanese fleet at Midway, failures in this area were disastrous. An extreme example this may be, but an equivalent programming logic applies to the routine operation of fleets, as well.

Fleet operations are supposed to be able to influence their context. This aspiration should shape deployment patterns. They should not be so rigid as to allow an adversary to predict what's coming, when. 'That's a great way to run a shipping line,' General Mattis told the US House Armed Services Committee. 'It's no way to run a Navy.'[16] But sometimes it is. President Roosevelt's dispatch of the Great White Fleet in 1907–1909 or the much trailed global trip of the *Queen Elizabeth* Carrier Strike Group in 2021 were effective as demonstrations of intent. Moreover, predictable scheduling makes the maintenance of *materiel* and of people much easier. Allies and partners need to know your plans as well. A carrier battle group can't normally just turn up at some port and expect an impromptu welcome.

Nonetheless, flexibility also needs to be built into the process. All too often, as the US Navy's Chief of Naval Operations, Admiral Gilday pointed out in 2020, 'the real world gets a vote, right?'[17] Careful planning is easily disrupted by unforeseen events and related demands, to which navies have to react. The Royal Navy's fast and effective response to the totally unexpected Falklands crisis of 1982 was one excellent example of improvisation and adaption. Less dramatic perhaps was the US Navy's success in responding to the Covid-19 crisis of 2020 when individual ships had to be taken temporarily out of service and ships on station could not access facilities ashore. Planned operating schedules had to be adapted, and deployments stretched from seven months to nine. Crews had to work even harder than usual.

In 2020–2021 all these considerations led the US Navy to explore the concept of 'Dynamic Force Employment' – as a way of balancing predictability and flexibility without consuming too much readiness. But success depends on a navy's 'can-do attitude' (which isn't always either felt or justified) and on the fact that sufficient readiness has been generated and sustained in the first place.

13.4 Maintaining and Sustaining a Navy's *Materiel*

Maintaining the fleet's platforms, weapons, sensors and systems is a question first of making good the consequences of operational wear-and-tear and secondly keeping its

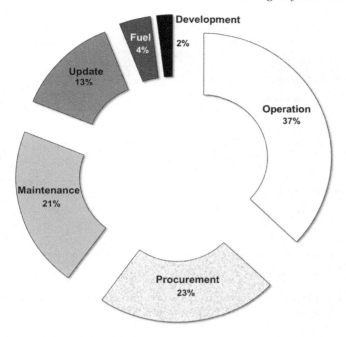

Figure 13.1 Naval Cost Distribution.

Source: Kirchberger, Sarah, *Assessing China's Naval Power: Technological Innovation, Economic Constraints and Strategic Implications* (Heidelberg: Springer, 2015).

overall standards permanently up to the level that the changing military-technical context requires. The fleet has to be able to move with the times.

13.4.1 Restoring and Maintaining Existing Capability

At the most basic level, all the components of the fleet have to be regularly serviced to compensate for operational wear and tear and to make them as good as new. The costs of this can very often equal and even exceed the costs of acquiring a ship in the first place, although they can usually be spread over a much longer period and so make less of a hole in the naval budget in any given year. (See Figure 13.1)

Broadly, the older the ship the higher the cost of maintaining it, relative to its overall 'through-life cost.'

Responses to this can reflect some very basic ways of thinking about the ship. The most important is really to differentiate between the acceptance of the initial acquisition costs and its almost always higher through-life costs if the ship is to be considered as a long-term fleet asset. The possibly very long operational life of a successful warship underlines the benefit of a 'cradle to grave' approach that runs from inception to ultimate de-commissioning. (See Figure 13.2.) Even so, there remains the chance of another quiet 'conspiracy of optimism' about the scale of tomorrow's maintenance costs rather than today's and how they are to be met.

In balancing these costs a further issue arises. Should the ship be regarded as a throw/give-away or, on the other hand, something worth further investment? Two

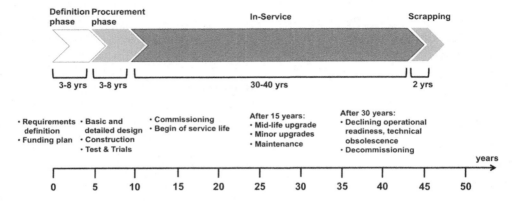

Figure 13.2 The Naval Life Cycle.

Source: Kirchberger, Sarah, *Assessing China's Naval Power: Technological Innovation, Economic Constraints and Strategic Implications* (Heidelberg: Springer, 2015).

different maintenance philosophies can be picked out. Count-Duke Olivares and his colleagues in the Spanish Navy of the early 17th Century concluded from the very high cost of 'careening' a ship that it made more sense for warships to be worked to death and when they reached the end of their inevitably shortened useful operational life, replaced by new build. For many years, the Japanese Maritime Self Defence followed the same line of thinking by limiting the life of their submarines and automatically replacing them at the 16 year point.

This had the advantage of providing the submarine builder with a steady and predictable programme; it would also help them to introduce modifications in a planned way. Although the Japanese did not do this for constitutional reasons, a navy following this line could further represent itself as 'one careful owner' and sell on a used submarine or warship to another navy. The savings though will be modest because the agreed price will usually reflect the buyer's acceptance of high maintenance/ adaptation costs.

In his break-neck campaign to recover the French navy in the early 1790s, Jeanbon Saint-Andre tried a variant of this approach – a form of cannibalisation. He had the upper decks hacked off ships-of-the-line in a poor state which couldn't be maintained cost-effectively in the desperate conditions of his times. Instead he had them turned into useful frigates. This exercise in naval recycling was in effect a halfway house between thinking of the ship as either disposable or worth substantial further investment. A common and less dramatic version of this approach is to keep on older ships but relegate them to less demanding duties.

The more conventional alternative in fleet maintenance is to try to make the unit as good as new and accept the high investment costs that this is likely to require. Ideally, this would be based on an honest original assessment of what the real through-life cost of a warship is likely to be, and for such servicing costs to have been taken into account from the start. While it is true that most of a platform's eventual maintenance costs are in effect set in its very early stages of platform design, through-life planning is not easy because it is hard to anticipate what technological modifications the ship will need through its career; given the major perturbations in the market that are almost certain to be encountered, and so estimating the economic costs of those modifications is difficult too.

It's a moot point which of these two approaches to maintenance is more risky. For this reason, navies tend to preserve their options and engage in a fluid mix of the two, building more platforms and/or effectively extending the lives of existing ones. The Danish fleet delivery programme already referred to is a good example of this. Alongside the recent acquisition of the *Iver Huitfeldt* and *Absalon* classes of high-end frigates, the older *Rasmussen* and *Thetis* classes of patrol frigates have been refitted and upgraded, the latter's giving it another 10–15 years of useful life until eventually to be replaced by new build from the late 2020s.[18]

Clearly and as was discussed in Chapter 9, effective fleet maintenance requires access to the necessary dockyard facilities, foreign or domestic. To ensure this support, the dockyards and their people and the naval acquisition systems and the defence industries with which they work have to be sustained over time as well as the fleet's *materiel* and people.

Maydman was clear about this. He lamented the way the dockyards sometimes neglected unfavoured ships, especially those built by someone else, leaving them '… rotting and decaying shamefully for want of careful preventions.'[19] He noted the cost-effectiveness of refitting ships and keeping them up to standard rather than building new ones. Indeed, the invaluable role of routine dockyard ship maintenance is often under-appreciated when compared to the more glamorous business of building and launching new ships. In the First World War, for example, Devonport dockyard alone refitted or repaired 25 dreadnoughts, super-dreadnoughts and battlecruisers, and 50 cruisers, many of them more than once. This programme dwarfed the new build programme in warships of this type.[20] Apart from battle and other related damage, the biggest single problem they had to deal with was the 'condenseritis' that resulted from much high speed steaming. Clearly the efficiency of dockyards in ship refits and of naval defence industries in servicing weapons, sensors and systems is a critical element in fleet maintenance; accordingly, their readiness matters too.

Maintaining capability is essentially an anticipatory process about what will need to be done and when. It is no use waiting for systems to break down or wear out before seeking their replacement – or, as is sadly often done, disguising this reality by unrealistically and belatedly extending a ship's operational life until its replacement arrives. All too often this simply results in greatly reduced capability and higher cost than hoped for.

Accepting and planning for the necessity and the costs of maintenance is easier if they can be anticipated. One interesting recent avenue for this is the notion of diagnostic or 'adaptive' maintenance which is designed to exploit the capacity of Artificial Intelligence to identify the components, and possibly procedures of use, which cause operational wear-and-tear, and to cope more exactly with its consequences. These days this kind of diagnosis can be done by the ship or even remotely from ashore; both approaches help the dockyard prepare for the refit before the ship arrives and so expedites the process.[21] At least in theory.

By contrast, historically, circumstances would often require the ship to maintain itself, especially when operating a long way from home. Provided that the ship was capable of carrying the necessary stores, its crew was expected to do a great deal to mitigate the consequences of operational wear-and-tear themselves. Ships these days still have to be able to do this to some extent. Indeed during the Covid crisis, when access to dockyards was more restricted, 'mid deployment voyage repairs' at sea became more common. The advent of 3D printing may also help with lower level maintenance tasks.

In a similar vein, access to nearby shore-side facilities when the ship is operating on some distant station reduces the need to return home, and the time-on-task that the voyage home can waste. Lower level maintenance can be conducted in commercially available 'places' but more advanced servicing and, crucially, re-weaponing will usually demand access to a proper naval base. The continued importance for many navies of forward operations on a global scale explain the residual enthusiasm for such places and bases in the Indian Ocean as Diego Garcia, Singapore, Bahrain, Djibouti and Duqm (Oman), for example.

The political complications this shore-side reliance may entail, however, can lead to alternative options of investing in the kind of 'sea-basing' that accompanying support ships can supply. This was first developed in a major way by the US Navy in the Pacific War (1941–1945) and copied to the extent their resources allowed by other navies since. The more a navy wishes to maintain a forward presence a long way from home, the more essential this kind of at-sea support actually is, but the more demanding it is too. It requires the supply fleet to transition from being essentially a civilian-manned 'freighting service' delivering needed goods to places and bases; instead it becomes an active part of the fleet, providing constant operational support. The 1982 British Falklands Task Force, operating in the ferocious waters of the South Atlantic and under the constant threat of attack depended absolutely on such support. Towards the end of the campaign, after weeks of danger and arduous effort, Admiral Woodward gloomily wrote in diary, 'We are now on the cliff edge of our capability, with only three ships lacking a major OPDEF (Operational Defect) ... Frankly if the Args could only breathe on us, we'd fall over.' Fortunately for the British the Argentine Navy and Air Force were in an even worse state, but the comment underlines the importance of afloat support and the dangers of neglecting it.[22]

13.4.2 *Moving with the Times and Enhancing Capability*

Very often during the ship refit process, the opportunity is taken to replace components with new ones likely to increase the platform's capability, not just restore it to what it was, when new and better. This more ambitious kind of maintenance is aimed at keeping the fleet up with evolving technological possibility and making sure that due advantage is taken of potential military-technical advances. Hopefully this will improve the ship's capacity to respond effectively to the operational challenges it will face.

Being able to do this will depend in large measure on a navy's capacity to innovate in technological research and development, or benefit from someone else's efforts, and in its capacity to implement the result effectively. This applies as much to the maintenance of *materiel* readiness as it does to its initial development. This has always been a critical element in the operational success of navies, and an obvious and easily identifiable explanation for their failure. For both reasons the topic of how navies should innovate technologically has been a topic of enormous interest to historians and all too often the subject of much criticism about the alleged innate 'conservatism' of naval leadership.[23]

The result of such academic industry is a vast quarry of processed experience which in theory should help today's technological innovators avoid the apparent mistakes of the past, provided they have the opportunity, time and energy to explore it. As a rule, they don't, relying instead on the output of historical research institutes inside and outside the service, on bespoke research reports on identified topics of interest and on the individual enthusiasms of the historically minded both within and outside their ranks.

Seeking the guidance of the past in maintaining the capacity to innovate fleet *materiel* is, however, fraught with difficulty, not least because historians themselves usually disagree about the causes of success and failure in particular instances. Also many of them do not think their advice should be proffered in the first place. Even so, most would agree with Sir Julian Corbett that investigation of the past does at least generate the questions that ought to be asked, if not the answers that should be followed. Moreover, previous experience suggests some of the general approaches (rather than specific recommendations) to the problem of technological innovation that seems to help.

Having attentive decision-makers who are well aware of what that experience is (and that will include the experience of others too) is therefore a good starting point. Keeping a close and informed eye on current and possible future technological development and on the places and people producing it is a good idea too. Many navies set up research institutes to do the watching for them and are receptive to their conclusions. Bearing in mind, though, how many radical ideas turn out to be not so radical after all, a degree of caution before heavily investing in brilliant but as yet unproven technological projects seems wise. From this perspective, it often seems better to be a 'fast follower and quick exploiter' rather than a technological revolutionary.

When developing naval aviation and nuclear propulsion respectively the US Navy's Admirals William J Moffett and Hyman D. Rickover on the other hand demonstrated the advantages of long-term and single-minded top-down leadership. Both of them also showed how important it was to adapt institutions and procedures so they could make the most of tomorrow's technology, while properly exploiting today's. Readiness also requires recognising when things are going wrong and a new approach is needed. The example often used is the failure of the torpedoes of US submarines in 1941 due to faulty depth settings and exploders; institutional reluctance to respond effectively to technical reality resulted in two years of wasted operational effort.[24]

Since new technology usually arrives in a process of incremental and evolutionary slither rather than in one of the dramatic jumps which transform everything overnight, maintaining readiness is more often largely a matter of building adaptability into standard operating procedures than it is of conducting root and branch institutional change. All the same, actually implementing technical innovation in order to enhance fleet capacity over time, rather than just piously acknowledging the possibilities, will usually demand significant institutional flexibility.

One such example might well be the current interest in the idea of disaggregating the overall tonnage and firepower of the fleet amongst a larger number of smaller craft in what is currently known as 'Distributed Maritime Operations.' A key part of this is the narrower notion of 'Distributed Lethality' by which firepower (usually in the form of missiles and sensors) is spread around the fleet much more widely than before, perhaps onto less conventional parts of the battleforce such as amphibious vessels and even support ships. This is certainly quite a significant shift in assumption about what 'concentrated force' can mean. Once it was taken as relating to a navy's biggest and most important combatants, its capital ships, whether they be battleships or carriers;

now technology offers an alternative vision of the battle force. It is weapon and sensor-centric rather than platform centric. Distributing your force over a larger number of smaller units may well provide alternative more resilient deployment options, especially in situations of hazard.

This might be uncomfortable for some to accept because superficially at any rate it seems such a change, but it might also be an avenue towards a more sustainable future. This is because budgetary pressure has increased interest in 'organisational arrangements that maximise decision efficiency, weapons effectiveness and the attainment of the strategic goal.'[25] Recently such arrangements have focussed on the effects needed rather than on the various platforms delivering it. 'This approach' says Australia's Admiral Barrett,' maximises the commonalities that derive from integrated systems, and facilitates the flexibility and agility that are key to contemporary and prospective seapower.'

Another such possibility, also increasingly discussed is the potential of unmanned systems, the extensive use of which would represent even more of a departure from conventional ideas about what 'the fleet' may come to mean. Still more radical is the evolving concept of the 'battle system' where conventional combatants in the shape of surface ships and submarines figure less dominantly than they did, their functions being complemented, or even taken over, by cyber, space-based systems and unmanned vehicles, the sustained readiness of which also has to be a key element in the mix. (See Figure 13.3 A Battle System.) Implementing any of these visions of the naval

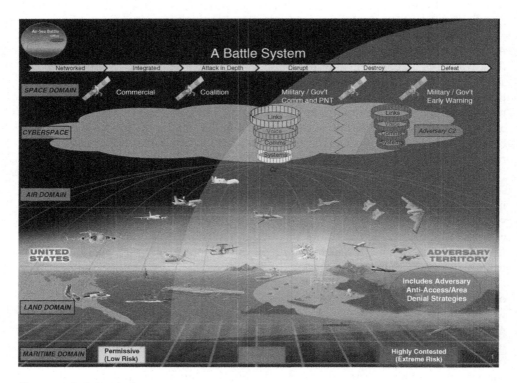

Figure 13.3 A Battle System.

Source: US Dept of Defense.

future will clearly require significant adjustments to habits of thought and the conduct of business. All of this of course cycles back into the preoccupations of fleet designers discussed in Chapter 12 and in part depends on the success of their mission.

13.5 Maintaining and Sustaining a Navy's People

As was shown in Chapter 11, senior sailors tend to say that their navy's most important resource is its people, and it follows that they have to be maintained and sustained over time just as much as the equipment which they operate. Mainly, this requires attending to the same recruitment, retention and training issues as were discussed earlier, but over a longer time frame. Maydman identified the two key elements in maintaining a constant and reliable work-force, namely getting them in the first place, and then treating them fairly so they stayed for as long as needed. Hence his recommendations for a seminary for seamen and measures of recruitment other than 'pressing' reluctant recruits. Hence his concern for good treatment of sailors on board and of the sick and wounded.

Ideally whatever is done from this point of view should be in harmony with whatever the maintenance of the equipment requires. The increasingly common practice of double-crewing ships is an example of such an ideal. Especially when the ship in question is forward-based, crew rotation provides greater career stability and less time away for a ship's people while enabling the Navy to get the most operational sea-time-on-task out of its platforms. Expedients of this kind partially explain why modern, efficient navies sometimes do indeed seem able to achieve more with less.

Sadly, there are hidden dangers as well as manifest advantages in such solutions. Commanders sometimes struggle to meet their commitments with the assets at their disposal and have to resort to such expedients as sending ships off for longer periods of deployment than usual, even 'double-pumping' them from time to time.[26] While the *materiel* might well be able to cope with this, its effect on crew morale, training and readiness can be dire. The U.S. Navy had a spate of serious accidents at sea in 2017 that subsequent investigation showed to be the direct result of a lack of training that in turn derived from ships being too busy meeting too many operational commitments. If the operational tempo only allows sailors 30 hours of sleep a week, accidents and declining standards will result. 'Programmatics' clearly needs to reconcile efficient deployment schedules with the demands of training. There are, for example, concerns that the OPRF system referred to earlier might lead to a box-ticking approach to required objectives that stifles creativity in training.[27] Clearly the demands of the recruitment, employment, training and retention issues referred to earlier have also to be catered for.

People's retention in the service in part depends on the navy providing them with an acceptable work/life balance. Unduly long deployments makes this more difficult. These days being away for 270 days entitles a US ship the dubious privilege of being able to fly the 'Homeward bound' pennant on its return. This contrasts strongly with the common practices of the days of sail when people could be away for years at a time. Famously, Nelson once spent over two years without setting foot on land. Moreover, in days when a ship of the line returned to port, its crew would not necessarily expect to be treated with much consideration; as we saw earlier, Henry Maydman complained about their not being released on leave to see their families and other such on-board instances he thought more characteristic of the 'inhumanity of the Egyptian task-masters.'[28] Always sensitive to the interests of his people, Nelson would doubtless have approved of the US Navy's desire to work towards a 'deploy to dwell ratio' of 2:1, but would probably have been quite startled to see how far a great navy, 200 years after his time, would feel it necessary to go in this regard. 'By increasing and monitoring these deploy-to-dwell thresholds,' said the then Defense Secretary Mark Esper in October 2020, 'we are working to make sure every warfighter and unit gets adequate time to recover from their last deployment, is well trained and prepared for their next one, and on a more personal note, experiences more of the important moments in their families' lives.'[29] Nelson would have understood, however, that volunteers need to be treated differently than pressed men.

This level of consideration needs to be set against the requirement to get as much availability as possible out of the navy's deployable people. Here the US target was to reduce the 'undeployability' level down to 5% of the total, an ambitious target apparently met in 2020 by improving training schedules, the efficiency of medical treatment, the availability of childcare and so forth.

Squaring all these personnel circles, and the high costs they produce, requires adaptation and an innovative approach, and this may take many different forms. Making better use of reservists can help. Technology also is seen as offering solutions, if for example in the shape of unmanned and other 'smart' systems it allows navies to make more cost-effective use of the people available through reduced ship complements.[30] 'The new generation of tech-savvy millennials' said the Royal Canadian Navy's Vice Admiral. Craig Baines,' is well placed to seamlessly transition to a state-of-the-art navy designed to best operationalize both human and technological functions.' But making effective use of this generation requires enhanced technical and staff training, the imaginative use of simulators, and often the deliberate shift of training from shore to sea. 'As part of this,' Admiral Radakin stated 'we have refocused on the front line, reduced our admirals and headquarters staff by 40%, and prioritized filling gaps at sea.' As another exercise in reducing the ratio between 'tail and teeth' to the benefit of the latter, the Indian navy is re-exploring the operator-maintainer concept. which aims to amalgamate the roles of the tactical operator and technical maintainer…The aim,' said Admiral Karimir Singh, 'is to evolve into a lean, technology-oriented force.'[31]

But of course there are disadvantages with many of these devices. Reducing shore-side complements can also cut the posting opportunities which improves the work-life balance by enabling people to live at home with their families for a while. It may mean the transfer of the actual supporting 'tail' functions to sea, which could disadvantage those of the 'teeth.' This could well involve increases in crew size, something most navies would rather avoid. On the other hand, reduced crew size may be a disadvantage when responding to manpower intensive tasks such as responding to humanitarian disasters; more generally it can increase pressure on the remaining individuals when at sea. Fewer people means fewer opportunities to post people ashore in support of the navy's wider international commitments – and fewer people at the head office back home to do the thinking about the navy's present and future.

Such considerations explain why some should conclude that however expensive people are, a few more of them would be nice. Thus, very understandably, Adm Giuseppe Cavo Dragone, of the Italian Navy:

Today, and even more in the future, personnel strength and quality remain crucial. We are therefore discussing the possibility of an increase in personnel to respond effectively to all the requirements of the country, the NATO Alliance, and the international community.[32]

13.6 Fleet Maintenance: Conclusion

There have been several references to the 'Tsar's last armada' which Admiral Rozhestvensky led across the world to catastrophe at the Battle of Tsushima in 1905. Its grisly fate at the hands of the Japanese all too graphically illustrates the penalties of failure in fleet maintenance. The fleet itself, as Captain Semenoff re-marked above, could not properly be so called. Especially after the decrepit 3rd Armoured Squadron joined, it was an incoherent mixture of ships of different ages, types and levels of performance, almost impossible to wield as a single unit. 'This is a miserable fleet,' the Admiral told his wife. 'One has to order five times to do some most trivial thing and then to check five times more whether they have forgotten the order or not ...'[33]

Its state reflected a series of failings. The decision to include ships that the Admiral thought too old, and did not want, was the consequence of the Tsar and the High Command confusing fleet numbers with fleet quality. Poor maintenance in the dockyards meant that even before the fleet had left the Baltic for its 18,000 mile long voyage around the world, ships were reporting serious operational defects. In part this was the consequence of low standards of skill on board. In the fleet's first coaling, three Danish colliers were seriously damaged by clumsy ship handling. Morale amongst officers and men was shaky, especially after the fleet's humiliating brush with a group of trawlers from Hull which the look-outs thought were Japanese torpedo boats. The Royal Navy aggravated this by the brutally faultless professionalism with which it harried the fleet off what it thought its premises and monitored its every move thereafter. A shortage of time and shells meant there was no opportunity for firing or any other tactical practice en route. By contrast, Admiral Togo waiting calmly for the Russians to appear had ample opportunity to prepare and compensate for the op-erational wear and tear his fleet had suffered in the first few months of the war.[34]

The Soviet Navy's Admiral Gorshkov writing 70 years later was quite correct in attributing many of these defects to the nature of the regime itself. 'State, economic, political and military backwardness' he said, plus 'the complete misunderstanding by Czarism of the importance of sea power ' was ultimately responsible for the disaster. Russian industry was in fact expanding at this time, but the technological rewards for the navy had yet to appear. Socially and politically, however, there were major pro-blems and these were inevitably reflected in the Navy. 'Each warship' concluded the historian Constantin Pleshakov, 'was a miniature replica of Russian society.'[35] As such relations close proximity made the differences in the conditions of officers and men brutally obvious; relations between suffered accordingly. Investment in the proficiency and conditions of the navy's people' after was neglected. The officer corps itself was riven with disputes. There were certainly exceptions when individual ships or parts of ship fought well, (or, later revolted more reluctantly or politely), but demoralisation, even disaffection was all too close. Training and morale at all levels and ship cohe-siveness all suffered in consequence. Although Rozhestvensky's fleet did very well even to reach Japanese waters, its maintenance and support deficiencies in both *materiel* and personnel made its defeat a near certainty.[36] In theatre, the Japanese navy was superior in every respect.

Those deficiencies were no accident. They reflected grave weaknesses in all aspects of the fleet's shore-side infrastructure and point to the need to maintain and sustain all aspects of this as well, very possibly with approaches similar to those covering the fleet's *materiel* and people. One major deficiency the Russians suffered from, especially in their Far East, was very limited dockyard facilities in comparison to the Japanese. Another was supplies of all sorts. The situation in Vldivostock was so dire that Rozhestvensky had been told to take what he needed with him. On top of all his other problems, he was therefore encumbered with a lot of supply ships less for the voyage itself than for his activities after he arrived. All this was evidence of the regime's inability to get the Pacific Fleet's infrastructure up to the necessary standard and keep it there.

This failure in turn was bound up in the characteristics of the Russia of the time, characteristics which greatly limited its predisposition for maritime power. One of these was slowness in learning from previous mistakes; typifying this, the regime's fixation on fleet numbers which had contributed to the disaster also led to Russia's buying back from Japan, ten years later, some of its useless ships that the Japanese had captured, despite professional naval advice to the contrary.[37] Because all aspects of effective fleet maintenance depend so much on stable social and economic conditions over a long period of time, the navies of countries without them, suffer accordingly. For them, maintaining the fleet will be much more difficult than buying it, being given it or even building it in the first place. This is as true now as it was then. It also explains why advocates of the development of maritime power will frequently conclude that major social and economic reform at the national level should precede or at least accompany it. The next chapter provides a good example of this.

Notes

1 Maydman, *Naval Speculations*, op cit, Preface, 5.
2 Parker, Geoffrey, 'The *Dreadnought* Revolution of Tudor England,' *Mariner's Mirror*, Vol. 82, No. 3 (August 1996), 269–30.
3 Juana Manuel and German Santana-Perez, 'The Fishing Sector in the Atlantic Oceanic Islands and its Role in the Economy of the Canarian Archipelago under the Ancien Regime,' *Mariner's Mirror*, Vol. 107, No. 2 (May 2021), 146–63.
4 Ronald O'Rourke, *Navy DDG-51 and DDG-1000 Destroyer Programs: Background and Issues for Congress*, CRS Report No. RL32109 (Washington, DC Congressional Research Service, 2020) https://fas.org/sgp/crs/weapons/RL32109.pdf.
5 'The International Commanders Respond,' *Proceedings of the US Naval Institute*, Vol. 147/3/1, 417 (March 2021).
6 Barrett, *The Navy and the Nation*, 61; Maydman, *Naval Speculations*, 325.
7 Quoted in Ballantyne, Ian 'North Atlantic -RN Top Priority,' *Warship IFR*, November 2019, 3.
8 Barrett, *The Navy and the Nation*, 61.
9 Megan Eckstein, 'Submarine Force Changing Training, Acquisition to Focus on Warfare Against Sophisticated Adversary,' *U.S. Naval Institute News*, 25 November 2020.
10 Toremans, Guy, 'Maintaining Peace on the Oceans is a Matter of Trust,' *Warships IFR*, January 2020, 10.
11 Seminoff, Capt. Vladimir, *The Battle of Tsu-shima* (London: John Murray, 1906), 10.
12 Adm Jonathan Greenert, 'Remarks at Center for Strategic and International Studies, Washington,' 19 May 2014.

13 Christopher P. Cavas, 'Carrier Bush Under the Gun to Deploy on Schedule,' *Defence News,* 29 August 2016.
14 Guy Toremans, 'Danes devise a fleet...,' *Warship IFR,* December 2019.
15 Guy Toremans, 'Epic Voyage of Norway's 'Grey Lady,' *Warship IFR,* November 2019, 31.
16 As quoted in Larter, David B., 'The carrier Eisenhower Gets Set for a Dubious "Double Pump",' *Defense News,* 26 September 2020.
17 As quoted in Megan Eckstein, 'No Margin Left: Overworked Carrier Force Struggles to Maintain Deployments after Decades of Overuse,' (USNI NEWS, 12 November 2020).
18 Toremans, Guy 'Danes Devise a Fleet....'
19 Maydman, *Naval Speculations,* 74–6.
20 Duffy, 'William James' Record,' op cit, 127.
21 My thanks to D. Max Jones for this insight.
22 Discussed at greater length in Till, Geoffrey, *Understanding Victory: Naval Operations from Trafalgar to the Falklands* (Santa Barbara: Praeger, 2014), 145–8, 161–2, 184–5.
23 Understanding the dynamics of innovation should start with history-based studies. A good example is Murray, Williamson and Millet, Alan R., *Military Innovation in the Interwar Period* (Cambridge: Cambridge University Press, 1996).
24 This theme is explored in Frank Hoffman, *Mars Adapting: Military Changes Under Fire* (Annapolis: Naval Insituite Press, 2021).
25 Barrett, *The Navy and the Nation,* 55.
26 A US phrase alluding to the need to send a ship, normally a carrier out for two seven month plus deployments in a 36 month cycle, without a major maintenance period between them.
27 Filipoff, Dmitry, *Losing the Warrior Ethos,* CIMSEC, 5 March 2018.
28 Maydman, *Naval Speculations,* 105–7.
29 Defense Secretary Mark Esper, Remarks on Military Readiness, to Heritage Foundation, 15 October 2020.
30 See, for example the Commanders comments from Argentina, France, Jordan, Spain and South Korea in 'The Commanders Respond, 2021'.
31 Comments from Canada, the UK and India, in 'The Commanders Respond, 2021'.
32 Comments from Italy, in 'The Commanders Respond, 2021'.
33 Quoted in Pleshakov, Constantin, *The Tsar's Last Armada; The Epic Voyage the Battle of Tsushima* (New York: Basic Books, 2002), 213.
34 Pleshakov, *The Tsar's Last Armada,* 184–5.
35 Ibid, 117–19.
36 Mitchell, *A History of Russian and Soviet Sea Power,* 234–66.
37 Timirev, *The Russian Baltic Fleet,* 56–9.

14 A Conclusion with Chinese Characteristics

Previous chapters have explored the recurring patterns that have characterised, and maybe still do, attempts to build maritime power, stage by stage. This one will attempt to draw the process together by looking at how just one country appears to be handling it now. Its focus on the present may confirm the validity of recurring patterns deduced from the past.

China seems a particularly apt candidate for this role since in many ways the challenge seems, rather like Maydman's England, to be teetering on the edge of maritime greatness. Indeed, given the obvious differences between the two situations, the unexpected similarities seem worth a comment or two for what they may portend about the future. In any event, given the past, current and forthcoming importance of China, a concluding look at its past and present maritime experience seems to make sense as a window into the global future. This brief review of China's experience will be condensed into four subject areas that nonetheless follow the order of earlier chapters, hopefully further illuminating some of their more important themes.

14.1 China: A Disposition towards the Maritime?

14.1.1 Maritime Geography

Geographically, modern China does not seem at first to conform to normal expectations about the way in which a country's topography can suit the development of maritime power. Its land borders, especially in the north, have been a constant source of strategic threat, not least to the survival of the regime itself, and so have tended to dominate its military thinking.[1]

Despite its 6000 km of coastline and 3000 or so islands, China's access to the world ocean is hemmed in by the first and second island chains. Much of the significance of strategic geography lies in the eye of the beholder. From a Western perspective, a chain of islands could simply mean a long line of such features; for China, on the other hand, chains are associated with imprisonment. Geopolitically, the resultant 'C-shaped Encirclement'[2] seems to severely constrain China's future. Moreover, to switch metaphors, the currently unsatisfactory status of Taiwan as seen from the mainland means that that island acts as a particularly objectionable cork in its maritime bottle.[3] Amongst other things, the island's re-possession, would allow the Navy the advantage of immediate access to deep water. And then, of course there is the so-called Malacca Dilemma addressed earlier; such more distant geography makes China's trade vulnerable to unfriendly interception.

DOI: 10.4324/9781003100553-14

Chapter 2 showed, however, that the Chinese, have done their best historically to compensate for these physical disadvantages by making the very best use of their massive rivers and internal waterways. It also explored the extent to which, these days, they are attempting to change their physical setting through the development of the very ambitious Belt and Road Initiative (BRI). This could fully exploit the country's potential as a 'rimland' state able to bridge the primarily maritime and continental worlds.[4] In its arguably unique capacity to do this, China could indeed be the 'exceptional' country it often claims itself to be. Geography it seems can be changed, and doing so has high priority.

Alongside the BRI as a way of attending to the country's geographic constraints, China's deepening relationship with Russia and its evident determination to consolidate its borders with the Indian sub-continent can all be seen as a way of reducing its potential landward vulnerability. China's assertiveness over the islands and features of the East and South China seas, and the militarisation of its holdings in the latter area will likely improve China's relative security in the near seas and possibly act as a jumping-off point for a growing presence in more distant ones – as part of its 'stepping-out' process. Nor does China exhibit any sign of relinquishing its long-term aim of (re)absorbing Taiwan, in fact quite the opposite. Indeed many would argue that this is the ultimate reason for China's naval expansion.

The paucity of China's domestically available raw materials, particularly oil and gas, together with an urgent need for foreign markets and growing concerns about the country's food security are all pushing China into a more maritime future, in a way not previously experienced. Nonetheless for China the dilemma of deciding defence priorities between the coast and the northwest remains, as it always has. This was particularly marked in the 19th Century when China faced serious territorial and maritime threats at the same time.[5]

Such geographically-induced dilemmas in powers with strong maritime interests, but landward ones too, are commonplace. Even Maydman's England, advantaged by its geography in many other ways, also had to attend to its equivalent land vulnerabilities, especially in Scotland and Ireland. The English could never entirely dispose of their territorial preoccupations. Sometimes, as in Marlborough's wars in Maydman's times, or in the First and Second World Wars, these could even predominate.

Although England's immediate concerns were with what Maydman referred to as the nearby 'Brittish seas,' the acquisition of Gibraltar and Minorca extended its reach further afield, as part of the Royal Navy's 'stepping out' process. In their establishment of bases outside the First Island Chain, most obviously Djibouti, but also places such as Gwadar in Pakistan,[6] the Chinese seem to be following suit. Both countries showed the same propensity to adjust their geography on a more than local scale and in the way Mahan recommended and so showed themselves to be more than merely regional maritime powers.

14.1.2 Society and Government

At first, and maybe second, glance, the nature of Chinese government and society China also does not seem to conform to the usual pattern expected of countries developing their maritime power. Its culture is often said to be settled, cautious, and continental in character. 'China remains,' says the noted scholar Hu Bo, 'a country governed by the mentality of agrarian civilisations.'[7] Particularly amongst the peoples of the north, *yang* the character of 'ocean' meant 'foreign,' 'outlandish,' non-Chinese, and, as a modifier, is still used in that way.[8] As was shown in Chapter 2, with its Confucian disdain for profit-making through trade rather than land, the government's preference and institutional practice were quite often actively hostile to maritime endeavour; because it involved interacting with barbarians, it was seen as a source of unsettling un-Confucian ideas thus threatening social harmony and perhaps the regime itself. Hence China's much discussed retreat from the sea after the last of Zheng He's famous voyages in the 15th Century. This retreat was marked by regulations banning ships with more than two masts and severe restrictions on the Emperor's subjects going abroad. Such was quite different from the entrepreneurial free-booting approach of Maydman's England.

True though this is, this Chinese lack of sea-mindedness was by no means universal in terms either of time or location. The peoples of China's south were markedly more maritime in their approach. The Tang dynasty traded strongly, making the most of the Confucian recommendation that there should be 'indulgent treatment of men from a distance, provided that they paid proper respect' and agreed to the establishment of an effective colony of 200,000 Persians, Arabs, Indians and Malays at Guangzhou to conduct China's maritime trade. There were periods, especially under the Song dynasty, when maritime endeavour was taken much further and positively encouraged by the regime since some exotic products (such as *lapus lazuli* for the porcelain industry) were unobtainable in China; moreover foreign trade, and especially the export of porcelain and silk, was seen as a source of governmental revenue just as it was elsewhere. Accordingly, the Southern Song Chinese themselves challenged Arab and Persian trade dominance and greatly expanded the navy, and so did the Ming dynasty's Yongle Emperor.[9]

Periodically the disadvantages of neglecting maritime opportunities became painfully obvious but were all too often suffocated by the sheer weight of the established, conservative, social practice and expectation on which dynastic security depended. Under foreign pressure, significant social change, however, gathered speed through the 19th Century, as a main plank of the 'self-strengthening movement' and partly under the dubious aegis of the Dowager Empress who encouraged the coming of electricity, the railroads, ironclads and other modern developments culminating in the 1908 abolition of the totally stultifying civil service examination system.[10] The extent to which China modernised and westernised is obscured by the fact that the Japanese did it faster and by China's long agony of revolution and war into the third quarter of the 20th Century. Part and parcel of these developments, nonetheless, was the emergence of a fledgling navy.

As shown in Chapter 2, it is widely argued that there is a natural synergy between liberal democracy (or at least having comparatively free and open societies for the time), economic success and a great navy. This proposition is largely derived from a review of the experience of Athens, Maydman's England, Genoa, the Netherlands and the United States. But in truth the success of Germany's economy and the power of its navy in the early 20th century and of China's a hundred years later could be seen as a major reservation in this thesis. President Xi's China is not a liberal democracy and, concluding that its 'state capitalist/party-state-capitalist system' is superior, mostly does not want to be; its booming sea-based economy and naval strength are nonetheless undeniable. In fact, Mahan himself entertained considerable doubts about the benefits of democracy from a navalist point of view, as was also shown in Chapter 2.

The question is whether Wilhelmine and Nazi Germany, the Soviet Union and maybe President Xi's China should be regarded as exceptions to the rule, or at least evidence of its weakness; on the other hand, the ultimate failure of the first three regimes could be seen as confirming it. If China nonetheless makes it as a sustained and successful maritime power, it will then have confirmed its exceptionality in yet another way.

Regardless of this broader question, the nature of China's maritime development in the future rather than the present will doubtless continue to reflect future developments in the nature of the regime, whether there is a further slide into or, as some predict,[11] a retreat from, autocracy. Whether more or less autocracy would help or hinder the long term development of maritime power, remains an open question.[12]

14.1.3 A Maritime Economy

By contrast, China does most definitely adhere to the usual pattern in the close association between the development of its naval power and the 'blue' aspects of its national economy. Its trade to GDP ratio is higher than that of the United States and even Japan; in part, this is the consequence of the deliberate adoption of an export-led growth model for faster economic development. Its success led to the generation of capital which has supported very high levels of investment in projects abroad. How things will develop as the country instead turns to a 'dual circulation economy' fostering domestic consumption and technological development while still facing many internal challenges remains to be seen.[13] Even so, some analysts, however, anticipate a doubling of the 'blue' parts of the Chinese economy by 2049.[14]

China is resource-poor and needs access to the world's raw materials as well as its markets.[15] Its burgeoning population and disproportionately limited supply of good agricultural land creates a food security problem. This explains China's turn to the resources of the sea, and the development of the world's biggest fishing fleet, comprising a fleet of a million or so fishing vessels employing some 13 million people, and taking 30% of the world catch.[16]

China also benefits from a maritime characteristic much emphasised by Mahan – the possession of a substantial, modern and effective merchant shipping fleet. In August 2018, after an increase of over a third since 2014, The China-owned shipping fleet overtook Japan's to become the world's second largest after that of Greece. By the end of 2018, it stood at 7744 ships totalling 170 million gross tons. Although global in reach, Chinese shipping mostly operates out of three main economic zones, Bohai Bay, the Yangtze River Delta and the Pearl River Delta. These three zones house nine of the world's 20 biggest and busiest ports and also some of its very largest shipping companies, mostly state-run.[17] All of this makes China a major hub of maritime exchange that is central to the national economy, profitable and world-wide in its impact and reach.

China's need to trade with the rest of the world (in striking contrast to the more autarchic economy of the Soviet Union in Cold War days) has also led to its maritime endeavour being globalised through the massive Belt and Road Initiative (BRI) discussed in Chapters 2 and 5. Whether or not the BRI is really the 'win-win' project the Chinese claim it to be,[18] China's economic dependency on safe shipping operations provides a further justification for the expansion of its naval capacity to defend them. This perfectly echoes English concerns in Henry Maydman's day.

But two major differences nonetheless appear. The first is the sheer scale of China and its maritime endeavour. In many ways its rejuvenation is simply a process of returning to the historic normal. As late as 1799 when the Qianlong Emperor died, China represented some 30% of the world's population, its GDP was five times that of Britain and France combined and six of the world's ten biggest cities were to be found within its borders.[19] Nowadays, there is a huge debate about the real extent of Chinese defence expenditure as a proportion of GDP, but simply in consequence of the simple size and annual growth of that GDP, perhaps now the world's biggest, the budgetary resources available for defence in general and the navy in particular are very considerable.[20] Although the cost basis of the two defence budgets are very different and so hard to compare, American defence spending is much higher, however.

The second major difference is the way in which the entrepreneurial instincts of China's current citizens have been married to high levels of state and party control of the economy, producing a 'state-capitalist' system at variance with the disorderly bottom-up market-driven economic style of Elizabethan England or the Dutch Republic or the 'contracting out' style of the Genoese. Against this, though, previous chapters have shown plenty of evidence of 'liberal' state-directed maritime endeavour in peace as well as in war, when leaving things to the market seemed unlikely to deliver what was needed. President Roosevelt's 'New Deal' and re-armament programme during the Second World War are just the most obvious example of this.

China might be much nearer the 'statist' end of this private-public spectrum than Maydman's England (and in fact, under President Xi's 'grand steerage,' moving that way too[21]) but it is nonetheless on the same spectrum. While it is not yet clear whether this will help China's ambition to shift its economy from scale to quality,[22] its party-state-capitalist system gives it important short-term advantages in the conduct of complex and massive projects like the BRI or the development of its maritime power.

14.1.4 Naval Forces

From a historical perspective, modern China's capacity to generate impressive naval capability is hardly surprising given its human, economic and scientific resource base. In the past, it was a matter of choice when this potential was realised. Sometimes, the maritime endeavour had low priority, and the state seemed content for the conduct of trade to be left in the hands of foreigners, especially those from Arabia and Southeast Asia – as during the Tang dynasty for example. But when maritime priorities were higher, as in the 15th Century, the era of Zheng He's famous voyages, China showed itself capable of quickly delivering world-beating ships, weapons and naval technology.[23]

From this perspective, the extraordinary advances in the quality and quantity of Chinese naval development, which have caused so much alarm regionally and in the West, are only to be expected. Until recently much of this was heavily dependent on foreign expertise, some gained illicitly, some by the ingenious reverse-engineering of military products obtained from abroad, some through normal commercial collaboration with others and an increasing amount through major state investment in research and development. The need for this and the comparative lack of purely home-grown technological innovation, for which China has sometimes been accused, may be attributed in part to previous neglect and the existence of more urgent priorities. Again, there is nothing exceptional or distinctively Chinese about any of this aspect of maritime development, except, perhaps that the country's 'catching up rate' is faster than many expected.

Delivering a clear-cut answer to the perennial question of the extent to which China should be regarded as a maritime country is hard. There is little doubt that for much of the time its major preoccupations were land-based, but that did not mean that its maritime interests were completely ignored.[24] Like all other countries, England included, China constantly shuttled up and down the maritime-continental spectrum depending on the circumstances of the time. The one constant in this was change, and nowadays the maritime impulse is extremely strong,[25] but that should not obscure the country's residual continental concerns. 'Our nation is a continental power,' President Xi, himself made clear in an important speech in July 2013, 'and an oceanic power possessing a wide range of strategic maritime interests.'[26] Being maritime or continental is no more a binary choice for China than it is for any other country. China is both and always has been; indeed as a 'rimland country' as already described these characteristics are mutually supportive.

But President Xi's comments are important for a second related reason too. China also *needs* to be a maritime power; as discussed in Chapter 2, this means not just acknowledging its maritime interests but being in a position to defend them. This is now the aim, generally espoused.[27] Definitions of what that means exactly naturally differ, even amongst China's maritime community, but the general consensus is that the capacity to defend its interests is crucial to the country's future, requires extensive effort and covers both the commercial and the military sides of the 'maritime affair.'[28]

Its naval aspect is especially important because, 'Today, and for a long time to come our country's national interests are expanding mainly in the sea.' The authoritative *The Science of Military Strategy* then drives the point home: '… national security is threatened mainly from the sea, [and so]…the focal point of military struggle is mainly in the sea.'[29] Admiral Wu Shengli, then Commander-in-Chief of the Chinese navy was crystal clear about what history shows to be the consequence of not realising that. The 'weak ocean consciousness' of the fading Qing dynasty led to the complete and humiliating naval defeat then at the hands of the Japanese in the war of 1894–1895 and the disasters that followed. The past must be studied, its lessons learned so that nothing similar could happen again.[30]

14.2 Context and Vision: China's Place in a Maritime World[31]

The steely determination to develop China's maritime power emerges very clearly from the discussion of President Xi's decidedly top-down approach in Chapter 4. That this strikes a chord with the Chinese public is equally clear, not least in the country's social media. The question that arises is why this is so? The economic incentives identified earlier already pointed to a need to cater for China's rights and maritime interests in distant seas, but is that it? Is there anything else about China's domestic and international context that has encouraged such maritime endeavour? And to what extent are these responses typical of countries in roughly China's position?

This is not the place for an in-depth analysis of China's security policy, a subject generating whole libraries of books with competing interpretations,[32] but three aspects of this can nevertheless be picked out as significant for naval development. The first, for China as for all others, is the extent to which its maritime security policy is framed by its perception of the security environment – its view of what other countries have done, are doing and might do.[33] What is particularly evident for China, though, is a lively sense of historic threat, whether justified or not. From the Chinese point of view many of the trials and tribulations that the country faced during the 19th Century can be traced back to the intrusions of European sea-based powers that started in the 16th Century and grew in substance thereafter, culminating in the two so-called Opium wars with Britain. The later intervention of the United States and still more of Japan, as just discussed, greatly aggravated a problem finally and very painfully exemplified by the multinational response to the so-called Boxer rebellion of 1905. This all resulted in a series of disastrous military defeats, the loss of much sovereign territory, the complete collapse of a centuries-old China-centred regional order, major social disruption, the wasting of China's economy and eventually in 1911, the collapse of the imperial system. Revolution, civil war and a vicious war with Japan followed, all costing countless Chinese lives. Arguably, the current status of Taiwan and foreign attitudes to it is seen as the most painful hang-over from this unhappy time. Given this long and searing experience, a sense of threat bordering on paranoia and an urge to develop the country's maritime power to guard against continuing sea-born threats seems hardly surprising.

Secondly and equally understandably, there is a strong sense in China of a need to reverse and recover from the consequences of a 'century of humiliation.' It is significant that President Xi, a leader deeply imbued in the tenets of China's historic culture,[34] frequently talks of the 'rejuvenation' of China, and of the resumption of its proper place in the international order. A glorious past should be balanced by a glorious future. This is the so-called China Dream as articulated in the 2010 best-selling book of that title by Colonel Liu Ming Fu, of the Chinese National Defence University.[35] To some extent a counter-narrative to the 'Peaceful Rise' vision of Zheng Bijian[36] the China Dream urges strength against the many threats and challenges, both domestic and international, that China faces, calling for a greater emphasis on building up the country's military power. A country with a strong economy but a weak military is a plump sheep waiting in the market for its fate. Such strength of feeling helps explain pride in the nation's naval achievements and the assertive so-called great power 'wolf warrior' tactics characteristic of Chinese policy in recent years. 'China is a big country,' the then Chinese Foreign Minister, Yang Jiechi, reminded his Southeast Asian colleagues in 2010, 'and other countries are small countries and that is just a fact.'[37] The underlying message was clear: 'We're back; get used to it.' In short, China's naval expansion can be seen as a consequence, not just of strategic considerations, or even economic ones; as well it can be seen as an expression of identity, a demand for international recognition, rather like that of Wilhelmine Germany.[38]

Finally, for many Chinese, the perceived relative decline of the West from the Great Recession of 2008 onwards, coupled with the disastrous consequences for it of the Covid pandemic seem to provide China with a unique opportunity to assume its rightful place in the international order. That sense of opportunity is fuelled by the apparently stellar relative performance of the Chinese economy for the past couple of decades, the country's technological prowess, American preoccupations with the costs and consequences of unwinnable wars in Iraq and Afghanistan and the palpable divisions, both domestic and international, in the Western camp. In short, China should challenge the existing maritime order now, because it can.

In a country as vast as China there are many different stakeholders in the maritime endeavour. They include the Party, its institutions and leaders, the Ministry of Foreign Affairs and other Government bodies, the navy, the China Coast Guard, the other services, local provincial authorities, resource companies and netizens empowered by the social media. Their views can be far from identical, even hard to reconcile.[39] Some Chinese participants have even doubted whether China has a national maritime strategy at all. 'China does not have a clearly defined ocean strategy at the national level,' complained Rear Admiral Yin Zhuo in 2011 when Chairman of the Expert Committee on Navy Informationalisation. Some agencies were only concerned with economic issues when 'naturally the navy has its own ocean strategy considerations, but these are all actions by certain departments and not at the national level.'[40] Nor is flat disagreement impossible, although the nature of the Chinese system discourages overt dissent from party conclusions and much discourse on maritime matters within China remains opaque to outsiders. As a result, there is room for interpretation and 'sharp divergences in perceptions regarding China's maritime strategic objectives,'[41] amongst foreigners and so in the way that other countries should react to them.

Nonetheless, senior policy-makers seem very aware of the importance of the sea to China and of possible tensions between the urge to expand their maritime power and the official 'Peaceful Rise' narrative so beloved of government spokespeople. They have to steer a course accordingly and under President Xi in particular show every sign of developing an overall and integrated national policy of the sort urged by Admiral Yin. 'The more complexities the party faces and the more arduous the tasks it undertakes,' President Mr Hu Jintao apparently told his successor Xi Jinping in 2012,' the more imperative it is for the party to strengthen its discipline and uphold centralised leadership.'[42] Rarely can advice have fallen on such receptive ears.

The impact of its domestic and international environment on the prospects of maritime development is distinctive and unique to each country. Nonetheless, there do seem to be some common elements. Like China, Maydman's England certainly had threats, both foreign and domestic, to be faced and was aware of the likely consequences, (including possible 'regime-change') of failing to deal with them. England too was developing a sense of its place in the world, and also the growing confidence that derived from economic success and strategic opportunity. In both cases, as well, their responses to the situation became part of the context against which other countries had and have to respond. And so the process goes on.

14.3 Maritime Advocacy, Priorities and Integration[43]

'Strength in Unity,' is something of a guiding principle in Chinese policy, and a focus on the integration of all aspects of national effort certainly seems to apply in the maritime sphere. As we have seen, Maydman certainly thought everything of maritime consequence should be made to hang together '... under one interest...like a well twisted cord, made up of many threads' such that even the weakest would derive '... a considerable strength' from the support of the others.'[44] Moreover, just as in Maydman's England, there seems a strong element of ensuring regime survival in all this. Like William III, President Xi is ultimately responsible for everything.

The strong top-down push for maritime power exemplified by President Xi and discussed above means that there is little need for more advocacy of the general policy by anyone else in policy-making circles. All the same, China, like any other country has a multitude of other demands on its resources and, as was just shown, there is a multiplicity of priority choices within the maritime domain as well. Inevitably there is a distinct 'maritime lobby' comprising various military, industrial and regional groups.[45] Typically, reconciling these part complementary, part competitive viewpoints is handled by the formation of 'Small Leading Groups' usually chaired by the Party's Chairman, President Xi. The appropriate Small Leading Group scopes the problem and provides the necessary guidance for subsequent implementation.[46]

It is particularly difficult for outsiders fully to understand the security decision-making process within the markedly opaque Chinese party and governmental systems and so to know how priorities are decided and then resourced, but several issues do seem fairly clear.

The first is that, as in Maydman's England, there's a major problem with corruption in officialdom and the military such that decisions may be made for the wrong reasons. Accordingly President Xi has made the extirpation of corruption something of a personal crusade. For him the obvious benefits would be a more efficient administrative system, the better use of available resources, better-prepared fighting services and, most probably, a strengthened political position as the date of an election for his third presidential term approaches.

There is also a very strong contemporary accent upon the efficient integration of the various levers of national power and national interest. The result is the Chinese concept of 'Comprehensive National Power' to which much attention is paid. Applied to maritime policies, it should correct what has seemed fractious and uncoordinated in the past. The resultant maritime benefits of a 'whole of nation' rather than simply 'whole-of-government' approach are manifest in China's resourcing and conduct of the Belt and Road Initiative (BRI) as discussed in Chapter 5. This approach maximises the inevitable linkages between industrial, economic, financial, diplomatic and military activity and makes the most of the mutual support they can offer each other. Inevitably, both Chinese policy-makers and foreign analysts differ in the relative weight that are and/or should be attributed towards these various sets of motivation, but all agree they are intertwined. The range of instruments extends into cultural activity, the selective use of history and even underwater archaeology in the service of the BRI and China's claims in the South China Sea. The effectiveness of this approach contributes significantly to the development of China's maritime power and partly explains why other countries, and especially the United States, Japan and India are so suspicious of the BRI while doing their best to emulate the methods used in its advance – at least to the extent their very different systems of government allow. For them too, the connections between military/naval and geopolitical considerations on the one hand and commercial ones on the other, in areas such as energy, are so obvious that a properly integrated approach appears nothing more than common sense.[47]

The same kind of emphasis on the unity of opposites is also evident within the military domain. This emerged as President Xi took forward the campaign to improve inter-service cooperation that was mentioned in Chapter 6. There were a variety of reasons for this. Probably the main incentives were to consolidate party control, hopefully without impeding operational effectiveness. Since 1949, this 'red *versus* expert' issue has always posed something of a dilemma for China. In 1959, for example, the Navy's then Commander Peng Dehuai was dismissed for espousing conventional naval views and the subsequent Cultural Revolution (1966–1976) is reckoned by some as having put naval development back by 20 years.[48] Currently, the issue is handled pragmatically; the Political Officers responsible for ensuring ideological rectitude in the military are also expected to be professionally competent in naval terms. Nonetheless, the issue has not entirely gone away, and has proved more of a problem for China than for most other countries.

Electronics paying no regard to ideological purity however, there remains a need to take account of the crucial new cyber, space and electromagnetic domains of warfare. This further underlines the importance of policy integration in the military area.[49] Institutional reforms which have accelerated under President Xi were and are intended to correct the very obvious lack of 'jointness' between China's various military services, their lack of operational agility and the overweening influence of the Army. Given residual tensions, vested interests and the simple fact that so many people are being 'let go,' it will probably take years, or even decades, before these reforms deliver the effects their advocates anticipate. The process began long before President Xi and will outlast him. In much of this, China is no different in its hopes, expectation and performance than any other country – except once again in the matter of scale.

The new emphasis on the maritime and aerospace domains of war has benefited the Navy in many different ways. Its loss of more than a tenth of its people in the reforms was compensated by taking in much of the Army's amphibious forces as part of the plan to expand the size and role of the Marine corps. In common with the other services, its Commander-in-Chief no longer sits on the Central Military Commission and has now become a 'capability deliverer' rather than an operational commander (a common global trend). The Navy appears to have special authority for the protection of China's maritime rights and interests in the South and East China Seas. It now leads the new, joint, and especially important Southern Theatre Command and for the time being at least runs its Far Seas Protection operations more or less independently. Moreover, these have now been accorded such a high priority that the other services all seem to be trying to get into the expeditionary act.[50]

The elevation of the Navy is not a culmination but simply the latest and especially significant stage in a long, historic and probably near-inevitable trend that long preceded President Xi. Arguably as something more than a mere 'coastal appendage of the ground forces', it started in the early 1950s with the independent requirement to protect fishing boats and merchant ships against attack from Taiwan. Remarkably, 1958 even saw the beginning of a determined campaign to build nuclear submarines and develop a sea-based nuclear deterrent.[51] The downfall of the continentalist Gang of Four in the mid-1970s cleared away many of the impediments to naval development which mushroomed from 1979 into Deng Xiaoping's campaign to reform China and open its economy to the world.[52] From that time on, the Navy's prospects as an autonomous blue-water force, the naval component of a newly invigorated joint force and as the leading authority in the conduct of interagency operations at sea have all steadily improved.[53] Current alarm at China's naval rise is a least partly due to a failure to appreciate that it is the culmination of a very long process.

Naval strength, though, is but one part of China's national power. Integrating all aspects of this led to the creation of a State or National Security Council. This was also set up to deal with the increasing difficulty in a globalised world of distinguishing between internal and external security threats, a point rammed home by the Covid-19 pandemic. Policy has to handle the mingling of the two and the agencies set up to do so, including the Navy, need the appropriate representation.

All this is entirely consistent with the 'Three Warfares' approach famously advocated in 1999 by Colonels Qiao Liang and Wang Xiangsui which sought to link hard and soft power by integrating military methods of persuasion with propaganda campaigns, psychological pressure and the selective use of international law.[54] This approach has been steadily implemented ever since, even though the relative military weakness that first inspired it (alongside the country's long and sophisticated strategic culture) has much diminished.[55]

For all their fascination with the theories of Mahan,[56] the Chinese appear to have taken to heart the admonition of Sir Julian Corbett that there's much more to maritime power than grey painted ships with numbers on the side. While this is becoming quite common around the world, the Chinese do seem to be taking this comprehensive view one stage further than most. While their rivals now mull over the capabilities of the new domains of competition, conflict and war (cyber, space, electromagnetic) as constituents of the system, the Chinese, looking through the opposite end of the telescope as it were, are thinking more about the requirements of the system as a whole, and shaping the constituents accordingly.

14.4 Naval Policy[57]

Within the constraints of the Chinese system, the inspirational effects of Admiral Liu Huaqing's vision of his country's naval future were investigated in Chapter 7. In subsequent years, Admiral Liu's original 'vision' was gradually amplified by his successors and accepted by his political masters, its place in the military scheme of things clear in a series of Defence White Papers.[58]

This process was accompanied by something of a public relations campaign on Chinese television, that was part of a cultural shift into 'blueness.'[59] The *River Elegy* series of 1988 enthusiastically urged abandoning 'the mentality of a servile, static and defensive people who always hug to mother earth to eke out a miserable living, rather than boldly venturing forth on the dangerous deep blue sea in search of a freer, more exalted existence.' The 'Yellow River mentality' must be abandoned and 'sea consciousness' encouraged. Admiral Tirpitz would have approved, but the party was not so sure. The implicit association of seapower with initiative and free enterprise was a bit unsettling and in the aftermath of the Tiananmen Square upheaval of 1989, the series was banned.[60] The basic proposition of the series, though, was not.

The whole process was sustained by careful analysis of the lessons of the maritime past including China's past successes and failures, not least its losing engagements with Japan.[61] Buttressed by such studies, there is much to be said for the view that 'China must be the most self-aware rising power in history.'[62]

Comparing China's maritime rise with that of both Wilhelmine and Nazi Germany, indeed, is a much-discussed issue both inside and outside the country, not least because of the catastrophic consequences of those German efforts. Arguably all three instances can be seen as a means of seeking international recognition of what the country, or at least the regime, believes to be its proper place in the world. The key difference, though, might prove to be China's greater industrial and strategic capacity to secure its goals, coupled with a determination to avoid the mistakes the Germans made.[63]

The Chinese Navy's consequent vision of its future is not articulated in the detail, extent and sometimes lunatic candour characteristic of American naval discourse. Instead it has to be inferred from fairly bland public statements, and the nature of its patterns of procurement and activity, inevitably with a corresponding lack of granularity. Nonetheless its broad outlines, all that are required here, seem fairly clear. Most importantly, the Chinese Navy seems to have come to some fairly specific conclusions about what it needs to do and so what it needs to have – the essential foundation for any navy's bid to plot its future course. The fact that it is noticeably reticent about its construction intentions, obviously makes for a level of uncertainty about the nature and level of China's naval ambitions, which could well lead some to exaggerated estimates of threat. But, it could have the opposite effect too. Either way, what China is thought to be doing becomes a major influence on the development policies of other navies because it has such an influence on their strategic environment.

For all that, the general consensus of opinion amongst China navy watchers is that its strategic missions have now developed over time into five main groups and these were all somewhat ambiguously referred to, rather than fully described in the 2015 Defence White Paper.[64]

- When applied to the defence of the near seas, the requirement 'to resolutely safeguard China's maritime rights and interests' means to support its sovereignty rights/claims in the East and South China Seas, and associated access to related resources. 'To resolutely safeguard the unification of the motherland' would seem to require the deterrence of Taiwan's drifting towards putative independence by, if necessary, demonstrating an unequivocal capacity to prevent it.[65]
- Lest other countries seek to intervene in these matters, China has expanded its 'offshore waters defence' mission into a more active form which others describe as an anti-access/area denial strategy within the first and second island chains. This requires, in the words of an earlier Defence White Paper of 2004,[66] 'the building of the Navy, Air Force and Second Artillery force to seek balanced development of the combat force structure, in order to strengthen the capabilities for winning both command of the sea and command of the air, and conducting strategic counter strikes.' The notion of 'counter-intervention' also requires the capacity '... to maintain strategic deterrence and carry out nuclear counterattack.' Naturally, China's strategic thinking is informed by its interpretation of the naval and defence policies of the United States, its allies and partners.[67] As the range of the threat increases, the Chinese Navy can be expected to follow it by moving forward from the mainland.
- 'With the growth of China's national interests...the security of overseas interests concerning energy and resources, strategic sea lines of communication (SLOCs), as well as institutions, personnel and assets abroad, has become an imminent issue.' Accordingly, the need to 'safeguard the security of China's overseas interests' means the Navy now has the demanding mission of 'open seas protection' well beyond the second island chain. Quite a few Western experts were surprised by the speed with which this aspiration has been addressed.[68]
- The Navy's need to engage in operations other than war has been stressed for many years. Accordingly it needs 'to participate in regional and international security cooperation and maintain regional and world peace.' 'Soft' naval activities of this sort, through the 'power to attract,' buttress China's 'Peaceful Rise narrative.' The Navy's global presence allows it to benefit from a special authority in the conduct of humanitarian and non-combatant evacuation missions.[69] Such maritime operations other than war are presented as part of 'China's grand strategy for peaceful development,' providing 'public goods' in the maintenance of good order at and from the sea, and 'bringing harmony, security and prosperity to neighbours.'[70] Such operations are to be conducted in an 'open, pragmatic and cooperative spirit.'[71] Like all sailors everywhere, the Chinese Navy considers itself particularly appropriate for, and good at, such missions.

- Finally, the Navy also has more domestic responsibilities which include the need to guard against 'infiltration, separatism and terrorism so as to maintain China's political security and social stability.' This includes an appreciation of the need to conduct emergency rescue and disaster relief, at home as well as abroad, especially in the light of the 2008 Sichuan earthquake disaster. '[S]upport for national economic and social development,' has always been one of the duties of the Chinese military.[72]

The Chinese Navy's expanding set of missions strongly suggests that it is following exactly the same trajectory of development as England's in the 16th and 17th Century. Maydman's initial focus was on what he termed the 'Brittish seas' but through the 18th Century the Royal Navy went on to consolidate its earlier capacity to operate in regional seas like the Mediterranean and in much more distant ones too. So did the Portuguese, the French, Dutch and Spanish. The Americans followed suit – although its early forward operations against Britain and in the Mediterranean telegraphed its global missions from the start. The Imperial German Navy and in due course the Soviet Navy did the same. Of course, most navies do *not* do this, but this would seem less strategic abstinence, more that they simply do not have the necessary resources. As a rule, those that can, do. Manifestly, the Chinese Navy can and does.

Any claim that China might be exceptional in this regard (and so true to narrower strictly defensive and local interpretations of its 'Peaceful Rise' and 'non-hegemonic' narrative) is still further undermined by its abandonment of the Party's earlier ex-pressed distaste for foreign bases and aircraft carriers. Until quite recently both of these were officially regarded as inherently offensive and so typically Western since they provided their possessors with an enhanced ability to interfere in other peoples' affairs.[73] Entirely predictably, China has now reversed course and joined their number. However there seems little doubt that China will also follow the general precedent in making its 'far seas' efforts contingent on its confidence that it can handle 'near seas' challenges, while at the same time being wary of the risks and costs of such ambitious far seas endeavour.

Turning to the related issue of fleet design, these expanded missions mean that,

> It is necessary for China to develop a modern maritime military force structure commensurate with national security and development interests ... so as to provide strategic support for building itself into a maritime power.[74]

This range of tasks means that China needs to develop a balanced fleet. Accordingly, the Chinese navy, like any other, has to make potentially tricky choices about fleet design priorities. Those choices find physical expression in the platform and weapon capabilities which provide probably the least ambiguous evidence of China's future naval intentions.

14.5 Naval Administration

First, though, China's ability to build, maintain and operate the balanced fleet it thinks it needs should be sustained by its administrative efficiency in making the best use of the maritime resources at its disposal. In this, it will likely benefit from President Xi's drive against corruption and for military reform because these have always been problems for the Chinese navy, as for many others. In China's case though it is particularly vexatious because it implies less than perfect control of the military by the Party.[75]

As in the other branches of the Chinese military, the navy's system for the procurement of equipment has been reformed. Its acquisition system comes under the joint General Armaments Department and operates a series of Five Year Plans, supported by a web of research and development programmes conducted by special national defence key laboratories in places like Wuhan and, especially, Qingdao. Progress benefits from a comprehensive national defence mobilisation system and a much higher degree of civil-military integration between the defence industrial base and private commercial concerns than is now commonly the case elsewhere, but which is still often considered insufficient.[76]

14.6 Maritime Synergy

As was shown in Chapter 3, Henry Maydman took a keen interest in all sectors of England's maritime economy and advanced his recommendations about how they could all be encouraged to support national purposes, both commercial and strategic. Not for nothing did he engage in 'discourse' on the country's 'oeconomy.' Since his time many other countries have come to the same conclusion. Nowadays the wisdom of developing the 'blue economy' is both public and commonplace.

But what is perhaps especially characteristic about the maritime policies of contemporary China is the very strong emphasis now being given to the effective integration of the various components of an increasingly impressive blue economy. What looks like the single-minded pursuit of maritime synergy serves both commercial and strategic purposes. Through the 1980s, under Deng Xiaoping, the marine economy was prioritised and invested in, growing at a rate of 18% a year. By 2010, it accounted for some 10% of national GDP, the aim being to double or even treble this achievement.[77]

Ship-building, merchant shipping and the fishing industry are the main components of this very variegated sector of the national economy, and there have been huge investments in all of them. Each of them offers considerable economic benefits to the country, and strategic benefits too.

Ship-building and the Maritime Defence Industrial Base (MDIB). Maydman was perfectly well aware that developing an MDIB would yield both commercial and strategic benefits. As in many other countries since his time, China's leaders think the same. Their results though are distinctive first and most obviously for their scale, for the extent to which they are state-directed and maybe for the degree of their success.

Particular stress was given to ship-building. Initially this was of the basic 'metal-bashing' variety but became more technologically sophisticated and efficient over time. It also became more expensive as China began to lose its initial comparative advantage in low wage costs. Recognising the need for higher standards, the Chinese devoted resources to the training of naval architects and marine engineers, producing in 2009 seven times more of them each year than did the United States. As upgrading became necessary in order to encourage innovation, shipbuilding was further reformed from 2013, accelerating after the publication of the 2015 Defence White Paper. Reform was aimed at reducing the fragmentation and relative lack of domestic competitiveness that has plagued the Chinese industrial base and which has created vested interests that had been a problem in the past.[78]

The shipbuilding industry remains dominated by two big consolidated state-run concerns, the China State Shipbuilding Corporation (CSSC) and the China Shipbuilding Industry Corporation (CSIC) both of which are also active in the Belt and Road Initiative (BRI). The shipbuilding industry also benefits from official encouragement of the use of Chinese owned merchant ships for imports and exports wherever possible (China's version of England's Navigation Acts). The Chinese see strategic as well as commercial benefits in all this. They apparently pay less attention to the common view in the West that given their distinctive technological requirements merchant-ships and warships must continue the historic trend towards divergence that started centuries ago. Their ship-building industry manages to produce high-quality warships and the world's greatest output in merchant-ships at the same time.

The China State Shipbuilding Corporation, in its yards at Shanghai is building LNG carriers, container ships and oil tankers, together with top-line warships such as the Type 052D and O55 destroyers, amphibious warfare vessels and the Chinese Navy's third and fourth aircraft carriers. A new state-of-the-art Shanghai shipyard at Changxin is shortly to complete.[79] All this underlines the advantages to be expected from its strategy since 2014 of 'Military-Civil Fusion.'[80]

Nonetheless in China as elsewhere, and as discussed in Chapter 12, the concept of the fleet has widened from it being a mere assembly of ships, submarines and sea-based aircraft into networked systems of platforms, weapons and sensors, many of them land, air, space or cyber-space based. This means that actual ship-building now takes up a smaller proportion of the MDIB than it used to in Maydman's day. It is recognised in China as elsewhere, that a much wider range of industrial prowess is required.

In turn this requires the candid identification of areas of technological weakness that need to be addressed in the light of the navy's strategic needs or the country's commercial ones. Sometimes this can be sparked of by a developing challenge posed by the United States, Taiwan or another of the country's neighbours. On other occasions particular events will highlight a developing need; the 2008 earthquake in Szechuan, for example is held to have shown a need for the procurement more locally built heavy-lift helicopters. By 2010 China's interest in developing a range of capabilities including computer network operations, precision-strike missiles, integrated air defence and counter-space operations, submarines, stealth fighters and UAVs – amongst others – were becoming apparent.[81]

China's huge population and burgeoning economy mean that a lot of human and financial resources can be thrown at the correction of identified weaknesses or at possibly promising areas of advance. This enables the building of a large number of state-supported research agencies and industrial conglomerates specialising in particular naval or general defence areas. In the fast-evolving world of hypersonics for example, China by 2020 had created 25 universities and research institutions with at least ten attached hypersonic wind tunnels for test purposes.[82] Many of these have the status of universities also tasked with the education of future generations of defence designers and engineers of one sort or another on a similarly large scale. Operating in a state-capitalist system they are less constrained by the requirement to make a profit than their western counterparts.

The strategic, and possibly commercial, benefit of this generous level of support is that when choosing which avenue to pursue in a particular project, China can often back more than one horse in the race, and sometimes all of them. Such a broad front advance multiplies the prospect of eventual success, if at a cost. This appears to have been the philosophy behind their building of four different classes of destroyers at the same time in the late 1990s.[83] The downside of this is that it produces a rather heterogeneous fleet structure, with, for example in 2010, 16 different classes of destroyer and frigates, which must complicate maintenance and the management of spare parts.[84]

Aside from the strategic benefits a capable MDIB confers, there are economic advantages too. The more China makes what it needs, the less reliant it is on imports of foreign made defence equipment which is often expensive and comes with irritating strings attached. Increasingly China is also moving into the arms export business, especially now its products are beginning to lose their 'agricultural' reputation while retaining their price advantage. This gets away from the problems of 'monopsony' (of these big industrial concerns having only one customer).[85]

Already by 2014, China's biggest defence electronics conglomerate, the China Electronics Technology Corporation was reporting a major shift in its business in radar, electronic warfare, missile warning and air defence systems business from supplying the needs of the Chinese military to exports.[86] This also has the benefit of increasing Chinese strategic influence with the customers. Much the same mixed benefit comes from the display of examples of Chinese industrial prowess in the defence sector at international exhibitions and in large military parades. Showcasing their products like this exhibits natural pride in their achievements, earns the interest and respect of possible customers and can be a means of sending pointed messages to potentially unfriendly countries.[87]

Neither the ease nor the speed with which China has developed its MDIB should be exaggerated, however. Until recently, and with only a few exceptions, China was considered by most experts in this field as more of a 'fast follower' than a major innovator. It started a long way behind the Russians, European countries and, especially, the United States but has been gaining ground on them in recent years.[88] Both the opportunities offered and the continued challenges faced are exemplified in China's much-discussed carrier programme, one of its most ambitious projects.

This perhaps started in 1984, with the acquisition of the veteran Australian carrier HMAS *Melbourne,* theoretically for scrap. While Admiral Liu Huaqing was an early and enthusiastic proponent of a carrier programme, Jiang Zemin was evidently only somewhat reluctantly persuaded of the need by the military members of the Central Military Commission.

Even though he was finally won over, such an ambitious programme was, and remains, challenging for China's MDIB. China started a very long way behind the Americans especially but also other carrier operators like the British, French and Indians and as yet has very limited building and operational carrier experience. The programme has been costly and the learning curve steep.

China's course through these challenges was cautious, incremental and methodical. Not for them the risky and ambitious leap into unknown technological futures characteristic of the US Navy's *Zumwalt* programme or even the Littoral Combat Ship project. The first move was to buy the old ex-Russian *Varyag* from Ukraine, apparently to be used as a floating casino in Macau; appropriately hedging their bets, the Chinese then took advantage of a golden opportunity for some inspired 'reverse engineering.' The result was the ship's transformation into the 'technology demonstrator,' trials platform and training carrier, the *Liaoning*. The project required extensive investment in everything from the construction of support facilities ashore, to two-seat trainer aircraft for its pilots. The *Liaoning* duly provided the experience, building and operational lessons necessary for the first locally built carrier, the *Shandong* which was commissioned in January 2020 from the Dalian shipyard. Carrier no 3, then took the project forward with greater size, the possibility of nuclear propulsion, and catapult-assisted take-off, very possibly arrested recovery and perhaps even the EMALS electromagnetic catapult system being developed by the Naval University of Engineering. Future carriers will be larger, more advanced, with conventional take-off and landing facilities, and maybe nuclear propulsion too.[89] The development and prospective operational use of Chinese carriers can be expected also to encourage advances in other associated areas, such as the space programme, telecommunications technology, missile engineering and so forth.

Nonetheless, however methodical the Chinese may be, technical difficulties and matters of cost still intrude.[90] The development of associated carrier aircraft is still a major problem since China's aviation industry has been heavily reliant on imported aircraft and especially aero-engines. The current far from ideal carrier fighter mainstay is the J-15 'Flying Shark' a heavy reverse-engineered derivative of the old Russian Su-33 Flanker fighter. Nonetheless substantial progress has been made, dependence on foreign expertise greatly reduced and the capacity for innovation so long aimed at finally arriving, even in this most demanding of sectors.[91]

Summarising, China has now become the world's second largest arms producer. Thanks to a deliberate and conscious policy of encouraging defence innovation guided by various agencies set up under the Central Military Commission, heavy spending on Research and Development, the sometimes illicit acquisition of foreign expertise and the benefits of its 'Civil-Military Fusion' project, it is fast closing on the United States in terms of quality of the product as well as numbers. Chinese experts freely acknowledge, however, that substantial problems remain.[92] Its continuing problems with aero-engines are one example. Others, plus a possible lack of perceived urgency, may help explain why China's development of nuclear propelled ballistic missile firing submarines (SSBNs) has been so slow, until recently.[93]

Overall Chinese experience shows that there are challenges and costs for countries seeking to develop an MDIB as well as opportunities. The resources available for industrial advance are finite and their use for this sector will, at least to some degree, be at the expense of others. Effectively balancing all this requires a strategic approach. Like their equivalents everywhere, China's naval leaders are aware of the need continually to improve the defence acquisition, technology and industrial system, reconciling the need for innovation and risk-tolerance with sensible caution and an appropriate awareness of cost. What distinguishes them, though, is the extent to which they see the process as a whole – one of the benefits, perhaps of their complete lack of the free-market fundamentalism that has so often hobbled the efforts of their Western counterparts.

Merchant Shipping. Much the same can be said for the merchant shipping industry sector of a blue economy, which was discussed earlier. Again this is no accidental development, but rather the consequence of deliberate and conscious party/state direction that goes back to the '4 Modernisations' outlined by Deng Xiaoping in 1979. He recognised the commercial benefits that a large and efficient merchant shipping industry (as a complex of ship-builders and maintainers, shipping operators and ports) can bring, especially for a country heavily dependent on sea-based trade.

There are considerable strategic benefits too. China's experience in port development and operations and its accumulated capital allows heavy investment abroad. It has established interests in two-thirds of the world's top 50 ports, partly through the BRI.[94] This brings strategic benefits as well as commercial ones. The more directly military benefits of a strong national shipping fleet were demonstrated by the British in the Falklands campaign and discussed in Chapter 8. The Chinese paid close attention to this. Accordingly, a strong connection is maintained between China's navy and its fishing and merchant fleets. Trawlers, ferries and freighters are all subject to mobilisation, often have military features built into them and retain standing assignments to military or militia forces as and when necessary.[95] This is especially true of Ro-Ro ships that might be of use in a Taiwan contingency.

All the same, China's economic dependency on sea-based trade also represents a key strategic vulnerability, a characteristic it shares with other countries with significant maritime interests.[96] Again, China's development of its merchant fleet is distinctive only in its speed, scale and degree of central direction.

The Fishing Industry. With its huge population and above average appetite for sea food, it is hardly surprising that China has the world's largest fishing fleet, as already mentioned. The economic benefits that this brings in terms of employment and national revenue are considerable. Much of this also applies to the country's neighbours in the south and north-east Asia. In consequence, the pressure on fish stocks in the South and East China seas threatens their sustainability, competition between fishing fleets has become acute, fishing boats have to go further out for catches both regionally and globally and the economics of fishing is getting increasingly challenging.[97] Although significant reductions in the fishing fleet would seem sensible environmentally, neither China nor its neighbours are taking this line. Presumably, this is because the industry creates a powerful vested interest that no government, whatever its political hue, can afford to neglect.

Instead, Chinese authorities, especially local ones, subsidise rather than rationalise their fishing fleets by supplying fuel and GPS navigational equipment, facilitating the transition to tough steel rather than wooden-hulled vessels and so on.[98] In return, much of China's huge fishing fleet has been turned into a paramilitary 'Peoples' Militia,' trained to serve the state's strategic purposes as well as its commercial ones. The plenitude of radio aerials many of them seem to have, helps them provide extra eyes and ears at sea. Their steel hulls are useful in 'shouldering' foreign vessels out of the way. In this way, the ship becomes the weapon. With their assistance, the conduct of so-called 'grey zone operations' becomes much easier and more effective. In such ways China's fishing fleet provides a key element in the defence of what China sees as its sovereignty in the South and East China Sea. Training takes place between May and August each year and its expenses are seen as a worthwhile investment by regional and national authorities. Vietnam has adopted the same policy.

Coastguards, the law and the assertion of authority. Moreover this same integrative approach that appears so distinctively Chinese also applies when it comes to dealing with the unavoidable ambiguities in the maritime enterprise that were raised in Chapter 9. China supports the maritime rights and interests given such emphasis in its declarations of its policy towards the sea, with a programme of legislative action and the establishment of a powerful coastguard force, a programme unusual only in its extent and purposefulness.[99]

This programme accelerated in the early 1990s with the development of a substantial body of domestic law relating to the sea, supporting, or, as some would argue, apparently aiming to supplant, international law. This process, which began with the

February 1992, *Law of the Contiguous Zone and Contiguous Zones* is continuous. China's *Maritime Police Law* which came into effect in February 2021 attracted media attention because it authorised the use of force by the China Coast Guard. In fact, in itself this is not problematic; international law provides the world's other maritime law enforcement agencies with this right. Ambiguities in what is considered the 'proportionate' use of force, and its manner of use, might cause trouble though. This new law, if too zealously applied, could well exacerbate the already very troublesome issue of the exercise of their rights of freedom of navigation by other countries. Worse still, attempts to enforce Chinese domestic law in areas in the South and East China seas where Chinese sovereignty is in dispute with other countries and even considered illegal under the UN Convention of the Law of the Sea would violate international law and could trigger US defence obligations to Japan and the Philippines.[100] For all the possibly malign consequences of *The Maritime Police Law* as part of the 'three warfares approach' discussed earlier, China does at least set an example in demonstrating the importance of backing up its maritime policy with a supportive set of laws and regulations, which is frequently neglected elsewhere.

China has also developed institutions and administrative systems with the same effect, as shown by its creation of a municipality or 'administrative city' on Woody island in the Paracel islands to further its sovereignty claims in the area.

Monitoring and implementing much of this is the function of the China Coast Guard (CCG). Created as late as 2013, the CCG took on many of the functions and much of the authority of the 'five dragons' that, once, 'stirred up the sea,' namely the set of disputatious and uncoordinated maritime law enforcement agencies that preceded it.[101] Reporting to different ministries, the now defunct 'dragons' were an almost accidental consequence of strategic inattention until fairly recently. Their inefficiency was seen to make it more difficult for Beijing to maintain what it considered its sovereign rights in the South and East China seas and to maintain the good order necessary for the sustainable enjoyment of their resources. Vested interests (such as wage differentials between the agencies) made the rationalisation process neither quick nor easy. Its final stage was only completed, five years later, in 2018.[102]

The result was a coast guard force that is now very substantial indeed, both in the number of its vessels and often their individual size, inherent power and coercive behaviour. Numerically the world's biggest coast guard, the CCG employs some 40,000 people and operates a fleet variously estimated at between 600–1200 vessels, some of them very large indeed.[103] In 2016–2017, it commissioned three 10,000 and 12,000 ton 'cutters. 'Armed with 76 mm H/Pj 26 rapid fire naval guns, two auxiliary guns and two anti-aircraft guns, these vessels should certainly be able to handle the odd Vietnamese fishing boat. More to the point perhaps, they are over twice as big as anything other claimants to the features of the South China Sea have in either their navies or their coast guard agencies. Accordingly, with their smaller consorts, newly militarised local features and the often remarked coercive way in which they are increasingly being used, such powerful vessels help China shape the contest for sovereignty in these much disputed local waters. The greater range and endurance of the larger ships will also allow the CCG to contribute to the defence of China's maritime rights and interests and the maintenance of good order in distant seas.

Not the least significant of the 2018 wave of reforms was the fact that the CCG was put once more under the control of the People's Armed Police (PAP) which itself reports to the Party's Central Military Commission, chaired by President Xi. This move demonstrated how important the Chinese consider their offshore maritime interests to be, further reveals the extent of their whole-of-government approach but also indicates a worrying trend towards the militarisation of maritime security. In consequence, the CCG works very closely indeed with the navy and, below it with the Peoples' (Fishing) Militia. They operate in what is sometimes called a 'cabbage leaf' or 'onion-ring' formation of concentric layers of protection around disputed features with fishing boats/militia as the first layer, supported by the CCG as the second, and further out by the Navy. This was all demonstrated in the HYSY-981 oil-rig incident off Vietnam in 2014 and also appeared to show that the Navy was in overall charge of its conduct.[104] Their combined effectiveness in the South and East China Sea demonstrates that there is indeed power in unity, especially when you have a lot of everything.

14.7 Preparing the Navy's People

As was shown in Chapter 11, the Chinese navy's approach to the relative importance and training of its people largely echoed the experience of the world's other navies. However, one distinguishing characteristic over the past decade or so has been the energy devoted, with President Xi's active encouragement, to making training 'combat-realistic...able to fight and win battles.'[105] This reflected concern that, to judge by comments made by the staff at Beijing's National Defence University standards were 'not high as compared with that of the armies of the world's military powers.' The Chinese appear well aware, not least in the wake of the disastrous loss of Ming submarine No. 361 in 2003, which killed the whole 70 man crew, that their operational experience is far less than that of their main competitors and that this has consequences.[106] All such reflections justify substantial effort in the improvement of standards.

Accordingly, training exercises are bigger, more frequent and more ambitious in scope and much less 'scripted' than they used to be. Specifically they now often involve cooperation between elements of China's three fleets, are more joint and increasingly also include foreign forces. Typically, while China's marines are optimised for operations in the tropical conditions of the South China Sea, they now also learn to cope with the very different challenges of winter training at a base in inner Mongolia.[107]

Similar reforms have been aimed at the navy's professional military education system. The Navy has eight single service academies for initial training which include those specialising in ships, submarines or naval aviation. As elsewhere, efforts have been made to integrate their efforts better, make wider use of simulation, get university-level accreditation, and so forth.[108] Above all, the aim appears to be to get rid of the 'Five Cannots' or 'Incapables' discussed in Chapter 11. Instead, given the need to 'master joint operations under modern high-tech conditions,' officers and sailors needed 'keen political insight,' a 'deep strategic mind' and mastery of 'high-tech operational theories and compatible science and technology.'[109]

As always it is very difficult for outsiders (and probably for insiders too) to assess the comparative effectiveness of this training, short of war.[110] After the steep learning curve provided by the navy's participation in the international counter-piracy effort off Somalia, the Navy's operational performance now commands respect from others. Because the Navy now spends more time at sea, it can follow the Western emphasis on training at sea, rather than mainly ashore. Its personnel to-ship ratio now pretty much conforms to those standards as well. Unsurprisingly the professional quality of officers and ratings is going up.[111]

Anecdotal evidence also suggests higher levels of personal initiative and less constraint from the political officers. Thus even in 2011, when Admiral Gary Roughead, then US Chief of Naval Operations visited the Chinese fleet, he was impressed at the degree of change already evident.

> ... [M] early encounters with the PLAN... were obviously very controlled engagements and [with]... officers who had not been exposed to the normal visitation and give and take that we have. Then most recently ... being able to engage young officers who are truly operators, who would look at me and answer questions in English without looking at any one else.'[112]

Some even suggest that younger officers might be becoming rather too free thinking and independent, perhaps leading to gung-ho escalatory attitudes and actions in disputed waterways. This could be a conscious reaction to the perceived 'softness' and lack of 'wolf character' lamented by the likes of the author Jiang Rong in 2004 as a possible consequence of a delicate generation preciously raised under China's previous 'one child policy.'[113] Hence the abiding importance of the military's guidance by the Party.

14.8 Designing and Maintaining a Balanced Fleet

To meet the country's strategic objectives, China needs a balanced fleet capable of serving the five rough sets of missions noted earlier, namely,

- Safeguarding maritime rights and interests
- Active defence (including strategic nuclear deterrence)
- Far Seas Protection
- Maritime operations other than war
- Domestic support.

Chinese fleet designers, like those in any other navy, operate with finite resources and so cannot avoid the necessity of choice. They have to balance first the relative extent of their investment in these five mission areas (which means adopting some form of priority between them) and secondly between the various assets they each need. This last choice is complicated by the facts that resources are finite, that some capabilities essential for all missions are not centred on platforms (but instead on networking, cyber operations, etc) and that most platforms are useful for more than one mission area. Even nuclear ballistic missile firing submarines or long-distance supply ships may be of value for more than, respectively, the active defence/deterrence and far seas protection missions that most readily come to mind. Hospital ships, likewise, are not limited to their main current humanitarian assistance and disaster relief (HADR) role. They also have diplomatic value and would no doubt come in handy at times of conflict.

From the Chinese perspective, the 'protection of maritime rights and interests' in the East and South China seas requires a capacity to back up fishing boats, the Peoples Maritime Militia and the China Coast Guard and so requires naval forces with sufficient combat-credibility to see off well-armed interlopers if necessary. A strong Militia and China Coast Guard, of course, frees up the Navy for other missions.

Because these 'near seas' are so central to the defence of China's homeland, this task merges with the requirement for 'active defence,' namely the provision within the first and second island chains of concentric rings of sea denial/control capabilities that get denser the closer a potential aggressor approaches the Chinese coast. Land- and space-based air, missile and electronic warfare systems make up much of this battle system, but high-quality hi-tech surface units and conventionally powered submarines all capable of contesting sea are also necessary. Such no doubt underlie China's procurement of ships like the Luyang II/III)Type 52 C/D and the large Type 055 destroyers, the Type 054 A Jiangkai II guided missile frigate and the Type 056 Jiangdao-class corvette. The serial production of these ships testifies to their mature technology and general purpose utility. New Chinese ships follow the universal trend of being bigger, more capable and presumably more costly than their predecessors. At 1500 tons, for example, the Jiangdao class corvettes are much larger and better armed than the patrol boats they are replacing.

One of the most remarked features of recent Chinese naval development has been a strong emphasis on building up a new amphibious capability. Given the Chinese focus on Taiwan and the control of islands and other features in the South and East China Seas, the aspiration to create a large amphibious fleet and up to 100,000 marines seems hardly surprising, save for its scale and speed.[114] Ths fleet now includes the Type 071 Yuzhao class LPDs (Landing Platform Dock) and the Type 081 LHD (Landing Helicopter Dock) assault ships. The size of the force, its stationing at the Chinese naval base at Djibouti, and occasional deployments and exercises with other countries in the Mediterranean and Indian Ocean, however suggest it will have a major role in the 'Far Sea Protection' mission area as well.[115] Moreover, other navies have shown how useful amphibious warfare capabilities are for HADR.

Even more analytical attention has been paid to China's ambitious carrier programme. Given China's access to land bases, most analysts conclude that while carriers might be of residual use in the Active Defence mission area (perhaps threatening Taiwan from the East for example) their real function is likewise in Far Seas Protection and no doubt also for 'general purposes of greatness.'[116] Like amphibious warfare forces, carriers require escorting battle groups of frigates, destroyers, and supply ships (like the Type 901 large combat ship) especially when operating far from home. These operations put a special premium on the range provided by nuclear propelled attack submarines (SSN) such as the *Shang* class, operating either independently or in support of a carrier battle group. No doubt this explains their early appearance in the Indian ocean. However, SSNs would also be of use in the middle and outer rings of China's active defence.

Taken together such a fleet positively balanced for the Active Defence/Deterrence and Far Seas Protection mission areas would provide such a range of capabilities as to be more than sufficient for everything else that the Chinese navy might be called upon to do. Moreover, a Chinese MDIB capable of delivering the necessary platforms, weapons and sensors is also increasingly able to export its products abroad, providing yet another means by which China can seek to secure its strategic interests and thereby consolidate its maritime power.

The Chinese Navy with its 350 ships (and submarine) battleforce, which includes 130 major surface combatants is now generally recognised to be the world's largest, but this does not mean the world's most effective. China's own naval analysts are well aware that they have started from far behind, technologically and operationally, and are in the business of catching up. The smaller US Navy (currently at some 295 ships) retains a significant advantage in areas such as carrier operations, the quality of its SSNs and its ASW capabilities. Nonetheless the gap is narrower than it was and the Chinese have an impressive track record in making faster progress than outsiders have sometimes expected.[117] Though clearly not (yet) the most powerful, its appearance must give competitors serious cause for thought, which is, presumably, one of China's main objectives, given its perception of its place in the world.

But, finally, building a balanced fleet is one thing, operating and maintaining it over time is quite another. Assessing China's capacity to sustain its naval aspirations in the longer term is not easy.[118] For the time being this must remain a real challenge for China, given its limited bank of overseas bases and of constructional and operational experience, especially when compared to that of its possible adversaries. The varied nature of its fleet poses something of a problem in terms of spare parts and refits.[119] Having built so many ships so fast, means it will face a 'block obsolescence' problem in the future, perhaps at a time when its demographic, societal and environmental challenges have become more serious, as some predict.

14.9 Conclusion

The fact that so many parallels can be drawn between the apparently totally different situations of England in the late 17th and early 18th Centuries and China in the late 20th and early 21st Centuries suggests first that there are indeed some valid and recurring patterns in the development and maintenance of maritime power, and secondly that for all its self-perceived 'exceptionalism' and unique geographic and other circumstances, China appears to be broadly taking the same course as many other navies have done in the past and are doing now.

In particular, the Chinese do seem to illustrate the advantages of regarding the Navy, in Admiral Tim Barrett's terms as a 'national enterprise.' The Admiral defined this as a two-way street of mutual trust and support between the navy and the nation. '[T]he Navy is an intrinsic national capability,' he said,

> intimately connected to the social, economic, industrial and educational drivers of national well-being. The modern Navy has to be a national enterprise, bringing together the private and public sectors of the economy to deliver a fundamental national objective – security above, on and under the sea.[120]

To do this sustainably, though, the navy cannot simply be a consumer of the nation's financial, human and industrial resources, it needs to be a partner too. Indirectly its success in its defence mission will facilitate the continued growth of those resources by helping provide the international context in which they can flourish. More immediately and directly the Navy should contribute to those national resources. A continuous building programme and its associated demand for high-tech manufacturing skills will support the development of a sophisticated defence industrial base, whose qualities will spill over into the civilian economy and wider society. In partnership with the national education sector, it will develop its own people and eventually release them to the benefit of wider society. 'We take recruits,' said the Admiral, 'and turn them into leaders – leaders who enrich both the Navy and the community at large.'

Provided they are properly recognised, these two-way linkages should help secure support from government and society and strengthen the bond between the people and their navy. By sustaining them, '… the Navy serves as custodian of our national values and national identity.'[121] This is undoubtedly a high-minded, even idealistic conception of the navy as a national enterprise. All the same, alongside the provision of effective military force capable of defending a country's strategic interests at and from the sea, the ability to sustain this kind of vision of a navy is an important indicator of how well, and how sustainably, that country has been in developing its maritime power. Indeed, in the long run, it may be the one that really matters.

Of course, Admiral Barrett's book, and perhaps this one too, gives the impression that developing maritime power is simply a calm, logical, clear-sighted top-down process, coolly linking ends, ways and means. All too often though, it is instead a process of 'muddling through' and of lurching from one crisis to another under the pressure of events. It is hard to avoid the conclusion, though, that the more it seems like the first and the less like the second, the more successful it is likely to be.

How successful the Chinese will ultimately be in their bid to become a first class maritime power will therefore in part depend on the international context at their time, on the strength of the economy, on how China's relationship with the sea has developed in the meantime and perhaps above all, on the nature of the regime and its capacity to deal with the many demographic, social, economic and environmental challenges coming the country's way in the rest of the 21st century.

Whether the Chinese will achieve success to the extent of Henry Maydman's England remains to be seen. But whatever the result, China has shown itself to be well aware of the need to consult its own experience and that of other countries, in order to identify the pitfalls as well as the opportunities in developing its maritime power and growing its Navy that await. Given the validity of such patterns, the present and future importance of China and the fact that in the words of Senior Captains Yan Yiouqiang and Cheng Rongxing back in 1997, 'the 21st century is going to be a maritime one,'[122] other countries would seem to need to plot their own maritime courses accordingly.

Notes

1 Swanson, Bruce, *The Eighth Voyage of the Dragon: A History of China's Quest for Seapower* (Annapolis: Naval Institute Press, 1982). The Imjin war with Japan over Korea in the late 16th century was one of several early exceptions. See Swope, *A Dragon's Head*.
2 The title of an influential 2010 book by Air Force Colonel Dai Xu, discussed in Kirchberger, *Assessing China's Naval Power*, 40–5.
3 Hu, *Chinese Maritime Power*, 6, 13, 17, 47–60; Yoshihara, Toshi and Holmes James R., *Red Star over the Pacific: China's Rise and the Challenge to U.S. Maritime Strategy* (Annapolis, MD: Naval Institute Press, 2018), 83–7.
4 Peter Dutton has shown how strongly influenced by geo-political thinking influential Chinese academics/officials were from the 19th Century onwards. Li Hongzhou and Xu Jiyu were amongst the advocates of seapower. See his 'Securing the Seas: China's Quest for Maritime Security Through International Law of the Sea,' PhD Thesis King's College London, 2021. Harvard University Press, forthcoming.
5 Swanson, *The Eighth Voyage*; Horner, Charles, *Rising China and Its Postmodern Fate: Memories of Empire in a New Global Context* (Athens: University of Georgia Press, 2009), 74–5.
6 Hao Zhou, 'China to Run Pakistani Port,' *Global Times,* 1 February 2013. This article quoted Lin Boqiang, a prominent Chinese academic in saying that one reason for the switch from a Singaporean to a Chinese port operator was that the latter would be better

able to develop its strategic rather than merely commercial potential motivations, though, both are doubtless in play. The varying reasons for the development of Gwadar and Djibouti are explored in Peter A. Dutton, Conor M. Kennedy and Isaac B. Kardon in the China Maritime Studies Institute Maritime Reports no 6 and 7, April 2020. See also Helmoed-Romer Heitman, 'China and Namibia reportedly discuss naval support base,' *Janes Defence Review,* 26 November 2014.

7 Hu, *Chinese Maritime Power,* 230; also 18, 31, 146, 226–35.

8 Huang Weijiya, 'Arrival of the Ocean people,' *China Daily,* 19–25 September 2014.

9 Levathes, Louise, *When China Ruled the Seas* (Oxford: Oxford University Press, 1994).

10 Jung Chang, *Empress Dowager Cixi: The Concubine who Changed* China (London: Vintage Books, 2013).

11 David Shambaugh, 'The Coming Chinese Crack-Up,' *Wall Street Journal,* 9 March 2015; Lily Kuo, '"He Killed the Party and the Country" – Insider Attacks China's Xi,' *The Guardian,* 19 August 2020.

12 Gresh, for example, suggests autocracy makes long-term planning easier. Gresh, *To Rule Eurasia's Waves,* 131, 161.

13 Dargnat, Christian, 'China's Shifting Geo-economic Strategy,' *Survival,* Vol. 58, No. 3 (June–July 2016), 63–76.

14 Hu, *Chinese Maritime Power,* suggests a share of 30%, 260.

15 Ibid, 25.

16 Zhang Honzhou, 'China's Food Security: Sourcing from the Seas,' *RSIS Commentary,* 2012, 213.

17 Yoshihara and Holmes, *Red Star Over the Pacific,* 52–61; UNCTAD Review of Maritime Transport, 2020, Figures 1:11; (Hellenic) *International Shipping News,* 13 September 2018.

18 Hu, *Chinese Maritime Power,* 37–44.

19 Horner, *Rising China,* 68–9.

20 See SIPRI Military Expenditure Data Base available at http://www.sipri.org/research/armaments,milex/milex_database. China claims its spending is currently 1.3% of GDP. Guo Yuandra, 'China's Defence Budget Stays Moderate and Restrained: NPC Spokesperson,' *Global Times,* 22 May 2020.

21 Lingling Wei, 'Xi Ramps Up Control of China's Private Sector,' *Wall Street Journal,* 10 December 2020.

22 Naughton, Barry, *Fateful Decisions: Choices That Will Shape China's Future* (Stanford, CA: Stanford University Press, 2020).

23 Levathes, *When China Ruled the Waves*; Ball, *The Water Kingdom,* Chapter 5.

24 The difficulty is revealed in the ambiguities that emerge in the conclusions of the classic text Cole, Bernard D., *The Great Wall at Sea: China's Navy in the Twenty-First Century,* 2nd ed. (Annapolis, MD: Naval Institute Press, 2010), 89–90, 201–2.

25 Yoshihara and Holmes, *Red Star Over the Pacific,* 100–118, makes the contemporary impulse very clear.

26 Xi Jinping, 'We Must Advance Our concern for Understanding of and Strategic Management of the Ocean' 31 July 2013, quoted in Yoshihara and Holmes, *Red Star Over the Pacific,* op cit, 118.

27 Bickford, Thomas J., *Haiyang Qiangguo: China as A Maritime Power* (Washington: Center for Naval Analyses, March 2016).

28 Liu Cigui, (then Director of the State Oceanic Administration) 'Striving to Realise the Historic Leap From Being a Great Maritime Country to Being a Great Maritime Power,' *Jingji Ribao,* online November 2020. Quoted in Bickford, *Haiyang Qiangguo,* op cit.

29 *The Science of Military Strategy* (Beijing: Military Strategy Research Department of the Academy of Military Science, 2013), 209. In effect this institution is the Central Military Commission's main think-tank. See also Fravel, M. Taylor, 'China's Changing Approach to Military Strategy: The Science of Military Strategy From 2001 to 2013,' Massachusetts Institute of Technology: Political Science Department, Research Report No 2016–15, April 2016.

30 Wu Shengli quoted in Rhodes, Andrew, 'Same Waters: Different Dreams: Salient Lessons of the Sino-Japanese War for Future Naval Warfare,' *Journal of Advanced Military Studies,* Vol. 11, No. 2 (Fall 2020). The article emphasises the resurgence of interest in this war, which included a mass-market film.

31 See Chapters 3 and 4, above.
32 Lai-Ha Chan, 'China's Vision of Global Governance: A New World Order in the Making or Old Wine in a New Bottle?,' Conference paper, RSIS Conference on 'China's Role in global and Regional Governance,' March 2011 is an excellent concise introduction. Kirchberger, *Assessing China's Naval Power* provides a balanced overview.
33 Cole, *The Great Wall at Sea,* op cit, lays this out very clearly from 1949, 7–18.
34 Lanxin Xiang, 'Xi's Dream and China's Future,' *Survival,* Vol. 58, No. 3 (June–July 2016), 53–62. The push for rejuvenation can be seen in the 19th-century 'Self-Strengthening Movement' and the writings of Liang Qichao (1873–1929).
35 Liu Ming Fu, *China Dream: The Great Power Thinking and Strategic Positioning of China in the Post-American Age* (Beijing: Zhongguo, 2010).
36 Zheng Bijian, 'China's "Peaceful Rise" to Great Power,' *Foreign Affairs,* September/October 2005.
37 Cited in Kirchberger, *Assessing China's Naval Power*, 20.
38 Murray, Michelle, 'Identity, Insecurity and Great Power Politics: The Tragedy of German Naval Ambition before the First World War,' *Security Studies,* Vol. 19, No. 4 (2010).
39 Linda Jakobson, *China's Unpredictable Maritime Security Actors,* Lowy Institute Report, December 2014.
40 Quoted in James Holmes, *China's Maritime Strategy Is More than Naval Strategy,* Jamestown Foundation China Brief, 8 April 2011.
41 Linda Jakobson and Rory Medcalf, 'The perception gap: Reading China's Maritime Strategic Objectives in Indo-Pacific Asia,' Lowy Institute Report, June 2015.
42 Quoted in Peh Shing Huei, 'Hu Defends Track Record, Calls for War on Graft,' *Straits Times,* 9 November 2012.
43 See Chapters 5 and 6.
44 Maydman, *Naval Speculations,* 267.
45 McCaslin, Ian Burns and Erickson, Andrew S., 'The Impact of Xi-Era Reforms on the Chinese Navy,' in Saunders et al. (Eds), *Chairman Xi Remakes the PLA,* 127. See also Chapters 13 and 14.
46 Hu, *Chinese Maritime Power*, 246.
47 Wojtek M. Wolfe and Brock F. Tessman, 'China's Global Equity Oil Investments: Economic and Geopolitical Influences,' *Journal of Strategic Studies,* Vol. 15, No. 2 (April 2012), 175–96.
48 Cole, *The Great Wall at Sea,* 10–13.
49 Saunders, Phillip C. and Wuthnow, Joel, 'China's Goldwater-Nichols? Assessing PLA Organizational Reforms,' *Strategic Forum* (Washington: National Defense University, April 2016); Saunders, Phillip C., et al., *Chairman Xi Remakes the PLA* (Washington: National Defense University, 2019). The new 'Strategic Support Force' has been set up to integrate these new domains.
50 McCaslin, Ian Burns and Erickson, Andrew S., 'The Impact of Xi-Era Reforms on the Chinese Navy' in Saunders,' *Chairman Xi Remakes the PLA,* 143.
51 Lewis, John Wilson and Litae, Xue, *China's Strategic Seapower: The Politics of Force Modernisation in the Nuclear Age* (Stanford: Stanford University Press, 1994).
52 Muller, *China as a Maritime Power,* 53, 61, 89–91, 174.
53 McCaslin and Erickson, 'The impact of Xi-Era Reforms,' 129–52.
54 Quiao Liang and Wang Xiangsui, *Unrestricted Warfare* (Beijing: literature and Arts Publishing House, 1999).
55 Sangkuk Lee, 'China's 'Three Warfares': Origins, Applications, and Organizations,' *Journal of Strategic Studies,* Vol. 37 (2014), 198–221.
56 Holmes, James R. and Yoshihara, Toshi, *Chinese Naval Strategy in the 21st Century: The Turn to Mahan* (London: Routledge, 2008).
57 See Chapters 7–13.
58 An admirably concise account of this process may be found in Erickson, Andrew S., 'China's Naval Modernization, Strategies and Capabilities,' in Bekkevold, Jo Inge and Till, Geoffrey (Eds), *International Order at Sea: How It Is Challenged, How It Is Maintained* (London: Palgrave, Macmillan, 2016), 63–92. Also, Cole, *The Great Wall,* 174–8 and Yoshihara and Holmes, *Red Star,* 111–18, 133–40.

59 Rhodes, Andrew, 'The 1988 Blues – Admirals, Activists and the Development of the Chinese Maritime Identity,' US *Naval War College Review*, Vol. 74, No. 2 (Spring 2021).

60 Wang, Irene, 'Propaganda takes back seat in Feted CCTV Series,' *South China Morning Post*, 27 November 2006, referenced in Erickson, 'China Naval Modernization.'

61 Paine, S.C.M., *The Sino-Japanese War 1894–5: Perceptions, Pride and Primacy* (New York: Cambridge University Press, 2003); Rhodes, Andrew, 'Same Waters, Different Dreams,' *Journal of Advanced Military Studies*, Vol. II, No. 2 (Fall 2020).

62 Mark Leonard, *What Does China Think?* (London: Fourth Estate, 2008), 84 quoted in Kirchberger, *Assessing China's Naval Power*, 22.

63 These issues are explored in Murray, Michelle, 'Identity, Insecurity and Great Power Politics: The Tragedy of German Naval Ambition before the First World War,' *Security Studies*, Vol. 19, No. 4 (2010) and Xu Qiyu, *Fragile Rise* (Cambridge, MA: MIT Press, 2016).

64 State Council Information Office of the People's Republic of China, *China's Military Strategy*, May 2015. http://eng.mod.gov.cn/Database/WhitePapers/index.htm. For the earlier period, Muller, *China as a Maritime Power*, 218–31.

65 Hu, *Chinese Military Power*, 77–8.

66 State Council Information Office of the People's Republic of China, Defense White Paper, December 2004. http://english.people.com.cn/whitepaper/defense2004

67 McKenzie, Peter W. and Easton, Ian M., *Chinese Views of the Air Sea Battle Concept: A Preliminary Assessment* (Washington: Center for Naval Analyses, Maritime Asia Project, 2012).

68 Bhaskar, Cdre C. Uday, 'Strategic Sustainment? China's Ships, Silk Roads and Indian Ocean Presence,' *Jane's Navy International*, December 2014; Hu, *Chinese Military Power*, 23, 25; Cole, *The Great Wall*, 199; Yoshihara and Holmes, *Red Star*, 7–8.

69 Saunders Philip C. and Wuthnow, Joel, 'Conclusion: Assessing Chinese Military Reforms,' in Saunders et al. (Eds), *Chairman Xi Remakes the PLA*, op cit, 723–5.

70 Hu, *Chinese Military Power*, op cit, 33–7, 53, 74–7.

71 *The Science of Military Strategy*, op cit, 217–8.

72 Scobell, Andrew, et al. (Eds), *The People's Liberation Army and Contigency Planning in China* (Washington: National Defense University, 2015) is a useful reminder of how seriously China takes this task.

73 Scobell, Andrew and Beauchamp Mustafaga, Nathan, 'The Flag Lags but Follows,' in Saunders (Ed), *Chairman Xi Remakes the PLA*, 178; Hu, *Chinese Maritime Power*, 3, 258–9.

74 State Council Information Office of the People's Republic of China, *China's Military Strategy*, May 2015. http://eng.mod.gov.cn/Database/WhitePapers/index.htm.

75 Leigh-Anne Luce and Erin Richter, 'Handling Logistics in a Reformed PLA,' in Saunders et al. (Eds), *Chairman Xi Remakes the PLA*, op cit, 269–71.

76 Zhang Yunzhuang, 'China's Military Procurement and its Operational Implications,' *Journal of Strategic Studies*, Vol. 35, No. 6 (December 2012), 887–96.

77 Erickson, 'China's Naval Modernization,' op cit.

78 Jon Grevatt, 'China looks to reform its defence-industrial base,' *Jane's Defence Weekly*, 17 June 2015.

79 'Chinese shipyard launches first large floating work dock,' *Global Times*, 19 May 2020; Liu Xuanzun, 'China's Top Warship Maker Builds New Shipyard, Phase 1 Project to Complete by 2023,' *Global Times*, 5 January 2021.

80 Alex Stone and Peter W. Singer, 'China's Military-Civil Fusion Strategy: What to Expect in the Next Five Years,' *Defence One*, 18 February 2021.

81 Wendell Minnick, 'China's 10 Killer Weapons,' *Defence News*, 9 April 2012.

82 Andrew Tate, 'China testing intercontinental HGC, says USNORTHCOM commander,' *Janes Defence Weekly*, 26 February 2020.

83 Kirchberger, *Assessing Chinese Naval Power*, 193–4.

84 Ibid, 237; Cole, *The Great Wall*, 132.

85 Kirchberger, *Assessing Chinese Naval Power*, 78.

86 Reuben F. Johnson, 'Chinese Defence Electronics Firms 'Closing the Gap' on Competition,' *Jane's Defence Weekly*, 13 May 2014. At the time much the same could be said for the supply of unmanned vehicles. Wendell Minnick, 'Chinese UAV Development Challenging Western nations,' *Defence News*, 29 April 2013.

87 Kerry Herschelmann, 'Analysis: Parade Reflects China's New Sense of Place in the World,' *Jane's Defence Weekly,* 9 September 2015. In the parade of this year, the DF-10, DF 21-D and DF 26 anti ship ballistic missiles made their first appearance.

88 Kirchberger, *Assessing Chinese Naval Power*, 164.

89 J. Michael Cole, 'China' Developing EMALS-Type System,' *Jane's Defence Weekly,* 6 May 2012.

90 Compare David Axe, 'China Goes Nuclear for Carrier No 3,' *Warships?,* August 2019 and his 'China's Plan for 6 Aircraft Carriers just "Sank",' *The National Interest,* 9 December 2019.

91 Michael Raska, 'China's Military Aviation Industry: In Search of Innovation,' in Tai Ming Cheung (Ed), *The Chinese Defense Economy Policy Briefs: Sector-by-Sector Assessments and the Role of Military End Users,* (San Diego: Institute on Global Conflict and Cooperation, 2013).

92 Kirchberger, *Assessing Chinese Naval Power,* 164; US Defense Department, *Military and Security Developments Involving the People's Republic of China* (Washington DC: Department of Defense, 1 September 2020); Kania Elsa B. and Laskai, Lorand, *Myths and Realities in China's Military-Civil Fusion Strategy* (Washington: CNAS, 28 January 2021); CSIS: China Power Report, *How Developed Is China's Arms Industry?* (Washington DC: CSIS, February 2021).

93 Robert Karniol, 'Thorny Issues Dogging China's Submarine Strategy,' *The Straits Times,* 4 June 2012; Andrew Tate, 'China may be struggling to build up sea-based nuclear deterrent,' *Jane's Defence Weekly,* 2 June 2016.

94 Gresh, *To Rule Eurasia's Waves,* 11.

95 Gady, Franz-Stefan, 'China Prepares Its 172,000 Civilian Ships for War,' *The Diplomat,* 23 June 2015.

96 Hu, *China's Maritime Power,* 10–11.

97 Cole, *The Great Wall,* 52–3.

98 Reuters, 'China Trains 'fishing Militia' to Sail into Disputed Waters,' *Gulf Times,* 2 May 2016.

99 Ryan Martinson, 'Early Warning Brief Introducing the 'New, New' China Coast Guard,' *China Brief,* 25 January 2021.

100 Raul (Pete) Pedrozo, 'Maritime Police Law and the Peoples' Republic of China,' *International Law Studies,* Vol. 97 (February 2021).

101 Lyle J. Goldstein, *Five Dragons Stirring Up the Sea: Challenge and Opportunity in China's Improving Maritime Law Enforcement Capabilities* (Newport RI: CMSI Red Book 5, 2010); Cole, *Great Wall,* 78–82.

102 Anguang Zheng, 'Integrating the China Coast Guard with the PLA Navy,' in Bowers, Ian and Koh, Swee Lean Collin (Eds), *Grey and While Hulls: An International Analysis of the Navy-Coastguard Nexus* (Singapore: Palgrave Macmillan, 2019).

103 Compare Zheng, 'Integrating the China Coast Guard,' 27–9 with Takuya Shimodaira, 'The JMSDF and JCG: Towards Cooperation and Contribution,' in Bowers and Koh (Eds), *Grey and White Hulls,* 39–41.

104 McCaslin and Erickson, 'Xi-era Reforms and the Chinese Navy,' 149; Yoshihara and Holmes, *Red Star over the Pacific,* 169–83.

105 Blasko, Dennis J., 'Going Through the Motions,' *Jane's Defence Weekly,* 9 October 2013.

106 Cole, *The Great Wall,* 196.

107 Herschelman, Kerry, 'Chinese marines get a taste of cold weather training,' *Jane's Defence Weekly,* 19 March 2014.

108 Erickson, *China's Naval Modernisation.*

109 Mark R. Cozad, 'Toward a Joint more Combat-ready PLA?' in Saunders et al. (Eds), *Chairman Xi Remakes the PLA,* op cit, 218. Also David M. Finkelstein, 'Breaking the Paradigm,' in ibid, 59, 76.

110 Cole, *The Great Wall,* 210.

111 Ibid, 130, 118, 123; Muller, *China as a Maritime Power,* 89–91.

112 Admiral Gary Roughead, Interview with *Financial Times,* 18 January 2011.

113 Kirchberger, *Assessing China's Naval Power,* 241.

114 Gabriel Dominguez, 'China planning to vastly expand size of marine corps,' *Jane's Defence Weekly,* 1 March 2017.
115 Newsham, Grant and Koh Swee Lean Collin, 'Can China Copy the US Marine Corps?' *The National Interest,* January 2016.
116 Richard D. Fisher, 'Chinese Media Acclaim Liaoning's Growing Combat Capability' *Jane's Defence Weekly,* 19 August 2016.
117 Office of the Secretary of Defense, Annual Report to Congress, Military and Security Developments Involving the Peoples Republic of China 2020.
118 Rick Joe, 'Hints of Chinese Naval Ambitions in the 2020s,' *The Diplomat on Line,* 24 December 2020; Christopher P. Carlson, 'China Maritime Report No 10; PLAN Force Structure Projection Concept: A Methodology for Looking Down Range,' *CMSI China Maritime Reports,* 2020, 10. https://digital-commons.usnwc.edu/cmsi-maritime-reports/10
119 Cole, *The Great Wall at Sea,* op cit, 68, 197.
120 Barrett, Vice Admiral Tim, *The Navy and the Nation: Australia's Maritime Power in the 21st Century* (Melbourne; Melbourne University Press, 2017), 1–2, 57.
121 Barrett, *The Navy and the Nation,* op cit, 74.
122 Quoted, Cole, *The Great Wall,* 184.

Selected Bibliography

Official

Dhowan, R.K., Admiral (approving authority); Chief of Naval Staff, "Ensuring Secure Seas: Indian Maritime Security Strategy, Indian Navy: National Security Publication (NSP 12), *Ministry of Defence*, 10 October 2015.

Dunford, Joseph F. General, US Marine Corps, Commandant of the Marine Corps, Greenert, Jonathan W., Admiral, Chief of Naval Operations, Zukunft, Paul F. Admiral US Coast Guard, Commandant of the US Coast Guard, *A Cooperative Strategy for 21st Century Seapower: Forward, Engaged Ready*, March 2015.

European Union Maritime Security Strategy (Brussels, 24 June 2014). Available at https://data.consilium.europa.eu/doc/document/ST%2011205%202014%20INIT/EN/pdf

Fundamentals of Maritime Operations: Netherlands Maritime Military Doctrine (The Hague: Defence Staff, 2014).

National Ocean Strategy 2013–2020 (Lisbon: Directorate General of the Sea, 2013). Available at https://www.msp-platform.eu/practices/national-ocean-strategy-2013-2020

Netherlands Defence Doctrine (Den Haag: Defensie Staf, 2005).

Politica Nacional de Oceano y de los Espacios Costeros (Bogota: Colombian Ocean Commission, 2013).

'Russian Federation Marine Doctrine' Press Release, Office of the President of the Russian Federation, 26 July 2015 on amendments to the 2001 Doctrine.

US Defense Department, *Military and Security Developments Involving the People's Republic of China* (Washington DC: Department of Defense, 1 September 2020).

Wijegunaratne, Vice Admiral R.C., *Sri Lanka Navy's Maritime Strategy 2025* (Colombo, 2016).

Books, Chapters and Articles

Abulafia, David, *The Great Sea: A Human History of the Mediterranean* (Oxford: University Press, 2011).

Abulafia, David, *The Boundless Sea: A Human History of the Oceans* (Oxford: Oxford University Press, 2019).

Allen, Kenneth and Clemens, Morgan, *The Recruitment, Education and Training of PLA Navy Personnel* (US Naval War College: China Maritime Studies No. 12, 2014).

Andrade, Tonio, *Lost Colony: The Untold Story of China's First Great Victory over the West* (Princeton: Princeton University Press, 2011).

Aselius, Gunnar, *The Rise and Fall of the Soviet Navy in the Baltic, 1921–1941* (London: Frank Cass, 2005).

Ball, Philip, *The Water Kingdom: The Secret History of China* (London: The Bodley Head, 2016).

Barlow Jeffrey, G., *The Revolt of the Admirals: The Fight for Naval Aviation 1945–1950* (Washington: Naval Historical Center, 1994).

Barnett, Correlli, *Engage the Enemy More Closely* (London: Penguin, 1991).

Barrett, Vice Admiral Tim, *The Navy and the Nation: Australia's Maritime Power in the 21st Century* (Melbourne: Melbourne University Press, 2017).

Bartlett, W.B., *Vikings: A History of the Northmen* (Stroud, Gloucs: Amberley, 2019).

Baugh, Daniel A. (Ed.), *Naval Administration 1715-1750* (London: Navy Records Society, 1977).

Baxter, Stephen B., *William III and the Defense of European Liberty 1650–1702* (New York: Harcourt, Brace & World, 1966).

Bekkevold, Jo Inge and Till, Geoffrey (Eds), *International Order at Sea: How it is Challenged, How it is Maintained* (London: Palgrave Macmillan, 2016).

Benton, Lauren and Perl-Rosenthal, Nathan, *A World at Sea: Maritime Practices and Global History* (Philadelphia: University of Pennsylvaniia Press, 2020).

Black, Jeremy, *Rethinking Military History* (London: Rowan and Littlefield, 2004).

Black, Jeremy, *Naval Warfare: A Global History Since 1860* (Lanham: Roman and Littlefield, 2017).

Blake, Robert, *Disraeli* (New York: St Martin's Press, 1967).

Bland, Douglas, *The Administration of Defence Policy in Canada 1947-85* (Kingston: Ronald P. Frye, 1987).

Boutilier, James A., 'Get Big or Get Out: The Canadian and Australian Decisions to Abandon Aircraft Carriers' in Frame (Ed), *Reflections on the Royal Australian Navy*.

Boutilier, James A., *RCN in Retrospect 1910-1968* (Vancouver: University of British Columbia Press, 1982).

Boyd, Andrew, *The Royal Navy in Eastern Waters: Lynchpin of Victory, 1935-1942* (Barnsley: Seaforth Publishing, 2017).

Bowers, Ian and Koh, Swee Lean Collin (Eds), *Grey and White Hulls: An International Analysis of the Navy-Coastguard Nexus* (London: Palgrave, 2019).

Bratton, Patrick, 'Pannikar, Geography and Sea Power' in Vijay Sakhuja and Pragya Pandey (Eds), *K.M. Pannikar and the Growth of a Maritime Consciousness in India* (Delhi: IWCA, forthcoming).

Brown, Cecil, *Suez to Singapore* (New York: Random House, 1942).

Buger, Christian and Chan, Jane (Eds), *Paving the Way for Regional Maritime Domain Awareness* (Singapore: RSIS, 2019).

Byers, R.B., 'Canada and Maritime Defence: Past Problems, Future Challenges' in Douglas (Ed.), *RCN in Transition*.

Chang, Jung, *Empress Dowager Cixi: The Concubine Who Changed China* (London: Vintage Books, 2013).

Childs, Nick, *The Age of Invincible* (Barnsley: Pen and Sword, 2009).

Churchill, Winston S., *The Second World War: Vol III, The Grand Alliance* (Boston: Houghton, Mifflin Company, 1950).

Churchill, Winston S., *The Second World War: Vol IV, The Hinge of Fate* (Boston: Houghton, Mifflin Company, 1950).

Churchill, Winston S., *History of the English-Speaking Peoples. Vol III, The Age of Revolution* (New York: Dodd, Mead & Company, 1957).

Clulow, Adam, *The Company. The Dutch Encounter with Tokugawa Japan* (New York: Columbia University Press, 2013).

Coffey Thomas M., *HAP: The Story of the US Air Force and the Man Who Built It* (New York: The Viking Press, 1982).

Cole, Bernard D., *The Great Wall at Sea: China's Navy in the Twenty-First Century*, 2nd ed. (Annapolis, MD: Naval Institute Press, 2010).

Cole, Bernard D., *Asian Maritime Strategies: Navigating Troubled Waters* (Annapolis, MD: Naval Institute Press, 2013).

Colombage, Jayanath, *Asymmetric Warfare at Sea: The Case of Sri Lanka* (Saarbrucken, Germany: Lambert Academic Publishing, 2015).

Corbett, Sir Julian, *Some Principles of Maritime Strategy*, 2nd ed. (London: Longmans, Green, 1911) – reprinted with introduction by Eric Grove (Annapolis: Naval Institute Press, 1988).

Cordesman, Anthony H. and Wagner, Abraham E., *The Lessons of Modern War: The Gulf War* (Boulder: Westview Press, 1996).

Cormack, William S., *Revolution and Political Conflict in the French Navy 1789-1794* (Cambridge: University Press, 2002).

Crook, Malcolm, *Toulon in War and Revolution* (Manchester: Manchester University Press, 1991).

Cubitt, David, *Lord Cochrane and the Chilean Navy 1818-23* (Santiago, Chile: Museo Maritimo Nacional, 2018).

de Custine, the Marquis, *Empire of the Czar: A Journey through Eternal Russia* (New York: Doubleday, 1971).

Dor-Ner, Zvi, *Columbus and the Age of Discovery* (New York: William Morrow & Co, 2103).

Douglas, W.A.B., Sarty, Roger and Whitby, Michael, *No Higher Purpose* (St Catherine's, ONT: Vanwell Publishing Ltd., 2002).

Douglas, W.A.B., *The RCN in Transition, 1910-1985* (Vancouver: University of British Columbia, 1988).

Duarte, Erico and Barros, Correira de, *Manuel Navies and Maritime Policies in the South Atlantic* (London, Palgrave, 2019).

Dye, Peter, *The Man Who Took the Rap: Sir Robert Brooke-Popham and the Fall of Singapore* (Annapolis, MD: Naval Institute Press, 2018).

Ehrman, John, *The Navy in the War of William III, 1689-1697* (Cambridge: Cambridge University Press, 1963).

Erickson, Andrew S., Goldstein, Lyle J. and Lord, Carnes, *China Goes to Sea: Maritime Transformation in Comparative Historical Perspective* (Annapolis: Naval Institute Press, 2009).

Falconer, A.F., *Shakespeare and the Sea* (London: Constable, 1964).

Farrell, Brian P., *The Defence and Fall of Singapore* (Stroud, Glouc: Tempus, 2005).

Ferguson, Robert, *The Hammer and the Cross: A New History of the Vikings* (London: Penguin, 2010).

Forbes, Andre (Ed.), *The Naval Contribution to National Security and Prosperity* (Canberra: Sea Power Centre, 2013).

Frame, T.R., Goldrick, J.V.P. and Jones, P.D., *Reflections on the Royal Australian Navy* (Kenthurst, NSW: Kangaroo Press, 1991).

Frankopan, Peter, *The New Silk Roads: The Present and Future of the World* (London: Bloomsbury, 2018).

Friedberg, Aaron L., 'Globalisation and Chinese Grand Strategy', *Survival*, Vol 60, 2018, 7–40.

Friel, Ian, *Henry V's Navy: The Sea-road to Agincourt and Conquest 1413–22* (Stroud: The History Press, 2015).

Gilbert, Gregory P., *Australian Naval Personalities* (Canberra: Sea Power Centre, Papers in Australian Maritime Affairs, No. 17, 2006).

Gilbert, Gregory P., *Ancient Egyptian Sea Power and the Origin of Maritime Forces* (Canberra: Sea Power Centre, 2008).

Gilbert, Gregory P. and Michelle, Jellett (Eds), *Australian Maritime Issues, 2009* (Canberra: Sea Power Centre, Papers in Australian Maritime Affairs, No. 32, 2010).

Gilbert, Gregory P. and Nick, Stewart, *Australian Maritime Issues 2008* (Canberra: Sea Power Centre, Papers in Australian Maritime Affairs, 2008, 2009).

Glendinning, Victoria, *Raffles and the Golden Opportunity* (London: Profile books, 2018).

Goldrick, James, 'Carriers for the Commonwealth' in Frame (Ed.), *Reflections on the Royal Australian Navy*.

Goldrick, James, *No Easy Answers* (New Delhi: Lancer Publishers, 1997).

Goldrick, James and Haines, Steven (Eds), *Maritime Strategy for Medium Powers in the 21st Century* (Woodbridge, Suffolk UK: Boydell & Brewer, forthcoming).

Goodman, David, *Spanish Naval Power, 1589-1665: Reconstruction and Defeat* (Cambridge: Cambridge University Press, 2002).

Gordon, Andrew, *The Rules of the Game; Jutland and British Naval Command* (Annapolis, MA: US Naval Institute, 2012).

Gorshkov, Admiral Sergei, *The Seapower of the State* (London: Brasseys, 1979).

Graham, Gerald S., *The Politics of Naval Supremacy* (Cambridge: Cambridge University Press, 1965).

Gray, Colin, *The Leverage of Sea Power* (New York: The Free Press, 1992).

Gray, Colin S., *The Navy in the Post-Cold War World: The Uses and Value of Strategic Sea Power* (University Park, PA: University of Pennsylvania Press, 1994).

Gresh, Geoffrey F., *To Rule Eurasia's Waves: The New Great Power Competition at Sea* (New Haven: Yale University Press, 2020).

Griffiths, Ann and Lerhe, Eric (Eds), *Naval Gazing: The Canadian Navy Contemplates Its Future* (Halifax: Dalhousie University Press, 2010).

Guan, Kwa Chong, 'East India Companies in the Long Cycles of Asian Maritime Trade' in Stephanie Yeo (Ed.), *Encounters and Connected Histories, The East Indies and Singapore before 1819* (Singapore: National Museum of Singapore, 2020).

Guan, Kwa Chong, Heng, Derek, Borschberg, Peter and Yong, Tan Tai, *Seven Hundred Years: A History of Singapore* (Singapore: Marshall Cavendish, 2019).

Guttridge Leonard, F., *Mutiny: A History of Naval Insurrection* (New York: Berkeley Books, 1992).

Haas, J.M., *A Management Odyssey; The Royal Dockyards 1714-1914* (Lanham, MD: University Press of America, 1994).

Hadley, Michael, 'The Impact of Public Policy on a Naval Reserve Division' in Boutilier (Ed.), *RCN in Retrospect*.

Hadley, Michael L., Huebert, Rob and Crickard Fred, W., *A Nation's Navy: In Quest of Canadian Naval identity* (Montreal: McGill-Queen's University Press, 1996).

d'Hanens, Albert, *Europe of the North Sea and the Baltic; The World of the Hanse* (Antwerp: Fonds Mercator, 1984).

Harding, Rebecca and Jack, *The Weaponization of Trade; The Great Unbalancing of Politics and Economics* (London: Publishing Partnership, 2017).

Hattendorf, J.B., *England in the War of Spanish Succession* (New York: Garland Publishing, 1987).

Hattendorf, John B. and Leeman, William P. (Eds), *Forging the Trident: Theodore Roosevelt and the United States Navy* (Annapolis, MD: Naval Institute Press, 2020).

Hattendorf, John B. and Unger, Richard W. (Eds), *War at Sea in the Middle Ages and the Renaissance* (Woodbridge: The Boydell Press, 2003).

Haydon, Peter, 'Sailors, Admirals and Politicians: The Search for Identity after the War' in Hadley (Ed), *A Nation's Navy*.

Healey, Denis, *The Time of My Life* (London: Penguin, 1990).

Hennessey, Michael A., 'Fleet Replacement and the Crisis of Identity' in Hadley (Ed), *A Nation's Navy*.

Hennessey, Peter and Jinks, James, *The Silent Deep: The Royal Navy Submarine Service Since 1945* (London: Penguin, 2015).

Herwig, Holger H. and Goldstein, Lyle J. 'Imperial Germany: Continental Titan, Global Aspirant' in Erickson and Lord (Eds), *China Goes to Sea* (Annapolis: Naval Institute Press, 2012).

Holmes, James R., Winner Andrew C. and Yoshihara, Toshi, *Indian Naval Strategy in the Twenty-First Century* (London: Routledge, 2009).

Holmes, James R. and Yoshihara, Toshi, *Chinese Naval Strategy in the 21st Century* (London: Routledge, 2008).

Hone, Trent, *Learning War: The Evolution of Fighting Doctrine in the US Navy, 1898-1945* (Annapolis MD: Naval Institute Press, 2018).

Hoppit, Julian, *A Land of Liberty? England 1689-1727* (Oxford: Oxford University Press, 2010).

Horner, Charles, *Rising China and Its Postmodern Fate: Memories of Empire in a New Global Context* (Athens: University of Georgia Press, 2009).

Hu, Bo, *Chinese Maritime Power in the 21st Century: Strategic Planning, Policy and Predictions* (London: Routledge, 2019).

Johnson-Allen, John, *They Couldn't Have Done It Without Us: The Merchant Navy and the Falklands War* (Woodbridge: Seafarer Books, 2011).

Kamer, Henry, *Empire: How Spain Became a World Power 1492-1763* (London: Harper Collins, 2003).

Kennedy, Paul, 'Naval Mastery: The Canadian Context' in Boutilier (Ed.), *RCN in Retrospect*, pp. 15–33.

Kennedy, Paul, *The Rise and Fall of Great Powers* (New York: Random House, 1987).

Ketchum, Richard M., *The Borrowed Years* (New York: Random House, 1989).

Kirchberger, Sarah, *Assessing China's Naval Power: Technological Innovation, Economic Constraints and Strategic Implications* (Heidelberg: Springer, 2015).

Knight, Roger, *Britain Against Napoleon: The Organisation of Victory 1793-1815* (London: Penguin Books, 2013).

Knighton, C.S. and Loades, David (Eds), *The Navy of Edward VI and Mary I* (Franham, Surrey: Ashgate for the Navy Records Society, 2011).

Knighton, C.S. and Loades, David, *Elizabethan Naval Administration* (Farnham, Surrey: Ashgate, 2013).

Kuehn, John T., *Agents of Innovation; the General Board and the Design of the Fleet that Defeated the Japanese Navy* (Annapolis: US Naval Institute, 2008).

Lambert, Andrew, *The Crimean War: British Grand Strategy Against Russia 1853-6* (Manchester University Press, 1990).

Lambert, Andrew, *Seapower States: Maritime Culture, Continental Empires and the Conflict that Made the Modern World* (New Haven and London: Yale University Press, 2018).

Lambert, Craig, *Shipping the Medieval Military: English Maritime Logistics in the Fourteenth Century* (Woodbridge: The Boydell Press, 2011).

Lambert, Nicholas A., *Australia's Naval Inheritance* (Canberra: Maritime Studies Program, 1998).

Lavery, Brian, *The Conquest of the Oceans* (London: DK Books, 2013).

Lerhe, Eric, 'Getting the Personnel and Capital Mix Right' in Griffiths and Lerhe (Eds), *Naval Gazing*.

Levathes, Louise, *When China Ruled the Seas* (Oxford: Oxford University Press, 1994).

Lewis, John Wilson and Litae, Xue, *China's Strategic Seapower: The Politics of Force Modernisation in the Nuclear Age* (Stanford: Stanford University Press, 1994).

Li, Nan, *Chinese Civil-Military Relations in the Post-Deng Era* (Newport RI: USNWC China Maritime Studies, 2010).

Liang, Quiao and Xiangsui, Wang, *Unrestricted Warfare* (Beijing: Literature and Arts Publishing House, 1999).

Liu, Huaqing, *Memoirs* (Beijing: PLA Press, 2004).

Liu, Ming Fu, *China Dream: The Great Power Thinking and Strategic Positioning of China in the Post-American Age* (Beijing: Zhongguo, 2010).

Lloyd, Christopher, *Lord Cochrane: Seaman – Radical-Reformer* (London: Longmans Green and Co, 1947).

Lo, Jung-Pang, *China as a Sea Power 1127–1368 (1957)*, edited and with commentary by Bruce A. Elleman (Hong Kong: Hong Kong University Press, 2012).

Lund, Wilfred G.D., Vice-Admiral Howard Emmerson Reid and Vice-Adm Harold Taylor 'Wood Grant: Forging the New "Canadian Navy"' in Whitby (Ed.), *The Admirals*.

MacDougall, Philip, *British Dockyards in the First World War* (Transactions of the Naval Dockyard Society, Vol. 12, August 2019).

Mahan, A.T., *The Influence of Sea Power Upon History 1660-1783* (Boston, MA: Little, Brown and Company, 1890).

Mahan, A.T., *Lessons of the War with Spain* (Boston: Little, Bowen & Co., 1899).

Mahan, A.T., *The Interest of America in Sea Power* (Boston: Little, Brown & Co., 1906).

Mahan, Capt. A.T., *Naval Strategy: Compared and Contrasted with the Principles and Practice of Military Operations on Land* (Boston: Little, Brown & Co., 1911).

Mahan, A.T., *Sea Power in Mahan relation to the War of 1812* (Boston: Little, Brown & Co., 1918).

Marder, Arthur, *Old Friends New Enemies: The Royal Navy and the Imperial Japanese Navy* (Oxford: Clarendon Press, 1981).

Marsetio, Adm (Ret) Prof Dr, *Archipelago Leadership* (Citereup, Indonesia: Defence University, 2019).

Massie, Robert K., *Peter the Great: His Life and Work* (New York: Alfred A. Knopf, 1980).

Mawdsley, Evan, 'The Russian Navy in the Gorshkov Era' in Phillips Payson O'Brien (Ed.), *Technology and Naval Combat in the Twentieth Century and Beyond* (London: Frank Cass, 2001).

Mawdsley, Evan, *December 1941: Twelve Days that Began a World War* (New Haven: University of Yale Press, 2011).

Maxtone-Graham, John, *The North Atlantic Run* (London: Cassell, 1972).

Maydman, Henry, *Naval Speculations and Maritime Politicks* (London, 1691).

McCabe, Robert, Sanders, Deborah and Speller, Ian (Eds), *Europe, Small Navies and Maritime Security* (London: Routledge, 2020).

McCranie, Kevin D., *Mahan, Corbett and the Foundations of Naval Strategic Thought* (Annapolis, MD: Naval Institute Press, 2021).

McKenzie, Peter W. and Easton, Ian M., *Chinese Views of the Air Sea Battle Concept: A Preliminary Assessment* (Washington: Center for Naval Analyses, Maritime Asia Project, 2012).

Mecollari, Captain (Rtd) Artur, *Shaping the Future Albanian National Maritime Security Strategy*, 2nd ed. (Tirana: National Centre for Security and Defence, 2014).

Menon, Rear-Adm, *Maritime Strategy and Continental Wars* (London: Frank Cass, 1998).

Middlemiss, Dan W., 'Economic Considerations in the Development f the Canadian Navy since 1945' in Boutilier (Ed.), *RCN in Retrospect*, pp. 254–279.

Miksic, John, *Singapore and the Silk Road of the Sea 1300-1800* (Singapore: National Museum, 2014).

Millis, Walter (Ed.), *The Forrestal Diaries* (New York: The Viking Press, 1951).

Milton, Giles, *Big Chief Elizabeth* (London: Sceptre, 2000).

Mitchell, Donald W., *A History of Russian and Soviet Sea Power* (London: Andre Deutsch, 1974).

Montefiore, Simon Sebag, *Potemkin: Catherine the Great's Imperial Partner* (New York: Vintage Books, 2005).

Moretz, Joseph, *Thinking Wisely, Planning Boldly: The Higher education and Training of Royal Navy Officers, 1919-1939* (Solihull: Helion, 2015).

Morgenstern, George, *Pearl Harbor: The Secret War* (New York: Devlin & Adair, 1947).

Morris, E., *Corregidor: The End of the Line* (New York: Stein and Day, 1981).

Morriss, Roger, *The Foundations of British Maritime Ascendancy* (Cambridge: University Press, 2011).

Muller, David G., Jnr, *China as a Maritime Power: The Formative Years: 1945-1983* (Lexington, VA: Rockbridge Books, 2016).

Murfett, Malcolm, *Naval Warfare 1919-1945: An Operational History of the Volatile War at Sea* (London: Routledge, 2009).

Murray, Michelle, 'Identity. Insecurity and Great Power Politics: The Tragedy of German Naval Ambition before the First World War,' *Security Studies*, Vol 19, No 4, 2010.

Murray, Williamson and Millet, Alan R., *Military Innovation in the Interwar Period* (Cambridge: Cabridge University Press, 1996).

Nicholls, Bob, *Statesmen & Sailors: Australian Maritime Defence 1870-1920* (Balmain, NSW: Balmain, 1995).

O'Brien, Phillips Payson, *How the War Was Won* (Cambridge: Cambridge University Press, 2018).

Octavian, Amurulla, *Indonesian Navy, Global Maritime Fulcrum and ASEAN* (Jakarta: SESKOAL Press, 2019).

O'Dea, Christopher R., 'China Has Landed,' *National Interest*, 31 October 2018.

Ormrod, David, *The Rise of Commercial Empires* (Cambridge: Cambridge University Press, 2003).

Overy, Richard, *Why the Allies Won* (New York: W.W. Norton and Company, 1995).

Padfield, Peter, *Maritime Supremacy and the Opening of the Western Mind* (Woodstock and New York: The Overlook Press, 1999).

Paine, Lincoln, *The Sea and Civilization: A Maritime History of the World* (New York: Alfred A. Knopf, 2013).

Paine, S.C.M., *The Sino-Japanese War 1894-5: Perceptions, Pride and Primacy* (New York: Cambridge University Press, 2003).

Palerie, Prabhakaran, *Role of the Coast Guard in the Maritime Security of India* (New Delhi: Knowledge World, 2004).

Palssson, Hermann and Edwards, Paul, (Trans and Introduction) *Orkneyinga Saga: The History of the Earls of Orkney* (London: Penguin Books, 1981).

Panikkar, K.M., *India and the Indian Ocean: An Essay on the Influence of Sea Power on Indian History* (London: G.Allen & Co, 1945).

Paquette, Gabriel, *The European Seaborne Empires* (New Haven: Yale University Press, 2019).

Parker, Geoffrey, 'The *Dreadnought* Revolution of Tudor England', *Mariner's Mirror*, Vol 82, No 3, August 1996, 269–30.

Parry, J.H., *The Spanish Seaborne Empire* (London: Hutchinson, 1971).

Pay, John and Till, Geoffrey, *East-West Relations in the 1990s: The Naval Dimension* (London: Pinter Publishers, 1990).

Peden, G.C., *British Rearmament and the Treasury* (Edinburgh: Scottish Academic Press, 1979).

Peyrefitte, Alain, *The Collision of Two Civilisations: The British Expedition to China 1792-04* (London: Harvill, 1993).

Phillips, Carla Rahn, 'Why Did Anyone Go to Sea?' in Benton and Perl-Rosenthal (Eds), *A World at Sea* (2020).

Plutarch, *Parallel Lives* (Berlin: Loeb Classical Library, 1914).

Poirier, General Lucien, *Strategie Theoretique II* (Paris: Economica, 1987).

Polmar, Norman, Brooks, Thomas A.andFederoff, George, *Admiral Gorshkov: The Man Who Challenged the U.S. Navy* (Annapolis: Naval Institute Press, 2019).

Postlethwate, Malachy, *Universal Dictionary of Trade and Commerce* (London, 1757).

Powley, Edward, *The Naval Side of King William's War* (Hamden, Conn: Archon Books, 1972).

Pryor, John H., 'Byzantium and the Sea' in Hattendorf and Unger (Eds), *War at Sea in the Middle Ages and Renaissnace* (2005).

Rafferty, Mathew Taylor, '"The Law is the Lord of the Sea": Maritime Law as Global Maritime History' in Benton and Perl-Rosenthal (Eds), *A World at Sea* (2020).

Ranft, Bryan McI and Till, Geoffrey, *The Sea in Soviet Strategy* (Basingstoke: The Macmillan Press, 1989).

Rhodes, Andrew, 'Same Waters, Different Dreams', *Journal of Advanced Military Studies*, Vol II, No 2, Fall 2020.

Rhodes, Andrew, 'The 1988 Blues- Admirals, Activists and the Development of the Chinese Maritime Identity', US *Naval War College Review*, Vol 74, No 2, Spring 2021.

Roberts, Jennifer T., *The Plague of War: Athens, Sparta, and the Struggle for Ancient Greece* (Oxford: Oxford University Press, 2017).

Rodger, N.A.M., *The Command of the Ocean: A Naval History of Britain 1649-1815* (London: Penguin, 2006).

Rose, Susan, 'A Re-appraisal of the King's Ships in the Reigns of Richard I and John, 1189-1216', *The Mariner's Mirror*, Vol 106, No 1, February 2020.

Roy, Vice Adml Mihir K., *War in the Indian Ocean* (New Delhi: Lander Publishers, 1995).

Roy-Chaudhury, Rahul, *Sea Power and Indian Security* (London: Brasseys, 1995).

Roy-Chaudhury, Rahul, *India's Maritime Security* (New Delhi: Knowledge World for IDSA, 2000).

Sakhuja, Vijay, *Asian Maritime Power in the 21st Century* (Singapore: ISEAS, 2011).

Salonia, Matteo, *Genoa's Freedom: Entrepreneurship, Republicanism and the Spanish Atlantic* (Lanham: Lexington Books, 2017).

Saunders, Phillip C., et al. *Chairman Xi Remakes the PLA* (Washington: National Defense University, 2019).

Sawyer, Peter, *The Oxford illustrated History of the Vikings* (Oxford; Oxford University Press, 1997).

Scobell, Andrew, et al. (Eds), *The People's Liberation Army and Contingency Planning in China* (Washington: National Defense University, 2015).

Seligmann, Mathew (Ed.), *Naval Intelligence From Germany: The Reports of the British Naval Attaches in Berlin, 1906-1914* (Farnham: Ashgate for the Naval Records Society, 2007).

Seligmann, Matthew, Nagler, Frank and Epkenhans, Michael (Eds), *The Naval Route to the Abyss: The Anglo-German Naval Race, 1985-1914* (Farnham: Ashgate for the Naval Records Society, 2015).

Seminoff, Capt. Vladimir, *The Battle of Tsu-shima* (London: JohnMurray, 1906).

Semenoff, Capt. Vladimir, *Rasplata (The Reckoning)* (London: John Murray, 1913).

Sharman, J.C., *Empires of the Weak* (Princeton: Princeton University Press, 2019).

Sharman, J.C., 'Power and Profit at Sea', *International Security*, Vol 43, No 4, Spring 2019.

Short, John Rennie, *The World through Maps: A History of Cartography* (Toronto: Firefly Books, 2003).

Smith Jeffrey, A., *Themistocles: The Powerbroker of Athens* (Barnsley: Pen and Sword Books Ltd, 2021).

Sobel, Dava, *Longitude* (London: Harper Perennial, 2011).

Sokolosky, Joel, 'A Question of Balance: Canada and the Cold War at Sea, 1945-1968' in Frame (Ed.), *Reflections on the Royal Australian Navy*.

Sokolsky, Joel, 'Canada and the Cold war at Sea' in Douglas(Ed.), *Boutilier RCN in Retrospect*, pp 209–232.

Southam, *Jane Austen and the Navy* (London: Hambledon and London, 2000).

Soward, Stewart, 'Canadian Naval Aviation, 1915-69' in Boutilier (Ed.), *RCN in Retrospect*.

Speller, Ian, Mulqueen, M. and Sanders, Deborah (Eds), *Small Navies: Strategy and Policy for Small Navies in war and Peace* (Farnham: Ashgate, 2014).

Stevens, David, 'HMAS Australia: A Ship for a Nation' in Stevens (Ed.), *The Navy and the Nation*.

Stevens, David, *Maritime Power in the 20th Century: The Australian Experience* (St Leonards, Australia: Allen & Unwin, 1998).

Stevens, David (Ed.), *The Royal Australian Navy* (Oxford: Oxford University Press, 2001).

Stevens, David and Reeve, John, *The Navy and the Nation: The influence of the Navy on modern Australia* (Crows Nest, NSW: Allen & Unwin, 2005).

Stohs, Jeremy, *The Decline of European Naval Forces: Challenges to Sea Power in an Age of Fiscal Austerity and Political Uncertainty* (Annapolis, MD: Naval Institute Press, 2018).

Stradling, R.A., *The Armada of Flanders: Spanish Maritime Policy and European War 1568-1668* (Cambridge: Cambridge University Press, 2003).

Strauss, Barry, *The Battle of Salamis: The Naval Encounter That Saved Greece – and Western Civilisation* (New York: Simon and Schuster, 2004).

Stripp, Alan, *Code Breaker in the Far East* (Oxford: University Press, 1995).

Sumida, Jon Tetsuro, *Inventing Grand Strategy and Teaching Command: the Classic Worlds of Alfred Thayer Mahan Reconsidered* (Baltimore: Johns Hopkins University Press, 1997).

Swanson, Bruce, *The Eighth Voyage of the Dragon: A History of China's Quest for Seapower* (Annapolis: Naval Institute Press, 1982).

Swinson, A. *Four Samurai* (London: Hutchinson, 1968).

Swope, Kenneth M., *A Dragon's Head and a Serpent's Tail: Ming China and the First Great East Asian War, 1592–1598* (Norman, OK: University of Oklahoma Press, 2009).

Symonds, Craig, *Navalists and Antinavalists: The Naval Policy Debate in the United States, 1785-1827* (Newark: University of Delaware Press, 1980).

Thucydides, *The Peloponnesian War* (London: Penguin, 1969).

Till, Geoffrey, *Understanding Victory: Naval Operations from Trafalgar to the Falklands* (Santa Barbara: Praeger, 2014).

Till, Geoffrey, *Seapower: A Guide for the 21st Century,* 4th ed. (Abingdon: Routledge, 2018).

Timirev, Adm S.N., *The Russian Baltic Fleet in the time of War and Revolution, 1914-1818* (Barnsley: Seaforth Publishing, 2020).

Toll, Ian W., *Six Frigates: How Piracy, War and British Supremacy at Sea gave Birth to the World's Most Powerful Navy* (London: Michael Joseph, 2006).

Tomlinson, H.C., *Guns and Government: The Ordnance Office under the later Stuarts* (London: Royal Historical Society, 1979).

Twitchett, E.G., *Life of a Seaman: Thomas Cochrane, 10th Earl of Dundonald, 1775 to 1860* (London: Wishart & Co, 1931).

Urbina, Ian, *The Outlaw Ocean: Journeys Across the Last Untamed Frontier* (New York: Alfred A. Knopf, 2019).

Valdaliso, Jesus M., 'Delayed Adjustment: Economic Crisis, political change and state intervention in the Spanish ship-building industry, about 1795-1990', *The Mariner's Mirror*, Vol 15, 4 November 2019, 461–479.

Vale, Brian, *The Audacious Admiral Cochrane* (London: Conway Maritime Press, 2004).

Wade, Geoff, 'The Zheng He Voyages: A Reassessment', *Journal of the Malaysian Branch of the Royal Asiatic Society*, Vol 78, No 1, June 2005.

Waters, Conrad (Ed.), *World Naval Review 2020* (Barnsley, Seaforth Publishing, 2019).

Weatherford, Jack, *Genghis Khan and the Making of the Modern World* (New York: Three Rivers Press, 2004).

Wedin, Lars, *Maritime Strategies for the XXi Century: The Contribution of Admiral Castex* (Paris: Nuvis, 2016), 207–213.

Weinland, Robert, 'Developments in Soviet Naval strategy' in John Pay and Geoffrey Till (Eds), *East-West Relations in the 1990s: The Naval Dimension* (London: Pinter Publishers, 1990).

Weir, Gary E. and Boyne, Walter J Boyne, *Rising Tide: The Untold Story of the Russian Submarines that Fought the Cold War* (New York: Perseus Books, 2003).

Wheeler, James Scott, *The Making of a World Power; War and the Military Revolution in Seventeenth Century England* (Stroud: Gloucs: Sutton Publishing, 1999).

Whitby, Michael, 'Vice-Admiral Harry G. DeWolf: Pragmatic Navalist' in Whitby (Ed.), *The Admirals*, pp. 213–246.

Whitby, Michael, Gimblett, Richard H. and Haydon, Peter (Eds), *The Admirals: Canada's Senior Leadership in the Twentieth Century* (Toronto: The Dundurn Press, 2006).

Wijegunaratne, Vice Adm R.C., *Sri Lanka Navy's Maritime Strategy 2025* (Colombo: Ministry of Defence, 2016).

Willis, Sam, *The Struggle for Sea Power: The Royal Navy vs the World, 1775-1782* (London: Atlantic Books, 2018).

Wills, Steve, *Strategy Shelved: The Collapse of Cold War Naval Strategic Planning* (Annapolis, MD: Naval Institute Press, 2021).

Wilson, E., 'The Limits of Naval Power: Britain after 1815', in P. Kennedy and E. Wilson (Eds), *Navies in Multipolar Worlds: From the Age of Sail to the Present* (London: Routledge, 2020).

Wise, Michael, *Travellers' Tales of Old Singapore* (Singapore: Marshall Cavendish, 2019).

Wohlstetter, Roberta, *Pearl Harbor: Warning and Decision* (Redwood City, CA: Stanford University Press, 1966).

Wuthrow, Joel, *China's Other Army: The People's Armed Police in an Era of Reform* (Washington: National Defense University, China Strategic Perspectives, 14 April 2019).

Xu, Qiyu, *Fragile Rise* (Cambridge, MA: MIT Press, 2016).

Yamamto, Fumihito, *The Japanese Road to Singapore: Japanese Perceptions of the Singapore Naval base 1921-1941* (PhD Thesis), National University of Singapore, 2009.

Yoshihara, Toshi and Holmes James, R., *Red Star over the Pacific: China's Rise and the Challenge to U.S. Maritime Strategy* (Annapolis, MD: Naval Institute Press, 2018).

Index

Absalon 267
Adams, John 62–63
Adaptability 254
Admiralty Office 194
Advocacy 122
Aegospotami 86
Aeschylus 130
Afghanistan War 111
Africa 175
Afro-Americans 213
Agreed jurisdiction 173
Agriculture 7, 28
Aircraft carriers 31, 133, 243, 248, 297
Albania 12
Alcibiades 86
Algerine pirates 63
Allies 92
Amazon River 22
Amboyna massacre 62
Amsterdam 61
Ancient Greece 84–86
Anti-ship missile projects 255
Antisubmarine warfare 145, 206, 222, 231, 298
A.P. Moeller/Maersk 93
Argentine Navy 268
Armada de Chile 144
Aroztegui, Martin de 236
Artificial intelligence 29, 255, 267
ASMAR. *See* Astilleros y Maeanstranzaa de la Armada
Astilleros y Maeanstranzaa de la Armada 145
Athenians 6, 11, 84–86
Athens 6, 84–86, 209
Atomic bomb 94–95
Audette, Louis 207
Austen, Jane 197
Australia
  description of 37
  National Ocean Office of 77
  Naval Shipbuilding and Repair Sector Strategic Plan of 2002 146–147
  ocean policy in 77
  Oceans Policy of 77
  Royal Australian Navy 232
  ship-building in 146–147
  submarines in 245
  warships from 145
  Weapons Systems Research Laboratory 150
Axis 92

BAE Systems 152
Baines, Craig 272
BAKAMLA 73
Balanced fleet 233
Ballinn, Albert 129
Ballistic Missile Defence 242
Ballistic-missile firing submarines 124, 243
Bangladesh navy 134–135, 137
Bank of England 152
Barnet, Corelli 90
Barrett, Tim 37, 215, 270, 298–299
Basque Country 7
Bataan peninsula 101
Battle Force 2045
  allocating responsibilities 252–253
  delivery planning 252
  distributed maritime operations 248
  electronic maneuver warfare 249
  expeditionary advanced base operations 248–249
  fleet's missions and tasks 247
  Integrated Naval Force Structure Assessment versus 250
  mix 252
  overview of 246–247
  programme resourcing 249–250
  readiness 251
  task requirements 248–249
  technology 249
Battle of Coronel 147
Battle of Jutland 130
Battle of Lepanto 251

Battle of Marathon 84–85
Battle of Namur 53
Battle of Salamis 86, 97
Battle of the Atlantic 131
Battle of the Boyne 47
Battle of the Downs 238
Battle of the Red Cliffs 23
Battle of Thermopylae 85
Battle of Trafalgar 217
Battle of Tsushima 29, 273
Battle system 270
Battlefleet 240–241
Battleships 95, 130, 200
Baugh, Daniel 199
Beachy Head 56–57
Beaverbrook, Lord 92
Bellinger, Martin 101
Belt and Road Initiative 24, 37–40, 92–93, 277, 279, 284, 290, 293
Berlin Wall 84
Betts, Richard 81
Bismarck, Otto von 122
Black, Jeremy 188, 191
Black Sea 22
Board of Commissioners 53
Bolivia 8
Botero, Giovanni 236
Bottom-up approach 74
Boxer rebellion 282
Brahmos hypersonic missile 146
Braunschweiger frigates 216
Brazil 144, 192, 194
BREXIT 113
Brezhnev, Leonid 127
BRI. *See* Belt and Road Initiative
Bribery 51, 196
Britain. *See also* England; London; United Kingdom
  armaments production by 92, 148
  battleship production 95
  BREXIT 113
  Committee of Imperial Defence 127
  competing service agendas in 109–110
  defence spending in 83
  exports by 129
  geographic isolation of 87
  Gibraltar seizure by 22
  GNP in 33, 83
  governments of 82
  in Malaya 101
  Manchester School 31
  Maritime Defence Industrial Base in 147, 152
  maritime resources in 88
  maritime success in 12
  maritime supremacy of 87
  mercantile importance in 30

National Security Strategy of 112
  population of 24–25
  resources-commitments problem 82–84
  Royal Navy of. *See* Royal Navy
  ship-building in 152
  strategy-making 52
  war industries in 92
British Civil Service 195
British Falklands Task Force 268
British Pacific Fleet 207
British Treasury 83
Brock Report 208
Broke, Philippe 218
Brooke-Popham, Robert 102, 104, 107–108
Brown, Charles Q. 213
Bugis 27
Bullion 7–8, 33
Bunga Mas Lima 157, 254
Bureaucracy 200
Burma 91
Bushnell, David 62
Byng, Admiral 205

Canadian navy 131–132, 151, 204–207, 219, 272. *See also* Royal Canadian Navy
Canary Islands 259
Capacity building 180
CAPE. *See* Cost Assessment and Evaluation Office
Cape Verde islands 61
Cargoes 169, 191
Casa de la Contratación 7
Castex, Raoul 45
Catalonia 7
Catherine the Great 65
CCG. *See* China Coast Guard
Central Committee of the Party 127
Central Military Commission 292, 294
Central Military Committee 125, 128
Chang I 23
Charles X 66
Chatham Chest system 57
Cheng Rongxing 299
Chernavrvin, Admiral 35
Chesapeake Bay 22
Chile 7–8, 144–145, 192–193, 213
Chilean navy 144–145, 192, 213
China
  agrarian economy of 71
  agricultural pursuits in 28
  as arms producer 292
  Belt and Road Initiative 24, 37–40, 92–93, 277, 279, 284, 290, 293
  Central Military Commission of 292, 294
  civilian maritime community in 93
  comparative advantage of 289
  comprehensive national power 284

corruption in 284, 288
COSCO 93
Cultural Revolution 284
Defence White Papers 112–114,
    286–287, 289
Deng Xiaoping 125, 128, 285, 289, 292
fishing industry in 158, 161, 279, 293
Five Year Plans 289
fleet design in 296–298
fleet maintenance in 296–298
GDP of 280
General Armaments Department of 289
geography of 276–277
government of
    description of 277–279
    sea-mindedness of China affected by 28
Huawei 93
hypersonics in 290
Indonesian investment by 73
land bases for 297
landpower of 24
Liu Huaqing 122–126, 128, 204, 216,
    286, 291
maritime advocacy for 283–286
Maritime Defence Industrial Base in
    289–292, 297
maritime economy of 71, 279–280
maritime endeavors in 28
maritime geography of 276–277
Maritime Police Law 294
maritime power in 70–71, 74–75, 78,
    86, 281
maritime synergy in 289–295
merchant shipping in 157, 279, 292–293
military capabilities in 290
military reform in 288
Ming dynasty of 28, 278
modern
    maritime power in 70–72
    military strategy in 70–71
    top-down approach in 70–72, 283
naval administration of 288–289
naval development in 297
naval forces of 280–281
naval personnel in 225–226, 295–296
naval policy in 286–288
naval strength in 285
Navy of. *See* Chinese Navy
near sea active defense of 126
Opium Wars 40
People's Liberation Army Navy 122,
    125–126, 131
port development in 86, 292
reform programme in 115
after Revolution of 1949 86
as Rimland country 24
rivers of 22–23

Russia and 277
sea-mindedness of 28–29, 278
sea trade in 28
seapower of 22–24
ship-building in 128, 289–290
ship procurement by 297
silk roads 38
small leading groups in 284
society in 277–279
Song dynasty of 23, 28, 39, 196
Tang period of 28
*Technical Standards for Civilian Ships To
    Implement National Requirement* 157
Three Warfares 285
Xi Jinping of 37, 70–71, 74–75, 78, 92, 115,
    278, 280–281, 283, 285, 294
Yuan dynasty 39
Zheng He 23, 28, 39, 278
China Coast Guard 71, 74, 93, 175, 179, 282,
    293–295, 294, 296
China Electronics Technology
    Corporation 291
China Marine Surveillance 74
China Shipbuilding Industry Corporation 290
China State Shipbuilding Corporation 290
Chinese Navy
    Belt and Road Initiative effects on 39
    description of 280–281, 285
    First Island Chain effects on 21
    growth of 9, 12
    in Indian Ocean 146
    maritime power of 71, 285
    missions of 288
    personnel issues for 225–226
    public image of 211
    size of 297
Choiseul 37
Chola empire 134
Christianity 6
Churchill, Winston 47, 53, 94, 104, 108, 231
Civil-military relations 114–115, 128
Civil War
    American 26, 64
    English 5
    US Navy during 64
Civilian cargo ship 35
Clerk, John 55
CMA CGM 93
Cnut 8
Coastguards
    of China 71, 74, 93, 175, 179, 282, 293–295,
        294, 296
    description of 35, 175–176, 179, 282
Coastline
    failure to defend 22
    maritime power and 20–21
Cochrane, Lord 193, 196–197, 199, 201, 213

Cod Wars 168
CODELCO 144
Colbert, Jean-Baptiste 36, 47, 78
Cold War 84, 135, 153, 204–205, 246, 250, 263
Collegiality 201
Collingwood, Admiral 193
Colombia 77, 97, 149, 172, 243
Columbus, Christopher 81
Commanders
  description of 271
  Maydman's writings about 55
Commercial aristocracy 26
Commissioners of the Navy Board 199
Commissioners of Victualling 53–54, 198
Committee of Public Safety 239
Common operational picture 174–175
Competing service agendas 101–110
Comprehensive national power 284
Confucius 28, 278
Conjunct Expeditions 55
Constructor-customer relationship 150
Continental
  countries as 11
  maritime versus 10
Continental powers 23
Cooper, Alfred Duff 108
COP. *See* Common operational picture
Copper 144
Corbett, Sir Julian
  description of 10, 87, 260, 286
  Some Principles of Maritime Strategy 34, 88
Cordoba 190
Corregidor 101
Corruption 51, 196–198, 284
COSCO 93
Cost Assessment and Evaluation Office 247, 250
COTECMAR 149
Council of War 236
Countries. *See also specific country*
  coastline of 20–21
  maritime geography of 20–24
  maritime success of 91
  population of 24–25
  sea-dependence of 27
Covid-19 pandemic 153, 221, 232, 264
Coward, Noel 107
Credit financing 152
Crime
  countering of 173
  in fishing industries 159
  oil theft 171
Crimean war 91
CSIC. *See* China Shipbuilding Industry Corporation
CSS Alabama 26

CSSC. *See* China State Shipbuilding Corporation
Cuban missile crisis 130
Cultural Revolution 284
Curzon, Lord 11
Custine, Marquis de 67
Cutlass Fury 222

Dakar class submarines 149
Daniels, Josephus 219
Danish Navy 215, 242, 267
Dark Vessel Detection Programme 174
DARPA 150, 201
de Tourville, Admiral 47
Deepwater 167, 181
Defective coordination machinery 107–109, 115–117
Defence Research and Development 153
Defence White Papers 96, 112–114, 286–287, 289
Defense Industrial Base 144
Degradation, of environment 171, 173
Democracy, maritime power and 6, 19, 26, 278
Deng Xiaoping 125, 128, 285, 289, 292
Desert Storm 116
Despotic governments
  maritime power and 26–27
  in Russia 67
Destroyers 240, 297
Development, Concepts and Doctrine Centre 110
Devonport Dockyard 198
Distributed maritime operations 248, 269
Djibouti 157
Dockyards 29, 54–55, 186–187, 267
Doenitz, Admiral 94, 251
Dolphin class submarines 149
Domestic agriculture 7
Doria, Andrea 190
Dragone, Giuseppe Cavo 272
Dreadnought 200
Dual use technology 147
Duke of Marlborough 53
Dutch 61–62
Dutch East Indies 88–89, 91, 103
DWP. *See* Defence White Paper
Dynamic force employment 264

Earl, Thomas 45
Earl of Nottingham 50
East China Sea 71, 179, 287, 293, 296
East India Company 61, 69, 91, 145
Economic competition 38
Economic cooperation 38
Economy
  maritime. *See* Maritime economy

national
   Maritime Defence Industrial Base
      benefits for 147
      maritime industries for 86
Ecuadorian Exclusive Economic Zone 161
Edward III 189–190
Edwards, William 25
Egyptians, Nile River exploitation by 22
Electronic maneuver warfare 249
Elizabeth, Queen 12
EMALS electromagnetic catapult system 292
Encomienda system 7
England. *See also* Britain; London; United
   Kingdom
   Deptford shipyard of 65
   economic growth in 25
   maritime geography of 277
   maritime interests of 12
   maritime power of 49
   maritime success of 12
   medieval 189
   Navigation Acts 30–31, 56, 290
   William III's influence on 47
English Channel 20
Environment
   degradation of 171, 173
   sea as 169–170
Esper, Mark 252
Essay on Naval Tactics 55
Estai 177
Ethnic minorities 213
Euphrates River 22
Eurasian landmass 23–24
European Carrier Group Interoperability
   Initiative 262
European Convention on Human Rights 178
Eurybiades 85
Exclusive Economic Zone 131, 161, 177
Expeditionary advanced base operations
   248–249
Expertise 222–223

Falklands 113, 116, 147, 155–156, 231,
   264, 293
Far East 104
Far East War Council 108
Far Eastern Combined Bureau 106
Farming 7
Farquar, William 70
"Fat Leonard" scandal 221
Federalists 63
Ferdinand of Aragon, King 81
Financial resources 51
First Island Chains nos 21
First World War
   demobilisations after 84
   Royal Canadian Navy in 131, 204

Fish trafficking 174
Fisher, Jacky 123, 200, 240, 253
Fisher, John 198, 254
Fishing
   declining fish stocks 168
   illegal, unregulated, and unreported
      167–168, 173
   sustainable 167
Fishing industries
   capturing of ships 160
   in China 158, 161, 279, 293
   as community 159
   crime in 159
   environmental damaging practices in 159
   food security from 159
   importance of 158–160
   integration of 161–162
   international tensions in 159
   management of 161–162, 167
   Maydman's writings on 157, 159, 162
   military value of 160
   in North Sea 158
   objectives of 161
   overview of 157–158
   paramilitary value of 160, 293
   political significance of 158
   in Revolutionary America 160
   seamen from 159–160
   support for 52
   sustainable 167
   wealth from 158–159
Fishing Protection Service 131
Five Year Plans 289
Flanders Frigate 237
Fleet. *See also* Ship(s)
   balanced 233, 240–243
   battle system for 270
   capability of 265–271
   logistics of 54
   maintenance of 259–274, 296–298
   materiel 264–271
   in medieval England 234–235
   missions of 247
   operations of 264
   readiness of 260–262
   regeneration of 238–240
   in Spain 235–238
   tasks of 247
   technological challenges 260
Fleet design
   in China 296–298
   difficulties in 230–233
   in France (1789–1794) 238–240
   Maydman's writings about 55, 233
   in medieval England 234–235
   process of 244–246
   in Spain 235–238

summarising of 254–255
Fleet-in-Being 55
Fleet logistics 54
Fleet Operations Sea Training 216, 223
Flyvefisken (Flying Fish) programme 242
Force Z 102–103, 243
Forrestal, James 116
FOST. *See* Fleet Operations Sea Training
4 Modernisations 292
France
    arms industries in 148
    British Royal Navy blockade of 20
    fleet design in, from 1789 to 1794 238–240
    maritime power of 22
    Secretariat General for the Sea 179
    William III and 47
French Navy
    British Royal Navy versus 56
    description of 55
    Navy Executive Committee of 132
    in 1789–1794 238–240
Frigates 236, 238, 242, 263, 267
Fruean, Brianne 27
*Fundamentals of Maritime Operations:
    Netherlands Maritime Military
    Doctrine* 138

Galapagos marine reserve 161
Galleys 209–211, 234–236
Gang of Four 125, 285
Gas 167
General line of policy 36, 50
General Purpose Frigate programme 151
Genoa 7, 190
Geo-politics school 23
Geography
    Belt and Road Initiative effects on 39
    maritime. *See* Maritime geography
German Navy 130
Germany
    armaments production by 92
    Army of 123
    atomic weapons development 94–95
    battleships of 130
    Bismarck's unification efforts in 122–123
    exports by 129
    High Sea Fleet of 22
    Nazi 26, 96, 279, 286
    Tirpitz's contributions to naval policy
        122–131
    U-boat force 94
    V1 94–95
    V2 94–95
Gibraltar, British seizure of 22
Gilday, Mike 204
Global Maritime Fulcrum 72, 94
Globalization 9

Glorious Revolution 46, 51, 165, 195
Goldwater-Nichols Act of 1986 110
Good Order at Sea 166
Gorshkov, Adm Sergei 67, 122–131, 253, 273
Governance
    integrated 180–182
    maritime power affected by 24–29, 36,
        40–41
    Maydman's writings on 48
Governments
    of Britain 82
    Chinese
        description of 277–279
        sea-mindedness of China affected by 28
    despotic 26–27, 67
    financial support from 152
    of India 145–146
    mixed approach used by 150
    sea-mindedness affected by 28–29
    in trade 31
    unpredictability and 94
Grace Dieu 234
Graham, Gerald 12
Gran Memorial 218
Grand Canal 22
Grand Strategy 81
Gray, Colin 4, 11
Great Patriotic War (1941–1945) 124, 127
Great Recession of 2008 83, 282
Greece 192, 195, 198
Greeks 35
Greenpeace 171
Greenwich 215
Gresh, Geoffrey 9
Gretchko, A.A. 127
Grey zone operations 217
Gross domestic product 30
Grotius, Hugo 62
Guadalcanal 31
Guidance 122
Guipuzcoa, Admiral 214
Gulf and Inland Waters, The 22
Gulf of Guinea 157, 169
Gulf of Siam 102
Gulf of Thailand 167
Gulf War 31
Gunpowder revolution 153
Guzman, Gaspar de 236

HADR. *See* Humanitarian and Disaster
    Response
Haixun 179
Hamburg-Amerika line 129
Hamilton, Alexander 63
Hamilton, William 20, 46
Hanse trading system 7
Hanseatic League 60–61, 123, 158

Harry de Wolff 260
Hart, Adm 'Betty' 103
Hawaii 101
Healey, Denis 113, 231
Henry V 190, 234, 240
Henry VIII 191
High Sea Fleet 22
High Stakes: The Environmental and Social Impacts of Destructive Fishing on the High Seas of the Indian Ocean 171
History of the English-Speaking Peoples 47
HMAS *Melbourne* 291
HMS *Duncan* 216
HMS *Inflexible* 147
HMS *Invincible* 147
HMS *Ocean* 144, 251
HMS *Prince* 263
HMS *Prince of Wales* 103, 232, 243
HMS *Queen Elizabeth* 152, 231–232, 251, 264
HMS *Repulse* 243
HMS *Shannon* 218
Hoffman, Frank 254–255
Hollweg, Bethmann 127
Homogenisation 117
Hornaday, William 70
Hospital ships 296
House of Commons 51, 54
House of Orange 61
Howe, Admiral 239
Hu Bo 277
Hu Jintao 283
Huawei 93
Huitfeldt frigates 242
Humanitarian and Disaster Response 243
Huq, Nurul 136
Hypersonics 290
HYSY-981 oil-rig incident 295

Illegal, unregulated, and unreported fishing 167–168, 173
IMET. *See* International Military Education and Training Programme
Imjin war 4
Imperial German Navy 288
Imperial Russian Navy 263
Income per capita 30
Independent Commission on the World Oceans 169
India
    Chief of the General Staff in 116
    conquest of 2
    Department of Military Affairs in 116
    Europeans' conquest of 2
    government of 145–146
    land-based invaders in 2
    Maritime Agenda of 77
    Maritime Defence Industrial Base in 146

maritime interests of 3
National Security Council 95
navy of 134
ocean-centred policy in 77
Panikkar's writings on 2
Research and Development in 145
sea-based threats to 2–3
sea trade by 32
ship-building in 145
sovereignty of 2
warships for 137
India and the Indian Ocean 2
Indian Mutiny 91
Indo-Pakistan wars 136
Indonesia
    BAKAMLA 73
    China's investment in 73
    Global Maritime Fulcrum in 72–73, 94
    maritime diplomacy in 73
    maritime power in 72–74, 110
    population of 72
    shipping industry in 73
Indonesian Navy 73
Industrial capacity 154
Industrial Revolution 29
Inflation 232
Inflexible 147
Influence of Sea Power, The 33
Information sharing 174–175
Informed outsiders 95
INFSA. *See* Integrated Naval Force Structure Assessment
Inner Crescent 23
Integrated governance 180–182
Integrated Naval Force Structure Assessment 247, 250, 252
Integrated Review of 2020 112
Intelligence Preparation of the Operational Environment 244
Intergovernmental Panel on Climate Change 171
International Convention for the Prevention of Pollution by Ships 178
International Maritime Exercise 2019 222
International Maritime Organisation 174, 178
International Military Education and Training Programme 222
Invergordon mutiny 215
Invincible 147
IPCC. *See* Intergovernmental Panel on Climate Change
IPOE. *See* Intelligence Preparation of the Operational Environment
Iranian Revolutionary Guard Navy 254
Iraq War 111
Ireland 87
Isabella of Castile, Queen 81

Island Chains 21, 126
Israel 149
Itagui Naval Complex 144
Italian Navy 272
Iver Huitfeldt 152, 242, 267

Jacobites 47
James II 46–47
James Shoal 131
Japan
    Korea invasion by 4
    maritime power of 25, 89
    maritime resources of 89
    military strategy of 90
    naval forces of 89
    population declines in 25
    warships of 214
Jefferson, Thomas 63
Jesus Maria 234
Jiang Zemin 126
Jiangdao class corvette 297
Job satisfaction 216
Jointness 100–109
Jokowi, President 72–75, 78, 94, 181
Jones, George C. 207
Jones, John Paul 62
Junta de Armadas 235–237
Junta de Ejecucion 235, 237
Jurisdiction 173
Justinian 166

Kadir, Abdullah Bin Abdul 69
Kaifeng 23
Kalibr missiles 249
Kamorta class ASW corvette programme 145
Kangxi Emperor 28
Kaplan, Robert 9
Kennedy, Paul 92
Khan, Genghiz 11
Khota Bharu 106
Khrushchev, Nikita 124–125, 127
Kiel canal 22
Kilo submarines 243
Kimmel, Adm Husband E. 106
King, Adm Ernest J. 88, 213
King, McKenzie 133, 209
Kirchberger, Sarah 154
Kiribati 167, 170
Kline, Jeff 252
Korea
    Japanese invasion of 4
    North 246
    South. *See* South Korea
Kwa Chong Guan 39

Lambert, Andrew 12, 75
Land power

of China 24
    sea power and 11, 22, 36, 90
    technological advances in 23
Landnam 6
Laureium 85
Law of the Contiguous Zone and Contiguous Zones 294
Layton, Adm Sir Geoffrey 108
Leach, Adm Sir Henry 113
Leadership 107, 113–115, 223–224
Leningrad 89
Leverage of Sea Power, The 4
Ley del Cobre 144
Liaoning 291
Liberal democracy, maritime power and 6, 19, 26, 278
Limburg 169
Littoral Combat Ship 242, 249–250, 291
Liu, Adm Huaqing 122–126, 128, 204, 216, 286, 291
Liu Ming Fu 282
London
    Singapore and 108
    Woolwich arsenal of 149–150
Long Range Anti-Ship Missile 255
Louis XIV 36, 109
LRASM. *See* Long Range Anti-Ship Missile
Luce, Adm Stephen B. 64, 219
Lysander 86

MacArthur, General Douglas 88, 103
Macdonald, Angus L. 207
Machine learning 29
Mackinder, Halford 23, 171
MacMunn, Gen George 81–82
Madison, James 63
Madrid 8
Mahan, Alfred Thayer
    colonies and 8
    description of 64
    despotic governments 26
    general line of policy 36, 50
    governance and society 24–29
    Gulf and Inland Waters, The 22
    Influence of Sea Power, The 33
    maritime geography and 20–24
    maritime power and 30
    naval forces and 33–34
    sea power elements of 19, 52
Majahapit empire 72
Malacca 46
Malacca Dilemma 276
Malay Peninsula 69, 105
Malaya 89, 91, 100–109
Malaysia
    15-to-5 project 253
    Exclusive Economic Zone 131

maritime vision in 77
National Security Council 95
Royal Malaysian Navy 157, 253
Malaysia Ocean Policy 2011–2020 77
Malinovsky, R.Y. 127
Manchester School 31
Mao Zedong 71, 125–126
Mappa Mundi 24
Mar-Portugal Strategy 76
Marine resources. *See* Maritime resources
Maritime
  continental versus 10
  countries as 11
  definition of 10
Maritime advocacy 11, 283–286
Maritime Affair 82
Maritime Agenda 77
Maritime authority 170–178, 293–295
Maritime case
  follow-up for 96–97
  representation for 96
  resource availability 90–93
  selling the sea 86–88
  strategic reality 88–90
  sufficient representation for 96
  uncertainty 93–96
Maritime Command 205
Maritime Defence Industrial Base
  in Brazil 144
  in Britain 147, 152
  in Chile 145
  in China 289–292, 297
  description of 143
  development of 147–148
  economic advantages of 291
  foreign suppliers 148
  in India 146
  maintenance of 147–148
  national economy benefits of 147
  reasons for investing in 146–149
  setting up 149–151
  in South America 144–146
  state owned enterprises 149
Maritime diplomacy 73
Maritime disorder 171–172
Maritime Doctrine of the Russian Federation, The 181
Maritime domain awareness 174
Maritime economy
  of China 71, 279–280
  maritime resources and 29–30
  metrics of 41
  naval forces and 32–33
  sea-mindedness and 27
  in Singapore 25
  society and 25
  in William III's reign 56

Maritime geography
  of China 276–277
  galleys and 234
  Maydman's writings on 48
  in Russia 68
  sailing ships and 234
Maritime identity 76
Maritime India Summit 77
Maritime industries
  description of 86
  fishing. *See* Fishing industries
  merchant. *See* Merchant shipping
  national economy affected by 86
  naval forces and 36
Maritime interests
  defending of 173
  definition of 10
  development of 11
  domestic influences on 58
  of England 12
  of India 3
  international influences on 58
Maritime law enforcement agencies 35
Maritime Ministry 96
Maritime Police Law 294
Maritime power
  in ancient Greece 85
  artificial 60
  Athenian 84–86
  being maritime versus 10
  in China 70–71, 74–75, 78
  constituents of 19, 24, 71
  cyclical nature of 3, 5
  declines in 5–9
  despotic governments and 26–27
  development of 4–5, 10–11, 30, 49–56, 76, 78, 84–86, 107, 144–154
  of England 49
  foresight for 78
  framework for 20
  of France 22
  funding for 85
  geography in 20–24
  governance effects on 24–29, 36, 40–41
  of Hanseatic League 60–61
  importance of 1–16
  improvements in 19–20
  in Indonesia 72–74, 110
  land power and 11
  liberal democracy and 6, 19, 26, 278
  Mahan's writings on 30
  Maydman's writings on 1, 49–57
  metrics of 40–42
  mixed approach to 74–75
  in modern China 70–72
  as multidimensional 100
  natural 60

naval forces and 33
navy as 4
in Netherlands 61–62
Panikkar's writings on 2
population influences on 24–25
public policy declarations about 97
relativity of 10
resources for development of 84–86
in revolutionary America 62–64
in Russia 64–68
sea power and 10
sea trade and 30–32
security benefits of 4
in Singapore 69–70
society effects on 24–29, 40–41
in Southeast Asia 107
of Spain 7
terminology associated with 10
tiers for 49–56
top-down approach to. *See* Top-down
    approach
trade and 30–32
virtuous circle of 3, 31, 87
Maritime resources
    allocation of 51–52
    in Athens 85
    gas 167
    of Japan 89
    loss of 171
    maritime economy and 29–30
    for maritime power development 84–86
    Maydman's writings on 48–49
    metrics of 41
    oil 167
    of Russia 89
    trade and 3
Maritime security
    Corbett's conception of 35
    description of 166
    Mahan's conception of 35
Maritime security policy 281
Maritime Strategy, The 125
Maritime synergy 143, 289–295
Maritime trade 3. *See also* Trade
Maritimeness 40, 42
MARPOL Treaty 178
Marquis de Montesclaros 236
MARSEC 166, 231
Marshall Islands 167
Martec's Law 201
Material readiness 262
Mauretania 129
Maydman, Henry
    administrative efficiency 188
    British Royal Navy 5
    description of 45, 188, 259
    dockyards and 54–55

fishing industry and 157, 159, 162
fleet design and 55, 233
governance and 48
living conditions and 214
Maritime Affair 82
maritime geography and 48
maritime power and 5, 12, 49–57
maritime synergy and 143
merchant shipping industry and 154–155
military mix and 52–53
modern applicability of 57–58
national policy and 50–51
naval forces and 49
naval personnel and 55
naval policy and 53–56
Naval Speculations 1, 13, 45–48, 188, 193
resource allocation and 51–52
running of ships and 55
ship commander's task according to 55
Singapore and 45–46
society and 48
strategy of means 57
tiers for maritime power development 49–56
top-down analytical approach of 58
trade and 48–49
McKenzie, Hugh 246
McKinsey Report 171
MCM. *See* Mine counter-measures
McNamara, Robert 110
McNeill, William 151
MDA. *See* Maritime domain awareness
MDIB. *See* Maritime Defence Industrial Base
Medieval England 234–235
Medway 22
MEF. *See* Minimum effective force
Mehmet II 78
Merchant shipping
    A.P. Moeller/Maersk 93
    in China 157, 279, 292–293
    CMA CGM 93
    description of 154–155
    Maydman's writings on 154–155
    narrative of 155–156
    of Royal Navy 155
    societal effects of 157
    Spain 7
    support for 52
    traditional view of 156
Merz, William 250
Mesoamerica 10
Middle Kingdom 28
Middleton, Charles 75
Mikkelsen, Torben 263
Military capability 116
Military education. *See* Professional military
    education
Military mix 52–53

Military power 116
Military-technological developments 191
Milizia da Mar 210
Mine counter-measures 222, 242
Ming China 4
Ming dynasty 28, 278
Minimum effective force 73
Mining 7
Ministry of Defence 109
Ministry of War 109
Mission analysis 244
Mitchell, Gen Billy 139
MLEAs. *See* Maritime law enforcement
  agencies
Modern China
  maritime power in 70–72
  military strategy in 70–71
  top-down approach in 70–72, 283
Modern state, naval administration benefits
  for 37
Modi, Narendra 181
Moffitt, Adm Rowan 244
Molyneux, Thomas 55
Monopsony 150
Monsoons 20
Morriss, Roger 192
Mountbatten, Lord 116
Mughals 139
Multinational cooperation 180
Murray, Leonard Warren 207
Mutinies 83, 91, 215

Nanda, S.M. 139
Napoleonic wars 84, 197, 251
Naresh Chanra committee 116
National character, sea power and 25
National economy
  Maritime Defence Industrial Base benefits
    for 147
  maritime industries for 86
National maritime security system 181
National Ocean Office 77
National Ocean Strategy 2013–2020 75–76
National policy objectives 50–51, 81
National Security Council 95, 285
National Security Strategy 112
NATO 133, 242, 262
Naval administration
  agencies involved in 53–54
  auditing system 54
  of China 288–289
  future orientation of 192–193
  modern state and 37
  qualities of 192–201
Naval advance 131–133
Naval Establishments Enquiry
  Committee 198

Naval expertise 199
Naval forces
  changes and challenges for 34–36
  development of 37
  historical description of 34
  Mahan's writings on 33–34
  maritime economy and 32–33
  maritime industries and 36
  maritime power and 33
  maritime trade and 3
  Maydman's writings on 49
  metrics of 41–42
  in military-maritime package 35
  needs of 36–37
  operational efficiency of 34
  purpose of 34
  technological influences on 35
Naval leadership 132
Naval personnel
  career prospects for 215
  in China 225–226, 295–296
  education of 216–224
  ethnic minorities 213
  job satisfaction of 216
  living conditions for 205
  maintenance of 271–273
  manning of 209–211
  Maydman's writings about 55
  motivation of 206–208
  number of 205–206
  preparation of 295–296
  quality of 206
  readiness of 262
  in Royal Canadian Navy 206–207
  on Spanish galleys 209–211
  support for 208–209
  sustaining of 271–273
  training of 216–224
  volunteers 211–212
  women 212–213
  working conditions for 214–215
Naval Planning Process 244–245
Naval policy
  deciding on 53–56
  Gorshov's contributions 122–131
  Liu's contributions 122–131
  Maydman's writings on 53–56
  Tirpitz's contributions 122–131
Naval power
  administrative angle of 186–202
  government and 36
  revolutionary America as 63
Naval revolution 4–5
Naval Shipbuilding and Repair Sector
  Strategic Plan of 2002 146–147
Naval Speculations 1, 13, 45–48, 188, 193
Naval strategy 53–56

Navalism 152
Navigation Acts 30–31, 56, 290
Navy
　Adams' writings on 63
　administration of. *See* Naval
　　administration
　Australian 232
　Bangladesh 134–135, 137
　Brazilian 194, 198
　Canadian 131–132, 151, 204–207, 219, 272.
　　See also Royal Canadian Navy
　Chilean 144–145, 192, 213
　Chinese. *See* Chinese Navy
　clarity of purpose for 138
　collegiality in 201
　corruption in 196–198
　costs of 6, 151, 265
　Danish 215, 242, 267
　definition of 189
　expensiveness of 5–6
　financing of 151–154
　French. *See* French Navy
　German 130
　importance of 9
　India 134
　Indonesian 73
　life cycle of 266
　loyalty to 195–196
　maritime power through 4
　medium 12
　military advantages of 4
　monitoring of 198
　as national enterprise 1, 37, 298
　New Zealand 233
　Pakistan 134–136, 230
　people of. *See* Naval personnel
　permanency of 193
　procurement planning by 240
　public image of 211
　Royal Australian 232
　royal fleets versus 189
　of Russia 68
　in 17th century 4
　in 16th century 4
　smaller 12, 253–254
　South Korean 149
　Sri Lanka 134–135
　strategic direction of 34
　technological influences on 35
　trade protection by 31, 87
　unit cost and complexity of 151
　US. *See* US Navy
　women in 212–213
Navy Board 53–54, 188, 200
Nazi Germany 26, 96, 279, 286
Nelles, Percy W. 207
Netherlands. *See also specific Dutch entries*

　maritime power in 61–62
　ship-building in 65
Netherlands Defence Doctrine 133, 138
New Deal 280
New Zealand 104, 233
Niazi, Muhammad Amjad Khan 230
Nicholas I 67
Nile River 22
Nimitz, Adm Chester 88
Nord-Deutscher-Lloyd 129
North Korea 246
Northern Sea Route 46, 65
Norway 7
"Not-invented-here syndrome" 201
NPP. *See* Naval Planning Process
NSC. *See* National Security Council
Nuclear propelled attack submarines 297
Nuclear weapons 124

Oarsmen 209–210
Ocean Alliance 93
Ocean policy
　in Australia 77
　in Colombia 77
　in India 77
OFRP. *See* Optimised Fleet Response Plan
Ogarkov, Marshall 128
Oil 167, 171, 232
Oil-producing countries
　sea transportation by 27
　Tanzania 171
Olivares, Count-Duke 240, 266
Operation Barbarossa 89
Operation Crusader 104–106
Operation Matador 102, 106
Operational efficiency, of naval forces 34
Operational Testing and Evaluation 245
Operations and Maintenance 224–225
Opium Wars 40, 282
Optimised Fleet Response Plan 263
Oracle of Delphi 85
Ordnance Board 53–54, 188
Orkneys 6
Orthodox Church 66
Ostfriesland 139
Ostland 7
OT&E. *See* Operational Testing and
　Evaluation
Oto-Melara 146
Overy, Richard 92

Pakistan
　navy of 134–136, 230
　warships for 137
　Western 136
Palk Strait 136
Panama canal 22

Panikkar, K.M.
  background on 1–2
  India and the Indian Ocean 2
  maritime power and 2, 5, 77, 88
PAP. *See* People's Armed Police
Paramilitary force, fishing industry as
  160, 293
Parker, Geoffrey 259
Parkinson, Cecil Northcote 195
Parliamentary Defence Committee 114
Patani 106
Patriotism 193
Pax Britannica 91
Pearl Harbor 89–90, 100–109
Pelham, Henry 83
Peloponnesian War 97
Peng Dehuai 284
Penguin 149
People. *See* Naval personnel
People's Armed Police 294
People's Liberation Army Navy 122,
  125–126, 131, 225–226
People's Maritime Militia 295–296
Pepys, Samuel 199–200, 218
Pericles 86
Perry, Oliver Hazard 145
Persians 84–85, 93
Persians, The 130
Personnel. *See* Naval personnel
Peru 8, 192, 195, 198
Peter the Great 50, 65–68, 95
Philip II 192, 214
Philip III 236
Philip IV 236
Philippines 88–89, 100–109
Phillips, Tom 106
Phoenician Women, The 130
Phoenicians 35
Phrynichus 130
Pickering, Victor 27
Piracy 157, 159, 168–169, 295
Piraeus 93
Pirates 63
Pitt, William 75
PLAN. *See* People's Liberation Army Navy
Plan Dog 108
Playfair, Major General 106
Pleshakov, Constantin 273
Plunder, by Vikings 6
Plutarch 84–85
PME. *See* Professional military education
Poirier, Gen Lucien 45, 57, 244
Politburo Standing Committee 128
Pollution 167, 171
Polynesians 27
Population
  of Britain 24–25

  of Indonesia 72
  of Japan 25
  maritime power affected by 24–25
Port Facility Security Code 177
Portugal
  Action Plan of 76
  description of 2, 5
  Independent Commission on the World
    Oceans 169
  Mar-Portugal Strategy 76
  maritime character of 76
  maritime identity of 76
  National Ocean Strategy 2013–2020 75–76
Pososhkov, Ivan 67
Postlethwayt, Malachy 32
Potemkin, Prince 65–66, 68, 95
Power. *See* Maritime power; Naval power;
  Seapower
Prins, Gwythian 139
Private enterprises 150
Professional military education
  benefits of 219
  description of 295
  differences of view on 218–220
  levels of 221, 224
  in Royal Canadian Navy 219
  topics included in 220–221
  training and 217, 220
  at US Naval War College 219
  of US Navy 295
Programmatics 262–264, 271
Punt 22
PVO-Strany 124

Qianlong Emperor 28, 95, 280
Qiao Liang 285
Qing dynasty 96

Radakin, Adm Sir Tony 260
Raffles, Stamford 26, 46, 69–70
Raleigh, Walter 29
Rasmussen 267
Reagan, Ronald 125
Red Sea 22
Regional Seapower Symposium 143
Resources
  allocation of 51–52, 111
  financial 51
  insufficient 103–105, 110–112
  marine. *See* Maritime resources
  sufficient 137–138
Resources-commitments problem
  in Athens 84–86
  in Britain 82–84
  coping mechanisms for 86–97
  management of 86–97
  selling the sea 86–88

Revolution in Military Affairs 124
Revolution of 1789 239
Revolutionary America 91. *See also* United
    States
    British Royal Navy 74–75
    fishing industries in 160
    maritime power in 62–64
    as naval power 63
Revolutionary War 22
RFA. *See* Royal Fleet Auxiliary
Richardson, James O. 108–109, 253
Richmond, Herbert 12
Rickover, Hiram 199, 224, 253
Rimland 23
Rivers 22
Ro-Ro ships 293
Rodger, Nicholas 90, 189
Roosevelt, Franklin D. 88–89, 109, 280
Roosevelt, Theodore 64
Rose, Susan 189
Roughead, Gary 296
Rowers 210
Roy, Mihir 179
Royal Air Force 101–102, 111, 232
Royal Australian Navy 232
Royal Canadian Naval Volunteer
    Reserve 212
Royal Canadian Navy 132, 204–207, 219, 272
    abolishment of 205
    Cutlass Fury 222
    Family Support Centres 214
    in First World War 204, 208
    history of 132, 204
    personnel in 205–208, 224
    in Second World War 205
    volunteers in 205, 212
Royal Fleet Auxiliary 155
Royal Malaysian Navy 157, 253
Royal Naval Hospital 57
Royal Navy
    after American Revolutionary War 74–75
    financing of 5, 87
    Fleet Operations Sea Training 216
    French blockade by 20
    French Navy versus 56
    greatness of 12
    Henry VIII and 191
    Invergordon mutiny of 215
    investments in 87
    merchant shipping support 155
    organisational structure of 53
    population growth effects on 24–25
    Procedure Alpha 211
    revolution of 5
    Royal Air Force and 111
    sea-based trade protected by 87
    T31 Frigate 242

    in 17th century 235
    Thursday Wars 223
    Type 42, 231–232
    underfunding of 83–84
    of Victorian era 200
    William III's 51–54
    women in 212
Rozhestvensky, Admiral 273
Russell, Lord 47, 56
Russia
    Catherine the Great 65
    China and 277
    Crimean war with 91
    Custine's visits to 67
    despotism in 67
    explorers 65
    Gorshkov in 122–126
    Kilo submarines 243
    Main Operations Directorate 138
    *Maritime Doctrine of the Russian
        Federation, The* 181
    maritime geography in 68
    maritime power in 64–68, 274
    Navy 124
    navy of 68
    Peter the Great 50, 65–68, 95
    PVO-Strany 124
    17th century exploration by 65
    silk industry of 66
    societal resistance to change in 67
    St Petersburg 66–67
    SU-33 Flanker fighter of 292
    top-down approach to maritime power in
        64–68
Russian Federation Navy 131

Sa'ar corvettes 149
Sabah incident 112
Safety of Life at Sea 177
SAGAR. *See* Security and Growth for All in
    the Region
Sailing ships 235
Saint-Andre, Jeanbon 239, 266
Saltykov, Fedor Stepnovch 65
Samoans 27
Sane, Jacques-Noel 239
Santiago 28
Sao Tome 61
Sargon 34
Scandinavians 7
Schools of seamanship 239
Schumpeter, Joseph 201
Science of Military Strategy, The 281
Scorpene French diesel submarine 144
Scotland 87
Sea
    authority of 170–171, 293–295

battles on 34
as data set 170
deterrence on 175
disorder at 168, 171–172
as environment 169–170
infantry fighting at 191
legitimate authority of 170–171
Polynesians' attitude toward 27
resources of 3
security at 166
as sovereign jurisdiction 166–167
strategic control of 4
territorialising of 3–4
tourism industry of 170
trade uses of 3
as transportation 168–169
writings about 9–10
Sea-blindness 72, 75, 139
Sea-consciousness 75
Sea control 101
Sea lines of communication 40, 240, 287
Sea-mindedness
    of China 28–29, 278
    countries with 27–28
    declines in 6
    description of 60
    governmental influences on 28–29
    maritime economy and 27
Sea of Azov 65
Sea robberies 169
Sea trade. *See also* Trade
    in China 28
    maritime power and 30–32
    protection of 87
    Royal Navy protection of 87
Seapower
    character of the government and 25
    of China 22–23
    development of 25
    elements of 19, 45–46, 52
    geography impact on 23
    land power and 11, 22, 36
    Mahan's elements of 19, 45–46, 52
    maritime industries as element of 30
    maritime power and 10
    national character and 25
    natural 11
    organic 11
Second World Ocean Assessment 171
Second World War
    aircraft carriers in 31–32
    armaments production in 91–92
    Britain after 84
    Canadian navy in 131–132
    demobilisations after 84
    Japanese warships in 214
    maritime power and 2

Secretariat General for the Sea 179
Secretary of the Navy 62
Security and Growth for All in the
    Region 181
Self-worth 215
Semenoff, Wladimir 263, 273
Semmes, Raphael 26
Seven Years War 194
Seventh Research Academy 128
SHADE. *See* Shared Awareness and
    Deconfliction Centre
Shandong 292
Shang submarines 297
Shared Awareness and Deconfliction
    Centre 174
Shared interests 173
Ship(s). *See also* Fleet; Warships
    specific ship
        battle system for 270
        British 56
        Chinese procurement of 297
        life cycle of 266
        performance of 263
        retrofitting of 267–268
        shore-side facilities for 268
        technological changes in 29
        through-life costs of 246
        Vikings' concepts of 6–7, 27
        in William III's reign 56
Ship-building
    in Australia 146–147
    in Britain 152
    in Chile 145
    in China 86, 128, 289–290
    in India 145
    in Netherlands 65
    in South Korea 149
    technological changes in 153
Ships taken up from trade 191
Sichuan earthquake 288
Signals Intelligence organisations 105
Silk industry 66
Silk roads 38
Singapore
    as commercial port 70
    defending of 101
    description of 20–21
    economy of 25–26
    Hornaday in 70
    London and 108
    loss of 105
    maritime economy in 25
    maritime power in 69–70
    Maydman and 45–46
    National Maritime Security System of 181
    National Security Council 95
    in 19th century 25

Raffles in 46, 69–70
society in 25
top-down approach in 69–70
Slaves 8, 210
SLOCs. *See* Sea lines of communication
Smaller navy 253–254
Soares, Mario 169
Society
    maritime economy and 25
    maritime power affected by 24–29, 40–41
    Maydman's writings on 48
SOEs. *See* State owned enterprises
SOLAS. *See* Safety of Life at Sea
Somalia 157, 159, 169, 295
Some Principles of Maritime Strategy 34, 88
Song dynasty 23, 28, 39, 196
South America 8
South Asia navies 133–137
South China Sea 71, 112, 125, 131, 158, 173, 287, 293, 295–296
South Korea
    Defence Acquisition Programme Administration 246
    ship-building in 149
South Korean Navy 149
South Sea Bubble affair 83
Southeast Asia 103, 109, 282
Sovereignty
    of India 2
    of sea 167
Soviet Union. *See also* Russia
    Gorshov's contributions to naval policy 122–131
    Navy of 89, 124, 130
Spain
    economy of 33
    farming life 7
    fleet design in 235–238
    force concentration issues for 22
    maritime decline in 8
    maritime power of 7
    merchant marine of 7
    Monarchy of 7–8
    private enterprises 150
    South America and 8
Spanish galleys 209–211
Sparta 90–91
Spartans 85
Special Report on the Ocean and Cryosphere in a Changing Climate 171
Spooner, Margaret 107
Spykman, Nicholas 23
SRF. *See* Strategic Rocket Force
Sri Lanka
    description of 12
    exports from 32
    navy of 134–135

warships for 137
Srivijayan empire 72
St Edmund 155
St Petersburg 66–67
Staff training 217
Stalingrad 89
State authority 172
State owned enterprises 145, 149
Steamships 199
Steregushchiy corvettes 249
Strategic Defense Initiative 125
Strategic Rocket Force 124
Strategy of means 57
Streltsy rebellion 65
STUFT. *See* Ships taken up from trade
SUA. *See* Suppression of Unlawful Acts
Submarines 35, 65, 94, 124, 126, 129, 136, 146, 149, 232–233, 243, 245, 266, 269, 290, 295, 298
Subrahmanyam, K. 115
Suez canal 156
Sukma, Rizal 72
Sultanate of Johor 46
Suppression of Unlawful Acts 177
Sustainable fishing 167
Swedish Naval Warfare Centre 223
Swope, Kenneth 188

T31 Frigate 242
Taiwan 285, 290
Tamandare corvettes 144
Tamil community 134
Tamil Sea Tigers 135, 137
Tampa 177
Tang dynasty 38
Tang period 28
Tangredi, Sam 148
Tanjung Priok 73
Tanker war of 1981–1988 168
Tankers 169
Tanzania 171
Technical Standards for Civilian Ships To Implement National Requirement 157
Technology
    Battle Force 2045 249
    land power affected by 23
    naval 135
    in ship-building 153
Temasek 46
Terrorism 169
Thailand 46, 89
Thalassocracy 11
Thatcher, Margaret 113
Theatre of Military Operations 124
Themistocles 82, 84–86, 88, 90, 93–94, 96–97, 139, 209
Thetis 267

30 x 30 Blueprint for Ocean Protection 171
Thomas, Shenton 101, 108
Three Warfares 285
Thucydides 11, 84–85
Tiananmen Square 286
Tidd, Kurt 172
Tigris River 22
Tirpitz, Admiral 122–131, 286
Top-down approach
  bottom-up approach and 74
  description of 82
  in Indonesia 72–74
  of Maydman 58
  in modern China 70–72, 283
  in Russia 64–68
  in Singapore 69–70
Torrington, Lord 56
Tourism industry 170
Trade. *See also* Sea trade
  conflicts over 32
  government involvement in 31
  maritime power and 30–32
  maritime transportation of 3
  Maydman's writings on 48–49
  mercantilist perspectives on 32
  Navy protection of 31, 87
  prosperity and 38
  silk roads 38
  Western views on 32
  wind effects on 20
Trafalgar 251, 263
Training 216–224
  costs of 224–225
  importance of 217–218
  professional military education versus
    217, 220
Transportation, sea for 168–169
Trident Group of 1980 246
Triremes 209
Tsarist regime 29
TSR-2 strike-reconnaissance aircraft 111
Turbot war 177
Tuvalu 170

U-boat force 94
*UK National Strategy for Maritime
  Security* 114
UN Convention on the Law of the Sea 135,
  166, 169, 173, 178, 294
Uncertainty 93–96, 105–107, 112–113, 192
UNCLOS. *See* UN Convention on the Law
  of the Sea
United Kingdom. *See also* Britain; England
  Development, Concepts and Doctrine
    Centre 110
  National Security Council 95
United Nations

Convention on the Law of the Sea 135,
  166, 169, 178, 294
  International Maritime Organisation 178
  Second World Ocean Assessment 171
United States. *See also* Revolutionary
  America
  specific US entries
  competing service agendas in 109–110
  DARPA organisation of 150, 201
  Department of Defense in 116
  maritime decline in 9
  maritime power of 22, 88
  National Defense Strategy of 2018 247
  revolutionary, maritime power in 62–64
  uncertainty of 104
Urbina, Ian 176
US Air Force
  description of 213
  US Navy and 111, 116
US Army 101, 110
US Chief of Naval Operations 143, 263
US House Armed Services Committee 264
US Marine Corps 110, 247
US Naval Institute 260
US Naval War College 64, 219
US Navy
  Adams' writings on 63
  Afro-Americans in 213
  aircraft carrier building by 31
  Battle Force 2045. *See* Battle Force 2045
  in Civil War 64
  fleet growth 250
  in Hawaii 101
  Littoral Combat Ship 242, 250
  N7 branch of 138
  Naval Planning Process of 244
  in Pacific War 268
  in Philippines 101
  professional military education of 295
  in revolutionary America 62–63
  Secretary of the Navy 62
  size of 298
  US Air Force and 111, 116
  Zumwalt programme of 291
US Pacific Fleet 103
US Sealift Command 156
US Senate Armed Services Committee 148
USS *Chesapeake* 218
USS *Constitution* 218
USS *Yorktown* 147
Ustinov, Dimitry 128

V1 94–95
V2 94–95
Varangians 22, 65
Vereenigde Oostindische Compagnie 61
Vestland 7

Victualling Board 188
Victualling Office 194
Vikings 190
  plundering by 6
  sea power of 11–12
  ships as symbols of 6–7, 27
Villaret-Joyeuse, Admiral 239
Villela Barbosa, Marine Francisco 194, 199
Vision, maritime
  in Australia 77
  in China 281–283
  in Colombia 77
  of countries 75–78
  in India 77
  in Malaysia 77
  need for 60
  in Portugal 75–76
Volunteers 211–212

Wang Xiangsui 285
War industries, in Britain 92
War of 1812 22, 63
War of Spanish Succession 51, 53, 84
War of the Pacific (1879–1884) 8
War on terror 251
Warren, Peter 160, 254
Warships. *See also specific warships by name*
  civilian cargo ship versus 35
  conditions on 54
  operational life of 265
Washington, George 62
Weapons Systems Research Laboratory 150
Widodo, Joko 72–74
Wilhelm II 127

Wilhemine Germany 26, 279, 286
William III
  departmental system created by 51
  description of 47, 50, 83, 283
  resource allocation under 51
Winds 20
Witt, Johan de 61
Women 212–213
Women's Royal Naval Service 212
World War. *See* First World War; Second
  World War
Wrongdoers
  apprehension of 175–176
  prosecution of 176–178

Xi Jinping 37, 70–71, 74–75, 78, 92, 115, 278,
  280–281, 283, 285, 294
Xu Yuan 196

Yamashita, General 107
Yan Yiouqiang 299
Yang Jiechi 282
Yangxi River 22–23
Yemen 169
Yin Zhuo 283
Yuan dynasty 39

Zaporogian Cossacks 65
Zenteno, Jose Ignatio 194, 199
Zheng He 23, 28, 39, 278
Zhukov, Marshal 128
Zumwalt destroyer 249
Zumwalt programme 291

Made in the USA
Coppell, TX
13 November 2022